A Strange and Blighted Land

GETTYSBURG:
The Aftermath of a Battle

Gregory A. Coco

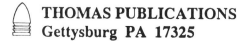

THOMAS PUBLICATIONS
Gettysburg PA 17325

Published by THOMAS PUBLICATIONS
            P.O. Box 3031
            Gettysburg, Pa. 17325

ISBN-1-57747-041-9

LC # 94-60303

Cover design by Ryan C. Stouch

Cover illustration: "Scene in the woods at the northwestern base of Big Round Top" by James F. Gibson. (USAMHI)

For
C.L.S.

I have questions—
She knows everything.

I speak strangely—
But she understands.

CONTENTS

◆ ◆ ◆

Chapter IV

The Woods are Full of Them

Chapter V

The Sacred Sod

Appendix

PREFACE

◆ ◆ ◆

"A Time of Triumph and Desolation"

A former army officer, John Howard Wert, enscribed the following words upon his examination of the aftermath of the battlefield of Gettysburg:

> A battle has never been described by the most brilliant writer so as to give the reader a full conception of its intensity of both splendor and horror. It must be seen and experienced to be understood. But if the most skilled of word-painters have failed to adequately describe the rage of battle, how utter must be the failure to describe the field of conflict when the passionate strife has ceased— when the splendor, the pomp and the circumstance of battles magnificently stern array have gone, and only the horrible remains in its ghastliest and most terrible forms.[1]

As a young man and just prior to his enlistment into a Pennsylvania infantry regiment, Wert had lived only 2 1/2 miles south of the county seat of Gettysburg along a major route leading into that borough. During the summer of 1863 Wert saw his share of destruction, bloodshed, suffering and dying. For months after the furious battle he helped to care for a portion of the torn and bleeding men who remained in field hospitals throughout Adams County. And, as the summer months waned into fall, he witnessed the deaths of many of those men. In times between his household and farm chores, and the constant extra duties thrust upon him in the tragic aftermath of battle, Wert would wander through the woods, fields, meadows, and hills to view the scenes of carnage and strife, and even occasionally to pick up relics and mementos of the struggle. The area which had recently been a battlefield was then an ever-changing panorama of countless never-before-seen and felt experiences of both dread and secret delight, of sadness and exhilaration. It brought out in him a most morbid sense of curiosity and a myriad of heightened emotions. The dreaded became almost commonplace, and in his youthful quest for knowledge and adventure, Wert certainly pushed from his mind most of the melancholy array of horrors around him. The sounds and sights of that vulgar field surely altered his view of the world, and he probably entered the army in 1864 mentally already an old man.

In a somewhat broader sense, this is what my book is about. It will be a return to those dreadful and dreary days as eyewitnessed by J.H. Wert and others. This current picture will be different of course, as it will be seen through the eyes of others only. Through them, the horrors of a battlefield infused everywhere by the corrupting corpses of humans and animals can be seen. Although it will be impossible to smell the pungent stench of death, its presence may be made known. And if our ability to hear the cries of the thousands of wounded is limited, then at least we can know why they screamed and thrashed about in agony. Not one of us will actually hold the shovel that heaps the dirt over the fetid remains of a rotting corpse, but our minds, given the tools, can reenact with mental images and recreate the setting and all of its hideous spectacles.

And there will also be other less gruesome visions. The dilemma of the many prisoners of war and deserters, the guarding and clean up of the battle area, the throngs of visitors searching for missing relatives and souvenirs, the quartermaster details collecting weapons and disposing of dead horses, all make up an interesting and colorful tableaux for us more than 130 years later. There is truly much fascination and drama here. The story of the aftermath of Gettysburg can never be less than enthralling to one who was not present in those dark days of triumph and desolation. These subsequent pages are filled with topics to amaze and attract anyone. The reader must simply turn these pages and absorb the words of men and women who were there. Your mind will do the rest. And like mine, your vision of Gettysburg will be forever changed.

Gregory A. Coco
Bendersville, PA
November 27, 1994

FOREWORD

◆ ◆ ◆

Gettysburg. Few names invoke such instant recognition throughout the entire world as does this one, being synonymous with Waterloo, Stalingrad, and Normandy. Proof of this fact is in the immense amount of literature produced concerning this landmark engagement. In the over 130 years since, Gettysburg has become the most intensely studied and scrutinized battle in American, if not world, history. Hundreds upon hundreds of books have been published, along with thousands of other accounts from newspaper and magazine articles to journals, diaries, and letters. These describe, seemingly to the most minute detail, every aspect of the battle; from the campaign, to the commanders, their decisions and the implications of those decisions, to the in-depth descriptions of the horrendous combat. And even today, more books and published works are produced yearly for an evergrowing interested public eager to learn more.

Yet, of all of these publications none, until now, have dealt fully with the saddest and most tragic aspect of the battle: its aftermath. Most narratives of the battle completely ignore the aftermath, or at best give it a brief or cursory description, tending instead to concentrate on the glory and pageantry of war. It seems as if this terrible phase of warfare has been nearly forgotten. Why? Gettysburg civilian J. Howard Wert probably gave the most concise reason when, nearly fifty years after the battle, he wrote:

> When the splendor, the pomp and the circumstance of battle's magnificently stern array have gone, then the horrible and the ghastly only remain and remain in their most terrible forms.

Simply put, this phase of the battle is too brutal, too shocking, too depressing for the average reader.

Gregory Coco's *A Strange and Blighted Land* does the opposite, making the savage reality of war starkly clear. "Such is war;" wrote one eyewitness, "destroying all that we hold dear; desecrating all that we most reverence, polluting all that we most love and cherish." Yet, no meaningful understanding of what occurred at Gettysburg can be complete until this important phase is studied.

Over 160,000 armed combatants struggled for three days over more than twenty-five square miles of rolling Pennsylvania farmland. When the fighting had ended, over 51,000 casualties had been suffered (10,000 dead or mortally wounded, 30,000 wounded, 10,000 missing or captured). While these numbers are staggering, they obviously do not even begin to convey the reality of the aftermath. It is nearly impossible for the modern reader, especially for one who has never seen combat, to fully comprehend the horrors of war.

Gregory Coco has come as close as possible to bringing the reality of the aftermath to us. J. Howard Wert gives us a typical scene:

> All was a trodden, miry waste with corpses at every step, and the thick littered debris of battle-broken muskets and soiled bayonets, shattered caissons and

blood-defiled clothing, trodden cartridge boxes and splintered swords, rifled knapsacks and battered canteens. When a description of a scene such as was presented on these fields...is attempted, words have lost their power and language is weak.

Drawing upon seemingly countless, varied and previously unpublished sources, nearly all of them primary, this book examines virtually every facet of the aftermath. One of the worst of these was the dead. A Union soldier recalled the Confederate dead along Cemetery Ridge:

No words can depict the ghastly picture...the men lay in heaps, the wounded wriggling and groaning under the weight of the dead among whom they were entangled....I could not long endure the gory, ghastly spectacle. I found my head reeling, the tears flowing and my stomach sick at the sight. For months the specter haunted my dreams...

The condition and treatment of the over 21,000 wounded who overwhelmed the area was another unforgettable horror, as one newspaper recorded:

No one that has never visited or witnessed...a field of battle...can form any conception of the claims of the wounded....This town...is literally one vast and over-crowded hospital...several thousands are lying, with arms and legs amputated, and every other kind of conceivable wound, in tents, on the open field, in the woods, in stables and barns, and some of them even on the bare ground, without cover or shelter....Oh! the horrors of this cruel war...

Even the sickening smell of the battlefield is there, as one soldier later wrote, "...over all, hugging the earth like a fog, poisoning every breath, the pestilential stench of decaying humanity."

Not all of the aftermath is so morbid and sorrowful, however. The redeeming qualities of humankind were also evident at Gettysburg, especially during the recovery efforts. Hundreds of volunteers, along with many local civilians, assisted the wounded. Thousands more gave willingly their money and time. Former enemies treated each other with kindness and compassion. Catastrophe always seems to bring out both the best and worst of humanity.

This and more is included in *A Strange and Blighted Land*, such as the burial of the dead, the establishment of the Soldiers' National Cemetery, the fate of the Confederate dead, the military medical practices and procedures during the Civil War and at Gettysburg, the impact of the battle upon Gettysburg and Adams County, the role of the U.S. Sanitary and U.S. Christian Commissions, the cleaning up of the battlefield, the role of the U.S. Quartermaster Department, the transformation of the battlefield into an American Shrine and much more.

The myriad of recollections Coco relies upon, including soldiers of both sides, wounded participants, doctors, military and volunteer nurses, civilians, newspaper reporters, curiosity seekers, school children, and countless others, allows the reader to have a complete and comprehensive understanding of the aftermath. Since this subject has been so long ignored, many "facts" have been accepted at face value. Yet, by careful sleuthing and diligent research Greg Coco tackles these stories, disproving many, while verifying and adding hard truth to others.

A Strange and Blighted Land fills the great void that has existed and will stand as *the* definitive study of the aftermath of the largest and bloodiest battle ever waged in the Western Hemisphere. It underscores the harshest realities of war; realities we should never forget. As one eyewitness stated:

> The tide of human misery around...Gettysburg swelled high as never before, perhaps, in all our land. We saw the horrors of war, enough to make the heart ache and revolt at the inhumanity of man to man.

Eric A. Campbell
December 1994

ACKNOWLEDGEMENTS

◆ ◆ ◆

The author is indebted to the generosity, advice and guidance of many good people who not only brightened and enhanced life for me in the course of the researching and writing of this book, but also provided assistance to and hard work towards the final outcome of the project.

In particular I am grateful to Cindy L. Small for the countless hours of typing, word processing, editing, constructive criticism and proofreading of the manuscript. My thanks to her goes far beyond a mere deep appreciation for her labor, but even more so for her personal encouragement, patience and dedication. Truly, this book would have remained only an elusive dream without Cindy's resolve, input and tenaciousness, and I will forever remain in her debt because of it. Thank you Cin; you may not have actually written this book, but you did everything else!

Further acknowledgement goes out to the following individuals for important contributions, various kindnesses and direct aid:

Eric A. Campbell, author and historian, for his insightful and all inclusive Foreword.

Lynn W. Myers, Spring Grove, PA, for the professionally drawn maps and sketches, and positive attitude toward all my requests.

Charles R. "Hap" Hazard, Owings Mills, MD, an old army comrade, for the delightful chapter illustrations.

Steven C. Hollingshead, Hollidaysburg, PA, formerly of the U.S. Special Forces and now a professional photographer, for hours of dedicated photography work both at Gettysburg and elsewhere, and in particular his documentation of the John B. Linn collection.

Scott D. Hann, Mays Landing, NJ, for the special trip to Gettysburg to provide photographs of Lieutenant Abbot and others.

Gladys C. Murray, Centre County Library and Historical Museum, Bellefonte, PA, for her research and photographic assistance with the John B. Linn collection.

Enid and William Craumer, Gettysburg, PA, the owners of the old George Bushman farm, for a warm welcome, and tour of their beautiful and historic property, and assistance in obtaining photographs of bloodstains and relics from its hospital period.

Patricia Weaver Newton and Jamie L. Newton, Gettysburg, PA, for kindly allowing me the use of an unpublished 1862 Jennie Wade tintype, and other local Gettysburg related material.

Additionally, for photographic support, I would like to thank and recognize: William A. Frassanito, author and historian, Gettysburg, PA; Steven J. Wright, curator of the Civil War Library and Museum, Philadelphia, PA; Andrew Larson, General Lee's Headquarters Museum, Gettysburg, PA; Brian A. Bennett, Scottsville, NY; Pat, Chet, Sam and Wes Small, The Horse Soldier Civil War Shop, Gettysburg, PA; Thomas W. Howard, Richmond, VA; Harold

J. Small, Gettysburg, PA; John R. McCabe, Springfield Armory National Historic Site, Springfield, MA; Michael Vice and Paul Shevchuk, curators, Gettysburg National Military Park, Gettysburg, PA; Kathleen R. Georg Harrison, senior historian, Gettysburg National Military Park, Gettysburg, PA; Michael Rhode, Paul S. Sledzik, Ron Kikel and Joan Redding, Otis Historical Archives, National Museum of Health and Medicine, Washington, D.C.; Gordon L. Jones and Ted Ryan, Atlanta History Center, Atlanta, GA; Eileen F. Conklin, author and historian, Smithsburg, MD; author Earle J. Coates, Columbia, MD; Blake Magner, Collingswood, NJ; Timothy H. Smith, Gettysburg, PA; Doris and W. Richard Best, Chambersburg, PA; Marilyn Felix Campbell, Carmel, IN; Steven Bartel, Los Angeles, CA; Sarah Rodgers, Fairfield, PA; Charles Rhodes, Gettysburg, PA; and Henry Deeks, Acton, MA.

For research assistance I am honored and pleased to thank and edify the achievements of these friends and acquaintances:

D. Scott Hartwig, author and historian, Gettysburg National Military Park, Gettysburg, PA; Dr. Walter L. Powell, historian and author, Gettysburg, PA; Philip Baron Ennis, Lancaster, PA; Dr. Charles H. Glatfelter, Timothy H. Smith, and Elwood W. Christ, authors and historians, Adams County Historical Society, Gettysburg, PA; Cindy A. Stouffer, author, Gettysburg, PA; John L. Andrews, Licensed Battlefield Guide and Visitors Center Supervisor, Gettysburg National Military Park, Gettysburg, PA; Greg White, Smyrna, GA; Len Rosa, Gettysburg, PA; Timothy K. Krapf, Licensed Battlefield Guide, Gettysburg, PA; David T. Hedrick, curator, Special Collections, Gettysburg College, Gettysburg, PA; James M. Cole, Licensed Battlefield Guide, Gettysburg, PA; Anthony M. Nicastro, Licensed Battlefield Guide, Gettysburg, PA; Grace L. Grogaard, Maryland Historical Society, Baltimore, MD; Daniel C. Toomey, author and historian, Linthicum, MD; and Lewis Leigh, Jr., Fairfax, VA.

And lastly my gratification to Mary Hush, Jim Thomas, and Dean S. Thomas of Thomas Publications, for their interest and dedication which insure that all the company's books become quality productions.

Again, to all, I am appreciative of your extraordinary accommodation and support. I hope you are as pleased with the outcome of your efforts as I am.

G.A.C.

Photo Credits

◆ ◆ ◆

(WL) Walter Lane
(USLC) United States Library of Congress
(SDH) Scott D. Hann
(LHW) Leander H. Warren
(HCC) Hanover (PA) Chamber of Commerce
(LL) Lewis Leigh, Jr.
(JB) J. Barnes, *Pictorial History of the Civil War*
(WT) Walter Taber (*Battles and Leaders of the Civil War*)
(TWH) Thomas W. Howard
(PBE) Phillip B. Ennis
(MSHCW) *Medical and Surgical History of the Civil War*
(EF) Edwin Forbes
(LC) Logan Clendening
(MGP) Marion G. Phillips
(PCW) *Philadelphia in the Civil War*
(HSC) Herb S. Crumb
(MJPA) Matilda J. Pierce Alleman
(HD) Henry Deeks
(CLS) Cindy L. Small
(JBB) John B. Bachelder
(DST) Dean S. Thomas
(AMH) Anna M. Holstein
(EM) Edward Marcus
(EC) Elizabeth Crim
(GNMP) NPS Photographic Archives, Gettysburg National Military Park
(SCH) Steven C. Hollingshead
(FL) Frank Leslie's *Illustrated History of the Civil War*
(ER) Emil Rosenblatt
(SPB) Samuel P. Bates
(NB) Nell Baynham
(ARW) Alfred R. Waud
(GAC) Gregory A. Coco
(FLB) Frank L. Bryne
(DAS) Daniel A. Skelly

(CWLM/BM) The Civil War Library and Museum/ Blake Magner
(CCLHM/SCH) Centre County Library and Historical Museum/Steven C. Hollingshead
(MCW) Gettysburg National Military Park's Museum of the Civil War
(TL) Time-Life Books, Inc.
(HCAC) History of Cumberland and Adams Counties
(OHA) Otis Historical Archives
(REW) Richard E. White
(ASGA) Adams *Sentinel and General Advertiser*
(EJC) Earl J. Coates
(JWM) John W. Muffly
(JRW) John R. White
(MI) Michael Insetta
(TGF/LWM) T.G. Field/Lynn W. Myers
(SGE/LWM) S.G. Elliott/Lynn W. Myers
(AL) Andrew Larson
(ACHS) Adams County Historical Society
(WAF) William A. Frassanito
(SGW) Sara G. Walters
(USAMHI) U.S. Army Military History Institute
(CV) *Confederate Veteran* Magazine
(JAR) J.A. Ragsdale
(JCM) James C. Mohr
(RN) Ralph Newman
(JSH) John S. Heiser
(TSF) The Small Family (Pat, Chet, Sam and Wes)
(HJS) Harold J. Small
(NA) National Archives
(MFC) Marilyn Felix Campbell
(WD) U.S. War Department
(AHC) Atlanta History Center
(HC) Howard Coffin
(HKD) Henry K. Douglas
(RK) Ron Kikel

INTRODUCTION

◆ ◆ ◆

In the year 1860, the United States of America was made up of thirty-three states and the District of Columbia, with a population of approximately 31,443,000. Of this number, a few less than 4,000,000 were slaves. When eleven Southern states seceded from the Union during 1860-1861 they formed a confederacy which counted about 6,000,000 white persons, excluding those sympathetic to the North in each state, especially border states. The remaining Union states then held somewhere around 20,000,000 people. Thus, according to census figures, the Confederate States would have had available for military service about 1,000,000 males; the United States could draw from just under 3,500,000 men of military age.[2]

The American Civil War began on April 12, 1861, in Charleston Harbor, South Carolina, and is generally accepted to have ended on May 26, 1865, when a representative of General E. Kirby Smith surrendered the Army of Trans-Mississippi to Federal authorities. During those four years, one month, and 14 days over 10,000 battles, skirmishes, and other engagements were fought. These many armed encounters (including water and sea actions) were participated in by just under 2,800,000 Federal troops and around 750,000 Confederates.[3]

As a further breakdown of these forces, there were, according to Colonel Boatner, at least 16 Union and 23 Confederate "operational organizations" that were known officially or unofficially as an "army." These nearly 40 field armies were usually named after the department or the territorial area in which they operated. Furthermore, armies were normally headed by the general who commanded the territorial organization.[4]

Both southern and northern field armies were normally divided into units called corps, divisions, brigades, regiments, and companies. In 1861, an authorized infantry company consisted of 100 men and three line officers. Therefore, a regiment of 10 companies regularly numbered 1,000 enlisted men plus their commissioned officers. A brigade of five regiments would then consist of 5,000 men. A division of 3-4 brigades would hold 15-20,000 individuals, and so forth. However, by 1863 and the time of the Battle of Gettysburg, most companies averaged only about 35 soldiers. These reduced figures then spiraled on upwards (toward corps level), reducing regiments to approximately 350 men, brigades to 1500-1800 muskets, and so on. Most losses were due to battle casualties, disease, desertion, and the assignment of men to extra duties or details, etc. At Gettysburg the Union Army was represented by 51 brigades of infantry (238 regiments), seven brigades of cavalry (29 regiments), and 65 artillery batteries (358 cannon). The Confederate army consisted of nine infantry divisions (37 brigades of 170 regiments), five brigades of cavalry (22 regiments), and 67 batteries, totaling 266 guns.[5]

The Gettysburg Campaign began on June 3, 1863, and ended in middle to late July. During those weeks about 100,000 Federals and 85,000 Confederates participated in nearly 18 battles and skirmishes; the largest and most significant being the Battle of Gettysburg itself. In that major conflict, which was the greatest of the 10,000 engagements of the Civil War as previously noted, roughly 93,500 Union and 75,000 Confederate troops took some part.[6] They were members of General George G. Meade's Army of the Potomac, and General Robert E. Lee's Army of Northern Virginia. After a three-day battle which was fought on July 1, 2, and 3, 1863, both sides suffered the loss of over 40,000 dead, mortally wounded, and wounded. The casualties which are listed below are all considered approximate, although "official" in nature:

The Battle of Gettysburg (only)

	Federal	*Confederate*
Engaged	85-88,000	70-75,000
Killed	3,155	3,903
Wounded		
(& mortally wounded)	14,529	18,735
Missing	5,365	5,425
Total losses	23,049	28,063[7]

Here it may be of interest to read what the local population knew of the battle's casualties. On August 7, 1863, the Gettysburg *Compiler* printed: "We have unofficial but reliable information that General Lee lost in the battles of Gettysburg fully 6,000 killed; 10,000 wounded taken with him on foot and in wagons; and not less than 12,000 in prisoners and deserters, making a total loss of not less than 35,000—He crossed but 41,000 men over the Potomac on his retreat....But a month ago he crossed...with over 80,000 men. General Meade's loss at Gettysburg was about 4,500 killed, 10,000 wounded and 4,000 captured."

◆ ◆ ◆

"Before the Storm"

Gettysburg and Adams County in June 1863

...[This area is] the most thoroughly improved which I ever saw. There was not a foot of surplus or waste territory....Wheat, corn, clover, half a dozen varieties of grass, rye, barley—all in full growth and approaching maturity—met the eye at every turn, all enclosed in rock or strongly and closely built wooden fences. Apples, cherries, currants, pears, quinces, etc., in the utmost profusion, and bee hives *ad infinitum*. The barns were, however, the most striking feature of the landscape, for it was one bright panorama for miles.[8]

Private John C. West,
4th Texas Infantry
June 26, 1863

The warm months of 1863 were, as usual then and now, the busiest time of the year for the farmers and merchants of Adams County. This growing and prosperous county, with its abundance of neatly laid out villages and towns, was nearing 65 years old. The largest borough in the county was named Gettysburg, and its population numbered 2,400 people, while its age was 20 years older than the county proper. The two armies which entered that peaceful landscape in 1863 naturally caused a serious disruption of the normal tranquility of the area, with their 165,000 fighting men and noncombatants, 6,500 supply wagons, 1,800 ambulances, 1,900 artillery caissons and limbers, 630 cannons, and over 90,000 horses and mules.[9]

The men who fought the largest and most destructive battle of the war in such delightful and peaceful surroundings surely never forgot what they had seen and admired there before many of the farms and villages were overrun, plundered and desolated. Therefore, a quick overview of the makeup of the county and the town of Gettysburg in that never-to-be-forgotten summer seems appropriate at this time.

Adams County, all 618 square miles of it, was then populated by 28,000 white Pennsylvanians and 474 African Americans, of these 6,674 were taxables. The Caucasians were almost all descendents of Scots-Irish and German settlers and their descendents who came to the area between 1740 and 1840. The 30 boroughs, villages, hamlets, and settlements were connected by numerous farm roads and turnpikes, three of which were hard surfaced. A dozen of these thoroughfares entered and crisscrossed the county seat of Gettysburg much like the spokes of a wheel. Surrounding the towns and intertwined within a collection of streams and creeks, woodlands, small forests, rolling hills and low mountains, were nine million dollars worth of farm land, dotted over with $100,000 in cattle, sheep, pigs, horses, and other less valuable livestock.[10]

Gettysburg's own citizens and the other residents of the county were justly proud of an impressive total of 15 cart, wagon, and carriage industries, 148

Gettysburg from Benner's Hill on the Hanover Road. (GNMP)

school houses, 75 churches, a private seminary and college, 16 lumber mills, nine blacksmith shops, 40 flour mills, 23 leather tanning establishments, four copper and sheet iron works, nine lime kilns and much more—a grand total of 119 manufacturers at a real value of $650,000, all of which employed several hundred people. Gettysburg alone boasted three weekly newspapers, two drugstores, two marble works, one bank, one savings institution, a fire insurance company, seven attorneys, and several doctors—44 diverse businesses in all.[11] The county was also conscious of and proud of the fact that out of 5,400 males eligible for military service, over 2,000 had already voluntarily answered the call to "save the Union," with 200 from Gettysburg alone.[12] A few of those early volunteers inadvertently returned to Adams County with the mighty Army of the Potomac to halt the invasion of Lee's army; a handful saw combat quite near to their own or their parents' houses and farms, and some were wounded on familiar ground; a small percentage remained forever there at home, killed or mortally wounded in action.

This then is a superficial glimpse of Adams County, Pennsylvania, *"before the storm."* Our gaze will now narrow and begin to focus on the *aftermath* of the clash of two great armies at Gettysburg.

Bivouac of the 9th Massachusetts Battery near Gettysburg on July 4, 1863. (LC)

I

THE BATTLEFIELD
IN THE AFTERMATH

"No pen can paint the awful picture of desolation, devastation and death that was presented here to the shuddering beholders who traversed these localities....Death in its ghastliest and most abhorrent forms everywhere. Festering corpses at every step....It was a hideous and revolting sight."[13]

So wrote John Howard Wert of his visit to a portion of the twenty-five square mile battlefield on July 6, 1863. This horror was what had become of one lovely section of his picturesque county, and these scenes were visible but a mere mile-and-a-quarter from the front door of his family farm on White Run. The region had become "a land of trouble and anguish,"[14] and Wert in his memory had forcefully summed up what the Duke of Wellington uttered after Waterloo almost 50 years earlier: "Nothing except a battle lost can be half so melancholy as a battle won."

And the battle had indeed been a victory. With only a sum of approximately 24 hours of *actual* combat during Wednesday, Thursday, and Friday's actions, of July 1, 2, and 3, 1863, Lee's confident and boastful forces had been fully and fairly whipped, and were in the determined process of clearing out of Adams County and other nearby sections of Pennsylvania. By the fifth of July the Rebels were sullenly retreating toward the Potomac River and safety; and General Meade's eight corps soon took up pursuit, just as quickly as the commanding general could stabilize the battle area and rest and refit his hungry and exhausted soldiers.

The Union and Confederate battle lines by July 6 were mostly abandoned. The Yankees' stalwart position during the fighting of July 2 and 3 was three to four miles of connecting hills, low ridges, fields, woods, and meadows in the rough shape of a large hook a mile south of Gettysburg. Just to its rear, a vast network of field hospitals, wagon parks, supply and prisoner depots had been temporarily laid out, and many of these places were still in use by 22,000 wounded and their many attendants left behind. After July 1 the Confederates, too, had their own "hook shaped" position, a distance much longer, perhaps six or seven miles including the town of Gettysburg. This line had barely encroached onto and around the flanks of the Union hook. This type of information however, was all generally unknown history in the weeks succeeding the battle. There were no armies, nor thousands of battered, worn out soldiers present, but throngs of inquisitive and determined visitors were fast taking their places.

John Howard Wert, his wife Emma Aughinbaugh, and daughter Anne, about 1885. (ACHS)

Sightseers Flock to the Field

Throughout time, for good or bad purposes, the curious have always flocked to any type of horrific calamity or tragic event. Liberty Hollinger, living on Gettysburg's York Street, noticed that it was not long after that the "town began to fill with friends and strangers, some intent on satisfying their curiosity, and others, alas! to pick up anything of value to be found. Blankets, sabres, and guns and many other articles were thus obtained and smuggled away or secreted."

Ironically, she was dismayed to find that some of her family's friends and acquaintances, "who were normally always welcome at their house," were not often what they appeared to be. She said all in her home were amused, and even saddened that some visitors *claimed* acquaintance in order to have a "stopping place."[15] She was certainly not the only witness to the almost immediate influx of local citizens and travellers to the recent battleground.

For whatever reason, civilians did come in great numbers, some arriving even before the Union army departed to chase the fleeing Rebels. A fraction of these people were local farmers who, being from nearby communities, took the opportunity afforded them to view a spectacle which could be seen but once in a lifetime. Others, because the National army was not yet in full control of a

"Citizen visitors in flocks came to see the field...." (FL)

7

plan to protect the military arms, equipment, and hospitals on such a huge former battleground, came to exploit the advantage of thousands of acres filled with government and civilian plunder and loot left behind, and the discarded spoils of war yet unguarded. Or, as Lieutenant Frank Haskell put it: "Of course there was not the slightest objection to their taking anything they could find now; but their manner of doing it was the objectionable thing."

A Gettysburg youth, Daniel Skelly, reported that his town, "...was filled up every day by people coming from all over the country—fathers, mothers, brothers, sisters hunting their wounded or dead and the scenes...were indeed distressing."[16]

One volunteer nurse was a preacher from Massachusetts, and like the officer above, found little remorse in many of the citizens. As he walked through the streets of the town on July 7 he found, "...ladies sitting in their open doorways talking, laughing, as though nothing had happened..."[17] while another soldier, a private detailed to bury a few of the dead, merely recorded: "Citizen visitors in flocks came to see the field and Army."[18]

As the days passed into late July, more and more of the sightseers turned out to be in deadly earnest in their searches for a friend or relative who had been hurt or killed in the fighting. But always intermixed with these sad cases, and usually outnumbering them unfortunately, were the onlookers whose main goal was to fulfill a desire to stand and behold and touch the macabre in all of its most bizarre forms.

In truth, there was a prosaic sort of pattern to the wanderings of these transients. Even within a few days of the end of the military contest, many of the spectators who congregated, whether for legitimate purposes or for idle inquisitiveness onto the blighted fields around Gettysburg, usually resorted to a self-guided tour of the battleground. This tour was almost never in the correct sequence of events as they had taken place, but more of a kind of rambling, disjointed jaunt to the famous or main points of interest. It was much too early for anyone to really comprehend what had occurred on these bloodstained fields, but it took no serious historian to determine that whatever had happened there was big, serious, and important. So within the simple everyday lives of the common masses and even the well-to-do and better educated people who travelled to the war-damaged town, and the trampled fields surrounding it, all appreciated immediately that such an opportunity would not come again in their lifetime.

◆ ◆ ◆

Cemetery Hill

The journey through the battlefield in those days almost always began at Cemetery Hill. It mattered little that the hill only became a valuable military focal point of concentration late on July 1. This hill was pre-eminent to early travellers because of its location alone. From it one could see clear across the village, and distinguish distant objects and battle sites, for the foliage around Gettysburg in 1863 was much less dense and abundant than it is today. No buildings or water tanks or tourist attractions blocked the view then, and a main thoroughfare, the Baltimore Pike, transversed its summit. The pike which cut through the hill, separated the main elevation and private cemetery itself from East Cemetery Hill, then known as Raffensperger Hill after the pre-war owners, Rebecca and Peter Raffensperger. Nearby and on the very crest was the solemn and stately Evergreen Cemetery capped with a neat but newly shattered gatehouse that had been occupied both as a temporary headquarters and field hospital. Most important, though, was the hill's use by large segments of the Federal army's artillery and infantry, which gave them a decided advantage of positions. It was obvious, even to a novice, that the heights were the most valuable part of the line, and it had stood firm and was held defiantly against the Rebel invaders.

On top of the 500 foot eminence, earthworks and artillery "lunetts" had been hastily thrown up by the defenders and a rough barricade was constructed to block the turnpike. The need for materials in preparing these defenses was so great that an early sightseer remembered the "curious looking breastworks" made of soldiers' haversacks and knapsacks filled with dirt by the men and piled up for protection. That visitor, Thaddeus Lowe, the famous balloonist for the Union army, said that because they had no spades or shovels, the "boys had scooped up the earth with their hands, filled their [knapsacks, etc.,] and coolly awaited the onset."[19]

One of the first recorded visits to this illustrious and commanding rise was made by special artist, Edwin Forbes who was covering the war for a New York

"...[N]ear the entrance of the Gettysburg Cemetery stood a two-story brick building with an archway through the center...." (GNMP)

based "illustrated" newspaper. Forbes had arrived at Gettysburg even while the shooting was still in progress. Here, he relates his initial look across the battlefield.

> Riding up the road toward the cemetery I was enabled to get an extended view of the Union line of battle and the position of the enemy's forces. To the left of the turnpike near the entrance of the Gettysburg cemetery stood a two-story brick building with an archway through the center which gave entrance to a small graveyard of a few acres. Scattered among the head stones and monuments, some of which had been broken by the enemys shells, were several batteries of 12 pounders, powder-blackened and covered with mud and dust....The village beyond was strangely silent and the streets deserted. To a casual observer it had the appearance of Sunday.[20]

Inherently, the brick cemetery gatehouse became a consistent landmark to those early curiosity seekers. But to Elizabeth Moser Thorn, it was primarily her home. This situation was even more complicated because her spouse, Peter Thorn, who was the normal caretaker of Evergreen, was then serving in the 138th Pennsylvania Infantry Regiment in Virginia. So, along with her aged father, she had to maintain the cemetery property during the war years. Returning to the gatehouse on July 7 Mrs. Thorn found that, "there were no window glass in the whole house. Some of the frames were knocked out and the pump was broken. Fifteen soldiers were buried beside the pump shed. I went to the cellar...everything was gone but three featherbeds, and they were full of blood and mud." Eventually Thorn dug graves for 105 soldiers inside the cemetery property and ridded the grounds of 34 horse carcasses, and she was six months pregnant at the time.[21]

Elizabeth M. Thorn in 1855. (NB)

Joseph H. Foster was a second preacher on the scene, this time from New Hampshire. One week after perusing the battered field he reiterated that the cemetery "monuments are broken by shot, scarred by bullets, or thrown over by bursting shells; the pretty iron fences are thrown down or smashed up, the flowers, and bushes, and trees, planted by loving hands, are broken and trampled, and thick around are scattered all the other marks of fighting....Such is war; destroying all that we hold dear; desecrating all that we most reverence, polluting all that we most love and cherish."[22] And still another preacher, this one a Methodist named Leonard M. Gardner, rightly believed that he was one of the first nonmilitary persons to arrive on Cemetery Hill. Coming directly from the south, he remarked that, "no civilian was allowed to go up to the front on Cemetery Hill." Since this was quite early on July 4, he and artist Forbes may have been very near each other. Gardner noticed too that the Baltimore Pike was backed up with traffic, saying:

"The scene presented along the way was wonderful to behold. The road was crowded with ambulances, luggage wagons, and soldiers on foot and horseback all the way to Cemetery Hill."[23]

In contrast, just three days hence, there was little difficulty in riding or walking up to the hill. A Chambersburg, Pennsylvania, resident stood there on July 7 and spent a few minutes canvassing the small burial ground. He later aired his thoughts:

Upon Cemetery Hill, within the enclosure where rest many of the former residents of Gettysburg, the evidences of the terrible strife were painfully visible. Many of the tombstones and monuments had been laid down, either to prevent their being defaced and broken, or to form sheltering places from the iron and leaden hurricane which had concentrated from one hundred and twenty guns upon that place. The silent sleepers in that city of the dead, all unconscious of the terrible conflict going on all about them, uttered no protest against the temporary and necessary desecration of their last resting place. Several of the monuments in this cemetery were defaced by shot and shell.[24]

Jacob Hoke, who penned the lines just inscribed, was partially correct in his assessment of the monuments in the cemetery. Several people other than Hoke thought that the granite stones and marble memorials had been purposefully "laid down." The reason was explained by Charles Coffin, a correspondent from the *Boston Journal*, who revealed that while joining in for supper with General Oliver O. Howard at the gatehouse on the evening of July 1, he had seen a squad of Union soldiers moving about the cemetery taking down the statuary and grave ornaments and flattening individual headstones. Howard informed Coffin that it had been ordered by him, "to protect his soldiers from splintering stone which would make a deadly hail if enemy shells fell among the graves, and to save the markers from being defaced."[25]

Also, near the looming and distinctive hill but more out beyond the northeast slope, was a writer for a Philadelphia paper, who stood and exclaimed on July 6:

Here many of the rebel dead yet lie unburied, every one of their pockets turned inside out. Many rebel wounded lie in the wood adjacent, and the air is polluted with a heavy sickening, disgusting stench. Thanks for the heavy rain we have had, carrying off much of the blood, otherwise I do not see how people could live here. As it is, it is the most disgusting atmosphere I ever breathed, or thought it possible human beings could live in.

A soldier heartily agreed. In an understatement made on July 4, he was quick to rejoin that the "scenes were horrid and the unattractive employment peculiar to those people who are spending their first day on a rough sea, was popular among military visitors gratifying morbid curiosity."[26]

One of the very best descriptions of Cemetery Hill was written two days later on Thursday of that week, by Thomas W. Knox, a correspondent for a New York newspaper. He had an eye for detail and his narrative describing this particular part of the field is worth recording in its entirety.

> Passing out of Gettysburg by the Baltimore turnpike, we come in a few steps to the entrance to the cemetery. Little of the enclosure remains save the wicket gateway, from which the gates have been torn. The neat wooden fence first thrown down to facilitate the movement of our artillery became absorbed for fuel and in various other uses, as the soldiers made their camp on the spot. A few palings scattered carelessly around are all that remain. The cemetery was such as is usually to be found near thrifty towns of the size of Gettysburg. None of the monuments and adornings were highly expensive, though all were neat, and many of them bordered on the costly. The place was kept with considerable care, as is evidenced by the few traces of horticulture that remain. The eye is arrested by a notice prominently posted forbidding the destruction or mutilation of any shrub, tree or stone about the place, under severe penalties. The defiance that war makes against the civil law, and the overthrow of many of society's customs, is forcibly apparent as one peruses these warning lines.
>
> Monuments and headstones lie here and there overturned. Graves, once carefully tended by some loving hand, have been trampled by horses' foot until the vestiges of verdure have disappeared. The neat and well trained shrubbery has vanished, or is but a broken and withered mass of tangled brush-wood. On one grave lies a dead artillery horse, fast decomposing under the July sun. On another lie the torn garments of some wounded soldier, stained and saturated with his blood. Across a small headstone, bearing the words "To the memory of our beloved child, Mary," lie the fragments of a musket shattered by a cannon shot. In the centre of a space enclosed by an iron fence and containing a half dozen graves a few rails are still standing where they were erected by our soldiers and served to support the shelter tents of a bivouacking squad. A family shaft has been broken in fragments by a shell, and only the base remains, with a portion of the inscription thereon. Stone after stone felt the effects of the *feu d'enfer* that was poured upon the crest of the hill. Cannon thundered and foot and horse soldiers trampled over the sleeping place of the dead. Other dead were added to those who are resting here, and many a wounded soldier still lives to remember the contest above those silent graves.[27]

In the cemetery was another prominent sign which must have caught the eyes of many participants throughout the three day engagement. Its official message read:

"Driving, riding and shooting on these grounds strictly prohibited. Any person violating this ordinance will be punished by fine and imprisonment."

While the battle was in progress, Lieutenant Colonel Edward S. Salomon of the 82nd Illinois Infantry pointed out this sign to General Howard, the Eleventh Corps commander. As Howard was reading it, a shell struck the board, knocking it to pieces. The general, not losing his composure, quipped: "Well, the ordinance is rescinded: I think the shooting can go on."[28]

A Massachusetts officer also made mention of this famous sign, but misquoted it in this version: "Within the gates of the old 'Evergreen Cemetery,' ...was a sign bearing the following inscription: 'All persons using firearms in these grounds will be prosecuted with the utmost vigor of the law.' With what a grim smile must that insatiable demon, war, have greeted this injunction of the simple residents, while glutting his appetite during the carnage among the tombstones that marked the dead villagers of Gettysburg."[29]

Another individual memorial, as the one to "Mary" above, came under the scrutiny of several different observers. It was that of a local man who had been a casualty of one of the 1862 battles near Richmond, Virginia. One of the persons who noted this marker wrote: "The top of a large stone, marking the grave of a soldier killed at Fair Oaks, was broken by a shot or shell."[30]

A reporter, however, penned a more eloquent version:

> How quiet, and yet how sad everything was. Here, among the monuments and flowers above the dead, lay our wounded and dying, and behind the iron railings of the burial places all the engines of war waited for the conflict. In one of the enclosures a marble slab marked the resting place of an orderly sergeant killed at Fair Oaks. Alas! how little did his mother think, when she laid him there to rest by his peaceful home, that his comrades would ever do battle over him, and crimson with their blood the myrtle on his grave.[31]

Curiously, a day or two before July 1 when the fighting would rage over these same graves, Alice Powers, a town resident, remembered how the cemetery was usually visited on those peaceful summer evenings by citizens of Gettysburg, and "where, during the battle the headstone of Sergeant Fred Huber, killed at Fair Oakes, was broken off by a solid shot, and the grave of a German soldier, Charlie Havermil[?], who met his death on a southern field, was torn up by a shell which exploded in it."[32]

A tombstone shattered by Confederate artillery fire. (GAC)

The broken headstone of Sgt. Fred Huber, 28th Pennsylvania Infantry. (GAC)

Yet another reporter was present on July 8, who was a "special correspondent" for the Philadelphia *Daily Evening Bulletin*. This man, known only as "J.R.D.," left his impression of the cemetery in an article printed by that paper on July 9, 1863.

> The once beautiful "Evergreen Cemetery" now presents a sad appearance...[as] the fire of the enemy's artillery was constantly directed upon it with a view of driving us back from its crest. The ground about our guns was literally strewed with shot and shell; tombstones erected over the remains of beloved relations were thrown from their position or broken into fragments; graves were turned up by plunging shot; tasteful railings and other ornamental work around the lots were badly shattered and even the beautiful archway over the entrance to the sacred enclosure was splintered and penetrated. Thank Heaven the desecration was not the act of Union soldiers.

Unlike the basic news style of "J.R.D.," Lieutenant Frank Haskell waxed somewhat more on the poetic side when he voiced his feelings concerning a slow ride across the hill on July 4:

> How these quiet sleepers must have been astounded in their graves when the twenty pound Parrott guns [of Taft's New York battery] thundered above them and the solid shot crushed their gravestones! The flowers, roses and creeping vines that pious hands had planted...were trampled upon the ground and black with the cannon's soot. A dead horse lay by a marble shaft, and over it the marble finger pointed to the sky. The marble lamb that had slept its white sleep on the grave of a child, now lies blackened upon a broken gun-carriage. Such are the incongruities and jumblings of battle.[33]

Lt. Frank Haskell viewed the battleground on July 4. (FLB)

Time, of course, has a way of healing most scars, especially any blemish on the natural setting. And so it was at Cemetery Hill. Within only a month a Baltimore man, Ambrose Emory, who was in sympathy with the Southern cause countered most of the other accounts when he explained on August 18, 1863: "I did not find the destruction about the Cemetery as near as bad as represented but few of the tombs or monuments were broken. Some were thrown down as a protection from the shot and shell. Had the cannonading from the Confederate guns on this city of the dead been such as was reported by the Northern sensation writers, not a stone would have been left upon another."[34]

In August, 1865 a passerby casually remarked:

The view from the top is beautiful and striking....

It was a soft and peaceful summer day. There was scarce a sound to break the stillness, save the shrill note of the locust, and the perpetual click click of the stone-cutters, at work upon the granite headstones of the soldiers' cemetery. There was nothing to indicate to a stranger that so tranquil a spot had ever been a scene of strife....

...[Here] the tombstones have been replaced, the neat iron fences have been mostly repaired, and scarcely a vestige of the fight remains.[35]

Menchey's Spring to Spangler's Spring

From the elevated heights of Cemetery Hill, maiden wayfarers commonly followed the contour of the hill downward in a southeasterly direction across Raffensperger's Hill toward Culp's or Raspberry Hill, and in the process they often passed a small spring owned by Edward Menchey, then on over to a little knoll called McKnight's Hill, where a Maine battery had been posted during the battle.[36]

Correspondent Knox was one who ranged over this route July 6 when he decided to take a path through the diminutive "hollow" between the pair of hills, Cemetery and Culp's. There, he explained, "much blood was poured out between these two swells of land. Most of the dead have been buried where they fell, or gathered in little clusters beneath some spreading tree or besides clumps of bushes. Some of the rebel dead are still uncovered. The first that meets my

Menchey's Spring where Thomas Knox found his first corpse. (GAC)

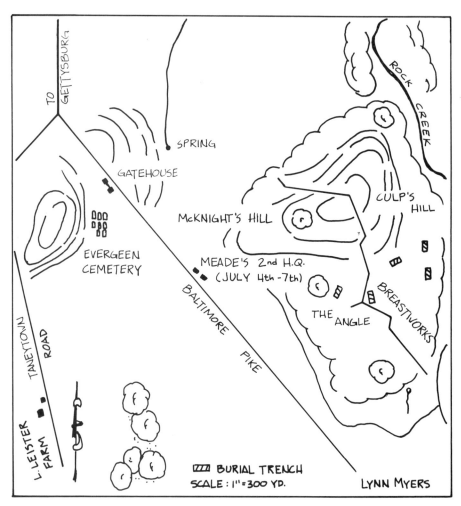

Cemetery Hill, Culp's Hill, and surrounding area.

gaze I come upon suddenly, as I descend a bank some three or four feet in height, to the side of a small spring. He is lying near the spring, as if he had crawled there to obtain a draught of water. His hands are outspread upon the earth and clutching at the little tufts of grass beneath them. His haversack and canteen are still hanging to his side and his hat is lying near him. His musket is gone...."

A few paces from the spring and that forgotten corpse, the reporter found another body with its arms thrown upward just as the former soldier had received the killing ball. The dead man's clothes were not torn, no blood was visible, and his face, though swollen, showed no expression of anguish. About twenty yards further on was one particularly grisly scene; a body cut in two by a shot or shell. "[T]he grass around him is drenched in his blood, that even the rain...has not washed away. His gun is shattered in pieces...."

Moving on, Knox spied another Rebel who had been struck while in the act of aiming his weapon. "His hands are raised, the left extended beyond the right, and the fingers of the former partly bent, as if they had been grasping the stock of a gun. One foot is advanced before the other....To appearances it did not move a muscle after receiving its wound."

Knox's next find immediately attracted special attention by its singular features. The face was intensely discolored, but the hands were..."as delicate as those of a lady and of snowy whiteness. With the exception of the face the body is but little swollen, and there are no signs of the commencement of decomposition. Several bodies...show blackened faces, but no others than this display such a contrast between the color of the face and hands....All possible positions in which a dying man can fall can be noticed on this field."[37]

Most reflections written by visitors who entered the wooded sections on and around Culp's Hill centered upon feelings of gloom and dread, mixed with surprise and wonder at the severe damages inflicted upon the trees along the Northern army's entrenched line of battle. These woods, as one soldier noted, appeared to be "bullet-stormed." One such witness, a correspondent from Ohio, pronounced that the trees were nearly all dead for 300 yards out from the Federal line. He called this area, "the deadened woods." Still another likened the effects of so many fired Minié balls on the timber as being, "...shot into the trees in clusters like wine grapes." A shadowy, cheerless sensation pervaded nearly all of the accounts composed about this segment of the dreary, corrupted field.

Jacob Hoke who lived 30 miles west of Gettysburg has left us with a vivid description of the parts of Culp's Hill which were within the Union's lofty bastion. After proceeding only a short distance into that expanse near the knoll just discussed, he stumbled upon the mangled and torn leg of a Confederate that had been cut from the body by a shell. Close to this partially buried corpse was a bloodstained pocket bible. Entering the musty smelling and shattered forest, he could easily discern places where wounded men had lain, by looking for branches and leaves that had been gathered up for a bed; these places were all thoroughly saturated with blood. Everywhere, "[p]aper, envelopes, bits of letters, shreads of clothing, pieces of photographs, muskets, bayonets, ramrods, knapsacks, haversacks, caps, old shoes and blankets, and many other articles, were scattered....The trees were riddled with balls. We saw an iron ramrod so fastened in a tree that we could not pull it out. It had evidently been fired from some musket and buried itself so deeply that we failed...to extract it. Long trenches, heaped over with fresh earth, told where tens, twenties and fifties of rebels were interred."[38]

The human blood-soaked spots depicted by Hoke had a special meaning to Captain Jesse H. Jones of the 60th New York Infantry who had been on the firing line at Culp's Hill on July 2 and 3. In that same month in 1866, a full three years later, Jones returned to the field and wandered over the old earthworks along the top of the hill and its adjacent ridges. An unusual phenomenon mesmerized the captain. Everywhere that he had remembered where blood from his comrades' wounds had freely flowed out upon the ground, he there saw a peculiar type of plant growing with startlingly blood-red berries. He called them "choke berries," and he affirmed that they were growing nowhere else. He went to several unmistakable spots where several of his men had bled, and there were the berries, and no other place. He returned in 1883, 1886, 1893 and 1895 and these plants were not then present. Jones could not explain the mysterious occurrence.[39]

The low mounds of earth which snake their way through this area today, from James McKnight's hill, now called Stevens Knoll, to Spangler's Spring, are not the remains of the actual defenses constructed by Union troops in 1863. The originals were built of fence rails, cord-wood, felled trees, stones, etc. against which earth was thrown or piled. These works were quickly and permanently dismantled soon after the battle by farmers who wanted to reclaim much needed building and fencing materials. The present-day earthworks were reconstructed by the Gettysburg Battlefield Memorial Association long after the war, and are on the site of the first barriers but lack the correct materials, as well as the bulk and massiveness of the Civil War era protective structures.

There are two prominent, almost 90 degree, "angles" in this line of defenses. Near the first "angle" which is just opposite the head of a narrow valley, stands the monument of the 29th Pennsylvania Infantry. John Wert, a 22-year-old farmer's son who spent many hours in early July exploring this

area, remembered that on the large flat rock where the 29th's memorial presently sits, he saw the mangled and shredded parts of a soldier who had literally been blown apart by a shell. Mingled in with the fragments of this former human being were a few shattered pieces of a daguerreotype photograph. Wert could not refrain from picking up and saving the broken photograph and often wondered as he gazed upon it, "...what aching heart of wife, or mother, or child in distant home, they represented."

Wert also recounted that in that locale almost an entire forest of full grown trees had been destroyed by the discharges of musketry, and some individual trees, he said, were literally shot out of existence. Wert recounts even more:

The large flat rock where J.H. Wert saw the "mangled and shredded parts" of a soldier. (SCH)

All who visited this spot...were impressed with the wonderful appearance here presented. None who saw it can ever forget how the trunks of all the trees...were riddled from the ground up, for twenty feet, so that scarcely a vestige of the original bark or its color could be seen....No pen can describe the appearance of these woods. Those who did not see the wonderful sight can never realize it. The life was shot from every pore of these trees as effectually as from the men in gray who were piled beneath them. The latter were buried in wide, yawning trenches, all along that marshy valley as it extends toward Rock Creek....The former [trees] quickly rotted and were prostrated by every wind upon the graves of the brave, but misguided men beneath, mingling dust with dust. Neither man nor tree, that stood before the...[rifle] fire that swept that valley of death, could live.

J. Howard Wert has just presented us with a truly astonishing description of the "angle" in the Yankee line on Culp's Hill and the ground in front, but he was not finished. He further revealed that on no other spot of the battlefield were dead men piled as thickly as they were there at the angle of the works and down in the little marshy valley. Continuing: "An area of perhaps four acres was so thickly covered with the dead that it was scarcely possible to walk anywhere without treading on them....[O]n the other side, the Confederate dead were piled against the works almost as high as the rampart itself....In some places the dead lay three deep."[40]

No better or more graphic depiction exists of the sadness which seemed to hang like a thick mist among the shot-torn woodlands and bullet-splattered

An "angle" of the Union earthworks below Culp's Hill, where the Confederate dead "were piled...almost as high as the rampart itself." (SCH)

boulders of Culp's Hill and its numerous small ridges and gullies, than the following which was observed by nurse Sophronia Bucklin on her lonely trek here shortly after the hostilities had ended.

> I visited the battle ground on several occasions—the first time soon after the conflict, when the evidences of the horrid carnage...lay on every hand in fearful sights....
>
> Earlier in life it would have been almost impossible for me to walk over such a field of horror, but I had grown familiar with death in every shape. Yet, when right above my head, at one place, so close that it touched me, hung a sleeve of faded army blue—a dead hand protruding from the worn and blackened cuff—I could not but feel a momentary shudder.
>
> Boots, with a foot and leg putrifying within, lay beside the pathway, and ghastly heads, too—over the exposed skulls of which insects crawled—while great worms bored through the rotting eyeballs. Astride a tree sat a bloody horror, with head and limbs severed by shells, the birds having banqueted on it, while the tattered uniform, stained with gore, fluttered dismally in the summer air.
>
> Whole bodies were flattened against the rocks, smashed into a shapeless mass, as though thrown there by a giant hand, an awful sight in their battered and decaying condition. The freshly turned earth on every hand denoted the pits, from many of which legs were thrust above the scant covering, and arms and hands were lifted up as though pleading to be assigned enough earth to keep them from the glare of day.[41]

Lieutenant Frank Haskell was also fascinated by the desolation of Culp's Hill, and even though slightly wounded he rode his horse there on Monday, July 6, and commented: "...[T]he trees were almost literally peeled, from the ground up some fifteen or twenty feet, so thick upon them were the scars the bullets had made. Upon a single tree, not over a foot and a half in diameter, I actually counted as many as two hundred and fifty bullet marks. The ground was covered by the little twigs that had been cut off by the hailstorm of lead."[42]

Ambrose Emory of Baltimore, who passed by the same "peeled" trees as noted by Haskell, remembered one other small oddity which no other eyewitness attested to. He observed that, "[o]n the trees were the names of several regiments—Ohio, Pa. N.Y. (3rd Wisconsin) & others."[43] The soldiers it seemed, had personalized their battle stations.

A portion of the "bullet-stormed" woods at Culp's Hill. (GNMP)

Among the few "off duty" military men tramping over Culp's Hill, along with a handful of nonresident civilians on sightseeing excursions throughout this torn and blighted landscape, were also a smattering of home-grown provincials plodding to and fro there both in and out of the woods. One of these latter types was Christian Benner, the son of a farmer who lived less than one half mile northeast of the summit of the hill. He testified that soon after the fighting ended on or about July 4 he had seen where, "...a Rebel sharpshooter had climbed up in a tree...and buckled himself fast to a limb with his belt. 'He was picking off our men...and of course it wasn't easy for them to make out where he was because the thick leaves hid him. But at last they noticed a puff of smoke when he'd sent a bullet in among them...[and] that was the last shot he fired. They aimed at the place the smoke came from and killed him, and after the battle, I'll be dog-goned if he wasn't still in the tree hanging by his belt.'"

A few days hence, on Tuesday the seventh, this young man and his father were notified by a neighbor that a dead man had been found in the woods below Culp's Hill and east of Rock Creek. Benner remembered what transpired next: "So Father and I took a mattock and a shovel and went along with Mr. [Zachariah] Tawney to the spot where he'd come across the body. There it was all bloated up, seated leaning against a tree. We had to make the grave a rod [16 1/2 feet] or so away on account of the tree roots. It was impossible to handle the man to get him there, he was so decayed like, and we hitched his belt to his legs and dragged him along, and no sooner did we start with him than his scalp slipped right off. We just turned him in on his side and covered him with earth."[44]

Returning again westward across Rock Creek, on July 4 a man who had acted as a guide for the Union army prior to the battle, Leonard Gardner, was taking a short ride on that day from Cemetery Hill toward Culp's. Almost immediately he passed a party of civilians lifting a dead soldier out of a shallow grave, in order, "...to take his body home." Passing into the trees he came to the now familiar breastwork built by the Twelfth Corps. Gardner described this long line of earthworks as a "...crib of logs...five feet high and several feet wide. Into this large stones were piled until it was full." He was amazed at the "length and solidity" of the structure, even more so when told that it had been constructed in only a few hours. Gardner continued his narrative with these intriguing images:

> It was now late in the evening....A light fog was rising in the woods and I rode for some distance outside of the entrenchment. At length I came to where a curve of the hill made an angle and saw one of the saddest sights to behold in life. About twenty-five or thirty dead men were lying in all positions on the ground. Some of them in groups huddled together. One especially attracted my attention. It was a boy apparently about twenty years of age. He lay with his head thrown back and his shirt pulled open in front. He had a beautiful face, jet black hair and skin as white as marble. The rain had washed the blood from his body and immediately above his heart was one small dark spot where the bullet entered that put out his life. I could not help thinking of the anxiety of some southern mother about the same boy who would wait and hope to hear that he had escaped the scourge of battle, only to be plunged in grief at last to hear that she would see his face no more.[45]

The remains of the breastwork built by the Twelfth Corps. (GNMP)

One among this same cluster of dead men could have been an old soldier specifically mentioned by Edwin Forbes on July 4. Soon after a hasty breakfast the artist "rode toward Culp's Hill," where he found the "...enemy's dead...lying pitifully among the rocks, singly and in numbers, some with upturned faces. Near the extreme right of the line where the flanking fire of the infantry and artillery had struck the enemy, bodies were piled in heaps. There was a point near the angle of the works...where some of the enemy had fallen within ten feet. And one, a gray-haired veteran of sixty, had died within a yard of the line."

Forbes further explained that the musketry fire had..."barked the trees until they were white, which with drooping limbs that had been cut by the bullets gave the woods a weird and dismal appearance."[46]

Remarks made by visitors concerning a particular or individual sighting of a deceased soldier are much rarer than the usual generalities noted by most of the constantly exploring soldiers and citizens. Connecticut corporal, H.D. Chapman, like Forbes above, made mention of a distinct Rebel corpse on that same day. Touring the infamous killing ground out away from the entrenchments, Chapman perceived where the Confederate bodies were "...massed in large numbers, [and] the sight was truly awful and appalling. The shells from our Batteries had told with fearful and terrible effect upon them and the dead in some places were piled upon each other and the groans and moans of the wounded were truly saddening to hear. Some were just alive and gasping but unconscious....I saw a letter sticking out of the breast-pocket of one of the Confederate dead, a young man apparently about 24. Curiosity prompted me to read it. It was from his young wife away down in the state of Louisiana. She was hoping and longing that this cruel war would end and he could come home. And she says 'our little boy gets into my lap and says now Mama I will give you a kiss for Papa. But oh how I wish you would come home and kiss me for yourself.'"[47]

A comrade of the corporal, and likewise from the 20th Connecticut, a regiment which had beaten back the Rebels at Culp's Hill, was John W. Storrs. His sightings were more general in nature, but they stand apart by the extreme vividness of his superb mental pictures, which are very clear even for being composed years later:

> The dead lay all about, some with a smile upon their faces, and others horribly contorted as if the death agony had there been photographed or modeled in clay. [One] was seen with his back against a tree, with arms folded calmly across his breast, and but for the swollen appearance of his face might readily have been taken for one asleep. He had been mortally wounded. Placing his musket against a tree he calmly, as it seemed, and resignedly sat down to die. In another place, a soldier had been engaged in bandaging the limb of a wounded comrade and was himself instantly shot dead, his body falling upon his friend and both dying together.
>
> Perhaps one of the most realistic pieces of battlefield statuary, a companion piece for the first one named, was that of a confederate soldier who was sitting with his arms folded about his musket, and with his head drooped down as if a sentinel who had sat down to rest and had fallen asleep. It was, in fact, hard to realize that it was not so, until laying the hand upon the body it was found to be cold in death.[48]

Strange as it may seem, on July 5 while assisting burial details on Culp's Hill, a 16-year-old Gettysburg native, John H. Rosensteel stumbled across what may have been the exact Southerner just described by Storrs. This Rebel corpse was "propped against a tree in a sitting position," with a rifle-musket laying across his legs. Rosensteel buried the body and kept the weapon as a souvenir. Ironically, this relic may have become the focus of one of the great private museums in the United States. John Rosensteel, who remained a bachelor until his death in 1924, eventually opened the popular "Round Top Museum." It was later sold to his nephew George D. Rosensteel, who operated a larger version of the museum until it was purchased by the National Park Service. If you visit the Gettysburg National Military Park Visitor Center and the Electric Map, (the map was opened by Rosensteel in 1939), you will view a part of John and George Rosensteel's huge collection which may have begun when John pulled a musket from the death grip of a Rebel soldier on Culp's Hill.[49] This very weapon was one of the most visited exhibits on display in that museum and is still part of the present U.S. Government acquisitions.

As we complete the meanderings at Culp's Hill, through the eyewitness testimonials of these early explorers, we must not ignore the July 6 commentary of former acquaintance Thomas Knox. After stopping at Cemetery Hill, Little Round Top, and General Meade's headquarters site at the Leister farm on the Taneytown Road, he concluded his visitation by walking over "a secession of elevations and depressions" on which the now familiar Union defenses had been constructed four days prior. About twenty feet from one section of these bold and foreboding earthworks he discovered a Rebel's coat and a bloody blanket, along side of which was a soldier's pocket testament printed in Atlanta, that contained the name of John H. Congreve of an Alabama regiment. Continuing along into the forest itself he came upon piles of camp debris, such as clothing, shelter tents and rubber blankets. A little way back from these log barricades Knox found in a "quiet nook," where the earth was not as rocky, the graves of several Federals slain in the battle. Further down the hill and nearer to Rock Creek he espied a, "long mound of Yellow earth." "Upon [a]pproaching this...I find it to be the resting place of a portion of the rebel dead. Close by it the side of a tree has been scraped and neatly smoothed down. On the spot has been placed the following inscription: *"Forty-five Rebs Buried to the Right."* An index ☞ points to the mound. Further down the valley is another mound close by the bank of the stream."

In his travels, Mr. Knox, too, has given us a good feel for the look of the woods at the time of the battle. He painted them as being made up of trees of good size and quality, with the forest floor free from underbrush. The limbs of the trees were from ten to twenty feet high, and as he claimed, offered, "no screen to the approaching foe."[50] The floor of the wooded ground did not remain barren forever. In the fall of the year it quickly became covered with a thick carpet of leaves, making walking not only uncertain, but as nurse Bucklin once revealed, slightly uncomfortable. She composed this gruesome piece after a visit to the "hill."

> Every advantageous position was marked with torn turf, lopped tree boughs, and the graves of the slain. Indeed, our whole way was lined with the narrow strips of earth, which rested over forms gashed with the implements of carnage....[T]he many [leaves], colored glories, yet green and tender having drifted down into the hollows, and over the trenches where dead men lay rotting. Sometimes bodies were so completely wrapped up with the fallen leaves that, unconsciously, I stepped upon them—the quivering of the loose flesh making my feet unsteady, and the thought of the awful pit below sending me away with no little amount of nervous terror.[51]

Returning to the account of New Yorker Thomas Knox who explained to his readers that he had already seen the whole battlefield of Shiloh, Tennessee, and the field over which General W.T. Sherman's men were repulsed at Chickasaw Bayou in western Mississippi. But Knox reported that, "[t]he traces of the fighting there are but slight compared to those on this ground. I find tree after tree [at Gettysburg] scarred from base to limbs so thickly that it would have been impossible to place one's hand upon their trunks without covering the marks of a bullet....The storm of bullets must have been as thick as hailstones in an ordinary storm. How a man could exist in it and come out unhurt is difficult to imagine."

Mr. Knox states here too, that not only did the trees display the effects of the shots but, "[t]he rocks wherever they face towards our breast works are thickly stippled with dots of white. On one rock, presenting a surface of about seven square feet, bullets have left their traces in little blurred spots, like a snow flake of the largest size. The missiles, flattened by contact with the rock, are lying scattered about in the leaves, most of them giving little sign that they have ever been musket projectiles."

Confederate bullet which splattered onto a piece of granite boulder near Culp's Hill, where the Twelfth Corps was positioned. (CWML/BM)

Ending his visit to the Culp's Hill region, Knox explored farther down to the far right flank of the U.S. position near Rock Creek at Abraham Spangler's spring. There he found lesser evidences of battle debris and damage, but commented on the novel ways sharpshooters on both sides ingeniously found cover to employ their clever and fiendish skills. He documented one such marksman who had converted a large hollow tree that faced toward the enemy. To give him cover the soldier had adopted a removable "knot" to use as a loophole for his rifle.

Like other first-time sightseers, Knox was much impressed with all he had seen. He summed up his notes with a patriotic pronouncement: "Strong men, who stood with blanched cheek and bated breath, half dreading to hear the result of the combat are to-day filled with exultation. To those whose valor stood [here] for the nations defense we will render our heartfelt thanks."[52]

Abraham Spangler's spring as it appeared to 1863 observers. (GNMP)

◆ ◆ ◆

The Round Tops

Visitation to Culp's Hill, undoubtedly was heavy in the days subsequent to the three-day encounter in and around Gettysburg. No less popular during those momentous weeks was the left flank of the old Yankee stronghold or "fishhook" line at the Round Tops, some two miles directly south of Cemetery Hill. There, heavy foot traffic tracked throughout the summer months and into the fall.

The largest eminence on this site appears to have been called Round Hill or Round Top by Adams Countians at the time of the battle. The smaller hill, though, actually a low craggy ridge, went by various and sundry names, such as Sugar Loaf Hill, Rock Hill, Granite Spur (also used in conjunction with the western face of Round Top), Rock Top Hill, Stoney Ridge, or Long Hill, while a few locals probably even called it by its present title, "Little Round Top."

As in all places on the field, visitors to the area near the Round Tops were present as early as July 4. A Southern officer, Colonel R.M. Powell of the 5th Texas Infantry who had been shot on July 2 in *front* of Little Round Top, was, two days later, lying in a field hospital *behind* that eminence. He sarcastically reported: "The big show was gone, but [the sight-seers] seemed content to look over the ground where it had been. A torn and bloody garment would attract a crowd, which would dispense only to concentrate again to look at a hat perforated by bullets....The habiliments of the men and variegated plumage of the women made an interesting scene. The typical farmer, the German costumed in clothes of the last century, the village belle and the country housewife, all moving in pursuit of the same object and animated only by idle curiosity, seeming without thought or care for the hundreds of suffering men lying so near them...."

Powell called this crowd, "a vast concourse...whole families with the baby."[53]

While most of the combat had taken place well below the summits of these two prominences (the highest being 785 feet above sea level, the other 650) documentation has been found in which certain narrators described the appearance of the summits and slopes of these hills themselves. For instance, one traveller who crossed over Little Round Top many months after the fighting noted that "heaps" of old clothing could still be distinguished behind the ridge where the wounded had first been examined by regimental surgeons at their forward or front line aid stations.[54]

Somewhat closer back to the days of the battle was the news report drawn up by correspondent Knox. He outlined for his readers that the main defenses on the Union left at Little Round Top consisted "...of a single line of temporary earthworks, and in a few instances of two lines. Behind them lay the debris of battle scattered everywhere. Pieces of clothing, tattered shelter tents, spoiled cartridges, canteens pierced by bullets, torn haversacks, broken muskets, sabres, bayonets, soldiers equipment—all were mingled in confusion—stained and saturated with loyal blood, the fragments of clothing torn from wounded heroes bore evidence of the terrible struggle. Behind the breastwork were the

A temporary stone breastwork on Little Round Top, behind which can be seen the "debris of battle." (GNMP)

graves of the fallen, dotted thickly around. The ground was deeply cut by the wheels of the artillery as it performed its evolutions on the field."[55]

The great ruts left by artillery pieces and limbers on the eastern slope of Little Round Top impressed another gentleman on July 18. After seeing to the reburial of his brother, Joseph, who had been mortally wounded on July 3 as a member of Battery C, 4th United States Artillery, John Campbell strolled along Cemetery Ridge to Little Round Top, where he collaborated Knox's recollection:

"On the southeast side the slope was 'gentle.' The opposite was steep and rocky. A field extended well up the south slope, terminating in a quagmire about 100 feet across. I saw where one gun carriage cut into the soft ground till the axle scraped the surface. Horse tracks were some two feet deep. At the upper side was an old rail fence. The wheels cut the panels in two and jammed the rail pieces down into the ground, the other ends sticking up like small posts. Above this fence was a thrifty growth of young white oaks. The axle of the carriage had run over one as large as my leg and bent it to the ground and skinned it from near the butt for 20 feet toward the top."

As fascinating as the first part of Campbell's account reads, the ensuing paragraph remains one of the classic descriptions ever penned of a scene on that gory field.

On the north side of Big Round Top and near the summit I saw the whitening bones of a Johnny who had killed and wounded 17 of our men during the night. He rolled a rock as big as a bushel basket ahead of him, while he crawled behind it. He could see our men toward the sky, while they could see only the flash of his gun, which they shot at all night. At the dawn he could not retreat, and our boys "got him." They could not dig a grave there. They cut brush and laid it across him...and carried dirt and weighted down the ends of the brush. His head had rolled down hill some 10 feet; his shoes with the bones of his feet had fallen sidewise and lay there. A soldier (convalescent) of the Pennsylvania Reserves, who was on the top that night, and whose brother was killed by this rebel, showed me and explained as above.

One final remark of John Campbell portrays the stark and festering battlefield unusually well. He proclaimed that, "[e]very fence and bush was black with flies, but not a crow or buzzard [was] to be seen anywhere."[56]

When J. Howard Wert asserted that, "[a]t Gettysburg every form of the battlefield's horrors was present over extended miles—on verdant meads, beside meandering brooks, in narrow chasms and defiles, along the public highways, in dense and tangled thicket, in the grand old forests, and on hilltops,

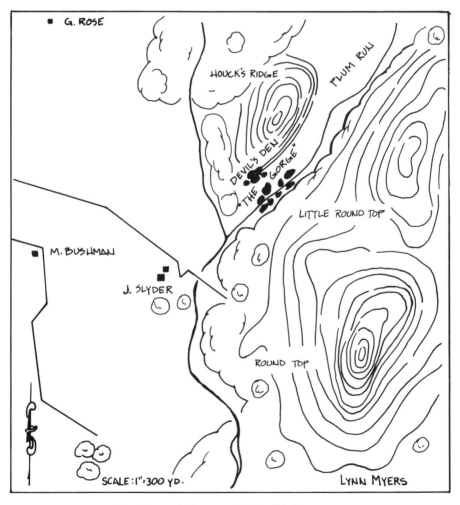

The Round Tops and Devil's Den area

bleak and bare, strewn with rocks in massive piles,"[57] the one area which fit several of those poetically descriptive places was certainly the neighborhood of Little Round Top. A different author, Professor Jacobs of the local college, did not simply generalize about the hill. He became much more specific when he wrote the following:

"In front of Little Round Top, amongst huge rocks, lay all summer long the decaying bodies of half a dozen or more of rebels who had probably belonged to Hood's division, and having been wounded on July 2...may have crept into...these rocks for shelter....There they died undiscovered, and when found they were so far gone in decomposition that they could not be removed." Jacobs went on to underscore the fact that the hill, "...has from the first been looked upon as a point of deepest interest, and visitors to the battlefield have not failed to go to see it."[58]

An unidentified letter writer to a Harrisburg newspaper provided that paper's readers with a view similar to the one above:

> The battle field around the quiet town of Gettysburg will be an object of absorbing interest to many of our citizens for weeks to come. We visited the scene of strife on Thursday [July 9] and can truly say that it is the saddest commentary on human ambition it has ever been our lot to behold. Any one anxious about the definition of the word glory will find the answer in the valley in front of Round Top, where numbers of bodies lie bleaching in the sun on the gray granite rocks, in every stage of decomposition, doomed to lie there exposed to the elements in every conceivable position that men killed outright will assume in their fall. Their anxious friends will never even know the horrible condition that death left them in.[59]

During the warm and muggy night of July 3, one of the first humans to view the carnage on the slopes of Little Round Top was a private of the Fifth Corps, Army of the Potomac. His Massachusetts regiment was on picket duty that day a short distance down the western side of the hill. Just after midnight he and a friend walked into the place the professor would venture into weeks later. This soldier, Robert G. Carter, testified that the moon "shed a dim and sickly light over the ground," and the eerie locale was, "partially obscured by a fog or haze that settled about us." All around Carter and his companion could be distinguished the bodies of the dead and dying: "We could reach out and touch them." His morbid adventure continued:

> Every possible part of the equipment of a soldier of either army lay mingled with both the rebel and Union dead. Caps and hats with the red Maltese cross [the corps badge of the 1st Division, 5th Corps] were mixed with the broad sombrero of the Texans. Haversacks, canteens of tin and wood, every kind of a rifle or musket, blankets, cartridge-boxes, and bayonet-scabbards, all strewed the ground....The bodies were in every conceivable position, some with hand uplifted and teeth clinched, others with a smile of peace, as though death had come gradually and without pain, giving them time to prepare for the dread and unknown future. The majority had a settled, determined expression, as though they had a revengeful feeling in their hearts. Some were in the act of tearing cartridges, or loading and reaching for the rammer. All [were] called forth in a moment to the mysterious hereafter. We came suddenly upon a young boy caught and stiffened in the forked branches of a small cedar, looking like a

statue of marble, with its upturned face to the sky. His cap had dropped off, and his whole appearance was so natural, that it seemed impossible that he was not alive. It startled us so that for a few moments [we] walked along in silence.[60]

The southwest side of the hill was hideous indeed. A few days after the above was related, a Philadelphia civilian named John Foster arrived in Gettysburg with the Christian Commission to assist the wounded in the Second Corps field hospital. He accentuated that the slope "was one horrid waste," and that unburied corpses had been lying there for days, and scores of living but wounded Rebels were crouching among the rocks unable to move. Foster recounted that, "[i]n some places bodies, caught in the thickets as they fell, were still hanging mid way between the summit and the hills foot, dense clouds of insects hovering over them. Broken guns, shells, cartridges, and fragments of rebel uniforms were scattered every where!"[61] And it should be kept in mind that Mr. Foster was verbalizing these visions at least *seven* days after the battle had ended.

About the same time as the preceding description was taking place on July 9, 1863, correspondent "J.R.D." of the Philadelphia *Daily Evening Bulletin* stood on the same southwest part of the hill saying that there, "[f]ifty dead rebels were buried in front of the position of the Twentieth Maine and Forty-fourth New York, and the Eighty-third Pennsylvania [here] brought in nearly a hundred of the enemy's wounded."

One other witness, who was present on the field from August 18 to the 25th, inscribed these next sights, indicating that the horrors were diminishing somewhat, but were still very much in evidence. This Baltimorean, Ambrose Emory, commented that there were bodies still on Round Top and Little Round Top, "lodging in the crevasses," where they were becoming food for vultures, and their "bleached bones a sad spectacle of the ruin and desolation that has been brought upon a once happy country." In closing Emory forcefully verified:

Alas, this is no fancy sketch; the writer...was over the whole battlefield, and here upon this Round Top has he seen these scenes—men not half buried. It may be a skull, an arm, a leg protruding from the ground, barely in many instances covered over. I have seen the body slightly covered, and the skull being outside the grave. In other instances the body being on the ground and piled over with stones. In some parts of this place you will find the stones removed and there lies what was once a human being...endowed with all the senses of man, a human skeleton, perhaps the Father of once a happy family, the stay of a widowed mother, an only son. Such my friends, are some of the scenes of a battlefield.

And only a moment later in his ramblings, Emory encountered "[w]ay down in one corner of a field and near the base of the round top, was the grave of [a] Texas Soldier named M. Price 5th Texas, [Marshall Prue] his round about [jacket] was lieing alongside of his grave."[62]

Even after the passage of a year, in the fall of 1864, one traveller to Gettysburg easily found manifestations of the hard struggle on the Round Tops. After driving his carriage eastward and over from the Emmitsburg Road, Isaac Moorhead's party and guide, John G. Frey, reached the base. "Dismounting among the rocks," he said, "we saw some bones of a rebel, with shreds of his 'butternut' clothing. We passed through the woods filled with rocks, and ascended the [Little] Round Top. The summit is clear of trees, but they are scattered on the sides. On a large rock near the summit is chiseled this inscription: 'Col. Strong Vincent fell here com'g 3d Brig. 1st div. 5th corps, July 2d, 1863.'"

Moving ever onward and down the side of the hill, the men picked their way still further. Moorhead renewed his story. "Here, in a secluded spot among the rocks, I found the bones of a rebel just as he had fallen. Picking up one of his shoes to remove the string, to tie together some little trees, the bones of his foot tumbled out. It was a 'Georgia state shoe.' made from canvas....From among his ribs I picked up a battered minie ball which doubtless caused his death. Moving aside a flat stone, Mr. Frey showed us the grinning face and skull of a rebel. Some of them in this rocky part of the field have very shallow graves."[63]

These remains were not the only ones which were still in evidence there, for in June 1866 a party of tourists "...found a perfect skeleton, which the rain had washed out of its bed." They also admired the, "...little protections which our sharpshooters had put up for themselves...the stone breastworks also, and dented into these enduring rocks are the marks of shell, the black rays of their explosion, and the scars of the glancing shot."[64]

Much like the two Philadelphia civilians had alluded to earlier, this next account portrays the field below Little Round Top less than 48 hours after the end of hostilities. It was composed by Amos Judson of the 83rd Pennsylvania, and he left an impressive image for us to contemplate.

> I counted...over forty dead bodies within a circle of fifty feet in circumference. They laid in every conceivable position among the rocks in that low swampy ground, some crouched behind the rocks as if about to fire, some lying upon their faces, and some stretched upon their backs, like corpses laid out for a funeral, as if they had determined to observe the propriety of attitude even in the hour and article of death. The rains had, during the interval, descended and the hot sun had beat down upon them, and they were now swollen and turned black with mortification, and millions of maggots could be seen rioting upon

The carving documented by Isaac Moorhead. (SCH)

"They laid in every conceivable position among the rocks in that low swampy ground...." (GNMP)

their flesh, Ah me! though I, could the fathers, mothers, and the wives of these unfortunate men suddenly appear and gaze upon the forms they had once fondled in their arms, they would curse to the bitter end the traitors who had brought the desolations and miseries of this war upon their once happy households.[65]

Periodically, a few objects were sighted that were not so totally gruesome. One vision more peculiar than horrid was seen on the sixth of July by a detachment of U.S. sharpshooters who were encamped near the base of the hill. While there, one of the men mentioned seeing the body of a horse that was killed in the fight on July 2. He declared that, "[t]he horse must have been shot dead and fell with its legs under his body, in upright position. It was a large bay horse and the body had swollen and the rain had smoothed the hair so it fairly shone and the neck was arched very much like the neck of a very proud live horse. On the whole, it was a very noble looking horse, notwithstanding it had been dead two or three days."[66]

Facing off in the general direction of Big Round Top, the southwestern approach to Little Round Top was defended during the battle by a segment of Colonel Strong Vincent's Brigade of the Fifth Corps. That brigade had been assaulted by members of General Law's and Robertson's Brigades of Hood's Division, and some of their men had fallen here in death, very close to the bodies of their adversaries. On July 5 a unit of Vermont troops held a temporary position near this spot. One of its members, Wilber Fisk, took a moment from his duties to overlook the recent field of action. In his recollection this part of the ground was said to be covered with jagged rocks and huge broken stones of every conceivable shape, and as he expressed, was

...the ugliest looking place for a battle, or for anything else that one could easily select....I saw but a small portion of it, but I saw all I wished to. The rebel dead and ours lay thickly together, their thirst for blood forever quenched. Their bodies were swollen, black, and hideously unnatural. Their eyes glared from their sockets, their tongues protruded from their mouths, and in almost every case, clots of blood and mangled flesh showed how they had died, and rendered a sight ghastly beyond description. My God, could it be possible that such were lively and active like other people so shortly previous, with friends, parents, brothers and sisters to lament their loss....I turned away from the heart-sickening sight, willing to forego gratifying my curiosity rather than dwell upon the horrors of that battle-field. I thought I had become hardened to almost anything, but I cannot say I ever wish to see another sight like that I saw on the battle-field of Gettysburg.[67]

At this point in our narrative some readers may wish to follow in the footsteps of Private Fisk and leave these unpleasant memories behind. For those of you who choose to read on it is just my intention to guide you even deeper into the hellish aftermath of Gettysburg. Therefore, contemplating on what one man felt, that "[t]hese scenes are still vivid on the page of memory, and the rememberance causes a shudder of horror still," let us move forward.[68]

This last quoted person was a soldier in the 12th New Hampshire who was present at the base of the famous hill when he wrote the above on July 6. None of the bodies in that region had been buried, he remembered. "The dead lay here so thick that it was with difficulty that we could walk without stepping on the lifeless forms. The features of all had turned black and maggots were crawling in and out of the gaping wounds. The boulders had protected the lower part of the victims and nearly all the death wounds were in the head or upper parts of the bodies. Nearly all of them had their pockets turned inside out showing that human ghouls had here robbed the dead."

He, like the previous sharpshooter also remembered the animals, noting that some wounded horses were "...looking with almost human faces at one for relief."[69]

Another unusual and singular related aspect to the many Confederates killed near the Round Tops was expressed by a member of the 16th Michigan, an infantry regiment which had been engaged on Little Round Top late on the second day of fighting. On July 5, as he and others were collecting serviceable weapons from among the bodies, they discerned something in abundance besides cast off rifles. Next to and inside the knapsacks and haversacks of the dead were, "[f]ragments of mutton, veal, crocks of butter, lard, preserves, baskets containing delicacies from the cellars of the wealthy farmers in the vicinity...[d]ressing apparel which could do them no earthly good, such as old bonnets, fashioned after old patterns, babies' shoes, young misses' gaiters, featherbeds, in fact everything stealable could be found here in profusion."[70]

A Gettysburg bank clerk who had become familiar with the region of Big Round Top because his uncle owned a farm there, was Thomas Duncan Carson. He estimated, too high, surely, that about 1,800 dead were buried in the vicinity of this heavily fought over tract of ground, and that many wounded had been discovered later who had crawled off to die alone. On July 7 Carson came across two of these fellows, one of whom had a compound fracture and had remained alive for days by sucking water from nearby mud to quench his terrible thirst. The many graves in that location were quite eerie according to Carson. Being so shallow, they gave off a phosphorescent light after dark which exuded from the earth above the buried bodies. In his remembrances, he correctly played down the popular notion that buzzards and vultures were everywhere feeding upon the remains of horses and men. In reality, Mr. Carson explained, there were in actuality *none* of these creatures present, as all had been frightened away by the tremendous noise of hundreds of cannons and thousands of muskets, and the acrid smell of so much gunpowder.[71]

Remarkably, even as late as the end of July, a number of corpses still remained above ground. A student from Mount St. Mary's College in Emmitsburg, Maryland, found them on Round Top; "[s]oldiers with their hands and feet sticking out of the ground, I do not say out of their graves for they had none, but were buried, if buried they were, where they lay by throwing a little dirt over their bodies; but the worst sight that I saw was a Con[federate] that had not been buried at all, most of his body was decayed, his head was disconnected from his body and on the whole presented a most horid[sic] sight; I covered him with his blanket which I found a short distance from him...."[72]

Six years after the battle there were likely no more skeletons in view, but battle damage was much in evidence. R.H. Conwell affirmed that on Little Round Top, "the bullet scars are still visible on the rocks, while several large flat stones near which officers were killed have been engraved with their names and the dates of their deaths. The stone wall which the troops threw up as a breastwork is still entire, and the trees have not yet outgrown their wounds."

The trees were always a curiosity. Thirty-one years later, all of the worst manifestations of war in front of Little Round Top had been obliterated by time and the elements, except a few of these scarred, venerated old trees which had once stood so healthy and strong. Sophie G. Keenan paid a memorable homage to these wooden victims:

> There stand oaks, still green and vigorous, through whose hearts tore solid shot or fragments of shell in the second day's fight. It is easy to trace the direction from which the storm came by the fact that the hole is small and clean cut where the ball entered and large and jagged at its exit, though the live bark has skimmed over the edges of both wounds. Scores of trees that survived a cannon ball were killed by the awful volleys of musketry that rained upon the valley, stripping them of bark, so that upright and firm-rooted as ever, they died of starvation.[73]

A Parrott shell in a section of tree from Big Round Top. (CWML/BM)

Plum Run, Devil's Den, and Houck's Ridge

Shifting the focus west, we now cross what is presently termed the "Valley of Death," but is in reality the tiny Plum Run Valley, and out toward today's Houck's Ridge, named after its proprietor, John Houck who owned it in 1863. Then south into Devil's Den, or the "Devil's Trap" as an 1878 visitor called it, which was a large outcropping of boulders that is the southern terminus of that ridge. In these places the exploration of the field as it was just after the battle will continue. At Devil's Den, as can be surmised, the sights were always a mixture of both morbidity and curiosity while, in a way, thrilling for early explorers. On July 9 as a prime example of the disagreeable sights there, a man counted over 70 Confederates still scattered around and unburied among the giant granite rocks.[74] While nearby and to the east, the debris of battle became thicker and more shocking.

Just a few yards east and south of the den runs a rocky gorge where Plum Run tumbles along and away in its journey down toward Rock Creek and then to the Monocacy River in Maryland. Within days of the fighting, J. Howard Wert toured the area and described the next scenes with the realism of one who had to have been there. Said he:

> In charging across the piles of rocks at Plum Run many dead and wounded fell in the chasms between. The heavy rains that followed the battle washed down and lodged in these places other corpses from positions higher up the flat. These bodies were never recovered, but gradually decomposed, whilst the bones were washed away or covered with rubbish. More than a month after the battle in one of these chasms was presented the hideous spectacle of the remains of five rebels piled upon each other just as they had fallen in a place from which it would have been impossible to extricate the bodies.[75]

Wert made no mistake in his speculation that the corpses would never be removed. In late 1864, Isaac Moorhead was pointed toward the grave of a Confederate by his guide John Frey. The grave was just at the mouth of Devil's Den, and the poor soldier's boots were lying nearby just within the den. Mr. Frey explained to Moorhead that this particular Rebel had been killed by two of Berdan's sharpshooters on July 2 because he had been the one who had shot Colonel Strong Vincent.[76]

Jacob Hoke was one of the true "pioneer" visitors to Devil's Den, a place where on July 7 he saw "...among the huge boulders, unburied confederates. They were black and bloated, eyes open and glaring, and corruption running from their mouths....some of our party had not seen the like before. They were shocked and horrified." Nearby were scores of dead horses. Hoke mentioned that a few had "...huge holes in them, and pools of blood had formed in the hollow places. They were swollen and putrid, and the stench was horrible."[77]

A description of the swampy ground east of the den, in the den itself, and in the little woods north of it, was penned by Frank Stoke, 1st Battalion Pa. Militia on guard at the general hospital near Gettysburg in October, just over three months after the engagement. He wrote to his brother describing:

[a] perfect storm of balls swept through these woods from our batteries which felled the trees in every direction. Between this woods and Stony Ridge [Little Round Top] is an open field, blue swamp mud and very rocky. This the Rebels had to cross....Along the middle of this swamp there is a chain of the largest rocks I ever saw; it seems as though nature in some wild freak had forgotten herself and piled great rocks in mad confusion together. This place is known as the "Devil's Den." The Rebels in passing over the rocks were shot and fell down between the rocks into the stagnant water and blue mud....When I visited this place...I clambered down to these miserable looking beings. I almost strangled from the effects of the smell caused partly by the decomposed bodies. The crevice is from ten to fifteen feet deep. It is dangerous to pass over these rocks. Some skeletons of late have been hooked up with iron hooks attached to long poles. You will remember the Rebels buried their own dead here. Scarcely any graves were dug here. They dragged them to where they could throw them into some crevices and tumbled them in and threw a few stones on them and thus left them. The visitor is shocked at every step while passing over this vast charnel house. As soon as the bodies began to decay the stones began falling down among the skeletons thus exposing all that each grave contains. It is not pleasant to the finer feelings of the human breast to see the frames of men ([even] if they are enemies) in every position conceivable. Here all the arms and legs that were shot off were not gathered and buried, but are lying about among the rocks. I saw in a circle of one rod, four legs lying with shoes and stockings on. While hands lay withering in the sun.[78]

The fascination shown by many sightseers to the den is once again illustrated by Sergeant White, one of the sharpshooters who had battled on Round Top on July 2. On the fourth of July he and some fellow soldiers "...took a look at the Devil's Den where a rebel's body was down in the cleft of the big rocks and was so bound in between the stones that it was impossible to get it out." White recounted an additional eye-catching moment a little farther away when he and his companions saw, "...a rebel's body standing up almost straight beside a big rock. His rifle lay over on top of the stone and his arms were extended on top of the rock. From appearance, I should think he was about to fire when he was hit and instantly killed, falling forward on to the stone and as his body swelled, it straightened up so as to be in a standing position."[79]

One of the crevices in Devil's Den where dead Rebels had been thrown for burial. (SCH)

A Michigan volunteer, using his own peculiar style of spelling, wrote how he had been told after the battle that there were 170 deceased Southerners found in and around the den. He concluded, that, if "...Devels Den was ever ocupied with the devels imps it was then." This soldier, James Houghton, believed that, "...the name of this place orriginated years before the Battle from its rough apearance. [I]t is only about 10 or 12 rods in length with the most Prominent side fasing East towards Little Round top."[80] Houghton was historically correct in his views on the naming of the den. It *was* a pre-war designation. Local legends through the years had interpreted that the name came about due to various creatures who had resided within the small caves therein. In one case the appellation was said to have been conceived because of a large black snake that had once lived in its dark, moist crevices. Supposedly, another origin was that a fearsome black bear had at one time made his or her home there in the deep fissures. Furthermore, one other source explained that the den was christened by the early settlers simply as "The Big Rocks." Emanuel Bushman who lived in the vicinity knew it as "Raccoon Den" because three of these large creatures called it home and were very protective of their lair, once inflicting severe damage to the flesh of an unwary explorer named Degroft. Joseph Sherfy, another farmer who dwelled nearby asserted that in his lifetime a large boulder of 20 tons was knocked apart or split open by lightning. Lastly, for a scientific point of view, geologists have written that the rock material itself "...is an outcrop of a diabase sill that about 180 million years ago intruded the Triassic sandstones and shales that floor the broad Gettysburg plain."[81]

So in leaving Devil's Den behind, the memoir of Gettysburg resident Daniel Skelly comes to mind. He recalled it as being one of the saddest sights of his day's visit to the field on July 6. Near the den on the low ground nearby, he encountered, "...twenty-six Confederate officers, ranking from a colonel to lieutenants, laid side by side in a row for burial. At the head of each was a board giving their names, ranks and commands to which they belonged. A short distance away was another group of thirteen arranged in the same way. They had evidently been prepared for burial by their Confederate companions before they had fallen back, so that their identity would be preserved, and they would receive a respectable burial."[82]

Daniel A. Skelly, who described "one of the saddest sights" at Gettysburg. (DAS)

◆ ◆ ◆

Upper Plum Run Valley to Sherfy's Farm

We shall now transfer our realm of attention to a large tract of ground which encompasses several hard-fought-over farms or portions thereof which were on ground generally in a northwest direction from Little Round Top and Devil's Den.

Basically pyramidal in shape, this piece of the battlefield includes the upper Plum Run area, the Dorothy and George Rose property (220 acres plus the centrally located wheat field planted by the Roses' relative), the Abraham and Catherine Trostle farm, Mary and Joseph Sherfy's farm including their peach orchard, and other places near to and along the "lower" Emmitsburg Road. These sites were relatively easy to approach through a variety of means and ways by early visitors. The whole section was generally flat, was only a short distance south of the town, and was contiguous to a fairly well maintained road.

Thursday, July 9 found just such a person, who had pursued his own approach, standing on the Emmitsburg Road near Sherfy's peach orchard. While there, this unnamed gentleman discovered the peach trees completely riddled with musketry, and nearby a piece of woods clearly showed the ravaging track of artillery fire. Trees ten inches in diameter were badly severed by solid shot or shells, and in several instances shells were still embedded in the tree trunks. This was exactly the case of a large old cherry tree in Joseph and Mary Sherfy's yard, which exposed one complete side of a 12-pounder cannon ball for decades afterwards. Along the road this man stumbled upon, "the first Rebel unburied. He was shot apparently while attempting to climb the fence. His legs still on the fence and his face in the mud." In a field adjoining the orchard he counted at least 17 more Confederate bodies all in "a forward state of decomposition."[83]

An old cherry tree complete with embedded cannonball sat on the north side of the Sherfy house and was a famous landmark for many years. (GAC)

38

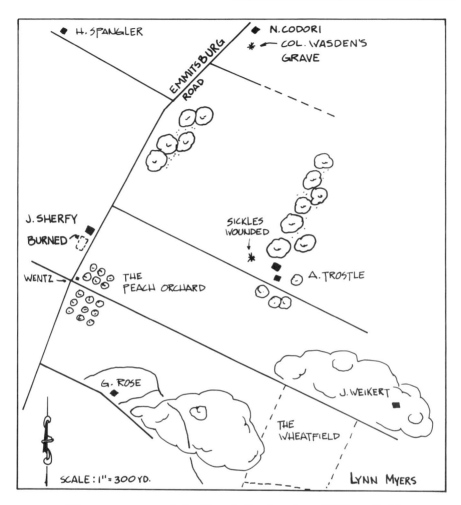

The area around the Peach Orchard and Wheatfield.

Three days prior another spectator to this locale was Lieutenant Colonel McCalmont of the 142nd Pennsylvania Volunteers, who on July 6 marched with his brigade across the ground which bordered the Emmitsburg Road. In a letter home, he narrated these sad spectacles:

> The ground was still marked with newly made graves, with the bloated and disgusting bodies of horses with their mouths open and eye-balls protruding. Many human bodies were still unburied and the faces were black and the teeth grinning horribly. The trees were shattered by shot and shell. Wheat fields were trodden down. War had done its work; and the air was terribly offensive with the odor of thousands of rotting bodies. It was a relief to reach the outside of the terrible scene, to come again among beautiful farms, and through fields of ripe grain....[84]

Michigan Private Houghton traversed this section on a mission to locate a friend who had been killed on July 2. Although his spelling left much to be desired, his macabre sense of humor and powers of description are not in any way diminished. "...[W]hen we arived at the wheatfield we found men there busily ingaged in burrying the dead....[O]n the bank near the [burial] trench lye[s] a large Rebel Sargent. one of our mineys balls had passed through His Head so quick that it dislocated all the Confederacy there was in it and it was gradually oozing out onto the Ground for the flies to Diagnosis."[85]

Much like Dan Skelly described, and somewhere between Rose's wheatfield and Houck's Ridge, (near where Colonel John R. Brooke's Brigade of the Second Corps had done its fighting on July 2), a July 9th witness saw in a gully, "laid in all the ghastly stages of decomposition, twenty-eight rebel officers without a particle of ground to cover them; near them three others, apparently thrown down in haste, lay jumbled in a pile promiscuously. The woods at this place were literally riddled with balls. We found that there was a literal meaning in the phrase, 'a storm of bullets.'"[86]

Southwest of the notorious wheatfield is a small marshy, stream which flows around and beyond the Rose buildings and then southeastward on through the woods below and into Plum Run. J. Howard Wert called this stream "the west branch of Plum Run," and proclaimed that it was thoroughly,

...clogged with the dead bodies of Confederates cut down by the fire of [infantry]...and [the] terrific missiles of Bigelow's artillery.... Immediately after the battle were heavy rains, and in this valley, so much was the course of the stream obstructed that great ponds were formed where the waters were dammed up by the swollen corpses of the Southern soldiery. The writer wandered over these fields immediately after the fierce strife had ceased, and the vivid impression of the horrible sights there beheld can never be effaced from the memory. Death in its ghastliest and most abhorrent forms, everywhere. Festering corpses at every step; some, still unburied; some, hastily and rudely buried with so little of earth upon them that the appearance presented was almost as repulsive as where no attempt at burial had been made. All the fields and woods from the Emmettsburg [sic] road to the base of Round Top were one vast hideous charnel house. The dead

The "west branch of Plum Run," which became clogged with Confederate bodies. (GAC)

"The dead were everywhere."
Confederates awaiting burial somewhere on the Rose farm. (GNMP)

were everywhere. In some cases nothing but a few mutilated fragments and pieces of flesh were left of what had been so late a human being following his flag to death or victory.

In the garden of the Rose house in full view...nearly one hundred rebels were buried. All around the barn, even within the house yard, within a few feet of the doors, were, in numbers, the scantily buried followers of the Confederate cause. Two hundred and seventy-five were buried behind the barn; a rebel colonel [Hance, 53rd Georgia] was buried within a yard of the kitchen door. No pen can paint the awful picture of desolation, devastation and death that was presented here to the shuddering beholder who traversed these localities July 4, 5 and 6, 1863. Fences and fruits of the earth had alike disappeared before the withering besom of destruction. All was a trodden, miry waste with corpses at every step, and the thick littered debris of battle-broken muskets and soiled bayonets, shattered caissons and blood-defiled clothing, trodden cartridge boxes and splintered swords, rifled knapsacks and battered canteens. When a description of a scene such as was presented on these fields...is attempted words have lost their power and language is weak.[87]

In recalling the Massachusetts batteries spoken of by John Wert, such as the one commanded by Captain John Bigelow, we also find Robert Carter's reminiscence, and it is easily as descriptive.

...[T]he scenes of that spot...still linger on our memories....Masses of Kershaw's and Wofford's Brigade advanced up to the muzzles of these guns, which had been loaded either with double shotted canister or spherical case, with fuzes cut to one second—to explode near the muzzles—[termed "rotten-shot" by artillerymen]—had literally [been] blown to atoms—and in a moments brief space into eternity. Corpses strewed the ground at every step. Arms, legs, heads, and parts of dismembered bodies were scattered all about, and sticking among the rocks, and against the trunks of trees, hair, brains, entrails, and shreds of human flesh still hung, a disgusting, sickening, heartrending spectacle to our young minds. It was indeed a charnel house—a butcher's pen—with man as the victim. One man had as many as twenty canister or case shots through different parts of his body, though none through a vital organ, and he was still gasping and twitching with a slight motion of the muscles, and vibrations of the pulse, although utterly unconscious of approaching death.

Private Carter inferred that these hideous sights were seen, "...along the lane at the northwesterly edge of the 'Wheat Field,'" a small dirt road which led over to the Emmitsburg Road. He finally ended his nightmarish tour by exclaiming: "It is awful!"[88]

John Blair Linn was a 31-year-old attorney living in Union County, Pennsylvania. Linn was known by his peers as an amateur historian, and quite a good one it appears. The rumors circulating about the battlefield at Gettysburg stirred in him a need to go and see for himself what had occurred there. He left for the field on July 6, and kept a diary of his experiences until July 11. Once he arrived in the town he walked down the Emmitsburg Road and past the Sherfy place then out to the Rose farm. Along the way Linn chronicled many absorbing scenes, especially sights around the stone buildings owned by the Rose family, then being managed by John Rose. Here is his entry for Wednesday, July 8. Please note that minor punctuation in this account, as in other quotes, has been added for clarity.

We soon came to marks of a fearful contest, hats with holes in them, rebel canteens, over-coats, torn clothing, dead horses, broken gun cartridges, letters, torn knapsacks and haversacks strewed the road. About a half mile from town was the grave of Colonel J. Wasden, 22 Georgia Volunteers....This was on the left of the road a little further on and more to the left were 15 unburied rebels. We walked up to look at them, they were swollen large as giants [and] black in the face, but seemed to me to have an individuality which would render recognition by their friends even then possible....Saw the graves of D.W. Cross Co. E 15th Massachusetts, J. Bradley Co. I 15th Massachusetts. Further on passing along [near a] parapet made of fence rails, mud, and knapsacks filled with earth on the right side of the road. We came to what was once Joseph Sherfy's peach orchard. The house was terribly used up by shell....Four feather beds...were soaked with blood and bloody clothes and filth of every description was strewn over the house....Their (Sherfy's) barn was burned down during the fighting. We proceeded about 1/2 mile beyond to [the] farm of Mr. Rose his

John B. Linn left a most descriptive account of a visit to the Rose property. (CCLHM/SCH)

***Burials on the Rose farm west of the house. The second soldier from the
left may be Capt. T.J. Warren, 13th South Carolina or T.S. Gasden, 15th
South Carolina. (GNMP)***

brick [stone] house and large stone barn are to the left of the road [about the]
width of a field from it. Here to the North of his barn we counted 33 graves of
12th South Carolina Volunteers. They were only slightly covered with earth
and you could feel the body by pressing the earth with your foot. One man's left
hand (J.B. Robins Co. I 8 S.C.V.) stuck out of the grave looking like an old
parched well worn buck-skin glove. A little further on across the fence was the
grave of J.W. Weldon 53rd Georgia, near him was that of Capt. J.M. Debond 53
Georgia co. I. On the other side of the barn and lane under a pear tree was the
grave of Capt. T.J. Warren, 13th South Carolina Vol. and in his garden Mr. Rose
told us were buried 10 superior officers colonels, majors, etc. That morning he
had removed them for fear of injury to the water of his well to a ravine in the
woods 1/2 mile East of the house where he placed their head-boards beside
them and left them unburied not having the strength or means to bury them.
He pointed up to his wheat field and said over 50 rebels were lying in there still
unburied. The rain slacked up and we returned picking up some letters, cards
and cutting off some buttons for relics of the fight. On our way in Goodman
picked up an Enfield rifle for a trophy. I found a testament with the name T.C.
Horcraft, 34th Regt. N.Y.S.V. Excelsior eagle and shield, on the next leaf was
written "David Mitchell" 105 Virginia Regt. I picked up a letter from a boy to
his father evidently stained with his father's blood contents very interesting,
it is among the relics I have from the field. Also one from a girl to her lover.[89]

A second person who, like John Linn searched this exact ground, was
Ambrose Emory. He too took an almost perverse interest in the graves of
deceased Southerners. One month and ten days after Linn, Emory's pencil was
put to paper in a small notebook and composed these lines.

The "Horcraft" testament picked up by J.B. Linn. (CCLHM/SCH)

The "bloodstained letter" mentioned by John Linn. It was written on June 17, 1863, from "Milo Centre," New York, by the son of 44-year-old Private Joseph Hollowell, of Company B, 126th New York, who was killed on July 3. (CCLHM/SCH)

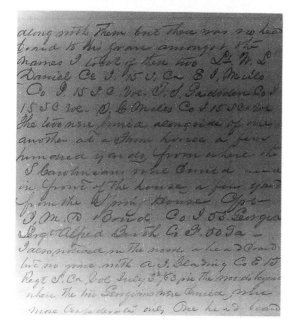

A page from the diary of Ambrose M. Emory. (GAC)

In passing over the field in front of the Round Tops, I came across the graves of 35 Confederates of the 15th South Carolina Regiment There was a Lieut Col buried along with them [J.W. Hance, 53rd GA.] but there was no head board to his grave amongst the names I took of these [were] Lt W.L. Daniel Co I, 15 S. Ca, E I. Mills Co I. 15 S.Ca Vol., T.S. Gadsden Co I 15 S C Vol., S.C. Miles Co I 15 S C. Vol. The two were buried alongside of one another at a Farm house [Rose] a few hundred yards from where the S. Carolinians were buried and in front of the house a few yards from the Spring House. Cpt. I.M.D. Bond Co I 53 Georgia Sergt Alfred Berth Co I 50 Ga ——

I also noticed in the woods a head board but no grave with A.I. Glading Co E 15 Regt. S.Ca. Vol July 3d/63 in the woods beyond where the two Georgians were buried, were more Confederates. One head board could I make out and that was Sergt J.L. Davis Co. D 11th Ga.[90]

The spring house on the north side of the Rose farmhouse near where many South Carolina and Georgia soldiers were buried. (GNMP)

In the identical location as above, I.O. Sloan, a U.S. Christian Commission delegate, came across the same types of destruction as had John Linn. In this letter to his supervisor, Sloan chronicled his discoveries:

It would be impossible to give you a picture of all that we saw on the different parts of the field where the contest raged. The dead were scattered in all directions. On one part, which was covered with rocks of all sizes and shapes, affording, as we would suppose, a perfect protection to all who secured a place near them, we saw hundreds of dead bodies, men of the south, who had come to devastate and subdue the north. These were stretched out cold in death, and the wonder to us was how our men had fired upon them in such seemingly impregnable positions. As we went on, we came to a house where it was said a

Mr. [John] Rose lived. Here everything was torn to pieces. Many shells had passed through the house. The enemy had destroyed all the furniture. Clothing were scattered about, drawers emptied, and everything torn, and broken, and thrown into the utmost confusion. I should judge, from the dead bodies we saw in the yard, that South Carolina chivalry had been at work.—They all were of regiments from that state. They covered every part of the yard. As we passed around we saw a young lad in search of buttons. He was cutting off one here and there. Just as we passed him we heard him exclaim, "Why, that man's alive. See how he breathes!" We turned and sure enough, he was breathing, but evidently near his end. He had been shot through the head. He was wholly unconscious, and had lain there through all the hard rain of the previous day and night....[91]

Mr. I.O. Sloan saw a "young lad in search of buttons." (GAC)

Daniel Skelly also passed by Colonel Wasden's well-marked and prominently displayed grave on the south side of Nicholas Codori's barn near the Emmitsburg Road. In writing of a July 6 trek he took over the battlefield, Skelly revealed that there were still unburied Confederates on this farm, possibly duplicates of ones viewed by John Linn and Ambrose Emory previously. Skelly testified that they were, "...lying on their backs, their faces toward the heavens, and burned as black as coal from exposure to the hot sun." A bit further to the southeast he came to the Trostle house which he found entirely deserted. "In their kitchen" Skelly said, "the dinner table was still set with all the dishes from the meal, and fragments of food remained, indicating that the family had gotten up from their meal and made a hurried getaway."[92]

The sixth of July proved to be a popular excursion day for many people. After leaving Gettysburg on that day, Thomas Knox walked south along the Emmitsburg Road where he "...found an orchard in which the fighting appears to have been desperate in the extreem. Artillery shot had ploughed through the ground in every direction, and the trees did not by any means escape the fury of the storm. The long balls of iron...a modification of the Whitworth projectile, lay everywhere scattered....At one time I counted twelve of these bolts lying on a space not fifty feet square. I was told that the forest in rear of our position was full of these shot that passed over our heads in the time of the action."

Knox looked in on a farmhouse between Little Round Top and Seminary Ridge, or the present day Warfield Ridge. It may have been owned by either the

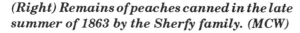

(Above) "Given me by Mr. Sherfy's daughter, the peach orchard riddled with balls and the house awfully abused. July 8, 1863, J.B. Linn." (CCLHM/SCH)

(Right) Remains of peaches canned in the late summer of 1863 by the Sherfy family. (MCW)

Sherfy family, Peter Rogers or David Klingle; in any event, this particular house had changed hands several times during the fighting, so he was told, and it bore the marks of hard use. He discerned walls that were pierced with shot and shell, many of the latter exploding within, making the premises a scene of utter devastation. Glass windows were shattered by rifle bullets on every side of the structure and the woodwork bore mute testimony to the struggle. The sharpshooters had been in every room, which added to the disorder caused by the explosion of shells. Knox hinted that what the missiles spared, the soldiers had destroyed.

Quoting Knox: "In the orchard in rear of the house was the position of the rebel batteries....Fifteen of their horses lie dead on the ground, swollen to an enormous size. As yet the citizens have made no attempt to bury the putrefying horses."[93]

Isaac Moorhead definitely visited the small residence of Susan and Peter Rogers in late October 1864. While driving south along the Emmitsburg Road Moorhead commented on Colonel Wasden's grave and the fields surrounding it, where he was told that 1,600 Rebels had been hastily interred. This information was probably correct, as General James Longstreet's July 3, 12,000 man assault had crossed over these fields only to break apart along the stone and earthen walls atop Cemetery Ridge. At the house of Rogers, which was on the west side of the road, Moorhead was shown about the farm by a small boy who was the grandson of Peter and Susan. The house was much disfigured and torn up by shot and shell. In the words of Mr. Moorhead, these explosive projectiles had, "entered the house from Cemetery Hill and Round Top, one bursting in a bureau and pinning a portion of the contents to the log walls, where they still remained. A piece of shell was stuck in a leaf of the table.

A minie ball struck just over the clock. A rebel sharpshooter was killed on top of the house, and tumbled down in front of the door. Another died of exhaustion on the steps. Many were found dead in the yard. In a field behind the house several were buried; the feet of one stuck up through the ground. His skull was bare."

On the return ride to Gettysburg, Moorhead announced that his entourage had passed a place where, "four rebel colonels were buried in a row." He remarked that from their position on the field he believed them to be General Lewis Armistead's officers.[94]

Peter Rogers was the same gentleman, who with his long silvery hair hanging over his shoulders, had cheered along the Union First Corps as it marched past his tiny farm on the first day of the battle. In a tremulous voice he had cried to the exhausted marching men: "Whip em boys, this time, if you don't whip em now, you'll never whip em." And a month after Moorhead came to the Rogers' place, Mr. Rogers was shot in the abdomen after an argument over flowers with an ex-soldier who was on his way to the rededication of the National Cemetery in Gettysburg on November 19, 1864. The old man recovered, (he died in 1870 at age 75), and the Marylander who fired the gun went to jail.[95]

Two years following the battle, in August 1865, John Trowbridge rode on horseback from Gettysburg down to view the Round Tops. On the way he paused on the Sherfy farm at what he called the "historical peach-orchard." He explained that "[t]he peaches were green on the trees then; [July 2, 1863] but they were ripe now, and the trees were breaking down with them. One of Mr. Sherfy's girls—the youngest, she told me—was in the orchard. She had in her basket rareripes to sell. They were large and juicy and sweet,—all the redder no doubt, for the blood of the brave that had drenched the sod. So calm and impassive is Nature, silently turning all things to use! The carcass of a mule, or the godlike shape of a warrior cut down in the hour of glory,—she knows no difference between them, but straightway proceeds to convert both alike into new forms of life and beauty."

Interestingly, by 1896, a Confederate veteran of the Georgia Troup Artillery claimed; "all that is left of the famous peach orchard is one tree, and it is in rather a delapidated condition."[96]

From the peach orchard eastward, about half way to the Trostle barn, lies a large and mostly flat piece of ground, which was heavily contested by both armies in 1863. It came under the critical eye of the chaplain of the 71st New York on July 4. Writing to his sister on the following day, he framed this account: "It was the most terrible battle field I ever beheld. The stench was almost unendurable, and the dead lay everywhere. In one place more than 30 were gathered together and the look of their bloated, blackened corpses was a thing to murder sleep. I saw where two confederate officers had tried to screen themselves behind a stump, but a shell passing through had taken off both their heads."

About the time that Chaplain Twitchell was wandering about, a lieutenant of the 10th Massachusetts was also regarding the shocking sights on this segment of the field. He underscored the grisly scene: "I thought I had seen the horror of war before, but the like of this battle is seldom seen. Men, Horses,

Cannon Cassions, and all the implements of war piled up in almost inextricable confusion. Men with heads shot off, limbs shot off, Men shot in two, and men shot in pieces, and little fragments so as hardly to be recognizable as any part of a man. [W]e passed yesterday 9 dead Rebels in one heap in the road probably killed by one shell, and dead Rebels were scattered everywhere and yet the ground was dotted with single graves and pits full of them."

This officer also eyed one, "[p]oor fellow [who] lay upon the field with his entrails scattered all about by a cannon shot....[his] mother & sisters will look in vain in the far off Florida for his return....["][97]

Earlier in the chapter, a notation was made by an eyewitness that Mr. Sherfy's barn was destroyed during the fighting of July 3. A soldier in the 77th New York also passed by this burned out building on the 5th of July. He gave a much more sobering viewpoint of the damaged structure in his remembrance:

> As we passed the scene of the conflict on the left...[there] was a [nearby] scene more than usually hideous. Blackened ruins marked the spot where, on the morning of the third, stood a large barn. It had been used as a hospital. It had taken fire from the shells of the hostile batteries, and had quickly burned to the ground. Those of the wounded not able to help themselves were destroyed by the flames, which in a moment spread through the straw and dry material of the building. The crisped and blackened limbs, heads and other portions of bodies lying half consumed among the heaps of ruins and ashes, made up one of the most ghastly pictures ever witnessed, even on the field of battle.[98]

Obviously, from its condition and location, this barn attracted much attention. A member of the 15th New Jersey saw it on July 5, when he and his companion were told "that it had been full of wounded men. We could distinguish the charred remains of several, but could not tell whether these had died in the barn, before the fire, or had perished in the flames. Some bodies, with clothing partially burned, were those of Union soldiers....["][99]

One "poor fellow lay upon the field with his entrails scattered all about by a cannon shot...." (GNMP)

William T. Livermore, who was a volunteer in the 20th Maine Infantry was camped with his regiment just in rear of the "peach orchard" on July 6. In a letter to his brother on that day Livermore not only described the burned barn, but provided future historians with an 1863 look at the surrounding meadows and woods between the Trostle farm and Seminary Ridge. His letter was headed "Camp in the field near Gettysburg Penn:"

We advanced [on July 5] in line of Battle about 2/3 of the way across the field and halted exactly where a barn was burned the day before set on fire by our Artillery we saw it burn. We stacked Arms and were ordered to throw up a breast work. We went about it in good earnest took the underpinning which was 4 feet high to the old Barn stones And rails and in a few minutes had a breast work breast high where our Brigade could hold [off] a Div of any troops. But what a sene was before us or how would a man that had not been seared by the horrors of War have felt to look upon the sene. There is where the hottest of the fight took place and the Barn was fill of dead and wounded which had been sent on fire and burned and there was the skelitons of men some all burned up others half burned some with only their clothes burned off. On the same ground that our Regt occupied was where the 149th [114th] Penn Zouaves red Breeches as we call them fought. There was as many as 30 or 40 lay dead there of that Regt. They had laid there 3 days in hot July weather. And I wish I never could see another such a sight. It is nothing to see men that have just been killed. But every man was swolen as large as two men and purple & Black. After building our Breastwork we were told to go over the field and get the guns while the Pioneers & detailed men by hundreds were burying the dead. I started immediately for the Rebel line of Battle where they formed behind a fence and there was where the Rebels left their things. I followed it about half a mile and it was a solid row of Blankets knapsacks haversacks cartloads of bread some that they had stole. There was cartloads of everything that soldiers carry left & I got what things I wanted. It was some sport to overhaul there things I found in one 43 sheets of writing paper this is some of it taken from our people. I think though some was Reb as you will see hereafter I got 30 or 40 envelopes in the same, nice stockings & shirts that never was put on. I walked til I was tired and sick of the sights. To speak safely there was a thousand dead horses that were all swolen and the smell of the horses & men was dreadful. That whole field as far as we went was as I might say covered with dead of our own & Rebels where we were there were more of our men that lay there than there was of the Rebels but we know they took a great many back farther to the rear & burried them. But to our right where they advanced on our Artillery the ground was covered with them. The ground every foot of it was covered with men, horses clothing cartridge boxes canteen guns bayonets scattered cartridges cannon balls everywhere. Caisons stood where the horses were instantly killed by a cannon ball and they piled up on the pole just as they were killed in some places on the bigness of your house there would be 8 or 10 horses & from 3 to 8 men where there guns stood one place in particular where the 5th [9th] Mass Battery stood within 3 rods of a house. 19 horses lay in the bigness of your Barn yard. Some with there head others there legs & some there thighs tore away. this is a great story & I would not have believed if it I had not seen it myself. They had to leave the guns but they were not captured by the Rebs. The man that owned the house would not leave it it was riddled but I saw him when I came back. Our dead were striped of their shoes and some of other clothing we found some Rebels dead with there hands tied but did not know what it was for unless they tried to desert. one we found with a handkerchief tied over his mouth. he was wound[ed] mortaly and they did it to keep him from hollaring. After what I have written you have no idea of the sene nor I did not much til this battle. you look at it on too small a scale.[100]

"Cais[s]ons stood where the horses were instantly killed by a cannon ball...." (GNMP)

The Trostle farmhouse after the battle. William Livermore claimed that, "19 horses lay [there] in the bigness of your barn yard." (GNMP)

In 1866, Henry Boynton, formerly lieutenant colonel in the 35th Ohio Infantry made his own personal observation of the peach orchard, which stood just southeast and across the road from Sherfy's barn, and some of the surrounding land. There at the little crossroads he stood, along with a group of congressional people from Washington, and said: "The [peach] trees are still alive, though a tangled mass of dead branches still strews the ground. From this point east to Round Top, the ground had been hotly contested, and rocks and trees, and the rank green above the graves showed traces of it still."

A few of the "countless graves" seen by Henry Boynton. These stood along the road leading from the peach orchard to Little Round Top. (FL)

Boynton and his party had ridden down along the Emmitsburg Road. There, paralleling the pike, he discerned that,

> in the water washed gullies which ran beside it, were many relics of the battle. Hats, shoes, bits of harness, shreds of clothing, cartridges, cap boxes, haversacks, tin plates, battered cups, scraps of gum blankets—in short, all the rubbish of a battle was scattered everywhere in great profusion. Torn from the dead or cast aside by the living while charging, or in the retreat, they were from both armies alike. There was the slouched hat of the rebel, and the blue cap of the Union soldier....[The] fields were all waving with harvest. The grass had closed over the almost countless graves, and their mounds had melted away, or corn and the lesser grains bent above them. Still, the deep green spot in the turf, the few hills of corn more luxuriant than their neighbors, or the dark color of the oats, and the ranker growth of the wheat, told where vegetable life had drawn rich nourishment from the dead.[101]

Emmitsburg Road, Cemetery Ridge, the Leister Farm

For the present, the compass will point us northward to the upper reaches of the Emmitsburg Road above the Nicholas Codori farmhouse and fields, and to its termination at the intersection of the Taneytown Road at Cemetery Hill. From there we shall turn further to the south and out toward Cemetery Ridge and to that the portion of the slight ridge known as the "angle." This ground is just north and surrounding the "copse of trees" where Longstreet's famed assault buckled against the Federal line of battle on the afternoon of the third of July. Some of our meanderings here will also encompass the Abraham Brien farm, "Judge" David Ziegler's small woods, the Lydia Leister farm which became General George G. Meade's headquarters, and other sundry features and sites near at hand. This whole area was known to the Union army at Gettysburg as their "left center." Interestingly though, one person who was a correspondent covering a visit to the field by President Rutherford B. Hayes in May 1878 called the "angle," "the geometrical centre of the occupied land" of the Susquehanna Indian nation. While on his assignment with the chief executive he reported this piece of information to his editor in Philadelphia:

> Near where the surge of Pickett's men broke into ripples as they charged against one stone wall and one wall of fire is a hundred-ton boulder that bears the clearly marked butt, blade, and handle of a tomahawk. This carved prophecy of the Susquehannas...brought me face to face at sunrise with a ragged, raw-faced foot-pad, who bent over the [Indian] sign, was muttering: "It's so, it's so; they foresaw the great battle, a curse to the white man, to boys in blue and gray." Such a character, with elbows bent at cracking angle over Indian mystery, is not seen every day, even at Gettysburg, and I couldn't understand him until he told me that, he, once was [a soldier] with Hancock, now a tramp, had traveled miles to see the mark again and speculate, as he had often done...whether this thing in the stone did not cause the great battle of the North and the breaking of rebellion's backbone. Superstition was everywhere [as I glanced] from the man of brown rags to the purple and yellow spotted butterfly...balancing above the protruding end of a human bone.[102]

Many writers of letters, diaries, or memoirs have endeavored to picture the severe losses and the miserable appearance of the land encompassing the "angle," which was named for the 90 degree bend in the rock fence that ran below the crest of Cemetery Ridge in one of Peter Frey's farm fields. This is probably one of only two places documented by eyewitnesses at Gettysburg as having bodies literally piled up on one another. Charles Wainwright, the First Corps' chief artillery officer, explained just how rare this phenomenon actually was on a Civil War battleground. On July 4 after riding through the neighborhood of Cemetery Ridge near the "angle," he wrote in his diary:

> Outside the wall the enemy really lay in heaps; far more so at least than dead often do on the battlefield, for historians draw largely on the imagination when they talk of heaps of slain, and rivers of blood. There was about an acre or so of ground here where you could not walk without stepping over the bodies, and I saw perhaps a dozen cases where they were *heaped* one on top of the other. A captain lay thus across the body of a lieutenant-colonel. Both, especially the latter, were very handsome men. A wounded reb told me the colonel's name, but I have forgotten it....[103]

Two members of Colonel Hiram Berdan's sharpshooter regiment walked across Cemetery Ridge on the rainy morning of July 5. They encountered ambulances bringing in the Confederate wounded which literally blanketed the fields out toward the Emmitsburg Road. Passing to the right of their regimental bivouac, the two men recognized the clear and obvious use of "double shotted canister" on the attacking Southerners, which had killed several hundred Rebels who were laying "almost in piles, and most of them terribly mutilated." One of the sharpshooters suggested: "It was a gruesome sight and a sight not to be forgotten."[104]

This next piece was composed by a soldier who on July 3 had served with his regiment, the 111th New York, right along the northern end of the stone wall on Cemetery Ridge near the Brien farm. Just after the action on that

Wednesday and right about sunset, he ventured a look at the contested field in front of his unit's position, stating:

> No words can depict the ghastly picture. The track of the great charge was marked by bodies of men in all possible positions, wounded, bleeding, dying and dead. Near the line where the final struggle occurred, the men lay in heaps, the wounded wriggling and groaning under the weight of the dead among whom they were entangled. In my weak and exhausted condition I could not long endure the gory, ghastly spectacle. I found my head reeling, the tears flowing and my stomach sick at the sight. For months the spectre haunted my dreams, and even after forty seven years it comes back as the most horrible vision I have ever conceived.[105]

Less than fifty hours later Jacob Hoke, the aforementioned civilian who was traversing the battlefield, paused near the stone wall at the "angle" and there presented his version of what lay on both sides of the ridge:

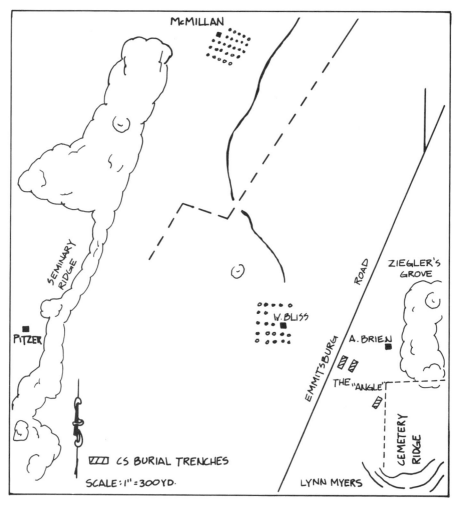

54

Emmitsburg Road looking toward Nicholas Codori's house. (GNMP)

The "angle" area, northward toward Abraham Brien's farm. (GNMP)

Cemetery Ridge near the "copse of trees" after Pickett's Charge. (EF)

Muskets were piled up along a fence like cord wood. There must have been ten thousand in one of those ranks. Dead horses lay all about the house where General Meade had his headquarters, and from that place all along down to Round Top scores of them were seen....All along the Emmittsburg road pools of blood were seen. When passing where Pickett's assaulting column crossed the road, the ground was like the floor of a slaughter house. In the low ground beyond Codori's, dead confederates yet lay unburied. One lay dead in a stable near Codori's house, and a grave was being dug for him when we passed.[106]

A Vermont staff officer named George Benedict stood directly in front of the Union position at the "copse of trees" and repeated much of the same type of description:

In the open grounds in front of our lines on the centre and left, multitudes of the dead of both armies still lay unburied, though strong burial parties had been at work for twenty-four hours. They had died from almost every conceivable form of mutilation and shot-wound. Most of them lay on their backs, with clothes commonly thrown open in front, perhaps by the man himself in his dying agony, or by some human jackal searching for money on the corpse, and breast and stomach often exposed. The faces, as a general rule, had turned black—not a purplish discoloration, such as I had imagined in reading of the "blackened corpses" so often mentioned in descriptions of battle-grounds, but a deep bluish *black*, giving to a corpse with black hair the appearance of a negro, and to one with light or red hair and whiskers a strange and revolting aspect. In the woods on our right, where the long musketry fight of Friday forenoon raged, I found the rebel dead (our own having been mostly buried) literally covering the ground. In a circle of fifty feet radius as near as I could estimate, I counted forty-seven dead rebels. The number of the enemy's dead in two acres of that oak grove, was estimated at 2,000, and I cannot say that I think it exaggerated.[107]

Near about midnight of July 3, another New Englander, Maine private John Haley, was on picket duty in that heavily contested area. He recalled this scene with obvious horror:

The dead lay everywhere, and although not a half day has passed since they died, the stench is so great that we can neither eat, drink, nor sleep. Decomposition commences as soon as life is extinct....The dead are frightfully smashed, which is not to be wondered at when we consider how they crowded up onto our guns, a mass of humanity, only to be hurled back an undistinguishable pile of mutilated flesh, rolling and writhing in death.

No tongue can depict the carnage, and I cannot make it seem real: men's heads blown off or split open; horrible gashes cut; some split from the top of the head to the extremities, as butchers split beef.[108]

It is clearly apparent and obvious from quotes such as these, that even hardened veterans were overwhelmed by the sickening and revolting aspect of what humans were capable of inflicting on one another.

Lieutenant Haskell, who had taken his own very active part in repulsing the Pickett-Pettigrew force, strode along the ridge on July 6, reflecting on the already immortalized spot.

I looked away to *the group of trees*—the Rebel gunners know what ones I mean, and so do the survivors of Pickett's division—and a strange fascination led me thither. How thick are the marks of battle as I approach—the graves of the men of the 3d division of the 2d corps; the splintered oaks, the scattered horses— seventy-one dead horses were on a spot some fifty yards square near the position of Woodruff's battery, [in Ziegler's woodlot] and where he fell.

I stood solitary upon the crest by 'the trees' where, less than three days ago, I had stood before; but now how changed is all the eye beholds. Do these thick mounds cover the fiery hearts that in the battle rage swept the crest and stormed the wall? I read their names—then, alas, I do not know—but I see the regiments marked on their frail monuments—'20th Mass. Vols.,' '69 P.V.,' '1st Minn. Vols.' and the rest....So I am not alone. These, my brethren of the fight, are with me. Sleep, noble brave...your resting place, hallowed ground.[109]

One other onlooker along that bloody ridge who is already very familiar to us, also testified as to the presence of specific graves, a knowledge of this kind is quite rare on a Civil War battlefield. Thomas Knox found traces of the ponderous artillery fire, he counted twenty-seven dead horses on a little more than one acre of ground. The trees were shattered, as he put it, "in that peculiar splintering manner that marks the course of a projectile through green wood." Nearby he particularized the presence of a large pile of muskets and cartridge boxes that had been collected from the field, adding: "My next advance to the left carries me where the ground is thickly studded with graves. In one group I count a dozen of the 20th Mass., near by those of the 137th New York [*sic*], and close at hand an equal number from the 12th New Jersey."[110]

On July 9, a few yards south of where Knox reported these identified graves, was another visitor who chronicled the neat burial mounds of several soldiers, all being plainly marked. They were Sergeant A.F. Strock, Captain Andrew McBride, and Lieutenant Sutton Jones, all of the 72nd Pennsylvania Infantry who had died within the "angle" on July 3.[111]

Thomas Knox also proclaimed the fact that breastworks of all kinds were visible all the way from the center of the U.S. line to Round Top. Stone fences were used, he observed, but there were mainly rails from wooden fences heaped up and covered with dirt, plus earth and trees simply thrown up independently or together.

James F. Clarke, unlike others roaming the battleground, seemed more taken with the personal aspect of the dead Confederates near this locality. He wrote of seeing "[i]n a field not far off...what looked like a man. I went up, and found a man, in the rebel uniform, lying on his back, his face black as coal from exposure to the sun, his hand white, and held up toward me in an attitude which seemed to say, 'Help me!'....So I walk on, looking at one and another each lying in a different attitude, each attitude seeming to show the last thought and seeking which was in the mind of the poor fellow as he died. To us these men are only rebels, but each of them had a home, mother, wife, children. They look out of their cabin-window...and say, 'When will he come back?' The little children say, 'When will papa come back? and what will he bring me?'...Poor, desolated homes, South as well as North! Long will they look, and look in vain, for the return of those dear to them as ours to us, who lie undistinguished, cumbering the bloody field."[112]

Jane Boswell Moore was a nurse voluntarily employed at the Union's Second Corps hospital. She took a few hours off from her duties on July 26 to sightsee along Cemetery Ridge and then transcribed her experiences to G.S. Griffith in Baltimore:

> In one spot on the battle-field are three or four broken down pieces of artillery, struck and disabled whilst flying across the field—the open [limber] boxes lie here half filled with the missiles of death. We counted about one hundred unexploded shells, thus arrested in the work of destruction....We walk along the low stone wall or breastworks...the hillocks of graves—[and] the little forest of headboards scattered everywhere....Oh how they must have struggled along that wall, where coats, hats, canteens and guns are so thickly strewn; beyond it two immense trenches filled with rebel dead, and surrounded with gray caps, attest the cost to them. The earth is scarcely thrown over them, and the skulls with ghastly grinning teeth appear, now that the few spadefuls of earth are washed away. In these trenches one may plainly see the rise and swell of human bodies; and oh how awful to feel that these are brethren—deluded and erring, yet brethren. Surely, no punishment can be too great for those, whose mad ambition has filled these graves![113]

On July 4, Private James Houghton, finding himself without duties to perform, secured a pass for himself and friend George Tracey, in order that they might explore the battlefield. The two comrades began on Cemetery Ridge where Houghton, using his own phonetic spelling, declared:

> We started out going over a portion of the ground where Pickets great charge terminated. in many places it was inconvenient to walk without steping in clots of Human blood. it was Rebel Blood so it did not seam so bad. we so[o]n came to [a house, possibly the Rogers' farm] it was sayed at the time that this House was the farthenist point that General Picket reached in his grate charge and that He ran into this house and sheltered Him self from the Bullets while His men went farther on towards our line. the Family had left their Home for their safety. the Doors were left wide open so we steped in....in the middle of the flore sat an old fashond X leged table and a fiew old fashioned web bottom chairs of the most anshant [ancient] life. the House was merely a board construction with a Leanto on the back side.[114]

Houghton and his comrade sharpened their axes at the house then continued on south toward the Rose farm and the "wheatfield."

Near where these Michigan privates had made their explorations along the upper Emmitsburg Road and Cemetery Ridge, Gettysburg civilian Dan Skelly, two days later, recited his impressions of the northern most section of the ridge at Ziegler's grove. Skelly revealed in his memoir how the little woods, "...showed the effects of the Confederate artillery fire. Good-sized trees were knocked off and splintered in every imaginable way. The bodies of horses that had been killed were lying about."

Skelly continued his travels about 300 yards southeast to the Lydia Leister farmstead along the Taneytown Road.

> The sight around Meade's headquarters...was terrible, indicating the exposed position it occupied, subject to every shot and shell that came over the ridge above it. Around the house and yard and below it lay at least 12 or 15 dead horses....
>
> A short distance below the house there was a stone fence dividing a field. Across this was hanging a horse which had been killed evidently just as he was

jumping the fence for its front legs were on one side and the hind legs on the other....

In the front room of the house was a bed, the covers of it thrown back, and its condition indicated that a wounded soldier had occupied it.[115]

Meade's headquarters was another common destination for numbers of tourists examining the Gettysburg landscape. The best version of it was drawn up by John Trowbridge in August 1865. After tying his horse at the gate he ventured in to meet the inhabitants. Trowbridge characterized the house as no more than a tiny square box "...having but two little rooms on the ground-floor, and I know not what narrow, low-roofed chambers above." Continuing, he narrated: "Two small girls, with brown, German faces, were paring wormy apples under the porch; and a round shouldered bareheaded, barefooted woman, also with a German face and a strong German accent, was drawing water at the well."

This kindly woman was Lydia Leister and she invited him into her "neatly scoured house," where her story unfolded. Mrs. Leister was a widow with six children, one was in the army, but she did not remember their ages. To Trowbridge, the woman conceded how she had lost "a heap" during the fight 25 months previous. The house had been robbed by the soldiers, her stock of hay was stolen, the wheat crop was trampled, an orchard was broken down and all the fences were torn up and burned. Several shells had crashed into the little abode and did severe damage. Seventeen dead horses were left on her land, five of these had been burned near a peach tree which died because of the fire. Lydia

The home of Lydia Leister used by General Meade during the battle.
(GNMP)

Leister declared that the dead horses had also spoiled her spring, but affirming that nothing much had been received from the government for the destruction. However, the bones of the horses were sold for 50 cents per hundred pounds, and all together seven hundred and fifty pounds were collected. Trowbridge concluded his visit with this remarkable thought, which could be pertinent to many of the average citizens of Adams County:

"This poor womans entire interest in the great battle was, I found, centered in her own losses. That the country lost or gained she did not know nor care, never having once thought of that side of the question."[116]

Going backward some pages, it may be recalled that Frank Stoke had written his brother an interesting and descriptive letter in the month of October. In one paragraph he described several features still prevalent on Cemetery Ridge even four months after the afternoon attack of July 3. His thoughts began by revealing that he had seen eight holes made by cannon balls through the house used as Meade's headquarters, and that eight horses still littered the yard here. Walking westward from the house and over the low ridge Stoke illustrated the following, which will be the final view in this chapter of the infamous ridge:

> At this point the Rebels fought with desperation and were slaughtered by scores, three hundred yards from our works. At this point any part of the human frame can be picked [up]....When I was last there the fields had the appearance of a vast bone yard. A few weeks ago the bodies became so decomposed that the heads would drop off the men—would drop from the slightest touch. Since then the heads have been kicked like footballs over the field. The stench here is still intolerable. But we pass on over graves and dead horses, while the ground is almost carpeted with knapsacks, haversacks, canteens, hats, caps, blankets, in fact everything that goes to make up the horrors of a battlefield. The blankets that have been left on the fields [were] used to bear off the wounded and are dotted with blood. Many of the hats and caps are besmeared with brains.[117]

From the Taneytown Road through Gettysburg

Our next concentration of aftermath descriptions will come from the northern base of Cemetery Hill near the junction of the Taneytown and Emmitsburg Roads, then up to where the Emmitsburg Road meets the Baltimore Turnpike, and on into the village of Gettysburg itself.

Just below Cemetery Hill on its northwest side and along the upper Emmitsburg Road ran a stone wall during the battle, and afterwards the remains of the fierce struggle could still be encountered there. Thomas Knox saw barricades and other evidences still in place on July 6 and he explained:

> A portion of our sharpshooters took position behind this wall and erected traverses to protect them[selves] from a flanking fire should the enemy attempt to move up the road from Gettysburg. These traverses are constructed at right angles to the wall, by making a 'crib' of fence rails, two feet high and the same distance apart, and then filling it up with dirt. Farther along on the road I find the rails from the western side of the road piled against the fence on the east

so as to form a breastwork two or three feet in height....This defense was thrown up by the rebels at the time they were holding the line of the roads.

Just behind the aforementioned stone wall was a natural and gradual sloping upward of the land toward the crest of Cemetery Hill. Upon this north side of the hill a field of wheat and another of corn had been planted before the battle. However, three days after the contest Knox disclosed that,

the wheat was fearfully trampled by the hurrying feet of the dense masses of infantry, as they changed their positions during the battle. In the corn field artillery had been stationed....Hardly a hill of corn is left in its pristine luxuriance. The little that escaped the hoof or the wheel, as the guns moved from place to place, has since been nibbled off by the hungry horses...not a stalk of wheat is upright; not a blade of corn remains uninjured: all has fallen long before the time of harvest. Another harvest in which death was the reaper, has been gathered above it.[118]

Much later, Henry Boynton, while inspecting the Emmitsburg Road as it entered the town, remarked that,

the marks of the fight are seen along the main street through which the 11th Corps fell back on the first day. Hanging signs are shot through, one scarcely larger than a foolscap page having the marks of four shot from a musket and one from a pistol, all showing that the balls were fired toward the enemy. Window shutters were riddled, and in such a way as to show that they were half opened, and the brick walls of the dwellings in various directions were spotted with the blue of lead. Rising toward Cemetery Hill these marks became more frequent, and one little two story house had over a hundred shot marks in its front, although it was sheltered from all but the random fire. Along the road the fences had been repaired, or built anew....Whenever the old lumber was used it showed its honorable scars.[119]

In keeping with Knox's account is this short missive drawn from the memoir of Lieutenant Samuel Boone of the 88th Pennsylvania, who saw, "a business sign across the pavement [on Baltimore Street] had 15 bullet holes in it."[120]

A different traveller approaching the borough from the south portrayed some of the same carnage as seen by Colonel Boynton above, but this man John Linn, encountered it much sooner after the battle on July 7. Venturing into the southern end of Gettysburg he first espied some standard military debris and pocketed a few relics including a small amount of Confederate money, a cartridge and a box of cannon fuzes made in Richmond,

"Window shutters were riddled..." *(GAC)*

Virginia. Linn next approached the grave of a soldier who supposedly had been a member of the 2nd Louisiana Infantry. Above the grave on an oak tree was carved "W.P.D." In the adjacent woods he discovered a concealed Rebel cannon carriage. Nearby were some dead horses, and Linn inscribed in his diary that, "the stench was horrid." Inside the town itself, and behind the Reformed Church he noticed the fences were, "perforated with balls." Linn specified, too, that within the village the smell of putrefied blood was "very disagreeable."[121]

Leonard Gardner rode down from Cemetery Hill onto Baltimore Street early on Sunday, July 5. He may have been one of the first civilian nonresidents to view the tattered borough after the battle. Between the dominating hill and Breckenridge Street, "the dead lay unburied and the ground was strewn with abandoned muskets, knapsacks, canteens and other accoutrements of war. The houses were marked with shot and shell on both sides of the street. Some with ugly gaps in the wall and others with a well defined hole where the cannon ball entered. A frame building particularly attracted my attention. It stood in a position facing the Union front and the weather boarding from the top to within a few feet of the ground was literally honey-combed with the Minie balls. No boards were torn or displaced but thousands of neat round holes marked the places where the balls entered."

At Breckenridge Street a barricade had been thrown up across the street. Passing through an opening in it Gardner continued up Baltimore Street where

A piece of Confederate money, a cartridge, and a fuse box accompany the original journal of J.B. Linn. (CCLHM/SCH)

A fence near Baltimore Street shows "its honorable scars." (GNMP)

(Above) The Jacob Stock House. "...[O]ne little two story house had over a hundred shot marks in its front...." (SCH)

(Left) Artillery shells made "ugly gaps in the walls." Some were simply repaired, others were later enshrined. (SCH)

he beheld "[a] scene of desolation and death...presented all the way. The unburied dead and the mangled remains of human bodies, mingled with the debris of broken gun carriages, muskets, bayonets, and swords, which lay around in confusion on that lonely street in the quiet Sabbath morning, was one of those pictures of desolation which will never fade from my mind."[122]

An occupant of the town during the Confederate occupation from July 1 through the fourth was Liberty Hollinger, her house sat on York Street, east of the square. The memoir she wrote illuminated that many once orderly houses were left in confusion by the Rebels. "[B]eds had been occupied, bureaus ransacked and [the] contents scattered over the house. The larders had been searched for eatables and nothing remained that the soldiers could find use for."[123]

The wanton looting and vandalism inflicted upon the town was also illustrated by a Gettysburg male, Albertus McCreary. He confessed that after the conflict there were some "sorry-looking homes in our neighborhood." In a friend's house everything had been cut to pieces or destroyed in some way. "Pieces of furniture were burned and broken, a desk had been destroyed, bookcases knocked down, and the books torn and shattered. To add more to the disorder and destruction, the soldiers had taken a half-barrel of flour, mixed it with water to make a thin paste, put into this the feathers from feather-beds, and thrown it over everything—walls, furniture, and down the stairways."

Alongside one of the village houses he found two dead Confederates, and inside the house were two more, one was lying on a bed, the other on the floor. Commenting on the many other bodies present, McCreary underscored that the stench was so bad that every one, "went about with a bottle of pennyroyal or peppermint oil."[124]

An unknown reporter, quoted in the Lancaster *Daily Express* for July 10, 1863, described the damage to the borough in detail:

> The people of Gettysburg probably suffered more from the rapacity of the rebels than those of any other town in Pennsylvania. A week's occupation gave the scoundrels ample time to exercise their pilfering propensities. Stores were ransacked and emptied of their contents, but in many, such articles as could not be used, were destroyed, and the buildings abused and defiled. Dwellings too were entered, and where men's clothing could not be procured, that of women and children was taken into the streets and roads, torn into fragments and cast aside. The houses of some of the professors in the educational institutions hereabouts shared the same fate; and from one store here even the clocks were taken out and destroyed. Everything eatable and drinkable was secured by the rebels, and such was their unlimited stealing that they did not even extend the courtesy of offering Southern shinplasters....

Entering the borough from the York Turnpike onto York Street on July 8, William Helffrich, one of the many rambling preachers in the area, perceived that the "whole thing was a melancholy sight....The town was wrecked; the windows and doors of the houses were smashed, brick walls had been pierced by cannon-balls—through one wall and out the other...."

All around were examples and evidences of the strife, especially abundant numbers of Rebel corpses beginning to quickly putrefy. Helffrich saw thousands of stacked rifles, too, but one particular facet caught his eye the most. He embodied that fascination into these words:

"The dead horses were all still unburied. They were starting to become bloated and thereby all assumed the same position. As they swelled up, the uppermost hind leg lifted into the air. This happened in every case, and all those legs sticking-up in the air gave the battlefield an incredible aspect."[125]

Similarly are the observations of a special correspondent for the Philadelphia *Public Ledger*. This reporter arrived on July 5 from the east, also along the York Turnpike.

> As we neared the town, we saw the fences down, and easily traced the tracks of battle through the grain fields, while on the roadside and on the fields could be seen quantities of dead horses, the decaying bodies of which filled the air with a sickening stench. Not a live thing could be seen as far as the eye could reach, save a long cortege, which seemed creeping along on the hillside to our right. The charred remains of a railroad bridge, destroyed telegraph poles, blackened masses of railroad cars lying to the right of the road, while on both its sides the homes of the poor which dot the entrance to nearly all large cities, I found to be closed, or a door, shutter or part of the fence carried to the adjacent field to form shelters for the sharpshooters from the bullets of the foe.[126]

In the early morning hours of Tuesday, July 7, Jacob Hoke meandered his way through Gettysburg. Throughout the battered town he passed the sleeping bodies of teamsters and ambulance drivers who were overcome with exhaustion. At the railroad depot on Carlisle Street, three or four disabled parked cannons caught his eye, one having been hit square in the muzzle by a solid shot. Makeshift hospitals were everywhere, but he took time to visit only one, at the county courthouse. Oddly, Hoke made no mention of any particular physical damage to the borough.

This cannon or a similar one caught the attention of Jacob Hoke. (TL)

In much the same vein, were the observations of James Clarke, who between July 4 and July 6 had traveled from Boston to Gettysburg to search for a friend who was wounded in the battle, Lieutenant Colonel H.S. Huidekoper of the 150th Pennsylvania. Arriving on the sixth, Clarke remembered Gettysburg to be a small place but with everything in utter confusion. His feelings were that the village "had not suffered severly from the thousands of shell and shot which had been fired directly over it from the [over six] hundred cannon in position." But Clarke did show amazement at the huge number of wounded which thronged the public buildings and even some private dwellings.[127]

The town had indeed been very fortunate. In a local newspaper printed on July 20, a report surfaced that the heaviest losses in the county were those who lost houses or barns or both by fire, "including [t]he house and barn of William Bliss, all their contents, the house and barn occupied by Mr. Comfort, (the old McClean property) the house and barn of Alexander Currens; the barns of Messors. John Herbst, Henry Spangler, (formerly Amos Plank's) Alexander Cobean, and Joseph Sherfy; in the barn of the latter and around the hay stacks were about twenty wounded Philadelphia Zouaves, [the 114th Pennsylvania Infantry] who perished in the conflagration. The sufferers have our warmest sympathies."[128]

The *Star and Banner* of July 2 pronounced one other building burned by the Southerners on June 26, when they passed through the village several days prior to the battle. It was the warehouse of Daniel Gulden located six miles east of town. The structure had contained 2,000 bushels of wheat, 3,000 bushels of oats and other articles and groceries. The loss was estimated at $5,000.

In his memory of those days, William McClean, an attorney who lived on East Middle Street next to the church, mostly recollected the smell. He noted that there were so many dead, "it was found very difficult to dispose of them, and there were not crows or buzzards enough to act as their executors. Consequently they rotted where they lay, and the atmosphere was, as a result, vitiated and corrupted. When you would open the windows for the morning air, you would be assailed by the foul odors which arose all over the field. We citizens became gradually acclimated to it, but some visitors coming from a pure atmosphere into this were poisoned, and went home and died."[129]

Matilda J. Pierce, also known as "Tillie," was a 15-year-old youngster who lived on Baltimore Street in 1863. She specified that her house was occupied by Rebel sharpshooters, and the brick structure was hit many times, including seventeen bullet holes on the upper balcony, one other hole through a pane of glass, while the back porch, fences, and such were similarly riddled. Her cellar and the houses around her family's property were severely ransacked by the Confederates.[130]

On looking back, Mary Horner of Chambersburg Street was reminded of the terrible plague of flies, and the curious fact whereby "not a song of a bird met our ears for weeks after the battle."[131] A neighbor of Mrs. Horner's voiced that, "when the wind blew from the south and west in the evenings, the stench was so overpowering that for a number of evenings all windows had to be closed." This last quoted female was Jenny Eyster Jacobs, who blamed the repulsive and sickening odors for the death of Charles A. Baer of Norristown,

Pennsylvania. He was a friend, and similar to many other visitors not acclimated to the odors, Baer was stricken ill on his return home, according to Jacobs, brought on by the putrid atmosphere. Like Horner, she also remarked on the scarcity of birds in the area.[132] A woman who did not live too far from Mary Horner complained to a friend in a letter on July 22: "I wish you could be here now, 'tis not the same quiet old place it was when you were here. The streets are always full of strangers, soldiers, ambulances and government wagons."[133]

Sarah King must have been an unusual case. She did not have the need to harbor any serious complaints about what she found when returning home on July 4, after having fled the town when the Confederates approached. While she was absent, the Rebel invaders had kindly taken care of her aged father when he became ill. She also could discover very little touched in her residence. King explained: "My room seemed to be as I left it with the exception of a little pile of gray rags. I didn't pay much attention to it at first it was so small. My curiosity was at length aroused. I could not imagine what I had left lying on the floor. I discovered it was the remnant of pants and a hat. Then I looked in a trunk where my husband kept his clothing and a fine blue suit, a Xmas gift, was missing and I suppose these gray rags were left in exchange. I gathered them up on a stick and threw them out in the street."[134]

Alice Powers brought up an important factor not normally considered by storytellers in those days. She saw fences destroyed in the town limits, and arms and household goods scattered everywhere, and dead horses and men lay thick in the streets and on the sidewalks, but what concerned her the most was "the well made gardens [had been] trampled in the stampede of retreat," on July 1. Powers concluded by exclaiming: "No wonder hands were wrung and tears flowed at the dismal sight for many depended on these large gardens for a living."[135]

Gettysburg photographer Charles Tyson, like Sarah King, had abandoned his house for safety on July 1. On July 3, he was informed by a friend that his place was now "gutted." Anxiously returning on July 5 to his house and studio along York Street he was surprised to find "...nothing wantonly destroyed. My secretary was ransacked and the contents scattered over the room. In the parlor we found a small heap of ashes, the residue of burned papers and letters....Upon removing the ashes we found the carpet uninjured....We found several bundles put up ready to be carried off, but which were left behind. All my clothing was taken and several rebel suits left in [their] place....with this exception, we missed very little, indeed, outside of the cellar and pantry, which was pretty well cleaned up."

Photographer Charles Tyson found "nothing wantonly destroyed" by the Southern army. (HCAC)

Tyson's photographic gallery itself was generally undisturbed, as we have just learned, but a shell was embedded below a front windowsill, and a bullet had broken two windows. The Rebels had also emptied a barrel containing a solution of 95% alcohol, using 8 oz. bottles on the premises to carry it away.[136]

Two weeks after the Confederates evacuated Gettysburg, residents and visitors alike were still imbued with remnants of the fighting that had occurred in the streets on July 1. One was Emily B. Souder, a nurse who had recently arrived in town. She was surprised to encounter on Chambersburg Street, "wrecked caissons and wagon-wheels." There were also, "broken windows, the mark of bullets and cannon-balls, the scattered and battered stone walls, the carcasses of dead horses steaming in the sun...all tell of what has been so recently the battle-ground." Souder concluded with these remarks:

"The atmosphere is truly horrible, and camphor and cologne or smelling salts are prime necessaries for most persons...."[137]

◆ ◆ ◆

Herbst's Woods to Blocher's Hill

It was a natural thing in 1863 and afterward for the battlefield tourist to travel from the streets of Gettysburg on farther out into the farmland north-west, north or northeast and through the fields and woods of the First Day's battleground.

Now, in the preceding part of this chapter, we have concentrated our observations on many and various parts of the field, most of which are now incorporated into the national military park. These places were usually south and east of the village, such as Cemetery Hill, Culp's Hill, Little Round Top, Devil's Den, the farms encompassing the "peach orchard" and the "wheatfield," the fields along the Emmitsburg Road, and so forth. Following, through the eyes of those who ventured long before us, our tour continues across Seminary Ridge and Oak Ridge, also to Pennsylvania College and the Lutheran Semi-nary, and Edward McPherson's old farm, John Herbst's woods or the "Railroad woods" as it was called in 1863, plus the incompleted railroad bed paralleling the pike, Oak Hill, and Moses McClean's farm, and more places north of the Gettysburg borough, including the Almshouse, Blocher's Hill and the environs of Rock Creek.

The battle began a few miles northwest of Gettysburg on the east side of Marsh Creek early on July 1, 1863. By six o'clock in the evening of that same day, it was winding down across the crowded streets and alleys of the borough and out toward Cemetery Hill, where we began this aftermath pilgrimage many pages ago. Ironically, some people even today do not realize how vicious and hard-fought the battle of July 1 really was. Then, as now, many saw it as merely a prelude to the "real" fighting of July 2 and 3. While in actuality, July 1 was a "bloodier" day than July 3 and was quite close in casualty figures to July 2, even with fewer numbers of men engaged in combat on that first day.

Ruefully, this information does not alter the fact that if we include a cross section of the early sightseers to Gettysburg, it is believed that a somewhat smaller portion took the time to experience and describe the July 1 ground.

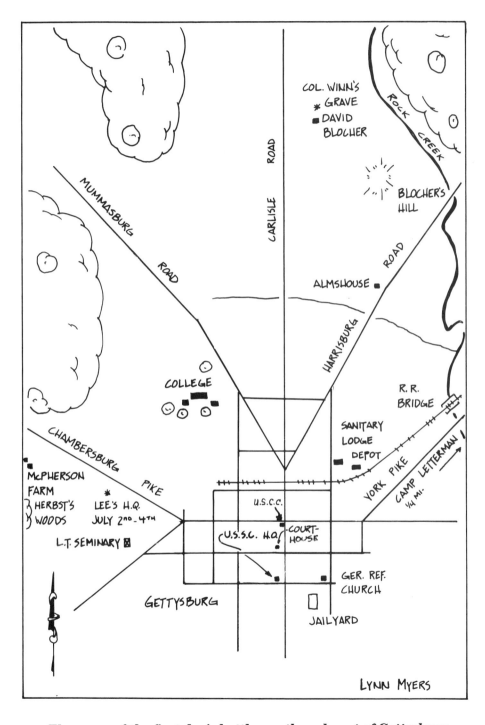

The scene of the first day's battle, north and west of Gettysburg.

Nonetheless, there remains for us several good accounts alluding to that section of the field. These will be examined next.

With the battle only one-third completed between the two armies in the early evening of Wednesday, July 1, one soldier was already presented with many sad, melancholy and hideous sights on that part of the battlefield.

Private Joel A. Walker, 45th Georgia was ordered to proceed to the land around the Edward McPherson farm late on July 1 with a platoon of men detailed as a burial squad. One of the first corpses stumbled upon was in Herbst's woods south of the McPherson's farm buildings. It was that of a man aged about 30, who had apparently torn up the letters and photograph of his betrothed, a young woman from South Carolina. Walker suggested that the soldier had not died suddenly, but had methodically destroyed the precious remembrances of his love before his death to prevent them from becoming curiosities to some uncaring ghoul.

Lying near the South Carolinian was a "little boy" as Walker described him, "...dressed in the full uniform of a Cavalryman, and as he lay he was a dethroned statue of Apollo. Beautiful as a young god, with a face white and clear as a girl's, his right hand resting peacefully across his breast and his left holding his cap. I found nothing to indicate his name....He was not over fifteen years old and had evidently died as he fell."

After burying this teenager, which was a rare sight indeed, especially when the average age of a soldier at Gettysburg was 24 to 25 years old, Walker came

The Edward McPherson farm as it must have appeared to Private Walker and others in 1863. (GNMP)

to another corpse which presented a somewhat unusual sight. "[A] white hankerchief [was] suspended over the face of a dead man. We approached to find that in the hour of his death some kind friend had fastened this hankerchief to a few straws, which kept the sun from burning his face, and his death had been so calmly [*sic*] he had not broken down the frail canopy. He was from Charleston, S.C., and bore the rank of captain, but his name was nowhere to be found."

Seventeen years later in the year 1880, veteran Joel Walker made a return visit to Gettysburg, this time as a civilian. Walking out to McPherson's Ridge, which was no longer owned by that family, he was able to locate the same grave, now empty, that he had dug so long before for a group of seven dead Union cavalrymen, including the fifteen year old noted above. He could easily make out the sunken depression in the ground. Ex-Rebel Walker sat there for a while and contemplated the tragic events and vivid pictures remaining in his brain from that bloody day so long before.

One of his thoughts of that time in 1863 involved an "orphan." After completing their duties at midnight, Walker's men lay down to rest in McPherson's farmyard. He declared that sometime after he fell asleep a confused and hungry calf ambled by, its mother having been killed during the day by a stray bullet. Walker recalled how the calf, "evidently a pet of the household...[had] wandered about during the whole of the night, bleating and moaning piteously for its dam. There was not a sound on the earth except the weary stepping of its tired limbs, and when it came over to where I was lying and touched its cold nose to my hand I felt that it was indeed a cruel fate....It fell to the lot of a little calf to speak more eloquently than all the rest of war's sacrifices."[138]

Another Confederate soldier named Berkeley was likewise engaged on a pioneer detail only this duty was the breaking down of fences for the easy movement of artillery. He was working first along Oak Ridge and then at the Pennsylvania College campus a few hours after Walker dozed off near the lonely calf. Berkeley related this story in a personal diary:

> This morning on getting up I saw a sight which was perfectly sickening and heart-rending in the extreme. It would have satiated the most blood-thirsty and cruel man on God's earth. There were [with]in a few feet of us, by actual count, seventy-nine (79) North Carolinians lying dead in a straight line. I stood on their right and looked down their line. It was perfectly dressed. Three had fallen to the front, the rest had fallen backward; yet the feet of all these dead men were in a perfectly straight line. Great God! When will this horrid war stop?

Subsequent to the above scene depicted on the John Forney farm west of Oak Ridge, but this time on the college grounds, the same artilleryman saw "the body of a yankee, which had been cut in two. The head, arms and about one-half of his ribs had been thrown against a fence, and the remainder with his heart and entrails was sticking to the top rail, while some 10 feet off the lower part of the body had been thrown into a mud hole in the road."[139]

On July 4 and three days after the above-quoted Confederates had retreated with their comrades from Seminary and Oak Ridges, William

The John Forney farm west of Oak Ridge where a soldier saw 79 North Carolinians lying dead in a perfect line. (GNMP)

Gettysburg from Oak Ridge, looking across the town, college, and some of the first day's battlefield toward Culp's Hill. (GNMP)

McClean, a Gettysburg attorney, walked out to the McPherson farm (then rented by John Slentz) to assist any wounded who remained there. On his way along the Chambersburg Pike, McClean could hear distant artillery firing. Once out of town, he passed "parties engaged in burying the dead in the fields where they fell. One, [a] dead soldier in blue was lying along the side of the turnpike, black and swollen from the heat and rain, disfigured beyond recognition."[140]

Entering McPherson's conspicuous stone and wood barn, McClean went to work assisting the many injured men who had not seen a friendly face since being wounded several days before.

About a mile or so beyond where McClean struggled to care for the wounded, a black woman discovered near Herr's ridge that several bodies had been dumped in the well of one of the local farmhouses as a quick and easy way of burying some of the dead. She later explained that the water in a nearby well had begun to make people ill. When it was cleaned out, the workers found it contained pieces of human bodies, such as a piece of wrist and a thumb, that may have been amputated at one of the field hospitals.[141]

J. Howard Wert went over these same ridges and farms on July 5. He revealed that the dead there were very much decomposed, as they were among the first to be slain.

> All that could be done was to throw some earth over the corpses where they had fallen. Often a very few inches of earth was the only covering, through which portions of the body and clothing were visible after the first heavy rain. Oh! the ghastly horrors of those sickening burials of valiant men. Here, and here, and here, and there, and everywhere, at the head of the rude mounds was a piece of a cracker box—and on it in lead pencil; "Unknown—14th of Brooklyn," or "Unknown—95th N.Y.," or as you moved from the pike into the grove, "Unknown—24th Michigan."

Wert not only denoted the Union dead, but said that mixed and mingled with the Northerners were also many corpses still dressed in gray. Returning to Wert's memoir:

> As you crossed Willoughby's run and proceeded toward Marsh Creek, they [the Confederates] were more numerous, many having after the battle of the 1st, been removed to the rear; and dying there. Nearly all were most scantily buried, if you may dignify the few shovels-full of earth thrown over them with the term burial. In some cases where numbers were thus slightly interred, swine were found revelling in the remains in a manner horrible to contemplate.[142]

Just about the time John Wert was contemplating the dreadful mutilations on McPherson's ridge, a Confederate officer witnessed a similar scene near the Harrisburg Pike, which was clear to the east across the Union battle line of July 1 and near a small knoll called Blocher's Hill. He noted that it had been more than three days since the fighting, and the "pioneer corps and burying parties had not been able to complete their work...."

This officer was Robert Stiles and he and his men were forced to endure a revolting few hours in an uncomfortable spot while readjusting and straightening their battle lines. Here, in one of the most graphic depictions written after the battle, he explains:

> The sights and smells that assailed us were simply indescribable—corpses swollen to twice their original size, some of them actually burst asunder with the pressure of foul gasses and vapors. I recall one feature never before noted, the shocking distension and protrusion of the eyeballs of dead men and dead horses. Several human or unhuman corpses sat upright against a fence, with arms extended in the air and faces hideous with something very like a fixed leer, as if taking a fiendish pleasure in showing us what we essentially were and might at any moment become. The odors were nauseating, and so deadly that in a short time we all sickened and were lying with our mouths close to the ground, most of us vomiting profusely....

...[L]ate into the night the fearful odors I had inhaled remained with me and made me loathe myself as if an already rotting corpse.[143]

Not quite so forceful was a remembrance by Leonard Gardner, the temporary civilian Union scout who passed through Gettysburg on July 5. As he rode along the Chambersburg Pike he saw "many little hillocks" where the dead had been hastily interred. Halting at the Theological Seminary he learned that all of the rooms were filled with wounded, and at McPherson's farm more graves were scattered in every direction. From a pigsty nearby, Gardner heard a voice begging for help. So for the next day or so he assisted many injured and dying men, and often held their crushed limbs still while the army surgeons performed amputations. He declared that he felt no nausea from the offensive smell or the ghastly sight of the bloody appendages that collected on the earth at his side.

The following day was spent at the college where Gardner explained how all of the buildings had been turned into hospitals. Every room there was crowded with Confederates whom he said were "suffering from every form of injury, [and] wore a sad and dejected appearance."[144]

This same day and in a general location near John Herbst's woods, a woman named Elizabeth Beller as she was leaving Gettysburg, noticed that "one lone sexton had been hiding [burying] the black and swollen bodies as rapidly as he could, and yet dozens of them were still resting there. The postures in which they lay seemed to tell pathetic stories. One was lying with his arm under his head; another leaning over the neck of his dead horse, his right hand thrown caressingly around it, his hand resting on its head. At another place they seemed to be lying in a group, as though they had drawn near to each other for companionship. No face among them was recognizable, as these men had been among the first that were killed, and of course those nearest the town had been buried first."

The Chambersburg Pike looking west, with the Lutheran Theological Seminary visible on the ridge to the left. (GNMP)

While exploring the land on which the sexton diligently worked, Beller watched the approach of a man all alone. He seemed kindly, and so much different from most of the ill-tempered and selfish visitors she had encountered while in Gettysburg. Continuing, her narrative, Beller presents us with a strange conversation:

"This man of whom I speak, a gentleman, delicate and refined in appearance, walked thoughtfully around among the dead, and the sexton said to him: 'Are you looking for any one in particular, sir?' 'No,' said he, 'thank God, no, but get me a spade, my friend, and I will help you with this work it is awful and shameful, no one to even cover these boys of ours with leaves; the very birds would do that much for them, if I left them so.'"[145]

Just to the east of the scene just depicted stood the Seminary, and on July 10 an unidentified person walking along the ridge, contemplated the Rebel rifle pits which had been constructed there, plus the battered and perforated walls of the brick seminary structures, and the graves of five Pennsylvanians in the south yard of the main edifice, each marked with a neat headboard. This unknown person described these burial mounds as containing the bodies of Colonel R.P. Cummings, Lieutenant A.G. Tucker, and James Hill of the 142nd Regiment. Everywhere, he reported, dead Rebels were buried, their graves intertwined with heaps of battered muskets, knapsacks, cartridge boxes, blankets, and every article of clothing employed by soldiers in the field.[146]

While travelling in from the west along the Chambersburg Pike during the evening of July 6, Jacob Hoke crossed slowly over the barrier of the South Mountains. There on the summit he first observed signs of military occupation in the form of a line of breastworks thrown up on both sides of the road. Entering Cashtown there were evidences of many large army encampments, and the accompanying broken fences, slaughtered cattle, and other discarded martial debris. At Marsh Creek, which was just a few miles west of Gettysburg, Hoke took notice of a large number of hospital tents containing wounded Southern soldiers abandoned by Lee's army. Hoke pointed out that along the way, every house and barn and outbuilding had been improvised into temporary field hospitals. He testified:

> Men wounded and maimed in almost every conceivable way lay along the roadside, in yards and gardens. Some were propped against the houses, or supported against the backs of chairs with an arm or leg off and some having lost both arms.
>
> Dead horses lay along the road, and the people in some instances, were piling wood upon and burning them. In the fields west of Seminary Ridge...hundreds and even thousands of empty boxes were strewn. The contents of these boxes, in the shape of shot and shell, had been hurled against the gallant defenders of the Union, and sent hundreds into eternity and crippled and maimed others for life. Along the crest of Seminary Ridge, breastworks were thrown up, and from that place to the town, dead Union soldiers were seen partially covered with earth. Several had been put into the gullies made by water along the roadside, and their toes, hands, noses and, in some cases, their faces protruded from their slight covering of earth scraped from the pike. New made graves were in the fields on both sides of the road.[147]

"Dead horses lay along the road, and the people in some instances, were piling wood upon and burning them." *(FL)*

Immediately after the fighting had concluded, Jenny E. Jacobs toured the First Day's arena. Many years afterward, these indelible visions remained fresh in her mind:

"The Union dead on the field...were covered with only a few inches of soil. Portions of the body protruded, as the rain washed away the soil....Some of the books in the College Library were soaked with blood, as the wounded had used them to support their heads. Medical students I found on the field preparing skeletons, and in a cauldron [they were] boiling the remains of heroes."[148]

This last sentence may seem farfetched, but, in fact, New York relief agent, Dr. Theodore Dimon, in his official report of medical activities at Gettysburg succeeding the battle, confirmed that scientists were indeed gathering bones to be placed in the Army's new Medical Museum in Washington, D.C. Furthermore, a U.S. medical doctor had actually been ordered to Gettysburg to collect human specimens for this museum. This physician was Dr. John H. Brinton, a Union surgeon and major, who was in charge of setting up the museum itself. From Washington, D.C. on August 15, 1863, after his initial expedition to Gettysburg, Dr. Brinton explained in a letter to Dr. Henry Janes, who was in Gettysburg: "With regard to specimens—I sent you some liquor [to ship bones in]; if you want more write me. I had a letter a day or two ago from Dr. [Frederick] Neff, saying that he had buried a barrel of specimens. Now that is hardly the idea. I wrote to him to send it on Adams Express. Will you please direct that as a barrel or keg full [of bones] is collected that it be capped up & forwarded to [me]."[149]

One other interesting version of this situation was given by Marylander Frank Stoke. He portrayed in October what Brinton was trying to *undo* in August, saying that the "amputated limbs [of the wounded] are put into barrels and buried and left in the ground until they are decomposed, then lifted and sent to the Medical College at Washington."[150]

Ambrose Emory was present on August 24, 1863, in the localities where the First Corps had engaged General Hill's forces on July 1. He searched the woodlot owned by John Herbst which was a stone's throw from McPherson's

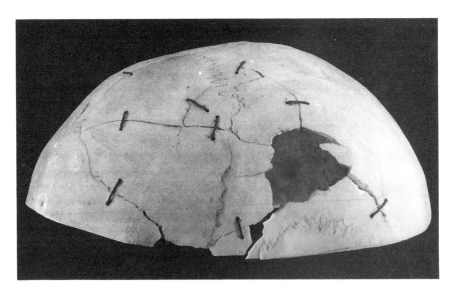

This U.S. Army museum specimen is a segment of cranium pierced by a musket ball at Gettysburg. The soldier was Private Phillip Pindell, 1st Maryland Battalion, C.S.A. He died on August 21, 1863. (OHA/RK)

farmbuildings. Here, Emory aired, "in this woods are the graves of many Federal soldiers. I noticed that most of them were Michiganders. I came across the graves of two Confederate soldiers buried together. They were L. Williams and M. Littrell of the 47 Va. Regiment. On this field I picked up a bayonet, brass epaulett, and one or two other little mementoes."

The next day was Tuesday the 25th and early on that morning Emory walked out to Oak Hill west of the college grounds,

> where the Confederates had their batteries planted in the first days of the fight here I picked up a 12 inch solid shot and a piece of shell and some cotton near where their battery was located, and a testament with the name of 'R.W. Davis, Virginia' written on the Fly leaf. Coming down this side of the hill I crossed over several fields where were buried Federals and Confederates....I picked up some twenty minnie balls, which had been dropped from some soldier's cartridge box. This battlefield, I should suppose, would traverse a space around in circumference at least 15 or 20 miles and you cannot pass over any portion of the ground but that you will come across the graves of the fallen.[151]

Much later in the month of October 1864, Isaac Moorhead could still find many traces and evidences of a battle. Walking along the Chambersburg Pike, he paused near "rebel lines where they crossed the road and turned to the left. Here again, through the fields and the woods, was all the debris of an army. I noticed that the shoes were mostly small sized and 'English make,' showing they had run the blockade.

"The lines were perfect, made of stone, and in absence of stone, rails covered with earth."[152]

Although we are not yet at the end of our story of the experiences and sights of eyewitnesses to the "Aftermath at Gettysburg," the general reader has probably concluded that one could soon have their fill of the many horrors which were visible on all parts of that blood-drenched field. And all may wonder, why did people come to view these spectacularly grisly scenes? For some, we believe, it was obviously a chance to see what would probably never be seen again on the American continent. In the nineteenth century, life had become fairly constant and predictable, and even dull in the larger cities. Therefore, average citizens who were simply small farmers in rural areas, would often go to great lengths and even expense to view unusual happenings or events. Everyone who visited such a distressing place as the recent battlefield at Gettysburg had their own reasons for coming. Some, as previously mentioned, came out of a morbid fascination or curiosity; others to search for a loved one or friend slain in battle or wounded in action, and who could still be lying helpless in a field hospital or even on the battleground itself. To help in answering the puzzling question, several commentators have left us with their impressions as to why the public at large was motivated to journey to such an unlikely and unpleasant region.

Michael Jacobs, a Gettysburg college professor, believed in reverse that it would have "indeed been well if the whole land had come, and had had their patriotism...rekindled anew at the sight of these blood-stained fields, those fresh made graves, and the mangled limbs and bodies of their fellow-citizens. Then [they] would have...more fully appreciated the unspeakable sacrifice at which the honor of the country and the safety of our homes and families have been purchased."

Jacobs went on to pronounce that these visitors were "drawn hither by an intense desire of assuring themselves, by the evidence of sense, of the certainty and the magnitude of the victory that had been achieved on that great field. By some this has been called an idle curiosity; but it surely deserves a better name. In a majority of instances...it was dictated by a laudable, a patriotic interest in the country's rejoicings. It was an impulsive outburst of almost irrepressible joy."[153]

Possibly so. But another man who was there made his comments with more cynicism: "Yet many look upon it [the battlefield] without emotion. Many walked about amid the horrid stench of the field unmoved. They turned over the rubbish, picked up bullets and fragments or shells for mementoes, but that was all —. They looked upon the dead, to be sure; but with no expression of pity if he were a federal soldier, and only a laugh or a curse if he were a Confederate."[154]

These last observations concerning early visitors were much more prevalent than Professor Jacobs' kindly thoughts just read. For instance, the provost marshal general of Meade's army merely stated: "[I] am thoroughly disgusted with the whole Copperhead fraternity of Gettysburg & the country about, as they came in Swarms to sweep & plunder the battle grounds...."[155]

One other infantryman, equally as sarcastic, summarized it like this:

No soldier was to be seen, but numbers of civilians and boys, and some girls even, were curiously loitering about the field, and their faces showed not sadness or horror, but only staring wonder or smirking curiosity. They looked for mementoes of the battle to keep, they said; but their furtive attempts to conceal an uninjured musket or an untorn blanket—they had been told that all property left here belonged to the Government—showed that the love of gain was an ingredient at least of their motive for coming here.[156]

In concluding this chapter we shall once again leave in our thoughts a short expression of what a recent battlefield was truly like. The next people quoted will have given us in a sentence or two the most overall unappealing aspect of such a spot. Our first illustration was written by correspondent Cooke. He remembered especially that, "the ground was trampled into a bog, and was covered with every conceivable thing....everything used in war or by soldiers, was scattered around in plenty. The grain and grass which once grew there, was almost ground to a jelly."

One soldier of the 27th Indiana recalled almost identically this feeling of utter desolation. Besides the terribly mutilated and disfigured bodies "now swollen and decomposed,—their lips as thick as one's hand, their eyes wide open with glossy, glaring eyeballs, unspeakably hideous and revolting..." there was something even more inhuman, more unsettling. He underscored that this particular aspect of war was not often thought of. It was, "that the surface of the ground, besides being everywhere gashed, seamed and trampled, is blackened, greased and besmirched, until one cannot think of remaining upon it or near it." The man concluded by asserting: "May God spare me from ever witnessing another such a scene I will never again go over a battle-field from mere curiosity, before the dead are buried."[157]

In summation, these witnesses believed that the appalling *filth* of the field of battle was the worst thing about it. The feeling that nothing should be touched, that everything was so sickeningly dirty that simply walking on the surface of the ground seemed obscene, and any normal and sensitive human being ought to be disgusted by the prospect.

If those of you who have read this far feel somewhat surprised or taken aback in any way by the things you have heard or visualized in this chapter it is only natural. For only imagine if you had been compelled to *experience in person* any of the above. Therefore maybe we owe to those who went through it that much; to care enough to be able to seek the bitter truth of war and all of its unspeakable and damnable horrors. Does it not seem right that if we as a society can send humans to battle, then should we not at least pay them the tribute of staring the evil of it straight in the eye? And for most of us that "staring it in the eye" is second-hand at best. That idea, then, is one of the small purposes of this book.

"A long black shadow"

II

THE BURIAL
OF THE DEAD

"Every name…is a lightning stroke to some heart, and breaks like thunder over some home, and falls a long black shadow upon some hearthstone."[1]

In the preceding chapter we dealt with the battlefield in quite a general way. The tour we followed with some of the first visitors to Gettysburg gave a much more vivid impression of the ground as a very unpleasant place. The stage has now been set for the next act of the play. Now the aim is to move from a general view to a more specific study of the various problems associated with a battlefield of such large proportions. Examples are many. The thousands of corpses of humans and carcasses of animals congested in a relatively small area; a shortage of time available for cleaning up the area; the problem of unpredictable weather; and finally, the fact that the two armies which caused this death and destruction, were then suddenly disengaged and had moved on to remote locations, and no longer were especially interested in the problems they had left behind.

To get a fair impression of the magnitude of the situation, let us once again review the numbers. By this, we mean the numbers of once living beings who on July 4 were strewn across the 25 square mile waste land. And in a forthcoming chapter, the wounded, the prisoners, and the clean up of the battlefield will be confronted in an equal way.

Immediately after the ending of hostilities at Gettysburg, official figures indicated that 7,058 officers and enlisted men were left dead on the field, and one woman in "a rebel uniform" was reported to have been buried by General William Hays' Second Corps.[2] If these casualties sound large, it is because they are. If they appear small, then you are probably not very familiar with average Civil War battle losses. It may be a good comparison to remember that the entire town of Gettysburg numbered 2,400 inhabitants in 1863. Even over 130 years later it consists of about 8,500. The nearest battle to compare with Gettysburg for *outright deaths* was Antietam with 3,900. Naturally in the

Private Alonzo Hayden, 1st Minnesota Infantry, did not experience the aftermath of Gettysburg; he was killed on July 2. Hayden was one of the first men to actually volunteer for service in the Civil War, doing so on April 15, 1861. (SB)

context of modern wars such as World Wars I or II, these *are* fairly small fatalities. One must remember that population totals were so much less in the 1860s. Until the industrial revolution, disease and war took enough of a toll to at best, keep the growth of populations to a "liveable level," or what would be considered to be a "repairable" level. But for battles in pre-1900 wars, these losses are substantial figures. Do not forget, too, that nearly 4,000 more men later perished of wounds inflicted at Gettysburg.

Furthermore, the slaughter of animals on the field was significant. At least 3,000 horses were killed outright. Many injured horses had to be destroyed; some were herded to a field near Rock Creek on the Union army's old right flank position and shot several weeks into July. There were also a number of mules killed, although that sum has not been fixed or even estimated. The citizenry itself lost heavily in livestock. There were certainly hundreds of partially eaten carcasses of cows, beeves, oxen, pigs and sheep, and various fowl spread thickly around. One informer underscored the offensiveness of these dead horses and oxen, which he said, "lie thick wherever the fight was hot. In one field fifty horses, in another the remains of more than as many oxen, and everywhere more or less. Some of these have been burned, others had earth heaped over them...."[3] Taken as a whole, it is easy to understand why a proportionate number of eyewitnesses called the whole ground for miles around, "a vast charnel house."

◆ ◆ ◆

The Natural Cycles of Life and Death

In the natural world, which we all are a part of, the rhythmic cycle of nature takes good care of any creature once it ceases to live. Particularly relevant to this idea was a quote by John Trowbridge where he illustrated the calmness and impassiveness of nature when dealing with death. He noted the process converts both a creature such as a bird or mule, as well as a human into new "forms of life and beauty." That is why death is final. Since there is no proof of a soul, why should it not be.[4] Our living bodies once deceased, provide rich humus for the soil which in turn enhances the growth of plants; and our decaying corpses give substance and life to various insects, as well as birds and other creatures both above and below ground. The cycle of life continues.

However, as true and normal as all this may be, when there is sensitive life still about, such as living humans, the lingering decomposition of corpses of people and animals does in fact soon become disagreeable in the extreme. Obviously then, it was always considered wise to prevent sickness or disease by rapidly covering these bodies. Had the battle been fought in a wilderness or remote rural area, the worry over the dead, except that of showing respect and decency to former living comrades, would have been given much less thought. Natural decay would have taken its slow methodical course and no living person would have been offended.

As we have discovered already, in many instances at Gettysburg, humans and horses were often *not* buried at all and did in fact, rot away on the surface of the earth. It is known from chapter one, that many were missed, purposefully left unburied, or improperly interred.

If a body was not buried, or was hastily and shallowly interred, what was the usual disposition of the corpse?

For one thing, contrary to popular belief, there were actually few airborne scavengers to do justice to the huge chore at hand. Most, if not all, of the vulture and buzzard population had gone away, fearful of the noise and smoke of thousands of weapons and human voices and the other intrusions present.[5] Both crows and other birds had likewise speedily vacated the scene of conflict. Many small animals were driven away too, although some corpses were probably partially eaten by roaming wild creatures, dogs, and also domesticated hogs, many of whom had not eaten regularly for a week or two due to the unsettling calamity in their midst.

As a matter of fact, several Gettysburg area residents remembered the damage hogs were capable of. One in particular related how he and his father found a dead Yankee soldier near the depot. They immediately placed the body inside a shed nearby, for fear the hogs would "tear him up that night," as many were running at large in those days. John Wert put the facts more coldly. He commented that, "[i]n some cases...swine were found revelling in the remains [of a corpse] in a manner horrible to contemplate."

A wounded New Hampshire soldier named Drake had the unpleasant sensation of watching as a hog tore the flesh from the bones of his recently amputated leg. It was eaten up before his eyes. He recalled that he could feel a sharp pain very clearly as it happened. Another injured officer named Inman who spent the night of July 2 in John Rose's wheatfield, had to fight off an aggressive horde of these creatures with his sword to keep them from helping themselves to his person and the dead men nearby.

David Wills, a local attorney attempting to gather support for a soldiers' cemetery at Gettysburg, wrote to the Governor of Pennsylvania that "attention has been directed to several places where the hogs were actually rooting out the bodies and devouring them."[6]

In the meantime and before any scavenger birds returned, many of the surface dead had been reduced to other substances that were less offensive by the never ceasing diligence of weather and insects. According to entomologists, this is how the latter organisms work:

"In the open air, for example, various blowflies and flesh flies lay thousands of eggs in a body's mouth, nose and ears within 10 minutes of death. The eggs hatch, usually about 12 hours later, into maggots that feed on tissues. When the maggots have finished, they move away from the body, cocooning in the nearby soil. A second wave of insects, usually beetles, comes to feast on the now drying skin. Later, still more insects, such as spiders, mites and millipedes, arrive to prey on bugs already at the site or to work at the remains."[7]

Scientists believe that these insects, such as the common green fly are attracted by a "universal death scent." Since insects have been on the earth for almost 300 million years they have had a long time to perfect and enhance these skills. As you have just read most of the first attacks upon the corpse are made by the flesh fly or blowfly, both of whom are excellent scavengers and who lay their eggs in dead animal and human tissue. The blowfly has the metallic bluish or green color most of us are familiar with. And as a sidelight, the reader may be interested to hear that these flies, which can carry so many diseases, lay an average of 500 eggs each in two to seven batches. It is estimated that a deceased 1,000 pound horse may hold up to 400,000 fly larvae, more than enough to accomplish at least a part of the "dismantling" of the creature.

There is an obvious common knowledge that swarms of flies by the literal millions settled over everything near Gettysburg. However, relatively few sources have been found which actually mention that fact in writing. This was probably due to the idea that the problem of flies in general was such a normal everyday occurrence in those days. People took it for granted that these insects were about in huge numbers, and therefore they went almost unnoticed. You may remember when Mary Horner exclaimed: "The flies exceeded them all!" meaning that of all the terrible experiences she had witnessed at Gettysburg, these bugs were the worst. And again, John Campbell, already quoted, related that, "every fence and bush was black with flies...." More common though to the literature of the day was not so much the mention of the mature creatures themselves, but the sight of the fly larvae, or maggots, which not only consumed the flesh of dead bodies, animal and human, but also tormented the injured men when they were deposited into a large majority of the unbandaged, uncared-for wounds.

So when all was said and done, the problem of dealing with the dead was a completely overwhelming one. Eventually someone, some living human being, would have to attend to the dirty business of cleaning up the mess. One such person was the soldier who epitomized the general consensus as he encountered each new corpse: "We would cover our faces tightly with our hands and turn our backs to the breeze and retch and gasp for breath."[8]

For the next several pages the story of this unhappy time will be told.

When the Confederate Army began to abandon the vicinity of Gettysburg late on July 4, it had not taken time to bury all of its dead. That task was immediately transferred to the Federal army, the townsfolk, and other Adams Countians who were already engaged in putting the thousands of uncovered Union bodies underground. In a report issued in October General George Meade stated that there had been 2,890 Confederates buried by his army at Gettysburg.

This number did *not*, however, include the hundreds of deceased buried by the Rebels themselves, or enemy bodies disposed of by the Eleventh and Twelfth Corps in early July. As an example of the large numbers that were interred during and immediately after the battle, one only has to look at General William Hays' report dated July 17, 1863. In it he claims his command alone, the U.S. Second Corps, buried 18 Union officers and 369 enlisted men, and 60 Confederate officers and 1,182 enlisted men in front of Cemetery Ridge between July 2 and July 5. And there are many diary and personal letter accounts by Northern infantrymen who, like the unknown member of the 147th Pennsylvania, simply wrote: "Sunday July 5. Buried 42 rebels in one grave and 31 rebs in another."

Furthermore, the provost marshal general, Marsena Patrick authorized and contracted with Samuel Herbst of Gettysburg to bury the remaining Federal and Confederate bodies. General Patrick did not have an easy time procuring the services of common civilians to perform this unpleasant task. After a July 5 meeting with General Meade at army headquarters in the house of Philip Pfieffer on the Baltimore Pike, Patrick was ordered to go into town to organize burial parties. He later wrote: "Had a great deal of difficulty in getting hold of some respectable parties to do any thing with, the people being nearly all Copperheads [meaning Southern sympathizers]....I called together the leading citizens (Union) at [David Wills'] office, made the necessary arrangements & Set a man at work." [Samuel Herbst][9]

To all Citizens,

Men, Horses and Wagons wanted immediately, to bury the dead and to cleanse our streets, in such a thorough way as to guard against a pestilence. Every good citizen can be of use by reporting himself, at once, to Capt. W. W. Smith, acting Provost Marshal, Office, N. E. corner Centre Square.

Notices such as this did little to entice local people into taking part in what was "a most unpleasant task." (ASGA)

Together the sum of Confederate corpses placed into the ground by all means probably added up to at least 3,903, a figure usually given for the number of Southerners killed in the battle, with 3,155 on the Northern side. Captain William G. Rankin, an assistant quartermaster, was the officer directly responsible for completing these remaining early burials, including any of the Union troops not interred between July 1 and 3 by either Rebel or Yankee forces. All in all the problem was formidable. One soldier emphasized it best: "[The dead] were on every side of us....They were so many it seemed a gigantic task...."[10]

Captain Rankin and his small band of pioneers were also directed to collect and safeguard all government and captured property, a complicated situation which will be covered in more detail later in this book. Two of the men assigned to assist Rankin were Captain Henry B. Blood and Captain William W. Smith, who received orders to report to Gettysburg after the battle, and did so by 4 p.m. on July 7. Between July 8 and 12 these officers and several squads of prisoners buried 367 Confederate dead and about 100 horses. Blood also burned some horses on July 11 along the Emmitsburg Road.[11] Apparently by that date, most of the bodies of Federals killed in action had already been dealt with.

But what of these initial burials? Just how were they accomplished, both between July 1 and 3 and also in the days directly following the battle?

Officially, strict regulations existed for the proper burial of the dead, but rarely could these specifications be followed to the letter. In one unusual case at Gettysburg oddly enough, the military maxims were followed exactly that way. Dr. John H. Brinton, on special duty for the U.S. Surgeon General, was in the town in early July. Near one church he "observed a number of new made graves, arranged with the greatest precision, each one of them being provided with a head board and foot board, made of shingles, the former bearing the

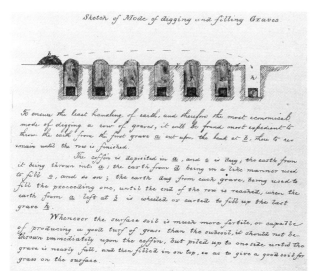

The official "Mode of digging and filling Graves." (NA/EJC)

name, rank, company and regiment of the man beneath. The head boards were exactly alike, the lines for the inscription and the styles for the lettering being alike in all cases." Brinton was astonished at this regularity in a sea of so much discord and confusion. All of the interments he had seen so far had been very haphazard. He later found out that a U.S. Volunteer officer, Surgeon Thomas H. Bache had made these precise arrangements.[12] As can be expected with hundreds to be buried, and from 50 to 100 men dying every day in the surrounding field hospitals, actual reality often foreshadowed any normal and decent obligation or instructions.

Coming in contact with death in such large quantities left an unerasable mark on even the most hardened gravedigger, and almost everyone who saw the faces, features, and postures of these former living beings that were now only hideous corpses, was shocked and amazed at the pitiful nature of the spectacle. A New Jersey soldier may have best summed up the overall atmosphere that existed as these early interments were carried out:

> Burial parties were sent out, and those who could get away from their commands went out to view the scene of carnage, and surely it was a scene never to be forgotten. Upon the open fields, like sheaves bound by the reaper, in crevices of the rocks, behind fences, trees and buildings; in thickets, where they had crept for safety only to die in agony; by stream or wall or hedge, wherever the battle had raged or their wakening steps could carry them, lay the dead. Some, with faces bloated and blackened beyond recognition, lay with glassy eyes staring up at the blazing summer sun; others, with faces downward and clenched hands filled with grass or earth, which told of the agony of the last moments. Here a headless trunk, there a severed limb; in all the grotesque positions that unbearable pain and intense suffering contorts the human form, they lay. Upon the faces of some death had frozen a smile; some showed the trembling shadow of fear, while upon others was indelibly set the grim stamp of determination. All around was the wreck the battle-storm leaves in its

wake—broken caissons, dismounted guns, small arms bent and twisted by the storm or dropped and scattered by disabled hands; dead and bloated horses, torn and ragged equipments, and all the sorrowful wreck that the waves of battle leave at their ebb; and over all, hugging the earth like a fog, poisoning every breath, the pestilential stench of decaying humanity.[13]

The First Interments

Several people have left behind excellent remembrances of how these burial parties actually worked. William Baird of the 6th Michigan Cavalry was excused from duty with his regiment on July 4 and was ordered on July 5 "to assist in gathering up the dead that had not been buried and burrying them." Baird declared that it was a "very trying job as they had become much decomposed. [O]ur stretcher was made of two poles sixteen feet long with a strip of canvass sowed to them in the middle long enough to carry a man.

[I]t took two men to carry this and a third man went along with a Pike Pole. We would go to the windard of the dead man, laying down the stretcher the Man with the Pike Pole would roll the dead man onto the stretcher the other two men would carry him off to the place of interment...."

Private John Parker illustrated this particularly nasty fact. He recalled that on July 5 a party under Lieutenant John G. Kinsley of the 22nd Massachusetts encountered bodies so repulsive and decomposed that, "[r]ails were run under them and when reaching the trench, they were allowed to slide off."

Using poles or fence rails to roll the rotting corpses onto litters or into graves was a very common approach to avoid handling the grim remains. Robert Carter had a similar experience when he affirmed that the dead "were so far decomposed that we had to run rails under the bodies, which, as they slid into the trenches, broke apart, to the horror and disgust of the whole party, and the stench still lingers in our nostrils. As many as *ninety* bodies were thus disposed of in one trench...most of them were tumbled in just as they fell, with not a prayer, eulogy or tear to distinguish them from so many animals."[14] This expression of absolute uncaring or lack of feelings by gravediggers seemed to be a notable feature of the business. Steven A. Osborn, 145th Pennsylvania, portrayed this view somewhat lightheartedly when he composed his memoir in 1915 of the burial of a dead comrade on July 4, 1863. After searching the ground, he and a companion came to the corpse which had been shot squarely in the forehead between the eyes, and the brain had,

> run down to the ground.
>   ...[W]e made a stretcher of two small poles and some straps or body belts found nearby, and with [Lt. Joseph L.] Linn ahead and I behind we made the trip by resting now and then. We were feeling very solemn and sad as we thought, but on reaching the place where they had just commenced the trench in which to bury the dead they told us he was wrong end to, and on turning him around one of the straps broke and pitched [the corpse] all twisted up into a heap. This was more than Linn and I could stand and we gave vent to our grief in a roar of laughter. You say, oh how wicked! All I have to say in reply is that

we were in a wicked business and it wasn't best for us to look at that side of the question or go without a good laugh too long at any one time. I believe Lieut. Linn and I brought the first one to the trench for burial at Gettysburg cemetery.[15]

One articulate Confederate wounded prisoner awaiting medical aid at the Twelfth Corps hospital had a similar sentiment when he explained that,

the dead are laid out in long rows, with their naked faces turned up to the sun, their clothes stiff with the dried blood, and their features retaining in death the agony and pain which they died with; and presently they are dragged forth and thrust into a shallow pit, with, perhaps, the coarse jest of a vulgar soldier for their requiem, and bloody blankets for their winding sheets. What a blessing it is that the gentle and tender loved ones at home are spared the sight of the last moments of their torn and mangled soldiers![16]

A Sergeant Meyer of the 148th Pennsylvania, who was placed in charge of a group of "pioneers," here describes his system of interring bodies and how his men operated smoothly as a team:

"Some of the men buried the dead thus laid in rows; a shallow grave about a foot deep, [was dug] against the first man in a row and he was then laid down into it; a similar grave was dug where he had lain. The ground thus dug up served to cover the first man, and the second was laid in a trench, and so on, so the ground was handled only once. This was the regular form of burial on our battlefields. It is the most rapid, and is known as trench burial and is employed where time for work is limited."

Meyer was present for the burial of some of the Confederates killed in front of the "angle" on Cemetery Ridge on July 3. He revealed that the "faces [were] black as charcoal and bloated out of all human semblance; eyes, cheeks, forehead and nose all one general level of putrid swelling, twice the normal size, with here and there great blisters of putrid water, some the size of a man's fist on face, neck and wrists; while the bodies were bloated to the full capacity of the uniforms that enclosed them."

He pointed out that almost all these corpses had been searched for valuables. Most often, Meyer said, the pockets "were cut open and rifled through the incision. The battlefield robbers were well known by the large amounts of money they had, and the watches, pocketbooks, pocket knives and other valuable trinkets they had for sale after the battle. All regiments had them."

Sergeant Thomas Meyer and his "pioneers" became experts in handling and interring corpses. (JWM)

The "Battlefield Ghoul." An unnamed man supposed to have been arrested at Gettysburg while robbing the bodies of the dead. (SDH)

The sergeant also explained: "First we collected the dead men into rows, as usual laying one against another, heads all one way, Union and Confederate in separate rows. Then some [of my detail] would collect and arrange [the bodies] in rows while the majority of men buried them in trenches as heretofore described. These burial trenches were dug here, there and everywhere over the field and contained three or four or fifty as the number of dead near required. Few of these men had anything about them by which they could be identified, and were buried as 'unknown.'"[17]

Meyer did not indicate it explicitly, but the way the bodies were "collected and arranged" in rows was to hitch the dead man's legs together with his belt or a piece of twine or rope, or pass the rope around the arms and chest and then drag the corpse to where a "row" was being assembled. That may explain why in some photographs taken of men killed in battle, one often sees the pants of the soldier pulled down off his waist or below his buttocks.

The whole process, as clearly related by Sergeant Meyer, was a most dismal chore.

Another sergeant who was on duty at Culp's Hill was in agreement. As Charles Blanchard strolled along the lines he, too, stumbled upon "some strange pathetic sights. I saw a Confederate soldier that a ramrod had passed through his body and pinned him to a tree, but the incident most vividly stamped upon my mind, was where I saw 108 Confederates put into a trench. Whisky had been issued to the Brigade Pioneers, as the stench was almost unbearable." Blanchard also observed that besides the pioneers, details were made from nearby infantry regiments to carry out the interments, and even citizens were pressed into service to assist these squads. The putrid smell of rotting corpses was an ever-present detriment to the burial gangs who canvassed the field. Sergeant Meyer of the 148th Pennsylvania commented on this vulgar aspect. "The stench on the battlefield was something indescribable, it would come up as if in waves and when at its worst the breath would stop in the throat; the lungs could not take it in, and a sense of suffocation would be experienced."[18]

An Ohio officer named Lieutenant Thomas Galwey explained in a postwar memoir how he remembered burials were completed along the Emmitsburg Road on July 5 which varies somewhat with Meyer's account. Large details were first made up from his corps and then the corpses were "brought into rows and counted, the Confederate and Federals being separated into different rows. At the feet of each row of fifty or a hundred dead, a trench is dug about seven or eight feet wide and about three feet deep—for there is not time for normal grave depth. Then the bodies, which are as black as ink and bloated from exposure to the sun, are placed in the shallow ditch and quickly covered with dirt."[19]

A common thread throughout these sources is the "black color" of a cadaver which was often described. However, one Pennsylvanian took that thought somewhat further as he was watching the burial parties at work. "One thing peculiar struck me," he related, "and that was the difference in appearance of the dead soldiers of the two armies. The rebel dead retained nearly their natural appearance, while our dead had almost invariably turned a very dark purple in the face. Why it was so I could not even guess."[20]

A Confederate present at Gettysburg gave his own recollection of how the burial process was completed in his army. He specified that, "a detail from each company was formed into a squad, and after arriving with spades or shovels they search the field for the dead. When found a shallow pit is dug, just deep enough to cover the body, the blanket is taken from around the person, his body wrapped therein, laid in the pit, and sufficient dirt thrown upon it to protect it from the vultures. There is no systematic work, time being too precious, and the dead are buried where they fell."[21]

An unknown writer of the 6th New Jersey has left us with a fine account of his experiences on a typical burial detail which went out on the field immediately after the fighting. At dusk on July 4 he was ordered to a wooded area just northwest of Little Round Top to bury indiscriminately both the enemy's and his own dead. He was also told to identify the bodies if possible, and to stay out until midnight. After arming his men with shovels and picks and a lantern they started out. The squad first came to a Rebel lieutenant with his arms folded across his chest. At the edge of a woods either on the John Weikert farm across from John Rose's wheatfield or on part of the Trostle place, they found a soft strip of land and there a grave was dug for the lieutenant's resting place. A little bit further they discovered three Union soldiers of the 1st Division, Fifth Corps. One of the men still held a portion of a paper cartridge tightly in his mouth where he had bitten off the end in readiness to load his musket. The dead man's pockets had been rifled and his shoes and stockings were stripped off. Next to him lay another private, also missing his hat, shoes and stockings. Inside a pocket of the soldier's uniform was a golden locket and a photograph of his wife or sweetheart, along with her name and address. The third body discovered was that of a Federal first lieutenant of artillery, also robbed of some of his clothing. Further degrading the corpse was the fact that one of his little fingers had been cut off, "as the print of a large seal-ring could yet be seen upon it." This officer was most likely Christopher E. Erickson of the 9th Massachusetts Battery who had been killed on July 2.

After completing these graves the party walked on. Moving through the dark woods with only the dim light of the lantern, our narrator suddenly tripped. As he fell, his hand came in contact with the cold forehead of a corpse. He was horrified:

My feet rested on another body, and my lantern was out. I felt for a match. I had none. But presently some of the men came up; the lantern was relighted, and the glare revealed a sight which I pray God my eyes may never look upon again. The body upon which my hand had fallen was that of a corporal; both legs were blown completely off. That over which I had stumbled was the body of a private with one arm severed, not entirely off, at the shoulder. Two trees of perhaps four inches diameter had been splintered, one about eight feet the other five feet from the ground, and had fallen right where the bodies lay. Within a circle of twenty feet from these trees I counted seventeen bodies, all, alas! with blue jackets on. I had hoped among so many to find some of the gray-backed ones.

How we buried these seventeen bodies you would not care to know.[22]

On that evening this informant also said they buried the remains of a 118th Pennsylvania soldier named Caldwell, who was identified by a silver medal found in his pocket and still clinched in the dead man's hand.

The work of burial parties at night definitely had a much more somber touch added to an already morbid and unpleasant task. One eyewitness recapitulated the feeling beautifully:

"Nothing could be more dismal and appalling than searching over a battle-field in a dark night for a friend or comrade. To turn up one dead face after another to the glimmering light of a lantern and see it marred with wounds and disfigured with blood and soil, the features, perhaps, convulsed by the death-agony, the eyes vacant and staring....Dismal, too, the sight of the dark battle-ground, with lanterns twinkling here and there, like the wisp on the moras."[23]

The U.S. sharpshooter W.S. White and a few fellow soldiers were sent out on the fourth after dark to search for their dead comrades. Having no stretchers, the sharpshooters resorted to carrying the men back by using two fence boards. By the time the group reentered Union lines in the pitch darkness, most of the men who were holding these "sacred burdens," had repeatedly fallen over the bodies of other slain men and inadvertently often dropped their cargo.

White remembered one vivid and eerie aspect of these nighttime duties. During the procedure of hunting for their missing friends, hundreds of dead Rebels were encountered who lay thick among the grass, the bodies lit up by an occasional lightning flash which exposed the cold stark faces of these upturned corpses. Later these burials were completed in the rear of Cemetery Ridge in total darkness with no light available from the moon or lanterns, and during the whole time, "there was a continuous shower and terrific thunder and lightening."[24]

Parties canvassing the grim but often surreal battlefield had many disheartening and melancholy pictures presented to them. One circumstance of the dreaded ground which was not always apparent or mentioned by burial details, was the fact that it could be

W.S. White vividly recalled his hours hunting for and burying the dead. (JRW)

a downright, in our parlance "creepy" job. Although we know that most soldiers in that century were not as highly superstitious as people are today, and in fact the sources available support this belief, still, venturing forth on such a blighted landscape as the Gettysburg battlefield at night, during a lightning storm, might unnerve the rational consciousness of even the most stalwart individual. Here is an example of the sheer terror which awaited someone who, already nervous, was ordered to sweep an area of the field in search of corpses to handle and bury. It was conveyed dramatically by a Connecticut enlisted man who was near Culp's Hill immediately following the battle.

> The dead lay all about, some with a smile upon their faces, and others horribly contorted as if the death agony had there been photographed or modeled in clay. As [our] burial party was going over the rebel field, suddenly some one shouted to a comrade, "Look out! There's a Johnny aiming at you!" And, sure enough, there he was, with his musket in position across a large stone and his face down on the breech. He had been struck in the forehead in the act of firing, and was instantly killed. There was not the slightest thing in appearance to indicate that the soldier's alarm was not well founded.[25]

Surprisingly, not all of the men assigned to pioneer duty buried the "killed in action" simply as cordwood, indiscriminately in large trenches, or in anonymous single graves. Some of the "squads," were really just individuals or groups of kindhearted soldiers out looking for a particular friend or comrade. Some men took a very tender and loving approach to the obligation of gravedigging. In the following account, a friend of Private Albert Frost, 3rd Maine, who had last been seen in combat in a wooded area west of the "peach orchard" about noon of July 2, went out to find his whereabouts. Believing him to have been killed, the soldiers sought to locate Frost's body, which they accomplished a few days later, declaring:

"We found him face down and with...the flesh eaten (in that hot climate) by maggots; but not so bad that we could still recognize him. When we went to bury him, all we could find to dig a grave was an old hoe in a small building. The bottom of the grave was covered with empty knapsacks, then we laid in our beloved brother and covered him with another knapsack, and over all put as much earth as we could find. The grave was dug at the foot of a large tree. We then found a piece of a hard wood box cover and cut his name on it with a jackknife and nailed it to the tree at the head of his grave." Private Frost, they had argued, was the best, most loved and most patriotic man in their company.[26]

The fate of the corpse of Private Albert Frost, whose face was consumed by maggots, was still better than most. (MI)

A second memoir conveys the same sense of decency to and devotion for one's companions as the story just examined. In this case, the burials were being performed on the edge of the infamous grain field northwest of George Rose's farmbuilding and near Little Round Top. The speaker was Private Houghton of the 4th Michigan.

> The principle part of the dead was carried on stretchers to the woods west of the Wheatfield for interment. [A]ll the paines possible was taken in their burial. . trenches was dug and the bottom was neatly covered with blankets and their remains was carefully an neatley layed side by side. blankets was torn into and made a roll to put under Each ones Head then blankets was spread over them and tucked down closely so no dirt could not tuch them. in some cases their Blo[o]dy garments were removed and washed and dried on limbs of treas then Replased.[27]

Houghton's description of cleaning the uniforms of blood, dirt, etc., then replacing the clothing of the deceased before burial is highly unusual, and has not been illustrated in any of the first-hand testimonies and sources available. Evidently these men were friends of the deceased and had the time to take more than normal care of their beloved companions. It seems a most sad and heartbreaking display, yet beautiful in the extreme.

How different the above is to this statement: "The burials of the battlefield at best seem shocking and sacrilegious as compared with the respect for the dead paid in our own homes. But, where the Confederate dead fell thick in the valley between the Round Tops, there was a special pathos in the mode of their interment. A large tract here is entirely destitute of surface soil. It is a massive bed of round, syenite stones of varying sizes. The dead bodies were collected in groups of three or four and stones, sometimes intermingled with brushwood, thrown upon them until a little mound had been formed, which, often, only partially concealed the decomposing corpses beneath."

May we not then understand why over two-thirds of the Southerners killed and buried at Gettysburg were simply marked "unknown." And as the author of the above conceded: "Hundreds of weeping, watching, hoping mothers in Virginia, Georgia, Alabama and every state of the confederacy never knew aught of a loved son but that he was last seen at the Peach Orchard, the Wheatfield, the Bloody Angle [sic], frowning Round Top, or rocky Culp's Hill of a Northern land."[28]

One such situation could have been the story of Sergeant James McLaughlin, of Company I, 21st Mississippi. McLaughlin, aged 30, originally from Canada, had been living near Carson's Landing, Mississippi, when he enlisted in 1861. He served through all the battles from Lee's Mills in April 1862, to the Seven Days' battles, the Antietam Campaign, Fredericksburg, and Chancellorsville. On July 2, 1863, at Gettysburg Sergeant McLaughlin was killed, somewhere between Joseph Sherfy's peach orchard and Abraham Trostle's farmhouse.

In the weeks and months that passed into years from that tragic day in July, McLaughlin's body, name and memory disappeared from the face of the earth. If or when he was buried is not known. He was not one of the five or six 21st Mississippi still in identified graves resting on the battlefield when the Southern remains were disinterred and removed to the South between 1871 and 1873. Of the eighteen to twenty 21st Regiment's deaths at Gettysburg, he, like more than half of the others, was never identified and possibly not even found. When a "Confederate Death Roster" was published in 1981, his name was missed and was not included. Only his service records in Washington, D.C. state that he was "killed in action on the field of Gettysburg." No regimental history exists to tell the story of his last moments, or to enlighten us as to whether a comrade tenderly buried his corpse. And no one is aware to our knowledge if a letter from his captain or a fellow soldier reached his anxiously awaiting friends or family in Sunflower County, Mississippi, nor anyone remaining in Canada.

Does his skeleton still lie on the field in a mass grave below the earth of the "peach orchard," where 40 Confederates were said to be interred and never recovered by Dr. Weaver in the early 1870s? Or were his bones shipped to Richmond or elsewhere with hundreds of others, unmarked and unmourned? As in so many of these forlorn examples, no one will ever know.[29]

There is no question that the Rebel dead were handled much less delicately than their Union counterparts. For one thing, the Federals in victory held control and responsibility of the field itself, and naturally took greater pains to inter their men more humanly. Moreover, even Confederate prisoners ordered to entomb their own comrades did a poor job, as is in this exemplification by Frank Stoke:

"It will be remembered that from the ["angle"] along our entire left the Rebel prisoners were made to bury their dead. They dug long trenches about ten inches deep, then would lay from fifty to one hundred in each trench, then throw clay along the middle of the rows of men leaving the head and feet entirely exposed."[30]

This is not a condemnation nor a very surprising scene, since the Southerners as already described, had made very little effort to inter Yankees much less their own brethren killed on the July 1st battleground. Being in control of that part of the battlefield until July 5, they let many of the Union bodies rot, and it became the painful duty of U.S. squads late on July 5 through July 7 to cover these almost totally decomposed corpses, where some of the most revolting remembrances of all who visited Gettysburg were encountered.

When forced by orders to undertake this tough and unpleasant chore, mainly because there were not enough Northern troops or civilian laborers to complete the distasteful chore, some of the Rebel prisoners, "went into this work with reluctance and murmuring, others did it cheerfully, saying, 'It is just what we have compelled the Yankees to do for us.'"[31]

Mapping the Grave Sites

When a soldier's grave was fortunate enough to have been properly marked, it was a boon to military authorities, cemetery officials, and most especially the family and friends of the deceased. Early wanderers through the battlegrounds often made note of particular graves that were identified and of course, therefore were more likely to have caught their attention. This was the case of Franklin Myre and Hugh Holmes of Co. B, 99th Pennsylvania whose burial sites were spotted by a Harrisburg resident on July 9 between Little Round Top and Houck's Ridge.[32] There are many existing accounts in which individual soldiers killed in battle or who had died of wounds in hospitals, were specifically mentioned in diaries, letters or memoirs written after a visit to the field. These along with correspondence sent home by comrades to the families of these victims, provided some small help in locating a grave site days, weeks, or even months after July 1863. Unfortunately, those few collected names were but a handful when speaking of the nearly 11,000 dead and mortally wounded of Gettysburg. In one single instance, a Confederate grave was documented on two separate occasions by a journeyer to Gettysburg. One may believe this 5th Texas Infantry soldier, Private Marshall Prue, should most certainly have been among the "known" Confederate dead transported south in 1871-1873 by Dr. Rufus B. Weaver, whose efforts will be discussed shortly. Remarkably, he was not. Prue's grave, although clearly marked, and specifically seen on two occasions by two distinct people, like his fate, simply disappeared from the face of the earth.[33]

A counterpart to Prue's story was the saga of another Confederate's grave, that of Colonel Joseph Wasden of Georgia. His burial spot was remarked upon by three or four passers-by, and his grave, both well preserved and marked, survived—until he was shipped to Savannah, Georgia, in 1872.[34]

A sample of the random recordings of identified graves may prove interesting to the reader.

In one important instance, Ambrose Emory, noted in chapter one, identified eight or ten graves near the Rose house in August 1863. He jotted down the names of Captain Bond, 53rd Georgia, Sergeant Berth, 50th Georgia, Private Gadsden, 2nd South Carolina, among others, and said he viewed 34 of the 15th South Carolina's burials.[35]

John Linn lingered near the burial sites of several soldiers on July 8, including Privates Cross and Burdsley of the 15th Massachusetts, J.B. Robbins, 8th South Carolina and Captain Warren, 13th South Carolina, their graves all being either along the Emmitsburg Road or on the Rose farm property. A day or so later he mentioned General William Barksdale's grave and that of Captain Forster's 148th Pennsylvania, side-by-side near the Taneytown Road. A mile or so eastward and on the Baltimore Pike he spotted beside a rock the burial places of Thomas Redshaw and John Perry, 20th Connecticut.[36]

John Linn plucked a souvenir wild rose which grew over the grave of John Perry, 20th Connecticut, along the Baltimore Pike on July 9. (CCLHM/SCH)

Out near Blocher's Hill just west of the Harrisburg Road, a "Dr. Bradford" from Beaver County, Pennsylvania, recalled seeing the sites of Captain Moore, 17th Connecticut and Lieutenant W.H. Beaver, 153rd Pennsylvania. While along Cemetery Ridge within the Union lines the doctor recorded the identified graves of Private James Clay and Captain G.C. Thompson, 69th Pennsylvania.[37]

O.C. Brown, a member of the 44th New York Infantry chanced upon the well marked grave of Lieutenant E.L. Dunham, which had been prepared near the garden fence of farmer Leonard Bricker on the Taneytown Road. Brown wrote to the family of Dunham with this information, enclosing a peach leaf from the tree under which the body rested.[38]

Ofttimes letters similar to the one written by Brown were accompanied by not only a memento but also a hand-drawn map made up especially to assist the family in locating the grave. A perfect example is this letter composed by a member of the deceased's unit:

Gettysburg Pa, July 4, 1863

M. Braddock, Esq.

Dr. Sir,

I have to announce to you the painful intelligence of the death of your son Stephen [of Battery C, 1st West Virginia Artillery]. He fell on Thursday P.M. while fighting gallantly. He was a good, brave and reliable soldier and his loss will be keenly felt and deeply deplored by the Battery. You have the warmest sympathies of every member of this command in this your hour of tribulation. A cannon ball struck him under the right eye completely carrying away over half [of] his head....I also send a plan of the ground near the grave. With sentiments of profound sorrow I remain

Very Truly
T.G. Field[39]

Such illustrations of personal records made to identify graves were rarely available and do not denote any systematic way in which *known* burials were tracked. According to the evidence available, the military did not keep a single ledger listing and locating *all* Confederate and Union graves on and around the Gettysburg battlefield. Nonetheless, we do know that a detailed map was commissioned for this purpose. The man responsible was probably Attorney David Wills of Gettysburg who was the agent for the Commonwealth of Pennsylvania authorized to collect the Union dead from the field and have them sent home for burial if the family requested it.[40] This unusual map, which originally measured approximately two feet by three feet, may have been drawn up in about the middle of July 1863 by S.G. Elliott of Philadelphia.[41] Unfortunately, no one today can be sure of the accuracy of this map. One of its failings is that it lumps many of the burials together, and does not clearly qualify if the indicated number of graves in various locations is the exact count or a generality. In some cases it appears that Elliott overestimated the number of remains present in certain areas such as the Rose farm, or that, worse yet, he did not in fact ever physically count them at all. Consequently we are left with more questions than answers when studying this map. One final and

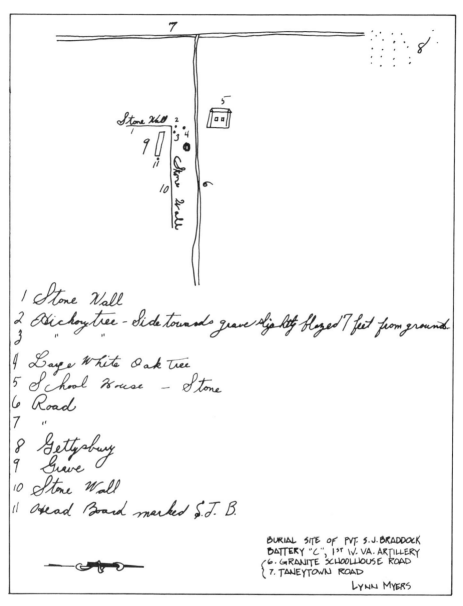

1 Stone Wall
2 Hickory tree - Side towards grave slightly blazed 7 feet from ground
3 "   "
4 Large White Oak Tree
5 School House — Stone
6 Road
7 "
8 Gettysbury
9 Grave
10 Stone Wall
11 Head Board marked S.J.B.

BURIAL SITE OF PVT. S.J. BRADDOCK
BATTERY "C", 1ST W. VA. ARTILLERY
6. GRANITE SCHOOLHOUSE ROAD
7. TANEYTOWN ROAD

LYNN MYERS

A sketch of the grave location for Stephen Braddock. (TGF/LWM)

important flaw is that he only *identifies* by name about 14 graves, one of which, as it were, happens to be an incorrect identification.

There is one other map which was purported to locate the graves of fallen soldiers. This particular diagram was commissioned by the State of New York upon the recommendation of Mr. John F. Seymour, general agent of the state for the relief of sick and wounded soldiers.

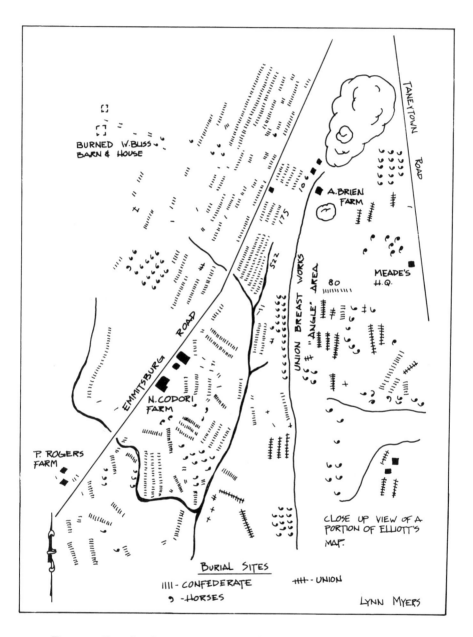

Recent sketch of a portion of the "Elliott Map." (SGE/LWM)

Dr. Theodore Dimon, a former Army surgeon of the 3rd New York Artillery who was then a relief agent for New York, was sent to assist the wounded in Gettysburg. Dr. John M. Cuyler, a U.S. Medical Inspector, suggested to Dr. Dimon that "[a] record should be made of the names and place of burial of the soldiers who may die, and a map should be drawn indicating the location of their graves."

Dr. Dimon revealed in a communication written July 16, that, "[i]n regard to our dead, I would say that I made a map, enlarged from the county map of the whole district of the battle-field, and procured a careful record of the names and plans of burial of our dead soldiers, referring to the map for the places of burial. This record contains all whose remains can be identified....This map and record is presented with this report."[42]

Presently as far as anyone is aware, that map has not been located, unless it is hidden somewhere in the archives of New York State. Dimon merely stated that he had deposited the map with a burial roll and report, "at the No. 50 Howard Street Soldier's Depot," in New York on July 31, 1863.

Dimon remained at Gettysburg until July 30, during which time another person compiled a similar map, only this one plotted the locations of all major field hospitals in the 25 square mile radius of the battlefield and town. It was hand-drawn by Andrew B. Cross who was a member of the U.S. Christian Commission, an organization organized in 1861 by the YMCA in New York City. This group was designated as a soldiers' relief society, working in conjunction with the U.S. Sanitary Commission during the war.

Along with the information and maps already portrayed, several other individuals took much time and effort to compose and manage records of soldier burials in the Gettysburg area. One of these persons was John G. Frey, a farmer who had served as a sergeant in Company B, 138th Pennsylvania Infantry. Frey acted as an early guide for friends or relatives of deceased soldiers seeking grave sites. Evidently, due to his excursions over the historic ground, he began to amass quite a list of Union names and burial places. Perhaps this made it easier for Frey to assist the searching, grieving persons whom he encountered, rather than to constantly have to question other farmers for grave locations. Mr. Frey's book is not complete, but he did compile a large and important number of soldiers. As listed, his manner of inventory was as follows: "J.R. Blake, Co I, 7th Ohio—J. Benner's cornfield;" or "L.A. Kelley, Co. B, 19th Maine—'Spanish Oak' near White Church;" and, "C.J. Crandall, Co. K, 125 New York on M. Trostle's farm near a sycamore tree, opposite 'Walnut Row,'" and so forth. In total, Frey's roster contains about 1100 names.

There is little doubt that if this catalogue was ever used by ordinary civilians or military authorities, it could have been of great assistance to families, or to the Soldiers' National Cemetery teams working to properly identify and reinter U.S. soldiers killed in battle at Gettysburg, or who had succumbed to their wounds in field hospitals.[43]

An equally important register of burials was devised and preserved by a local physician, Dr. John William C. O'Neal. O'Neal was a Virginian who was born in Fairfax County in 1821. For his early education he attended Pennsylvania College in Gettysburg and later received a medical degree in 1844 from the University of Maryland. O'Neal first settled in Hanover, Pennsylvania, but soon moved to Baltimore in 1849. In 1847 he married Ellen Wirt of Hanover. A son born to them, Walter H., became a doctor after the Civil War. After the Battle of Antietam O'Neal assisted many of the wounded near Sharpsburg, Maryland, as he did nine months later at Gettysburg.

Dr. O'Neal had relocated to Gettysburg a few months prior to the battle. He originally rented an office in the Wills' building opposite the bank on York Street, but in April 1863 O'Neal leased a new office at the northeast corner of Baltimore and High Streets.[44] The burial roll kept by the doctor seems to have developed while he travelled around the countryside making his regular housecalls.

O'Neal's first catalogue attempt contained only Confederate known or "named" graves. Like J.G. Frey, who registered just Union burials, O'Neal preferred to document Southern soldiers exclusively. Eventually his book held about 1,100 identified Rebel names and their grave sites, although one source estimated that there were only 500 identified Confederates and about 2,000 unknowns on the field in 1871.[45]

Dr. O'Neal's register was initially written in a "Physician's Hand Book of Practice" a small three inch by five inch "appointment" journal he probably kept on his person daily. Some of the burial entries are jotted in above or below and even *over* his normal accounts, prescriptions and patient schedules. As an example, on one page he places several Confederates, "[b]urried, Hunterstown Road, 1st House," one of whom was "J.H. McElroy, Co. A. 1st La. Reg," another was "Cpl. J.S. Scarborough, Co. A. 2nd Louisiana Infantry," and "John M. Stricker, Co. E. 21 Mississippi Vol Killed July 2, burried in woods on road to Crises" etc.[46]

This maiden attempt by O'Neal at recordkeeping in a tiny, cluttered, "appointment" book was later supplemented by a larger more detailed version in 1864.

Subsequently, Dr. O'Neal refined his handbooks even more, probably in 1866, and correlated all of the names and interment locations into a more proper record book. That last ledger was donated to the National Military Park in 1943. Additionally it contained information on the shipment of Confederate

Dr. John W.C. O'Neal. (ACHS)

remains to the South in the years 1871-1873. Totally this "final attempt" register held the names of his close surveys of the Confederate graves at Gettysburg both in 1863 and 1866. The 1866 list was an attempt to update the original work and to verify just how many *marked* Southern burial sites still remained viable three years from the battle. From studying the two compilations, it is readily apparent that the graves were being lost quite rapidly, and that the names on the headboards, rails, tree trunks, etc. were becoming harder and harder to decipher.[47]

For us to understand just how valuable these catalogues of names and burial placements were to the relatives and friends of a deceased soldier, it is enlightening to read the following. It was extracted from a letter to Dr. O'Neal from "Mrs. A.T. Mercer" of Supply, North Carolina requesting his aid in locating the grave of her 21-year-old son, Captain O.E. Mercer who was killed on July 1. She wrote in part:

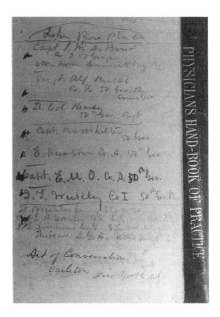

A page from Dr. O'Neal's "Physician's Hand Book" indicating Confederate marked graves on George Rose's farm. (ACHS)

"Our Wilmington papers bring the welcome intelligence to many bereaved Southern hearts that you have cared for the graves of many of our Confederate dead at Gettysburg, replaced headboards and *prepared a list of names*. May the Lord bless you is the prayer of many Southern hearts—Oh! we have lost so much. There are but few families that do not mourn the loss of one or more loved ones, and only a mother who has lost a son in that awful battle can and does appreciate fully such goodness as you have shown."[48]

Miscellaneous other registers, rolls, and lists were presumably maintained by organizations and individuals in the months following the battle. There is a personal "family kept" roster in existence which was made out in 1865 and penned in a small type of "notebook" found on his land after the battle by George W. Rose. In this twenty page, four inch by six inch booklet, Mr. Rose wrote down the identities of about fifty Confederates who were buried on his farm. Some of the entries included are: on page five he mentions "back of Privy, Sargt. Alfred Bird, Comp F 50 Ga," and "Weldon, between the t[w]o apple trees behind the washhouse," or "Capt Cunningham Comp C 2nd SCV in the field next to Sherfy orchard close to the fence," and so on.[49]

Lastly, two of the most thorough and well known compilations of these types evolved through the good work of Samuel Weaver and his son, Dr. Rufus B. Weaver. Samuel was the man hired by David Wills to supervise the disinterments of Union soldiers to the new "national cemetery" at Gettysburg.

After the death of his father, Rufus Weaver agreed in 1871 to manage the great task regarding the removal of thousands of Confederate remains to final resting places in the South. More will be presented on these two men and their efforts later in this chapter.

◆ ◆ ◆

Marking the Graves

No list, roster or register of the dead at Gettysburg would have been possible without the crude, wooden headboards and other various means by which graves were temporarily marked and or distinguished. To enhance the importance of correct identification markers placed over soldiers' graves, we shall read how one visitor felt on the subject. He was 37-year-old artist and teacher John B. Bachelder of New Hampshire who arrived at Gettysburg sometime between July 5 and 7. His memoirs emphasize not only the usefulness of headboards, but the equal significance of the burial list. In a letter to Governor Curtin of Pennsylvania on August 10, 1863, Bachelder stated:

> I have been engaged since the battle at this place in making drawings of its various phases for historical pictures. I am now occupied upon a general view representing something over twenty square miles, on which I show each road, house, field and forest, in a word everything that could effect the tide of battle or be of interest to the public. I propose to publish a supplementary sheet, with proper reference to the general view, giving the name of every soldier whose grave is marked and showing, its position....
>
> I am obliged to carefully canvass every rod of the ground, to get all the names. I find that a large proportion of them were written with lead pencil and by the rains beating the fresh earth upon them have already become nearly effaced. And before the coming autumn many will be entirely obliterated. Massachusetts sent a committee on here to remark the names of her sons that had fallen in battle; they spent several days but finding they had the whole ground to canvass they have left the remainder with me. As I said before I visit every enclosure and take every name. I now propose to the Executives of different States for a fair compensation to good men to go with me and remark every name that may need it, and when necessary put up new headboards. The expense will be but a trible, and though entirely distinct from my business I will see it well done if left in my charge. I commenced to remark them gratuituously, but find it will take me about three times as long to go over the ground. Yet I cannot bare [*sic*] to leave a name un-marked which another rain may blot out from its friends forever...."[50]

These grave markers and inscriptions went from simple initials written in pencil on a board or scribbled onto a tree trunk to more elaborate means, such as a brass plaque nailed to the headboard, or even, as is in the case of Captain David Acheson, 140th Pennsylvania Infantry, the initials and regimental number chiseled into a large boulder at the head of a temporary battlefield grave. The "classic" headboard and the type best known from the Civil War was much like the one discovered on a farm west of Gettysburg in 1888. The *Compiler* of May 29 gave the find a couple of inches of space:

(Left) The original headboard from the grave of Lt. Walter A. Wallace, 24th Michigan, found in John Herbst's woodlot. (WAF)

(Below, left) The temporary burial site and chiseled inscription "DA 140 P.V." on a rock several hundred yards north of Rose's wheat field. (GAC)

(Below) Captain David Acheson had one of the most durably marked graves at Gettysburg. (SGW)

RELIC.- Mrs. Clayton Hoke, some time ago, found, near the Chambersburg turnpike, a piece of white pine board, about nine inches square, marked as follows:

Capt. J.M. Gaston.
Capt. T.G. Clark and Son.
42d Miss. Vols.
Killed July 1st, 1863.

The marking is very distinct; looks as if the letters had first been cut with a sharp-bladed pocket knife, and the lines afterwards followed by a pointed piece of iron or coarse wire heated. This notice of the relic is made with the hope that it may meet the eye of some one directly interested.

In continuing, the reader may need to understand that the "christian" cross representing this religion was rarely, if ever used on graves in the United States in the 19th Century, just as churches did not use a cross on the cupola or steeple. The use of the cross is an oddity anyway. Although it dates back many years prior to Christianity as a pagan symbol, it is a more modern sign of that religion except in the Roman Catholic Church. In fact, in the earliest Greek manuscripts available which recount the Christian "gospels," the word "cross" is not even used to designate how the Jewish prophet Jesus was executed. The word in the very first Greek transcripts is actually "stake" or "upright pale," which of course is how many early civilizations *impaled* their criminals. The actual word "cross" interestingly, is written nowhere in even the *oldest* biblical documents.[51]

Therefore, people searching for the graves of loved ones, or just merely passing by them on other errands, would have seen a variety of signs to indicate a burial, such as fencerails at the head of graves, pieces of boards from ammunition or ration boxes, roof shingles, leather cartridge box flaps nailed to a post or tree, regulation wooden grave markers, including very precise black painted letters and numbers noted earlier, piles of stones over the site, the name chiseled into a nearby rock or boulder, floor boards ripped out of houses or barns, or a piece of paper or "pasteboard" attached to a tree or post, and even more. The official means of identification and recognition furnished by the U.S. Government was the use of "walnut or locust headboards on which the name etc. was burnt into the wood."[52]

Since soldiers in the Civil War were not issued "identification discs or tags," or as they are called now, "dog-tags," it was always a difficult and often an impossible job to identify the remains of a deceased battlefield casualty. Military men could however, *purchase* these discs or pins from army sutlers, or other mercantile establishments catering to soldiers' needs. Under the *best* circumstances, where friends, or regimental comrades with time aplenty were in attendance at the burial, the needs of the dead were better met, tags or not.

Increasingly as more time passed from the time of the battle, interest in and attention to these rural burials, especially those of the Confederates, waned. Then came vandals, family members searching for *particular* dead, ravaging and hungry animals, plows cutting through graveyard areas, wood cutters and their wagons crisscrossing the sites, farmers moving to and fro over their fields, visitors on foot, horseback and in carriages, heavy rains, melting snows, storm washouts, and the normal heavy leaf pile up in autumn—all slowly but certainly wore down both the markers, as pitiful as they were, and the crude graves themselves.

One other early commentator did see the interred laid out in well defined sites near the "angle" along Cemetery Ridge. These were obviously Union graves that he defined:

"Care had been taken to place a headboard at each grave, with a legible inscription thereon, showing whose remains are resting beneath. The headboard is usually made from the remnant of a box that may have served its purpose and become useful as a box no longer. In a few instances they appear to have been made from fresh lumber, with special reference to their present use. On one board the comrades of the dead soldiers had nailed the back of his knapsack, on which his name was painted. On another was a brass plate [a clothing stencil] bearing the soldiers name in heavily stamped letters."[53]

Certainly and clearly there was more care given to the interment of the Federal dead. Lamentably, even one of the local newspapers had to admit that for every grave having been distinctly marked, just as many were not. On July 21, a short article was printed purporting that already upwards of 700 coffins had been built in Gettysburg by a local undertaker to facilitate the removal of bodies to their Northern homes. But, as the paper explained, the town was filled with anxious visitors and inquiring relatives. "Some have to go away cheerless and unsatisfied, the last resting-place of their friends not being identified, from the vast amount that were hurried into their mother-earth, without a mark to tell who lies there. This is painful to a father, a mother, a wife, a sister; but such is the inevitable consequence of a fearful and tremendous battle, like that of the three days of Gettysburg."[54]

Another similar description came from Joseph Foster of Portsmouth, New Hampshire, who collaborated that news story on or about July 19. "The saddest marks are the graves of those killed. They are in all directions, sometimes singly, sometime in little groups of from 3 to 12. Some are marked with a board, carefully cut with the name and regiment, others have merely a stick with the initials scratched on it, and still others have no mark whatever to show who sleeps there. The graves are generally very hastily dug not more than 18 inches deep, and coffins of course are out of the question." Often regiments had particular individuals who became quite proficient in the specific duty of "cutting headboards." Sergeant E.P.M. Bragdon, 10th Maine, who was assisting Dr. H. Ernest Goodman at the Twelfth Corps hospital, directed his men into squads to accomplish various tasks at this facility. One of these squads, he said, was designated to "provide head-boards and to letter them. Josiah Smith and Ephraim C. Benson were especially apt in cutting the names of the dead upon wooden head-boards improvised from cracker boxes."[55]

A rare Gettysburg battlefield grave marker preserved by the family of Lt. Livingston. (WL)

A cavalry officer present near where Foster meditated on July 7, drafted a few words to the effect in his diary that, "our men were buried in good order and the most of the graves have a board at their head with their name Regt. & Company written upon it."[56]

Curiously, one of the burial mounds noted above, had these sentiments carefully added: "please do not pull up this board."[57]

One Confederate cautioned that in his experience *any* sign or marker inscribed in any way could eventually be lost. He warned that "[s]ometimes friendly hands cut the name and the company of the deceased upon the flap of a cartridge box, nail it to a piece of board, and place [it] at the head, but this was soon knocked down, and at the end of a short time all traces of the dead are obliterated."[58]

Marshal Prue, the Texas soldier called attention to some pages back, had a piece of rail fence unpretentiously driven in at the head of his grave, his name merely written thereon with a lead pencil. The author of the Prue sighting, also rejoined that "it is gratifying to see the respect shown, when opportunity is had, in the burying of individuals in spots, under trees, by a rock, near a stream, places where they can be found, with the inscription on a board, or cut in a tree, or on a rock."[59]

The difference in the care and effort taken to inter the National dead versus enemy remains was remarked upon by Lieutenant Frank Haskell, who interjected that "[o]ur own men were buried in graves, not trenches; and upon a piece of board, or stave of a barrel, or bit of cracker box, placed at the head, were neatly cut or penciled the name and regiment of the one buried in such. This practice was general...." He further informed his brother to whom he was writing that Northern men were inhumed not long after they fell, and it was the work of their own comrades which gave them a decent burial, while the enemy's

A regulation Federal headboard from Gettysburg. (AL)

A piece of red shale used to mark the grave of a soldier who died at the Second Corps field hospital on the Jacob Schwartz farm. (GAC)

dead could not be provided for until after the hostilities had ended. By then the needed tools were absent with the army's departing wagon trains; haste was required due to the temporary nature of the work details who must soon return to their regiments, and of course no Federal soldiers knew personally any of the deceased Rebels. Therefore their entombments were not properly carried out. Haskell admits that had the Confederates won the battle, the results would have been just the opposite.[60]

One of the most unusual ways in which a grave was identified was the resting place of Private R.G. Gunn of the 17th Mississippi, who was probably mortally wounded on July 2 near Sherfy's "peach orchard." On his carefully placed headboard was a silver plate with this plea nicely engraved thereon: "OH, God preserve his body for friends." Gunn's body lay on the farm of John Crawford out on Marsh Creek, a hospital of General Barksdale's Brigade.[61] One wonders how the plaque was obtained or made in such an out-of-the-way location. Or, more curiously, did Gunn himself carry the plate with him throughout his service, to be used in just such a manner?

It may be interesting to contemplate this information. Out of the approximately 1,100 marked Confederate graves left at Gettysburg, at least 50 percent were incorrectly listed or identified by the various people we have already surveyed who kept personal registers. This disturbing statistic did not pertain only to the Southerners. Even on the Union side, many errors were made. By the time 3,500 bodies were reinterred into the Soldiers' National Cemetery between October 1863 and April 1864, a great percentage were erroneously identified in some way. Some examples will suffice to demonstrate how frequent misidentification was made in both U.S. and Confederate registers of the dead.

Initial Identification	*Corrected Identification*
"Lewis Frento"	Louis Torango (76th NY Inf)
"Lt. J. Ferretzy"	Julius Friederic (119th NY Inf)
"A. Sulgroof"	Elkanah Sulgrove (19th Ind. Inf)
"George Ketchler"	George Hitchelor (5th Mich. Cav)
"Harris Mahammer"	Harris Mahorner (11th Miss. Inf)
"R.S. McLaning"	R. Lewis McLaurin (18th Miss. Inf)
"William Sensolman"	William Sensebaugh (5th Tex. Inf)
"Clint Buchaler"	J.C. Burkhalter (61st Ga. Inf)
"Mr. Dungerdol"	John A.F. Dunderdale (9th Va. Inf)

These are just ten of the nearly three *thousand* names that were both inaccurately and accurately placed or inscribed on markers around the battlefield.

For one of the more unusual exemplifications of common errors made in grave identification, we reiterate the story of Private Stephen Kelly of Co. E, 91st Pennsylvania. He joined that unit in August 1861, and was mustered out three years later in Philadelphia. Several years after the war Kelly had occasion to visit the battlefield park and was surprised to find his own grave, (#A-88) nicely defined in the Pennsylvania section of the National Cemetery.

It is there today, but Kelly was not in it. He took the whole matter in stride and in good humor, and was once heard to say: "[E]ach Decoration Day I go up there and strew some flowers on the tomb of the man who is substituting for me."[62] But as to whom does lie forever in Kelly's place there under the sod and manicured grass at Gettysburg, no one will ever know. Here is just one of many who, although a name is nicely fitted to a grave, happens to be the wrong man.

Mistakes such as the Kelly case were not at all uncommon. On November 3, 1863, the Adams *Sentinel* included an article illustrating that very serious problem. This one, however, did have a happy ending.

Singular Case of Mistaken Identity

In the battle of Gettysburg there was engaged with the Union forces a young man, whose parents reside in Birmingham, Allegheny county, Penna. It was announced that he was among the killed in that sanguinary fight, and his friends proceeded to the battle-field to recover his remains. After some difficulty, they managed to recover what they were positive was his body, and brought it home and had it interred in the family burying ground. A few nights since, the house of the parents was visited by a young man from the army, who aroused the household. On entering the house what was the surprise and astonishment of the parents to discover in their visitor their deeply mourned son, whose remains they fancied were resting quietly in the cemetery. It turned out that the body brought on and interred there was that of a rebel, who wore in the battle a United States uniform and whose resemblance to the Union soldier was a very striking one.[63]

The best instance of this unhappy but familiar situation is the belief that at least three Confederate soldiers who even as this is written, still lie buried in the National Cemetery alongside and among their mortal enemies; a portion of the several thousand bodies of Union men who were slain at Gettysburg. These Southerners are: Private M.F. Knott, Company F, 1st Maryland Infantry Battalion, CSA, buried under the name M.F. Knott, 1st Maryland Infantry, USA; Private John T. Johnson, Company K, 11th Mississippi Infantry, reposing in the marked grave of John Johnson, Co. D, 11th Massachusetts, and Private Eli T. Green, Co. E, 14th Virginia Infantry, resting forever under the granite stone of E.T. Green, Co. E, 14th Pennsylvania. Major Benjamin W. Leigh, on the staff of General Edward Johnson, CSA, was buried in the "unknown" section of the cemetery but was removed in 1866 to Shockoe Cemetery, in Richmond, Virginia.[64]

There could be, and presumably are, more Confederates buried there, but it is unlikely we will ever know the exact number. It is not our purpose to discredit a man who did so much good work, but here read a remark made by Samuel Weaver who superintended the exhumation of Federal soldiers from the field for reinterment in the Soldiers' National Cemetery. He asserted this in 1864:

"I firmly believe that there has not been a single mistake made in the removal of the soldiers to the Cemetery by taking the body of a rebel for a Union soldier." And frankly, considering the fact that he successfully and decently removed and reburied 3,512 remains, that declaration is not very far off the mark.[65]

◆ ◆ ◆

Reinterment into the National Cemetery

Ultimately, there came a day when the bones and relics of battle, the mounds of graves, broken fences, and trampled crops, scarred trees and buildings, all began to be smoothed over by time and weathering, and by the husbandry and handiwork of men and women. And, if nothing else, everything is always put right again by nature. In the interim, though, in the first few weeks and months after the terrible battle, the landscape was no doubt a raw, foul and offensive setting which was both oppressive and unsettling to those who had occasion to traverse the storm-lashed streets and fields, the trampled and broken meadows and woods, and the gouged and rutted hills, ridges and knolls. Those were the weeks when local speculation was intensely focused on what should be done to rid the area forever of not only the debris and destruction of war, but more especially, the once human remains of the warriors who had fought over the ground. The many pathetic little mounds and gashed burial trenches were but an ever-present and gruesome reminder of the great price someone had to pay in fulfillment of the country's need and call. The constant and morbid scenes were uncomfortable and highly unnerving to some, and merely a bothersome inconvenience to others; but in any event the bodies would have to be permanently removed. Farming was to begin again very soon, and not only would many graves be in the path of the plowmen, but the constant stream of friends and relatives of these dead, or their representatives, the embalmers, as well as souvenir hunters and sightseers, were unremittingly in the path of these somber and practical agriculturists. Then there were the less utile folk who thought it an elementary right to give proper respect to those men who had died in defense of their country, and especially in this particular case, as defenders of the great Commonwealth of Pennsylvania.

In those days following the battle there had to have been many ideas batted around of just how to accomplish the task. Instinctively, most of it was just idle talk and conjecture, while some whose thoughts and emotions ran deeper began to take the problem very seriously. Soon their plans emerged and materialized into reality.

The Republican Governor of Pennsylvania, Andrew G. Curtin, then 46 years old, visited the field as early as Saturday, July 11; he undoubtedly saw and contemplated the more brutal aspects of the battleground, and certainly knew that Pennsylvania carried a law on its books since February 1862, *requiring* the state to care for its war wounded and the burial of its dead.

So by the middle of July 1863, several people in Adams County were already petitioning the governor, proposing ideas for a central, all in-

Governor Andrew G. Curtin. (USLC)

clusive cemetery for the Pennsylvanians killed in action or who had died of wounds received at Gettysburg. By then removals of soldier remains had steadily progressed for two weeks as family members of the slain sought to bring their men home to be reinterred in regional plots and cemeteries. The upsetting aspect of these ongoing removals, was due in part to the mood which manifested itself at that time to begin a general collection of bodies. That is, the worry over the chance of various health related problems arising, plus the high personal cost to families for embalming and transportation, and lastly, the reality that not every state like Pennsylvania was providing money to enable soldiers' corpses to be returned to loved ones. The number of men expressed home by private means, or by use of states' funds may never be fully known, but in all likelihood it was around 1,500.[66]

One of the first to broach this idea locally was Gettysburg attorney David McConaughy, the President of the Board of Evergreen Cemetery, who had already tended to the burial of more than 100 soldiers in that private cemetery. In a communication to Governor Curtin on July 25, McConaughy asked for support backing a plan to bury all of Pennsylvania's dead in the Evergreen Cemetery at the expense of the state. Ironically, at about that same time, on July 23, the mayor of Boston was urging his city council to purchase a plot of ground at Evergreen exclusively for the burial of Boston men killed in the battle.[67]

Meanwhile, ex-army surgeon Theodore Dimon, the aforementioned New York relief agent, had an inspiration of his own. Owing to the impracticality of having all of the deceased, "removed to their former homes, and especially in the case of the more distance States," he concluded and asserted to "present it [his idea of a central 'national' cemetery at Gettysburg] to several gentlemen from the various states interested, who were [then] at Gettysburg." There is little doubt from the evidence available that Dimon was indeed the first person to actually introduce the novel subject of instituting an all inclusive cemetery on the battlefield itself. At Dimon's request a meeting was held at the office of David Wills, who was another Gettysburg lawyer and Governor Curtin's specially appointed relief agent for the state of Pennsylvania.

"At the meeting," Dimon related,

> I presented a proposition that a portion of the ground occupied by our line of battle on Cemetery Hill should be purchased for a permanent burial place for the soldiers of our army who lost their lives in this battle, or who died here of their wounds; and that their bodies should be gathered from the fields in which they were interred and deposited in this burial place by regiments and States with proper marks designating their graves. It was proposed, also, that this should be done by joint action on the part of the executives of the States interested. The proposition met with approval. The Governors of New York, Pennsylvania, New Jersey, Massachusetts, etc. were written to, stating the proposal and the reasons for its adoption. Mr. Wills entered into negotiations for the purchase of the land, and I am since informed that Governor [Horatio] Seymour of New York has addressed Governor [Andrew] Curtin of Pennsylvania engaging to join him and the executives of the other States in purchasing this land and carrying out the proposed undertaking.[68]

Accordingly, on July 24, 1863, David Wills wrote to Governor Andrew Curtin, a correspondence which appears at least officially, to have started the momentum. In almost every contemporary and current account, David Wills has received the central credit for the conception of the Soldiers' National Cemetery. Let us remember however that there was already a law on the books in the United States, it was a year old in 1863, which authorized the President to purchase ground to be used for new "national cemeteries," thus providing an honorable resting place for soldiers who had died in service. By late 1863 there were at least twelve of these U.S. government cemeteries in existence across the country. Finally, we should be cognizant of the fact that the Soldiers' National Cemetery in Gettysburg did not become *United States* property until June 22, 1871.

Mr. Wills, the agent for Andrew Curtin, was 32 years old in 1863. He was the son of Ruth Wilson and James Jack Wills and had been born at Wilsonville, near present-day Bendersville, in Menallen Township, Adams County, Pennsylvania, where his father was a farmer and also owned a tannery. When David was thirteen years old, four years before his mother died, the family including one sister, moved to Gettysburg. There, Wills attended Pennsylvania College, graduating in 1851. He spent a year in Alabama as a teacher, then returned to Pennsylvania where he studied law under Thaddeus Stevens. In 1856 Wills married Jennie Smyser of Norristown, Pennsylvania, and set up a practice in Gettysburg, where he became very active in public affairs.

The Commonwealth's Governor Curtin was pleased with David Wills' labors and suggestions, and the plan, with the aid and support of other interested states, soon went forward.

During the months preceding the end of 1863, much had to be accomplished. In truth, work was already in progress. Only a few weeks prior to the day Attorney Wills began the process of establishing the soldiers' cemetery, a Gettysburg newspaper advertised:

> To All Citizens
> Men, Horses and Wagons wanted immediately, to bury the dead and to cleanse our streets, in such a thorough way as to guard against a pestilence. Every good citizen can be of use by reporting himself at once, to Capt. W.W. Smith, acting Provost Marshal....[69]

Very few "good citizens" volunteered, as we have already found out, and the burials had to be carried out by various and sundry other groups or persons.

Attorney David Wills. (HCAC)

So even as the first hurried burials were being completed or already slowly decomposing in the mid-summer earth of hundreds of temporary graves, David Wills and others were fulfilling their pledge and duty of finding a permanent site for these unfortunate mortals.

The first action was to find appropriate ground so as to be ready to move the corpses when colder weather arrived.

As we are now aware, David McConaughy had originally pressed the governor to use land within the boundaries of Evergreen Cemetery. He had in fact already made verbal agreements with several adjacent landowners to purchase additional space so as to expand the ground in order to take care of the influx of thousands of soon to be expected Northern soldier remains. David Wills was therefore placed in a quandary as he tried to purchase this same land already described and promised to the governor, but now "locked in" by McConaughy. As Wills tried to persuade the owners of the land on Cemetery Hill to break their agreements with McConaughy, as can be imagined, a bitter struggle resulted. Finally after much squabbling, and with letters flying back and forth to the governor, Wills had to accept defeat, so in August he began to search for an alternate site. The one finally selected was on the north end of Cemetery Ridge near the left center of the old Union battle line, on Judge David Zeigler's wooded property.[70]

Eventually, just after the middle of August an agreement was reached between Wills and McConaughy, mostly due to the pressure finally exerted by several local community leaders. McConaughy and the Evergreen Cemetery board agreed to sell to the state the land needed for the new soldiers' burial ground. A total of five plots was purchased, seventeen acres in all, for a fairly reasonable price which averaged about $175 an acre. During the battle, these plots had consisted of an apple orchard, a wheat field and a corn field, among others.

With all of the "haggling" now past and emotions settled, it was time to draw up a plan to indicate how the military cemetery would be laid out. With no clear idea in mind, Wills turned to the expertise of respected landscape gardener William Saunders, who was then an employee of the newly authorized U.S. Department of Agriculture. Saunders had been born in 1822 in Scotland, was a university graduate and had come to America before 1850. He spent his early years in the United States designing and laying out private estates and cemeteries. Saunders believed that in his Gettysburg proposal the grouping of soldiers by states was very important. He also stressed his idea that the overall area should be one of "simple grandeur," with the burials by state matched in harmony with the land and the natural surroundings, thus according *solemnity* to the whole design. He chose to avoid "intricacy and great variety of parts," and in particular Saunders insisted upon refraining from "introducing any inter-mixture or meretricious display of ornament."

His selection of a low semi-circle of graves grouped by state, officers and men on equal footing, with care taken in the selection of shrubbery and trees, walks, etc.; a plain yet beautiful centerpiece monument; the gateway and gatehouse built on a tasteful, but solid and sturdy design; all of these ideas coming together to form the "central theme."[71]

While the Saunders plan for the cemetery went ahead, David Wills and his committee made the more practical arrangements for implementing the many small and necessary details, and for the eventuality of "consecrating" the grounds. For the consecration, Edward Everett was chosen. He was a 69-year-old Harvard educated former clergyman and statesman, orator, and freethinker. Throughout his long and eventful life Everett had served as the President of Harvard College, the Governor of Massachusetts, a U.S. Secretary of State, the Minister to Great Britain, as well as a member of the U.S. House of Representatives and a U.S. Senator. Because Everett could not complete other previous engagements and have a speech prepared by October 23, which was the first date chosen for the dedication ceremonies, November 19 was finally selected for the event.

The extraordinary statesman, Edward Everett. (GNMP)

Meanwhile on August 10, an important order was posted in Gettysburg's newspapers, and on her streets and buildings. It hailed from Major General D.N. Couch's Headquarters of the Department of the Susquehanna at Chambersburg, Pennsylvania, and instructed that no disinterment of bodies would be allowed to take place during the months of August and September, or until authorized by that headquarters.[72]

In the interim, since the order made it impossible to begin transportation of the bodies until at least October, Mr. Saunders, Agent Wills and the committee continued to prepare the newly acquired grounds for receiving the bodies in the upcoming fall.

Although the order had been issued by Couch in August to halt the removal of bodies by Northern families, we know that up to that time and even later, up to 1,000 and possibly more remains had already been shipped to Pennsylvania homes and to other Union states. A specific example of one of the many soldiers who was found by friends and carried home, may be of interest to the reader, as so many similar moves were accomplished under varying degrees of difficulty.

On July 2, in the heat of battle, a young officer named Edward Stanley Abbot was mortally wounded on what is today called Houck's Ridge, a place west of the northern rim of Little Round Top. He was hit by a Minié ball in the right breast, the lead cut through the lung and lodged near his spine. Borne to the rear as quickly as possible, he was eventually driven by ambulance to the 2nd Division field hospital of the Fifth Corps, which was situated on the Michael Fiscel farm south of Gettysburg. This farm sat about one mile west of the Baltimore Turnpike where it passed the "White Church." Abbot died there on July 8, 1863, in a hospital tent while lying on a bit of straw on the damp, bare ground. When he was wounded Abbot was a lieutenant in the 17th U.S.

Infantry, a Regular Army regiment commanded by Lieutenant Colonel J.D. Greene. Stanley, as he was known by all, had enlisted on July 1, 1862, in Portland, Oregon. Earlier in life he had been educated at several fine schools, including the Boston Latin School, the Phillips Exeter Academy, and for a time at Harvard College. Until the war began, his desire was to become a writer.

On July 7, a day before his death, Abbot's older brother, Edwin H. Abbot of Boston received a telegram from him which stated: "Wounded in the breast. Doctor says not mortal. I am at Corps hospital, near Gettysburg. Expect to be in Baltimore in a few days. E. Stanley Abbot."

Edwin started at once for Gettysburg, but did not arrive until Friday the 10th, two days too late to see Stanley alive. After speaking to a number of soldiers and physicians concerning his brother's last days, Edwin finally sought out the grave. It was found "on a hillside, just

Lt. Edward Stanley Abbot. His grave was found by a brother on Michael Fiscel's farm. (SDH)

on the outskirts of the grove in which the [hospital] camp was pitched. [A] brook rolled round its foot in the little valley, while in the distance was Round Top, and the swelling landscape peculiar to that portion of Pennsylvania, —a family of hills, stretching far and near, with graves dotting their sides and summits. Here was the spot which, ten days before a lovely farm, was now populous with the dead."

Edwin Abbot tried diligently for five days after his arrival to procure a coffin so Stanley's body could be brought home. He confessed that the "condition of things at Gettysburg after the battle beggars description." Finally he was able to hire two men, a horse and wagon and so proceeded to the Fifth Corps hospital. The heavy-hearted story is continued here in Edwin's own words:

> My brother's grave was marked carefully with a wooden headboard, made from a box cover, and bearing his name, rank, and day of death. It was so suitable a place for a soldier to sleep, that I was reluctant to remove the body for any purpose. But the spot was part of a private farm; and as removal must come, I thought it best to take the body home, and lay it with the dust of his kindred. When my companions had scraped the little and light earth away, there he was wrapped in his gray blanket, in so natural a posture, as I had seen him lie a hundred times in sleep, that it seemed as if he must awake at a word.
>
> Two soldiers of the Eleventh Infantry, the companion regiment of the Seventeenth, had followed me to the spot,—one a boy hardly as old as Stanley, the other a man of forty. As the body was lifted from the grave, this boy of his own accord sprang forward, and gently taking the head, assisted in laying the body on the ground without disturbing it, a thing not pleasant to do, for the earth had received and held it for a week. I told them to uncover the face. They did so, and I recognized the features, though there was nothing pleasant in the

sight. I then bade them replace the folds of the gray blanket, his most appropriate shroud, and lay the body in the coffin. They did so; but again the boy stepped forward, and of his own motion carefully adjusted the folds as they were before. When we turned to go, I spoke to the boy and his companion. They said they knew Stanley, and knowing I had come for his body, they had left the camp to help me, because they had liked Stanley. "Yes," added the boy, "he was a strict officer, but the men all liked him. *He was always kind to them.*" That was his funeral sermon. And, by a pleasant coincidence, as one of the men remarked to me on our way back, the sun shone out during the ten minutes we were at the grave, the only time it had appeared for forty-eight hours.

In due time Edward S. Abbot was returned to his home in Beverly, Massachusetts, and the body was placed in the family plot; "a pleasant place among the trees on a sloping hill, where one can see the sea in the distance, and at times hear the waves upon the beach,—a spot he had often admired in former times...."[73]

Lt. Abbot was buried on this hillside overlooking a small creek. (SCH)

✛ ✛ ✛

October 1863 finally arrived and with it cooler weather. But there was also an added sense of urgency regarding the soon to be final destination of the multitude of dead soldiers who, unlike Abbot, still lay across the thousands of acres of battlefield farms and woods and the many field hospitals adjacent.

On the 13th of that month, David Wills wrote out a notice for the Adams *Sentinel and General Advertiser*. It read in part:

All the dead will be disinterred and the remains placed in coffins and buried...in the Soldiers' Cemetery.

If it is the intention of the friends of any deceased soldier to take his remains home for burial, they will confer a favor by immediately making known to me that intention.

After the bodies are removed to this Cemetery, it will be very desirable not to disarrange the order of the graves by any removals.[74]

Two days later another very important notice was placed in the local papers by Wills. For this one he also printed up broadsides to be hung around the county. It indicated that "sealed proposals will be received at my office...until the 22d inst....for the following two contracts, viz:

"1st. For disinterring the bodies on the Gettysburg Battle Field and at the Hospitals...and removing them to the Soldier's Cemetery....2d. For digging the graves, and burying the dead in the Cemetery...."[75]

The specifications for the work detailed in each contract were clearly spelled out and consisted of how and where to pick up the coffins (which, by the way, were provided by the quartermaster general of the U.S. Army), how to open the graves, search for the bodies, take out the remains, place the body in the coffin, mark the coffin, and cover the old grave, etc. The successful bidder of this first contract was instructed to make sure that the remains were definitely Union soldiers, and the contractor was allowed to transport no more than 100 bodies per day, and the work had to be commenced on October 26.

The second contractor was directed to dig the graves in the new cemetery where ordered in a manner stipulated and approved by William Saunders and

PROPOSALS
FOR THE REMOVAL OF THE DEAD ON THE
GETTYSBURG BATTLE-FIELD.

SEALED proposals will be received at my Office in the Borough of Gettysburg, until the 22d inst., at 12 o'clock, noon, for the following two contracts, viz:

1st. For disinterring the bodies on the Gettysburg Battle Field and at the Hospitals in the vicinity, and removing them to the Soldiers' Cemetery on the south side of the Borough of Gettysburg.
2d. For digging the graves, and burying the dead in the Cemetery.

☞The specifications of work for each contract, to be strictly complied with by the Contractor, can be seen and examined at my office.

DAVID WILLS,
Agent for A. G. CURTIN, Governor of Pennsylvania.

Gettysburg, Oct. 15, 1863.

PRINTED AT THE "SENTINEL OFFICE," GETTYSBURG.

One of Wills' printed broadsides, measuring 11" x 17" (MCW)

David Wills. The coffins had to be placed three feet deep. At the head of each trench an offset would be dug in the earth 20 feet long and two feet from the surface of the ground. On this offset a dry stone wall was to be built 18 inches in height and six inches from the surface for the placement of the granite marker which would contain the name, rank, company and regiment of the deceased. The coffins would be deposited side by side, with the original headboards to be attached when present and nailed upright and above ground to show the name and regiment of the soldier. In conclusion, bonds were to be secured and posted by both parties.[76]

On October 22 the bids were opened and tabulated. Wills had received 34, varying from $1.59 to $8.00 per body. The lowest bidder was Frank W. Biesecker who was selected to complete the entire job specified by the proposal. At the end of the completed process, Wills reported that the work by Biesecker was performed with "great care and to my entire satisfaction."

James S. Townsend of Rahway, New Jersey, who was named the "Surveyor and Superintendent of Burials," was hired by the cemetery committee to survey and lay out the grounds as designated by William Saunders, and to superintend the reburials *in* the cemetery. He personally measured the depth of every grave, for a total of 3,512 and the proper distance to be dug between each coffin. He also kept a log with the name, company and regiment of each of the remains as they were placed in the ground, and clearly marked the grave with a new headboard. The daily totals kept by Townsend were carried to Wills' office every evening to compare with the list that Samuel Weaver made of his days' work on the battlefield itself. These names and numbers, once they corresponded and added up were placed in correct order and then were affixed to a permanent register each day by Mr. Wills himself.

Samuel Weaver was a Gettysburg drayman (or teamster) who was hired by Biesecker as the superintendent for the exhuming of the bodies of Union soldiers on the battlefield. His teams delivered up to 100 bodies to Townsend's men in the cemetery each day. Weaver asserted that no grave was permitted to be opened or a body searched unless he was physically present. He was proud to report in 1864 that he "saw every body taken out of its temporary resting places, and all pockets carefully searched; and where the grave was not marked, I examined all the clothing and everything about the body to find the name. I then saw the body, with all the hair and all the particles of bone, carefully placed in the coffin...." He also verified that all headboards were retained, and a record of each soldier's identity, when available, was kept in a special notebook. Weaver explained that often he was able to learn the name of a former "unknown" by finding within the personal effects of the corpse such items as pocket diaries,

James S. Townsend. (LHW)

Samuel Weaver and one of the exhumation parties. (HCC)

letters, testaments, bibles, photographs, or written in pocket books, or on descriptive lists, express receipts, medals, uniform clothing pieces and equipment, such as belts or cartridge boxes. All money, watches and jewelry, or relics and any other articles of value were packaged up and labelled for the friends of the deceased. A collection of 287 such packets were turned over to David Wills, but it is not known how many of the packets were ever claimed, or where the remainder of them are presently located.

In his final report written in March of 1864, Samuel Weaver accused undertakers and even the sorrowing friends and family of the soldiers of "obliterating or destroying many originally well preserved graves, by opening them carelessly and leaving about the area open graves, bones, clothing, and hair." Weaver notified Wills that his crews were not responsible for these atrocities, as they had left each grave neatly closed over and levelled, and no body parts or clothing were allowed to be left on the surface of the earth.

Furthermore, Weaver described how not all of the bodies were discovered in the same stages of decomposition. The burials on the first days' field were particularly distressing as few had been properly interred, much less identified, due to the carelessness of the Rebels who had held that ground from July 1 to 5. Most of those found by Weaver's men were generally "dry skeletons." On other sections of the field he observed that "[w]here bodies were in heavy clay soil, or in marshy places, they were in a good state of preservation. Where they were in sandy, porous soil, they were entirely decomposed." He explained too that the Federals were not *all* buried in single graves. Frequently they, like many Confederates, had been interred in trenches or shallow ditches where all were laid side by side, with often as many as sixty or seventy corpses in one trench.

As to identifying whether the body was a Union or Confederate soldier when the grave contained no personal identification, Weaver resorted to a clothing check as a final determination. He could often distinguish a Rebel body from a Yankee by the fact that Rebels "never went into battle with the United States coat on. Also Southern clothing was often cotton, colored gray or brown, while U.S. uniforms were always blue wool....Shoes were completely different too." But the most significant factor was the underwear. Weaver learned that Confederate soldiers' undergarments were almost always made of cotton, while Northerners predominantly wore wool. "Taking all these things together" he concluded, "we never had much trouble deciding, with infallible accuracy, whether the body was that of a Union soldier or a rebel."[77] Unfortunately, we know that Sam Weaver did make errors, and as far as identities, he may have caused many of the mistakes himself. His hard work is readily apparent, but his spelling through lack of formal education, misidentified a fair number of Union remains. A letter written to his brother William, a photographer who resided in Baltimore, is interesting as it concerns the November 19th cemetery dedication program, and also illuminates his less-than-perfect orthography.

November 25, 1863

Brother I wish you could have been here on the 19th last at the dedication of the National Cemetery it was one of the largest assembling that ever met in our country with the exception when the battle was fought, it is supposed that there were not less than from 30 to 40,000 strangers present, & the order of the day was so excelent everthing was done in peace & harmony, I dident see one drunken man all day nor evening, though I was kept very buisey all day, in the fore noon I assisted Peter [Weaver] of getting a negative of the large assembly on the cemetery ground which I think is very fine, we have not as yet printed any shot of the negative. Peter went off to Hanover on last Sunday evening to attend to his car again [a traveling photographic studio], I suppose he has printed some shots of the assembly that was at the dedication of the 19th. I have had Peter at G. for 7 weeks taking negatives of the surgeons [and] the hospital tents at the General Hospitals, he has some very fine negatives, we have sold over 1000 shots up to this time, we have something like 75 different negatives, I intend as soon as all the dead soldiers are burried in the National Cemetery, to take a picture of the whole ground & also take a negative of the ground for each state, Brother it is going to make one of the pertiest cemetary in U.S. I have been employed by the government to superintend the raising of all the dead that fell on the battle fields at G. & all that died in the hospitals to the N. Cemetery in 20 days I sent 1285 If the weather remains favourable I think that I can have them all sent in by the first of Jan. Please let me hear from you soon, Yours in love & cc

S. Weaver[78]

The actual day-to-day operations of the crew members involved in the constant removals and reinterments were quite enlightening in their own right. For one of the better accounts left to us by a participant, we look to Leander H. Warren who was fifteen in 1863 and lived on Railroad Street in Gettysburg. Years later Warren, the last survivor of one of Weaver's gangs, recalled these compelling experiences:

I would drive to the railroad car (the white pine coffins were sent here from points in York County) and load six of the coffins on my wagon and then drive to the point where the bodies were being taken up. There I would unload the boxes and return to the car for another load. By the time I had returned, the first six coffins were filled, and they were then loaded on my wagon and I took them to the National Cemetery. On the return trip for more bodies I stopped at the car and loaded six more coffins to be filled while I took the next load of bodies to the cemetery.

Many friends of the dead soldiers came here to witness the disinterment of their loved ones and the new burial in the national plot. Many of the women— wives, mothers, or sweethearts—fainted or became hysterical when the bodies were uncovered. Many of them would be found with a limb or other part of their bodies missing. Many of the bodies were only skeletons while on others the decomposed flesh still clung to the bones. Most were almost unrecognizable.

Basil Biggs, colored, of Gettysburg, was given the contract for disinterring the bodies on the field. He had a crew of eight or ten negroes in his employ. Samuel Weaver directed Biggs' men and as each body was removed, Weaver went through uniform pockets with an iron hook and sought for any means of identifying the body....

Basil Biggs had a colored boy hauling with a team of two horses and he could haul nine coffins at a trip. I hauled only six. When the bodies were placed according to states in the cemetery, the men placed long signs over the graves indicating the state from which the soldiers had come. There were over 900 that were unknown and could not be identified in any way.[79]

As mentioned by Mr. Warren, one of Samuel Weaver's assistants was Basil or Bazil Biggs, one of the few African American residents of Adams County. Biggs was born in 1819 and died in June 1906. He had moved to the county in 1858 with his spouse Mary J. Jackson, and had lived in various places as a tenant, such as on the Edward McPherson and John Crawford farms. After the war he purchased the old farm of Peter Frey on the Taneytown Road. During the battle the Crawford tenant house he was living in was used as a Confederate aid station and Basil and Mary suffered a $1,500 loss of property and damage.

Generally the work went on in this specific manner. When Frank Biesecker won the contract he hired Samuel Weaver as superintendent for exhuming the bodies from graves on the field. Weaver would personally examine each body as Basil Biggs and his crew of eight to ten helpers raised the corpses and put them into separate coffins. Weaver then checked each soldier more thoroughly and identified any by name if possible, all the while keeping a detailed register. David Warren and his son Leander and possibly others, including Biggs' teams, transported fresh coffins to the battle ground grave sites, then back to the cemetery with the coffins and bodies. At the cemetery, Townsend, as superintendent of burials, marked each grave, while Frank Biesecker and John B. Hoke physically dug the holes and lay the dead then reposing in their new coffins into the newly-made graves.

Warren, who died in 1937, made one other pertinent observation. He declared that Biggs, who had a two-horse team, could haul nine filled coffins at a time, while he (Warren) with a one-horse team only took six at a time. But, as Warren claimed, "I hauled about as many as he did, because I could go a little faster and [did] not have as many coffins to handle."[80]

John B. Hoke, the gravedigger noted above, was another man who had been born locally in 1813. He was married in 1838 to Jane E. Boling, and died in Juniata County, Pennsylvania, in 1888. Little is known of Samuel Weaver, the drayman, except that he was born in Gettysburg in 1812 and died there in February 1871. His spouse was Elizabeth A. Rinehart and the couple had at least one child, Rufus Benjamin, who was born in 1841 and became a medical doctor. More on Rufus Weaver is forthcoming.

By November 2 the newspapers were spreading the exciting intelligence that "the removal of the dead into the Soldiers' National Cemetery is now in progress—Several hundred have already been transferred to their new resting place.

"The Massachusetts dead are being removed by Solomon Powers, the Boston committee having made a special contract with him for the work."[81]

This latter contract was a unique agreement and not part of the regular proposal let by David Wills on October 22. Solomon Powers, who died in Gettysburg in 1883, had opened the first granite quarry where he "dressed" its first granite block about 1838. A native of New Hampshire, Powers, who was not yet sixty during the battle, had, with his wife Catherine, cared for a number of critically wounded soldiers in the weeks following the fighting. How and why he procured a separate deal with Massachusetts is unknown at this time.

About two and a half weeks after the above notification, on a pleasant November 19, the handsome new cemetery was officially dedicated with about 15,000 people in attendance. A large wooden platform to hold the many officials, delegates and honored guests had been erected just southeast of where the sixty foot high soldiers' monument would be completed by 1869, with its five white marble statues representing war, peace, history, plenty and the Genius of Liberty. This beautiful monument, which was carved in Italy and is 65 feet tall, was in the beginning supposed to be placed in the extreme southwestern portion of the seventeen acre cemetery, but the plan was changed and it was later built in the rear center of the semi-circle of graves. Contrary to popular belief, the wooden platform where Edward Everett delivered a very detailed two-hour oration, which was followed by President Lincoln's "few appropriate remarks," was not situated where the soldiers' monument now stands. According to more recent evidence, it stood about fifty yards behind or southeast of it, in the private Evergreen Cemetery, somewhere it is believed, in the locale where Mary Virginia Wade, the young woman shot on July 3, is currently entombed.

By late December 1863 and early January of the new year, David Wills began placing more notices in the town newspapers. This time the reader saw:

The Dead on the Battlefield

Farmers are requested to leave at my office, in Gettysburg, a description of the location on their lands of graves of Union Soldiers. Many have been buried in secluded spots, and persons will confer a great favor by making known to me, or to Mr. Samuel Weaver, the locality of such graves....[82]

The work on the battlefield and at the field hospitals had ceased when the earth could no longer be easily handled. A few reburials were still carried out notwithstanding the off-and-on cold weather throughout the winter months. But all that season, as James Townsend made known, there were delays due to frozen ground, wet weather and frequent snows, so the burials continued longer than first expected as they continued into the spring.[83]

By the 15th of February 1864, the *Compiler* was able to report this:

"The bodies of about 3,100 Federal soldiers have been reburied in the National Cemetery. Several hundred are yet to be removed, the work upon which is steadily going forward, and will doubtless be completed by the first of April."[84]

Not long after all of the Union reinterments were completed, John Trowbridge strolled through the cemetery. As he walked the ground in August of 1865 with guide John L. Burns, Trowbridge reflected on what he saw and felt.

It was a soft and peaceful summer day. There was scarce a sound to break the stillness, save the shrill note of the locust, and the perpetual click-click of the stonecutters, at work upon the granite headstones of the soldiers' cemetery. There was nothing to indicate to a stranger that so tranquil a spot had ever been a scene of strife. We were walking in the time-hallowed place of the dead....

I looked into one of the trenches in which the workmen were laying foundations for the headstones, and saw the ends of the coffins protruding. It was silent and dark down there. Side by side the soldiers slept, as side by side they fought. I chose out one coffin from among the rest, and thought of whose dust it contained....I could not know....He sleeps with the undistinguishable multitude, and his headstone is lettered, "Unknown."[85]

Curiously, according to the June 27 *Compiler*, a California visitor to the cemetery in June 1864 complained that the wooden headboards crowning the graves in the Indiana section were identified only *in pencil*, and were fast becoming obliterated. It is evident by these comments that the stone cutters were not working fast enough to keep up with such fading transient records.

The final cost for the entire cemetery project came to over $80,000. Altogether 3,354 reinterments were completed by Wills' workmen, of which 1,664 were unknown by name, and 979 were unknown by both name or state.

By a legislative act the Commonwealth of Pennsylvania incorporated the ground on March 25, 1864, designating it the "Soldiers' National Cemetery." In this same month and just a few days prior to the incorporation, David Wills granted an interview to a Washington newspaper correspondent. The product of that meeting was picked up by the Adams *Sentinel* on March 22, 1864, and provides us with a summary of that attorney's work in progress near the end of a long and tedious undertaking.

THE GETTYSBURG DEAD

BALTIMORE, March 14—David Wills, Esq., of Gettysburg, the General Agent of Pennsylvania for the Soldiers' National Cemetery arrived here this morning on his way to Washington. He informed me that all the bodies of our Union soldiers have been disinterred, and carefully buried in their appropriate places in the new National Cemetery. The total number thus removed and interred is three thousand five hundred and twelve. About one thousand of them are unknown, and one-fourth of the whole number belong to New York.

Many of the Union soldiers have been recognized, their names having been discovered when removing them, from letters, photographs, medals, devices, clothing, and other things buried with them, as they were hastily thrown into ditches after the battle. Quite an amount of money was also found on them, both in coin and paper, in sums ranging from the fraction of a dollar up to fifty dollars. Thirty-six dollars in gold were found in the pantaloons pocket of one corpse, and thirty to forty dollars in garments of others, besides many relics, mementoes, &c. All this money and these relics have been taken care of by the committee, properly labelled, and held in safekeeping for the relatives, should they ever call for them. A fine hunting case gold watch and five or six silver watches were also found upon bodies whilst disinterring them.

The Cemetery Association will be organized as soon as the Pennsylvania Legislature passes an act of incorporation for that purpose now before it. Workmen are busily engaged improving the grounds, and will continue so doing until the cemetery is completed....

From evidence developed from the workmen and others engaged in removing the dead bodies on the battle-field, they are now fully convinced that not less than seven thousand Rebels lost their lives in this conflict, the bodies of whom are still there. In one space of three acres was found three hundred and twenty five Confederate slain; and elsewhere, in a single trench, two hundred and fifty more. A considerable portion of the battle-ground is likely to be ploughed up this spring and summer by farmers owning it, preparatory to planting corn and other grain. As a matter of course, the Confederate graves must be obliterated, and the trenches which now indicate their burial places. There is a strong desire with the people, in respect to humanity, to have these bodies, though of the enemy, respectfully and decently put away, in some enclosure where they may not be disturbed—where they can sleep in quietude. Many strangers from all parts of the country still continue to visit Gettysburg to behold the scenes and relics of the terrible conflict so triumphant in behalf of our country, and of republican liberty.

On May 1, 1872, the Secretary of War accepted legal title to the National Cemetery at Gettysburg for the United States of America, and today it is one of 130 such entities in the country, and as John Patterson has truthfully stated, "one of our nation's most precious shrines."[86]

Removing the Confederate Dead

There could be no mistaking the actuality that the Confederates had lost the battle. If you didn't believe it from rumors, newspaper reports, letters sent from the front, or the participants themselves, all that was needed to convince you was an excursion to the old battlefield at Gettysburg. Depending on what a person thought before his or her arrival, it became clearly apparent as one looked around that indeed the Rebels were most certainly *not* the victors in the July engagement. It became even more noticeable after January 1864 when the Soldiers' National Cemetery really began to take shape. Now the cruelest vision for visitors was to gaze upon only the several thousand forlorn graves left behind by the Southern Army. Everywhere one looked there were the small mounds, grassy and luxuriant in warmer weather, or barren and bleak during the winter months. An entire half year had passed and the little single rises of

The only known site of an actual Confederate burial trench still visible on the Gettysburg National Military Park. (SCH)

earth or the long more prominent burial trenches had begun to settle as the corpses below the surface decomposed bit by bit. The action of rain and snow, leaf cover, farm plows, wandering animals, idle and curious visitors, and vandals, had helped to erode or erase many of the Confederate grave sites.

The words are worth repeating of Henry Boynton after his visit to the ground around the "peach orchard" in 1866, then filled with these forlorn Confederate burials.

"The grass had closed over the almost countless graves, and their mounds had melted away, or corn and the lesser grains bent above them. Still the deep green spot in the turf, the few hills of corn more luxuriant than their neighbors, or the dark color of the oats and the ranker growth of the wheat, told where vegetable life had drawn rich nourishment from the dead."[87]

Affirming Boynton's description was Russell Conwell, who added: "But the graves of the rebel dead are there, dotting the fields for miles around, generally covered with clover."[88]

It was this state of affairs which prompted Gettysburg's *Sentinel* newspaper to print the following:

THE REBEL DEAD

There appears to be considerable feeling in and around Gettysburg that a place be set apart for the burial of the Confederate dead who are now buried promiscuously over the battlefield, or in the vicinity. The recent rains have washed the places where they are buried, and the bones are exposed; besides, which, in a short time the land will be put under cultivation, and no trace of their last resting-place will be left. Common humanity would dictate a removal to some spot, not in or about our own National Cemetery, but the purchase of ground somewhere, where Southern friends may, when the rebellion is crushed, and all is peace, make their pilgrimage here. Our State should not make the purchase, nor should it be expected; but if Southern people should express the desire and would carry it to completion, we should say let it be done for the sake of our common humanity. The hostility of the dead has ceased; and let them be in a spot where a father, a mother, a sister or brother, can visit their last resting place; "when this cruel war is over."[89]

Following this notice, the Adams *Sentinel* received a poem from a woman in Washington, Pennsylvania, who had read the article and commented that the "sentiments you express in regard to the 'Confederate Dead,' are humane, magnanimous, and to my mind, truly patriotic." Here are her poetic lines as published in that paper on March 15, 1864.

Oh! choose ye a place where the dead may rest,
 And gather their bones from the field,
On their nameless graves let the sod be press'd,
 For Death has their mission sealed.

Ye Southern dead, what a mournful past —
 Three years, so grim and gory —
Oh, would ye had clung to the dear old Flag,
 For HERS WAS OUR EQUAL GLORY!

But the past, the past, we may not recall,
 The past so fraught with sorrow,
Then let us pray that for each, for all,
 There may speed a peaceful morrow.

Yes, choose ye a spot where the dead may sleep,
 Nor storms their bones uncover,
A spot where their lov'd ones may come and weep,
 "When this cruel war is over."

A.S.M.

Those in Adams County who dared to write or even think of such treasonous ideas were at once branded Southern sympathizers or "Copperheads." To examine how real this feeling was we should read of the experiences of John Trowbridge who had traveled to Gettysburg in August of 1865. His visit was more than a year after the above kind sentiments were published. Trowbridge had employed John Burns as his guide. Burns was the eccentric 70-year-old former town constable who on July 1, 1863, had taken his place in the ranks of the Union army on the south side of the Chambersburg Pike, was "sworn in" as a volunteer soldier and fought alongside a regiment of Yankee First Corps veterans until he was disabled by three battle wounds. Of course he was fanatically anti-Rebel, and for the ten years he lived after the battle Burns constantly accused anyone in the county he did not like of being a traitor.

Hiking through the fields that day with Burns, Trowbridge found that to the old man, the Confederate graves represented nothing more than dead

Rebels... "and nothing more; and he spoke with great disgust of an effort which had been made by certain 'Copperheads' of the town to have all the buried Rebels, now scattered about in the woods and fields, gathered together in a cemetery near that dedicated to our own dead." Trowbridge, who was thinking through the situation as they ambled over the countryside, replied to Burns in this manner.

"Yet consider, my friend...though they were altogether in the wrong, and their cause was infernal, these, too, were brave men; and under different circumstances, with no better hearts then they had, they might have been lying in honored graves up yonder, [in the national cemetery] instead of being buried in heaps, like dead cattle, down here."

John Lawrence Burns.
(SPB)

In a private moment to himself, Trowbridge later mused:

"Is there not a better future for these men also? The time will come when we shall at least cease to hate them."[90]

If Trowbridge, a 38-year-old Bostonian who had spent most of the war years writing anti-slavery tracts, could feel so generous and kindly to dead Southerners in 1865, there probably was indeed a chance at a better future for the bodies of these men who had been slaughtered at Gettysburg. But when and how would it come?

The answer to the question put by John Trowbridge would come six years later. For us the process will be made clear as we continue to develop and study this chapter, because the next section reviews the events leading to the collection and removal of the Confederate dead from Gettysburg.

✝ ✝ ✝

As the years passed from the end of the Civil War in May of 1865 to the beginning of the next decade, hundreds of visitors still regularly made the pilgrimage to Gettysburg. Certainly not in the numbers in which they had come right after the battle, for the populace in general was sick and tired of war, war talk, and most anything dealing with battles or casualties. Even the families and friends of those who fell at Gettysburg or on the other 10,500 battle sites across the land, had to get on with the normal day-to-day business of living. Occasionally, though, a memory became too painful, or a question remained unanswered, or after too many nights robbed of sleep, someone was finally drawn to make the mournful journey to the famous Pennsylvania community and its battleground. There were times in those days when a person could walk the entire battlefield and meet only a few farmers hard at work, and see no other travellers at all. Frankly the interest after the war was not there, especially on the subject of Rebel graves, as few visitors ever travelled up from the Southern states. An indication of how little appeal there truly was in the thousands of Confederates interred at Gettysburg is apparent by this fact: Of the hundreds of photographs taken on the renown field between 1863 and 1900, only *one* photograph is known to have been taken of any Southerner's grave site, and this photograph was of an *empty* burial trench. No photographs exist of headboards of Confederate graves between 1864 and 1873, the year when the last body was removed to the South. And no photographs are seen dating from 1873 to 1900 when evidences of these graves and burial trenches still existed. (The exceptions are a few rough sketches in newspapers.) It has always seemed very peculiar that these photographers actively took pictures of the dead, the landscape, and later the monuments and memorials, but they constantly ignored the lonely and pitiful multitude of little dirt mounds ofttimes covered with clover and topped by a leaning, decaying headboard, which might contain a barely readable inscription. What a poignant scene that would have been. What beautiful and fitting poetry could have been written to accommodate such a view. A silent yet powerful blow could have been dealt the god of war, showing the finality, the futility and the somber reality of it all. And what a missed opportunity, not only for that contemporary photographer, but for all of us today.

Just how many of these graves did exist on the field between 1863 and 1871? No one can ever know for sure, but we can work up some approximations.

As part of a final report submitted in early 1864, Samuel Weaver disclosed that as he was "searching for the remains of our fallen heroes, we examined more than three thousand rebel graves. They were frequently buried in trenches, and there are instances of more than one hundred and fifty in a trench....I have been making a careful estimate, from time to time, as I went over the field, of the rebel bodies buried on this battlefield and at the hospitals, and I place the number at not less than seven thousand bodies."[91]

Unquestionably Mr. Weaver knew the field and the location of its many graves better than any man or woman alive. But *seven thousand* Confederate dead! Was it possible? Probably not, for these several reasons.

The number of killed and mortally wounded Southerners lost in the Battle of Gettysburg has been studied by various historians. The most widely accepted casualty figures seem to indicate that there were at least 4,500 Confederates killed or mortally wounded in the engagement but no more than 5,000.[92] However some statisticians have found it hard to believe that if there were definitely 5,100 to 5,200 Federals killed and mortally wounded at Gettysburg, (who for the most part were fighting on the *defensive*), why were only 4,500 Confederates felled *attacking* a superior defending force over the three-day period. Without question something seems amiss here, but this researcher, for one, does not have the answer, except to fall back on the reaction of author Edwin Coddington, who noted that many Southerners were often simply better marksmen.

Between 1871 and 1873 Dr. Rufus B. Weaver examined, boxed, and shipped to the South 3,320 remains. Now these figures presumably do not take into account the many graves at Gettysburg which were lost or obliterated, or the graves of Rebel soldiers who died in outlying areas far from the Gettysburg battlefield, such as on the retreat route. Nor do they reflect the Confederates who died of wounds at hospitals in Virginia once Lee's Army had successfully crossed the Potomac during the middle of July. Neither counted are the various Confederates who were mistakenly buried as Yankees, or those whose remains were privately removed to home cemeteries by Southern friends and relatives between 1863 and 1873. So adding all of these figures together and even haphazardly guessing at some numbers, the final count of the dead does come to about 4,500, which is the accepted figure already previously estimated. Casting any doubts aside, the answer may finally be that there is no mystery after all, and it all just happened that way and the numbers are relatively close and correct.

By now we know that a few individuals in the county kept the names of Confederate dead and the whereabouts of burial places for many of the Southerners left on or near the battlefield. The lists of Dr. John O'Neal and Samuel Weaver were the most complete, locating about 1,100 identified Southern graves. There is little evidence to indicate that during the remaining years of the war, 1864-1865, very many Southern families made the effort to have the bones of soldier relatives removed from Pennsylvania to graveyards below the Mason and Dixon Line. Those few who did must have been resolute souls indeed and filled with a strong determination, and having the monetary means necessary for the task that not many others in the Southern states possessed.

One very early account of this unusual dedication was kept by Dr. O'Neal in his memoranda book. In it he outlines a case where the father of Captain Samuel W. Gray, a member of the 57th North Carolina Infantry, began making inquiries about his son's resting place while visiting the field in the middle of November of 1863. The older man, Robert Gray, was from Winston, North Carolina, and was assisted by O'Neal in returning Samuel's remains to the Old North state.

Other rare early Southern removals included Virginia's General Lewis A. Armistead and Colonel Lewis B. Williams, Jr., 1st Virginia Infantry, also the bodies of General William Barksdale and Captain Isaac D. Stamps, both of Mississippi, Major Donald McLeod, 8th South Carolina Infantry, J.T. Adams, 14th Georgia, and the remains of Captains William Murray and William D. Brown of Maryland.[93]

In speaking of these maiden removals of both Union and Confederate soldiers, this question always arises. How were such corpses shipped home in a state of partial or total decomposition?

Both the 700 or more Union bodies and the known dozen or two Confederates who were transported from Gettysburg between the battle days and the early months of 1864, were due to the work of embalmers or undertakers and "professional" intermediaries like O'Neal and Weaver. At least six of these "morticians," besides the locals already in business, had set up shop in or near Gettysburg after the end of the conflict. Embalmers during the Civil War were often regular medical doctors or even army surgeons who used the craft as a "side-line" business to increase their income. The return in the embalming trade for some physicians was much greater than for that of their usual medical

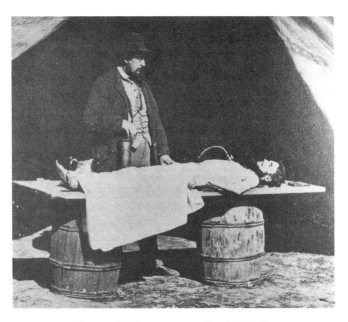

An embalmer at work. (USLC)

practice, with so many families anxious to retain for burial some physical portion of their deceased relatives who had succumbed to disease or by the deadly missiles of battle.

To insure the survival of the corpse on its long journey home, embalmers of the 1860s often used a preservative fluid which was a combination of zinc, chloride and arsenic. The blood was not normally withdrawn or "bled out" of the body as it is today; the embalming fluid was simply hand pumped into the cadaver. After this process the body was cleaned, dressed and fitted into a coffin, usually of wood, but zinc or copper was often needed for airtight shipment. One type of coffin available was a wrought iron "Fiske Burial Case" which weighed in at between 200 and 300 pounds. Since the embalming procedure was often inadequate (fluid did not always get to all parts of the body) a good coffin was necessary to control body spoilage, leakage and odor.

Some undertakers used a newer system whereby "a fluid holding in solution pounded glass and certain chemicals, was...injected into the blood vessels, and the subject at the same time [was] bled at the neck. The body thus became hard and stony, and would retain its form for years."

A visitor to a battlefield in 1862 observed one of these "operations" and glumly testified:

> I had occasion, in one of my visits to the depot, to repair to the tent of one of these embalmers. He was a sedate, grave person, and when I saw him, standing over the nude, hard corpse, he reminded me of the implacable vulture, looking into the eyes of Prometheus. His battery and tube were pulsing, like one's heart and lungs, and the subject was being drained at the neck...."If you could only make him breathe, Professor," said an officer standing by.

The dry skin of the embalmer broke into chalky dimples, and he grinned very much as a corpse might do:

"Ah!" he said, *"then* there would be money made."

Later one of these grim personages confided to the same witness:

I used to be glad to prepare private soldiers. They were worth a five dollar bill apiece. But, Lord bless you, a colonel pays a hundred, and a brigadier-general two hundred. There's lots of them now, and I have cut the acquaintance of everything below a major. I might, he added, as a great favor, do a captain, but he must pay a major's price. I insist upon that! Such windfalls don't come every day. There won't be another such killing for a century.[94]

Certain of the "patent coffins" were built with a compartment for ice in the lid which enabled the box to keep the corpse cool and fresh on its journey home.[95] Often as supplies for the wounded went to Gettysburg they were shipped in what was then termed an "arctic car," or ice car. On the return trip when they were empty these specialized train cars were utilized to transport filled coffins.

One resident of the town stated that he knew of two "embalming rooms" in Gettysburg, one located in a building on York Street near David Wills' house, and the other was in a brick schoolhouse on the Mummasburg Road (or Black's Turnpike) north of town.[96]

J. H. Wert remembered more generally that, "all around the suburbs of the town were pitched the tents of embalmers."

Very few of these characters are personally known to us by name. Two who are partially identified were "Drs. Lyford and Chambers [Chamberlain]" of 487 Penn Avenue, Washington, D.C. These undertakers were returning to the capitol city after working several months in Gettysburg, and an eyewitness placed them at one point in time at a farm where they spent the night in Bendersville, Pennsylvania, which was just north of Gettysburg.[97]

In addition to these two gentlemen, the New York *Herald* of Friday, July 24, 1863, printed an advertisement for the firm of Doctors Brown and Alexander, "embalmers of the dead," of New York City who were offering to, "exhume, disinfect and send home the bodies of deceased soldiers, thereby saving friends the expense and trouble of a journey to the battle field." Clients were urged to give "full particulars of regiment, company, location of grave, etc."

One person of said persuasion familiar to many Adams Countians following the battle was Dr. Cyrus N. Chamberlain, a U.S. Volunteers surgeon who operated

TO THE UNDERTAKER

OR FRIENDS WHO OPEN THIS COFFIN.

AFTER removing or laying back the lid of the Coffin, remove entirely the pads from the sides of the face, as they are intended merely to steady the head in travelling. If there be any discharge of liquid from the eyes, nose or mouth, which often occurs from the constant shaking of the cars, wipe it off gently with a soft piece of cotton cloth, slightly moistened with water.

This body was received by us for embalment in a *City Good* condition, the tissues being *so fully discolored* The embalmment is consequently *Good* The natural expression is *preserved*, on account of *the condition* in which it was received. The body will keep well for *any length of time*

After removing the coffin lid, leave it off for some time, and let the body have the air.

Drs. BROWN & ALEXANDER,
EMBALMERS,
WASHINGTON, D. C.

Instructions to the family of the deceased. (LL)

an embalming service at Camp Letterman east of Gettysburg. He was the officer in charge of all Sixth Corps field hospitals during the battle and was also in command of the U.S. General Hospital near Gettysburg, better known as Camp Letterman.

The cost of an average embalming could vary, and the price of transportation to the soldier's home was extra, but usually the total expenditure ran anywhere between $50 to $150.

This price also included removing the body from the ground, the embalming process itself, a zinc coffin, a wooden box to place it in, transportation to the depot, plus the express shipment fee to its final destination by rail or ship.[98]

A Connecticut soldier documented the price of this service as $15 for embalming, the box was $5 and the express to his state, $24. He denoted further that "[s]ince the battle, Gettysburg has been an extensive coffin mart & embalmers harvest field. the coffins were stacked on the streets blockading the sidewalks. these coffin speculators made an enormous profit but their harvest is now over...."[99]

One of the "speculators" in this business was a "Doctor F. Gardner" who was stationed at a cavalry hospital at Hanover. He was said to have made $1,000 embalming bodies in the month-and-a-half after the battle.

On July 19, Frederick Law Olmsted who was employed by the Sanitary Commission, wrote to his supervisor after being at Gettysburg that the dead, "are all buried, and a great business is being done in disinterring bodies for embalming and shipment North. There are half a dozen diff[t] embalmers competing for it."

The corpse of Sgt. John Christian, 7th West Virginia Infantry, was expressed to his home in Tyler County, WV, by Dr. Henry Janes. (LL)

Drs. Chamberlain and Lyford, undertakers, did a lively business following the Battle of Gettysburg. (GNMP)

Olmsted was surely correct, for we know that at least 1,000 coffins were shipped to Gettysburg in the week following the fighting.[100]

Emily Souder remembered being aroused from her sleep by "the sound ...[of] the perpetually passing wagons loaded with coffins, either going empty to the battle-fields, or returning with their sad freight."[101]

A Gettysburg carpenter who made coffins before the battle was Henry Garlach, whose shop sat on the west side of Baltimore Street. A wounded officer who recuperated at this house during July recalled that Garlach "as can be readily imagined, having at that time all the business that he could attend to."[102]

An example of the work carried on by these embalmers is manifested in the story of a partially decomposed corpse which was taken from its burial site very early after the battle and shipped home. It was the body of General Lewis Armistead, C.S.A., one of General George Pickett's brigade commanders who was shot twice on July 3 and died shortly thereafter at a Union field hospital.

Alfred J. Rider, the "regimental post master" of the 107th Ohio, was the man ordered to disinter General Armistead's remains. Dr. C.N. Chamberlain of Philadelphia, previously noted, embalmed what was left of the corpse. Rider's duties also included seeing to the burial of the dead at the Eleventh Corps Hospital, to recover and care for their effects, and enter their names into a record book. Rider also claimed that he heard Chamberlain say that the family of Armistead would probably pay a good price to have his body shipped home. The remains of the general were "four weeks" in the ground at that time and had been interred previously inside a rough wooden box.[103]

It was a common practice to embalm even long buried bodies because relatives of these soldiers wanted to make sure that the body they received was undoubtedly that of their son, or brother, or husband and furthermore to have the peace of mind that the deceased would forever lie near at hand in familiar surroundings. So, in the weeks after the battle there was, as one woman nurse commented, "a perpetual procession of coffins...constantly passing to and fro, [and] strangers looking for their dead on every farm and under every tree."[104]

In December 1865 about seven months after the ending of hostilities between North and South, Samuel Weaver was contacted by the mother of Captain George R. Bedinger, 33rd Virginia Infantry who was seeking her son's grave at Gettysburg. Mr. Weaver was unable to aid in her quest due to the lack of precise information to guide him to the site as Captain Bedinger's name, unfortunately, did not grace any of the burial registers available. But in that same month Weaver was able to assist the family of Colonel John A. Jones, 20th Georgia, who had good information that Jones had been buried on the John Slyder farm about 150 yards from the house under a cherry tree. So, Weaver was able to procure the body for them and have it transported to Georgia.[105]

Similarly, the records of the family of Colonel Henry K. Burgwyn, 26th North Carolina Infantry reveal that in the spring of 1867 his remains were returned to a cemetery in Raleigh. Burgwyn had been interred by his comrades, "N.E. of a medium sized stone farm house," under a walnut tree along or near the Chambersburg Pike, a few miles northwest of Gettysburg.[106]

The graves of two other Confederate colonels were discovered and the bodies retrieved and moved South during the war years or shortly thereafter. The first was John B. Magruder, 57th Virginia, and another was William D. DeSaussure, 15th South Carolina Infantry. Magruder was disinterred in October 1863, and DeSaussure's body was boxed and shipped some time before 1871.[107]

In another scenario, the body of Lieutenant Valentine W. Southall, 23rd Virginia Infantry was collected and returned to his sister, Lucy H. Wood through the efforts of Dr. John O'Neal, who was aided by a detailed map which was drawn in June 1869 by the chaplain who buried Southall. As we have seen, these maps were very important in the efforts to locate individual battlefield burial spots, but no one can know how many were drawn and used during the war years or afterward.[108]

In October 1869, a few months after Southall's family met with success, O'Neal assisted another distraught person who was the brother of Captain James H. Burns, 6th North Carolina. Captain Burns had been mortally wounded on July 2, and had died at a field hospital along the Hunterstown Road. How and where his body was found is explained by Dr. O'Neal in a letter to the brother, C.B. Burns:

"I found a grave (marked with his name) alone, back of the barn on the [Elizabeth Weible] place, the front teeth as you described. Sound. The clothing was all so decayed that I could not recognize them. The buttons were not brass guilt as you described, but military = The neck tie being silk was not fully rotted = So also a small military flag which I suppose he had pocketed as a trophy as also his shoulder straps. All of which I have...."[109]

One of the most interesting cases on record is that of 22-year-old Captain William L. McLeod of the 34th Georgia, who was mortally wounded on July 1, and then buried by his slave "Moses" under a peach tree on the farm of Jacob Kime along the Harrisburg Road. Sometime following the conclusion of the war, Moses and a family friend, John Prescott, travelled by wagon from Emanuel County, Georgia, to Gettysburg and retrieved the remains of McLeod. The body was placed in an oak coffin where it remained at his mother's wish adorning the parlor of the McLeod house until 1872 when the young officer's body was finally reburied in the family plot.[110]

There were presumably others whom O'Neal and Weaver aided, but the letters and records documenting the events are not available. In any event, the numbers removed before 1871 could not have been large, although enough requests surely came in between 1863 and 1871 to keep both of these gentlemen, and possibly others quite busy in their spare time.

Within five years of the end of the Civil War, it became obvious by articles appearing in newspapers throughout the Southern states, that a movement had begun and was underway to institute a formal arrangement to find, gather together, and transfer back to the Southland all of the Confederate dead still at Gettysburg. Why exactly this singular endeavor was born at that precise time cannot really be known. It may have been due to the emergence after the war throughout the South of many active groups which were loosely entitled, "Ladies' Memorial Associations." These were hard years for the South when most citizens had chosen to try and forget the war. However, a few people did not care to bury their heritage, and wanted to recall with pride its past military deeds, even if, and probably *because*, their side had lost. And since all organizations need purposes and goals, these societies picked as one of their main efforts, the honorable return to the South of all deceased Southern soldiers from Pennsylvania and elsewhere. In the early days of this movement, especially before 1870, most of the interest shown toward the lost dead was from the states that had the largest number of these associations, i.e. Georgia, North Carolina and South Carolina. Veritably, Rufus B. Weaver, who eventually became directly responsible for all removals of Confederates from Gettysburg, wrote to one society leader in 1871 and rejoined that, "[i]t seems very strange to me that Virginia who is so near and whose known list is not so great as yours [meaning Georgia] does not recall her dead. I have learned that they [have] ample means to accomplish the work and not to do so is paying a very poor and uncharitable compliment to her dead. I have sent South all the State lists and none but you, [Georgia] N.C. & S.C. have done anything. None of the others have even taken account of the lists as far as I know. If all could see what I have seen and know what I know, I am sure that there would be no rest until every Southern father, brother and son would be removed from the North."[111] It appears these organizations were often very loosely organized, and often made up almost exclusively of aging mothers of the men who had been slain in battle, or who had died of disease. They had little money or resources and were often ignored or frustrated in their attempts by the white male dominated state and Federal governments. But through it all these women somehow kept focused on their "sacred" quest and eventually were successful in preparing the legal and mechanical groundwork needed to put such intricate plans into operation.

It was late in the year 1870 when the various organizations which had cooperated in these, at best, loose-knit ventures, and were mainly from the few states mentioned above, were able to report that some monies had been appropriated from their state legislatures and the "ladies" associations themselves. A coalition of these groups then turned to a man they felt was best suited for the tremendous task, old Samuel Weaver himself. But sadly for the groups' efforts Weaver died in 1871, just as the wheels began to turn, leaving them in a quandary as how to proceed. Accordingly, after much deliberation, they asked his son Rufus B. Weaver who was a Philadelphia physician, to take up and complete the huge responsibility. At first the younger Weaver refused their offer.

Rufus B. Weaver had good reason to do so as he was a busy and focused young man. Born in Gettysburg in January 1841 to Samuel and Elizabeth, he received his degree from Pennsylvania College in 1862, and his medical degree from the Pennsylvania Medical College in 1865. Between 1867 and 1869 Dr. Weaver pursued his studies "with the purpose of becoming thoroughly informed regarding the teaching and methods" of clinical medicine. At the end of this interim of life in 1869, Weaver married Madeline L. Bender and soon became the Demonstrator of Anatomy at the Hahnemann Medical College in Philadelphia. A biography of him during that time purports that, "[a]fter his father's decease the records of [Confederate] burials came into [the] possession of Dr. Weaver and he having personal acquaintance with the land owners and an accurate knowledge of the location of individual graves and trenches, there was no other person possessing the information which would enable them to identify the respective graves."

After many months of pressure Weaver, who continued to complain to the representatives of these organizations that he was overburdened with his relatively new and important medical career, finally gave in. His biography also disclosed that these Southerners had expressed so keen a desire for their dead, and displayed such "anxious solicitude that the remains of all Confederate soldiers

Dr. Rufus B. Weaver at age 74. (ACHS)

should find a permanent resting place among their kindred, [so that] after frequent solicitations Dr. Weaver could not with propriety resist their appeals and consented to aid them at such intervals as could be spared from his professional engagements."[112]

During these many days of planning and uncertainty, a number of the Ladies' Memorial Associations were in hopes of stirring up additional interest in other places not yet committed to the vast undertaking. One tactic often successfully used can be clearly shown by an article which appeared in a Georgia newspaper in 1871:

The Georgia Dead at Gettysburg

Having been informed by a person who has visited the spot, that the following named Georgians [a nominal list was included] are interred at Gettysburg, and, unless removed by fall, the owners of the ground have given notice that they "intend ploughing up the land and grinding the bones for fertilizing purposes," the Savannah Memorial Association asks each of her sister associations in the State to come forward at once and assist her in removing these remains....[113]

How many of these compelling brands of articles may have appeared in various parts of the South in post-war days we have no way of knowing, but there is little doubt that they must have succeeded in electrifying not only the blood of true Southerners, but stirred up some serious interest as well.

Ploughing up the bones of dead soldiers. (JB)

The idea that all Northerners were preparing to make fertilizers out of the bones of Confederates who died in battle for their country was of course, a ridiculous thought, quite far from reality. Emotions aside, many citizens of the North and South had brought a more calm and sensible approach to the problem even much earlier. Here is a clear example of that from the New York *Express* which was reprinted in the April 11, 1864, Gettysburg *Compiler*:

RESPECT FOR THE DEAD

It has been announced upon semi-official authority, that the fields of Gettysburg, where the Rebel dead lie, are to be ploughed up. It is to be hoped that for decency's sake, at least, such report may prove unfounded. It is far more in accordance with the laws of civilized warfare, to pay proper respect to the buried remains, even of one's enemies.

A piece of ground should be set aside, and such of the bodies as are recognizable by marks on clothing, or otherwise, should have a separate burial, and a head board, though it be but rough wood, should designate the name and regiment, if known. The foe who so bravely contested the famed battle of Gettysburg, certainly need a better fate than the burial of a dog.

When the war is over, and the moment of calm reflection unbiased by heated passion and party malevolence shall return, many, very many heart-stricken wives and mothers will visit the Northern battle-fields on a search for the remains of lost loved ones; and who can describe the feelings of such, at seeing over the bodies of those they love, the corn or rye lifting its tall head, to preach of the uncalled-for vindictiveness of man! Let not this threaten desecration occur. Rather let the beautiful sentiment of the Golden Rule be carried out, and instead of retaliating for famed or real injuries, learn how doubly blessed it is to "return good for evil."

As indicated earlier, only the states of Georgia, North Carolina, and South Carolina had gone as far as to actually raise money for their state's participation in battlefield removals. Banking the whole venture on these few funds, Dr. Weaver, during the spring and summer of 1871, exhumed and shipped the first set of remains to Raleigh, North Carolina, a total of 137 Confederates; there were also 74 sent to Charleston, South Carolina; 101 to Savannah, Georgia; and a few others to Maryland.[114] Included in this opening delivery were seventy-three separate boxes made to individual families, among these were the bodies of Lieutenant Colonel J.W. Hance, 53rd Georgia Infantry, Colonel David R.E. Winn, 4th Georgia, and Colonel Joseph Wasden, 22nd Georgia.

During this first season Rufus Weaver discovered that the grand enterprise he had accepted was twice as hard and frustrating as he had expected. For one thing, he had some difficulty with an assortment of local farmers who demanded cash for the long upkeep of graves on their property. One in particular in this class was David Blocher who lived just north of Gettysburg near the Newville/Carlisle Road. He refused to let the bodies on his land be removed without advance payment. Eventually, due to the authority given to Weaver through the power and prestige of the associations, these remains were allowed to be taken, although it proved to be a time-consuming and frustrating process. Even after the body of Colonel Winn, the soldier in question, was sent home, it was found that Mr. Blocher still held possession of that officer's lower jaw containing a gold plate, to which was attached a set of false teeth. In time, and with a compensation of $5, (the initial asking fee was $10) Weaver obtained the jawbone from Blocher's son, Oliver.

Even with these delays, Dr. Weaver was still able to report to one of the association's presidents in October 1871 that the work had generally gone well, and that a predominance of the area landowners were good men, some few had even gone above the normal human respect for the dead and had taken both excellent and continual care of the Confederate graves on their farms.[115]

A month after the above cited letter was written, in November 1871, the secretary of the Hollywood Cemetery Memorial Association of Richmond, Virginia, wrote to Rufus Weaver that the association was ready to arrange and make contracts for the removal of Virginia soldiers buried in and around Gettysburg. Soon afterward this association tentatively decided to go a step further and pay for the exhumation and transportation south of *all* of the remaining Confederates interred there, not only the Virginians. Accordingly, on February 7, 1872, Weaver mailed the association a list of 400 names of identified Confederates who remained at Gettysburg, but these were only a fraction of the Southern soldiers still buried there. The doctor had acquainted the Hollywood group earlier with the knowledge that it would cost $3.25 per body to disinter, box, and ship each of the several thousand remains to Richmond. Since the Richmond association had only $4,000 in their coffers, a final decision could not be made at that time.

In the meantime this same Hollywood Cemetery society sent a delegate to Gettysburg in the form of ex-Confederate engineer captain Charles Dimmock, to assess the situation there. After his visit, Dimmock estimated that there were about 2,500 remaining Confederate soldiers still interred around the field. As a matter of record in front of the "angle" along Cemetery Ridge he specified that already the large old burial trenches were hard to locate, and, all around were "skeletons which had been ploughed up and now lay strewn about the surface." The disrespect shown these former Southern infantrymen by the Pennsylvanians shocked the captain, but he had nothing but high praise for the efforts of Dr. Weaver. After Dimmock's assessment was presented to the association, they authorized Weaver to proceed with the disinterments and certified that he would be paid through an agent in Baltimore.

The second year's exhumations began on April 19, 1872. Weaver was forced to labor eighteen to twenty hours a day to stay ahead of the normal spring plantings then in progress, and notwithstanding this tight schedule, he was still thoroughly conscientious in his daily field work. Late at night and after a full day's efforts, the doctor would arrange, label, and record all the human remains that had been exhumed; he

Charles Dimmock. (TL)

was often up long past midnight. Dr. Weaver believed that due to the poor conditions of some of the graves, "it required one with Anatomical knowledge, to gather *all* the bones, (which workmen could not do) and, regarding each bone important and sacred as an integral part of the skeleton, I removed them so that none might be left or lost." One may imagine how delicate and difficult his job was when the long burial trenches were opened, and the decaying bodies of dozens of soldiers had become intermingled and intertwined amidst the dirt and rocks and roots of the preceding eight to ten years.

The first shipment to Richmond arrived from Gettysburg on June 15, 1872. The cargo consisted of 279 wooden boxes containing 708 Confederate skeletons, 469 from that lot of soldiers were identified; 70 were from Virginia, 49 from Alabama, 34 from Mississippi, 28 from South Carolina, 18 from North Carolina, 11 from Louisiana, 8 from Florida, 7 from Tennessee, 4 from Texas, 4 from Maryland, 2 from Georgia, 1 from Arkansas, and 3 from unknown states. The majority of these remains came from the Nicholas Codori farm, and the hospital sites at the Jacob Schwartz, David Shriver and Emmanuel Pitzer farms, and the battlefield around the Moses McClean farm.

Several weeks later in early August another shipment arrived by steamer at the wharf in Richmond, comprising 882 more soldier remains arranged in 98 large boxes, only 19 of which were identified. These were from the farms of John Trostle, Nicholas Codori, John Crawford, Francis Bream, George Rose, Abraham Trostle, James Warfield, John Forney, Edward McPherson, David Hankey, William Plank, John F. Currens, and John Pitzer. Many of the bodies buried after the battle near Little and Big Round Tops, the Devil's Den, and in the Plum Run Valley and "Houck's Ridge" had been washed away, or lost and obliterated in some fashion, and Weaver was able to recover a total of only 49 in this area.

Hollywood Cemetery, Richmond, VA, where the remains of many Confederates killed at Gettysburg now lie. (TWH)

On September 9, 1872, 683 skeletal remains in 90 boxes were forwarded to the former Confederate capital by Dr. Weaver; he estimated that there were about 600 more to be recovered, and that so far he had packed and shipped 2,273 Confederates to Hollywood Cemetery. The good doctor was having more difficulties again as several farmers made demands to be paid for the bodies, as much in one case as $50 per grave. Due to these trying situations he could not complete the project that year, and so returned in the fall, to his teaching position in Philadelphia. So far Weaver had been paid $2,800, but as of October 1872 he was still owed $4,585.

Assuming that this outstanding payment would be met, Rufus B. Weaver's endeavors began again in the month of April 1873. Shortly thereafter a fourth shipment was readied for transport; it consisted of 333 remains in 35 boxes, which Weaver carefully prepared as usual.

Unfortunately, Dr. Weaver had not been informed that even as these dead were being reburied in Richmond, the Hollywood Memorial Association was in the throes of deep financial trouble. Charles Dimmock, their mentor and advisor had died, and the women of the association, short of money and lacking leadership, and probably partly due to a surplus of stubborn pride, failed to notify anyone of their serious situation, most especially the hard laboring Pennsylvania doctor.

June 28, 1873, was the day Weaver sent a fifth shipment to the city, this one holding 256 more complete skeletal remains. Following this delivery, the association would have owed Dr. Weaver $6,499. However only a mere $380

After the removals. A forlorn and gaping Confederate burial trench below Culp's Hill. (GNMP)

was paid to him at that time as a token gesture. In the second week of October 1873, the sixth and final boatload arrived in Richmond with only 73 bodies. All together there had been 2,935 Confederates exhumed; 40 known bodies were left in Joseph Sherfy's peach orchard, and hundreds more, he was simply unable to locate.

In all, 3,320 soldier remains had been recovered since 1870 from at least 116 separate sites on the battlefield and from outlying field hospital sites. At each one of these places the July 1863 graves had been dug originally in various rural locations as mentioned in the several burial registers, such as "north of A. Butts under cherry tree;" or "near Forney's place in a field under an apple tree;" or "near Benner's opposite a stone house;" or "Henry Spangler's near Right Wing under gum tree;" or behind "Jacob Schwartz's barn under walnut tree near creek," etc.

By the onset of the winter of 1873-1874, Dr. Weaver was in great need of the over $6,000 still due him for his long and tedious services rendered. He was strained financially because he had donated much of his personal savings to the medical college where he was employed which had recently suffered a crisis itself.

Rufus Weaver tried every courteous way he knew to entice the Richmond Association to honor their contract, but with no success. The Richmond Association of honorable Southern gentlewomen soon lost interest now that the dead had been returned, and the organization slowly began to disintegrate.[116] And perhaps, after all, the attitude may possibly have been that Weaver was simply just another Yankee.

Eventually the doctor was forced to abandon his claims to the money. In a letter written to Dr. John O'Neal fourteen years later, Weaver summed up his feelings:

"I tell you that the Association yet owe me, for that great work, including interest over ($11,000) eleven thousand Dollars! You have had an extensive correspondence with friends of the Confederate dead and I Judge that, from your acquaintance with many prominent personages of the South, most probably you might be just the one to exercise a favorable consideration in behalf of my interest in the above debt."[117]

No doubt, it is believable that when Dr. Rufus B. Weaver died in July 1936, the huge debt had still not been settled. It had most definitely not been forgiven.

The Forgotten Few

The final question which should be asked in this chapter is this: Did Samuel Weaver and Dr. Rufus B. Weaver find and remove *all* of the bodies of Union and Confederate soldiers killed or who died of wounds at Gettysburg? We know there were clusters of Rebel remains that would *never* be disinterred, such as the 18 Confederates buried in the environs of Carlisle, Pennsylvania; and many similar examples do crop up all through the areas traversed by Southern columns advancing or retreating across Maryland and Pennsylvania during the summer of 1863.[118]

The answer to part of the question is already known. It has been admitted by Rufus Weaver that some Rebels were overlooked or purposefully left out of the shipments to Virginia. Various observations as seen by articulate witnesses indicate that a fairly large number of Confederate graves were either lost, missed entirely, or erased by the actions of nature. In accordance with this knowledge Weaver placed one last notice in the county newspapers in April 1873, about the time he was beginning to collect the final Southern skeletons for passage to Richmond:

"Dr. Rufus B. Weaver is now finishing the work of exhuming the Confederate dead on the Battle-field, and desires information in regard to any bodies which may have escaped his notice."[119]

Even with such pleas entered in public circulars, a number of citizens chose not to respond. One farmer who failed to notify Weaver, or David Wills the man responsible for the collection of Union bodies, lived along the Baltimore Turnpike about one half mile south of the cemetery. This gentleman conveyed the fact to a visiting ex-soldier of the Union army that he *knew* the bodies on his property had never been collected. The farmer was Nathaniel Lightner, and his farm had been used as a hospital for the Second and Twelfth Corps. The veteran spoken of was Charles Muller, and in 1897 after talking to Lightner, he recalled:

"Mr. Lightner told me that all the dead that were buried on his farm are still resting on the ground and that none of them were ever took up."

One of the men buried there was a soldier of Co. B, 1st Minnesota Infantry, Private Augustus Koenig, nicknamed "Beerkeg" by the other men of his company, as not only had he been a brewer before the war, but he was shaped somewhat like a beer barrel.[120]

A woman seeing the field for the first time in 1894 may have summed up the answer to the question we are asking. She attested to the idea that there must have been many missing bodies, saying:

> Besides, no one may guess how many soldiers still rest where they fell. In some cases all traces were lost of the shallow trenches and scant graves into which the bodies of brave men were, perforce, hastily rolled, after lying for days unburied, beneath a July sun. In that time of triumph and desolation, inextricable confusion and terrible suffering, the wounded demanded the chief care and burial was rather for the sake of the living than of the dead.[121]

Obviously no one can or will ever know the whole truth of the matter. It will always be impossible to say how many of both Northern and Southern dead were missed, and the intriguing question will stay a mystery forever. Even the correct number of skeletons or parts of bodies found between 1863 and the present time is hopeless to determine as not all such discoveries were reported. And as to how many soldiers still lie on or near the battlefield today, that too will never be revealed, although estimates run from a few dozen to as high as 1,000 or more. Since there can never be a real solution to the problem, let us then glance at a few of the cases where bones and artifacts of soldiers were discovered between 1873 and 1934. What you are about to read in most instances is a very brief synopsis of the original news article or other source.

✝ ✝ ✝

October 1877—The bones of four Confederate soldiers were found just east of the old mineral springs area which is north of Willoughby's Run and south of the Chambersburg Road. They were taken up and placed in a "suitable spot." This find was probably the same noted by a correspondent of the Philadelphia *Weekly Times*, who wrote on June 8, 1878, that, "[y]ear by year, in the spring washes of storms and in the June work of the hoe, bones are dug up—some times single bones and again whole bodies. Last fall, said a farmer, six dead rebels came from under the crust near Willoughby run, and two others from the ground covered by the left wing of the enemy."

May 1878—The bones of a Union soldier were struck by a plough on the Nicholas Codori farm last week. Sergeant Nicholas G. Wilson, the superintendent of the cemetery, had them removed to the National Cemetery from along the Emmitsburg Road.

July 1878—The remains of a Confederate soldier were found one mile north of Gettysburg near Blocher's Hill. Along with the bones was an old glass daguerrotype photograph of a woman and two young girls. The body was believed to be a member of the 31st Georgia, Gordon's Brigade.

June 1881—Mr. W.H. Gelbach plowed up on his farm, which is west of the Emmitsburg Road and not far from David Ziegler's woods, the bones of at least twenty Confederate soldiers believed to have been from Lane's and Brockenbrough's Brigades. There were thought to be more in the area. All were exhumed and then reburied in a corner of his field. The burials were about 500 yards northeast of William Bliss' "burned barn" site.

May 1882—The remains of a Union soldier were ploughed up on the premises of Lydia Leister's farm which was used by General George G. Meade as his headquarters during the battle. The bones were transferred to the National Cemetery, and a cost of $1.12 was approved for a headstone which had the word "Unknown" cut into it. Cemetery superintendent N.G. Wilson requested this approval from his superior, Colonel C.W. Foster, assistant quartermaster in Baltimore, Maryland.

April 1885—Isaiah Trostle and James Young found the bodies of two Federal soldiers while out walking near Devil's Den. The remains were turned over to N.G. Wilson at the National Cemetery.

October 1885—The unidentified body of a soldier was found while workmen were removing a corpse from the Catholic cemetery. He was buried about 18 inches beneath the sod, and his breastbone had been crushed in by a piece of shell. Nothing in the grave indicated whether he was of the Union or Confederate army.

October 1885—William Smith while walking on East Cemetery Hill observed what appeared to be a bone protruding from the earth. Upon investigation he found it to be a human skull. It was handed over to Superintendent N.G. Wilson at the National Cemetery.

June 1886—D.A. Riley, the tenant farmer on the Nicholas Codori place ploughed up the bones of a soldier in the field over which Pickett's Division attacked on July 3, 1863. It was very near where Colonel G.H. Ward's monument of the 15th Massachusetts stands. Among the bones was a piece of skull with a bullet hole protruding at both sides, and also a thigh bone with a bullet imbedded in its lower end. A cap box full of percussion caps accompanied the remains. From indications present it was believed to be a Southern soldier.

August 1886—A human skeleton was discovered by Paul Kappes in Menchey's sand pit near East Cemetery Hill. The body was believed to be that of a Confederate, as the buttons were of Southern manufacture, and a bottle of ink, soundly corked and bearing a Richmond, Virginia label was found in the grave.

May 1887—While ploughing in the field on the west side of the Emmitsburg Road near the 12th New Jersey monument at the site of the old William Bliss farm, Frederick Peffer uncovered the remains of seven soldiers, "supposed Mississippians." The bones were reburied in the same area.

July 1888—William Heagy, who lives on the ground of the "South Cavalry Battlefield" along the Emmitsburg Road, reported the location of several soldiers' graves in his woods; whether Union or Confederate he did not know, but presumably the latter as the remains of the former were carefully collected shortly after the battle.

July 1888—Edward Leeper discovered the remains of two Confederate soldiers in a shallow grave while gathering herbs in Herbst's Woods (Reynolds' Grove) just south of Edward McPherson's farm. At first they were believed to be Union soldiers, but after investigation they were found to have been Confederates removed and buried there several years earlier. It was expected that more bodies might be found there.

July 1888—While showing the beauty of Devil's Den to a tourist, Jacob Mumper noticed a human bone protruding from the ground. He immediately procured digging irons and began an investigation. After going down about a foot he found the skeleton of a Confederate soldier. The remains were in good condition, that of a large man. All the bones were present except those of the right arm. In the grave were some Alabama and U.S. buttons, and a gold ring. (Another account of this find stated that the buttons were "Georgia" and added that a dozen bullets and a piece of shell were also found.) The body was reburied nearby.

December 1888—Mr. H. Speece, in digging a drain in Phillip Hennig's field west of Seminary Ridge uncovered the remains of a soldier. A few bones, pieces of blanket, a part of a leather belt, and several brass buttons, having on them the letter "I," (for infantry) were found in the grave.

July 1889—Workmen engaged in opening an avenue to connect Reynolds Avenue with Buford Avenue, unearthed the remains of a Union soldier. His body was interred in the National Cemetery.

August 1889—Dennis Twomey (or Toomey) and his Western Maryland track workmen found a well-preserved skeleton near the "railroad cut" northwest of Gettysburg. The remains were about a foot underground, and with them were found five U.S. buttons, several bullets, two iron heel plates and the heels of two shoes.

May 1890—While workmen were digging in rear of the lot belonging to the McClellan House hotel and near the railroad station along Carlisle Street, they unearthed the remains of a soldier. There was no identification present, but several Union buttons were in the grave. The Washington House hotel which stood along the southwest side of the tracks and at its junction with Carlisle

Street was used as a hospital during and after the battle. There was also an embalming establishment nearby for weeks following the fighting.

July 1890—the remains of a Confederate soldier were discovered while workers were digging sand at the sand bank on the old brick yard lane east of Cemetery Hill. Buttons indicated he was a Rebel.

November 1890—Charles E. Lady was crossing a field about 300 yards southeast of the old medicinal springs near Willoughby's Run south of the Chambersburg Road, when he noticed where a dog had been digging in the ground. Inside the hole were bones, and on closer inspection he discovered several skeletons thought to be Confederates.

December 1895—Employees of the Farrell Brothers who were macadamizing Hancock Avenue close to the High Water Mark monument, dug up a human skull and other bones and two shoes. With the remains was part of a Parrott shell, which probably caused the soldier's death. The bones were reinterred near where they were found.

September 1899—While closing the dirt road from Slocum Avenue to Spangler's Spring, Farrell's employees found on the southwestern side of Culp's Hill eighteen bodies of Union soldiers killed in the battle. Many relics such as belt buckles, etc. were with the remains, which were put into boxes and buried with the unknown at the National Cemetery. (The initial report of this find however, claimed the number of skeletons was seventeen.)

September 1899—While digging a drain in the meadow near Spangler's Spring, battlefield workmen unearthed the bones of a Union soldier, about two feet below the surface of the ground. There was also a U.S. belt plate, a knapsack, a cartridge box belt and several other articles contained in the shallow grave.

October 1899—In the process of excavating for the foundation of a new manufactory on Washington Street in Gettysburg, the laborers came across the bones of a body supposed to be a soldier killed in the battle, by reason of various articles found with it. The remains were taken up and buried in the National Cemetery with the 18 skeletons found in September near Culp's Hill.

September 1900—Fence builders digging a hole near John Slyder's stone house on the southern end of the battlefield came upon the bones of a soldier. The entire skeleton was soon uncovered and the park historian present declared that the man was probably a member of the 2nd U.S. Sharpshooters who had fought there on July 2, 1863. The bones were boxed up and delivered to the National Cemetery for interment. Supposedly, five Vermonters from this regiment had been buried near the house by their comrades after the battle, but never recovered.

August 1906—The various limbs of soldiers wounded in the battle which had been amputated by the surgeons at the Adams County Courthouse hospital were uncovered when enlargement and remodeling of the building was in progress. These bones of fingers, toes, legs and arms were given to Dr. E.W. Brickley for examination.

April 1910—The superintendent of the Gettysburg Water Company, Robert Caldwell, uncovered the remains of a Confederate soldier while doing some cleaning up on East Cemetery Hill. With the bones was found a table knife, spoon, and the frame of a pocket coin purse along with an Indian arrowhead.

This body was probably a member of either Hoke's North Carolina or Hay's Louisiana Brigade who made a charge on the hill, July 2. Many of these bodies were said to have been missed by grave-diggers in the early 1870s when the Southern dead were exhumed, and several have been found since; the most recent, about 1890 by Professor Louis Sowers. Sowers had discovered a body in the vicinity of Menchey's sand quarry when he noticed a shoe sticking out of the ground. Investigation revealed the remainder of the soldier. All these bones were reinterred nearby.

July 1911—The remains of three Union soldiers buried on the first day's battlefield were uncovered recently. The bodies were about 13 inches underground and were in an area

An original letter concerning the post-war discovery of a soldiers' remains. (GAC)

near the county almshouse, a position that had been occupied by General Francis Barlow's troops. A relic hunter digging in the ground for artifacts discovered the graves. With the bones were found two $5 gold pieces, a number of New York brass buttons, and two bullets. The three deceased soldiers were reinterred in the National Cemetery.

November 1914—Mr. William H. Johns found the bodies of two Union soldiers while digging a ditch on his property at the southwestern edge of town along Steinwehr Avenue extended. The larger bones were well preserved, and the boots of one were still intact. There was also present an old army hat, also a number of teeth, and a brass button. The last twelve months have resulted in the uncovering of a number of remains in various places on the field, and these occurrences are likely to happen many more times.

May 1915—The skeleton of an unknown soldier was unearthed at the foot of East Cemetery Hill by government workmen. The bones were principally leg and arm bones, the skull was not located. The remains were near Menchey's spring not far from the 41st New York monument. The find included a button, one U.S. belt buckle, a cap box, and other military items. A bullet was embedded in one leg bone.

August 1927—Approval was given by the Quartermaster General, U.S.A. to the park superintendent to remove and reinter two soldiers' remains. One was discovered on the side of Wadsworth Avenue about half way between its junction with Reynolds and Buford Avenues. The other was in the field bordering Reynolds Avenue on the east, a short distance south of the Chambersburg Road. The latter was found while excavating for the foundation of a monument. Both were believed to be Union dead, and were reburied as "unknowns" in the National Cemetery.

October 1928—The complete set of bones of a soldier was found by workmen in a hole on the north side of the Western Maryland Railroad cut a short distance east of Reynolds Avenue. There was nothing to indicate whether Union or Confederate. The remains were reinterred in the National Cemetery as an unknown soldier.

October 1928—The Ladies Hollywood Memorial Association of Richmond, Virginia reported to the superintendent of the Gettysburg National Military Park that the grave of a Confederate was known to be on the "left side of the street going west towards the Chambersburg Pike," and the association requested permission to have it disinterred for reburial in Hollywood Cemetery.

Summer 1933—After the occurrence of a large storm, the human bones of two Confederate soldiers were found in a deep gully or washout in the bean patch at the David Klingle farm along the Emmitsburg Road south of Gettysburg. The park historian present determined that these men had belonged to Wilcox's Alabama Brigade of Anderson's Division. The remains were boxed and given over for reburial to the Rose Hill Confederate Cemetery at Hagerstown, Maryland.

June 1938—Workmen engaged in digging trenches for water lines south of Gettysburg discovered parts of a skeleton and a Southern infantry blouse

The bones of a soldier who died at Gettysburg found several decades after the battle. (PBE)

button. The site of the grave was about 150 yards northwest of "the Angle" at a depth of 16 inches, with the head pointed to the west. It was thought to be at the eastern edge of a Confederate burial plot known to have been in this area. The bones were delivered to the Confederate Cemetery in Hagerstown.

1950s—Walter A. West reported that while a flower bed was being created near the old well on the southeast side of the Eisenhower farmhouse, the skeleton of a Civil War soldier was unearthed. Mamie Eisenhower allowed the remains to be left there and the bed was moved to a new location. It was noted by West and Mrs. Eisenhower that a Confederate dressing station had been in place at the well site during the battle. The 223-acre farm was then owned by Catherine and John Biesecker who had leased it to Adam Bollinger and his spouse in 1863.

Date Unknown—Samuel Robinson, a government worker at the national park, found at Spangler's Spring the portion of a skull three or four inches long and wide, one arm bone, and one leg bone of a Union soldier. With the remains was a U.S. belt plate, some small pieces of belt, part of a cap box, some percussion caps, and two pieces of leather from a bayonet scabbard.

Date Unknown—Another skeleton of a Confederate soldier was found along the tracks of the Old Tapeworm Railroad. The skull had a bullet hole and a bullet in it. The bones were reburied nearby.[122]

> No useless coffins enclosed their breast,
> Nor in sheet nor in shroud we laid them,
> But they lay like warriors taking their rest,
> With their martial cloaks around them.
>
> —poet unknown

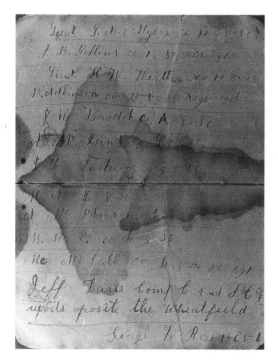

A water-stained page from George W. Rose's burial record. Found on the field at Rose's farm, it was used to record the gravesites of dead Confederates interred there. (MCW)

"A great rushing river of agony"

III

C.R. HAZARD 95

THE CARE OF
THE WOUNDED

"The tide of human misery around the little town of Gettysburg swelled high as never before, perhaps in all our land. We saw the horrors of war, enough to make the heart ache and revolt at the inhumanity of man to man. Yet all these ghastly wounds were received from the hands of their own countrymen."

"Sat. July 11, 1863—Leaving for [home]—For six miles on this side of Gettysburg we saw nothing but hospitals—barns, farmhouses, tents, etc.— Everywhere the Red Flag streamed."[1]

An Accounting

In the unpleasant aftermath of the battle people travelled to the war-torn environs of Gettysburg not only out of curiosity, or in search of the grave of a deceased friend or relative, but for other reasons as well. They were also impelled to make the difficult trip in order to locate a specific wounded person, or to bring aid or supplies to the injured multitudes in general, or to volunteer their services as nurses or attendants. John Howard Wert exemplified this class rather soundly in the following:

> Crowds came that were searching for husbands, sons, fathers, brothers, dead or wounded in that awful vortex of destruction. They came by the thousands...all on one common errand of love, all torn by the same agonizing feelings of doubt, which, in thousands of scenes was, too soon, dissolved in the certainty of despair.
> ...They came to search for their dead—to minister to their wounded. Some were successful, some failed. Some exhumed hundreds of bodies but never found the dead for whom they sought. Some found their loved ones in rude hospitals and hovered over them for weeks, with the gentlest ministrations, until partial health began to replace the palid hue; or, until death terminated all.[2]

When Wert and others spoke of "the wounded," or the "injured or maimed," just how many of these shot-torn and battered humans did they mean? If we return to the second chapter of the book we find that there were approximately 51,000 *casualties* inflicted during the three days of conflict. These are *casualties* only, and reflect, as we have said, the total number of killed, mortally wounded, wounded, missing in action, and prisoners of war. Very often at Gettysburg, a park ranger, battlefield guide, or some other knowledgeable person who works at the National Military Park will overhear some astonished visitor exclaim how they read that over 50,000 men were *killed* in the battle. For some peculiar reason it has seemed difficult for people to grasp the difference between the words "killed" and "casualties." It is now common knowledge to the reader that approximately 7,100 Union and Confederate soldiers were killed outright on the field of Gettysburg in three days of strife. Within several months of the engagement over 3,000 more men died of their wounds. Furthermore, approximately 27,000 were *wounded* in the battle. That last total is everyone who lived, plus the men who died later of their injuries. These 27,000 were only the wounded actually sent to field hospitals, treated and counted.

There were many hundreds on both sides who did not report their injuries for various reasons, and therefore are not listed in the compiled registers of men wounded at Gettysburg. In fact, within some personal military service files at the state or national level, there often does not appear a record of these varieties of wounds; most of which were very slight and usually were not ordinarily debilitating. Some of these injuries were not only unaccounted for, but could be, at best called unusual. Take these stories of two Union soldiers shot during the battle. One wonders how many other such curious wounds could be found, or how many men long after Gettysburg, and the other thousands of engagements of the Civil War were troubled by similar reoccurring problems:

A STRANGE WOUND

A Confederate Button Found in John Bowden's Leg Which Entered His Arm.

John Bowden, 55 years of age, a brakeman on the Baltimore and Ohio Railroad, residing in Baltimore, went to the Presbyterian Hospital yesterday and complained of a severe pain in his leg. No outward evidence of any injury could be discovered by the physicians, but, with Bowden's consent, they cut into the centre of pain and removed a large Confederate military button, which, when cleaned, looked as bright as new.

Bowden said that he was wounded in the arm at the battle of Gettysburg, but at the time the bullet could not be found, although the wound was probed several times by the hospital physicians. The Confederate button was the missile that inflicted the wound in his arm and had worked its way up through his body and down to the place where it was found and removed.

A CURIOUS RELIC OF GETTYSBURG

Rev. Edwin Wells, pastor of the Baptist congregation, at Mt. Carroll, Illinois, has obtained, recently, a relic of the great battle of Gettysburg, in a rather curious way, which is thus spoken of in a late number of the Chicago *News*:

"The Rev. E. Wells, pastor of the Baptist Church at Mount Carroll, was wounded in the left cheek at the battle of Gettysburg by what he supposed to be a spent ball. Two teeth were knocked out. The wound appeared so slight that he did not have it examined by a surgeon. About a month ago he felt pain in the region of his old wound and went to a dentist for relief. The dentist removed the rebel bullet, which had remained in the wound and the presence of which had never been suspected by Mr. Wells."[3]

As one Confederate explained, the true casualties of a battle can never be known. This was due to the vast confusion after any military engagement, especially one the size of Gettysburg, where the immediate need to restore order in the army was paramount. There were too, the heavy losses themselves, the many scattered commands and personnel, and the critical need to care for the many thousands of seriously wounded, the burial of the dead, and most important, the problem of a difficult and long retreat and pursuit into Virginia. He reviewed the problems:

...[And] for many weary days there was no time or opportunity to ascertain the losses. The hasty company lists forwarded to become the basis of the routine casualty returns of the Medical Department were...admittedly inaccurate and incomplete, but were allowed to stand, imperfect as they were, and were soon lost sight of in the pressure of other great events.

The unfortunate absence of the usual official statements of casualties and the overwhelming evidence of the inaccuracy of the medical returns, has impelled a resort, in part, to other evidence, that of participants, verbal and written...[which were often even more imprecise.][4]

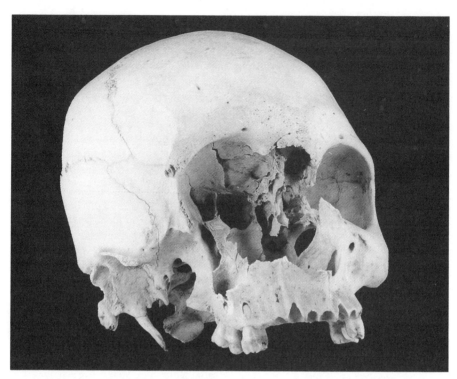

G.W. Bowles, Company G, 42nd Virginia, received a wound in the neck and a fracture of the inferior maxilla on July 3. He was admitted to a U.S. hospital on July 6 and died on July 13 in Frederick, MD. (OHA/RK)

In speaking of "the wounded," we generally mean *male* combatants; however, let it be known that at least one soldier who served in the ranks of the Confederate army at Gettysburg was an unnamed female. She was taken prisoner and with many other Rebels was sent to a military hospital in Chester, Pennsylvania. A witness who saw her there depicted the unusual event: "i must tel you we have got a female secesh here, she was wounded at getti[s]burg but our doctors soon found her out. i have not seen her but the[y] say she is very good looking. the poor girl [h]as lost a leg; it is a great pity she did not stay at home with her mother...."[5]

Regrettably, therefore, we must let stand the official number of wounded even though there are serious gaps in the accounting, a figure which is nominally stated at 27,238 men. The older count for the wounded at Gettysburg for many years was held as 33,264. General Meade's report of Union injured came in at 14,529, Lee's Confederates were placed at 12,709. The Army of Northern Virginia's tally has been revised and juggled with somewhat in the past few years but still stands at about 12,200. Let us safely say, for now anyway, that the wounded on both sides come to right around 26,708.[6]

Of this final number, United States Army Medical Inspector Edward P. Vollum recorded on July 29, 1863, that the sum of both Federal and Southern wounded *left at Gettysburg* was 20,342. His visual, on-site research at the time led him to believe that 6,739 Confederate wounded remained behind in the wake of Lee's retreat from Pennsylvania. The official revised compilation later had 6,026 Confederates abandoned in U.S. hospitals around Gettysburg. This was disputed by Dr. Jonathan Letterman, Medical Director of the Army of the Potomac, who contended on October 3, 1863, that there were really 6,802 Rebels in Yankee hands. This summary more closely matches that of Inspector Vollum, who also stated that his numbers did *not* enumerate the C.S. wounded then sequestered in hospitals at Carlisle, Chambersburg, Hanover, Mercersburg, and other sites far from the battlefield. In his synopsis, Medical Director Letterman suggests that the "total number of wounded thrown by that battle upon this department [is], twenty thousand nine hundred and ninety five."[7] Hence, when we speak in this chapter of the "care of the wounded" at Gettysburg, that topic will concern all 20,995 men, both Southern *and* Northern soldiers who were provided for in hospitals at and surrounding that village. In conclusion, one other interesting statistic may be worth recording here. Although historians do not agree and do not know the exact breakdown of Confederate casualties on each of the three days, we do have an approximate Union figure. They were: July 1—8,955 killed, wounded and missing, (4,308 wounded); July 2—11,630 total casualties, (8,528 wounded); and July 3—3,017 all total, (2,012 wounded). "Reportedly" the Confederate complete daily losses on July 1, were 5,643; July 2, at least 7,000 and on July 3, possibly 6,000.[8]

Dr. Jonathan Letterman. (GNMP)

Military Medical Practices

Before we proceed into an exclusive description of the wounded and hospitals which at Gettysburg were in place between July 4 and November 20, 1863, it might be prudent to provide for the reader a summary of general information on the medical corps and its operations during the Civil War years.

In 1860 the medical staff of the entire U.S. Army of 16,000 men consisted of only 30 surgeons and 83 assistant surgeons. Twenty-four of these men resigned their positions to support the Southern Confederacy at the beginning of hostilities in 1861. Ultimately, by the end of the war, more than 12,000 doctors had been on the payroll of the Union army at one time or another and in the Confederate States army 3,236 doctors served from 1861 to 1865. The budget of the U.S. Army Medical Department in 1860 was $90,000 but by 1863 it had risen to $11,594,000. Its total expenditure for the war was $47,400,000.

The war progressed vigorously into 1862 and that year produced so many thousands of diseased and injured soldiers that the medical departments of both armies were forced to add larger and more proficient staffs. As a matter of record, in 1860 the Federal army did not even have an ambulance service, so by 1863 the new medical director of the Army of the Potomac, Dr. Jonathan Letterman, instituted a complete reorganization of the medical corps including adding an ambulance corps to that army. On the other hand, the Confederate forces never did seem to reach the effectiveness of their Federal counterparts, and their system, although copied for the most part from the old U.S. Army regulations, was not always as up to date on new improvements, measures and techniques endorsed and employed by the Federal medical department.

During the time of the Battle of Gettysburg, the Union Army of the Potomac had more than 1,000 ambulances present for duty, while the Confederates carried with them to Pennsylvania about 400. Officially, or "on paper," an army of 100,000 men, would need about 600 of these vehicles or a train of ambulances about 25 miles long. During the campaign and battle there were about 650 doctors present with Northern commands and approximately 400 surgeons available to the Confederates. These Confederate medical officers were under the authority of Dr. Lafayette Guild, the medical director of the Army of Northern Virginia.

Each of the hundreds of regiments in both armies at the moment of the battle of Gettysburg had essentially the same organization. All regiments were supposed to be supported by a surgeon and one or two assistant surgeons, often called "acting assistants." From the ranks came several medical orderlies and/or hospital stewards. The army medical corps, like that of its fellow infantry, artillery, commissary or quartermaster corps, had wagon trains attached to them to move the huge quantities of baggage, supplies, tents, and medicines they needed on campaign. During any ongoing hostilities, the assistant surgeons at regimental level (a regiment averaged about 350 men at Gettysburg) kept pace with their units, whether infantry, cavalry or artillery, and maintained a close proximity to the men on the firing line. The first duties of these front line assistant surgeons were to organize aid or dressing stations near the fighting areas, while the surgeons of the regiments, who were thus delegated, rode back to select suitable spots for *field* hospitals at brigade, division or corps levels. The locations of these early "close by the front line" field hospitals were frequently poor choices and this fact was very apparent at Gettysburg. Taking account of nearly all the primary or initial field hospitals of the First, Second, Third, and Fifth Corps established near Gettysburg, almost one hundred percent of them were forced to move farther to the rear owing to the ever-present danger of stray or overshot artillery rounds. A civilian correspondent was the first to disclose that danger. At 7 AM on July 3, T.C. Grey of the New York *Tribune* wired a telegram to his editor, Sydney H. Gay. It was headed "H.Q. Army of the Potomac," and read in part: "...hospitals inside [the lines] are not safe and some are quite exposed."

The more secure and permanent designated field hospital localities were supposed to provide shelter from the elements in tents or in buildings such as houses, barns, or churches, and safety from enemy fire, plus a plentiful supply of water. These hospitals were also often contiguous to main roads where supplies and food could reach the doctors, their assistants, and patients and where ambulances hauling wounded could easily and quickly find their way there and back to the battle areas.

Meanwhile at the "primary stations" and near where the regiments were in action, the assistant surgeons prepared themselves for the expected and almost certain influx of wounded which were destined to be fed hastily into the medical system as the battle raged on in intensity.

One of the better sources which demonstrated how these combat front-line medical officers plied their trade, is here presented by Dr. William Taylor.

It was the custom of the assistant surgeons of our brigade to work together for the benefit of mutual help. As the troops advanced we kept with them and closely scrutinized the locality in the search for places suitable for [aid] stations. Noting trees, fences, straw-stacks, depressions of the surface, or whatever offered a show of shelter, and specially for gullies, which were the most desirable of all. It was necessary for these stations to be near the engaged men....

As the men moved forward to get into position they would not infrequently be under heavy fire, and we assistant surgeons had to maneuver against it the best we could....

We shifted our stations, when it became necessary, to conform to the movements of the fighting line....Our surgical work was usually very simple, though often there was enough of it to keep us fully and laboriously employed. It consisted chiefly of the application of plaster and bandages and the administration of stimulants and superintending the placing of the badly wounded in the ambulances for transportation to the field hospital. No elaborate surgical procedure was undertaken unless there was urgent necessity for it. Sometimes...[the] wounded men...would be scattered about [an extended area]...in out-of-the-way places, whither they had wandered. When the battle was ended....we had to hunt up these unfortunates—a duty willingly performed, though not infrequently an arduous one.[9]

The surgeons just described, who were doing duty both on the firing line and in the rear, were commonly equipped with chloroform or ether (usually the former), brandy, aromatic spirits of ammonia, bandages, adhesive plaster, needles, silk thread for ligatures, and the like. Amputating cases were also available and were supplied with catling (a long, thin-bladed knife), artery forceps, bone forceps, scalpel, scissors, butted probes, and tourniquets. In the field the assistant surgeons generally carried and made use of a small emergency case or pack called a "field companion," which was about the size of a common knapsack. Contained within this kit were most of the above items except in more limited quantities. The first aid administered by these forward area medical teams or individuals rarely went beyond the staunching of bleeding vessels and applying temporary dressings to the open wounds. When this service was completed, injured soldiers were directed immediately to the rear to a division ambulance collecting point where they were picked up by an ambulance team and then transported to a field hospital, which was usually out of musket range, but not always far enough from the deadly reach of stray artillery shells or cannonballs.

Before and during a battle, the ambulances of an army division were habitually drawn from the main ambulance park into what was known as a "collecting point." This location was generally in a fairly safe area about 300 to 500 yards behind the line of battle, back just far enough to be readily reached by the stretcher bearers. These latter named attendants were sometimes only musicians detailed from the ranks of regimental bands or some other similar

This surgeon's operating kit was presented to Dr. J.W.C. O'Neal by Mr. J. Edward Plank. It was left at his farm by Dr. Means. (ACHS/CLS)

rear echelon troops. However by 1863 litterbearers often held regular maintained positions in the army's ambulance corps. These men were often weighed down with heavy, blood-soaked burdens, and were frequently forced to make many tiring and dangerous trips, often under fire, out toward and back from the firing lines. With the end of normal hostilities, stretcher parties continued to run the gauntlet of enemy sharpshooters in search of wounded men previously missed.

In many cases, ambulances were driven by men who had been detailed from the line units, as were soldiers acting as nurses, cooks, clerks, attendants and so forth. But often the government simply hired civilian teamsters. In 1862, William A. Hammond estimated that if a separate "Ambulance Corps" was created it would immediately return 16,000 infantrymen back to their regiments. It had been calculated that 77 officers, doctors and enlisted men were needed to operate an army ambulance section, with 25 of these medical vehicles allotted to an average army division containing 5,000 to 6,000 foot soldiers. These picked men, having enlisted especially for the sole purpose of transporting the wounded would obviously have been better fitted for that rigorous duty than the musicians and convalescents in use in the early months of the war, who more often than not proved utterly worthless in bringing off the seriously injured. But it would not be until 1864 that an official army-wide Ambulance Corps was established. In the interim the army used a system Major Jonathan Letterman had set up shortly before the 1862 Battle of Antietam. It was indeed a good structure, but unfortunately was in use only by the Army of the Potomac.

Letterman's new and improved method provided for ambulances to be organized into separate division trains with a first lieutenant in command of

An army wagon fitted up as an ambulance. (MSHCW)

each train. A properly supplied medicine wagon also formed part of this unit, as well as a travelling forge, along with its own saddler and blacksmith, while the ambulances were supplied with handpicked drivers and stocked with stretchers, kettles, lanterns, beef stock, bed-sacks and kitchen utensils.

This plan or "Letterman system" was approved by General George B. McClellan in August 1862 and further ordered that the ambulance attendants and drivers be specially selected for their good moral character. They had to be active, efficient, and interested in the duty, and were to be drilled and inspected constantly. Ambulances would then be placed in the front of all wagon trains accompanying the army and could be used only for injured or sick troops, not as convenient resting facilities for tired officers, as an example. Stretcher-bearers and hospital stewards were required to wear distinctive green colored insignia on their uniforms, and only these medical corpsmen were allowed to remove the wounded. Furthermore, all ambulance drivers, vehicles and horses were arrayed under the control of an army division.

What follows is a quote from the report of Lieutenant Joseph C. Ayer who commanded the ambulance section of the 1st Division, Fifth Corps at the Battle of Gettysburg. He goes into more depth concerning the main duties and responsibilities of such a "section" in that battle:

> As soon as the division was placed in position all my stretcher men, under their lieutenants and sergeants, were sent to the front to follow their respective regiments; leaving one lieutenant and three sergeants in charge of the train. I conducted the train to a point two hundred yards in rear of the second and third brigades, where it was rapidly loaded with severely wounded. Owing to some misunderstanding there was a delay in locating the division hospital and the wounded men remained in the ambulances about an hour, when the hospital was established and the wounded unloaded. The ambulances then commenced regular trips to the battlefield and were constantly at work during the night.
>
> As soon as all the wounded were secured, orders came to me to remove all the wounded in the field hospital to one farther in the rear.

On Friday, July 3, Lieutenant Ayer and his little command continued the removal of the torn and bleeding men of his division to newly set up hospitals. He commented that by sunset of that day the horses had been in harness for 60 hours. Then at 10 PM Ayer was ordered back into the field to help carry injured of the Third Corps to the rear. At 9 AM the next day, July 4, they began work collecting Fifth Corps wounded who were then in other corps hospitals. He noted in his memoir that the Fifth Corps with about 35 regiments, had 81 ambulances available and did pick up and transport 1,300 of the 1,611 men hurt from that corps from July 2 through the fourth.[10]

For more on the subject, we see that the Union Eleventh Corps "ambulance train" at Gettysburg consisted of 100 ambulances, 9 medical (Autenreith) wagons, 270 men and 260 horses. The quartermaster-general of the U.S. Army, General M.C. Meigs ascertained that on July 4 the entire Army of the Potomac had 1,100 ambulances equipped and ready for duty.[11]

As an interesting sidelight, this Army of the Potomac's Ambulance Corps suffered the loss of one officer and four privates killed, and seventeen injured in the line of duty while moving about the field between July 1 and July 5. The conduct of these individuals, as it came under the scrutiny of others, was highly satisfactory overall. One officer who took especial notice of their work testified: "And many a time did I see the stretcher-carriers fired upon and wounded while bearing away the wounded... But they did not desist from their humane work; and many a time did I watch anxiously, fearing every moment to see him fall, our ambulance- lieutenant [John S.] Sullivan, of the 14th Indiana...as he coolly rode

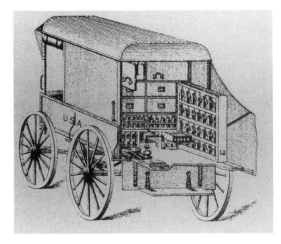

An Autenrieth medicine wagon. (MSHCW)

all over the field, sometimes in the thickest of the firing, and away to the front even of our pickets, on his errand of mercy, not satisfied to leave a single suffering man uncared for on the bloody field....All honor to such noble fellows...."[12]

The ambulances in use in 1863 were of several varieties, notably the "Finley" two wheelers and the four-wheeled "Triplers," named for the former medical director of the Army of the Potomac, C.S. Tripler. Other ambulance vehicles used during the war were called the "Wheeling" and "Rucker." The Confederates also had one known as the "Chisolm" field ambulance-wagon. As can be expected, the Union army was vastly better equipped with these vehicles than the Southern army. And all that can be said of the Confederate system in use at Gettysburg is that it was measurably much less efficient. The Rebels were forced by circumstance to make do with any and all wheeled conveyances they could gather together, such as supply wagons, civilian carriages, buggies, and freight wagons, etc.[13]

From the collecting points located several hundred yards behind the centers of combat activity, to the division field hospitals, the ambulance detachments usually had laid out a prescribed route. Small red flags or even hand-lettered signs were attached to trees, buildings and the like to direct the drivers to the hospitals, which were customarily set up in and around large farms, public buildings, or shady groves, all often situated on high ground near a good supply of water.

The large semi-permanent division field hospitals were always manned by a contingent of surgeons detached from the infantry regiments, or who were already an integral part of the brigade or division medical staffs. In preparation for the influx of wounded, medical wagons were ordered to the chosen sites, and the operating staff under the surgeon-in-charge readied their instruments,

Ambulances coming from the area of the Round Tops and moving toward the Baltimore Pike near Power's Hill. (EF)

tables, and supplies. Tents would be pitched if they were available; straw, water, fuel, blankets, and other necessary items were brought close to hand, and a rough kitchen was organized. Upon the arrival of patients, the operating surgeons and "dressers" took their places, with the operating tables often erected in rear of the medicine wagons, over which a canvas fly had been spread, and where instruments, dressings, anesthetics, and stimulants were stocked and in close proximity to the doctors and attendants.

As soon as an ambulance arrived or the walking wounded came in, an assistant surgeon known as a "recorder" made an entry for each soldier in a casebook, stating his name, rank, company, regiment and the nature of the wound or injury. If an operation was required the soldier was sent at once to the tables, otherwise he was directed or carried to one of the wards, where a dresser and other attendants or nurses took charge.

The structure of this arrangement continued unchanged, if it was not completely overwhelmed, as more and more disabled men were brought from the field. Operations were started and completed, wounds dressed, patients fed, and reports written and sent to headquarters, and eventually all the wounded men would be shipped to a main depot or general hospital at the army's supply bases which were located in specially designated cities and towns. All the while the field hospitals and ambulance trains were supposed to be subjected to close inspection, both during a campaign or battle and at other times necessary to insure proper attendance to regulations and efficiency.

A normal infantry division's hospital staff included the surgeon in charge, one assistant-surgeon designated as recorder, one assistant-surgeon posted to provide food and shelter, three medical officers to perform surgical operations, plus additional medical officers, hospital stewards and nurses to attend to the wards, dress wounds or administer food, medicine or stimulants as needed. There were likewise hospital guards, cooks, attendants, and volunteer nurses assigned to the division. Normally only proven physicians known for their operating skills were employed in these large field hospitals, and they were actually called "operators."

Besides the operating instruments and medical equipment already catalogued, the more permanent field hospitals had in stock many of the standard remedies of the day, including opium, morphine, Dover's powder, quinine, rhubarb, Rochelle salts, castor oil, sugar of lead, tannin, sulphate of copper, sulphate of zinc, camphor, tincture of opium, tincture of iron, tinctureopii, camphorata, syrup of squills, simple syrup, alcohol, whiskey, port wine, brandy, and sherry wine.

Most medicines were usually administered in a powder form or in the liquid state; some of the powders when stirred in water for the patient were bitter indeed. Tablets were not then in use, and pills were not always plentiful. Asafetida, valerian, and opium and its derivatives were about all the average Civil War surgeon had to relieve nervousness and pain and induce sleep. The majority of physicians utilized chloroform and ether during surgery, and sometimes nitrous oxide, but chloroform was the most prevalent in use. One of its earliest uses had been in March, 1842 when Dr. Crawford Long successfully administered this anesthesia in an operation performed on patient James Venable.

Very few serious operations were carried on during the war without the use of these anesthetics, although it was not uncommon for a soldier to refuse these stupefacients and, totally conscious, suffer the terrible pain of an amputation. This was a dangerous business too, because the doctor or attendant was putting the patient into what was literally a "chemical coma" using often unspecified or far from accurate measured amounts of chloroform or ether. It should be interjected here that even in the 1860s, doctors did not require soldiers to bite down onto a lead bullet during surgical procedures. In all of the sources consulted for this and other works, no such reference has ever been encountered.[14]

A case available to us which portrayed a soldier who chose, with good results, not to take anesthesia was that of Private Richard C. Phillips, 44th New York. After being wounded on Little Round Top he found his way back to the Twelfth Corps hospital where the doctor told him to lie down on the amputating table. Expecting to have the arm removed, Phillips was asked if he wanted to take chloroform. He answered "not till I knew how bad it was." The surgeon then took a knife and cut the ball, "which was just under the skin, and raised my arm and let it fall, and asked if it hurt much. I told him it did not. He said [you are] all right...."

A Confederate named Worley of the 5th Alabama Battalion was even more unconcerned about the use of chloroform. A physician who examined the ugly wound in his leg on July 1 prepared to administer the chemical. To this, Worley stoutly objected saying, "Cut off the leg Doc, but leave off the chloroform; if you can stand it I can."[15] In a final note, it may be of interest to read that in a study conducted during the war, the medical corps discovered that out of 8,000 cases where chloroform was used as the anesthetic, 37 patients died due to the product or its misuse, but in 8,000 cases where ether was used only four patients died.

During or just following a battle, aid stations, but especially division field hospitals, were often overwhelmed by the gross number of wounded. The small staffs of surgeons, nurses, and hospital stewards consequently were constantly working to keep up with these influxes.

Private Richard C. Phillips described his battlefield "operation." (MGP)

The story of the Second Corps hospital three miles south of Gettysburg where 4,000 wounded were directed by July 4 is a case in point. At this location only about a dozen attendants and doctors were in residence for the first few days of its opening, making that hospital a classic "hell on earth."

After the patient's arrival at a particular field hospital and often following a long wait, (a day or two was not out of the ordinary,) the wound would be examined and dressed. Wounds were never antiseptically treated, though, for it was long after 1865 that Sir Joseph Lister, the great English physician and others announced the discovery that something in the air was the cause of infections and disease, and which could only be killed by disinfecting wounds, surgeons' hands, instruments and bandages. Coming to this conclusion was not an easy one for the medical profession. In March of 1865 Lister, a 38-year-old professor of surgery at the University of Glasgow in Scotland, began to paint his patients with carbolic acid or phenol prior to an operation. Lister believed that the "exclusion of air" was what brought on the defeat or control of infections, and he soon commenced to spray the air with phenol. A contemporary of Lister was Dr. Lawson Tait, (both men had been students of Dr. James Syne of Edinborough) who thought that cleanliness was even more important than carbolic acid treatments. He began using clean rooms, bandages, instruments and scrubbed hands during his surgeries. Tait published a paper describing his methods in the *Lancet* of January 1871. But it was not until 1878 that Robert

Koch discovered that *germs* were the actual cause of infections, not the air itself.[16]

Amazingly, even careful handwashing by Civil War doctors was not a typical procedure. During surgical operations which often took place in the open air of a wooded grove or under a barn overhang or tent flap by operators who were usually ankle deep in mud and blood, filthy water, urine, fecal matter, bloody bandages and pieces of the human body. These hardened individuals plied their trade amidst the annoying drone and buzz of thousands of biting flies, the heat of the burning sun or the chill of a drenching rain, all the while wearing blood splattered uniforms and standing for hours hunched over old barn doors or kitchen tables used for operating benches. Sponges dabbed into wound after wound before and after amputations were tossed into filthy buckets filled with germ laden bloody water. The probing for lead or iron missiles and bone fragments was carried on with dirty instruments or fingers. One concerned surgeon, Dr. W.W. Keen, confessed that "we operated with clean hands in the social sense, but they were undisinfected hands....We used undisinfected instruments from undisinfected plush cases, and still worse used marine sponges which had been used in prior pus cases and had been washed only in tap water. If a sponge or an instrument fell on the floor it was washed or squeezed in a basin of tap water and used as though it was clean."[17]

It is no wonder that someone once said: "Possibly the surgeons, who bound up these wounds, alone can some day tell the world how savagely men fought upon the bloody field of Gettysburg."[18]

Most of the battle injuries between 1861 and 1865 were caused by round balls of pre-Civil War pattern or lead bullets known as Minié balls, which had been invented in the 1840s by Captains H. G. Delvigne and C. E. Minié of the French army. This newer type of projectile was hollow based and was produced in calibers generally from .54 to .72, some weighing well over an ounce and composed of pure soft lead. Capable of killing a man at over one thousand yards or more, the bullets caused large, gaping, ugly wounds. If the missile struck bone it never failed to fracture or shatter the bone's structure. These bullets

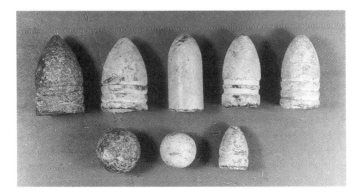

Musket and rifle small arms projectiles of the Civil War era; calibers .44, .58, .577, .69, and .72. (GAC)

also destroyed muscle, tissue, and arteries, often beyond repair. As described by one writer, the nature of the Minié ball's destructive capability was often horrendously complete; more precisely, it was a "blasting" of the tissue and bone, where the balls became a "terrible, crippling, smashing invasion of the sacred machine, splitting bones like green twigs and extravasating blood in a vast volume of tissue about the path of the projectile." If the minies hit *with enough speed* they split bone and shattered it into large fragments which in turn caused severe secondary lacerations inside the body, whereas the old style round ball had mostly sheared and chopped its way through the victim.[19] Humans shot in the abdomen and brain almost never lived, and the amputation of a damaged limb was often the cause of death itself, especially as surgeons examined the bullet holes with infected fingers and instruments. That so many men lived is probably due only to the fact that they were young and strong and had become toughened by the outdoor life of a soldier. In a normal group of Civil War soldiers injured in battle, bullets accounted for at least five times more wounds than that of artillery shells; canister was next on the list, after cannonballs and shells, and way below all of these crippling weapons of war in use then were bayonet and sword injuries, which were practically non-existent. Interestingly in returning to the *second* greatest cause of death or injury at Gettysburg, Dr. Henry Janes who was left in charge of the 20,995 wounded there, underscored that he found only 204 injuries were the direct result of artillery fire. Dr. Janes went even further and enumerated that of 245,790 "shot" wounds inflicted on U.S. soldiers during the Civil War, only 14,032 were caused by artillery projectiles.[20]

It is fascinating to learn, too, that of all of the wounds recorded during the war, about 20 percent were in the torso of the soldiers who were hit. In many such examples where the patient lived, the bullet or other missile was never removed. And approximately seventy percent of the remainder were shot in the arms or legs.

The amputations of severely damaged limbs became a common practice as well as a necessity, and a skilled "operator" with a good scalpel and sharp medical saw could remove a leg or arm in as little as half a minute, although that was certainly not the norm. With such huge numbers of wounded as were collected at Gettysburg and other battles, and with the work being carried on so quickly, one can understand why heaps of severed limbs soon grew very large near the operating tables, seemingly almost like unstacked cordwood. In general, somewhat more than one-third of the men who suffered a major limb amputation could expect to survive.

Typically, an ordinary operation/amputation might have proceeded in the following manner at any of the many operating stations in the dozens of field hospitals at Gettysburg. This hypothetical case involves a Confederate soldier with a gunshot to the leg who, let's say, is brought into General Longstreet's First Corps hospital or "infirmary corps station" at Francis Bream's tavern and farm on the Fairfield Road. Once the patient arrived, if he did not have to wait long due to scores of men ahead of him, a surgeon might administer laudanum, a liquid sedative to help calm the man's nerves. Upon being placed on the operating bench, morphine was injected into the leg wound using a "Wood's

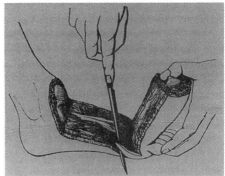

(Above) Instructional diagram used for a common Civil War amputation. (MSHCW)

(Left) Amputation of both thighs at the lower third. (MSHCW)

hypodermic syringe." Always surrounding the busy surgeon and the suffering patient were many other injured soldiers waiting their turn. A few screamed out in their delirium calling for their mothers or wives, others in shock lay still and quiet and pale. Near the crude, often makeshift operating table stood the overworked doctor who was splattered with clots of blood and pus and looked more like a butcher than a professional and educated physician. Swarms of fat green "blow flies" or flesh flies bit into soldiers' tender wounds, searching constantly for a warm place to lay their eggs, often even as the surgeon prepared to operate. This poor Confederate, now about to "go under the knife," felt fortunate he had only waited an hour before his turn. The torment quickened, both mental and physical, as the laudanum began to wear off, and he began to notice the pain in his leg more acutely. However, our Rebel was probably almost unaware of the filthy, sweat-drenched and blood-stained uniform he wore. But he did realize, as he lay upon the bench, that the fecal matter and urine that had collected in his clothes could be smelled clearly by himself, the doctor peering into his leg wound, and the hospital attendant who had cut off his trousers.

First the opening and skin around the Southerner's injury was washed with a cotton rag taken from a bucket of brownish water which stood nearby. Sponges in the Southern army *by this time* were long exhausted. Then with dirty fingers, the surgeon pushed open the large bloody opening, as he searched for bits of bone, cloth, or the bullet or iron fragment. Unable to find anything foreign, but noticing that the femur was shattered beyond repair, the doctor called for chloroform, and a "chisolm inhaler," an instrument which had been invented by Dr. Julian Chisolm. This inhaler was a cylinder with two tubes that fitted into the nostrils of the patient. This new method eliminated the pouring of chloroform onto a cone-shaped cloth, or simply dripping the liquid chemical through a cow's horn stuffed with cotton. These last two techniques placed the fluid directly onto the patient's face, which often burned the skin. Within a few minutes after the use of chloroform the soldier was limp. If the man had chosen not to use an anesthetic, which surprisingly quite a number did, he just gritted his teeth, screwed up his courage, and prepared for the severe pain, which was sometimes dimmed slightly by the use of whiskey or laudanum. The surgeon, using his scalpel then made an incision through the skin and muscle to the bone both above and below the wound leaving a flap of skin on one side. Finally a bone saw was employed which cut roughly but quickly into the large thigh bone until it was severed, the separated leg was then pitched onto a pile of similar limbs nearby. Afterward the arteries were tied off with horsehair, cotton or even silk thread, if available. Next, if this physician was knowledgeable and careful enough and after the arteries were secured, the end and edges of the bone would be scraped until they were quite smooth. Taking the sharp edge off the bone prevented it from working its way through the flap of skin. This flap was a large piece of skin cut into the shape of a half circle; it was left intact and hanging free until needed, then pulled taut over the stump and sewed closed, leaving a drainage hole. The stump was then bandaged with a piece of cloth well greased with olive oil. Over this was placed the Husband or isinglass plaster. Shortly afterward, our poor soldier groggily awoke and found himself lying under an apple tree on a few handfuls of straw, and if he was really fortunate, an army blanket. He was weak and confused and very thirsty and soon his pain grew stronger. By then the surgeon was already well into his next surgery.[21]

As busy as most medical people were, there was often at Gettysburg as elsewhere, opportunities for experimentation if a doctor found himself with extra time. As an example of this, in the 2nd Division, Fifth Corps hospital, Dr. John S. Billings had under observation six cases, in which the lungs of the gunshot victims had been *hermetically sealed*. Lamentably, all died within eighteen days. It was reported that this new type of operation was performed in order to give relief from dyspnoea (difficult, or painful breathing) and was first instituted by Dr. Benjamin Howard. The sealing took place by first paring the edges of the penetrating wound and holding them firmly together by means of two or three sutures; a pledget of lint (a small wad of wool, cotton or linen) was kept in position over the united lips of the wound by one or two strips of isinglass plaster, and the whole was coated over with collodion.[22] (*Isinglass* was a form of gelatin prepared from the internal membranes of fish bladders; it is a clarifying agent and adhesive. *Collodion* was a viscous solution of nitrated cellulose in a mixture of alcohol and ether—it dries quickly and forms a tough, elastic film over the wound.)

Secondary hemorrhages from wounds or after operations killed thousands of soldiers during the war and could begin even weeks after a battle. Tetanus or lockjaw was also a common peril prevalent following surgery and was often contracted from the filth of a farm yard, stable, or barn. Gangrene was susceptible in patients where the blood supply to a limb was obstructed by the injury. In severe bouts of gangrene the tissue begins to decay or rot. Often gangrenous limbs had to be amputated several times in order to halt the spread

Sgt. Michael C. McMurry, 125th New York Infantry wounded on July 2, lost his left arm at Gettysburg. (OHA)

of the decay and open the limb's vessels to freer blood flow.

After a stay of a few days to several weeks in a field hospital near the battlefield, the recuperating soldier could expect to be transported to a nearby city or town which had "general hospital" accommodations. From Gettysburg most patients were moved by train to major cities along the east coast. Some of those cities with general hospital facilities in operation by 1863 were Baltimore, Maryland, which had in its military hospitals 4,000 beds; York, Pennsylvania, 1,500 beds; Chester, Pennsylvania, 1,000 beds; Annapolis, Maryland, 2,500 beds; Philadelphia, Pennsylvania, 10,000 beds; and New York, New York, 5,000 beds. Pennsylvania alone had more than 15,000 spaces available for diseased or battle damaged soldiers. All major metropolitan areas throughout the North and South had large military hospitals. In Richmond, Virginia, for instance, 150 hospitals were in place throughout the war years. A more unusual feature of the Battle of Gettysburg was the use of a "general hospital" which was established right on the battlefield itself. So, for many wounded the next temporary stopover of a few weeks or months after a stay in a division field hospital was a trip to the U.S. General Hospital, called Camp Letterman, located along the York Turnpike. There they remained until the patient was

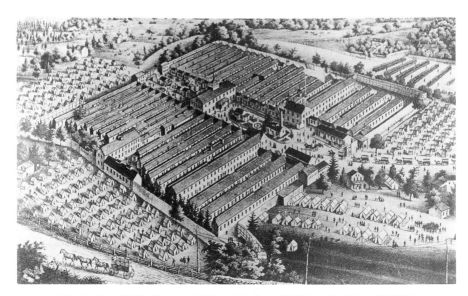

Satterlee U.S. General Hospital in Philadelphia. (PCW)

ready for rail transportation to a permanent hospital in one of the cities just noted, or was well enough to be discharged or even returned to his regiment. This concept of a general military hospital situated directly on a recent battlefield was extremely rare and Gettysburg had one of the very first of its kind. There will be more of interest concerning this large hospital in a later part of this chapter.

◆ ◆ ◆

Conditions of the Wounded

What were the conditions really like after the Battle of Gettysburg where nearly 21,000 seriously wounded remained to be cared for, especially considering the knowledge that there were only 106 Union doctors and a handful of Confederate surgeons in attendance? General Carl Schurz summed the problem up this way: "There are many who speak lightly of war as a mere heroic sport. They would hardly find it in their hearts to do so had they ever witnessed scenes [in a typical field hospital]. A war brought on without the most absolute necessity is the greatest and most unpardonable of crimes."[23]

In the next few pages, medical eyewitnesses and former combatants who experienced the grim realities of war will acquaint us with many long remembered scenes from those dreadful places.

We must also consider the irony that it was not always just the soldiers and medical people who suffered through fear, uncertainty and confusion. A historian for the county in 1886, described how the products of war affected ordinary people in and around Gettysburg during and after the battle, who were left with the worst vestiges of its brutality.

> To all this was the great tax upon the people of providing and caring for the wounded from the bloody battle-field of Gettysburg....People threw open their private houses; the churches, the schoolhouses, the public halls, and even the barns and stables, rang with the groans and agony of the shot, maimed and mutilated, that filled apparently every place, and still the field of death and agony could yet furnish more victims. The churches looked much as though they had been converted into butchers' stalls. The entire community became hospital nurses, cooks, waiters or grave-diggers. In this wide expanse of Christian charity, rebel and Union sufferers were cared for without material distinction. The Government ambulances commenced to carry away from the field their bleeding cargoes; soon every wheeled vehicle was at work bearing its loads of bleeding agony, filled with its pale sufferers garnered from the field where the cannon, the musket, the rifle and the saber had mowed their hideous swaths in living human ranks. Would these whirling wheels, in their quick trips back and forth as they dumped their loads of sufferers, never stop? What a swollen, great rushing river of agony! Literally half the surface of the entire county was a hospital, and every farm-house, barn, stable, outbuilding, for twenty miles square, was full to overflowing. The beds, the floors, the yards, everywhere, were they cared for, and behind them in the lines of battle, in the brush, by the side of the little spring streams where they had so painfully dragged themselves or sometimes been carried by their companions, were the uncollected dead and dying mostly. What a ghastly harvest to gather from the fair and peaceful fields of Adams County. And when the poor bruised and

maimed bodies were gathered in this widely extended hospital and laid side by side, what never-to-be-forgotten scenes were there. The pale sufferers, the flushed, feverish and raving maniacs, whose reason had given way as they lay upon the field suffering, and watching the stars, and welcoming the storm and rain, that came like pitying tears from heaven to soften their hardening, blood-clotted clothes, to moisten their horrid wounds and cool the raging fevers of their brows—Union and rebels, sons and fathers and brothers. Here the smooth-cheeked boy, the darling, the pet and hope of home; there the lusty man, yesterday in the prime of life and strength, in the midst of his suffering and pain turning to the grizzled-haired husband and father lying by his side, and who wanderingly talks of home, and addressed by name the different ones of his family, to feebly minister with his one yet sound hand to this pitiful sufferer, and in this charity for a moment forces himself to forget his own, still perhaps incurable, wounds.[24]

In like manner there is another summary of the awful situation, this one drawn up by a correspondent of the Philadelphia *Public Ledger*. He conveyed this version in that paper on July 15, just days after the combatants had forever forsaken the scenes of the late strife.

No one that has never visited or witnessed the vicinity of a field of battle, soon after the conflict has taken place, can form any conception of the claims of the wounded on the time, energy and means of the benevolent, who have been enjoying their ease and comfort in their quiet and peaceful homes. This town, and the vicinity within a space of country surrounding it of eight or ten miles, is literally one vast and over-crowded *hospital*. In the town itself every available space has been freely given up by the citizens to the sufferers, and yet on this, the *ninth* day after the battle, several thousands are lying, with arms and legs amputated, and every other kind of conceivable wound, in tents, on the open field, in the woods, in stables and barns, and some of them even on the bare ground, *without cover or shelter*. During a violent thunder gust, accompanied with high wind and heavy rain, on yesterday (Sunday) [July 5], some would have drowned, had not the most extraordinary efforts been put forth to prevent it. Amputated limbs could be measured by the cartload, and hundreds are dying. Oh! the horrors of this cruel war, brought on by the ambitious demagogues of the South! It beggars the descriptive energies of language, to convey an adequate conception of them!

The reporter then offers an excellent suggestion to his readers:

A word of well meant advice. Let no one come to this place for the simple purpose of *seeing*. To come here, merely to *look* at the wounded and dying, exhibits a most vitiated and disgusting taste. Besides, every such visitor is a *consumer*, and adds to the misery of the sick, by subtracting from the means that should be given exclusively to *them*. Let all that come, come with stores for the sick, and ready to work for them, but let all mere sightseers *stay at home*.

The people of Gettysburg proper most certainly had their share of difficult days surrounded by thousands of mutilated and hurting humans. Annie Sheads, a young citizen of the town, remembered that she could stand the cannons and bullets, but,

Oh! the anguish and agony after a battle is heart-rending. After the battle you could see nothing but ambulances all through the town and you could hear nothing but groans from the wounded and dying, and begging for a Dr and for water, every body was out giving them water as they went by. Those that were able to walk, walked on the side walk, with the blood coming from their wounds. Oh! how my heart ached for them. Every person went to work and done all they could for them. The town was full of wounded all the churches and all public buildings....I have been waiting on the wounded giving or rather feeding them, for they were not able to eat....some of them [would] beg me for just one spoonful, and then they would say God bless you. They died those to whom I now refer. My Mother is almost worn out, she had been attending to the wounded ever since the battle...there are still about three thousand here, they are moving them a mile out of town, as it is better for the wounded and better for the health of the town. The air is very impure, there are still a great many Confederates that are unburied and a great many horses that are lying around town.[25]

One government medical inspector, G.K. Johnston who was required to report on the situation of the wounded after the battle also declared:

There were some in churches, some in barns, some in tents among the fruit trees, some in tents in the fields, some under such shelter as a farmer would be ashamed to show for his cows. Some were under blankets hung over cross-sticks, and some without even so much shelter as that. There were some scattered groups of men outside the hospitals. It sometimes appeared as if an experiment had been made to see how many wounded could be crowded in a given space in a house.[26]

In one locale south of Gettysburg almost 3,000 Federals of the Second Corps lay on the ground along Rock Creek waiting for attention. An eyewitness observed:

The men here were in a terrible condition. They lay upon the damp ground, many of them with nothing under them. In this hospital there were an

"The wounded were everywhere." Barns were a favorite, though totally unsanitary, hospital environment. (GNMP)

unusually large number of amputations, the amputated stumps lying directly on the ground; except when now and then elevated a little upon a handful of straw or a bunch of old rags. Many of the men, perhaps most of them, were in want of clothing. Suitable food was not to be had. The surgeons were over-worked. There was an insufficient number of attendants....[Nearby] were nearly or quite a thousand rebels, most of them severely wounded...shrieking and crying for assistance continually....Destitute of clothing many of them nearly naked and covered with filth, without tents, lying in the mud...cursing, praying, begging their attendants or visitors to put an end to their suffering by taking their lives....[27]

In this same area just northwest of the Baltimore Pike at "White Church" a reporter in the July 16, 1863, issue of the Philadelphia *Daily Evening Bulletin* commented that in the "awful struggles" of battle and from subsequent wounds, the "clothing of many [men] was partly torn from them....[and] what few articles they had remaining were so covered with blood and dust that it was necessary to strip them entirely, so that many of the poor fellows are now in the hospitals, completely naked. The lady nurses are not permitted to enter some places owing to this fact." He added that the "wounds of many...have already been filled with larvae, so that [a] passing ambulance emits a most unpleasant stench. The condition of the rebel wounded in the barns is even worse than our own."

At a hospital of the Fifth Corps a few hundred yards west of the one just described was this scene:

At one place, near a fence, lay privates, corporals, lieutenants, majors, and colonels, from New York, North Carolina, Indiana, Mississippi, Connecticut, Georgia, New Hampshire, Alabama, Maine and Delaware, side by side on the

An early field hospital of the U.S. Second Corps near Rock Creek. (GNMP)

bare ground, or on a little wet straw; no distinction. Men were gathered around trees, with their heads toward the body of the tree; occasionally, when able, one sat up and leaned against it. They were in every condition, from the slightest wound to the man dying in agony, from the terrible mangling of a piece of shell.[28]

Unlike the town of Gettysburg which had been dealing quite well with its burden of pitiful, broken humanity, the various outlying field hospitals of both the Union and Confederate armies were not so fortunate. Spread across an area of close to 25 square miles, they presented a very different situation entirely, as here noted by a Christian Commission delegate:

In most of them there was not the face of a female to be seen, nor was there a surgeon nor a chaplain to minister to the wants of the bleeding multitudes that were groaning in pain and crying for help. Generally there was a nurse in charge of the men that were gathered into a dwelling house, or barn, or into a hastily constructed tent, or in the shade of some forest trees. Accommodations on beds and couches were afforded for but few among the thousands that needed them. Upon straw, and hay, and blankets, and overcoats, and upon the bare ground, by far the greater number of the sufferers were lying, and their cries...were deeply afflictive.[29]

Even four days later on July 7, another delegate's first sight of the wounded of both Federals and Confederates was of them "laying around in the woods, with scarcely a blanket to cover or lay under them, and all soaked with the daily drenching rains, with not even a sheltering tent to protect them from the weather, and many of them perfectly helpless from wounds, it was almost too much for me...."[30]

In barnyards and wagon-sheds, stables and barns the heavy rains which succeeded the battle had made the dirty ground even more offensive than normal. In many of these outbuildings the injured, who at least had an overhead shelter, were made even more uncomfortable with the flooding waters which spread rapidly and continually underneath their miserable "beds." One bystander related how a bundle of clean hay could not have been bought with all the gold in California. He also added these lines:

In the cow stable the filthy water of the dung-heap had dammed up and backed in upon [the men], saturating straw, blankets, and everything else within its reach....On account of the water most of the scanty hay had floated away, and left the poor sufferers lying upon the bare rails, sometimes without so much as the thickness of a single blanket between their emaciated bodies and the sharp, knotty wood. And these men were the *elite* of the Southern army—lawyers, planters, men of wealth, intelligence and refinement....[31]

Heavy rains which frequently followed a large battle were noticeably present within hours after Gettysburg's three-day combat. As one Confederate explained: "As usual after a big battle, rain came and this added to the gloom of our spirits."[32]

The *Compiler* of June 20, 1864, attempted to enlighten its readers on that very subject with this gem taken from a city newspaper:

Storms After Battle

The New York *Sun* is discussing that law of nature which produces rain and storm after battle, and particularly where much artillery is used. The same discussion has been the rounds of the French and German journals after every great battle, for rain or snow, it is said, after all great battles, is the rule and not the exception. For three years Americans have had opportunity to test the truth of the assertion, and the result has established the fact beyond all question, says the *Sun*, that great battles are followed by rain storms. While Napoleon was startling Europe with his military movements, the French Academy of Science directed its attention to the fact that a storm of rain or snow invariably followed his battles, and declared its faith in the truth of the noted rule now reaffirmed. Many doubted the accuracy of the statement, so the question was dropped, and it seems to have been left for solution as to the effects observed during our own unhappy war. It is stated that all the prominent battles fought by our armies thus far have been followed by a storm. Those who recollect the first Bull Run conflict will remember the storm that followed. After the battle of Fredericksburg the Rapidan became so swollen by heavy rains as to render the situation of our army, while waiting to cross the river, extremely critical. Later evidence of this is found in the severe storms of rain and hail that followed the recent battles in Virginia, whereby the operations of Gen. Grant were delayed a week or more by the muddy condition of the roads. The scientific men of the country are just now discussing the theory.

The sights and sounds emanating from the many field hospitals which dotted the landscape for miles in every direction were often monotonously and painfully the same. That statistic, however, will not prevent us from looking more closely into a few of those sad places.

Jane Boswell Moore endured them in person, while she dutifully nursed hundreds at the Union Second Corps hospital. Here she explains her experiences:

> Words utterly fall short in describing the appearance of those woods on the morning we reached the hospital....The site of the hospital, which had been hurriedly chosen was in a grove of trees on a piece of rising ground, surrounded nearly on all sides by a ravine, along which ran a creek near whose banks lay hundreds of wounded and dying Rebels, most of whom were exposed to the pitiless pelting of the storm....Shrieks, cries and groans resounded on all sides, not only from those in the tents, [and in the open air] but on the amputating tables, which were almost constantly occupied; and who could pass them without a dreadful shudder at those ghastly bleeding limbs heaped without, which the eye, however cautious, could not always avoid....Never will those scenes of suffering pass away; with terrible reality and vividness we feel that they must dwell in our memory forever!

Returning to the same hospital the next day [July 8], she happened through one of the First Corps establishments along the Baltimore Pike. There, Moore could only acknowledge that,

> ...language fails to depict the misery which was everywhere present. Scarcely had one man out of a thousand anything more than the ground, covered with an old blanket or an oil cloth, to lay on, and hundreds had undergone amputations since the battle. Miserable little shelter-tents alone protected

them from the rain, whilst numbers of the poor wretched Rebels had not even these, but were exposed through all the heavy rain of Tuesday night, with scarcely covering enough to keep warm in dry weather. All were clamorous for bread and butter; our own men were badly off; the Rebels begged piteously; the doctors were busily engaged in amputating; great piles of limbs being heaped up at the three different tents, and hundreds were suffering to have their wounds washed and dressed. The air at times resounded with moans and shrieks of anguish; men were employed all the time as grave diggers, and the dead lay at tent doors on the ground, as well as on the bloody stretchers, waiting burial.[33]

Alas, it should be remembered that not only the hospitals in the *field* were in bad condition, but also those in more stable and protected areas. To exemplify this, it was claimed that even inside Pennsylvania College's beautiful main edifice, one of the sturdiest structures anywhere near Gettysburg, the situation was far from good. And, unbelievable as it seems, this description of the place was written on July 17, a long time after the battle had ended, when the circumstances should have been much improved.

The writer was Nathaniel Davidson, one of the reporters for the New York *Herald*. While visiting the college he observed that the Rebel wounded had suffered many more amputations than the Federals, he responded further that the Confederates may have had well disciplined infantry corps, but that discipline did not carry over into their medical department. The main college building, Davidson revealed,

...is a large structure, very well adapted for hospital purposes, situated in the centre of beautiful grounds, with unobstructed circulation of air, and yet the atmosphere within was close and fetid, and the stench arising from wounds and filth was insufferable. The wounds of the patients were inflamed and the bandages dry. When asked where their nurses were, they said they only had one or two to each floor, and they could not attend them all. [There were approximately 900 Confederate wounded sequestered in and just outside this building.] In each corner was a pile of dirt, and the floors were wet from the careless spilling of water....We went into the yard and there were some two hundred slightly wounded and convalescent rebels, able to draw and cook their own rations, eating their breakfast. In our hospitals they would have been made to take their watches with the helpless as nurses; but they would not raise a hand to help their more unfortunate fellows.[34]

Some Confederates might have agreed wholeheartedly with this drab assessment. In fact, one did. An officer of the 47th North Carolina who was quartered in the college hospital wrote what follows in 1867, just two years after the war ended:

As a consequence of the small number of surgeons left with us, our men...suffered much....Thus for the first two weeks, there were no nurses, no medicines, no kinds of food proper for men in our condition, our supply being two or three hard crackers a day with a small piece of fat pork, with now and then a cup of poor coffee, and for men who were reduced to mere skeletons from severe wounds and loss of blood, the floor was a hard bed with only a blanket on it....

We each day became weaker and thinner until a certain point was reached, then if our wounds were curable, nature began to revive the wasted frame; if they were not, a little struggle, a low moan, and the poor emaciated skeleton, of what was once a man, was wrapped in a blanket and borne from our sight forever.[35]

These problems were not only contained in and near Gettysburg, but overflowed into communities outside of Adams County. Thirty miles away in Chambersburg, Pennsylvania, on July 10, a U.S. Sanitary Commission agent, Isaac Harris, found "...70 Reb patients under charge of Dr.(?) Hamilton M. Gamble—20th Va. Inf. (Reb) & nephew of Gov. [H.R.] Gamble of Mo. Hospital in horrible condition and without supplies of any kind, the patients lying on the bare floors, without covering of any kind, and even without dressing for their wounds and the entire place infested with vermin. The sight was sickening, in fact, the most horrible I have yet met with."[36]

As it turned out, the questionable "Dr." Gamble was not an M.D. and was in fact only a hospital steward.

The seventy Confederates Harris described were in some ways more fortunate than most wherein they at least had a medical attendant present. Ninety percent of the Rebel wounded did not have this luxury, as indicated by the president of the U.S. Sanitary Commission. He pronounced on July 14, 1863, that the Southern army had left behind over 6,000 wounded in 24 hospitals in a 12 mile radius of Gettysburg, but these men were "deserted by all but five of their own surgeons...."

This gentleman, Henry Bellows, also spoke of the roads being,

> thronged with wounded [Union] men, here on canes and there on crutches, not seldom with amputated arms, and heads still bleeding, making their way on foot from the corps hospitals two, three and four miles to the depot. At the hospitals themselves...the spectacle was intensely wretched. Men with both legs shot off—shot in the eye, the mouth, both hands gone, or one arm lost, were laying in rows that seemed pitiable and in wonderful patience, fortitude and patriotic pride, facing their sufferings. The rebels, as was just, had to wait their turn....Many, after six days, were looking forward to an amputation of their shattered limbs. The terrible destitution of many of the rebels will not bear description. It was too horrible for recital.[37]

Is it any wonder that a Federal staff officer could understand why some men were forced to commit acts of desperation. This lieutenant, Thomas Leiper, explained in a letter to his father that, "a rebel, badly wounded, after making several attempts to rise, committed suicide, by discharging his piece with the end of a stick, the contents entering his head."[38]

On July 5, Mary Cadwell Fisher of York, Pennsylvania, arrived at a field hospital at an unidentified site near Gettysburg. Her first feeling was the "thought [that] before this...I had learned all the horrors of warfare inside the walls of our crowded hospitals and from the continually passing trains of wounded....

"But here a new revelation of the brutality of war was presented to my eyes. Grouped beneath the trees we saw about five hundred men, who had hastily been removed beyond fighting limits. They were lying upon the ground, some of them literally half buried in mud. There was no shelter. Wounded, chilled, starving and racked with pain, how they welcomed us...."

The next morning Fisher and her cohorts were begged by a frantic surgeon to come to another hospital nearby. "Crossing two or three fields to a barn," she continued,

we found several hundred sufferers. No words can tell the horrors of that "charnel house of death...." The huge Pennsylvania barn [possibly that of Jacob Schwartz] was completely packed, so full that we could not step between the men; even the stables and lofts were crowded.

In all that ghastly array of human misery, between 300 and 400 men, there was not one whole individual. Every one had lost either an arm or a leg and in some cases both were gone. One poor wretch had both legs and his right arm torn off by a shell, and one had lost both arms and one leg. There was every conceivable form of wounds, cuts and bruises. What horribly mutilated faces looked up to us from the straw-littered boards which formed the only beds!...

Exhausted with loss of blood, faint with hunger, they turned to us with imploring looks, and dying eyes brightened at the sight of friends bringing food and aid....Many had to be fed like infants....I saw tears of gratitude run down the cheeks of men who would have died in the ranks without flinching as they received the food we so gladly gave.

In a week of helping the wounded Mary Fisher related how she had but once become, "utterly unnerved." On her way out of the hospital one evening Fisher depicted how she "suddenly came upon an amputation table. Beside it lay a ghastly pile of several limbs, just as they had been taken from the mangled

The barn of Jacob Schwartz was filled to capacity with "a ghastly array of human misery." (GAC)

bodies. I had seen the ground thickly strewn with dead bodies, had picked my way among them with calloused nerves, had stood on the brink of uncovered trenches filled with blackened corpses, had gone home at night with my skirts stained with blood, but there was a pathetic horror around those nameless hands and feet, none knowing or caring to whom they once belonged. It was so dreadful, so revolting, that my feet seemed paralyzed and I stood rooted to the spot with a horrible fascination."[39]

Another woman, Charlotte E. McKay, spent about six weeks in a corps hospital almost five miles from Gettysburg. There she collected supplies for about 1,500 men, and then made sure the rations were cooked. The only means available to prepare the food was to boil it in great camp kettles and caldrons suspended from cross pieces on upright poles over open, roaring fires. She and other volunteers tried desperately to procure a real cookstove, but to no avail. McKay endorsed the fact that while men died daily, good food stored in nearby tents could not be suitably cooked. Another problem was the lack of bedding:

"Our men were also suffering for want of sheets, the coarse army blankets being their only defense against the flies, and these were terrible on their wounds in the hot weather. I have seen men, with both hands disabled, crying in helpless agony from the tortures of these merciless little insects."[40]

Surgeon Daniel G. Brinton was engaged in his own medical work as a division surgeon-in-chief at the field hospital of the Eleventh Corps on the George Spangler farm, one mile south of Gettysburg. From July 1 through the fifth he was present at the hospital, describing his duties as "[v]ery hard work," and where,

[F]our operating tables were going night and day. On the 4th of July...the number in the hospital was 1000. A heavy rain came over in the afternoon and as we had laid many in spots without shelter some indeed in the barnyard where the foul water oozed up into their undressed wounds, the sight was harassing in the extreem. We worked with little intermission, & with a minimum amount of sleep. On one day I arose at 2 AM & worked incessantly till midnight. I doubt if ever I worked harder at a more disagreeable occupation. On the afternoon of the 3rd we were exposed to a sharp fire of shells. Several horses & one man were killed close to the hospital. Shells fell within 20 ft of the room where we were, and we were much in fear that the barn would blaze, which would have been an unspeakably frightful casualty....Among our wounded were three [U.S.] Colonels, [plus] Gen [Francis] Barlow, & Gen [Lewis] Armistead of the rebel army a fine man, intelligent & refined.[41]

A surgeon of the 77th New York named George Stevens also saw the Union wounded collected in great numbers and carried to the field hospitals, which he recalled were, "composed chiefly of hospital tents, some farm house with its large barns, serving as a nucleus for each. To these, thousands of our brave comrades were brought with mangled limbs, torn bodies or bleeding heads, yet, notwithstanding their terrible wounds, exhibiting their accustomed heroism. Long trains of ambulances were bringing in crowds of poor fellows with arms or legs torn to shreds, yet who never uttered a word of complaint, and who indeed appeared cheerful and some even gay."

Dr. Stevens resumed his narrative by mentioning a peculiarity or difference he perceived between Federal and Confederate wounded: "A Union soldier, if so severely wounded that he could by no possibility assume a cheerful countenance, would shut his teeth close together and say nothing. While a rebel, if he could boast of only a flesh wound, would whine and cry like a sick child." Stevens specifically stated that this contrast was not over drawn and that every surgeon who ever had the opportunity to observe this distinction in the bearing of the injured men of the two armies, could truthfully testify to this phenomenon.[42]

Emily B. Souder, a nurse stationed at the Second Corps hospital also remembered the conduct of some of the Confederates. She composed this in a letter home on July 20: "The rebels bear their suffering very differently from our men. Some of them, their officers, are intelligent and gentlemanly; but the privates are for the most part perfectly abject. They whine, and cry, and complain; and their own men, who have been detailed as nurses, *will not* wait on them. They may well be called 'white trash,' for they are lacking in nearly all those qualities that we respect and value."[43]

Frederick Law Olmsted was also impressed by the Southern style of handling discomfort. On July 19, corresponding with a Sanitary Commission agent, Olmsted suggested that the wounded Rebels, "expressed surprise at the kindness which they were treated when they came as invaders, and were as usual, peevish, childish, and exacting among themselves about their wounds and pains...."[44]

An unknown reporter for the Brooklyn *Eagle* gave his opinion on the matter in an article published by that paper on July 22, 1863. Said he: "A noticeable contrast was observed in the sentiment and demeanor of the Union and rebel soldiers. That of the former was one of honest pride in the discharge of his duty to his country, and of the beneficial results expected thereby; the latter was generally that of disgust for the service in which he had embarked, and the hopelessness of ultimate success. They were tired of the war. The officers, however, preserved the defiant attitude which has characterized them throughout the whole war."

Working at Camp Letterman General Hospital, which had been established in late July east of Gettysburg, Sophronia E. Bucklin made mention of the same sort of inclination of the Confederates with reference to their bearing and attitudes. She recollected that the Southerners in that large hospital numbered more than half of

Frederick Law Olmsted nursed the wounded at Gettysburg. (TL)

all the patients, and that they were "grim, gaunt, ragged men—long-haired, hollow-eyed and sallow-cheeked." Bucklin observed further that "[i]t was universally shown here, as elsewhere, that these [Rebels] bore their sufferings with far less fortitude than our brave soldiers who had been taught, in sober quiet homes in the North, that while consciousness remained, their manliness should suppress every groan...." She also deduced that a greater percentage of Confederates died at Letterman, even though they received the same care as the Federal soldiers. Bucklin could not explain why this was so.[45]

Returning to the care of the wounded on the battlefield itself, a volunteer surgeon, Dr. Francis M. Wafer of the 108th New York, had similar viewpoints. Employed in aid station duties at the Peter Frey farm on the Taneytown Road late on July 3, he counted vast numbers of Confederate and Union wounded who filled fully a quarter of an acre of ground around that stone farmhouse. Wafer attested that "[t]he enemy wounded were loudest by far in their outcries for help. I have found this to be invariably the case on subsequent occasions. This I am not prepared to explain unless it be that they had no confidence in our humanity & dreaded wilful neglect—but I can confidently and earnestly assert that I have never seen any distinction in their treatment."

Dr. Wafer was also troubled by the sad circumstance that prevented many of the Confederates from being brought in immediately from the deadly contested slope in front of Cemetery Ridge. There they lay hurt and unassisted because their comrades, the Southern pickets and sharpshooters, kept firing at the plainly visible Union stretcher-bearers. Therefore a day or more passed before these suffering Confederates could be collected.[46]

On July 10, John Foster, who was another volunteer member of the U.S. Christian Commission, was assigned to a division of the Second Corps hospital. While there he found almost every wounded man still in deplorable condition, especially the hundreds of Confederates whom he portrayed as dirty and almost all naked, and every one destitute of every basic human comfort. "[They] lay upon the ground," he exclaimed, "with pools of water all around them, often with channels the rains had made flowing under them in the hollow of the soil."

Foster blamed much of the problem on the Confederate surgeons, whom he said were "almost brutal in their treatment of the men left to their care." These Rebel doctors seemed to him neglectful and indifferent to the distressing condition of their own troops. In a barn on the premises which the Southern physicians had appropriated for their use, the wounded were packed so thickly on the ground floor that it was

> almost impossible for one to stir without communicating a shock to all. In the centre of the floor the surgeons planted a table for amputating purposes; and there in full view of hundreds of enfeebled wretches, the process of cutting, and carving, and butchering (for it was nothing else) went on day after day. The scene, as we saw it on more than one occasion, was horrible. It was torture for the faint, disheartened wounded, to lie, hour after hour, perfectly helpless, compulsory witnesses of the atrocities which these surgeons dignified by the name of "operations." During every minute of fifteen hours every day some sufferer was upon the table. Groans, shrieks, and curses constantly filled the air, the sound of the knife and crash of the saw blending continuously with the

din of agony. Legs and arms falling from the table to the floor beneath were raked out in armfuls, with every eye fixed on the spectacle, and carted away for burial.

Foster too conceded the oft-illustrated detail that "[g]enerally the spirit of our men was much better than that of the rebels; they submitted more willingly and bravely to necessary operations, and often, in fact, made light of sufferings from which the Southrons seemed to shrink in dismay."[47]

This same barn hospital (Schwartz's) situated within the Second and Third Corps' medical area was still full to capacity on July 9, when Major William Watson, a surgeon in the 105th Pennsylvania, saw 100 Rebels there "in a most distressing condition." He heard from old army surgeons that the wounds at Gettysburg were more serious and the amputations more numerous than in any previous battle. Watson himself had already performed more than 50 major surgical operations by July 7, once completing fourteen during one shift without leaving the table. He estimated a fearfully high mortality among the wounded, caused principally by gangrene, erysipelas, tetanus, and secondary hemorrhage. Dr. Watson expressed the sad intelligence that secondary operations were producing the high mortality rates, as most of these patients died very soon after.[48]

Although it may seem to appear that only the Confederates in the Second Corps hospital were in unusually bad condition and had received no aid, the truth is that both sides, including the National troops there, were suffering about equally. As a matter of record, a Yankee officer whose body was wounded three times waited in that place over six days to receive medical attention, excepting the minimal aid provided by his friends.[49]

An infantryman of the 15th New Jersey never forgot the horrors of what he had seen of the injured, maimed, and impoverished soldiers after Gettysburg. He retained in his mind until his death,

scenes at the hospitals [that] were often of the most shocking kind. The human body was wounded and torn in every conceivable manner. No description can portray the work of the surgeons at the amputating table. All the nights of the three days, they were busy with their dreadful work. Limbs were thrown in piles outside the hospital tents, and the sufferers were at first stretched in the open air, side by side. There were men with both legs gone; men shot through the lungs; men with bullets in their brain, still living; men with their torn bowels protruding. On the floor of a crowded barn sat a man in gray coat, swaying his body back and forth, with both eyes shot out, and his face all mangled. The tide of human misery around the little town of Gettysburg swelled high as never before, perhaps, in all our land. We saw the horrors of war, enough to make the heart ache and revolt at the inhumanity of man to man. Yet all these ghastly wounds were received from the hands of their own countrymen. The surgeons were very humane in their treatment, and seemed, in the discharge of their work, to know no difference between Union and Confederate soldiers.[50]

General Carl Schurz looked in on the Eleventh Corps hospital shortly after the battle and found the environment most depressing. He had a quite similar experience to the one Surgeon Daniel Brinton recalled just above. Schurz said:

The houses, the barns, the sheds, and the open barnyards, were crowded with moaning and wailing human beings, and still an unceasing procession of stretchers and ambulances was coming in. A heavy rain set in during the day—the usual rain after a battle—and large numbers had to remain unprotected in the open, there being no room left under roof. I saw the long rows of men lying under the eaves of the buildings, the water pouring down upon their bodies in streams. Most of the operating tables were placed in the open, where the light was best, some of them partially protected against the rain by tarpaulins or blankets stretched upon poles. There stood the surgeons, their sleeves rolled up to the elbows, their bare arms as well as their linen aprons smeared with blood...around them pools of blood and amputated arms or legs in heaps, sometimes more than man-high....Many of the wounded men suffered with silent fortitude, the fierce determination knitting their brows and the steady gaze of their bloodshot eyes....But there were, too, heartrending groans and the shrill cries of pain piercing the air....[51]

Can we ever again be surprised that a soldier once exclaimed: "It requires a man with a steel nerve and a case hardened heart to be a Army Surgeon"?[52]

To the men literally looking into the eyes of these surgeons from their places on the operating tables, the grave and unpleasant situation was a good deal worse for them personally. One wounded New York officer, Lieutenant Charles Fuller, indelibly remembered for years later how he felt before the operation which removed both a wounded leg and an arm that had been shot in the upper half. He pronounced that the surgeons, when they finally got around to him, after a long interval on the ground, first slit his uniform apart to get a better look at the wounds. They next applied some "adhesive straps" over the injuries, while holding a brief consultation on how to proceed with the surgery. As he waited, Fuller saw quite a few other patients laid down on the nearby table. There, after a few quick passages with a scalpel and saw, some rapid winding of bandages, the bloody job was complete. When his turn came Fuller was picked up and,

> placed upon the operating table. One of the doctors took a large napkin, or small towel, and, doing it up in tunnel shape poured a quantity of chloroform into it, and the tunnel-shaped napkin was immediately placed over my mouth and nose, and I was directed to take in good long breaths. This I did with a will, but it seemed to me an intermidable time before any anesthetic effect was produced. I suppose really it was a short time, but finally the effect came on and I well remember that my head seemed to swell out and increase to double its natural size. One of the last conscious impressions on my mind was produced by one of the surgeons sticking his fingers into the wound at my shoulder and saying that here was a fine opportunity for a re-section. [i.e., the surgical removal of part of an organ or bone, etc.]

When the lieutenant awoke from the effects of the chloroform, he turned his head and beheld a "large array of bandages at the shoulder, and that there was a very short apology for a leg on the same side." The operation had been performed at night by the light of two flickering candles, said Fuller, and the leg was cut off eight inches below the hip. As he was being removed from the table one of the doctors remarked: "Fuller, it won't do you any harm to drink all of the whiskey you can get hold of." Later, another surgeon entered the hospital tent where the lieutenant was lying and gave he and others there a good dose of morphine, which Fuller conceded, quieted them all down and made everyone feel quite happy. A week or so afterward the original saturated and caked bandages were removed and replaced for the first time. When they were lifted off, scores of maggots were discovered squirming about in the dead flesh of his wounds, whereas Fuller related, these insects were producing "an activity greater than I had ever observed. This caused the goose pimples to go up my back in a lively manner. I apprehended that these animals might penetrate my body and I would become a mass of wigglers...."

Fuller was soon relieved to hear from a volunteer surgeon, that a little diluted turpentine would quickly dispose of them, and that the lieutenant had more important worries at the moment than a few wormy creatures. Eventually the young officer was taken from the field hospital to a house in Gettysburg

Lt. Charles Fuller met a cruel fate at Gettysburg. (HSC)

where he remained for two weeks. From there it was on to his home in Sherburne, New York, where he lived for over 40 years.[53]

As was just outlined, some men were fortuitous enough to receive at least fundamental medical attention. Elsewhere, the wounded backed up so quickly that the conditions for those waiting were appalling at best. In this next, which is a description of a Third Corps hospital shortly after the battle, an officer of the 124th New York attempted to seek out the injured men of his regiment. The man was Major C.H. Weygant and he portrayed a nighttime scene producing some of the most somber and terrifying feelings imaginable, where nearly 3,000 wounded were helplessly lying in a large grove of trees behind the Union lines. In that grove the noises which filled the air were such that Weygant hoped he should never hear the like again. During the night he explored this unnatural place searching for his comrades, and later sketched this:

> The thick foliage caused dark shadows to fall upon these acres of mangled bleeding human forms. Away down through the trees flickering lights could be seen, the reflections of which fell with ghastly effect upon the corps of surgeons who, with coats off and sleeves rolled up, were gathered at, or moving rapidly to and fro about the amputating tables. After a moment's hesitation at the edge of the woods I resolved to attempt to pick my way through towards where I hoped to find the objects of my search, but as I moved on among those, for the most part, prostrate men, their groans and piteous appeals for help appalled me. Several in a state of delirium were shouting as if upon the battlefield, and others, believing I was a surgeon, besought me to stop just a moment and bind up the wounds from which their life-blood was ebbing. Presently a man I was about stepping over, sprang to his feet, shook in front of me a bloody bandage he had just torn from a dreadful, gaping wound in his breast, and uttered a

hideous, laughing shriek. This sent the hot blood spurting from his wound into my very face. Then he threw up his arms as if a bullet had just entered his heart, and fell heavily forward across a poor mangled fellow, whose piercing wails of anguish were heart-rending beyond description. I could endure no more, and wheeling about, hurried over the wounded and dying to the open field again, and returned to the regiment, glad that I had informed no one of my intended errand of mercy, for I was heartily ashamed of the weakness which had caused me to turn back.

Charles Weygant later met one of the men he had sought, who being seriously hurt was awaiting his turn on the tables at that hospital. The soldier claimed that he had endured eighteen hours of listening to "the horrid noise made by saws gnawing away human bones...."[54]

Certainly, there were feelings of pain and anger and frustration for the injured, but there were other hardships too. One such issue was the uncertainty and loneliness felt by men left alone in the early hours after the battle. Sergeant David E. Johnston of the 7th Virginia, who was shot during Pickett's and Pettigrew's attack on July 3 against Cemetery Ridge, exemplified these feelings:

About dark [of July 4] I was removed by ambulance to the shed of a farmer's barn, [Francis Bream's mill where the tenant in the farmhouse there was master miller William E. Myers] a mile or more away on [Marsh Creek], to the place where General [James L.] Kemper had been removed, the farmer placing him in his dwelling house....The shed in which I was placed was filled with the wounded and dying. Throughout that night and until a little before dawn, I spoke to no one, and no one to me, never closed my eyes in sleep; the surgeons close by being engaged in removing the limbs of those needed to be amputated, and all night long I heard nothing but the cries of the wounded and the groans of the dying, the agonies of General Kemper, who lay near by, being frequently heard. Everything in the barn was dark, but near dawn I discovered a flickering light advancing toward me; it was borne by John W. Grubb, of our regiment, who had been sent by our surgeons to look after me. Comrade Grubb was very kind to me, preparing for me a day or two later a bed and shelter in the orchard....[55]

Another Confederate, a Texan lieutenant named Barziza, was wounded in the fight for Little Round Top and was removed by U.S. troops to the Twelfth Corps hospital on the farm of George Bushman. He found that the Southern wounded were, "generally well treated, and were put side by side with the enemy's." And Barziza verbalized here almost poetically, that every building or shelter in the neighborhood, "was crammed; even hay-lofts were filled with the bleeding, mangled bodies. The surgeons, with sleeves rolled up and bloody to the elbows, were continually employed in amputating limbs. The red, human blood ran in streams from under the operating tables, and huge piles of arms and legs, withered and horrible to behold, were mute evidences of the fierceness of the strife."

Lieutenant Barziza ended his dreadful account by testifying bluntly and truthfully that,

[h]e who has never seen the rear of an army during and immediately after a battle, can form no idea of the scene, while the mere mention of a Field Hospital

to a soldier, brings up recollections of blood and brains, mangled limbs, protruding entrails, groans, shrieks and death. And when night comes upon them, and their wounds begin to grow chill, and pains shoot piercingly through them, then the deep and agonizing groans, the shrill death-shriek, the cries for water, opium, any thing, even death, make up the most horrible scene that can be conceived of. See that poor, bleeding boy turn his face to the surgeon and ask, "doctor, is my wound mortal." And oh! what shades of agony, despair and dread flit across his features, as he hears the reply, "I fear it is, sir!" There lies one mortally wounded, sleeping "unto death," under the influence of opium, which has been given in large quantities to let him die easy. Now, one goes off in a convulsive spasm, another with a shriek, which causes the hair even of a hardened soldier to stand on end....What a blessing is it that the gentle and tender-loved ones at home are spared the sight of the last moments of their torn and mangled soldiers![56]

No more honest depiction can be found than these few sentences, which bespeak so forcefully of the waste and misery and horror that is war.

A week or more into the wretched wake of that battle, a civilian doctor traveled to Gettysburg to assist the wounded as he had done before, ten months earlier at Sharpsburg, Maryland, following the Battle of Antietam. He was Bushrod W. James who lived in Philadelphia. Dr. James was assigned to a hospital near White Run, three miles south of Gettysburg which was very likely a Second or Third Corps facility. According to his estimates, in the general vicinity there were at least 7,000 wounded. James was employed as an "operator" while there, and recorded one aspect never before mentioned about this, the largest field hospital in the Gettysburg area. It was the revelation that a spring located near White Run creek became infected with pollutants from the hospital grounds after the stream overflowed during a heavy rain. This single spring was used for cleaning, drinking and cooking, and for more than a week everyone in the hospital camp became sick due to the infection in the water. Dr. James himself, gradually became very ill and much weakened from the effects of the hot, sultry weather, bad water, and hours on end at the surgical stations. He finally gave in and returned home where he suffered continuously for several weeks thereafter from the infliction caused by his exertions and environment. Thirty-two years later in 1895, Dr. James revisited the old hospital area where he had volunteered his services in 1863. There on a flat ridge overlooking White Run he examined the depressions still visible where the tent poles had been embedded. The hay and straw that had been used inside these tents had produced each year an enriched growth of hearty green grass showing plainly where the tent lines and avenues had stood. Nearby he could make out the worn channels dug into the ground under the operating tables so the blood and water could run out and away, and he could still recognize the mounds here and there which marked the holes where the amputated limbs had been buried. Standing there in the quiet and beautiful spot, with the clear sky above and birds singing in the trees, Dr. James recalled the terrible days he had spent at that site over thirty years before:

I live over again those weeks of sickening work, when the cut of the knife and the rasp of the saw seem to be grating upon my own overtaxed nerves, Oh, the horror! The misery! The terror of a battle!....I had read of all the battles and had pictured to myself the most horrible scenes that could be conjured by imagination, but no written nor expressed language could even picture the field of Gettysburg! Blood! Blood! and tattered flesh! shattered bones and mangled forms almost without the semblance of human beings! faces torn and bruised and lacerated until wife or mother could hardly have recognized one of them! groans and cries! screams and curses! moans and grinding teeth! And the horrible silence of torture beyond all expression! I have traveled through many countries and my memory is filled with vividly lovely, glorious and magnificent pictures, but sometimes these crimson-framed pictures of the battlefields of Antietam and Gettysburg return to me with such intense reality that all else for the time grows dim and almost fades away.[57]

"All else...grows dim and almost fades away."

Whenever one reads words such as those written by Bushrod James or others graphically similar there is always the acute inclination to believe or be aware that few people who today visit a battlefield park like Gettysburg can ever really understand what it was like to be in an actual battle, but more especially to be among the wounded of such brutal combat. If one thing is accomplished in this story of the aftermath of Gettysburg, it is the hope that we can dispel some of the pure nonsense and myth that has grown up surrounding the Civil War, and which is perpetuated even now by movies, novels, and battle reenactments around the country. The affairs of war are cruel, cold-blooded, and totally undignified, and no sane person should ever dream of purposefully being part of such barbarous acts against humanity. It is my wish that you who read these terrible descriptions, especially any presented in the first three chapters, would finally close the book feeling a great anger and distrust toward people who advocate war, as well as a deep hatred and fear of the thing itself.

In a stone farmhouse owned by the Weikert family south of Gettysburg on the west side of the Taneytown Road, surgeons of the Fifth Corps administered care to the wounded of their infantry divisions until forced to relocate the hospital to the vicinity of the Michael Fiscel farm. In the first-named house, a 15-year-old girl witnessed the unpleasant duties being attended to around her. Amputating benches had been placed near the sturdy house and the doctors were working diligently at them. This teenager, Matilda Pierce, had these vivid recollections:

I was looking out one of the windows facing the front yard. Near the basement door, and directly underneath the window I was at, stood one of these benches. I saw them lifting the poor men upon it, then the surgeons sawing and cutting off arms and legs, then again probing and picking bullets from the flesh....

I saw the surgeons hastily put a cattle horn over the mouths of the wounded ones, after they were placed upon the bench. At first I did not understand the meaning...[but] soon learned that that was their mode of administering chloroform, in order to produce unconsciousness. But the effect in some instances was not produced; for I saw the wounded throwing themselves wildly about, and shrieking with pain while the operation was going on.

To the south of the house, and just outside of the yard, I noticed a pile of limbs higher than the fence. It was a ghastly sight! Gaping upon these, too often the trophies of the amputating bench, I could have no other feeling, than the whole scene was one of cruel butchery.[58]

Meanwhile, several miles north of Weikert's house and inside the borough limits of Gettysburg, almost all of the public buildings, warehouses, churches, schools, and an array of private dwellings had been appropriated for the injured which had flooded in from the first day's battle arena. Fannie Buehler, a resident of the village, commented on sights and sounds within the Adams County courthouse which were "too horrible to describe. Limbs were amputated amid the cries and groans of suffering humanity...and often have I stopped my ears that I might not hear the groans of those poor unfortunate men, whom I could not relieve. Loads of arms and legs of these poor soldiers...were carted outside the town, and were either burned or buried. The Regimental Bands...[used to mute the distressing cries] came every afternoon and played patriotic airs in front of the hospital...."[59]

Teenager Tillie Pierce observed the "butchery" of the surgeons in a farmhouse east of Little Round Top. (MJPA)

Gates Fahnestock was among those who tried to alleviate the suffering of the desperately wounded men in the courthouse. He confessed that he almost fainted at seeing his first amputation there, but soon got used to the cruel but necessary surgery. His recollections were centered on the injured that had been congested into every available building, and also on the people of the town who "responded splendidly with anything they had—time, strength, material." Young Fahnestock's mother and their household cook and maid "were steadily cooking and sending over to the Court House, diagonally across the street...bread, cakes and delicacies."[60]

Many seriously hurt soldiers of both Lee's and Meade's armies unfortunately received very few delicacies during the long dreary days and weeks following the battle. One Rebel soldier in particular revealed just how bad the lack of food had gotten in some of the out-of-the-way Confederate hospitals. After being shot near Little Round Top on July 2, Private W.C. Ward of Alabama and a comrade were carried to a field hospital of Hood's Division at the John Plank farm southwest of Gettysburg. Deposited in an apple orchard, the two men had nothing to eat and no one to help them, so they patiently waited several days for assistance. Ward explained their predicament: "Great green flies in swarms of millions gathered in the camp, grown unnaturally large, fattened on human blood....Fever-smitten, pain-racked, there came to us another terror: we were to be devoured while living by maggots—creeping, doubling, crawling in among the nerves and devouring the soldier while yet alive."

Ward disclosed that his companion and friend, who was from Marion, Alabama, began to bleed one day from a damaged artery. A surgeon applied a tourniquet, but it repeatedly became dislodged by the movement of the soldier. During those times Ward would quickly place his thumb and finger around the artery to stop the bleeding. "For forty-eight hours," he underscored, "this struggle went on....The blood had accumulated in a pool from the point of his hip to his heel, and in that blood...the maggots were rioting in their gory feast and reveling in the poor fellow's wound. The noise they made as they doubled and twisted, crept and crawled, was that of hogs eating corn. Lying on his stomach, the soldier dipped away, by the aid of a spoon with which he fed himself, a half gallon of these terrible insects."[61]

Both Alabama infantrymen survived that singularly humiliating experience, but so many others like them did not. There were plainly just too many seriously injured men and not enough help, medical supplies, or food to go around in the first weeks succeeding the battle. Furthermore, even precious water was scarce for a time, especially for Confederates deposited in hospitals northwest, north, and northeast of Gettysburg. Many wells had been pumped dry by the contending armies with their thousands of thirsty men and animals, and the hospitals in these specified areas were not adjacent to any large bodies of fresh water such as Rock or Marsh Creek. Several examples by three Southern soldiers and one Federal will suffice to illustrate that problem. One, an artilleryman named Berkeley chronicled in his diary how he had to ride almost six miles northwest of town to find any potable water. And just northwest of Gettysburg again, an officer of the 23rd North Carolina had to station a guard with "fixed bayonet" to keep back a horde of men attempting to use a well which had already been pumped dry. He was afraid that their insistence and rough handling of the device would break the pump before the well could refill, stating: "The demand for drinking water was so much greater than the supply. Indeed the shortage of water near at hand seems to have added to the difficulties of the [military] situation for the Confederate leaders."[62]

Wounded Confederate Lieutenant John Dooley of the 1st Virginia who lay not far from two fairly large streams of water, Rock Creek and White Run, did not have it much better. He asserted: "I begin now to suffer from thirst, for the only water they bring us is from a neighboring run which is warm and muddy and has the additional properties belonging to human blood and dead bodies." Dooley was able to abstain from drinking for four days, then found some spring water, probably from the same source spoken of earlier by Dr. James, which, as we know later became polluted.[63]

A twice-shot Northern captain lying near the same White Run, recalled how on July 5 he became "seized with an awful thirst. Though the rain was pouring down my face and over my now totally unprotected body, I wanted water as I had never before wanted it...A stream of water was boiling, bubbling, and running within my hearing; my face and body were drenched; and yet it seemed as though I should die of thirst."[64]

✣ ✣ ✣

As we have come to recognize through the memories of many who were present in the summer of 1863, the landscape around Gettysburg for several weeks after the battle was not a very pleasant environment for anyone, and even more so for the 20,995 wounded of both armies who remained behind. The aid stations and field hospitals could be shocking places indeed—to visit, to work at, or especially if injured and left in one for treatment. When Vermonter Dr. Henry Janes, a U.S. volunteer surgeon, was placed by Director Letterman in total charge of every hospital at or near Gettysburg, he originally had over 100 separate sites to attend to. Several weeks into the month of July this number had dwindled to or had been consolidated into about 60 hospitals. On or about July 25, however, 16,125 wounded had already been transferred to other regularly established U.S. general hospitals in towns and cities along the east coast. Approximately 4,800 patients remained, these were banded together by August 1 into several active hospitals, namely the Lutheran Theological Seminary, the Union School on High Street and the railroad express office and warehouse in Gettysburg, and at Camp Letterman, a U.S. General Hospital on the York Turnpike, one mile east of town. The original 650 Union medical officers with Meade's army (13 of whom had been wounded and one killed) and the several hundred Confederate surgeons under General Lee, worked on their respective wounded until the Southern army retreated on July 4 and the Federal army began its pursuit around July 6. Of these 650 Yankee physicians, 106 were ordered to remain in Gettysburg by Dr. Letterman. These few doctors were reinforced by a contingent of Confederate medical men who remained behind under orders from Lee's medical director, as well as 50 extra surgeons requested by Dr. Henry Janes from the War Department, and 75 to 100 volunteer civilian medicos who arrived between July 4 and July 20.

Returning for a minute to the Confederate doctors who stayed to assist over 6,000 injured of their comrades, we know for certain that General McLaws' Division of Longstreet's Corps left at Gettysburg eight surgeons, two chaplains and 70 nurses and cooks, while still another such report indicates eight of these Southern doctors were later put to work in Camp Letterman. Other than these numbers, no source is available as to the total Rebel physician contingent in the Gettysburg hospitals, although one physician, Simon Baruch, remembered that 110 doctors and 15 chaplains were

Dr. Henry Janes was in charge of all military hospitals in the Gettysburg area. (HC)

moved from Gettysburg to prison at Ft. McHenry and other similar places. This figure is undoubtedly too steep, and may contain a number of attendants and nurses also. The sum for actual physicians is perhaps more like 20 to 30, although this is only a guess.[65]

The Confederate medical officers who were ordered or chosen to remain with those men unable to travel were as Baruch said ultimately sent to Fort McHenry Military Prison, Baltimore, Maryland, about August 10, when their services were no longer needed. A few espoused that their treatment in U.S. hands was often not very kindly. The majority were soon released on parole.

Dr. Janes did testify that in total he had used the services of about 250 "surgeons," all being under his command at one time or another in the weeks following the end of the great battle. As a sidelight, Janes had the use of only 46 ambulances and 32 wagons which had been assigned to him by Dr. Letterman to carry the wounded from the hospitals to the railroad depot for eventual transportation away from Gettysburg.[66] This sum turned out to be woefully inadequate.

Prior to the consolidations of hospitals and the establishment of Camp Letterman, the exact dispositions and locations of the main field hospitals of the various divisions and corps of both armies may be of interest. In the next section, this subject shall be examined.

◆ ◆ ◆

Union Field Hospitals

As promised, the following part will contain a catalogue list and description of the various field hospitals which grew up between July 1 and July 7 in and around Gettysburg. These "temporary" hospitals remained viable generally no later than August 15 with the few exceptions of those previously annotated. The larger field hospitals of the Union Army of the Potomac were segmented by corps and divisions. For additional or supplemental information on all of these hospitals, plus a compilation of many lesser known sites, please refer to *A Vast Sea of Misery: A History and Guide to the Union and Confederate Field Hospitals at Gettysburg*, which was published in 1988.

◆ ◆ ◆

Army of the Potomac

U.S. First Corps, General John F. Reynolds, containing the divisions of J.S. Wadsworth, J.C. Robinson, and T.A. Rowley.

The initial field hospitals of this corps were positioned as early as the morning of July 1st in the Lutheran Theological Seminary (which was primarily a large aid station) and inside the town limits, in churches, schools, warehouses, the railroad depot, express office, the courthouse, one hotel, and even a few private dwellings. A select few places used for these hospitals would include:

Lutheran Theological Seminary—All three brick buildings in use, plus tents were placed in the yards nearby; Edward McPherson farm buildings also connected with the 1st Division for a while, and other farms and houses in the locality. The seminary's main structure was converted into a more permanent hospital after the battle and some of its patients were Confederate officers including Generals Trimble and Kemper, although it was considered a Federal facility. One of the rooms served as a "clinic" where surgical operations were performed. Dr. A.J. Ward was surgeon-in-chief for a time there. The worst cases were kept in the basement until it was flooded, then 100 men were taken to the fourth floor, making a total of 173 wounded on July 6. In summation, about 500 injured soldiers had occupied the building, and it suffered $2,300 worth of damage during and after the battle.

Pennsylvania College—The president's house occupied by 10 to 20 men from the 2nd Division. Its main use however was as a Confederate hospital.

Adams County Courthouse—Soldiers of the 1st Division, for the most part, were in this 1859 structure. It contained about 250 patients, 77 of whom were amputation cases and 83 were shot in the body. All rooms, halls and the vestibule were utilized by the wounded. The courtroom was employed as the operating area; every bench had been pitched out of the windows to make room for patients.

Christ Lutheran Church—150 or more from the 2nd and 3rd Divisions were here. This is one of the most documented sites in Gettysburg. Wounded men were taken to the auditorium on the second floor as well as the main vestry. The amputating bench was located in an anteroom opening off the main hall. The church was closed about August 15, but 78 patients were still there on or about August 3, with many of the men using the pews as beds.

The Hanover, Hanover Junction, and Gettysburg Railroad Depot, and The Adams Express Office—These buildings were used by Cavalry Corps and 1st Division, First Corps, especially the 1st Brigade of that division. It was opened on June 30 by the cavalry corps, with Surgeon Abner Hard, 8th Illinois Cavalry in attendance. Surgeon Jacob Ebersole, 19th Indiana Infantry also spent some three days here with men of his brigade.

St. Francis Xavier Roman Catholic Church—The 3rd Division of the corps took over this church and the Presbyterian Church across the street; it contained about 200 wounded and as late as July 11 was under the charge of Dr. Philip Quinan, 150th Pennsylvania. This hospital, at one point, was described as in an utter state of confusion, with seriously wounded men lying about and being given little or no attention; no "intelligent" assistants or surgeons present, and even the food was insufficient. When the Confederates captured the town, Dr. Quinan; Dr. F.C. Reamer, 143rd P.V.; and W.G. Hunter, 149th P.V. were all made prisoners. The dead were removed to the basement where they were prepared for burial or shipment. Strangely, one operating table was situated in the cellar, and the doctors stayed in the two rooms adjacent to the altar. There was also another table in the entry, just at the large front double doors. Pew doors were removed and placed on top of pews for the wounded. Injured men also occupied the gallery (at least 14) on the south end of the church, as well as the area near the pulpit and altar. The hospital closed between August 7 and 15.

The United Presbyterian and Associated Reform Church—As noted above, was combined with St. Francis, Dr. James Fulton, 143rd Pennsylvania in charge for a time. The dead were buried in two trenches nearby, and operations appear to have been performed in the outside yard of the church.

The Methodist Episcopal Church—Very small number of injured here; some Sisters of Charity in attendance; this hospital closed about the middle of August.

The Washington House Hotel—Used by at least 50 or 60 New York troops of the 1st and 2nd Divisions for about two months. Drs. Theodore Dimon, a New York relief agent and Henry L. Farley of the 14th Brooklyn were in attendance for a time. It was struck by artillery fire on July 1. There was an "embalming house" adjacent. All three floors were in use including the third floor attic. Dr. Dimon claimed that when he arrived with his contingent of nurses, attendants and cooks, the hospital was in a disorderly and filthy condition.

The Union (Public) School, and another private school nearby were employed by a few Eleventh and First Corps men and some Confederates who occupied the top floor. This building was the main education facility for the 400 students of the borough of Gettysburg. It was in use as a hospital from July 1 to September 1, with about 60 patients present, generally from Meade's Cavalry Corps, and was headed by Surgeon Theodore T. Tate, 3rd Pennsylvania Cavalry, and then by Dr. W.H. Rulison, 9th New York Cavalry.

McConaughy's Hall—A store and warehouse on Carlisle Street. Some 1st Brigade, 1st Division men here, possibly occupied until September.

The Robert Sheads and Charles Buehler Warehouse—North end of village near the railroad—unknown as to who, exactly, employed it or who was in attendance, but housed "many wounded," including at least some from the 1st Brigade, 1st Division (definitely the 7th Wisconsin). The second floor was kept separate for operations, the limbs were pitched out of the windows.

The Robert McCurdy and Jeremiah Diehl Warehouse—Also near the railroad. The damage claims submitted for this place document it was used by Confederates who were "in complete possession."

The Alexander Spangler Warehouse—Some men from the 1st Brigade, 1st Division present, it was also near the railroad, on the north end of town. This warehouse, like the two above probably housed some Confederates as well, their units unknown, but likely General Early's Division. There were at least two men here from the 24th Michigan of the 1st Brigade, 1st Division.

Private Dwellings:

The numbers of wounded estimated to have been placed in *private houses* in Gettysburg are thought to be between 400 and 450. Many soldiers hurt on July 1 had simply been unable to continue due to their injuries to the division hospitals, or had been taken in for aid purposefully by generous and concerned citizens or to keep them from capture. For a presentation of many of these private structures and their owners and histories, again see *A Vast Sea of Misery*, pages 32-56. All private houses were ordered closed and evacuated by the 14th of July.

With the end of the first day's battle and the retreat of the U.S. First and Eleventh Corps, and the follow-up Confederate occupation of Gettysburg, a re-establishment of all First Corps hospitals was necessary.

Often, wounded Confederates found themselves helpless, and "in the hands of the enemy," as suggested by this 1889 painting by Thomas Hovenden (1840-1895). The scene is a Pennsylvania farmhouse near Gettysburg. (GNMP)

John F. Chase, 5th Maine Artillery, was wounded 48 times by an exploding U.S. caseshot and was cared for at Isaac Lightner's farm. (GAC)

Invariably, with the chaos and disorder inevitable in such a retrograde move, some hospitals were hurriedly reinstated without much thought or planning along the roads leading into Gettysburg from the south and southeast. Ultimately, the main hospitals of this corps took up new stations along the Baltimore Turnpike and behind Cemetery Hill and east of Cemetery Ridge. These permanent field hospitals covered a fairly large section of Mount Joy Township. The 1st Division and medical headquarters of the corps were in and near Mark's German Reformed Church, or the "White Church," and the Barbara and Isaac Lightner farm. All total they administered to 1,229 wounded. "Mark's Church" was named after Nicholas Mark who donated the land for the church. Mark was an early settler who built a brick house and sawmill near White Run in 1780. This farm was owned by Daniel and Lydia Sheaffer in 1863 about which more will be forthcoming in the "Third Corps" section. Surgeon George W. New, 7th Indiana, 1st Division, testified that his field hospital was at the "White Church" and the Lightner house and barn plus "others convenient." He added that on July 2 several hundred wounded Rebels were placed near the church "in a lawn and grove."[67]

The Lightner farm was in use from July 2 to 20. Some of the artillerymen of the First Corps Artillery Brigade were taken here, and it may have been also adopted by the Artillery Reserve. Both house and barn were filled with men and a bakery was set up on the premises. Lightner claims that a large number of hospital tents were erected on his property.

A U.S. Christian Commission map (*quod vide*) locates a Confederate hospital camp fairly near this church and just west across White Run on the farm of Aaron Sheely, which was taken over by General Marsena Patrick, Provost Marshal of the Army of the Potomac as his headquarters. It may or may not have been the same camp. A New York woman volunteer, Elmina K. Spencer, assisted as a nurse at the church hospital.

The 2nd Division occupied the Ellen and Peter Conover farm; 616 wounded were reported here including a few Confederates. It appears Stannard's and Paul's Brigades utilized these grounds.

The 3rd Division took possession of the Jonathan or "Jesse" Young farm where 1,279 wounded were cared for. The Young and Lightner farms were situated on the east side of the pike, while Conover's place sat on the west side.

Eliza W. Farnham and three other women drove in a field-ambulance through the First Corps area on July 7. On the way out she remarked that the "earth in the roads and fields is ploughed to a mire by the army wheels and horses...[and] straggling wounded line the roads, and rest against the fences....The putrid remains of slaughtered bullocks, the cast-off clothing of the dead and wounded, lie scattered around."

Shortly afterward, Farnham and her companions...

reached the place we were bound to, there appeared before us avenues of white tents under the green boughs, and many men moving about. But good God! what those quiet looking tents contained! What spectacles awaited us on the slopes of the rolling hills around us! It is absolutely inconceivable, unless you see it. There are miles of tents and acres of men lying on the open earth beneath the trees. I never could have imagined anything to compare with it. Dead and dying, and wounded, in every condition you can conceive after two days in such a rain of missiles. Old veterans who have seen all our battles, say that there never has been such firing anywhere for more than half an hour or so, as there was here for the greater part of nine hours. No wonder that men who were rushing upon and through and upon it, should be torn to pieces in every way.[68]

The division hospitals of the First Corps cared for 2,379 wounded, 260 of which were Confederates. Complete losses for the corps amounted to 3,987 out of somewhat less than 9,000 engaged; the wounded numbered 36 percent of the corps' total complement.

The medical director of the First Corps was Surgeon Theodore J. Heard, U.S. Volunteers. The medical officer in charge of all hospitals was Surgeon A.J. Ward, 2nd Wisconsin Infantry.[69]

U.S. Second Corps, General Winfield S. Hancock, containing the divisions of J.C. Caldwell, J. Gibbon, and A. Hays.

All aid stations and field hospitals of this corps were originally located in and around several small farms, a school and "groves" along or near the Taneytown Road, immediately south of Gettysburg. The 1st Division was first settled in "an opening of the woods, along the crossroad from the Taneytown Road to the Baltimore Pike" (now called Granite Schoolhouse Road), with headquarters for the corps at the Granite Schoolhouse itself. Another source specified that a large number of wounded of the Second Corps were placed about a quarter to a half mile north of Sarah Patterson's farm, and in a little dell among some large boulders where a small stream ran between the Taneytown Road and Baltimore Pike. One of the men who died in this latter site was brigade commander, Colonel Edward Cross.[70]

The 2nd Division hospital was established in the stone barn and within the confines of an orchard on Sarah Patterson's farm on the east side of the Taneytown Road. The 3rd Division hospital camp was pitched near another barn on the same road, possibly one owned by William and Lydia Patterson. The 1st Division hospital was "shelled out" of its position by overshot artillery early in the battle and forced to shift to a spot near William McAllister's sawmill on Rock Creek along and east of the Baltimore Pike. A surgeon stationed at the 1st Division hospital, Dr. W.W. Potter, affirmed that the new location was "covered by a hill near a stream of water..." which describes the mill area perfectly.[71]

When these hospitals were permanently relocated due to Confederate cannon fire on July 2, they were transferred to a spot about two miles southeastward on to the west bank of a sharp bend in Rock Creek east of the Anna and George Bushman farmbuildings.

Ambulance officer Thomas Livermore who was ordered to select the above position, attested that this site was, "a mile and a half down the stream from the crossing of the Baltimore Road...the left bank was a hillside and the right bank was level and low...." He claimed the terrain was quite good, and defended it later when it was flooded, noting that the men lying so near the stream should not have been allowed by their attendants and nurses to have been there.[72]

A U.S. Sanitary Commission source however, identified the new camp as "situated on the banks of Rock Creek, in tents, about eighty rods [1,320 feet] north of the house indicated on the map [q.v.-drawn up by the Commission in early July] as that of Isaac Schriver."[73] This farm name is obviously incorrect. In 1863 the house of Isaac T. Shriver was owned by Lewis A. Bushman, and the most reliably accepted ground of the Second Corps hospital's first position along Rock Creek was at least three-quarters of a mile (about 3,900 feet) *northeast* of the L.A. Bushman buildings.

The new Second Corps hospital which had been picked by Livermore and sat in a large grove of trees along the creek, later proved to be very detrimental to the wounded, for it was placed on very low ground and soon became flooded, then remained muddy after severe rains fell between July 4 and 6. The 1st and 2nd Divisions occupied the north side of the creek, and the 3rd Division was deployed on the south bank, which put many injured men in danger of drowning. Several reports of deaths due to the high water have come from various sources, which leads one to believe that several soldiers were indeed drowned in the unexpected flood of rising water which overflowed the banks of both White Run and Rock Creek, although this was denied by Dr. Dwinell, the surgeon in charge.

One eyewitness, Dr. Theodore Dimon, characterized his viewpoint on July 15, saying that the 1st and 2nd Divisions were up on a steep hill covered with woods, while the 3rd Division crowned a second open hill farther south. His description could actually have been the last move of the corps which will be plotted next.[74]

After the flooding and due to so much heavy timber surrounding the hospital which kept the air from circulating and the ground from drying out, those in authority decided to relocate the hospitals of the Second Corps once again. This final move took place on or about July 22 when the hospital equipment and patients were transported across the creek to "a large clear field of second growth clover." A nurse wrote that it was on a "beautiful ridge, open to sun and air, [and] forms a hollow square....It is a lovely spot. A bright stream flows close to the encampment, and the water is good."[75]

This last move near Rock Creek to fresh and healthier tracts of land was to the 300+ acre farm of Jacob Schwartz, whose barn had been pointed out as containing at least 100 Confederate patients.

Now to sum up the four positions of this very large and important hospital. The first locations were behind the Union battle lines on farms along the Taneytown Road and out toward the Baltimore Pike at Rock Creek. The second site was south of the pike on the west bank of Rock Creek in a curve of the creek near its junction with White Run. The third position was southeast across Rock Creek on a steep hill covered with woods and encircled by the creek, with the 3rd Division on an open hill some distance farther south. The fourth and final camp was on an open, grassy slope in a clover field, the three divisions united on the three sides of this slope, with the Confederates moved in and adjacent to this same area. The final change was perpetuated due to the third position being too small to accommodate all of the tents; plus all of the divisions were so spread out it made supply difficult; and trees obstructed the circulation of pure air, and did not allow the ground to dry out after rain.

The huge Second Corps hospital remained in operation until August 8, on which day the last man was sent to Camp Letterman. There were 3,260

Supply tents and quarters for the staff of the Second Corps hospital. Surgeon Dwinell is in the dark suit, center, leaning against a tree. (GNMP)

registered wounded in the three divisions; of these, 952 were Confederates. In total, 437 died there including 192 Southerners. There were so many deaths that at least four burial yards were cordoned off. The number of army doctors present was approximately seventeen on and off during the four weeks and at all four sites from July 2 to August 8, plus eight or nine more "contract surgeons," and several Confederate doctors, with approximately 30 volunteer civilian physicians in and out at various times. According to Dr. Justin Dwinell who ran the hospital, members of this last category were not reliable, except perhaps for a half dozen. He portrayed most of these men as the type who came to "cut off limbs," and Dwinell could not even entice them to dress a simple wound or the "stump" of an amputation.[76]

The medical director of the Second Corps was Surgeon A.N. Dougherty, U.S. Volunteers, with Surgeon Justin Dwinell, 106th Pennsylvania Infantry in charge of the hospitals themselves.

U.S. Third Corps, General Daniel E. Sickles, containing the divisions of D.B. Birney and A.A. Humphreys.

This corps was in action periodically from noon on July 2 to about seven o'clock p.m., and the majority of its losses occurred during a three to four hour span of that day.

Very little is known about the earliest positions of the Third Corps field hospitals. As army historian Louis Duncan commented, the writers of that era, in placing aid stations or field hospitals, "had an exasperating, indefinite manner of mentioning 'a house near the road,' or 'a grove beside a small stream.'"[77]

The general consensus is that the opening combat casualties of this corps were taken to houses and barns along the Taneytown Road, and as usual to groves of trees or unnamed farms or wooded areas along brooks or small streams between that road and the Baltimore Turnpike. The case of Major General Daniel Sickles is a perfect example of the unsubstantiated and undocumented locations for hospitals as found in both armies. Current and known research files describe at least a dozen or more distinct spots where Sickles, who was the *commander* of that corps, was removed in order to have his severely crushed leg amputated after it had been struck by a cannonball about 5:30 p.m. on July 2. We know for sure that he was eventually taken to Lydia and Daniel Sheaffer's brick farmhouse a few hundred yards south of White Run on the

General Daniel E. Sickles. An amputated leg gave him immortal fame. (GNMP)

west side of the Baltimore Turnpike. To indicate the confusion of many writers when it came to placing hospitals, here are a few samples of the types of commentaries left us as to where Sickles' leg was surgically removed. These could also have been places where other Third Corps wounded were brought for aid during the afternoon fighting of July 2:

"[Daniel Sheaffer's]...brick house still stands in its heavy age, and it was in it that General Sickles' leg was amputated on the evening of July 2, 1863" (J. Howard Wert, Sheaffer's then neighbor, 1907).

"[I] saw the noble chieftain [Daniel Sickles] borne with shattered leg to the somber brick house on the Baltimore pike, at that time occupied by Daniel Sheaffer..." (J. Howard Wert, 1886).

"...they took him over there to Rock Creek, where the corps hospital was, and there the leg was amputated by Surgeon [Thomas] Sim. I administered the chloroform" (Joseph H. Hopkins, Chaplain, 71st New York Infantry, July 1863).

"In a moment I was removed from the ground [where I was wounded] to the field hospital. On the Baltimore Pike that night, in the gloaming, Dr. [J.T.] Calhoun cut off the useless limb" (General Daniel E. Sickles, August 1882).

"A twelve pounder solid shot...shattered his right leg....[H]e was removed a short distance to the rear to a sheltered ravine and amputation was performed low down in the thigh by Surgeon Thomas Sim, U.S. Vols., Medical Director of the 3rd Army Corps" (Surgeon George T. Otis, Surgeon General and Curator, Army Medical Museum, Washington, D.C., 1870).

(Left) Lydia and Daniel Sheaffer's house where Sickles spent the night of July 2, 1863. (GAC)

(Center) The Trostle barn overshadows the rock where Gen. Sickles was carried after being struck by a 12-pounder solid shot. (GAC)

(Bottom) The crushed leg bones of Daniel Sickles. (OHA)

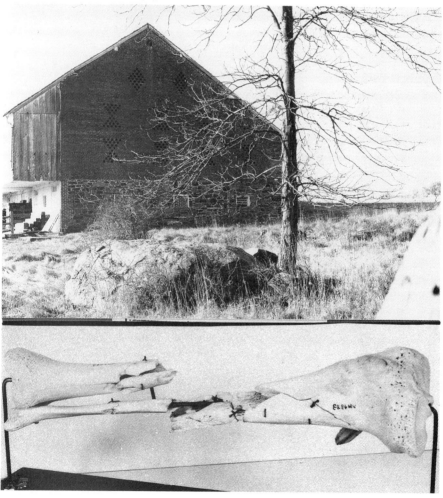

"He was struck just below the knee by a shell, and his leg so badly shattered that it hung merely by a shred. He was carried to a wheat field in the rear, where amputation was performed under the influence of chloroform..." (Thomas Cook, Correspondent, New York *Herald*, July 7, 1863).

"General Sickles was carried about a quarter of a mile to the rear, where his leg was amputated" (E.L. Townsend, former field officer, Third Corps, Army of the Potomac, August 1903).

"[East-southeast of the George Bushman farm buildings was the hospital of the Second Corps]...Leaving this, we cross the creek eastwardly, climb a high hill, and find the hospital of the Third Corps, in a delightfully airy and shady situation....It was here that General Sickles' leg was amputated..." (Nathaniel Davidson, Correspondent, New York *Herald*, July 24, 1863).

"It seemed to me a long while before a halt was made [of the ambulance containing General Sickles]....It was fast growing dark, and the scene and actors need not be recalled. [In a Third Corps hospital, "behind Round Top"] an improvised operating table, candles in bayonets, lanterns, sponges, the odor of medicines, of chloroform, a few idlers who belonged elsewhere—all are vaguely assembled in uncertain memory certain only of the distant sounds of the continuing battle" (Henry E. Tremain, staff officer, Third Corps, 1905).

General Oliver O. Howard's brother, Rowland B. Howard, who was a volunteer nurse with the Christian Commission had spent two nights in the Sheaffer house during the battle. On a return tour of the field in May 1887 he went back to the house to reminisce. *Later*, and *not at* Sheaffer's house, Howard said he visited, "the spot where I saw Gen. Sickles immediately after amputation" (Rowland B. Howard, Boston, MA, June, 1887).

"[We] took him to [an] old Penna. Bank or stone Barn and Dr. [M.J.] As[c]h I think and others amputated his leg" (W.H. Bullard, Musician, Co. C, 70th New York Infantry, 1897).

"An ambulance was sent to bring the General to a less exposed position. He suffered much pain during the ride. Upon being informed that the mutilated portion of his leg must be amputated, he replied, 'Do with me as you please.' Chloroform was administered, and the operation successfully performed....

"It was then thought best to have him carried to the rear to some house, that he might rest quietly....He was taken to the house of Mr. Shaffer on the Baltimore road" (Unnamed Correspondent, New York *Times*, July 18, 1863).

"While passing to the [Third Corps] hospital with [a wounded] soldier, we passed the table where General Sickles was having his leg amputated" (Stephen P. Chase, Private, 86th New York Infantry, undated memoir).

"[Our] farm was occupied by a portion of the Army of the Potomac, and on the second day of July 1863 Maj. Gen. Sickles was carried to the house in consequence of a wound which resulted in the amputation of a leg, he remained over night..." (Lydia and Daniel Sheaffer, war damage claims petition, January 11, 1868).

"About two miles below town on the Baltimore pike we came to the stone house of the [toll] gate-keeper, Henry Hoke. To this house Gen [Samuel K.] Zook was brought, wounded through the breast....Just below this house, at Mr. Bushman's Gen. Sickles had his leg amputated" (Attorney John B. Linn, diary entry for Thursday, July 9, 1863).

(The "Bushman" house mentioned above was possibly the "J. Bushman" house which was noted on an 1858 Adams County map, one-third of a mile southeast of the Hoke place on the north side of the pike.)

"Mrs. Christopher Young, whose farm was on Taneytown Road near the Round Tops, was a volunteer nurse during the...Battle of Gettysburg....Union officers forced [the family] to move out of the farmhouse during the battle....It was here...that the general's leg [D.E. Sickles] was amputated. Her mother made tea and toast for him after the operation. The farm home of the Youngs was known as Granite Dale" (Gettysburg *Times*, December 17, 1952).

(The Christopher B. Young farm, was possibly owned by Sarah Patterson in 1863. This place, which is today still covered by many granite boulders, was used as a hospital by the Second Corps on July 2. The connection here with the general is both very interesting and significant and should be researched in greater detail in the future. It does seem more likely that Sickles' leg was amputated somewhere in this particular locality where several Second and Third Corps hospitals were flourishing.)

"[On July 3] the family continued to travel [along the Baltimore Pike] but stopp[ed] at a farm house about two miles farther on. The farmer [Henry Beitler] and his family had departed and the house was vacant. [We] took possession and stayed there until Sunday, July 5. A barnyard was used as a hospital and the wounded soldiers who required surgical attention were operated upon in the barnyard....General Sickles had his leg, shattered by a shell, taken off at that emergency hospital" (George D. Thorn, son of Evergreen Cemetery caretakers, Elizabeth and Peter Thorn, Gettysburg *Compiler*, July 9, 1932).

(Henry Beitler's old farm sits between one-half and three-quarters of a mile south of Daniel Sheaffer's house, at the junction of the Low Dutch Road and the Baltimore Turnpike.)

There are several other references to Sickles' amputation site which due to space limitations will not be printed here, such as "in an ambulance," "behind a rock" and "then and there." One source revealed that the operation was completed in the Abraham Trostle house which was only a few dozen yards behind where the general was wounded and directly on the battlefield.

The previous diversion is but an example of the mystifying circumstances regarding hospital locations. Even so important a personage as a corps commander can be easily lost in the shuffle, as to where he was at any given time, in the chronicle and chaos of the battle story.

When artillery rounds began to fall among the scattered aid stations and field hospitals of the Third Corps, they forced a removal "further to the rear." Surgeon-in-charge of the 1st Division Jonas W. Lyman, remembered that many of the houses along the Taneytown Road had already been absorbed by the Second and Eleventh Corps as he searched for a possible site for his own hospital at 2 p.m. on July 2. He finally selected an "old barn by the roadside." This rough building was abandoned between 3 and 5 p.m. and Lyman chose another shelter at "a large stone barn." Neither of these farms have been positively identified.

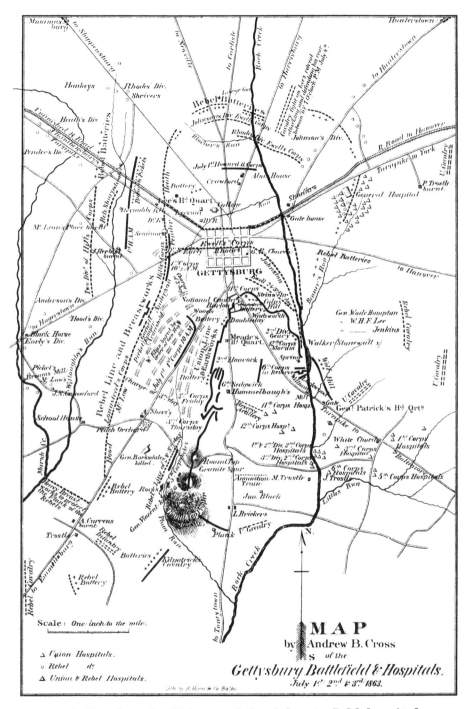

A map indicating the Union and Confederate field hospitals near Gettysburg. (HCAC)

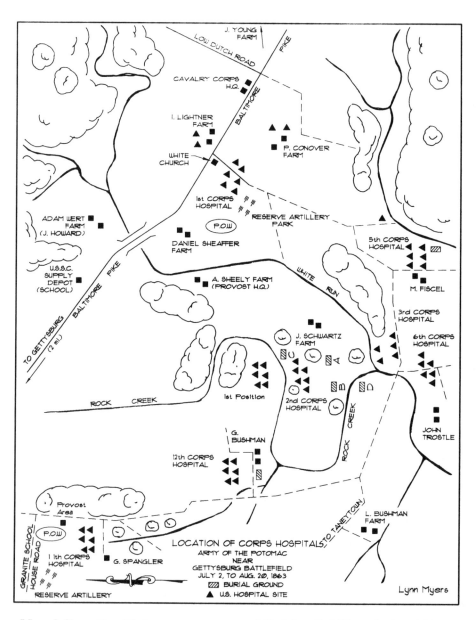

Map delineating Union army corps and division field hospitals. (GNMP)

Again, early on the third of July an order came to "pull up stakes" at his newer hospital. This time it was transferred, "across Rock Creek to an excellent site on a slope, with a fine stream of running water at hand."[78]

J. Howard Wert who in 1863 lived within the boundaries of several of these Union corps hospitals, earmarked the Third as running "through thick forests and along the bluffs of Rock Creek, White Run, and Two Taverns Run [Little's Run], it occupied not only the large farm of Michael Fiscel, but lapped over on several contiguous properties."[79]

As we have already shown, New York reporter Davidson fixed the Third Corps' permanent field hospital across Rock Creek "eastwardly" from the Second Corps' camp, on an airy, shady, high hill. He depicted it containing clean tents and pure air, "compared with the [fetid] atmosphere of town hospitals."[80]

The official U.S. government hospital marker erected near the area is more specific. It reads: "The Division Field Hospitals of the Third Corps were located July 2 in houses and barns along the Taneytown Road from the [Granite] Schoolhouse Road to the Mill Road [Blacksmith Shop Road]. During the night they were removed to the south side of White Run three hundred yards from its junction with Rock Creek."[81]

Mr. J.H. Douglas, the associate secretary of the U.S. Sanitary Commission lodges this hospital "on high ground south of [Jacob] Schwartz's house about one hundred rods [about 1,650 feet] above the junction of White's Creek with Rock Creek, on Schwietzel's farm."[82] "Schwietzel's farm" has unfortunately not been identified, unless it was confused by Douglas with Michael Fiscel's name in the conversational accents of the period. Owned by Matilda and Michael Fiscel in 1863, this particular parcel of ground just described contained some of the Third Corps' wounded, and many from the Fifth Corps.

Dr. Theodore Dimon documents the chief Third Corps hospital on what is today Goulden Road which runs west from White Church Road, then becomes Sachs Road at Rock Creek, and ends at the Taneytown Road. He asserted: "On the left of this road [Goulden] as you face east at this point [at the bridge on Rock Creek] is the Hospital of the 3d Army Corps, and on the right, the Hospital of the 6th Corps. The three Divisions [only two] of the 3d Corps have separate encampments in the same field, on a dry, airy hill, well policed, and the tents a proper distance from each other....I visited all parts of the extensive hospitals of this Corps, finding everywhere evidences of care and attention to the wounded."[83]

Mary A. Brady was a nurse attached to both the 1st and 2nd Divisions of the Third in late July. She established her work site west of the "White House Chapel" (as she called "White Church") on the "border of a wood." Brady maintained that "in all directions the fields are dotted with the graves of soldiers..." while at the hospital itself the surgeons had all things functioning in good order, with the ward doctors and even chief medical officers "dressing wound after wound, without ceasing."

She was generally complimentary of the care given to all of the men in the corps, but regarded the lack of straw to be one of the worst features in all of the field hospitals near Gettysburg.

Her tent sat adjacent to "a long row of tents, occupied exclusively by amputated cases...." Nearby were the rippling waters of a stream which had flooded soon after the battle, and as others have already admitted, she embraced the belief that "several rebels, wounded, [and] unable to help themselves, were drowned...."

Brady and her companions from Philadelphia had brought along a stove which was used daily to prepare food for her patients, including "custards, etc., green tea by the bucket full, chocolate, milk toast, arrowroot, rice pudding, beef-teas, and other delicacies. While completing their normal rounds the nurses had to "stand out in the wet, [for it rained very often throughout July] wearing gum boots and hoods, as the shelter tents are only a few feet high in the middle or apex, sloping down to the damp ground at the sides, and scarcely the length of a man."

Several well-known personages passed through this hospital and were catalogued by Mary Brady and others. They included Governor Andrew G. Curtin of Pennsylvania, the well-known philanthropist Dorothea L. Dix, and the eminent Philadelphia photographer Frederick Gutekunst and his assistant Mr. J. Marshall.[84]

By one estimate, Sickles' corps went equipped into action with 12,598 officers and men present for duty, however, other sources place the figure below 10,000. Two days later the rolls reveal 5,494 still present. Total losses of all killed, wounded and missing were 4,211. The 1st Division had 271 killed and 1,384 wounded; the 2nd, 314 killed and 1,562 wounded. This latter division, commanded by General A.A. Humphrey, had the heaviest loss of any division engaged in the battle. These field hospitals cared for more than 2,550 wounded, 259 of these being Rebels. The hospital closed August 8, 1863. The medical director was Surgeon Thomas Sim, U.S. Volunteers, while the medical officer in charge of corps hospitals was Surgeon Thaddeus Hildreth, 3rd Maine Infantry.[85]

U.S. Fifth Corps, General George Sykes, containing the divisions of J. Barnes, R.B. Ayres and S.W. Crawford.

General George Sykes' Fifth Corps is similar to the Third in that it was in action very heavily on the afternoon of July 2. Almost two-thirds of their casualties were inflicted on this day alone. The primary aid station was positioned behind the Round Tops at the 102-acre Jacob Weikert farm, complete with a complement of doctors and eventually 750 patients. The farm, which the owner claimed was also used by the Second and Third Corps, was the province of the 2nd Division and a group of disabled Confederates from General McLaws' Division. A second farm probably in use by the corps was that of Sarah and Michael Frey, and no doubt there are one or more of still unknown whereabouts. The 1st Division was posted in a field to the rear of Big Round Top, and a little more than half a mile from its base. Surgeon Joseph Thomas declared that 250 or 300 men were collected and brought to that field and "placed in long rows, with no reference to the nature or gravity of their injuries, nor condition of rank."[86]

This was presumably the field south of the Weikert farmhouse and on the west side of the Taneytown Road. Assistant Surgeon John S. Billings left a good account of his work at the Weikert place. He said he was ordered to a large stone house and barn near the base of Round Top, and there established a field hospital. Billings noted with satisfaction that,

[a] good fire was blazing in the kitchen stove, and a large quantity of dough was mixed up, the bakepans were greased, everything was ready for me. I immediately set my attendants at work baking bread and heating large boilers of water. In five minutes I was joined by the other medical officers detailed for the hospital. The ambulance train reported fifteen minutes later, and with it were three Autenreith [medicine] wagons, and by the time operating tables were set up and materials for dressing arranged, the wounded began to pour in.

I performed a large number of operations, received and fed 750 wounded, and worked all that night. An agent of the Sanitary Commission visited me in the evening and furnished me with a barrel of crackers and some lemons. Of stimulants, chloroform, morphine and dressings, the Autenreith wagons furnished an ample supply.

On July 3d at 7 a.m., I was ordered...to remove the hospital one mile to the rear....The new site was a large grove of trees, entirely free from underbrush, on the bank of a little creek, about a mile from the Baltimore Pike.[87]

Billings counted eleven surgeons who stayed with him, of which eight became ill, including himself. He serviced 800 patients on July 4, some in 17 hospital tents encircling the farmhouse, which contained 75 of the worst cases, with about 100 more under "tent flies," and the remainder placed in shelter tents.

J. Howard Wert who lived nearby, testified that the new position of the Fifth Corps occupied ground "somewhat to the south and east of the Third Corps hospital....This hospital bordering at one point on the Two Taverns Run, [Little's Run] extended on either side of a public road, [now the White Church Road] through long stretches of forest...."[88]

The government hospital marker on site there indicates that the 1st Division was south of White Run on the Michael and Matilda Fiscel farm. The 2nd Division it says was 100 rods [1,650 feet] south of White Run near the house of Jane Clapsaddle. Her home sat near and east of Lousy Run, a small stream that entered Little's Run from the northeast. The 3rd Division was some distance away, about one-half mile west of Two Taverns, Pennsylvania, at the Ann and Jesse Worley farm, on a road now called the Barlow-Two Taverns Road.[89]

Louis Duncan is in disagreement on the actual site of the 1st Division. He puts it on a "Mr. Little's" farm, just north of the house and a little south of White Run. There were two "Little's" in the area in 1859, but they appear to be farther to the northeast, near Two Taverns. Since Duncan obtained this information from Sanitary Commission agent, J.H. Douglas, it could be again a possibility that Little's farm was confused with Fiscel's.[90]

Theodore Dimon visited the Union hospitals after the middle of July and narrated in a subsequent report that, "[f]ollowing the cross road mentioned [Goulden-Sachs Road] to the east for half a mile, and turning to the right [onto White Church Road] through the woods, the Hospitals of the 5th Corps are found on the banks of Little's Run." Correspondent Nathaniel Davidson designates these hospitals simply "at some distance east of the Third, in the same piece of woods...." And the aforementioned Sanitary Commission agent Douglas, totalled 1,400 wounded Federals at these three division camps, including 75 Rebels.[91]

Another surgeon present at the Fifth Corps hospital and in the neighborhood of the Fiscel farm was Dr. A.M. Clark of White Plains, New York, the acting surgeon-in-chief of the 1st Division. He explained that during the battle his hospital had to be removed to "a large grove between the Baltimore and Taneytown Roads, about one-and-one-half mile in rear of the field, (and near the house of a Mr. Fussell?) [Fiscel]." Clark, unlike Douglas added up the patients there at 1,780 including a "considerable number of Confederates."[92]

Fiscel's large barn and small house were given up totally for the use of the injured, mostly of Colonel Vincent's 3rd Brigade. There were 65 of the worst cases of the whole corps in that barn. Several physicians were in attendance around the buildings such as Drs. A.M. Clark, Cyrus Bacon, William H. True, and several others. At least 186 burials were counted in the graveyard of this hospital which was in a lonely spot, east of the barn "at the edge of a woods," and overlooking a stream.

The three division hospitals folded their tents on August 2 having sheltered in the realm of 1,600 patients; i.e. 1st Division, 594; 2nd, 802; and 3rd, 181, not counting the 75 Southerners. The medical director of the corps was Surgeon John J. Milhau, U.S. Army, and the medical officer in charge of the corps hospitals was Surgeon A.M. Clark, U.S. Volunteers.

One of the U.S. Government's hospital markers and a view of a portion of the Fiscel property. Today the farm is a golf course. (SCH)

Fiscel's sturdy barn held the worst medical cases of the Fifth Corps. However, it is now only a memory. (GAC)

U.S. Sixth Corps, General John Sedgwick, containing the divisions of H.G. Wright, A.P. Howe, and J. Newton.

The loss of this corps at Gettysburg was relatively small; only thirty men were killed and approximately 185 wounded. The troops of this corps had made a forced march of 100 miles in four days, during which in one stage the corps pushed on for 35 miles with hardly a break. Arriving too late on July 2 to be of much combat service, they were placed in reserve status, but did suffer some casualties during the next 24 hours. The Sixth Corps division hospitals were established all together on the 165 acre farm of John and Suzannah Trostle, John was the son of Michael and Ruffine Trostle of Mt. Joy Township. His house and barn were on the south or eastern bank of Rock Creek about 1,700 feet below (south-southwest) the junction of that creek and White Run. A 37th Massachusetts soldier, James Bowen, presented for posterity a precise layout of the hospital: "[The wounded] of the Third Division occupied a thatched shed without flooring; the Second were quartered in a barn adjoining, in conjunction with some wounded [Southern] prisoners, while the First Division more numerous, took possession of a large barn nearer the house. In the latter building [John Trostle's house] the wounded officers of the Corps found accomodation." Bowen's one complaint was a serious lack of food. It was so scarce that he and others resorted to combing the nearby fields and meadows for blackberries with which to supplement the poor diet.[93]

Dr. Dimon observed that this hospital, due to having so few wounded, gave each injured soldier excellent attention, purporting that every "individual case was specially attended to, and every pain taken as if each was the only wounded man under treatment."[94]

The Sanitary Commission summarized the three divisions of the Sixth in this array: the First at and around the house of John Trostle; the Second and Third, "in tents nearby."

To the end, this hospital eventually cared for about 315 wounded, a handful of Confederates, and a few from other corps.[95] One hurt Rebel officer in residence there was Captain Benjamin Little, 52nd North Carolina who was given, "every attention and through that, [they] saved my life."[96]

There were about seventy burials on Trostle's property, eleven from Lee's Army. Although not known for certain, the camp probably closed operation in early August, as did most of the other major field hospitals. The medical director was Surgeon Charles O'Leary, U.S. Volunteers, and the medical officer in charge of the corps hospitals was Surgeon Cyrus N. Chamberlain, U.S. Volunteers, who it is believed worked as an embalmer when he was not otherwise employed as a physician.

U.S. Eleventh Corps, General Oliver O. Howard, containing the divisions of F.C. Barlow, A. von Steinwehr, and C. Schurz.

Supporting the right flank of the First Corps on July 1 the Eleventh pushed forward two divisions, the First and Third to engage the Confederates north of Gettysburg. Most of this corps' casualties were suffered on one day. The opening influx of wounded were carried by ambulance or made their way on foot to the Adams County Almshouse, Pennsylvania College, the Evergreen Cemetery gatehouse and churches and other public and private buildings in Gettysburg.

Two of the structures so adapted were the Trinity German Reformed Church on the corner of Stratton and High Streets, and the Union Public School a block away to the west.

In the Almshouse, which was a temporary site only, Dr. J.W.C. O'Neal, a Gettysburg physician performed some medical work during and after the battle. This large group of brick structures was occupied by "many" wounded from the 1st and 2nd Brigades, 1st Division, and the 3rd Division, Eleventh Corps, and that corps' artillery. The patients there probably included a few Confederates.

After July 1 all three divisions banded together when the hospitals were being regrouped. All then were encamped in the close vicinity of the Elizabeth and George Spangler farmbuildings south of Power's Hill. Power's Hill is just west of the Baltimore Pike about one and one-quarter miles south of Cemetery Hill. Witnesses describe three operating tables in use which made the Spangler barn "more resembled a butcher shop than any other institution...." This building was completely full of injured men from one end to the other, including the hay mows, the cow stable, the horse stalls, the wagon shed and loft. The Confederates were placed earlier, for the most part, in the wagon shed which later became the surgeons' quarters.

During the heavy rains of July 4 and 5, the foul water in the barnyard "oozed up into the [patients'] undressed wounds, the sight was harassing in the extreme."[97]

A New York *Herald* reporter located this hospital "nearest the town, and is composed of a large barn and numerous tents of various descriptions and contained between 700 and 800 patients. Its situation is airy and the cases as comfortable as it is possible to make them...."[98]

Elizabeth and George Spangler and their farm which was occupied by the medical establishment of the Eleventh Corps. (GNMP)

Theodore Dimon, for the New York General Relief Agency, found on his official inspection that the Eleventh's site was dry and sat on an airy knoll. He interjected that a few wounded had been deposited in a large barn and

> there was a sufficient detail here of surgeons, who appeared to be zealous in the performance of their duties....Several good women were encamped here, cooking for, and nursing the wounded, and the relatives of the soldiers, in considerable numbers, were each caring for a brother or son. The wounded lay upon stretchers, or upon ticks filled with hay or straw. Shirts and sheets were provided....Food of good kind and variety and well prepared was furnished.
>
> Pads, compresses, and other appliances to relieve position or support painful parts, urinals, bed pans, basins, dishes, lanterns, etc., etc., had been freely distributed by the Sanitary Commission.[99]

Two other narratives were not as complimentary to the surgeons as Dimon had been. One, a private in the 17th Connecticut Infantry, recounted on July 7 how numerous wagon loads of delicacies for the wounded arrived, but "these are mostly gormandized by the gluttonous surgeons in charge who gorge themselves while many a poor fellow is lying in want."[100] The second was a preacher named Schantz, who asserted that some of the "wrappers" (nightshirts or hospital gowns) he brought solely for the use of patients, were later seen being worn by the medical staff.[101] This type of disconcerting activity, was very common. Charles Muller, a wounded soldier at the Second Corps hospital recalled bitterly that a large group of preachers and their friends and families took precious time and materials to build an uncommonly long picnic table on the hospital grounds, and while hundreds of hungry, suffering, dying men lay all around them, this pious assemblage sat down to a huge and bountiful feast eating the very provisions that had been sent to the thousands of wounded there. Muller claimed that from then on he lost all respect and had no further use for any preacher on earth.[102]

As with most of the others, this Federal corps facility continued in operation until early August. By the time of its closing the camp had cared for more than 1,400 wounded, 677 in the 1st Division, 507 in the 2nd, and 684 in the 3rd Division, with about 100 Confederates in residence too, including General Lewis Armistead who died there. Another physician said the corps took over 1,600 casualties, with 800 sent away between July 1 and 9.

The medical director was Surgeon George Suckley, U.S. Volunteers, and the officer in charge of the hospitals was Surgeon J.A. Armstrong, 75th Pennsylvania Infantry.

U.S. Twelfth Corps, General Henry W. Slocum, containing the divisions of A.S. Williams and J.W. Geary.

This corps, paralleling the Third, had only two divisions in combat and most of its heavy fighting occurred on the right flank of the Northern "fishhook" shaped line near and on Culp's Hill. Due to the strong entrenchments which were constructed and the very defensible nature of the terrain, the 1st Division bore only 406 wounded and the 2nd, 397.

In the beginning the two divisions separated their hospitals, but ultimately combined them upon the farm land of George and Anna Bushman. Early on, amidst the fighting itself, the field hospitals and larger aid stations had been arranged along the Baltimore Turnpike west and southwest of Culp's Hill. One in particular settled onto the Abraham Spangler farm, then being tilled by his son Henry and his wife, Sarah. Another site was probably that of Nathaniel Lightner on the west side of the pike, and the farm, grist and saw mills of William McAllister, all of which stood between the road and Rock Creek. An area near the mills was set aside to treat wounded Confederate prisoners being sent down the pike for safekeeping at Westminster, Maryland. Further on, just at the crossing of the creek, the houses and outbuildings of Peter Baker, George Musser, and G. Flemming Hoke were likely taken for the same purposes.

Eventually, the two divisions were posted permanently on the Bushman farm, both near the buildings and north of the house. The Bushman place was just off the road running south from Power's Hill (presently Hospital Road), to the lower crossing of Rock Creek along Sachs-Goulden Road.[103] The Twelfth was the only corps of the Union army which was accompanied by its medical supply wagons and ambulances as it marched into the engagement at Gettysburg. All of the other corps in following the orders of General Meade left their supply wagons back in the rear and had only ambulances in tow. Because of the Twelfth Corps' advantage of having medical and supply wagons, one surgeon remarked: "It is with extreme satisfaction that I can assure you that it enabled me to remove the wounded from the field, shelter, feed them, and dress their wounds, within six hours after the battle; and to have every capital operation performed within twenty-four hours after the injury was received."[104]

The George and Anna Bushman farm used by the Twelfth Army Corps as their main field hospital. (GNMP)

Private Eldridge Sherman, 55th Ohio Infantry, wounded on July 3, may have been attended to at the Bushman farm hospital. (OHA)

If one looks over any good map of the battlefield, it is quickly perceived that the location of the Twelfth Corps obviously should have been taken for use by the Second, Fifth, or Third Corps. As a matter of record the Twelfth did succor a number of wounded from these corps, including 125 Confederates. One of the Confederates recalled that this hospital "consisted of the barn, and other out-houses of a farm, sheds, etc., besides a great quantity of hospital tents which were afterwards pitched." On July 10 A New York *Herald* correspondent counted 460 patients in residence, with already 100 amputations completed, all under the direction of Dr. Artemus Chapel, chief medical officer of the 1st Division.

The main house, built of stone, was used as a dining facility for the surgeons and attendants. North of the house and barn, tents were erected in rows on "each side of an imaginary street running up in the field....The tents on the west side of the street were allotted to the Second Division, and those on the east side to the First Division." Sergeant E.P.M. Bragdon, 10th Maine Battalion, recorded that the basement of the barn was crowded with Confederate wounded, and he personally saw to the placement of a cemetery for the dead of this hospital. It was, "fenced in a plat...in the field east of the house, one half was for the Blue, and the other for the Gray." There were about 13 surgeons in residence, with attendants, hospital stewards, cooks and nurses.[105]

After a tour of the premises, Surgeon Dimon specified that the wounded of the Twelfth Corps were positioned near a bend of Rock Creek, at a farmhouse and large barn, and that they "looked cheerful and hopeful, and spoke grate-fully of the care taken of them."[106]

This hospital shut down its operations on August 5, and all patients were either transported to Camp Letterman near Gettysburg, or sent on to more permanent hospitals in eastern cities. The medical people there had cared for in excess of 1,200 U.S. wounded and 125 Confederates, although two other sources place the figures at 1,006 and 1,139 respectively, for the number of Union troops attended to.

The medical director of this corps was Surgeon John McNulty, U.S. Volunteers, and the medical officer in charge of the hospitals was Surgeon H. Earnest Goodman, 28th Pennsylvania.

U.S. Cavalry Corps, General Alfred Pleasonton, containing the divisions of J. Buford, D.M. Gregg, and J. Kilpatrick.

The cavalry arm of the Army of the Potomac was partly engaged on all three days of the Battle of Gettysburg and throughout the six-week campaign. In the early part of the fight of July 1, their field hospitals were established at the railroad depot on Carlisle Street, the Presbyterian Church on Baltimore Street, and other structures in Gettysburg, including two small schoolhouses on High Street near the main "Union School."

On July 2 a cavalry engagement took place at Hunterstown, northwest of Gettysburg. There, several small aid stations were filled up almost immediately, including the Great Conewago Presbyterian Church, the Jacob Grass hotel, the J.G. Gilbert farmhouse, the Methodist Church, and the Jacob King house and store.

Fairfield, Pennsylvania,was the scene of a similar action on July 3 in which the resulting wounded were taken to St. John's Lutheran Church, the J.A. Marshall and Hugh Culbertson farms, plus a few other private residences in the tiny village. Also on July 3, there was a cavalry skirmish fought south of Gettysburg along the Emmitsburg Road, and the main cavalry battle which occurred east of Gettysburg some distance south of the York Turnpike.

Following the last named cavalry clash, which was a major confrontation between Generals Gregg and Stuart, the farms of Abraham Tawney, John and Sarah Rummel, Joseph B. Leas, J. Brinkerhoff, Isaac Miller, and others

Isaac Miller's farmhouse was one of Stuart's cavalry division hospitals.
(GAC)

sheltered the wounded. Many of the troopers who became casualties on any of the three days of battle surely ended up in various infantry corps hospitals; as did those injured who had served in the many artillery brigades of each infantry corps.

The cavalry hospitals cared for at least 300 wounded. The medical director was Surgeon George L. Pancoast, U.S. Volunteers, and the medical officer in charge of their hospitals was Surgeon W.H. Rulison, 9th New York Cavalry.

U.S. Artillery Reserve, General Robert O. Tyler.

The Artillery Reserve of the Army of the Potomac, consisting of about 100 pieces were first placed in an artillery park on July 1 or 2 in the fields and meadows west and north of White Church between that building and Daniel Sheaffer's farm and White Run. Within a day or so the reserve was moved to an artillery park on the Spangler farm southwest and across from the Granite Schoolhouse, with General Tyler's headquarters at or near Michael Frey's farmhouse on the Taneytown Road. The school was at least partially the site of an artillery hospital during the battle, with Dr. H.B. Buck in attendance.

One source places the reserve hospital out on the Baltimore Pike three miles from Gettysburg, in a "good dwelling house and barn." There were at least 200 patients there, some from units such as the 5th Massachusetts Battery and the 15th New York Independent Battery. Dr. Joseph D. Osborne of the 4th New Jersey Infantry was in charge.[107]

◆ ◆ ◆

Confederate Field Hospitals

When the Army of Northern Virginia left Pennsylvania in the days following the battle, we know that in its retreat more than 6,800 wounded Confederates were forced to remain behind. Through the passing of the years some historians have come to believe that the total number of General Lee's wounded was far greater than the 12,706 reported. Even the tally of the wounded of the Federal army may be somewhat inaccurate and is probably registered a little too low. But the Confederate problem is more serious, as their surgeons "were forbidden by orders to report slight wounds not preventing duty." This class of unreported injury may have been 10 to 15 percent of the whole. In any event the actual count can never be known for certain.[108]

Of the 6,802 *wounded* Rebel prisoners remaining at Gettysburg on July 4, about 1,800 were settled in Union hospitals, with the largest percent deposited in the Second Corps hospital, or approximately 1,000; the First Corps, about 260; the Third Corps, around 250 and so on. The balance, perhaps 5,000, had been collected by the Confederate medical establishment into nearly 25 field hospitals in close proximity to Gettysburg, and also farther out to the west, northwest, north, and northeast of the town limits.

The Southern army brought along very few hospital tents on its invasion, so it made greater use of farmhouses, barns, outbuildings, sheds, and private and public structures for their injured. (Reverend) Dr. Gordon Winslow was the U.S. Sanitary Commission agent responsible for inspecting the Confederate hospitals. His report was completed on July 22, 1863, and forwarded to J.H.

Douglas who was the associate secretary of the commission in Washington, D.C. In it Dr. Winslow declared that he had toured twenty-four separate camps which occupied an area of some twelve miles extant. In these field hospitals he recorded 5,452 wounded Confederates, whose injuries in a large proportion of cases, were severe.

"Amputations and resections are frequent," related Dr. Winslow. "The corps of Confederate surgeons are, as a body, intelligent and attentive. The hospitals are generally in barns, outhouses, and dilapidated tents. Some few cases are in dwellings. I can not speak favorably of their camp police. Often there is a deplorable want of cleanliness. Especially in barns and outhouses, vermin and putrid matter are disgustingly offensive."[109]

Gordon Winslow of the U.S. Sanitary Commission. (HD)

As a matter of record, the diverse corps, divisions, and brigades of the Army of Northern Virginia were issued numerical designations, but more frequently identified themselves by the name of a current or past commander. Therefore in this section of chapter three we too shall proceed on that basis. The Southern field hospitals were roughly located by divisions, as in the Union army, but often these camps were in reality brigade hospitals grouped together for mutual benefit or by circumstance. It is a fine distinction, true, but after a little study, one sees an actual, although subtle, difference.

◆ ◆ ◆

Army of Northern Virginia

C.S. First Corps, General James Longstreet.

McLaws' Division—General Lafayette McLaws, containing the brigades of J.B. Kershaw, P.J. Semmes, W. Barksdale, and W.T. Wofford.

This division reported 576 wounded left in U.S. hands, along with ten surgeons, two chaplains and 70 nurses and cooks. Federal figures differ, placing the number of their wounded remaining near Gettysburg at about 700; but these extra could represent the overflow from other divisions. Of this figure, 113 died. In the battle the entire division suffered 1,538 wounded, not including officers. Dr. F.W. Patterson, 17th Mississippi Infantry was in charge of this particular hospital, and General Longstreet's corps medical director was Dr. J.S. Dorsey Cullen. Dr. R.L. Knox and 75 attendants from the 17th Mississippi were also left to assist their comrades with injuries.

The hospitals of McLaws' Division were set up southwest of Gettysburg and adjacent to and along Marsh Creek which included Francis and Elizabeth Bream's farm on the east bank of that creek at its crossing of the Fairfield (or Hagerstown) Road. Bream's farm also answered to the name of the "Black Horse Tavern," and for many years had been an important traveller's rest along this insignificant thoroughfare. The old stone house on the premises was built by the McClellan family over 60 years earlier. Many of the injured of General J.B. Kershaw's Brigade ended up here. A few of the named Confederate doctors who worked there were James Pearce, H.J. Nott, Aristides Monteiro, and Simon Baruch.

The last named surgeon had strong memories of the morning of July 4. In the hospital at Black Horse Tavern were 222 *seriously* wounded men, ten orderlies, and three surgeons. Baruch, with his staff and patients, was captured by the Yankees, but all remained at the farm six weeks attending to the helpless men. Food was obtained from the U.S. Army and the Sanitary Commission through the courtesy of Dr. Gordon Winslow and all medical supplies came directly through a requisition signed by Dr. Letterman. One story Baruch related concerned two Maryland women who were chaperoned by an elderly English woman and remained at the Tavern where they served as nurses for the entire period the hospital was in operation. Later toward the end of August, Baruch, his companions, and almost 100 other Confederate doctors (he says), were sent to Baltimore as prisoners.[110]

The Bream farmhouse or "Black Horse Tavern." (GNMP)

The student of the battle should realize that the creation of these main C.S. division hospitals, like those on the Union side, did not change the fact that the Confederates, too, had aid stations or dressing or primary stations, the important but temporary smaller "field hospitals" immediately behind their battle lines. In the case of Longstreet's Corps these stations were situated directly on the ground in rear of the infantry regiments or brigades or on nearby farms. Examples abound, such as the situation at the George Rose farm. There, Dr. James B. Clifton of Semmes' Brigade cared for the wounded during the night of July 2. In other places emergency medical aid was given out at the James Warfield place, or

Surgeon Simon Baruch of the 13th Mississippi. (MCW)

on the farms of M. Bushman, P. Snyder, J. Slyder, S. Pitzer, J. Biesecker and the like.

Some additional brigade hospitals of McLaws' Division have been found. General William Barksdale's and General Paul J. Semmes' respective brigades were located at the John Crawford farm and tenant house on Marsh Creek, while the hospital of General W.T. Wofford's Brigade rested on the John and Margaret Cunningham farm. These last two farms were adjacent and separated by only a quarter of a mile; one sat on the west bank of the creek, the other on the east. Both were almost directly south of the Black Horse Tavern, about one-and-one-quarter miles, more or less. Mr. Crawford claimed that his farm of 289 acres was in use for five or six weeks and contained "hundreds of wounded." The Rebels he noted, occupied his stone house, barn, outbuildings, and farm grounds. One of the artillery hospitals of Longstreet's Corps was placed near a tenant house contiguous, (probably lived in by the Basil Biggs family) also owned by Crawford. All of these farms used by Longstreet's doctors still held the remains of more than 260 dead in 1871.

On Cunningham's farm of nearly 200 acres there were at least two Confederate doctors in residence, named Eldridge and Ransom, who in caring for the wounded there, also used his barn and house. The dead were buried in Mr. Cunningham's orchard, where he carefully tended them for nearly ten years. There were also a few Union wounded here who had been captured by the Rebels while fighting with the 4th Michigan Infantry and other units around the "wheat field" on Rose's property.[111]

Pickett's Division—General George E. Pickett, containing the brigades of R.B. Garnett, J.L. Kemper and L.A. Armistead.

Although in combat less than three hours on July 3, this division counted more than 1,200 wounded, most of whom were taken prisoner and ended up in the U.S. Second Corps hospital. The field hospitals of this division recorded 279 wounded under the charge of a Dr. Reeves. The brigade locations were in general south-southwest of the Black Horse Tavern on and near John F. and Elizabeth Currens' 105 acre farm, Francis Bream's Mill, (called the "Mineral Mills") and at the house of "Master Miller" William E. Myers. General James Kemper, who was one of Pickett's brigade commanders, was brought here and placed in Myers' house. The mill was between ten and fifteen years old in 1863 and was filled with Pickett's suffering men. Today the old building is long destroyed, unfortunately. In the 1870s over 40 human remains were removed from burial sites around the mill and farm.

Hood's Division—General John B. Hood, containing the brigades of E.M. Law, J.B. Robertson, G.T. Anderson and H.L. Benning.

Hood's was one of the largest single Confederate division hospitals and encompassed the John Edward and Sarah Plank farm of 220 acres. This site covered the west side of Willoughby's Run nearly three-quarters of a mile southeast of the Black Horse Tavern. Division facilities here originally contained 1,542 total wounded, with 515 of these abandoned by Lee, all under the care of Dr. F.A. Means of the 11th Georgia. A member of the family, Elizabeth Plank, remarked that the house, barn, porches, and grounds were filled with injured Confederates and it was in use for five or six weeks after the battle. As the men died, numbering around 105, they were buried in the Plank orchard. One wounded soldier brought here stated that three Baltimore women nursed the men at the farm. An officer of the 59th Georgia remembered that he was moved to Camp Letterman on the 12th of August. So this helps to date the closing of that hospital possibly at that time or not much later. Another farm just north of this place was owned by George Culp and was likely in use by this hospital. According to damage claims filed, Culp's was a field hospital for only a short time and unlike the Plank farm, this entire farm and buildings are now only a memory. A handful of other localities which could have been temporary hospitals for Hood's men, such as Culp's were: the Pitzer Schoolhouse, John Socks (Sachs) farm and mill, the Samuel Pitzer farm, and the Levi D. Maus property. Adjacent to John Edward Plank's was the William or Abraham Plank farm. The buildings of this latter site were 1,800 yards southwest of the J. Edward Plank farm. It was probably retained by Anderson's Brigade of the division as a good portion of the dead removed from there served in his organization. Included in these burials were men from Robertson's Texas and Arkansas Brigade, so we may safely assume that both of these brigades shared the same hospital.[112]

C.S. Second Corps, General Richard S. Ewell.

Early's Division—General Jubal E. Early, containing the brigades of H.T. Hays, W. Smith, I.E. Avery (Hoke's), and J.B. Gordon.

General Ewell's veterans were engaged in all three days of the battle. Little is known of General Early's hospitals, except that they held 806 wounded, with 259 left near Gettysburg under the charge of Dr. Louis E. Gott, 49th Va. Inf.

Between July 1 and July 4, Early's field hospitals were most certainly established behind his fighting lines north and northwest of town. These stations may have included the Josiah Benner farm on the Harrisburg Road just north of the Rock Creek bridge, Pennsylvania College, the Adams County

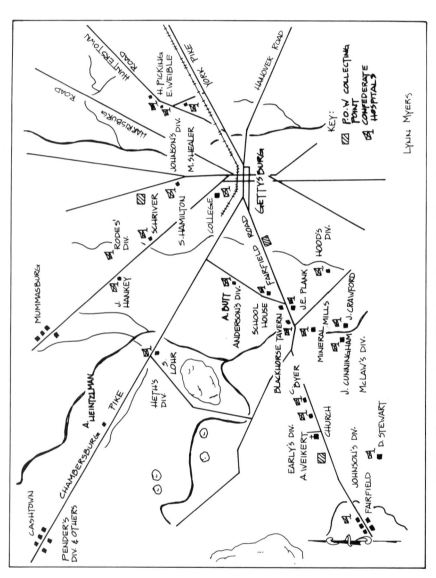

Major Confederate field hospitals in the Gettysburg area.

Almshouse, the Jacob Kime and Henry Culp farms, and conceivably the Christian and Susan Benner farm. The last two sites were out on the Hanover Road east of Gettysburg. In the same neighborhood but a little farther out of town stood the Daniel and Rebecca Lady farm which was employed by Ewell's artillery as a temporary hospital.

All three of the Pennsylvania College buildings may have accommodated some of Ewell's casualties, however we are positive that men of General Perry's (Lang's) Florida Brigade of Anderson's Division were quartered here, also at least one soldier from Pettigrew's Brigade, Heth's Division (both divisions were from Hill's Corps), and another man from Armistead's Brigade, Pickett's Division; a strange mixture indeed. On July 16 it was disclosed by a former student that 500 to 700 Rebels were still occupying the main edifice and had totally ruined the building. This damage included vandalism, for someone had smashed the glass cases in the foyer and stolen the college mementoes, specimens and souvenirs displayed there.

On July 4 Robert E. Lee gave the order to pull his left wing, Ewell's Corps, back westward from its original positions in Gettysburg and in front of Cemetery Hill and Culp's Hill, to a new defensive location north of General A.P. Hill's Third Corps along Seminary and Oak Ridges. This change involved Ewell's hospitals also. At that time we believe he appropriated the following farms for his wounded: John Crist's stone house and barn (for Hays' Brigade), standing several hundred yards north of the Chambersburg Road (which may have been in use since July 1); William Douglas' farm (for Hays' Brigade), seems unlikely, however, as it was *behind* Hood's Divisional operations area; Andrew and Susan Weikert's 97 acre farm (for Gordon's Brigade) on the Fairfield Road, which was commandeered for six weeks and contained 300 wounded; and Elizabeth and Christian Byers' 120 acre farm (for Avery's [Hoke's] Brigade) also on the Fairfield Road and used for five weeks, with 100 patients.

We must not forget, too, that when Ewell's Corps swung back upon Oak Ridge on July 4, many of their hospitals ended up on the Fairfield Road due to its function as one of Lee's retreat routes. In point of fact, one witness says that the entire road, on both sides, in fields, woods, and farm meadows was filled with ambulances and wagons, as the hospitals prepared to move southwestward back to Virginia. A source in General Ewell's Corps underscored that at 2:30 p.m. on Saturday, July 4, all of their wounded were being driven to the Fairfield Road and collected at the stone building of the Lower Marsh Creek Presbyterian Church in preparation for debarkation south.[113]

There were certainly other temporary field hospitals adopted by Ewell's Corps in the area, but these are presently unknown.

Johnson's Division—General Edward Johnson, containing the brigades of G.H. Steuart, J.M. Williams (Nicholl's), J.A. Walker (T.J. Jackson's old "Stonewall" Brigade) and J.M. Jones.

Like Early's Division, General Johnson's men were engaged at Culp's Hill. The division finished the battle with roughly 1,300 wounded and of these, 446 were left to their own devices after the retreat. Dr. William R. Whitehead took charge of these hospitals.

During the battle days of July 2 and 3 General Johnson's hospitals were mostly concentrated northeast of Gettysburg along the Hunterstown Road and east onto the York and Hanover Roads. There were injured Confederates at the Daniel Benner farm; Rebecca and Daniel Lady's farm (Jones' Brigade and some artillery); W. Henry and Catherine Monfort's 125 acre farm; the Martin and Amanda Shealer farm (Steuart's Brigade); John or Joseph Weible's farm (Steuart's Brigade); Elizabeth Weible's, (possibly Steuart's Brigade), this latter place was kept in use until the middle of August; the Charlotte and Henry Picking farm and schoolhouse, (Walker's Brigade); and possibly the Alexander D. Buehler and the David Jameson farms both on the York Pike, of which little is now known.

When Ewell's Corps was swung back to Seminary Ridge on July 4, Johnson, like Early, would have uprooted some of his hospitals out to the Fairfield (Hagerstown) Road or into Fairfield itself. In all likelihood the farm of David and Margaret Stewart was taken, as it sat about three quarters of a mile west of the "Marsh Creek" church. Other possible sites serving medical purposes in this area include the Joseph and Rebecca Mickley farm, and the homesteads of Elizabeth and William Harner and Rebecca and Henry Wintrode.

The Sanitary Commission claimed that one of Johnson's Division hospitals was *at* Fairfield on Middle Creek, which flows just east of the village. The Commission placed only 50 wounded at Fairfield, but indicates 135 of Johnson's men in hospitals *on* the Fairfield Road itself, under a "Dr. Stewart." Moreover, in his early 1900s medical study, Louis Duncan recites that on July 5 the Federal forces discovered 871 wounded in Fairfield under the charge of Dr. Benjamin F. Ward, 11th Mississippi Infantry and Dr. LeGrand J. Wilson, 42nd Mississippi Infantry." In Ewell's primary hospitals on the Hunterstown Road U.S. officers counted 311 Rebels left with Dr. W.R. Whitehead.[114]

Martin and Amanda Shealer's thatched roof barn was filled with injured Confederates of General George H. Steuart's Brigade. (GNMP)

Rodes' Division—General Robert E. Rodes, containing the brigades of J. Daniel, A. Iverson, G.P. Doles, S.D. Ramseur and E.A. O'Neal.

When General Rodes maneuvered his division into the heavy Union fire directed at him northwest of Gettysburg on July 1, it is doubtful he would have believed that by nightfall, 1,728 of his veterans would lie seriously wounded on that field. And, worse still, somewhere between 760 and 800 of these brave men were captured by Federal forces because they could not be transported back to Virginia. To those remaining in enemy hands he assigned four surgeons, six assistants, and 97 attendants along with ten days' rations. One of Rodes' main field hospitals under a "Dr. Hayes," was organized at Susan and David Schriver's 150 acre farm (used primarily by O'Neal's Brigade) along the Mummasburg Road northwest of Gettysburg. This hospital stayed intact for five weeks, the farm buildings themselves were utilized for a month and were reported to have been much abused and damaged by the occupation. Just up the road from Schriver's was the 250 acre farm of Elizabeth and Jacob Hankey. Since Jacob had died in 1860, the land was being cultivated by his eldest son, P.D.W. or "David" Hankey. Many of General Iverson's wounded were brought there, and neighbors remembered it being "thronged" with Rebels and pronounced that at least 1,000 Southern soldiers lay on this farm and at adjacent sites. One of these peripheral locations was a large grove of trees on a slight elevation which sat directly north of the Hankey property.[115]

Closer to Oak Ridge there is evidence that Rodes' troops made use of the farmsteads of Moses McClean and John and Mary Forney, as temporary aid stations/field hospitals; and definitely those of Sarah and John Hamilton, and Samuel Cobean. The latter two were situated on the west side of the Carlisle Road. One source describes the amputation of the leg of General Isaac Trimble as occurring in the Cobean parlor.

At least a portion of one of Rodes' Brigades, the one commanded by General Junius Daniel, is thought to have formed a field hospital on the Fairfield-Hagerstown Road at Jacob and Sarah Plank's 184 acre farm. In a damage claim filed in 1868, Mr. Plank conveys to authorities that the Rebels were there in large numbers, maybe 500 present for several weeks, and the house was filled with patients for 17 days. Looking at these figures, the inclination is that Plank's farm had to have been occupied by brigades other than just Daniel's. The Planks lived about three-and-one-half miles southwest of Hankey's place.[116]

C.S. Third Corps—General Ambrose P. Hill.

Hill's Third Corps was engaged chiefly on July 1 and 3, but participated in some fighting on the second. Its battle lines were along Seminary Ridge from the Lutheran Theological Seminary southward toward the Millerstown "crossover" road, now named Waterworks Road, which is a continuation of the National Military Park's "Wheatfield Road."

Anderson's Division—General Richard H. Anderson, containing the brigades of C.M. Wilcox, A.R. Wright, W. Mahone, D. Lang (Perry's) and C. Posey.

Anderson's Division officially listed 1,128 wounded and 840 missing; many of the latter were probably killed or wounded. Surgeon H.A. Minor, 8th Alabama Infantry, was detailed in charge of the 111 men unable to be transported out of Pennsylvania. Many of these injured men were driven by ambulance to Fairfield, but a large number remained in field hospitals east of Marsh Creek and along the Fairfield Road. One of the chief hospitals was on the farm of Nancy and Adam Butt, the buildings of which sat a few hundred yards north of the Fairfield Road on today's Herr's Ridge Road. We know that Samuel Herbst owned this farm several years before the battle, and on older maps his name is often associated with it during the Civil War era. Nevertheless, it is believed that by July '63, Nancy Butt and her spouse had purchased the farm. In any case, Wilcox's Brigade appropriated the farm as its hospital for about six weeks, and approximately 40 bodies were disinterred from the burial ground in the early 1870s.

Along the Fairfield Road, and about 500 yards south of Butt's stone house was a schoolhouse called the "Brick Schoolhouse" or "Butt's School"; here wounded members of Wright's Brigade were cared for. Across the road on the south side, was the farm of Allah and John Butt, which on the U.S. Sanitary Commission map is depicted as a Confederate hospital, and was likely a companion site in conjunction with the aforementioned places.

Heth's Division—General Henry Heth, containing the brigades of J.J. Pettigrew, J.J. Archer, J.M. Brockenbrough, and J.R. Davis.

At the end of all combat on July 4, General Heth's Brigades had sustained 1,905 wounded and many missing. Approximately 900 men lacking transportation, or too seriously hurt to be moved remained in the Gettysburg vicinity under the care of a small staff of surgeons when the Confederate army departed. Several reports included a "Dr. Smiley," or Dr. Benjamin F. Ward in charge. A contingent of Heth's Division's wounded was said to have been found at Pennsylvania College, but not the majority as is often claimed. There were in the realm of 700 to 900 Southern wounded sequestered at the college (853 is one figure given), many of whom had been part of Ewell's Corps. There is also information that a handful of the 5th Florida Infantry was cared for in the college edifice which, as was already proclaimed, would indicate a hospital of Anderson's Division of Hill's Corps. The surgeon-in-charge there was Dr. H.D. Fraser of South Carolina.[117] Union documents mention that 693 men were left behind from Heth's Division in the hospitals around Gettysburg.

A few of General Heth's men may have been housed at the Seminary for a short time; we know for sure that Generals Trimble and Kemper of Hill's and Longstreet's Corps, Major Henry K. Douglas of Ewell's Corps, and Colonel Robert M. Powell, 5th Texas Infantry, Longstreet's Corps, were quartered here for many weeks after the battle. Generally, however, it was a Federal hospital, still intact and occupied until almost September. Finally, the majority of wounded of Heth's Division were carried to farms along the Chambersburg Turnpike and at Cashtown. The normal infantry and artillery primary or "dressing stations" were definitely settled in "hollows" along Willoughby's Run and at the "mineral springs" south of the pike and near that stream. These low, protected areas, with a supply of good clean water, made ideal spots for collecting and caring for men injured early in combat.

The "Herr Tavern" and farm along the Chambersburg Road may have been taken as a temporary aid station for Pettigrew's Brigade. This farm and "public house" had been owned by Frederick Herr prior to the Civil War, but we know that Joseph Weible purchased the land and improvements in 1860. And too, along that turnpike, the houses or farms or outbuildings of Charles B. Polly, David Whisler (blacksmith shop), C. Schultz, G. Stover, and Daniel Polly possibly were implemented as aid stations, or as very temporary (one or two day) field hospitals. It is felt that Davis' Brigade might have had a dressing station at the farm of George and Mary Arnold (tenanted by John Horting), at the Fairfield Road crossing of Willoughby's Run, because several burials of the 2nd and 11th Mississippi turned up there. But the leading hospital associated with Heth's Division was placed on the 126 acre farm of "Major" Samuel Lohr. This Chambersburg Road medi-

The landmark Lutheran Theological Seminary's main edifice was in use as a hospital for several months after the battle. (GAC)

cal complex contained many of the disabled of both Pettigrew's and Davis' Brigades, and we know that Dr. B.T. Green, 55th North Carolina, and B.F. Ward, 11th Mississippi performed operations on the premises. In residence here were also a "Dr. Hubbard," Dr. LeGrand J. Wilson, 42nd Mississippi, Dr. L.P. Warren, 26th North Carolina, and Dr. Spencer G. Welch, 13th South Carolina of Pender's Division. From the information available it is in all likelihood that Hill's Divisions were wedged together in large hospitals between the Andrew Heintzelman farm and the Lohr place, a distance of perhaps a quarter of a mile, one on each side of the pike. In his damage claim Mr. Lohr specified that his farm was occupied by a "large number of rebels" for several

The springhouse of Samuel Lohr is all that remains of his farmstead. Hundreds of uninjured and wounded Confederates of Gen. Hill's Corps used the cooling waters which trickled through this old structure. (GAC)

weeks and the house, barn, and outbuildings were sorely damaged. According to the affidavit the family was unable to move back in until September 1.

Just beyond the Chambersburg Pike and almost one mile southwest of the "Herr Tavern" stood the house and small farm of Dr. Samuel E. Hall and his spouse, Ellen. Two of General Pettigrew's men were found buried there, which could indicate the presence of an aid station or short-term hospital. Hall's claim does not specify "hospital use" of his property, so he may have cared for the men himself.[118]

Pender's Division—General William D. Pender, containing the brigades of A. Perrin, E.L. Thomas, J.H. Lane, and A.M. Scales.

Federal fire power inflicted wounds on 1,312 soldiers which were then thrown into the medical facilities of William Pender's Division. Seven hundred of this figure remained near Gettysburg under the stewardship of a "Dr. McAden."

The division's leading hospital camp was formed around the nucleus of the Elizabeth and Andrew Heintzelman farm and tavern on the Cashtown-Chambersburg Pike, just northwest of Samuel Lohr's. Here in 1871, 100 Confederate graves still remained, a number which would denote a large concentration of wounded. The farm consisted of 82 acres, and the tavern went by the "Sign of Seven Stars," a name the tiny hamlet answers to presently. Just north of the tavern was the Christian Shank farm, where the barn and outbuildings were used by the Rebels, "for Hospital purposes for about two weeks." The Heintzelman property was occupied for close to ten days as a Confederate hospital, not the length normally associated with many of the others. It is possible these wounded were simply the first to be moved away or into Federal care. Another of Pender's Division hospitals was in the village of Cashtown; the locality was just south of Joseph Mickley's brick hotel on high ground south of a stream called Muskrat Run, and close by the road to Fairfield. In Cashtown 171 wounded remained under a "Dr. Wilson." In this village where General Robert E. Lee temporarily headquartered between June 30 and July 1, the houses or grounds of Elizabeth Mickley, Isaac Rife, Dr. William C. Stem, and others accommodated some injured. There is also evidence that a few of General McLaws' wounded men of the Confederate First Corps were encamped there somewhere in the vicinity.

Miles to the east, back toward Gettysburg, General Scales' Brigade of Pender's Division may have established a temporary hospital or aid station at the farm of Michael Crist near McPherson's Ridge, which was near his relative John Crist; the latter farm is believed to have been appropriated by General Early's Division. Michael Crist's stone house paralleled the "unfinished railroad" grade and was about 200 yards north of the pike; John Crist's was more northwest of Michael's, probably 500 yards farther on, but the house and barn are no longer standing.[119]

Over 200 burials are associated with these last two divisions. Many were removed in the 1870s by Dr. Weaver.

As in most cases, the locations of the greater part of the artillery hospitals, if they were separate from infantry, are unknown at this time.

By the time the hot, dry days of mid to late August rolled around, most of the Union and Confederate corps/division field hospitals had been officially closed by the U.S. Government, and the men either moved on to general hospitals in the eastern cities, or military prisons throughout the northern states. On the first of September there were no more than a few wounded soldiers, if any, confined in any of the aforementioned Gettysburg facilities and only a handful remained at the Union School in Gettysburg, the Lutheran Seminary, the Express Office and of course, Camp Letterman. Any seriously injured soldier whether wearing blue or gray, who could not make the passage to a permanent general hospital went straight to Camp Letterman U.S. General Hospital. As one nurse bluntly put it, that hospital "contained, in truth, the very dregs of battle from two armies."[120]

A total of 1,347 Confederates of the nearly 7,000 of their wounded abandoned in the Gettysburg area, went directly to Camp Letterman between July 15 and August 15. Additionally, 2,500 were transported to David's Island, New York, 1,100 to Chester, Pennsylvania, a few to Harrisburg, Pennsylvania, and several hundred slightly hurt men went off to Baltimore, Maryland, for prisoner exchange or confinement. Finally, many had died of their wounds, but those who recuperated were shipped off to military prisons.[121]

The plan to remove the large numbers of wounded from Gettysburg was set in motion almost immediately after the fighting ceased. Since the railroad tracks and the eastern bridge over Rock Creek had been destroyed by the Confederates prior to the battle, most of the early transportable victims of the combat were settled along the York Pike about one mile east of Gettysburg where the iron tracks of the railway curved toward the proximity of the pike. This railroad was a branch of the Northern Central and was named the Hanover, Hanover Junction, and Gettysburg Railroad, with a depot on Carlisle Street in Gettysburg as the terminus of this short line. From Gettysburg proper, the men were shipped to Hanover Junction then on to Baltimore, Philadelphia, or points up the east coast. By the 6th of July all bridges along the railroad had been repaired and the trains could then take on their human cargo within a mile of town, as previously mentioned. The first evacuations began on July 7. By the 8th, 1,462 patients had already been removed. Due to the more than 30 or 40 ambulances (and countless private conveyances) then running constantly, the wounded reaching the temporary depot on the York Pike before long, far exceeded the number of men who could be routed out. And a few days later one of the inspectors sent to the battlefield by medical corps headquarters brought along 50 additional ambulances which added to the influx.

The day of July 25 came around barely three weeks after the battle, but 16,125 wounded had already been sent away, including 12,000 from Gettysburg, 2,000 from Littlestown, Pennsylvania, and 2,000 by way of Westminster, Maryland. As an example of the expedient and ongoing transportation, on July 12 alone 1,219 men had been placed on the trains for Baltimore, 90 percent of them Confederate. On July 17 over 400 Southerners were sent to New York, in addition to 100 Union soldiers who made the same trip. An average of 800 men were being shipped each day. Inspector Edward Vollum had pronounced earlier that Surgeon J.D. Osborne, 4th New Jersey was detailed to adopt a system for the removal of these wounded. In applying this system it became necessary to have several trains, usually two or three, leave each day at irregular times. For instance on July 12, trains departed at 10 a.m., 12:15 p.m., and 5 p.m. Vollum's recommendations, as carried out by Osborne, were that "[e]very train of wounded was placed in charge of a medical officer detailed by Surgeon H[enry] Janes. Instruments, dressings, stimulants, etc., were furnished him....Each car was filled with a sufficient quantity of hay, and, on the longer routes, water-coolers, tin cups, bed-pans, and urinals were placed in them and guarded on the route by some agents of the Sanitary Commission."[122]

Even with such good intentions and a workable plan, not all of the transported patients received this type of treatment especially on the earlier trains. On or about July 18 a man travelling to Gettysburg to bring back a friend killed there, stated: "The cars in which they [the wounded] were conveyed were common baggage and cattle cars, covered on the floor with a thick layer of straw, on which the poor fellows were obliged to sit or lie during the weary hours of their ride of 50 to 150 miles."[123]

In the end, with even the best care and provisions available and in place, 4,217 very seriously injured men could not be immediately moved. Hence, the necessity of a general hospital on premises; so the idea and realization came about, and the establishment of Camp Letterman was implemented. Those who were unfit or untransportable included men with penetrating wounds of the head, chest, abdomen and pelvis. There were also a large number of long-term patients who had suffered compound fractures of the thigh, leg and arm. These soldiers were placed on stretchers during the time span of July 14 through late July, and from the hospitals in and around Gettysburg were hand-carried the several miles out to Camp Letterman. Their collection was with the utmost care, as these cases were singularly often desperate and very painful. A sergent in command of one of these detachments remembered that his men were only able to make two 3-mile round trips daily as the work and the heat were "exceedingly trying."[124]

In reference to this primary movement of the injured into Camp Letterman, Dr. William F. Norris, a First Corps surgeon, recalled that he was ordered to transport his patients out to the site from the Catholic church and elsewhere in Gettysburg on Thursday, July 23. By 7 p.m., Norris asserted that his entire complement of wounded was already in place at the new hospital, and many had been carried out on stretchers. Surgeon H. Ernest Goodman, 28th Pennsylvania who had been the chief of the Twelfth Corps field hospital was then in charge of the new hospital.[125]

◆ ◆ ◆

Camp Letterman

The name Camp Letterman has come to the reader's attention many times in the preceding pages. By now you are probably familiar in a general way, with the purpose of this unusual hospital camp and why it was needed. However, a little more detail on this interesting concept and that hospital itself may be enlightening to us all.

Camp Letterman was named in honor of Dr. Jonathan Letterman, medical director of the Army of the Potomac and was officially opened on July 22, 1863. It ceased its formal operation on November 20, 1863. With over 4,000 immovable patients finally brought together near the railroad, and who still remained lodged in a few outlying field hospitals, it was believed by Medical Inspectors Edward P. Vollum and G.K. Johnston, as well as Surgeon Henry Janes, that a United States *general hospital* should be planned, built, and maintained while and until most of these seriously hurt men were sent away. A camp ground of about 80 acres was therefore selected on an elevated wooded knoll south of the York Turnpike, and near the railroad one mile east of Gettysburg. This land was a segment of George Wolf's farm and the area where the camp was built was locally known as "Wolf's Field" or "Wolf's Woods." Before the war it had been enjoyed for its high scenic beauty, cooling spring water and shady environment by town residents, and was often employed as a community picnic spot. This was a perfect locale for hospital use, being only a short distance of about 500 feet from the railroad, and it was directly astride a major turnpike, with a source of fresh water in the form of a clear spring nearby, plus it was partially shady, but also open and breezy. By July 16 the grounds were cleared, drained and cleaned, and a few tents were pitched where over 400 tents would eventually be erected and occupied.

Within a few days of its beginnings a Christian Commission agent reported the site to be an "excellent situation." It was beautiful he said, with a skirt of woods on the northeast and on the southwest, supporting a good spring, and the ground gradually rolling so that rain and slop did not remain long. There he counted between 125 to 150 tents, which were large and well built, each able to hold 12 to 16 persons on the accompanying bedsteads and mattresses. We know too, that by August 10, the camp still mustered a total of 1,772 patients, one half of them Southern soldiers. Earlier on the 18th of July Letterman contained 1,600 wounded, plus 400 doctors and attendants; the only other hospitals in use then were the Public School, the Seminary, a few private houses and the Sheads and Buehler Hall or warehouse.[126]

On August 6 another U.S. Christian Commission delegate, James P. Ludlow, described the site of Letterman, as "high and beautiful." He depicted the camp as having six distinct rows of tents with avenues between them, with each row consisting of seventeen tents and each tent, when full, containing twelve patients. "With our haversacks loaded," wrote Ludlow, "with soldiers books, letter paper, pencils, envelopes, etc., etc., each delegate takes a tour of one row of tents, ascertaining what is needed, supplying it either from our haversacks or writing an order on our tent agent, which the tent nurse presents at our counter and is filled. Three rows of tents are filled with rebels, who as a class, stand in the ratio of four professing Christians to one such Federal."[127]

The tents that have been described were designed to be heated in the fall and winter if necessary, and were aligned in six double rows, ten feet apart, with several of the tents collected into a group and sectioned off into individual "wards" all with letter designations. Each tent held an average of between

8 and 12 patients. Quoted earlier, Dr. Norris recorded that one whole section of the camp was allotted to the First Corps' wounded, in all, 16 tents. That corps' section, for example, held 192 beds which were subdivided into wards, 48 beds to a ward, each under the charge of an assistant surgeon.[128]

Huge ditch latrines were dug some distance from the camp, and a large cookhouse was constructed of wood and canvas near the spring close to the turnpike. Also located near and behind or south of the main tented area was a "dead house," actually just another large tent used for corpses awaiting burial, with an embalming canvas pavilion near at hand. There was an "officers row" separated from the enlisted quarters, a large graveyard, with Union and Confederate sections, and other areas set apart for use by the medical staff, orderlies, attendants, nurses, hospital stewards and administrative personnel. Near to these stations was a designated portion of ground where the Sanitary Commission shelters were erected, reported by an eyewitness to be in "huge tents...spread beneath tall oaks and hickorys." The Commission required lodging for 38 persons, and in addition had store-tents and offices, plus a special kitchen which could be used to prepare the lighter diets which many of the patients depended on.[129]

It is impossible to know the exact number of staff members at this camp, other than the figure quoted above, but one source placed it almost as large as the number of patients.[130] It is recorded that Surgeon Cyrus N. Chamberlain, U.S. Volunteers was in command of the hospital, and under him were twenty-eight acting assistant surgeons, seven assistant surgeons and four surgeons, plus nine Confederate doctors who had temporarily remained behind in various field hospitals when Lee retreated. Those doctors and 18 Rebel nurses were under the jurisdiction of Surgeon L.H. Hill of Daniel's Brigade, Rodes' Division. Surgeon Henry Janes was the officer in charge of *all* hospitals in the Gettysburg area. Each medical officer had the responsibility for anywhere from 40 to 70 patients.[131]

Orders had come through channels in early August to begin closing all field hospitals in the Gettysburg vicinity and by August 7 as the old corps and division field hospitals were being shut down, there were already approximately 1,600 patients, half of them Confederates at Camp Letterman. In addition, there were nearly 200 still in the Seminary, 30 at the railroad

The cookhouse or camp kitchen at Letterman. (AMH/DST)

"Express Office" hospital near the depot, 70 more at the "Union School House," and as many as 450 patients housed in private dwellings. At the Lutheran Theological Seminary hospital all three brick school structures were in use, and of the 200 wounded there, 100 were Southern soldiers. Included too, were between 50 and 60 patients in tents standing alongside the main edifice on Seminary Ridge.

In October the number of wounded Confederates at Letterman exclusively, as documented by the provost marshal general of the Army of the Potomac, was 112 officers and 1,235 enlisted men.

On this date a Michigan chaplain who was visiting Camp Letterman described it in these words:

> The hospital is located on a rise of ground, skirted on two sides by an oak grove, as fine a spot as I ever saw. The tents are pitched in an open field, which descends gently toward the west and north. A fine spring, sufficient for a bountiful supply of good water is located near the cookhouse. There are about one-hundred and twenty-six tents already up, each of which is occupied by twelve persons. The prospect is that the area of the hospital will be materially enlarged, as tents are being put up daily. The patients are in good spirits....[132]

The patients probably *were* generally in overall good condition, considering their wounds. However, even as late as October 26, one sentinel at the camp illustrated the negative side: "When we first came here there were five thousand sick and wounded, so the steward told us; as high as seventeen die per day. It is heart-rending to pass through the streets and hear the cries of agony that burden the air; I have heard them when I was away from the hospital a half-mile. Those who die in the hospital are buried in the field south of the hospital; there is a large grave-yard there already. The dead are laid in rows with a rough board placed at the head of each man, (they are nearly all Confederates)...."[133]

In speaking of these Confederates it is known from records in the National Archives at Washington, D.C. that upon the opening of this hospital there were at least 250 Southerners present. The first recorded death of a Rebel there was on July 23. He was Clinton White, Co. H, 1st North Carolina Infantry. The last to die at Letterman was J.F. Drain, Co. A, 53rd Virginia on November 6, 1863.

Like all military hospitals, Letterman was under guard twenty-four hours a day. In the month of October and afterward the camp sentinels were made up of a Maryland company called the "Patapsco Guards" of Howard County, which had taken the place of the 51st Pennsylvania Militia Regiment, which in turn had replaced the 36th Pennsylvania Militia.

Another observer, this one writing in late August, was impressed with the culinary apparatus. He explained: "A number of tents were under the shade of the trees, and the cooking, baking and dining arrangements were within the grove. The cookery and bakery were conducted on an extensive scale. Provisions for preparing soup and cooking meat were ample and well arranged. In the department adjoining the cookery, persons were busily engaged in carving the boiled beef that was in preparation for supper. The bread, of which there appeared to be an abundance, was as white and nice as any seen at 'the baker's.'"

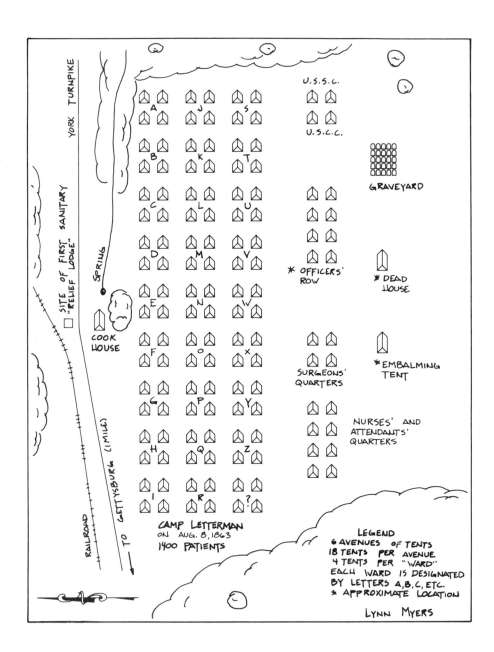

The U.S. General Hospital "Camp Letterman" sat along the York Turnpike one mile east of Gettysburg.

A few of the hundreds of tents erected at the general hospital. Gettysburg can be seen in the distance to the west. (GNMP)

A view of the U.S. Sanitary Commission headquarters within Camp Letterman. Superintendent of the Commission Dr. Gordon Winslow is seated to the right. (GNMP)

This same Christian Commission delegate declared that there were in residence 30 surgeons, a superintendent or medical director, seven division, and 26 ward surgeons, all quartered south of the main hospital grounds "in a lovely grove." Dr. Henry Janes, he interjected, was the superintendent, with Dr. Cyrus Chamberlain, the assistant-superintendent. There were also good living and working quarters for the Christian Commission which were housed in the southeast angle of the grounds, the same position cited for the Sanitary Commission. The U.S. Christian Commission's shelter allotment at Letterman included three single tents and one double tent. The double tent contained a counter and shelves filled with reading matter, and stocked there were catalogued supplies of assorted delicacies for the soldiers. In rear of this tent was a dining table for the sole use of the eight agents who remained on duty. All together the U.S.C.C. employed about 50 agents at Gettysburg from July 4 into the end of November.

While visiting the camp the above-mentioned agent viewed a surgical operation, one of many secondary procedures performed daily. His recollections are worth repeating:

> In the operating tent, the amputation of a very bad looking leg was witnessed. The surgeons had been laboring since the battle to save the leg, but it was impossible. The patient, a delicate looking man, was put under the influence of chloroform, and the amputation was performed with great skill by a surgeon who appeared to be quite accustomed to the use of his instruments. After the arteries were tied, the amputator scraped the end and edge of the bone until they were quite smooth. While the scraping was going on, an attendant asked: 'How do you feel, Thompson?' 'Awful!' was the distinct and emphatic reply. This answer was returned, although the man was far more sensible of the effects of the chloroform than he was of the amputation.[134]

Volunteer nurse Sophronia Bucklin who was engaged at Letterman throughout its several months' history, remembered that there were originally 500 tents in the hospital and this total was soon increased to many more. Ms. Bucklin added that wells had to be dug to supplement the water at the spring. And in speaking of water, Bucklin had a profound and distinct memory of how difficult it was to get the Southerners there to bathe; she perceived that a "hydrophobic fear of water" seemed to prevail in their ranks. And besides this quirk, the good nurse underscored that "when convalescent the rebels were even too indolent to pluck from their garments the vermin that seemed to be swarming in every seam...."

As Bucklin illustrated it, each day at the hospital had its own general system

***Nurse Sophronia E. Bucklin.
(OAN)***

One of the many operations performed at Camp Letterman. Nurse Sophronia Bucklin stated that one patient named Peter Brock was kept on the amputating table for three hours as the surgeons, "paused awhile to have their photographs taken...." (GNMP)

Prisoner of War Lt. Sanford W. Branch, 8th Georgia, recuperating at Camp Letterman on September 10, 1863 [lying down, right]. Severely wounded in the left lung, he wrote his mother that day: "I had my photograph taken today. How much pleasure it would give me to send it to you. I also walked today for the first time." (AHC)

and method of operation. Stimulants were first given out early each morning, followed by special diets which were prepared by the cooks. Next came the "wound dressers" who made their rounds, each being assigned to a particular section of each ward. Beef tea was passed out three times a day, the stimulants three times, and the extra diet three times, making nine visits total, which every male or female nurse was obliged to complete for all 200 men under that person's care. The soldiers' faces were washed, their hair combed, and sponge baths were performed only by male nurses, and extra drinks administered as required. She testified that each attendant had his or her own specific duties, and included the surgeons in charge, the hospital stewards, the ward surgeon, women nurses, ward masters, men nurses, wound dressers and the night watch; there was no conflicting or overlapping of work.

Sophronia Bucklin was intrigued by the fact that of the 22 Rebels who were under her care, thirteen died, a very high number she thought, who thereby joined the "1,200" dead that eventually populated the camp cemetery. (Her estimate is high.) She was puzzled at this statistic because the Southerners, she argued, had received the same assistance and attention as the Union men.

When Camp Letterman General Hospital was finally terminated in late November, it was Nurse Bucklin who wrote a most fitting and poetic eulogy concerning the historic old ground.

> The hospital tents were removed—each bare and dust-trampled space marking where corpses had lain after the death-agony was passed, and where the wounded had groaned in pain. Tears filled my eyes when I looked on that great field, so checkered with the ditches that had drained it dry. So many of them [the patients] I had seen depart to the silent land; so many I had learned to respect, and my thoughts followed them to other hospitals, and to the fresh battle fields, which would receive them, when health was fully restored.[135]

Another nurse who was assigned to Letterman in late July from the Second Corps field hospital was Cornelia Hancock. Her notations in letters written home manifest that the hospital was divided off into six avenues, with eighteen tents holding twelve men each on every avenue. Four tents together were called a ward, and each ward was designated by a letter of the alphabet. In early August she claimed that the cookhouse was preparing three to four meals a day for 1,300 men. Sentries were in evidence throughout the hospital grounds allowing no one inside the camp without a pass, and then only after 4 p.m. After dark, the militia guard rounded up all visitors and escorted them out of the area.

Hancock revealed that nearly every week Dorothea Dix made an appearance to check on the operations of her "nurse corps," and that the matron-in-chief of the general hospital was the very capable Mrs. Anna M. Holstein. Furthermore, Hancock believed and gossiped that many of the woman nurses were there simply to capture husbands, and those who were "good looking," often, "galavant around in the evening and have a good time."[136]

Anna Holstein, the matron-in-charge at Camp Letterman enumerated in her own reminiscences that by the 7th of August there were approximately 3,000 men who had been moved into the tents at the camp. She affirmed that nearly one-third of the camp were registered as Confederates, and that "rebel

Cornelia Hancock,
volunteer nurse. (SDH)

Justus Silliman was detailed as
a nurse at the general hospital.
(EM)

ladies" from, "Baltimore and other places were permitted to come and wait upon their own wounded." She reiterated however, that there was one emphatic rule in the hospital: i.e. that "no difference was permitted in the treatment of the two [sides]."[137]

One of the slightly wounded patients at the camp was Private Justus Silliman, 17th Connecticut. He was also detailed as a nurse there, and specified that the hospital contained over 700 "nurses and workmen," who could furnish the wounded with half a dozen kinds of food. He revealed that the cookhouse had in use, "five large boiler stoves, six large cooking ranges & three immense ovens besides innumerable pots & kettles, etc."[138] It is interesting to find that when the last of the hospital property was being packed and shipped away from the camp in February 1864, Captain H.B. Blood, Quartermaster at Gettysburg, accounted for the following with Dr. Janes: eleven Stoves or "Cauldrons," 119 Kettles, 353 iron bedsteads, 198 boxes of hospital property, 89 bales of hospital property, 30 chests and boxes, and 29 barrels of hospital property among other items. And this was only one shipment of many.[139]

In letters to his mother, Private Silliman described how every patient in camp received clean underclothing each week, but he complained bitterly however, about one incident which clouded the stay there for many convalescents. This unpleasant situation occurred at a large picnic prepared especially for the wounded men of both armies. On the appointed day of the festivities, the Rebel nurses (who he said, had been ordered by their government to remain behind and care for the wounded of their own army), rushed the tables and gobbled up most of the delicious foods, all the while elbowing out both Union and Confederate wounded. Ironically, while the Southern nurses gourged, a choir was singing popular songs of the day including verses such as "Down with the traitors," "We'll rout the rebel hoard," etc., which seemed to cause only slight embarrassment to the feasting "chivalry."[140]

On September 29 one of the local newspapers, the Adams *Sentinel and General Advertiser*, revealed that this great picnic or banquet as it was also called, had occurred on Tuesday, September 23, and some of the items brought in were 4,000 to 5,000 chickens, 20 to 30 hams, 50 tongues, uncounted oysters and pies, plus plenty of ice cream. The patients and attendants took part in foot races, greased pole and "gander pulling" contests, watched minstrel performers, while a band from York, Pennsylvania, played the favorite tunes of the era.

A New York soldier who convalesced here, Private Henry H. Smith, nicknamed "Razor Strop," of the 140th Regiment, scribbled a letter home on August 17. In it he gave the particulars of his health and his wounded leg, commenting that the doctors could not locate the bullet, but had given it a good hard painful try by using a set of forceps. Smith tracked rather humorously how, "[f]or many days, while I was under the influence of chloroform, I talked, they say, most incoherently. Shouted, preached, sang, etc. The fact is, I think they gave [me] five times as much as necessary."

In another part of this correspondence, Smith itemized his breakfast of August 18 which consisted of one slice of bread, a teaspoonful of sauce, and two tablespoonfuls of hash. Later he was able to supplement his diet by buying several dozen eggs, which were cooked and eaten on-site by he and his comrades. Smith also explained that there were good things at the camp too such as plenty of clean clothes like shirts, socks, drawers, as well as an abundance of reading material, etc.—but never enough food.[141]

On November 16, 1863, another Gettysburg newspaper published that there had been a total of 1,981 patients at Camp Letterman since July 22, (this may be incorrect, as most sources document that over 4,000 stayed there at one time or another) and 381 of these had died. Of 180 men tallied who had bullet fractured thighs, as one example, 65 percent were "cured." There had been three successful ligatures of the femoral artery performed in the camp, and it was found by the doctors that the treatment of fractured thighs was as good with or without amputation. As of November 15 only 60 patients remained, and the final one, according to the paper, was said to be going out November 17 to Cincinnati, Ohio.[142]

Finally, on November 20 all medical officers were relieved of their duties at this vast and important hospital. The last man was removed, the tents were struck, and the equipment and supplies either stored and or packed and transported to distant places. The closing process was not totally completed, though, until late February of 1864.

Fifteen years later in 1878, a historian of the Battle of Gettysburg inscribed his emotions concerning the once famous but now time-worn hospital grounds:

"Not withstanding the mournful memories of this hill, it is still a very charming spot. Its commanding location, its leafy shades of hickory and oak, its spring of delicious and pure water, indeed, all its surroundings, invite the traveller to pause and rest and ponder."[143]

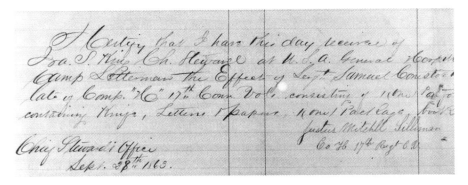

When his friend Sgt. Samuel Comstick died, Pvt. Silliman took charge of his personal effects. This is the actual receipt given at Camp Letterman, September 29, 1863. (GAC)

Camp Letterman's last tents were struck in late November 1863. (GNMP)

And finally, a resident of the area who had been just a youngster during the battle, critiqued the site in 1932:

"It has always been a wonder to me that the government, when it was acquiring the historic fields upon which the battle was fought and other sections now included in the reservation, did not buy this woods, one of the most historic and sacred spots on the field."[144]

Many of us still wonder. The government never did purchase any of the land where Camp Letterman had once stood, and one need only drive by today of what remains of "Wolf's Woods" to realize what a terrible mistake that was.

◆ ◆ ◆

Civilian Volunteer Aid Societies and Organizations

Within the confines of this book the reader has found material concerning the efforts by the government, local and visiting civilians, the U.S. Sanitary and Christian Commissions, and various other patriotic organizations to assist the 27,000 wounded of the Battle of Gettysburg in the weeks and months following the first three bloody days of July.

It is known that during the first hours following the great clash of arms, General George Meade had not allowed the order to be sent which would have brought up the large numbers of hospital supply wagons for seven of the eight corps of the Army of the Potomac. Consequently, only the Twelfth Corps was fortunate enough to have with it all of its supply wagons, which naturally helped to alleviate the sufferings of many men of that corps. The other infantry corps brought up only ammunition wagons and a few ambulances from the rear, along the crowded roads leading to Gettysburg. Medical Director Letterman was heartily frustrated by this turn of events as he and his 650 surgeons were unable to feed and properly shelter the victims of the hard fighting. As a matter of record, Letterman emphasized that even *during* the battle, hospital wagons and other supply vehicles were sent even farther to the rear than they already were placed. These wagons were parked initially between Union Mills and Westminster, Maryland, with Dr. John B. Brinton in charge, who was later appointed to the position of U.S. Medical Purveyor of the Gettysburg hospitals.

Both during and after the heavy combat in Adams County, Dr. Letterman contended that the need for tents, cooling apparatus, and food was critically felt. He emphatically stated: "The Medical Department *had* these means, but military necessity deprived it of a portion of them, and would not permit the remainder to come upon the field." The medical director said too, that without proper supplies, his department could no more take care of the wounded than the army could fight without ammunition.

On July 4, after much discussion, Director Letterman was able to persuade General Meade to order *half* of the seriously needed supplies, so eventually on July 5 twenty-five wagons reached the field at a very critical time. On the 5th and 6th Doctor Letterman ordered additional medical and hospital provisions and equipment from Baltimore and Philadelphia. Surgical stocks were not lacking, at least in the beginning. It seems it was only the many other vital accessories usually carried by the department which were missing and were deemed just as important as surgical apparatus.

Before he left to rejoin the army in its pursuit of Lee's crippled forces, Letterman left 106 doctors behind (of the 650 available), under the capable direction of Dr. Henry Janes, and then requested through channels that Surgeon-General William A. Hammond in Washington send Dr. Janes twenty more.[145] In one of his last acts at Gettysburg, Letterman made sure that hospital guards were posted, and assured the doctors that cattle and other foodstuffs, bed sacks, and various other important materials would be sent forward immediately.

After the battle, civilian doctors flocked to the field to "volunteer" their services, but Letterman and other military professionals found these types to be mostly adventurers looking for a chance to do only *surgical operations* — especially amputations. One surgeon who certainly felt this way was Dr. Dwinell of the Second Corps, who strongly voiced that these volunteers were unreliable, as a class. He complained that of the large number who reported to him to assist "only four or five were really [of] much benefit." He went on to describe how these "gentlemen" often showed up, got their fill of a free breakfast, watched the doctors for a while at work at the tables, then immediately disappeared. Dwinell portrayed them as mere opportunists who hated dressing wounds or "stumps," and declined to do anything "unless they can take off limbs."

Incredibly, one of these "emergency" medicos was actually discovered charging exorbitant prices for his services. A soldier had complained that he was made to pay $50 for an amputation.[146]

And Letterman himself summarized: "[I]t cannot be too strongly impressed...that an army must rely upon its own Medical officers for the care of the sick and wounded."

Returning to the all important medical commodities, obviously some supplies did arrive in a timely manner or were already available. An illustration of this can be seen by utilizing one set of the bills of lading signed for by the local agent of the Northern Central Railroad. These bills were for material that was delivered shortly after the battle to the army quartermaster for distribution to the hospitals. The items listed were as follows: 1,676 bedsteads, 360 stretchers, 12 caldrons, 11 cookstoves and fixtures, 122 kettles, 1 table, 321 buckets, plus 30 bundles, 348 boxes, 288 bales, 42 hogsheads, and 60 barrels of "hospital property."[147]

One more case in point is augmented by Surgeon Justin Dwinell who remembered that on July 3 he received at his hospital 6,000 rations of tea, coffee, sugar, crackers, soup, salt, candles, salt-pork, and 3,600 pounds of beef on the hoof. On the fourth, Dwinell was again delivered of the same quantity. Obviously from their bland content, these items were just the normal issue of commissary infantry rations. Some items on the list would not have been the best eatables for seriously injured men, but they were certainly better than nothing. Later, the doctor acknowledged that he acquired from sundry civilian groups donations of soft bread, wines and cordials, oranges, lemons, "light diet" foods and even comfortable clothing for his patients. He outlined however, that what was needed most were tents, straw, reliable transportation, and more shovels and axes.[148]

Upon his arrival along with an accompanying cattle herd, Dr. John Brinton established a temporary medical department supply depot out by the "White Church" on the Baltimore Pike. This was a perfect location to administer to the needs of the several large corps hospitals which had sprung up in that area, but this facility was only in service for a short time until a more reliable system of supply could be arranged.

Because of the unusually large number of wounded and sick after the battle, it can be rightfully assumed that the Federal government, meaning the *army* itself, could not provide for each and every object, article, or commodity wished for, or wanted and needed by wounded soldiers and their doctors, or the cooks, attendants and nurses who were scattered over miles of ground in more than 150 individual locations. Therefore, several beneficent groups, both secular and religious, took up the cause. Some of these organizations had been functioning since the war began, others sprang up periodically as the need or the calamity arose. A few of the scores of philanthropic agencies were: the Hospital Corps of Adams Express Company, the Fireman's Associations of Baltimore (one soldier called it "a secesh...organization"), the Patriot Daughters of Lancaster, the Ladies' Aid Society of Philadelphia, the Soldiers' Relief Society of Philadelphia, The Daughters (also called "Sisters") of Charity (25 individuals were present at Gettysburg from St. Joseph's at Emmitsburg, Maryland), the New York Soldiers' Relief Agency, the Germantown Field Hospital Association, the Indiana Soldiers Relief Agency, and the Benevolent Society of East Thompson (Massachusetts), as well as many other and varied independent sources and ordinary citizens.

In the last-named category, a good example is that of Lydia Smith, who was a kindly black woman living in Adams County. With an old broken down cart and horse she scoured the countryside for donations which were delivered to the suffering soldiery in the hospitals south of Gettysburg.

The Hospital Corps of Adams Express Company was quite unique and worth expanding upon here. Adams Express was a commercial freight company associated with U.S. railroad transportation, and was one of the largest freight movers in the world. During the Civil War it was the company which common soldiers, the U.S Army in general, and many private organizations such as the U.S. Sanitary Commission, relied on to haul everything possible, from personal mail to coffins containing the bodies of slain soldiers, and they operated to and from almost every city, army camp or town in Federally-controlled states or territories. On July 4, the superintendent of the company, S.M. Shoemaker wrote to Secretary of War Edwin Stanton and offered to set up a "hospital corps" within the company, to send "men, food, suitable comforts, etc." to the front (meaning Gettysburg), along with spring wagons to take in the wounded from the field. Stanton "heartily approved" this generous venture, and the "corps" did excellent service after the battle. Their headquarters in Gettysburg was in the storeroom of Michael Spangler in the southwest corner of the diamond or the town square, and Harry Eiglehart was appointed to be the local representative.[149]

Not all citizens donated goods; it is recorded in government invoices that dozens of farmers in the area sold food and fodder, hay and straw, and other necessities to the medical purveyor for use in the hospitals. One example was Peter Conover on whose farm was situated a division hospital of the First Corps. On July 4 he vended 75 gallons of milk, 350 pounds of mutton, 100 pounds of beef and 60 pounds of pork for $60.20 directly to Surgeon A.J. Ward, 2nd Wisconsin Regiment, the physician in charge of the First Corps hospital at that time.[150] Conover was one of many who used the ongoing medical emergency in order to profit; it was no doubt in the finest tradition of the American spirit.

One other positive and immediate route to obtain stores, was simply to order any idle enlisted man at any given hospital to take out a horse and wagon and go into the surrounding area stopping at all farms and collecting what was available. One such outing was completed by William Baird, 6th Michigan Cavalry. On July 4 he, "was given a Horse and Cart and sent out into the county for supplies for the Hospital, and met with the best of success in the way of Bread, Butter, Eggs, Fruit as well as sheets for Bandages...."[151]

The two most important organizations which were responsible for the greatest effort, time spent, hospital supplies gathered and services rendered were the United States Sanitary Commission and the United States Christian Commission. These names are familiar to us, but some may still be in the dark about their beginnings, histories, and duties. The following is a more detailed description of each.

The U.S. Sanitary and Christian Commissions

The United States Sanitary Commission was a civilian agency formed about three months following the beginning of the war in June of 1861, to assist the military in providing help and comfort to sick and wounded soldiers and sailors. Pastor Henry W. Bellows of New York City was elected president of the organization, and specified that the improvement of life for the soldier was their main objective. During the war the U.S.S.C. formed 7,000 aid societies throughout the North, with its central office established in Washington, D.C. and ten branch offices placed in other important cities. All of the 500 agents were unpaid, but included some of the country's best doctors, government and civic leaders, and businessmen. A variety of hired workers, such as field inspectors, nurses, cooks, and teamsters received small salaries. The Commission was involved in nursing, general hospital work, direct battlefield aid, the deployment of relief lodges near railway stations, and the donation of medicines, food, clothing, and personal items. From 1861 to 1865 this Commission raised and spent over seven million dollars, and gave out freely at least ninety-five million dollars' worth of supplies. Most of the money and goods were contributed or raised through "sanitary fairs."

Beginning in 1863 and arranged throughout the war, these fairs were popular attractions in the major cities. Generally a parade was held first, after which people crowded into the fairgrounds' buildings and tents to view exhibits

The U.S. Sanitary Commission fair in Philadelphia, June, 1864. (PCW)

and be fed and entertained, and to purchase donated merchandise at auctions. The fairs generated funds in amounts from $200 to almost $1.2 million which was raised at one New York City sanitary fair in 1864. By May 1864, and prior to the New York event, seven of these fairs had already been held and at least $1,000,000 had been raised.

On July 2, 1863, even as the fighting raged, four wagons of Sanitary Commission supplies had already reached the army at Gettysburg and were distributed "under fire." Another team of agents and several wagons that were on the way to the field were captured by a Confederate patrol as they drove through Maryland. Within a few days of the end of the battle (or by July 7), 12 wagons of medical goods and food reached the Federal army. These provisions were not simply handed out, but were issued to the medical officers from regular depots established near the battlefields. After the Gettysburg battle, the commission first set up its depot or storehouse along the Baltimore Pike in a schoolhouse called White Run School (almost one mile north of the White Church). It was centrally located and within reach of all Federal corps hospitals. When the first train reached Gettysburg shortly after the combat ceased, two of the railway cars in it belonged to the Commission. Each day for a week two additional cars arrived, and on July 7 a new storehouse was opened in the town itself. This "depot" was transferred from the White Run School to a better location on Baltimore Street and into the Samuel Fahnestock & Company store and warehouse. This large brick structure soon became crowded to overflowing with generous donations of miscellaneous supplies, which were distributed each morning to the division hospitals, both Union and Confeder-

The Fahnestock store and warehouse in Gettysburg, was for months packed with supplies for the outlying Federal and Confederate hospitals. (GNMP)

ate. Interestingly, the assemblage of Confederate surgeons who remained behind with their wounded was so impressed by the generosity of the Commission that toward the end of August twelve of them signed a letter directed to General Robert E. Lee. In it they expressed their gratitude to this organization and asked Lee to extend the same kindness to U.S. wounded in his hands.[152]

To lend a helping hand to the hundreds of injured men leaving Gettysburg from the hospitals daily, a relief lodge was constructed by the Sanitary Commission at the temporary terminus of the railroad. This lodge and terminus was located about a mile east of the village, and out along the York Pike, just north of where Camp Letterman would eventually be laid out in the middle of July. This relief lodge consisted of two large pitched tents, each of which could hold 75 men, and a field kitchen. For the pained and exhausted soldiers who were weary from hobbling and dragging themselves to this rail terminal, the relief lodge became a bright spot and an immense comfort while they waited for the trains to take them to permanent hospitals.

Meanwhile, as each incoming train pulled in for its cargo of soldiers, it brought in tons of ice, mutton, poultry, fish, vegetables, soft bread, eggs, butter, and other delicate foods, plus clothing and hospital furniture from many different locations around the country.

As of Friday, July 10, the burned-out bridge over Rock Creek had been repaired, so the Commission was now able to transfer its relief lodge to a second and better position. This site was nearly opposite and east of the Gettysburg railroad depot on Carlisle Street. The first lodge had provided hearty beef soup, coffee, and fresh bread to over 3,000 slightly wounded men and a few serious cases who departed the battlefield. One Commission physician was always present to administer extra medical care to these soldiers as needed. Within a day or two this new depot camp of the second relief lodge listed a doctor, seven assistants, several cooks, and a score of other attendants on its roster. Five more tents were erected including a "storehouse" tent; drains were dug and straw was brought in to provide temporary sleeping quarters for 150 men a day who were often forced to wait all night for a train leaving in the morning. From July 4 to July 14 about 5,000 Union and Southern soldiers had been succored at the two lodges. Subsequently, when fewer men were leaving each day due to the seriousness of their wounds, the Commission transferred its operation to Camp Letterman.

Cited below is a brief sample of the types and amounts of goods and foods and supplies brought in by the Commission on *July 1, 2, and 3 alone:*

Towels and napkins	10,000	Sponges	2,300
Tubs, basins, cups	7,000	Combs	1,500
Bandages	110 barrels	Fans	3,500
Shoes & slippers	4,000 pairs	Crutches	1,200 pairs
Butter	6,100 pounds	Eggs	8,500 dozens
Bread	10,300 loaves	Ice	20,000 pounds
Concentrated milk	12,500 pounds	Jellies	2,000 jars
Fresh poultry &			
mutton	11,000 pounds		

Sugar	6,800 pounds	Drawers	7,143 pairs
Shirts (woolen)	7,158	Shirts (cotton)	3,266
Mosquito netting	648 pieces	Handkerchiefs	2,659
Stockings	5,818 pairs	Bed Sacks	1,630
Blankets	1,007	Pickles	400 gallons
Codfish	3,848 pounds	Wine	1,148 bottles
Brandy	1,250 bottles	Tobacco	100 pounds
Catsup	45 jars	Preserved fish	3,600 pounds
Preserved meats	500 pounds		

Often some of the donated goods posted to the Commission were very personal in nature and were accompanied by messages from the donors. The Adams *Sentinel* issue of March 22, 1864, gave some examples:

Marked Articles

Some of the marks which are fastened on the blankets, shirts, &c., sent to the Sanitary Commission for the soldiers, show the thought and feeling at home. Thus-on a homespun blanket, worn, but washed as clean snow, was pinned a bit of paper, which said: "This blanket was carried by Milly Aldrich (who is ninety-three years old) down hill and up hill one and a half miles, to be given to some soldier."

On a bed quilt was pinned a card saying: "My son is in the army. Whoever is made warm by this quilt, which I have worked on for six days and most all of six nights, let him remember his own mother's love."

On another blanket was this: "This blanket was used by a soldier in the war of 1812—may it keep some soldier warm in this war against traitors."

On a pillow was written: "This pillow belonged to my little boy, who died resting on it; it is a precious treasure to me, but I give it for the soldiers."

On a pair of woollen socks was written: "These stockings were knit[ted] by a little girl five years old and she is going to knit some more, for mother says it will help some poor soldier."

On a box of beautiful lint was this mark: "Made in a sick room, where the sunlight has not entered for nine years, but where God has entered, and where two sons have bid their mother good-bye as they have gone out to the war."

On a bundle containing bandages was written: "This is a poor gift, but it is all I had; I have given my husband and my boy, and only wish I have more to give, but I haven't."

On some eye shades were marked: "Made by one who is blind. Oh, how I long to see the *dear Old Flags* that you are all fighting under."

The total cost of supplies for just *three days* was calculated at $75,000, and the above list of food and clothing is only one half of what came in. One may see by this very small table, why war is so costly, not only in lives and the implements of battle, but also in the millions of items like these which are rarely really accounted for. Within one month of the battle the *Compiler* of August 7, 1863, printed another selection of donations saying that the amount of fresh bread brought in by the Sanitary Commission was over 20,000 pounds; fresh mutton and poultry, 20,000 pounds; condensed beef soup, 10,000 pounds; condensed milk, 9,000 pounds; fresh butter, 5,000 pounds; eggs, 10,000 dozen; sweet chocolate, 4,000 pounds; shoes and slippers, 4,000 pairs; lemons and oranges, 300 boxes; and included were also carloads of boxes of sponges, bandages, lint, socks, miscellaneous clothing, wines, jellies, and many other foods and liquors.

The U.S. Sanitary Commission staff associated with the Army of the Potomac normally contained a contingent of 23 people; these being relief agents, inspectors, clerks, drivers, and a cook. After a battle had been fought, dozens more would be assigned for the duration of the emergency.[153]

One woman who worked at the relief lodge was Georgeanna M. Woolsey, who made these notes about her activities: "After the men's wounds were attended to, we went round giving them clean clothes; had basins and soap and towels, and followed these with socks, slippers, shirts, drawers, and those coveted dressing-gowns [called "wrappers"]. Such pride as they felt in them! comparing colors, and smiling all over as they lay in clean and comfortable rows ready for supper, 'on dress parade,' they used to say."

Nurse Woolsey also expressed her belief that the lodge was a first-rate temporary camping ground for the men awaiting transport, having five tents close by the town near the depot. It was pitched "in a large field directly by the tracks, with [an] unlimited supply of delicious cool water. Here we set up two stoves, with four large boilers, always kept full of soup and coffee, watched by four or five black men, who did the cooking, under our direction, and sang (not under our direction) at the tops of their voices all day—

'Oh darkies, hab you seen my Masser?'
'When this *cruel* war is *over*.'"[154]

The soup was always on, she remembered, but the dinners were varied with custard, baked rice puddings, scrambled eggs, codfish hash, corn-starch, soft bread, jellies, and tea, coffee, and milk.

Altogether this lodge provided 16,000 meals and sheltered 1,200 men overnight, with an average of 60 men per night for the three weeks the relief lodge remained open. The Commission even extended its care to a group of black men, many were ex-slaves and lived in a camp nearby. They had been hired by the government to work on the railroad and were provided with various foods and supplies to make their lives more comfortable.

In parting, Ms. Woolsey said that the last man to leave the lodge and depart by rail was a lieutenant originally from Oregon. He had lost a foot in the battle.

The United States Christian Commission was founded in New York City on November 14, 1861, by the Young Men's Christian Association. As this organization expanded throughout the North, it began to work more closely in conjunction with the U.S. Sanitary Commission for the general relief of soldiers and sailors. However, in the beginning, instead of merely providing physical comforts to disabled men, the U.S.C.C. felt it had a mission to cater also to the spiritual comforts, plus the moral and or religious needs of the men who requested it and sometimes those who did not. During the war years this group of citizens raised about $6 million to aid the army and navy.

At the Battle of Gettysburg two delegates from the Commission, J.G. Chamberlain and R.B. Howard were already accompanying the Federal Army of the Potomac. Southward back at Westminster, Maryland, a few newly

A Christian Commission delegate at work in the field. (JB)

assigned delegates to this force set up a temporary hospital to attend the hundreds of wounded who had crowded into that town from the battlefield seeking shelter, aid, or transportation. Shortly after the battle, the Christian Commission wagons brought stores to the Union Second Corps hospital south of Gettysburg, later adding the Third and Fifth Corps to their lists. One of their first patients was General Winfield S. Hancock, commander of the Second Corps, itself.

As one delegate pronounced: "[T]hus [we] relieved the wants of many a poor soldier, while pointing him to Jesus, before supplies or laborers arrived from any other source."[155] With Christianity, it seems, there is always the double-edged sword.

On the 4th and 5th of July a few more agents arrived and a headquarters was fitted out in the office of Robert G. Harper, editor of one of the village newspapers, the Adams *Sentinel*. Mr. John Shick's store on the southeast corner of the town square was acquired by U.S.C.C. Delegate Andrew Cross as their main supply depot. So by the 10th, there was a Sanitary Commission depot on Baltimore Street, a U.S.C.C. depot at Shick's, and one at Adams Express Company near the railroad station. The quarters for the Christian Commission agents *in* Gettysburg were adjacent to the house of George Little on West Middle Street, several houses in from the northeast corner of Washington and West Middle Streets.

On July 7, 30 additional delegates reached the battlefield along with eighty boxes of supplies, to add to the four to six people already engaged in working with the wounded. Eventually there would be 50 agents at Gettysburg.

The Christian Commission reportedly built an "eating saloon" to assist injured men waiting for the daily trains out of Gettysburg, and they claimed it remained open until the Sanitary Commission put up their own "relief lodge" as previously documented. Since there was always some jealousy and a spirit of competition between the two agencies, it is difficult, if not impossible, to extract who did what first. Stations of the U.S.C.C. were definitely established in each corps hospital except the Sixth, and later one more went in at Camp Letterman. These stations were usually a tent or two filled with supplies and necessities, with one or more agents present to help the wounded and issue the materials. In the 3rd Division of the Second Corps hospital, John E. Adams and J.B. Stillson manned the station alongside twelve other delegates. The other divisions had their own camps established, in much the same fashion. The Commission even provided some physicians to bolster the assigned government and army surgeons already in place.

In addition to the corps hospitals outside of town, U.S.C.C. delegates were employed in the borough churches, at the Seminary, in the College and Courthouse, and in other public and private buildings occupied as hospitals; others applied their know-how and experience to meet the needs of the wounded Confederates spread out in several camps which sat on the Cashtown Road and elsewhere. One delegate especially liked this work. He reminded his superiors that the Confederates were "especially accessible on religious subjects."[156] Other agents, most of whom were ministers, complained that a great number of the Yankees and Rebels were terrible "infidels," that swore off preachers, and had no religious needs or training. Feeling this same rejection, one Catholic nun made a reference to the nontheists, saying that the "spiritual deprivation of these Southern soldiers seemed even worse than their deplorable physical plight." She also retorted that they "knew no more religion than a Turk, no baptism—nor did some of them believe in Heaven nor hel [sic] only to live just as long as they could and enjoy life as it came." The preachers and sisters and other religious zealots were surprised that many of these men had never heard of a thing called baptism, and the subjects of the debate were often not simply poor ignorant farmers, but highly educated enlisted men or even officers. But what stunned the Christian delegates even more was the fact that so many of the soldiers simply had no knowledge of any god. "Not a single one of the men from Georgia or Alabama had previously received the rite of baptism. No hereafter did these ignorant creatures of God believe in."[157]

Quotes like these make one wonder as to the Commission's real purpose for being at Gettysburg, and brings to mind the words used by an overworked surgeon when he exclaimed, "I'd give 100 DD's [doctors of divinity] for one extra M.D. right now!"

What these orthodox people obviously did not realize was that in the years prior to and during the Civil War only approximately 25 percent of the citizens of the United States and Confederate States were actual professed Christians. This particular brand of religious myth had not yet really taken hold of society. That would come later, probably due to the determined work of these same types of fanatical people and those who came after them.

The true feelings of some of these hardened veterans do come out once in a while concerning the religious sermonizers.

A soldier in the Eleventh Corps hospital watched for a while as a preacher there was attempting to obtain food and other needed items for the large number of wounded men. This private was Reuben Ruch of the 153rd Pennsylvania and he commented that this was the only time in his life, "when I thought a preacher was any benefit to his fellow man." Later in that same hospital on Sunday, July 5, the same hard-working minister began to conduct religious services on the floor of the barn. He got down onto his knees and offered up a prayer to his invisible deity. And just as he was getting nicely started someone lying in the cow stable screamed out, "put the preacher out." The yelling continued and the service was cut short, and the hymn even shorter. Private Ruch admitted that it was never so hard to keep from laughing as at that time; but out of "respect" he controlled himself.[158]

In conclusion and in fairness, it must be reiterated that some men did appreciate the "spiritual" side of these ministers as they could be a comfort to men prone to religion and to those who were far from the support and love of their families. It is simply a fact, however, and must be stated, that millions of people in those days did not need religion, and got along happily without it, contrary to what many might otherwise choose to admit.

As is clearly apparent, both of these Commissions were absolutely necessary to provide the extra aid called for to care for the 22,000 seriously hurt men at Gettysburg, many of whom would have died without this added assistance that the government could not and did not administer. The Adams *Sentinel* exemplified these sentiments, saying on July 21 that both agencies, "have been doing noble work here. The thousands of wounded men...will ever bear in kind remembrance the untiring efforts of the members of the Commissions."

◆ ◆ ◆

Adams County Civilians in the Aftermath

When reporting on such a forbidding situation as the wounded in the aftermath at Gettysburg, one is tempted to publish nothing but positive aspects about the tremendous amount of kindness and goodwill shown toward the battle's casualties. After all, one might question, what purpose would it serve to bring out any of the negative aspects of human nature, for overall the decency and basic goodness of people did come through in its very best forms at Gettysburg. Inasmuch as this is certainly true, but in order to conclude with a balanced account we will continue to report the facts as they are known and appear in the testimony of eyewitnesses. Therefore in the next and last segment of this chapter, transcripts will be presented in which soldiers and citizens alike were struck by the greed, selfishness, and hard-heartedness of many of the citizens who lived on or in the vicinity of the battlefield. Before we begin, however, it should be reemphasized that the average civilian, especially those living in the town of Gettysburg itself, generally went far and above what would be considered normal obligations and responsibilities in the emergency that was the aftermath of this great battle.

As a sample of that sentiment, Robert G. McCreary, local attorney and volunteer delegate for the Christian Commission, made these comments concerning the criticisms which were directed against the citizens of his village in the weeks following the battle:

"Allow me here to remark, that the stories which have been published charging the people of this town with a want of hospitality toward the soldiers, are barely false. I do not believe any community has exhibited more generous devotion towards those thrown upon their hands....In every community there are heartless and sordid persons to be found, and doubtless there are such here; but they are exceptions."[159]

His words reflect the record very truthfully. But there is another side of the coin and the "exceptions" he mentioned are worth illuminating, purely because there were so many complaints, and all aspects should be examined.

Within the research files assembled for this study is a collection of over 75 negative comments toward Pennsylvanians, usually directed by the soldiers or medical personnel against the German inhabitants of the *county*. Curiously, there were not as many complaints toward the Gettysburg townsfolk. The poor "Dutch" farmers, however, did take a serious bruising in the memories of combatants or the outsiders who came to nurse the wounded.

Some of the earliest *printed* reports outlining the various detested activities of these "low minded, selfish, avaricious farmers," appeared in several July 1863 issues of the New York *Times* and other large newspapers. Correspondent Lorenzo L. Crounse of the *Times* in an article on July 9, denounced the men of Gettysburg for deserting their families before the battle; then when the fighting was over, he wrote that they came creeping back, not to assist the wounded or bury the dead, but to tender bills to the military authorities for damages to their property incurred during the invasion. Naturally the local newspapers countered these allegations with more balanced and rational accounts, or at least with a blind eye cast as to the truth of the charges.

Presented here are a few varieties of complaints beginning with a short description of the German people of south-central Pennsylvania as seen by a more fair-minded soldier.

"[T]he *Dootch* (who compose a considerable part of the population) retain their habits of economy and plain living acquired in the old country; they are not much inclined to activity and generally prefer denying themselves many privileges for the sake of taking life slow and easy."[160]

In spirit, these next quotes are not quite so gracious.

Surgeon Cyrus Bacon, 7th Michigan Infantry: "I regret to be required to make dispersion on the action of any people recognizing the Union. Yet it is my deliberate opinion that this part of Pennsylvania is not in the Union for no other Union place will fraternize [with] it. Thousands visited the battle field, yet for days I did not see the first act of charity from the people....The people seem to consider us lawful prizes, and are not only extortionate but give to us little real sympathy. A man comes after a bit with a few bundles of straw. $1.00 for a loaf of bread. Such items makes one indignant for the honor of his county.

"However, the people of the city of Gettysburg in some measure redeem this character of the county residents."[161]

Surgeon William Watson, 105th Pennsylvania Infantry: "The people in this district have done nothing for [the wounded]. I have yet to see the first thing

A typical Adams County farmer of the 1860s. (GAC)

brought in for the comfort of the wounded. Some farmers brought in some bread which they sold for seventy five cents a loaf. The brave army that has protected this State surely deserves better treatment...."[162]

Surgeon John H. Brinton, U.S. Volunteers: "The battle-ground occupied the farms which lay beyond the town for miles. A good many of the farmers were Germans,—I'm afraid of a low type and mean, sordid disposition. Their great object in this life, seemed to be to hoard money, and their behavior toward our troops and our wounded soldiers, was often mean beyond belief."

Brinton also related how he came upon a "mean-looking" farmer in a wagon hauling two wounded men to the hospital. The only way the farmer offered to help these soldiers they said, was if the men gave him a silver watch and some other personal items they carried.[163]

Mrs. "C.A. Ehler," civilian volunteer nurse: "That there were isolated cases of meanness and extortion is certain, for the men of our hospital told us how, after lying three days without anything to eat, and suffering great agony from their wounds, five wounded men were charged twenty-five dollars (all they had in the world) for bringing them two miles into Gettysburg in an uncovered wagon without springs, whose every motion they thought would put an end to their sufferings. The next day three of the number died."[164]

Lieutenant Ziba Graham, 16th Michigan Infantry: This officer was on the way back to his command on July 2 and stopped for a drink at Jacob Weikert's stone farmhouse on the Taneytown Road. There he noticed that the well crank had been removed from the well pump, and all the while there were 50 Rebel wounded in the yard of the house, desperately in need of water. He continued:

"I went into the house, found this man, a mean Dutchman, buried in the bosom of his family, and his family buried in the bowels of the cellar....I ordered him to give up the well crank. He first refused....I threatened to shoot him if he did not give me the crank; this brought it out of its hiding place back of the stairway. I went out, [and] watered the boys...."[165]

Captain Benjamin W. Thompson, 111th New York Infantry: "The patriotism of the neighboring farmers did not shine very brightly. A well to do farmer near us refused us straw for our men....Not a man or woman in the vicinity offered a hand to help or a drop of milk for the poor sufferers. I employed one of them to take the men of my company to the depot. He did it in half a day with one horse and wagon and charged twenty dollars for the service. But it was the best I could do."[166]

Private John W. Haley, 17th Maine Infantry: "After all we have sacrificed for them, the women have the contemptible meanness to charge us two dollars for a loaf of bread that could be bought for seventy-five cents in Rebel Maryland. Even the proverbally mean New England Yankee would blush to ask twenty-five cents for it. One old female sauerkraut had the sublime and crowning cheek to cut a loaf into twelve slices and ask twenty-five cents a slice."[167]

Georgeanna M. Woolsey, civilian volunteer nurse: "Few good things can be said of the Gettysburg farmers, and I only use Scripture language in calling them 'evil beasts.' One of this kind came creeping into our camp three weeks after the battle. He lived five miles only from the town, and had 'never seen a rebel'....'Boys,' we said, marching him into the tent which happened to be full of rebels...here's a man who never saw a rebel in his life and wants to look at you'....'And why haven't you seen a rebel...why didn't you take your gun and help to drive them out of your town?' 'A feller might'er got hit!'—which reply was quite too much for the rebels, they roared with laughter at him, up and down the tent.

"If any time you would like to swear, call your enemy a Dutch farmer—nothing can be worse....The Dutch farmers of Gettysburg have made themselves a name and a fame to the latest day, by charging our poor men...three and four dollars each for bringing all that was left of their poor bodies, after defending the contemptible Dutch firesides, down to the railroad."[168]

Colonel Charles S. Wainwright, First Corps Artillery: "Gettysburg may hereafter be classic ground, but its inhabitants have damned themselves with a disgrace that can never be washed out. Had it not been for the wounded and women and children left in it, I should rejoice had it been levelled with the ground....

"Instead of helping us, they were coming in shoals with their petty complaints of damages. One man wanted a dead horse removed out of his stable! Another demanded twenty dollars for bringing half a dozen wounded cavalrymen some seven miles....

"Hundreds from the county around, too, came down in their waggons to see the sights, to stroll over the ground, and gaze and gape at the dead and wounded. But not one lifted a finger to help the tired soldiers remove the one or bury the other."[169]

Private John W. Storrs, 20th Connecticut Infantry: "After satisfying themselves that there was really no further danger to be apprehended from the

Rebels, the fugitives of the people of Gettysburg came sneaking back and expressed their gratitude for the saving of their homes from destruction by charging wounded officers five dollars each for carrying them back two miles to the officers hospital, and five cents a glass for cool water for the parched and fevered lips of wounded soldiers. Others hurried to headquarters, before the dead had all been buried, whimpering and whining even to tears about the timber cut for breastworks, or the fence rails used to cook their defenders' meals, and wanting to know how they were to get their pay for them; as well as for the trampled wheat where there had been such agonizing struggle in defense of our common country during those bloody hours."[170]

"*J.R.D.,*" special correspondent for the Philadelphia *Daily Evening Bulletin*: "[Let] me make it a matter of undeniable history that the conduct of the majority of the male citizens of Gettysburg and the surrounding county of Adams, is such as to stamp them with dishonor and craven hearted meanness. I do not speak hastily, I but write the unanimous sentiments of the whole army—an army which now feels that the doors from which they drove a host of robbers, thieves and cut-throats were not worthy of being defended. The actions of the people of Gettysburg are so sordidly mean and unpatriotic, as to engender the belief that they were indifferent as to which party was whipped."

Lieutenant Robert S. Robertson, 93rd New York Infantry: "It was evidently a flourishing village, but I can't say much in favor of its inhabitants....Most of the rest left their homes, and many are coming back today only to find their houses in ruins, or else used as hospitals. Those who staid home are trying to make up for what they lost by the battle in exorbitant prices for food sold to the soldiers. They are a miserly crew, and have no souls or conscience where a penny is concerned. Some took the pumps out of their wells, and others charged the soldiers for the privilege of drawing water. I paid a dollar and a half for a small loaf of bread which could be bought in New York for 8 cents, and everything else they offered for sale was in like proportion. I heard one man grumbling because the army had used his rails to build rifle pits. Another had a dead mule in his door yard and wanted pay for burying it. Another presented to a Quartermaster a bill for 37 1/2 cents for a few bricks knocked off his chimney by a shell. For a joke, he was rendered from one to another without success, until at last he got to Maj. Gen. [Oliver O.] Howard, who had lost an arm in the service. The General, tapping his empty sleeve, said—'My friend, give it to your country, as I did this.' The old man left him quite dissatisfied, and the last I heard of him, he was still looking for the right man to pay the bill."[171]

Lieutenant Frank A. Haskell, 2nd Division, Second Corps: After viewing many early visitors on the field and how they greedily walked off with every piece of government property they could find, Haskell uttered: "I could now understand why soldiers had been asked a dollar for a small strip of old linen to bind their own wounds, and not be compelled to go off to the hospitals."[172]

General Marsena R. Patrick, Provost Marshal General, Army of the Potomac: "Came back to Head Quarters, thoroughly disgusted with the whole Copperhead fraternity of Gettysburg & the county about..."[173]

Lieutenant Benjamin F. Rittenhouse, Battery D, 5th United States Artillery: "It was about four o'clock in the afternoon of the 2d of July, when the Fifth

Army Corps commenced to move from near Rock Creek bridge to the left. While we were crossing a field, an old farmer approached me and said: 'I say mister, won't you all go and fight on somebody else's ground' It is needless to say that we did not accommodate him; I suppose he was an Adams County, Pennsylvania Dutchman, the meanest of all the mean men the Army of the Potomac ever met."[174]

Captain Dunn Brown, 14th Connecticut Infantry: "Our boys came back out of Pennsylvania with no very exalted opinion of the German inhabitants of that portion of the state....The people seem to be utterly apathetic as to our great national struggle, and careless of everything but their own property."[175]

Private Lewis M. Creveling, 149th Pennsylvania Infantry: "If the people of Southern Penna used the rebs no better than what they did us I think they would have left before our army arrived. We were treated just as good again in Maryland as we was while in Adams County, Pa. In Md we could get all the butter we wanted for 12 cts [cents] per lb, bread 18 & 25 cts a loaf, pies 10 cts, milk 5 cts a canteen ful and in many places they would take nothing. In Pa at every house would be 2 or 3 Dutch women with great loads of bread Butter Pies & milk, Bread 50 cts, Butter 25, Pies 25, milk 20 cts. They don't know enough to appreciate American Liberty. I would not [have] cared a dam if the Greybacks would had taken half of the dutch Sarpents to richmond."[176]

"Vox Populi," unknown correspondent, Lancaster *Daily Express*, July 6, 1863: "Here is a farmer who has twelve stray cows, all of which he had milked daily, in addition to his own, whose farm and crops have been protected from the hands of the despoiler, by the blood of the slain, and whose barn is filled with two hundred bleeding, dying patriots. Does he give them milk when they ask and plead for it? Yes. At *five* cents a pint! Does he give them *one* loaf of bread when they have saved for him *ten thousand?* Yes. At *forty* cents a loaf. Here is another who has been driven from his home by the invading hosts, who bought tobacco at eight cents a plug, and sells it to the wounded at fifteen. Bought letter paper at a cent per sheet, and taking advantage of their misfortune, sells it to the disabled at five—all this because they have unfortunately fell defending his home. They seem to be proud of the opportunity, and laugh at their cunning in counting their gains—it is *not* cunning, it is something *less* than duplicity.

This is sufficient to dampen the patriotism of any soldier....."

Here is one last thought from a Confederate. While on the invasion into Pennsylvania, this young infantry captain belonging to the 47th North Carolina remarked that he had often heard from Yankees he had met that the "people in that part of Pa., were the most cowardly in the world, which allegation may possess some truth in it..." Furthermore, he explained, the Rebels were very often *welcomed* in that section of the state, by the citizens, and most of them "expressed joy at the appearance of our army and many an old dutch lady said our comming would keep her old man and son out of the militia, which was called out by the Governor at our approach..."[177]

The idea that the Confederate army was welcomed in Pennsylvania as related by the captain may seem a bit far-fetched. But, unfortunately, there were local people who appeared happy to see the Rebel forces and actually assisted them in their pursuits. One of the former paid dearly for his actions, as seen in a news article published in the Gettysburg *Compiler*, February 8, 1864, but extracted from the Carlisle *Democrat* of Carlisle, Pennsylvania:

To be shot

A man named Isaac Fishel, a citizen of York county, was brought to Carlisle Barracks, on Saturday inst., under sentence of death, by court martial. Fishel was tried at Chambersburg, some days since, upon the charges of desertion, and of piloting Fitz Hugh Lee through York county, last summer and sentenced to be shot at this post. We understand he will be executed on the 18th last.

It is now stated that the sentence has been commuted to ten years imprisonment in the penitentiary of this State, or such other place as may be directed by competent authority.

All of the above quoted individuals would not have been surprised to find that even 25 years after the battle the stigma attached to many of the good citizens of Adams County and Gettysburg had not changed. The following was taken from a visiting correspondent of the *National Tribune* on July 5, 1888.

Gettysburg is a beautiful place, but most of the people are mighty queer. They were scattered so by the three days' fight that they hid in their cellars while the battle was going on. It had a depressing effect upon them, from which they seem never to have recovered. Ask a sarcastic visitor what the people do for a living, and they will answer: "Nothing. They live on the people who come here. They sell pretended relics and poor photographs. They take borders during the celebration days, and thus they get a revenue which seems to satisfy them."

The town is rather a poor place for the accomodation of such vast crowds of visitors as resort here on occasions like the present, [25th Anniversary of the battle] and the extortionate charges for board, carriages, and other necessaries, is outrageous. When you come to reflect that the battlefield covers an area of ground of 25 [square] miles, it will be seen that carriages are a very necessary institution in getting about. But they put up the tariff to such an extent that it would make a Niagara Falls hackman turn green with envy.

Indeed, these accounts present an altogether unpleasant indictment of the area and its citizenry.

"The woods are full of them"

IV

PRISONERS OF WAR,
STRAGGLERS,
AND DESERTERS

"Lee was repulsed—his panting, shattered, bleeding ranks were compelled to retire."

> Wm. P. Wilkin, Captain, 1st West Virginia Cavalry

"The number of colors and prisoners taken by us was really astonishing, hosts of the latter coming within our lines and giving themselves up."[1]

To clearly understand the prisoner of war issue during the Civil War we are fraught with two problems. One is the fact that the subject is still, even to this day, filled with sectional emotions and recriminations. Questions often crop up as to which side was the most brutal to its captives, or who operated the worst prison camps; and number two is that even after 130 years the available source material on hand and convenient to historians is inadequate at best, and is ofttimes both confusing and contradictory.

In this chapter we will treat the roles and concerns of the prisoners of Gettysburg with broad generalities. Topics included will be the actual numbers captured, when, if, and how some were paroled, where these captives were sent; then finishing out with a few personal and individual experiences. Likewise, we will observe what happened to the hundreds of POWs who remained on the field after the battle, and some discussion will be directed toward Union and Confederate stragglers and deserters who were marooned in Pennsylvania during or after the retreat or who remained of their own accord.

During the War of the Rebellion which was fought between 1861 and 1865, approximately 212,000 Northerners and 463,000 Southerners were captured in battles, sieges, skirmishes and naval engagements. Of these, 194,743 Federals and 214,865 Confederates were confined in military prisons. And of those who actually went to prison, around 30,000 Yankee and almost 26,000 Rebel soldiers died in captivity. (One source puts this last number at 30,716; 5,569 died of wounds, and 23,591 of disease.) The balance was released "on the field" or paroled on the spot. The best estimates claim that 12 percent of the prisoners in Federal hands died and that 15.5 percent of the captives in Confederate prisons died. By all accounts and according to many researchers, the North could have prevented many deaths in prison camps due to its wealth of medicines and the abundance of food and doctors.[2]

Prisoners

When the Battle of Gettysburg ended, both sides were found to have secured almost an equal number of prisoners. The Confederate Army of Northern Virginia reported the capture of 5,182 Unionists, although Lee once said the figure was between 6 and 7,000. Meade's Army of the Potomac had succeeded in taking from the ranks 5,150 of Lee's men, all *unwounded*. There have been, and will continue to be other estimates claimed, but in good faith we shall accept these figures for our purposes.

Colonel H.C. Alleman of the 36th Pennsylvania Militia Regiment, a ninety-day "emergency" unit sent to Gettysburg following the clash, was authorized to forward to the rear all wounded and prisoners, and to gather property from the field. In his report he collected many tons of the latter, as well as 12,061 injured Union soldiers in camps and field hospitals, and 6,197 similarly wounded Rebels, plus *3,006 Southern unwounded prisoners and "large numbers of stragglers."*[3] This last figure *may need to be added* in the future to the usual Confederate prisoner total that General Meade made public.

In the same vein, a correspondent for the Lancaster *Daily Express* visited the headquarters of the provost marshal general in Gettysburg on the evening of July 8, 1863. There he was told that up to that date, 11,000 C.S. prisoners had been taken, both wounded and uninjured, and that *no* artillery had been captured from the enemy so far.

Of the more than 5,000 Confederates who were seized during the battle, meaning those captured under combat conditions but *not* wounded, almost all ended up in Northern prison camps. Let us recall again that the total numbers of wounded and unwounded prisoners totaled in October 1863 as cited by General Patrick the provost marshal, was 12,867 enlisted men and 754 officers. But of the more than 5,000 Union men netted by the Southerners in the battle, somewhere between only 3,500 and 3,800 were committed to Southern prison pens, although several Confederate accounts place the sum that marched to Virginia as 4,000. Why so?

It is believed that the reason for this disparity is that approximately 1,500 U.S. prisoners were paroled *on the field* by General R.E. Lee's officers, and only the remainder were taken to the South. Of course, Lee ordered all the wounded Federals that he had captured left behind in his own field hospitals around Gettysburg. So it is necessary to eventually only tabulate the unknown numbers of Yankees who escaped the clutches of the Rebels while on their retreat from Pennsylvania, a sum unlikely to ever be arrived at.[4]

Included in these POW figures should be added several civilians taken as hostages for various reasons by the Confederates and who made the long walk to Virginia and were detained in miscellaneous prisons, but ended up at a holding camp in Salisbury, North Carolina. Although some names are incomplete, they were: J. Crawford Guinn or Gwinn; Alexander Harper of Greenmount, Pennsylvania; George Codori who died of pneumonia three days after his return in March of 1865; Emanuel G. Trostle; a "young Warner;" William Harper (Alexander's father) who died at Salisbury prison; "Mr. McCreary," postmaster at Fairfield, Pennsylvania; Samuel M. Pitzer; George Patterson and George Arendt. All, it is believed, returned home by the end of the war, except William Harper. Mr. Trostle, who was partially crippled came home in 1865 "feeling better than ever before."[5]

Surprisingly, some paroles were issued by General Lee even with the knowledge that his adversary General Meade would refuse to acknowledge them. As a matter of record, at 6:35 a.m. on July 4, 1863, Lee sent a message to Meade by flag of truce proposing an exchange of prisoners to be, "made at once," he said, "to promote the comfort and convenience of the officers and men captured by the opposing armies in the recent engagements...." Meade responded at 8:25 a.m. that, "it is not in my power to accede to the proposed arrangement."[6]

There was no reply from Lee, as he was in no position to argue the situation due to his perilous status at that moment. Meade may have desired to make an exchange, but he was bound by a general order which had been issued in September 1862 (G.O. #142) and had originated from a prisoner of war cartel arranged between General J.A. Dix, U.S.A. and General D.H. Hill, C.S.A. in July of that year. Known as the "Dix-Hill Cartel," this order stated that prisoner exchanges, by agreement, could only take place at Aiken's Landing, James River, Virginia, or at Vicksburg on the Mississippi River. It lasted only about a year, and was soon dissolved due to various disagreements between the parties. President Lincoln decided however, to adhere to this agreement, as he felt that paroles for the "convenience of the captor," should not be honored as in the case of Lee at Gettysburg.

Another directive which was in effect on July 3, 1863, was General Order No. 207 which had been issued through General Henry W. Halleck from the U.S. Secretary of War. This order declared that paroles and exchanges were to be regulated and enforced as above, but were not necessarily or absolutely forbidden. As it was explained by the Confederates to the Union captives at Gettysburg, anyone paroled on the field would be sent directly into Union lines at Carlisle, Pennsylvania, but they were warned that these parolees may not be accepted by the U.S. Government, which meant that the men would be returned directly to their regiments or batteries.

Due to this aforementioned compromise, an interesting local situation developed on the Gettysburg battlefield. A group of Federal captives encamped west of the town on July 3, were tantalized with the prospects of a parole by one of Lee's representatives. A prisoner and member of this assemblage was Private Roland E. Bowen, 15th Massachusetts, who recorded the scene as it unfolded:

> In the course of the day the Major in command of us read an order or rather an offer to us from General Lee offering any or all of us a parole if we desired. At this same time stateing that the Federal Government had issued an order prohibiting the recognition of any parole given on the battle field....
>
> Now this was a bumper. Many of the boys had not had any thing to eat for two days and were willing to do any thing to get out of that. Another says, but our Government won't recognize the parole and will put us in the ranks again, then if "Bob" catches us he will give us Hell. And so the argument went on....Finally it was proposed to leave it to General [Charles K.] Graham (who was a prisoner too). He at once advised us not to take any parole as it had been forbidden by the Government; this ended the "conflab."[7]

Bowen added that some of the men chose to take the parole anyway; he personally and foolishly, as he remembered, did not and spent more than four miserable months in dreary Belle Island prison at Richmond. General Graham, a brigade commander in the Third Corps, had been captured near the "peach orchard," and was later exchanged for General James Kemper of Pickett's Division.

In an experience similar to Bowen's, a member of the 157th New York, Jonathan W. Boynton, was taken in battle by Southern troops along the Carlisle Road about one-half mile north of the square in Gettysburg. He was then marched about three quarters of a mile to the Confederate rear, to a brick house along the same road (probably the Samuel Cobean farm), which was a collecting point for prisoners. There he and 1,500 other Union men awaited their fate. He said these men were soon joined by approximately 3,500 others. Boynton recalled that on July 3 they walked five miles further up the Carlisle Road where they were informed that paroles would be issued to those who chose to take them. One thousand men jumped at the offer, claimed Boynton; he did not, because prior to the campaign the soldiers were read a general order that declared that no paroles would be accepted by the U.S. Government. Therefore he and the remaining men were sent off to Virginia. Boynton disclosed later that he regretted his decision while "languishing in a southern prison."[8]

One of the infantrymen to accept the parole offered on the Carlisle Road was an unnamed member of the 14th Brooklyn. After being captured, he and about 75 men of his regiment were marched two miles past the enemy rear areas on July 1, to the headquarter site of General A.P. Hill, Lee's Third Corps' commander. Hill was described as "a man of middle age and medium size [and who] was dressed in a suit of gray clothes and could not, by his dress, be very readily distinguished from those around him." The general gave them the option to be paroled. The men were then divided into squads according to their regiments (there were about 2,000 prisoners in the group), and to accept parole had only to "answer as their names were called." They then pledged, "not to bear arms against the Confederate government until they were honorably released from the obligation they were about to assume." Ten of the 14th Brooklyn, our subject, and other parolees were placed into the hands of a Georgia regiment who showed good feelings toward their captives. It was at this time that the New Yorkers found out that General George Meade had replaced Hooker as their new commander.

The paroled men were then supplied with two days' provisions and started for Carlisle, Pennsylvania. Upon arrival there it took three hours of waiting before they were admitted into Union lines. From Carlisle these newly freed Federals were transported to Westchester, Pennsylvania, where a camp for paroled prisoners had been established, and where the citizens demonstrated great kindness to the men, making them as comfortable as possible.[9]

In retrospect, it appears that from all of the POW collecting points in the Confederate rear areas at Gettysburg, at least 1,500 U.S. soldiers did accept Lee's offer to be paroled, legal or illegal, dire consequences or not. These men were turned over to Union authorities and marched northward under guard to Carlisle then on to the state capital at Harrisburg. As the parolees moved off, a wounded Federal officer watched the Confederates as they continued to fill more than 500 wagons, ambulances, and other wagons with their wounded, "piled as thick as they could be," and began *their own* retreat southward.[10]

Interestingly, a column of Union parolees was sighted at Harrisburg by a U.S. Sanitary Commission agent Isaac Harris, on Sunday, July 5. He commented in his diary that "2000 paroled prisoners, mostly of the 1st Corps passed through on their way East today, which would seem to indicate that Lee was so hard pressed as to be unable to hold them."[11]

Harris was absolutely right. Lee was indeed "hard-pressed," and the supplies and guards needed to sustain over 5,000 superfluous men would certainly have been a drain on his resources; and not counting the obvious, he was also short of artillery ordnance, was deep in enemy country with the responsibility of saving a beaten and exhausted force which of course, had themselves and their own injured to think of first.

In the ordinary course of events nearly all of the 5,000 plus Confederate prisoners retained by the Northerners did reach Federal military prison camps in the Union states. There they bided their time until paroled, exchanged, or the war came to a close. If exchanged, such as the example made of General Graham, it was through a system that had been established on July 22, 1862. The arrangement regulated that one general could be released for one general, one private for one private, etc., or other various combinations thereof, such as one general for 60 privates, one colonel for 15 privates and so on. General Ulysses S. Grant ended this exchange structure in April 1864, because he believed it was a great disadvantage to the North, who unlike the South, could replace its losses more easily.

General Robert E. Lee, commander of the Army of Northern Virginia. (JAR)

The Southern captives taken at Gettysburg were quickly marched to Westminster, Maryland, then on to Baltimore or Washington by rail, and then finally transported by train to a great variety of prison pens, such as Fort Delaware, Delaware; Fort McHenry, Maryland; Point Lookout, Maryland; Fort Warren, Massachusetts; Rock Island, Illinois; Elmira, New York; Camp Morton, Indiana; Camp Douglas, Illinois; Camp Lafayette, New York; Camp Chase and the Ohio Penitentiary, Columbus, Ohio; Alton, Illinois; Old Capitol Prison, D.C.; and Johnson's Island, Ohio.

Ironically, on July 19 U.S. Secretary of War Stanton and General-in-Chief Halleck personally selected the site for a new prison camp at Point Lookout, Maryland, which would eventually hold 10,000 Confederates. This additional room helped substantially in alleviating the problem of overcrowding in many other prisons.[12]

A report made in October 1863 allocated most of the Confederate captives from the Gettysburg Campaign in prisons as follows:

Prison camp	Officers	Enlisted Men
Fort Delaware, DE	417	7,244
DeCamp General Hospital, NY	65	2,472
West's Building Hospital, Baltimore, MD	51	632
U.S. General Hospital, Chester, PA	83	1,049
U.S. General Hospital, Gettysburg, PA	112	1,235
U.S. General Hospital, Harrisburg, PA	14	111
U.S. General Hospital, Frederick, MD	12	124

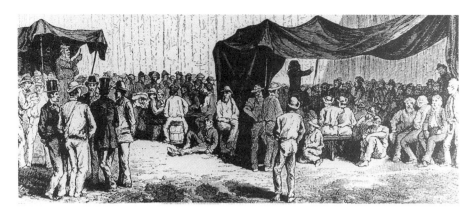

Confederate prisoners at Fort Delaware. (PCW)

The total number of Confederates placed in Federal custody during the Civil War and eventually in the *major* prisons was 175,496, of which 23,213 died. Some miscellaneous sites were: Newport News, Virginia; Louisville, Kentucky; Ship Island, Mississippi; St. Louis, Missouri; Camp Butler, Illinois; Hart's Island, New York; and New Orleans, Louisiana.

Surprisingly, by September 21, 280 of the captives at Fort Delaware had already enlisted into the U.S. service to fight Indians in the western territories, and a number of ex-Confederates who had taken the oath of allegiance were found to be employed in the city of Philadelphia.[13] By the end of 1865 almost 6,000 Southern captives chose the perils of frontier service to the cheerless confinement of Northern prison camps.

The numbers of Rebel prisoners at all points varied naturally, according to the month or year. But as an example, on September 8, 1863, the Adams *Sentinel* confirmed that there were in the vicinity of 27,000 Confederate prisoners then in captivity in nine camps and "other places." Names and totals given in the article were, Fort Delaware with 11,000; David's Island, New York, 3,000; Camp Douglas, Illinois, 3,270; Johnson's Island, Ohio, 1,683; and Camp Chase, Ohio, 2,000.

As to the 5,200 Union men captured by the Southern army at Gettysburg, it was estimated that approximately 2,500 were marched south to Williamsport, Maryland. There they were ferried or waded across the Potomac, then passed through Martinsburg, Winchester, and finally to Staunton, Virginia. In Staunton, rail cars were provided, and within a few weeks all of the captives were taken to Richmond.

Not all Yankee prisoners of war stayed long enough to reach Winchester or Staunton. Many escaped along the route or even before the march began. An early attempt at freedom was made by Benjamin Worth, 16th Maine Infantry. He was captured on July 1 on Oak Ridge and was ordered to join a work detail the next day carrying discarded muskets off the field. By July 3 he had gained entrance into a Rebel field hospital where he accessed some bloody bandages and bound up an imaginary leg wound. When the withdrawal began, Worth pretended to be unable to march so was left behind. He soon successfully made his way back into Union lines.[14]

In one communication, General John D. Imboden, who was in charge of Lee's retreating 17- to 20-mile long train of wounded, said that by July 9, "about 4,000 [U.S.] prisoners taken at Gettysburg were ferried across the river...and I was ordered to guard them to Staunton." (A few Pennsylvania citizens claimed that after counting Lee's wagons they agreed that the entire train was actually 31 miles long.) Imboden's figure appears inflated, but it is confirmed by some other Southern sources. Imboden's route took him from Cashtown to Greenwood, then to New Franklin, Greencastle, Hagerstown, and finally to Williamsport before crossing the Potomac into Virginia.

Initially however, it was the responsibility of General George Pickett's Division for the security of all Northern captives. Writing to a close woman friend about that time, the general confided: "Oh, the pity of it, guarding these prisoners [he confirmed the number at 4,000] through their own country, depleted and suffering mentally and physically as we are, and being forced to march forward with a speed beyond their own and our endurance." Pickett complained of the poor rations he and his captives shared; flour made into paste and baked on hot stones, and beef roasted on a stick. He called further attention to the sad circumstance that the Yankee prisoners seemed much more cheerful than his own men. On the 6th or 7th of July the Federals were turned over to General Imboden by Pickett at Monterey Springs. There the Rebels again offered the hungry captives a chance to accept a parole. Nothing much came of this offer but it was obvious that the Confederates did not want to feed and guard these cumbersome numbers any longer—it was simply too much of a drain on supplies and manpower.[15]

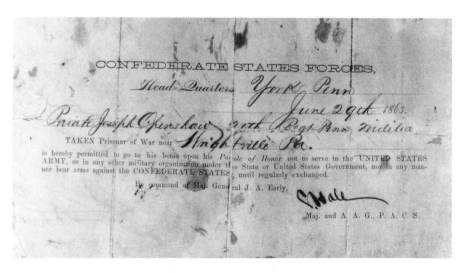

The Pennsylvania militiaman who received this parole was probably very happy to get it. (DST)

Once at Richmond a final disposition and distribution was made of the captives. Some remained at the Confederate capital, mainly the majority of the officers. In the city itself the Federals were quartered at Libby, Ligon's, Castle Thunder or similar converted tobacco factories or warehouses. At Richmond too was Belle Isle, a POW camp in the middle of the James River comprised of several acres of tents and occupied by enlisted men only (up to 6,000 at one time). If not confined at Richmond, the prisoners would have been shipped to Petersburg, Danville, or Lynchburg, all Virginia sites, or to Salisbury, North Carolina, Macon and Millen, Georgia, or Charleston, Florence, and Columbia, South Carolina. Since there were more than 150 places in use as military prisons in both the Union and Confederate states, there was an almost endless variety of locales to choose from. There were for instance, other "stockades" at Cahaba, Alabama, and Camp Ford and Camp Groce, Texas. Plus a large camp was eventually opened at Andersonville, Georgia, named Camp Sumter, in February 1864 to help ease the overcrowding in other prisons throughout the South.

According to figures released in November 1863, by the 18th of that month Union troops were dispersed in several Confederate prisons in Virginia, and these included some of the men taken during the Gettysburg Campaign. Those camps were:

Libby Prison	
(all commissioned officers)	1,044
Crew's Prison	453
Pemberton's Prison	1,115
Smith's Prison	928
Scott's Prison	1,082
Belle Isle	6,300
Hospitals	728
TOTAL	11,650[16]

◆ ◆ ◆

Collecting Confederate Stragglers

All along the Confederate withdrawal routes from the battlefield of Gettysburg, hundreds of stragglers from Robert E. Lee's army were picked up during the month of July by elements of the main Federal army, Pennsylvania and New York militia forces, and even armed civilians. Many of these lost, misdirected, or deserting Rebels were also rounded up north of the town and northwest toward and into the mountains. The number usually found quoted in newspapers even as early as Saturday, July 4 was "upwards of eleven hundred stragglers" corralled by Union patrols. Of course, this was not counting the thousands of battle captures or the many wounded who had fallen into Federal hands in the three days previous.

In one curious but not unusual instance, not only did Union troops take a captive, they also recovered his plundered loot. In the August 3 Gettysburg *Compiler*, this notice read:

An Owner Wanted

A Silver Plated Tea Urn and Pitcher taken...from a rebel prisoner and susposed to have been stolen from some citizen of Adams, Franklin, Cumberland, or York counties, have been left in my hands to be reclaimed by the owner, who can have the same by proving property and paying cost of advertising.

July 27, 1863	J.R. Welsh Waynesboro, Pa.

In the town of Gettysburg itself and nearby, scores of bewildered, drunk or uncaring Southerners were easily overhauled. These demoralized, helpless and unfortunate beings were abandoned or had sneaked away, and were the normal "flotsam and jetsam" of a great army which was in partial disarray at that moment. Inside the town limits on July 4 along Baltimore Street, occurred a sample of these activities. Mr. James Pierce, who lived nearby, picked up a discarded musket when the Rebels fled, and went through his neighborhood collecting stragglers and "deserters." He netted four or five before he noticed that the weapon he so boldly brandished about was empty.

And on the same morning in another instance, Charles Tyson of Gettysburg saw a Southern soldier coming out of his house on York Street carrying a stolen overcoat. Tyson pronounced that the Reb had "overslept himself," and was promptly arrested.[17]

A pertinent comment worth mentioning here has come down from a surgeon who was engaged in caring for an injured officer in Gettysburg. He was Dr. Robert Hubbard and from a window overlooking Baltimore Street on July 9 he witnessed this: "While I have been writing a squad of about 200 rebel prisoners passed by & I am told that the woods are full of them."[18] His words rang true, as other commentators agreed with Hubbard's assessment.

Another similar report was written in the personal diary of John B. Linn, Esq. He remarked on July 11 while at Gettysburg that "John Vanderslice [is] here with 12 prisoners ten of them Amish they seemed glad to be taken. Crowds of rebels in the mountains giving themselves up on 1st opportunity."[19]

All the while cavalry units were active in procuring even greater numbers of Southerners and their vehicles and equipment.

For instance, the 1st West Virginia Cavalry (U.S.) with only 100 men made a charge in total darkness on July 4 which was ordered by General Kilpatrick himself. The night lacked the low light of either moon or stars, while heavy black clouds sent down rain at intervals. This blind attack netted 1,200 captives, 1,001 horses and mules, and over two hundred wagons loaded with baggage.[20]

A day later on July 5 near Greencastle, Pennsylvania, a group of 653 officers and men, mainly wounded, were captured by Colonel Lewis B. Pierce, 12th Pennsylvania Cavalry, along with 100 wagons, two cannons, and 300 horses and mules. And on that same day, a 200-man detachment of Union volunteer cavalry cornered a wagon train of 100 vehicles and around 1,000 Southerners all of whom were taken captive. Going back 24 hours, General Judson Kilpatrick's Yankee horsemen surrounded nearly 1,000 Confederates at Monterey Pass above Fairfield. Then less than 12 hours later his men swooped down on a C.S. ambulance and supply train collaring 150 wagons and

1,360 wounded and others. These last were from Ewell's Corps and the incident took place near Smithsburg, Maryland. Shortly afterward 100 more were taken at Leitersburg in the same general area. All of these injured prisoners were shipped directly to hospitals in Frederick. On that same day, Sunday the fifth, the sheriff of Franklin County arrived in Harrisburg and turned in 11 wagons and a group of prisoners captured in his locale.

About this same time Sergeant Andrew Buck of Company F, 7th Michigan Cavalry transcribed in his memoranda book the good news that a part of his regiment had just picked up over 100 wagons and 500 Confederates in "Mountain Dale" pass. Most of the prisoners of war were either sick or wounded, he confirmed.[21]

A spectator to one of these episodes was David Powell of the 3rd West Virginia Infantry (Union) who recorded a curious turn of events in his diary on or about July 5: "Late in the evening we were ordered to Mercersburg, PA. Our cavalry had struck a retreating column of Lee's army & captured 110 wagons, 2,500 horses, & 1,500 of the enemy, near and half of them were wounded & in the wagons. At Mercersburg the wounded were taken out & put in houses for treatment. Those able to march were put in line and I was ordered to command the guard put over them. I marched them back to Franklin & there many of them were paroled & went out to seek work among Pa. farmers."[22]

A witness to this or a similar affair explained that a small force of New York and Pennsylvania (Militia) Cavalry under Captain John W. Jones had encountered an immense train of Rebel ambulances and wounded eleven miles out from Mercersburg on the Hagerstown Road near Cunningham's Tavern. On that day which was July 5, they "pitched into the middle of the train" and "gobbled up" three pieces of artillery, one hundred wagons, three buggies, four hundred mules, one hundred horses, and 747 prisoners, mostly wounded. Forty-eight hours after this event, men of the 71st New York State Militia on their way to Funkstown, Maryland, passed a column of "two or three thousand prisoners." Their colonel cautioned his militiamen to "avoid any demonstration." One soldier said the order was unnecessary for, "[our] hearts were full of sympathy for these hatless, coatless, shoeless and ragged poor fellows."[23]

Three days later in the Clear Spring Valley near Fort Loudon, Pennsylvania, 700 Southerners and 11 wagons were seized. And on that very day a local newspaper warned citizens that "hundreds of Confederate deserters and stragglers" were discarding their uniforms for civilian dress and taking employment in the surrounding farms during the harvests. General D.N. Couch, in his final report issued after the campaign, stated that his troops rounded up 1,341 Confederates, 500 "taken under arms, 400 wounded, and the remainder stragglers and deserters. This does not include quite a number who escaped through the mountains and went north, being aided in this by the citizens."[24]

On July 9 even more straggling Rebels were taken near Chambersburg by a detachment of the 1st New York Cavalry.[25] In like manner, far to the north near Bendersville, Pennsylvania, a clearly very lost supply or ordnance train of 10 wagons and 100 Southern soldiers fell into the hands of a portion of the same New York cavalry unit scouting in Menallen Township, twelve miles above Gettysburg.[26]

Not all of the Confederates who were then being rounded up stayed completely under Yankee control. One who did not was Private Berkeley Minor, captured among a train of wounded that was overtaken by Federal cavalry one wet night. During a heavy rain only minutes after being taken he walked up to a Confederate comrade nearby and "whispered to him that we might easily slip through the fence [along the road] unobserved." Waiting until the guard's back was turned they quickly fled from the road and into the woods. It took a day or two but eventually Minor and his new friend circled around the huge Northern force and regained the rear of General Lee's army. At one point they were helped along by a farmer near Leitersburg, Maryland, who by chance was a Southern sympathizer. His name was David Beck, and Minor recollected he had a "bitter grudge against the Yankees."[27]

The entire region from northern Maryland and across the line into southern Pennsylvania, a front of some 75 to 100 miles long, was then swarming with United States regular and volunteer forces, supported by various and sundry militia and "emergency" units. Most of these troops constituted men under General Couch, and amounted to 7,600 at Waynesboro, 12,000 at Chambersburg, and 6,700 at Mercersburg. All were primarily engaged in nipping at the tail and flanks of Robert E. Lee's long, and thinly spread out trains of commissary supplies and wounded, including their protective screens of cavalry. Reports were in circulation everywhere that the mountains were "thick as fleas" with individual Rebs and small groups of Confederates who had been cut off, misdirected, lost, or abandoned by the fleeing gray columns. These enemy soldiers encompassed groups of men who were concealing their identities as previously discussed. By July 14 the Confederates were well into their crossing of the Potomac River at Falling Waters; there the rear guard of the Army of Northern Virginia lost 2,000 more of their troops in defending that vital escape route, besides 200 sick officers and enlisted men left in Williamsport and other villages close by. From the constant reports of these large groups of prisoners being taken, one might have conceived that Lee's whole army was disintegrating.[28] The fact was, that a segment of these accounts are contradictory and/or redundant. However, no one could deny that the Army of Northern Virginia was losing heavily, and frankly, was somewhat in a dangerous predicament.

By July 30, most of the Southerners captured directly in the Battle of Gettysburg or taken on the retreat, were already in diverse prisons, hospitals, or local jails. Testimony quite often appears in various newspapers of the time, prior to that date, providing the reader with information on the whereabouts of many of these captives. One eyewitness quoted on July 4 was a cavalryman who watched as 3,500 Confederates under guard were filed through Westminster, Maryland. On July 5 a large city newspaper informed its patrons that 2,300 C.S. prisoners of war had been marched from the North Central Railroad Station on Calvert Street in Baltimore to confinement at Fort McHenry.[29]

A day later the New York *Times* printed these comments:

PRISONERS EN ROUTE TO BALTIMORE

Eight hundred and fifty rebel prisoners, largely composed of Alabama troops, captured from Longstreet's corps in Wednesday's fight, arrived here this morning. More prisoners are announced at the depot, and accounts from up the road say there are large trains at various points, on their way down, whilst there are said to be acres of them awaiting transportation.

Twenty-three hundred prisoners have just passed along Baltimore-street from the Northern Central depot, and 190 more are shortly expected, which will make 5,050 for to-day. This is but a small installment, it is said, of all who, are to come. While passing through the streets some parties had the bad taste to raise cheers of triumph, which induced the rebels to give their peculiar yell for JEFF and the Southern Confederacy. In addition to the 5,000, eight hundred and thirty passed through here on Friday night, which will make the entire number, so far, nearly six thousand.

Indeed, it did seem that the totals were increasing. A publication dated July 10 printed a piece commenting that 2,000 prisoners had arrived in Baltimore on the North Central; and on July 24, came the story of another group or possibly the same 2,000 Confederates (the majority were wounded) who were then in New York City and about to be transferred to David's Island in that city's harbor. Earlier the New York *Tribune* of July 5 had printed a forewarning of what was to be expected: "[Many] [p]risoners and guns taken...arrived at Baltimore. Acres of cars laden with prisoners blocked on the railroad."[30]

Back on the local scene, the Gettysburg *Compiler* of July 7 had this to say: "Ever since yesterday week large numbers of rebel stragglers are being brought into our town daily, picked up by our cavalry forces. We learn that quite a large number of them were captured whilst attempting to get away with horses, which they had stolen in the country. We have no doubt the military authorities will give the citizens an opportunity of identifying their horses and reclaiming them."

Even before the type for those sentences was being set a farmer ten miles north of Gettysburg had scribbled in his diary the same day: "Cavalry in Bendersville today. Pickets on our hill [called Liberty Hill in 1863] yesterday and today. Took some 6 or 8 prisoners."[31]

All these captures had another effect, as related by a soldier in one of the pursuing cavalry regiments west of Gettysburg. He jotted this in his diary for July 4: "We have been gathering in prisoners from the rebel army all afternoon. These were sent to the rear in such large numbers that we have but few men left in the regiment. The rest went back as escorts to prisoners. Our camp tonight is at Caledonia Springs."[32]

When one examines these and other similar personal accounts, plus all of the news stories and official reports, we are apt to believe, as noted earlier, that the entire Confederate Army of Northern Virginia had been captured or was in the process of being swept up. Many of these narratives were obviously misinformed, overlapped, or were plainly sensationalized. Notwithstanding, we must not be completely lulled by this knowledge. The plain truth does seem clear: that *thousands* of Lee's men had been roped in, either as verifiable prisoners of war, or as wounded who remained in hospitals near the battlefields around Gettysburg or in places like Chambersburg, Greencastle, Fort Loudon, Mercersburg, McConnellsburg, Frederick, Martinsburg, or anywhere in between. There were also, great numbers of deserters, lost or straggling men, and even small guerilla bands and individuals who remained in the wake of the

Confederate army hoping for a chance for plunder or robbery. When you recall that Lee gave up possibly as many as 24,000 of his troops listed as wounded, missing in action, or prisoners of war, that number is not insignificant. It is important to concede that many of the 7,000 to 8,000 wounded soldiers that Lee *claimed* to have taken back to Virginia, actually did not make it there. Scores were captured in cavalry raids, became lost or were purposely misdirected by civilians or captured by them. It is certain that not a few decided to drop out of the retreat due to physical and mental pain and stress from wounds, or plain exhaustion. And a fair number died along the retreat and were never heard from again.

Examples abound. In a letter to his sister, Chambersburg native Henry Reeves wrote on July 4: "The exciting event of the forenoon was the capture, by citizens near the town, of a dozen wagons, filled with rebel wounded, to the number of forty. These were part of an immense wagon train, of several hundred wagons, which had been moving south today by a road passing through Fayetteville. The wounded men expressed themselves as glad to be taken prisoners; they were tired of the long wagon ride."[33]

A farmer near New Franklin, Pennsylvania, Jacob C. Snyder had his own experience with abandoned soldiers. At about 10:30 p.m. on July 4, he was awakened to find his farmyard filled with injured Confederates who quickly took over a portion of his house. One of his neighbors was having kindred problems. Snyder explained:

> At the same time during the halt the men were [also on the farm of] Mr. Jeremiah W. George. At this place some of the men died and were buried, and others unable to go any further were left with Mr. George [including Lieutenant Colonel B.F. Carter, 4th Texas]. The graves of some that died there can yet be seen along the road; others are farmed over. Among those that were buried was Major [Donald McLeod] of South Carolina [8th South Carolina Infantry]. He was buried close by the well in a beautiful grove, and the grave was marked by a head-board bearing his initials.[34]

A sample of these continued losses comes from a Christian Commission delegate who counted at least 300 wounded Confederates left at Hagerstown and Williamsport, Maryland. This may seem a small number, but when added with others abandoned in the dozen or so villages along the retreat, and at the uncounted farms which parallel the roadsides, the sums do mount up. Another agent of this commission F.F. Shearer, said that there were "several camps" of Rebel prisoners on the Cashtown Road, and all were in a very needy condition, remarking: "As stragglers were picked up day after day, or found wounded lying in remote outbuildings, the necessities of these camps became greater and greater. When we remember that from eight to ten thousand of these prisoners fell into our hands, it will readily be seen that it was no slight task to take care of them."[35]

As these pages are being turned, the reader begins to form a picture of the many poor, tired captives dressed in faded, dirty and ragged blue or gray, many obviously dejected and forlorn, who wearily tramped along on muddy or dusty turnpikes and back roads, forcefully prodded toward some miserable prison camp which was far from comrades in the ranks and friends and family back home. Civilians along these routes of march, some for the first time especially in the north, were getting their first look at an enemy soldier, a real live *REBEL*. To give our own senses an appreciative view of these warriors with that "fresh from the battlefield" appearance about them, we shall look at the accounts of three eyewitnesses who saw first-hand Confederate soldiers who had invaded the United States and were now paying a stiff price for doing so. Artist Edwin Forbes begins with a description of some "just captured" soldiers; men he also sketched as they marched along.

> An hour later [after Pickett's Charge on July 3] the great struggle was over, and intelligence came that the enemy were beaten back with thousands of killed and wounded and a great number taken prisoners. Soon a long column of men were seen coming down the road from the direction of the cemetery. They were unarmed and as they approached it became evident that they were prisoners. The most of them were sturdy fellows dressed in a variety of clothing. Butternut and gray cloth predominated though some were partly clothed in blue uniforms which had probably been stripped from our dead soldiers at Chancellorsville or after some other battle. The officers were generally a fine looking set of men, bearded in most cases with resolute faces and a firm upright carriage, and as they moved along quietly, with the guards riding at each side of the column, one could not but feel a sympathy for [them]. The prisoners numbered several thousand, and they were finally halted in a vacant field about a mile to our rear.[36]

Artist Edwin Forbes sketched these Rebel prisoners on the Baltimore Pike south of Gettysburg on July 3. (EF)

Correspondingly, but not as complimentary was this writer who admitted that the Southerners

> ...[p]hysically...looked about equal to the generality of our own troops, [but] there were fewer boys among them. Their dress was a wretched mixture of all cuts and colors. There was not the slightest attempt at uniformity in this respect. Every man seemed to have put on whatever he could get hold of, without regard to shape or color. I noticed a pretty large sprinkling of blue pants among them....Their shoes, as a general thing, were poor; some of the men were entirely barefooted. Their equipments were light as compared with those of our men. They consisted of a thin woolen blanket, coiled up and slung from the shoulder in the form of a sash, a haversack slung from the opposite shoulder....The whole cannot weigh more than Twelve or fourteen pounds. Is it strange, then, that with such light loads they should be able to make longer and more rapid marches than our men? The marching of the men was irregular and careless;...Their whole appearance was greatly inferior to that of our soldiers.[37]

Lee's line officers were often better uniformed and more resolute than the average infantryman. (GAC)

And there was this, also not very flattering.

> I spend a good deal of time with the prisoners, privates and officers. The privates generally speaking, look most wretched—ragged, torn, bruised, mutilated, dirty. Their dress represents every style and color, butternut cloth, half uniforms, no uniforms, full of mud from the heavy rains. Many of them are miserably ignorant and unable to read or write. They represent almost all the Southern States, including Maryland, and belong to Hill's and Longstreet's divisions....Some of them are intelligent, susceptible of religious impressions....Many admit that the South was too hasty in seceding, and lost more than she could gain.

This composer summed up his piece by observing that some of the officers were, "unanimous in [their] intense hostility to the North, and determined to fight to the last man."[38]

In the preceding account by Edwin Forbes, he mentions a column of Confederates moving past him on the Baltimore Pike late on July 3. These were not the first to move southward, as other prisoners had been sent toward Baltimore as early as July 2. One contributor was Mary Shellman of Westminster, Maryland, who was certain she had seen the "first prisoners" come by, numbering about 500 as they marched through her town on that date.

She counted 1,100 more on July 4 in a single group, and throughout the day smaller squads walked past her house under guard.

Another resident of that Maryland town remembered that a temporary camp for these captives was provided in an open field "on the Fairground Hill, immediately to the left of the turnpike." This gentleman, Mr. J.W. Hering, felt sympathy for them because all were left without shelter standing or sitting in the pouring rain. During one period on the morning of either July 3 or 4, he counted from his window over 100 Confederate captives being "urged along like cattle." "These men," he ascertained, "were captured in battle. Many of them were without hats, some without shoes, clothes tattered and torn and in some instance stained with blood."[39]

Twenty-four hours later, Christian Commission Delegate Andrew Cross was on hand at Westminster and close by the depot. He noticed "a little farther along the track, under guard, stood about 1,000 Confederate prisoners, waiting to enter the cars for Baltimore."[40]

By 5 p.m. on July 3, the provost marshal general of the Union army, General Marsena Patrick, had already designated localities for several depots to be used by prisoners of war. Two days earlier as the battle began on July 1, he had been busy in camp near Taneytown, Maryland "overhauling trains & examining prisoners." At 2 a.m. on July 2 Patrick finally finished interviewing "a great many prisoners," so he moved forward to Gettysburg. At 6 a.m. on that date he established a central depot for Rebel captives, placing Colonel Richard Butler Price and the 2nd Pennsylvania Cavalry in charge. It is believed this depot was somewhere within the Union lines and south of Gettysburg, possibly alongside or adjacent to the Baltimore Pike. The most likely area was east of Meade's headquarters which was then at the Lydia Leister farmhouse on the Taneytown Road. Along about sunset on July 2, General Patrick confided in his diary that Captain William Becksmith of his staff had "found a place where we could keep a few prisoners." When dawn broke on Friday, July 3, General Patrick had over 2,000 Southerners in custody, and before night began sending these prisoners toward Westminster. Near the close of the day, Patrick moved his POW depot to rolling ground near "White Church" on the Baltimore Pike beyond White Run, placing his headquarters temporarily at the nearby bank barn of Aaron Sheely, the only large structure in the vicinity that was not in use as a hospital.

On the fourth he reestablished a "holding pen" near the front, and for the next several days Colonel Price's cavalry was sent out, "on all the roads & over the Battle field, to pick up Stragglers & prisoners, [and] wounded, from the Rebels...." Within two weeks General Patrick estimated that he had collected 1,500 additional prisoners in all; but even as late as August 7 he could write: "[A] large lot of prisoners brought in...."[41]

Confederate Prisoners

What became of most of the battle injured Confederates who were captured and sent directly to hospitals or prison camps is now generally understood. One question does still remain. Just what did happen to the scores of unwounded captives left behind in Gettysburg, or were caught shortly afterwards by roving Northern cavalry, armed civilians or militia? All such detainees eventually joined their comrades in military prisons, some sooner than others. A few of the miscellaneous hundreds taken later than the battle were forced into unpleasant employment on the field itself. These shall be examined further. It is believed that "two camps" were established for prisoners remaining in or near the town after the armies had departed. The locations of these camps have not been positively identified to date, however one citizen named William McClean related how early burial squads were made up of these Rebel soldiers. He specified that when not thus engaged, they "were kept in the jail yard, under guard." This yard was in the southeast section of town on the south side of East High Street across from the Public School, where the old prison building still stands.[42]

Civilian Albertus McCreary recorded in his memoirs the placement of another of these prisoner of war camps in the borough of Gettysburg. He testified that it was in and near a large barn at the "end of their lot," on the southwest corner of Baltimore and High Streets, and "used as a prison for Confederate soldiers; there were four hundred in it at one time." McCreary added: "The barn and yard around it were full of men. For food they gave them boxes of hard tack and water from our pump. This was all they had." After the departure of these Rebels, McCreary pointed out something they left behind. "Graybacks" or lice, thousands of them infested the barn, he said, until it was thoroughly cleaned out and whitewashed.[43]

Small detachments of provost guards were ordered to remain in town to secure the POWs and the battlefield itself, in conjunction with the tons of government ordnance and equipment then being collected from the field. Colonel R.B. Price's 2nd Pennsylvania Cavalry had been the unit initially detailed from the Army's provost marshal contingent to carry out the difficult mission of guarding the field, including all prisoners both wounded and not, and collect stragglers. This regiment was augmented with 100 infantrymen who were ordered to assist them in the herculean task.

On July 6 the 36th Regiment Pennsylvania Militia was added to this insufficient force, with Captain William W. Smith as acting provost

Colonel Richard Butler Price and his 2nd Pennsylvania Cavalry were the first to guard the thousands of Confederate prisoners flocking into Union lines. (USAMHI)

marshal in charge.[44] Smith's entire provost unit, of which more will be written in the next chapter, had an enormous responsibility. Not only were they commanded to collect government supplies, guard the field and its "treasures" from looters and souvenir hunters, and watch over prisoners who were burying the many dead men and horses, but they were also decreed to provide sentries for the numerous hospitals in operation around Gettysburg.

This last duty presented a whole new set of problems. In the main though, it consisted of preventing the Confederate prisoner patients, their assigned nurses and attendants from escaping. A few weeks after the battle one of the women volunteers at Camp Letterman proclaimed that the provost marshal had still not posted guards around the tents of the Rebel soldiers, whom she called, "a poor, degraded, deluded set of men." This nurse, Mrs. Ehler, added that the Confederates were much inferior in education and in cleanliness to the Union soldiers, but were devout Christians and read their bibles often. In her mind, this last quality made them equal to, if not better than, their Federal counterparts. Ehler testified that at the onset the nurses of the Southerners were mostly paroled prisoners. When the general hospital was opened in mid-July, Southern sympathizers flocked in to aid their countrymen. While assisting the wounded Confederates, Ehler noted that these non-Union people "furnished those who were slightly wounded...with citizens' clothes, and that by this means they escaped." After these furtive acts the provost marshal placed sentries at all tents occupied by Rebels and the care of these men came exclusively under the rule of Union nurses and attendants.[45]

Such bold escapes as just reported must have been more common than one might expect. An article concerning a similar venture appeared in the July 20, 1863 issue of the Gettysburg *Compiler*, which read: "We learn that on Thursday night last [July 18], a number of rebels who were connected with the hospitals in this place, managed to get hold of Federal uniforms, arms and horses, and in this disguise made their escape toward Dixie. Whether they succeeded in reaching their destination or not, is a matter of considerable doubt. We hope that they may be 'gobbled up.'

"PS—We understand they have been caught."

Two Southern prisoners who were not retaken and successfully reached home were Sergeant Charles Jones and Private Thomas C. Paysinger, both members of the 3rd South Carolina. While in residence at Camp Letterman in September they made a bid for freedom by asking to visit the grave of a "deceased brother" in the camp cemetery. Under this pretense Jones and Paysinger gained access to the burial grounds, and as soon as the sentinel turned his back they "jumped the fence into the woods and made the escape." These two intrepid fellows travelled down into Maryland and on to Richmond, Virginia, then eventually all the way to Columbia, South Carolina.[46]

Like many patriotic folks in Gettysburg, Mary Arnold Horner was unhappy with Southern sympathizers and the knowledge that they were allowed to bring in, "carloads of luxuries to their friends, and that there was no disposition to give a share to Uncle Sam's boys." She underscored too that "[s]ometimes...they brought citizen's clothing to enable their prisoners to escape, and if I am not mistaken, one surgeon was arrested with three or four suits of clothing on his person, conveying them to the College Hospital for this purpose."[47]

Liberty A. Hollinger had a duplicate reminiscence; except in this case she inadvertently aided the enemy. It began when four women from Baltimore boarded at her house for a few days after the battle. At the time no one believed that they were anything but good Northern people visiting wounded Federal soldiers. Hollinger depicted them as, "very delightful ladies and were well supplied with money. They spent [their time] out on the field and in the hospitals where the Confederate wounded were. We did not suspect their intentions at first, but when they began to try to buy up men's civilian clothes, and even women's clothing, we began to understand what they were about. As soon as my father learned what their real mission was, he insisted that mother must send them away."[48]

Confederates were still frequently able to escape, even without the help of others. One who successfully "flew the coop" was Lieutenant Thomas L. Norwood of the 37th North Carolina. Affectionately called "Big Tom," Norwood had been shot through the left shoulder, was captured, and ended up in the field hospital at Pennsylvania College. Finding no guards present, he garbed himself in an "academic gown" and walked away to the west in order to overtake his fleeing comrades. Norwood climbed over South Mountain where he met a farmer who offered to assist him. At the man's house Norwood shed his bloody uniform and dressed in laborer's clothes, and continued walking to Waynesboro where he ran directly into Union patrols. Pretending to be a local farm worker, Norwood was able to slip through enemy lines on July 9 and on to General Richard S. Ewell's headquarters. On the morning of July 10 "Big Tom" breakfasted with his commanding general, Robert E. Lee, and while so engaged passed on valuable information concerning the positions of Federal troops he had eluded on his week's adventure.[49]

The concerns of the citizens of Gettysburg began to be felt as more and more Confederates were seen wandering around in their midst. As their wounds healed some Southerners were able to walk about, and many of them even while still in U.S. hospitals were given temporary passes. This freedom was extended even though the threat existed for "unauthorized flights" from captivity.

One of the men fortunate enough to obtain a military pass was Lieutenant James F. Crocker of the 9th Virginia Infantry who had been wounded and captured on July 3 and brought to the U.S. Twelfth Corps hospital. While there he received permission to visit Gettysburg to order and to purchase a new uniform. Crocker had graduated from Gettysburg's Pennsylvania College in 1850, and was easily able to spend the entire day in the familiar town visiting old friends, college professors, and even a former "sweetheart;" and he finally did get around to finding a new suit of clothes. While standing on one of the borough streets talking to an acquaintance, Crocker was tapped on the shoulder by his old mathematics teacher, who kindly asked the lieutenant in a whisper not to talk about the war! The whole scene can hardly be imagined. It is one of those unique moments in history where nothing seems to make sense, yet it all falls into place like a comfortable puzzle—just one more instance of the absurdity of war, especially a civil war.[50]

Lieutenant Crocker was not the only Rebel thus privileged. Another similarly entitled person was Henry K. Douglas, a staff officer detailed to the

Confederate Second Corps. He too had been shot in the left shoulder like Lieutenant Norwood above, and was evacuated to a C.S. field hospital on the Henry and Charlotte Picking farm northwest of Gettysburg. Shortly thereafter Douglas fell into the hands of the Yankees, was paroled, and taken to the Lutheran Seminary to recuperate where he shared quarters with Generals Isaac Trimble and James Kemper, Charles E. Grogan A.D.C. and Colonel Robert M. Powell of the 5th Texas Infantry. Captain Douglas had friends in the area as well; he had graduated from Franklin and Marshall College in nearby Lancaster, Pennsylvania, in 1859. Douglas however, unlike Crocker, was forced to "sneak" a bit in order to leave his room at the Seminary Hospital. While in confinement he made friends with two local women, who had become great favorites of the Confederates because they treated the incarcerated Southern patients no different from

Confederate officer Henry K. Douglas had enjoyable experiences while a prisoner of war at Gettysburg. (HKD)

the Union men. In his memoir Douglas demonstrated how he often slipped out of the hospital, "...on occasional nights, when Dr. [A.J.] Ward was conveniently absent or not visible I would stroll with [the women] to make visits in the town, the [Confederate military rank] on the sleeve of my uninjured arm being artfully concealed by some little female headgear which I was directed to carry just that way, and marching between the sisters...we generally landed at Duncan's [possibly a tavern] and made an evening of it. It never seemed to occur to them that they were harboring a Rebel; and nothing occurred to me except their graciousness and attractiveness."[51]

The problem of these roaming Southerners did not go unnoticed. Complaints must have been lodged with the provost marshal and with the medical authorities, because on October 8, 1863, several comments and recommendations were made to Surgeon Henry Janes in a letter headed "York District Headquarters:"

"Surgeon Janes

"I am directed...to call your attention to the fact that Rebel Prisoners both officers & men were allowed to visit Gettysburg upon passes issued by you. It is reported that Rebel officers have been seen in town as late as 11 o'clock P.M. in company with females.

"It is not deemed conducive to the best interest of the service to grant such permits...."[52]

There are also good accounts available of soldiers who made several varieties of "escapes," not only from Federal authorities and eventual prison but from Confederate service as well. Here are two illustrations.

This first is an interesting narrative which came from a Gettysburg newspaper. It is the story of Private William Cranford who, as the paper denoted, "...deserted the Confederate army here, and was hidden by a farmer named Kuhns, in the Irishtown [Pennsylvania] area. When the armies went south Cranford remained here, worked as a carpenter and eventually married a young lady from the New Chester area, Miss Mary Spangler, daughter of George and Ninetta (Wolf) Spangler."

It seems that Cranford died in an accident in 1890 and was buried in the Spangler section of the New Chester cemetery. Left with four children his wife Mary soon remarried, this time to an ex-Union soldier named James Frederick.

What happened to William Cranford must have been more common than one would first be inclined to believe. Liberty A. Hollinger accented in her own memoirs that "[m]any romances were developed during the stay of the soldiers in Gettysburg. One of our most intimate girl friends married a southerner whom her mother had nursed back to health and happy life. A number of the young ladies were wedded to boys they learned to love while kindly ministering to them."[53] War and society's mores aside, the mere color of a uniform has not always deterred such affairs of the heart.

This next story is definitely a classic and may not have been possible except in our civil war. Nurse Anna M. Holstein here first summarized the situation in her reminiscences of service at Camp Letterman: "We found, in the rebel wards, the son of a former Secretary of State of New Hampshire, a conscript from Georgia; his life had been repeatedly threatened by them, if he dared to leave, or if he admitted he was a Union man." Shortly after, when most of the Confederate officers in his area of the camp were sent off to prison this "Yankee conscript" George Hadley made his identity known to the hospital staff, insisting that he would take his own life rather than leave the hospital as a Rebel prisoner. In Holstein's summary the young man was soon allowed to take the oath of allegiance at Letterman where he remained as a clerk. When his injury was healed enough to permit travel Hadley was sent home.

Except for Holstein's account, little else would have been known of this rare incident. However, a letter has recently surfaced which tells more of the story. It was written to the surgeon-in-charge of all hospitals at Gettysburg, Henry Janes, just as Camp Letterman was being closed forever. It is such an unusual tale that most of that correspondence will be quoted as written:

South Weare, N.H.
November 22, 1863

Dear Sir,
    I take the liberty of writing you a few lines about my son George L. Hadley now a prisoner of war at Gettysburg.
    I have made application to the Com[missary] Gen[eral] of Prisoners at Washington for his release on his taking the oath of allegiance, but the Department do not see fit at present to grant my request, but I am in hopes before long they will do so. I presume he has made you acquainted with the circumstances under which he went to the south, and how he was under the necessity of entering the rebel service.

I trust he will not be compelled to be exchanged, but may be permitted to remain within the union lines, and if possible away from the other rebel prisoners. He has written me of the kindness manifested towards him by yourself and other union surgeons....

...I have further to ask, that if he is not released before the hospital at Gettysburg is broken up, that you will continue to exert your influence in his favor. He has always been a kind and dutiful son. For more than two years we were cut off from all communication with him & now [he is] providentially left within our lines, it seems hard that he cannot be permitted to return and visit the home of his youth, his mother, sisters and brothers whom he has not seen for over four years. But we will wait in hope and confidence that in due time he will be restored to us....

Very respectfully,
Your obt. servant,
John L. Hadley[54]

As it is often said, if only we knew the rest of the story.

Deserters and Depredations

Stragglers, deserters, or those "absent from their commands without leave" were a major concern for both armies. In the next few paragraphs the problems caused by these men shall be examined, with the main emphasis on the Confederate army, principally because it was the aggressor and in enemy country. Moreover, it is not the intention of this section to overlook the same aspect within the Union forces, where straggling and absence without proper leave was at least as bad and often more of a troublesome situation.

Many of the 160,000 Federal and Confederate soldiers present throughout the six-to-eight-week campaign in Maryland and Pennsylvania committed many and varied depredations on the local populace. Of that fact there is not a shadow of a doubt. Vandalism, thievery, looting, drunkenness, and other forms of misconduct were and always will be a by-product of war, and wherever a military campaign is conducted these antisocial problems will most definitely occur.

Comments such as the following can be quite easily found throughout the annals and literature of the Gettysburg Campaign:

> The farms everywhere suffered the loss of oats, horses and cattle and etc. Horses were generally run off to the mountains, but the rebel cavalry have been scouring all the retreats so far as they could and have taken a great many. Some farmers were injured to the extent of thousands of dollars, through various stealing and destruction of fences and wasting of crops. Horses were sometimes turned into wheatfields. Cherry trees were cut down by the rebels to get the cherries, or the branches were lopped off. Orchards were destroyed; searches were made in farmhouses for hidden goods or for money. Clocks were taken as well as goods and money. Dishes were often broken through mere wantoness, and even the clock on the mantelpiece. One woman in the country had the dress she wore cut by them into strips. Feather-beds were ripped open and their contents scattered on the ground. A body calling themselves Independent

Rangers, and were responsible to no power higher than themselves, have been committing great depredations in the south-western part of the county, about Welsh Run.[55]

Of course, much has been made over General Lee's famous General Order #72 issued June 21, 1863, and with good reason. The instructions prohibited unprincipled acts of destruction and stealing while in Northern territory, and overall the "letter" of the order was fairly successfully complied with.[56] But Lee was no more adept at totally containing the ruthless nature of humanity than any other commander in history, and hundreds, even thousands of instances of disobedience to G.O.#72 were recorded by army participants and by civilians in their paths.

In the Chambersburg area, which was the very center of Lee's rear echelon activities, Jacob Hoke who was a respected and well thought of merchant underscored that although he could not be everywhere among the Rebels, he personally witnessed no cases of drunkenness. There were examples to be found, naturally. Hoke, himself, transcribed the findings of a military court-martial which

General Lee's Order #73 issued six days after #72 was copied by Dr. J.W.C. O'Neal into his 1863 Physician's Hand Book. (ACHS)

took place on June 25 in a Mennonite Church one mile north of Chambersburg. This tribunal tried, found guilty, and punished one officer and several privates for desertion and drunkenness on duty. Hoke emphasized: "If that kind of discipline had prevailed in the Union army there would have been fewer disasters from the use of intoxicating liquors."

Even with two general orders issued against it, and the presence of superior discipline and watchfulness in the ranks, indiscriminate plundering still did often occur, and heavy looting was a common practice in some organizations, particularly in General Imboden's command. Hoke recorded that "the taking of groceries, provisions, stationery, hardware, clothing, hats, boots and shoes, drugs, horses, cattle, corn, oats, hay, etc.," was expected in war times. But he also knew of persons in some instances, who were relieved of "watches, pocket-books, boots, etc., by stragglers, but never in the presence of an officer." Jacob Hoke said but one civilian was killed, Isaac Strite, who was robbed and murdered by Rebel stragglers. After the infamous act, Strite's body was concealed under a manure pile in his barn yard. No rapes have been confirmed during that campaign, which is not so unusual in the era of the Civil War, however, one would be naive to hold to the belief that none occurred in Maryland or occupied Pennsylvania between June 15 and July 30, 1863.

Even the Southerners themselves suggested that serious lapses in Lee's General Order #72 had taken place. Colonel Arthur Freemantle, a British observer with the Southern army complained: "So completely was the country through which the Confederate army passed robbed and plundered, that...farm labor had come to a complete standstill."[57] And anyone reading the reminiscences of Union prisoners of war marching southward with the Rebel army, will hear of the great trains of stolen loot accompanying that army.

One Chambersburg woman, however, was not as diplomatic as Mr. Hoke had been. She called these stragglers and Rebels in general, "dirty ragged lousy trash," whom she said had "robbed the country people of nearly everything they had & acted very insultingly."[58]

On the other side of the coin, one of our best sources for descriptions of the mischief manifested by Union soldiers is the diary of General Marsena Patrick, who held the important position as the provost marshal general of the Army of the Potomac. Patrick constantly complained throughout his memoranda book of the terrible behavior and havoc caused by scores of Yankees in the rear of Meade's vast army. It must be remembered that the hindmost portion of the Army of the Potomac contained thousands of men on duties not directly associated with combat roles such as cooks, blacksmiths, clerks, teamsters, orderlies and the like. These figures also do not estimate the other thousands (sources say 10,000) who were plainly absent without authorization from their regular commands. The U.S. trains alone consisted of 1,100 to 1,200 ambulances, 3,700 to 4,000 supply wagons, 360 artillery pieces, over 1,000 artillery caissons, limbers, and service vehicles, plus 45,000 horses, not counting

Rachel Bowman Cormany called the Rebels who inundated her community, "dirty ragged lousy trash." (JCM)

thousands of mules. This immense scattered flood of animals and vehicles made a convenient hideout for men who were not anxious for front line duties. If we throw in the localities containing dozens of field hospitals among a multitude of farms, one can see how easily a single soldier, bent on mischief or playing the coward, could outwit all of the provost guards ever assembled. A reporter for the Lancaster *Daily Express* summed up the problem perfectly when he wrote this on July 10, 1863:

> Several thousand men are counted among the missing [from Meade's army] but they are not prisoners—they are on a grand straggle, and the country from Frederick to Westminster, to Hanover, to Gettysburg, and back again to Frederick, swarms with loose men away from their commands—luxurating among the farm houses as long as their money lasts, and safe from the gobble of provost guards, of which, by the way nobody has seen lately.

A sample of some excerpts from Patrick's diary may indicate the magnitude of the problem:

> *June 25, 1863:* We have done nothing, Scarcely, except to pick up Stragglers of other commands....
>
> *June 30:* At a late hour I...sent for two Squadrons of Cavalry to go back to Frederic [sic] [Maryland] & clean out that town, which was reported full of drunken men & Stragglers....
>
> *July 3:* I never saw such artillery fire....It was terrific & I had my hands full with those who broke to the rear, but we succeeded in checking the disorder & organized a guard of Stragglers to keep nearly 2000 Prisoners all safe.
>
> *July 4:* Busy gathering men from their places of retreat & straggling....
>
> *July 7:* It was a very hard march of 30 miles & I had a rough time in driving up Stragglers, Officers & Men....
>
> *July 13:* The day has been rainy &...we have had a great deal to do with prisoners & all that kind of work....The Country is full of the employees of the Press, Christian Commission & curiosity hunters.
>
> *July 21:* Our Army is in no condition to fight another battle—The discipline is horrible. There is no responsibility any where, & Commanders of every rank, cover up the rascality of their Troops—There is a vast deal of Stealing of Horses, & depradations [sic] of all kinds.
>
> *July 23:* Officers & men are turned thieves & robbers—The whole country is full of stragglers & the Officers all permit it and say nothing—
>
> *Aug 1:* [The] outrages in the *Country* have been perfectly infamous....
>
> *Aug 3:* The Soldiery are overrunning the whole Country, especially the Cavalry....
>
> *Aug 4:* [We] succeeded in capturing ten men of the 6' [US] Cav[alr]y out on a robbing expedition & representing themselves as belonging to a patrol from me....[59]

It is perfectly clear from the recorded statements that General Patrick was at his wits' end. As a result, in late July he asked Meade to relieve him of his duties, a request which was turned down.

Returning to Patrick's July 3 entry concerning the disorder and "breaking" of the troops to the rear, there was another eyewitness to the scene described by the general. It is especially worth noting, as its very existence as a source is quite rare. The writer was a wounded Confederate officer who had been

General Patrick (seated, center) had uncounted problems with stragglers and deserters in his midst. (GNMP)

captured during Longstreet's assault against Cemetery Ridge on the final afternoon of the battle. He was deeply impressed with the moment:

> ...[I]t is astonishing how cowards can be made to fight, I saw that well illustrated during the fight [of July 3]. At one point, where we had carried a portion of the line, and were struggling desperately for the rest, I, with my own eyes, saw several officers standing in rear of their line of battle, with cowhides or whips in their hands, seizing every one that attempted to run, and whipping them back to the fight. I saw more than one strike the men over their heads with the butt of the whip, slash them across their faces, pull them by their collars, and kick them back to their positions. Another instance: —After my capture, I saw a squad of fifteen or twenty making for the rear, and just as they were crossing a road, General Patrick, the Provost General of the Army, came galloping along, and espied them. Riding up to them, he drew his sword, and asked where they were going, etc. Some said they were wounded, others said they had lost their guns; each had his tale, "No!" said General Patrick, "damn you, you are skulkers; go back to the line," [and] he commenced whacking them over the head, making the blood flow profusely, and forcing the skulkers to take the back track![60]

Lest the reader disbelieve this officer, Patrick himself once wrote in his diary: "Had a very hard time & had to use my riding whip more than I wished...."[61]

In support of what General Patrick had to say about the immense problem of stragglers and others absent from the Union ranks, is a piece from the pen of Whitelaw Reid a correspondent working for the Cincinnati *Gazette*. While resting near the post office at Two Taverns, Pennsylvania on July 1, Reid, who was en route to cover the activities of the army, wrote to his editor: "Drunken soldiers were still staggering about the streets, [of Frederick, Maryland] [when I left] looking for a last drink or a horse to steal, before commencing to straggle along the road..."

The previous night he spent in Frederick was even worse. Reid summed it up this way:

> Frederick is Pandemonium. Somebody has blundered frightfully; the town is full of stragglers, and the liquor-shops are in full blast. Just under my window scores of drunken soldiers are making night hideous; all over the town they are trying to steal horses or sneak into unwatched private residences or are filling the air with the blasphemy of their drunken brawls. The worst elements of a great army are here in their worst condition; its cowards, its thieves, its sneaks, its bullying vagabonds, all inflamed with whiskey, and drunk as well with their freedom from accustomed restraint.[62]

A former soldier had his own view of these scoundrels: "[A]fter the soldiers came the camp–followers. Imagine, if you please, the chronic straggler who avoids a battle because he is a coward. Make this armed coward drunk on stolen whiskey, give him a dozen or more armed companions as desperate, cowardly and drunken as himself and turn them loose into a peaceful community, every farmhouse near the highways filled with drunken loafers in uniform, compelling the farmers to keep constant watch, you will have a picture of the rear of a large army."[63]

Confederate prisoners or Union deserters, "going to Provost Head-Quarters under guard." (EF)

To complete the view of what often occurred behind the front lines, it is appropriate here to return to General Patrick who was faced with yet another bad situation, one compounded by the already critical problem of these "cowardly stragglers." He stated his case on July 9.

"During the recent engagements, large numbers of soldiers were passed to the rear, not only by surgeons, but by commanding officers, without specifying place; consequently, they were scattered over the whole country in the rear of the line of battle. Large numbers of enlisted men were also found beyond the line of fire, in charge of pack mules, officers' horses, mess establishments, and company and regimental property, as well as guards of general officers, pioneer detachments, entirely unarmed, regimental bands and field music, scattered all along the rear, all of which were on no duty whatever."

Patrick then proceeded to give his lengthy ideas for improving this intolerable mess, and ended his report by explaining that the teamsters and train-guards were "especially lawless in this respect, demanding food and committing depredations more than any other of our troops...."[64]

On July 12, 425 of these ruthless types who were a mixed bag of both Yankee and Confederate misfits, were turned over to the provost guard in Harrisburg. Considering what has been told of the misadventures and troubles of General Patrick, that group was surely but a small sampling of those still on the prowl.[65]

◆ ◆ ◆

Disaffection in the Rebel Ranks

In the preceding pages several spectators have told us of the presence of large numbers of Confederate deserters and stragglers roaming the countryside after Lee's defeat at Gettysburg; men who were more "anxious to get northward than to join General Lee."[66] Just how prevalent this noxious condition was is almost unknown. The topic has never been thoroughly investigated; sources on the subject are very weak, therefore the question will unfortunately not be dealt with as properly as it deserves in this chapter.

One of the best derivations available on deserters comes from Historian Bell Wiley, a man of high professional ability who studied the life of the average Confederate soldier in great depth and detail. Wiley found that "[i]n the wake of Gettysburg the highways of Virginia were crowded daily with homeward-bound troops, still in possession of full accoutrements; and, according to one observer, these men 'when halted and asked for their furloughs or their authority to be absent from their commands...just pat their guns defiantly and say "this is my furlough," and even enrolling officers turn away as peacefully as possible.'"

Wiley also demonstrated that the Confederate Assistant Secretary of War estimated in 1863 that the number of Southern soldiers "evading service by devious means, but chiefly by unauthorized absence, reached 50,000 to 100,000."[67]

Throughout the months following the battle, newspapers even deep in the heart of the Southern states (the Raleigh *Standard*, for example) published articles which openly opposed President Jefferson Davis and his government, and especially his failure to permanently establish a confederacy. There were calls from many quarters to secure a peace with the North. For instance even U.S. Secretary of War Edwin M. Stanton was notified by a Federal general at Fort Monroe on July 22 that a strong Union movement was growing in North Carolina and appeared to be prepared to "make a bold stroke for the severance of the State from the Southern Confederacy."[68]

The defeats of Vicksburg and Gettysburg written up in newspapers certainly had a negative impact on the morale of the South. Likewise, thousands of men were deserting the armies and coming home with sad stories of military hardships and defeat. The United States Commissioner of Prisoner Exchange, Colonel William Hoffman, claimed that there were 65,000 Rebel soldiers then in Union hands after these two recent Northern victories, and he indicated that deserters were flocking into Federal lines. The feeling was that for every Confederate who came freely into Northern control, nine others went straight home. One angry and disappointed Southern captive writing home from prison on or near July 25 attested that of the 700 comrades in prison with him only 200 still remained faithful to the cause. Five hundred had already taken the oath of allegiance to the U.S. This unhappy fellow continued: "Oh! how I have urged...those dishonored wretches to pause [in their decision to take the oath]...but they answered me, 'The Confederacy cannot gain her independence; Vicksburg has fallen, and why should I long waste my life in a useless undertaking.'"[69]

A particularly good case in point in describing the morale of the average Confederate soldier after Gettysburg has come down through the years from Major William W. Goldsborough of the 1st Maryland Infantry Battalion. He tells a story of how many men in the army personally felt when they reached their permanent camps near Orange Court House, Virginia, following the end of the campaign.

> But here...a new danger threatened the Confederate army, and one that never menaced it before. The army was threatened with disintegration. With its return to Virginia thousands of letters had been received from every part of the South from wives who made heart-rending appeals to their husbands to return home, even if for but a few days. Gaunt famine had so soon laid its cold hand upon these poor wives and their helpless children, and to whom were they to appeal but to their husbands...Furloughs were out of the question. Already the Federal army...was assembling but a few miles away, and if the appeals of these frantic men were heeded there would be few left to oppose the enemy. Was it a wonder, then, that they began to leave without authority? At first it was by twos and threes, and then, emboldened, in larger numbers. It is doubtful if during the whole campaign General Lee was more exercised than then, as he was powerless to resist them, and unable to prevent the exodus without resorting to extreme measures, which he was doth to do....

According to Major Goldsborough among those who departed the army were ten good men of the 3rd North Carolina Infantry who in leaving, retained their weapons as they expected to return after a brief visit to their loved ones at home. The adjutant of the 47th, Lieutenant Richardson Mallett, Jr., was sent after them. When he caught up to the men a struggle ensued, and the adjutant was killed. But even under this trying dilemma the men returned voluntarily to their regiment and reported the facts of the encounter, and the death of Mallett. The ten were arrested, and on the 6th of September after a court-martial and General Lee's approval of their sentence, they were all shot dead by a squad of their comrades. The major retorted: "Oh! it seemed so cruel that these poor, battle-scarred soldiers should thus die at the hands of their comrades, and among the assembled troops there was scarcely a dry eye...And the widows and orphans starved on. Such is 'glorious war!'"[70]

On the night of July 29 another group of fifty soldiers from several North Carolina regiments, deserted, and as General Lee claimed, they were responding to a "disgraceful peace sentiment" expressed in newspapers recently received from home. The commanding general then requested that Richmond authorities take extra efforts to recapture these men. The brigade commander of the deserters also urged that "every effort should be made to overhaul them..." for as he declared "if this should pass by unnoticed, many more will soon follow."[71]

During the Gettysburg Campaign per se, many Southern soldiers undoubtedly did desert for many and varied reasons. The army was present in both Maryland and Pennsylvania and these men found it easier than normal to accomplish this unacceptable deed, as many sympathetic people were present and willing and able to assist them in the act. Many desertions were convenient rather than planned, as when a soldier found himself left far behind by his unit or lost deep in enemy territory. After all it was deemed better to be paroled than to be confined in a Federal military prison. Therefore it became imperative to convince the authorities that they were truly "deserters." It is my personal conviction that many, but not all, of these desertions were most commonly due to a feeling of general disillusionment with the Confederate cause, and the betrayed hope of ever winning a peace settlement with the United States. A large segment of these troops was obviously also unhappy with normal military life and its inherent misery, hardships, and dangers.

As an early indication of the emotions of some Confederates, several paragraphs from the Adams *Sentinel* of August 18, 1863, are thought-provoking, especially if remembered that the people of Gettysburg and Adams County had ample time to speak and become acquainted with a large cross-section of Lee's army. All totalled, the county residents had as guests in their midst as many as 7,000 Rebels for a number of weeks, and some for as long as four months. Here is a segment of the article:

> A private letter received here from a prominent officer at Warrenton, says that a Rebel Lieutenant, who deserted from their army and came into our lines last Sunday, reports that great dissatisfaction exists among the North Carolina, Tennessee and Mississippi troops, particularly among the former, at the condition of affairs in their respective States. The North Carolina troops threaten to mutiny unless they are sent back to their homes. Once there, they say they will throw down their arms, and abandon the Rebel cause, of which they are heartily sick. It is only with great difficulty that the officers restrain the men.
>
> The disaffection also extends to the officers, and is increasing among the rank and file of the troops from the Southwestern States, who argue that there is no use of further resistance, since Vicksburg and Port Hudson have fallen

and the National troops have gained possession of the Mississippi. The Mississippi and Tennessee levies are also clamorous to go home. The defeat at Gettysburg seems to have completely broken the spirit of Lee's army, and the utmost apathy prevails among both officers and men. They have lost all hope of the South being able to achieve its independence. The men are almost unanimously in favor of peace at any cost.

Another article which elicits the same sentiments, but is more pointed toward the economic situation on the Southern homefront, was published on October 20, 1863, by the same paper. Although naming only the city of Richmond, it does portray the slow decay of the Confederacy from its heart outward.

> The rebel soldiers have no faith whatever in their government; they told us that their pay was not worth the snap of their fingers, and they would give *eight* dollars of their money for one of ours. A pair of boots in Richmond are worth from forty-five to fifty dollars, shoes from fifteen to twenty dollars; a pound of coffee, half rye, five dollars; sugar, three dollars; a pair of coarse pantaloons, forty dollars; and everything else in proportion. They have "bread riots" nearly every day; robberies and murders are committed almost every night, and you can see armed men stationed at the corner of every street, and all over the city to keep the peace.

The subject of the discontentment of the common soldier of the South was apparently very often on the minds of the local populace, especially if we follow the evidence provided by the regional newspapers. A lot of it was "wishful thinking" as people grew tired of the war. This article on that important topic was printed in the July 9, 1863, issue of the Gettysburg *Star and Banner* under the heading, "The Rebels Tired of the War."

"We have talked with multitudes of the rebel soldiers and find very many heartily sick of the war. They acknowledge themselves badly whipped; and seem desirous of finding a quiet home beneath the protection of the stars and stripes. They declare that General Lee deceived them, representing that they had nothing before them but raw militia. They [instead] found the veterans of the Army of the Potomac."

Union propaganda aside, there was more truth than presumptuous thinking in these patterns of statements.

Individual experiences with "dissolutioned rebels," are not hard to find in the thousands of first-hand accounts available to the interested researcher. A sample gleaned from a variety of sources will be worth investigating. The reader could judge from these writings and others available that there was a serious problem of low morale within the ranks of Lee's army. If such feelings existed among General Lee's proud veterans then it most certainly smoldered within the breasts of thousands of other Confederates who fought in the many other Southern field armies, the navy, on the homefront where militia troops operated, and naturally in the civilian population at large.

Beginning even before the Battle of Gettysburg and as early as June 27, during the height of the Confederate invasion, rumors were rampant that Southern soldiers were deserting in groups and singly now that they were safely on Northern soil. On that very day Rachael Cormany, a native of

Three Confederates photographed near Gettysburg. They were either captured prisoners, deserters, or stragglers picked up by Union patrols. (GNMP)

Chambersburg, Pennsylvania, wrote in her diary these prophetic words of things to come: "I pity some of [their] men for I am sure they would like to be out. At Dickson's they told me that 400 went at one time—gagged the guards and got off to the mountains and on to Harrisburg to help our men....J. [Jacob] Hoke told me this morning...that about 1000 had deserted." On July 4 Cormany saw 15 Rebels who came walking through town and were quickly made captives, commenting that they were "willing prisoners [who] had thrown their guns away before they reached [us]."[72]

Ten miles north of Gettysburg a farmer named William B. Wilson living at Bendersville, penned this in his diary for July 1: "Great Battle at Gettysburg. 2 deserters from the rebel army here this evening. Heavy cannoning all day at Gettysburg. A great many Rebels at Middletown [present day Biglerville] tonight."[73]

A day later on the morning of July 2 at about 2 a.m., Harriet Bayly who lived on a farm atop a low ridge just north of Gettysburg, heard a knock at the door. She found the caller was "a woebegone little 'Reb.' about 17 years of age, who said he had been in the fight the day before; that he belonged to a North Carolina [unit]; that his regiment was broken up and scattered; that he had been wandering around all night keeping away from pickets and fearing to seek shelter as he never intended doing any more fighting for the Confederacy.

"He was given a suit of citizen's clothes and remained with the family until the battle was over. He is now living on a farm near the battle field and the size of his family indicates that he has been more successful in peaceful pursuits than those of war."[74]

While assisting wounded Confederates during the night of July 3, Private Daniel G. Crotty of the 3rd Michigan stumbled upon an Irishman wearing the gray, who told Crotty that he was dying and regretted he had not died instead for the "starry flag," but misfortune had deemed it otherwise.[75]

Sergeant Joseph R. Balsley of the 142nd Pennsylvania Infantry had even a stranger meeting with a North Carolina lieutenant on the battlefield during the night of July 1. Balsley had been wounded and was lying on the damp ground, when the Southern lieutenant approached to give him water. In the process, the Confederate said to Balsley, "Well, Sergeant, never desert the old flag." Balsley went on to relate how he believed that a large number of the Confederate troops much like the kindly lieutenant, especially those from North Carolina, had not fully accepted the secession movement and were unhappy to be in rebellion against the United States. To Joseph Balsley, this utterance by the Rebel officer meant that he was sorry for leaving its folds.[76]

A higher ranking Alabama officer vented similar feelings to a Pennsylvania soldier on the slope of Little Round Top late on July 2. According to Amos Judson, Colonel M.J. Bulger of the 47th Alabama Infantry had fallen into U.S. hands after being wounded and "spoke and acted as if he was evidently tired of the war."

Quite late in the summer, in September, eight weeks after the battle, a member of the Patapsco Guards of Maryland who was engaged in the work of guarding hospitals and caring for injured horses, went to Cashtown, Pennsylvania for a break from the tedium of his battlefield duties. While there, this soldier, Hezekiah Weeks, and a few friends visited a tavern and general store. In the store they were surprised to find, "a squad of Confederate soldiers buying provisions." The Rebs were hiding out in the countryside, unable or unwilling to make the trek southward and across the Potomac River. After a friendly exchange, both groups went their separate ways, with no one molesting the other.[77]

In reality these uncharacteristic sentiments were much more frequently encountered by Northern people than the average Southern partisan would wish us to believe. They should not mislead us however, to paint an unfair picture of utter and total hopelessness within the South's forces. Commonly, for *every* officer who voiced regrets like that of Colonel Bulger, ten others acted otherwise. In my personal opinion the underlying sentiments of the average *enlisted* man versus the officer class would not be nearly so great, more like a fifty-fifty split.[78]

On July 2 Private Reuben Ruch of the 153rd Pennsylvania and a prisoner of war met a North Carolina "Johnnie" who was stationed as a guard in the hospital at the German Reformed Church on Stratton Street in Gettysburg. Ruch plainly remembered that the Rebel believed there was "no use fighting the North, for he had never seen such a rich country as Pennsylvania, and that our towns were yet full of men, in fact a fellow would not miss those that were in the army." When the "Tarheel" was pressed to remain behind as the Southern army retreated Ruch told him that the Northern boys would not kill him. The North Carolinian retorted that "the old flag [U.S.] was good enough for him, that he lived in a rented house, and never owned a negro, that he would take my advice and stay north but for one thing. He had a wife and two children...and if he did stay north, and the Rebels found it out they would use his family meaner than dogs...."[79]

This theme was often heard from the mouths of Confederates; the idea that the people and authorities of the South would retaliate swiftly against Northern supporters in their midst, or against traitors and deserters, was not an idle threat. To the people of that era it was a very serious intimidation. The Southern States during the Civil War, and frankly before and after it, could be a nasty, uncivilized place, where hot-bloodedness, ignorance, and meanness of many of the people, especially when spurred on by mob rule, was commonly known. More often than we might care to believe, these underlying qualities could escalate the danger of physical violence against innocent citizens who chose not to follow local sentiments. Indifference, jealousy and poverty anywhere else might bring out the same reaction, but in the South, with its long history of class sectionalism, and where wealthy men had complete power over millions of human beings, the situation was more unsettled than in the North. Even the post-war Western frontier could hardly match it for this low type of ugliness.

In a church on Chambersburg Street, a scene quite similar to Private Ruch's was enacted, this one near dusk on July 1. There, Private Austin Stearns, a member of the 13th Massachusetts began a conversation with a Confederate who had been wounded and taken to the Christ Lutheran Church. Stearns commented on the fact that the Rebel soldier was a very intelligent man who conceded he had been

> a union man before the war, and [had] done all he could to prevent his state from going out. He was one of the delegates to the convention that carried the old state out. After the secession of his state he said he went home and said he would have nothing more to do with politics. He carried on his farm and tried to live a peaceful life. The first year passed, and in the second year more men were wanted, so they came and without saying "by your leave" they took him and put him in the army....He said according to his ideas there was no cause for war, but being a Southern man, with all his interests, home, wife, children, and property there, he should continue to fight till the end, if not for his own sake, for those left behind who were dependent upon him.[80]

One of the guards stationed at a Gettysburg field hospital was George Liebig of Company K, 36th Pennsylvania Militia. On July 30 he penned a letter to friend John Caldwell reiterating that he had spoken to many of the Southern wounded and had obtained many of their opinions on "this fraternal war." Liebig continued: "They are all tired of it and wish it over; and they too with one answer are for union, their excuse for fighting is that the north has robbed them of their rights and that they are compelled to take up arms against the U.S. government."[81]

A preacher from Altoona, Pennsylvania, confided to his diary several similar observations relating to the attitudes of some of the injured Confederates he met.

> Friday July 10, 1863. I visited the 2nd Army Corps Hospital four miles from town where we saw sights never to be forgotten. The woods and creek bottoms were full of badly wounded rebels who piteously asked for water, medicine,

attention to wounds, etc. Amputations were rapidly taking place by rebel and Union doctors. Most of the wounded were North Carolinians and Georgians who were hurled against the impregnable entrenchments [of the Union line] and swept down like chaff. These men expressed abhorrence of the war and of their ambitious leaders who precipitated Secession. We labored in behalf of the Christian Commission until dark among these fallen foes.[82]

John B. Linn, who inspected the field from July 6 through July 11 compared the differences between the two classes of Southerners. Many whom he talked with at the College hospital, (he spoke of 900 present there), "were of the fighting South, bitter and relentless to the last, far different from the deserters and those caught in the mountains who seemed glad to be caught and anxious that this should be the last battle."[83]

At another of the hospitals near Gettysburg, a New York volunteer nurse remembered an emotional scene involving a wounded Rebel who was near death and was stretched upon the almost bare ground being attended by a surgeon and members of the Sanitary Commission.

The writer narrated how with feeble voice and tearful eyes, the Southern man returned his thanks, saying: "I was deceived, we were told the North was a country of cruel wretches who would give no quarter to a prisoner, and, under the belief that captivity would be worse than death, we fought. Had I known sooner what I now know, I never should have entered the Confederate army....This is harder to bear than my wound. My God, you are killing me with kindness!"[84]

A letter sent to David G. Porter from Sergeant Alexander McNeil, 14th Connecticut Infantry on August 16 presents us with some of the very typical feelings found in a large portion of the North Carolina soldiers and others fighting for the Confederacy. While at Gettysburg, McNeil "had a long conversation with a Captain of the 52nd North Carolina Regt. He was severely wounded & we carried him into our lines & laid him down. I gave him coffee to drink twice, while waiting for a stretcher to carry him to the Hospital. He was a sensible Intelligent man. He told me the South had been rough & harsh with the North Carolina troops all through, since the War commenced. He then told me it was because the State of North Carolina did not *Secede* quite soon enough to suit some of the other Slave States. He told me, too, that the State of South Carolina ought to be sunk. That, he said, was where the trouble commenced."[85]

The captain was close to the mark when he believed that his state was used harshly during the war. Specifically, it is known that at Gettysburg there were approximately 38 North Carolina infantry and cavalry units present in the battle. Their troops suffered 1,350 combat deaths. On the other hand, Virginia had 58 infantry and cavalry regiments available in the fight and reported 837 fatalities. From these figures alone, one begins to understand that perhaps the "old North state" was giving the Confederacy a bit more than its fair share. Coincidentally, if one looks at an article in an issue of the *Confederate Veteran* magazine of 1896, the statistics provided indicate that North Carolina suffered the deaths of 14,522 men killed in battle and 5,151 who died of wounds, while Virginia, who had more men in service, lost 5,328 men "KIA" and 2,519 mortally wounded. The military population in the two states in 1860 as follows: Virginia, 196,587, North Carolina, 115,369. During the war North Carolina raised 85 infantry and cavalry regiments and artillery batteries, while Virginia called up 197 units of all types.[86]

Dr. Theodore Dimon, one of New York State's relief agents, assisted many of the Confederate wounded and often related how he was informed repeatedly by Secessionist soldiers that "they could again live with us under the old Union." He depicted the story of one Mississippian who was so anxious to stay behind in the North that his request was granted; a rare occurrence indeed. Dimon disclosed that the Mississippi soldier was adamant and the surgeons felt it would cost him his life if he was forced to go with his comrades who were being transported to Philadelphia. Another sad remembrance for the doctor was a North Carolinian who was heard to cry out in his grief: "I thought I was fighting for liberty, and here I am dying like a dog."[87]

Mary Cunningham lived on her father's farm in July 1863 which was then in use as one of the field hospitals along Marsh Creek, west of Gettysburg. There she met a very young soldier of the Confederate army who wanted to desert and found help from her father, John Cunningham. The facts as told by Mary are as follows:

> At the withdrawal of the Confederates, all able to walk were ordered to leave....After they were gone Father noted a mere stripling with his head down on the meadow gate crying as if his heart would break. When Father asked the cause of his grief, he sobbed out that, "Our men are gone and now the Yankees will kill me." Father was a comforting person. He assured the boy that he wouldn't be killed, that there was food in Pennsylvania and it wasn't at all a bad place to be. Months later when the incident had quite gone from his mind, he received a letter from this boy: "Mr. Cunningham, what you told me about the Yankees is true—I'm in the Union army now."[88]

Christian Commission Delegate John Foster had his own memory of Private William Yearger of the 22nd Georgia Regiment. Yearger was wounded in the battle and earlier in the war had been terribly sad to leave home to fight with the South. He told Foster: "You can never know what we have suffered in our army. We thought when we enlisted that the life of a soldier was full of charms—even those of us who volunteered purely in obedience to popular clamor and not from any principle, thought we should not after all be so very badly off; but we have all long ago found out our mistake." Foster also discovered from speaking with these Southerners, who were mostly Georgians, that they believed the rebellion, "was inherently a struggle against oppression, a combat for independence." When told by Foster and others that the North had never injured, had never assailed nor thought of assailing the rights of the South, and the existing government stood solemnly committed to the mainte-nance of every right for every citizen, these Confederates "uniformly responded that they did not so understand it, that they had been educated to believe that the North was deliberately resolved to overturn Southern society, blot out its cherished institutions, and reduce its people to vassalage. When asked if their condition under 'Confederate' rule had been made better than it was in the days of Federal domination, they uniformly replied in the negative."[89]

On the afternoon of Monday July 6, Jacob Hoke and friends set out from Chambersburg to visit the battlefield around Gettysburg. At Fayetteville they encountered Federal cavalry gathering up straggling Rebels who were "footsore, tired and greatly discouraged." Hoke observed these men in large numbers all along the road. One of them, a North Carolinian, was offered a seat in Hoke's wagon. Hoke wrote: "He was so footsore and weary that he could scarcely walk....This man told us the usual story of nearly all the men we conversed with from his State—that he was opposed to the war, was in favor of the Union, had been dragged away from his family, and was resolved never again to fight in the cause he detested. Of his sincerity we had not a doubt. Poor fellow, his heart yearned for his absent wife and children, and he desired to know if there was any way by which he could have them brought north so that he need not ever return to his southern home."[90]

Dr. Robert Hubbard, a surgeon of the 17th Connecticut Infantry, was amazed at just how many Confederates were left behind by General Lee. He expressed these thoughts on the subject:

"It is impossible to estimate at present the number of wounded rebels which they left....The evidence of demoralization of the rebel army is strong—many expressing delight at falling into our hands & declaring that they will not go south again. We find daily large collections of their wounded in a wretched condition....We are doing all we can for them."[91]

Another associated with the Christian Commission and who spent countless hours with the Confederates was Andrew Cross, and he agreed that wounded North Carolinians were found abandoned in almost every direction. "How is it" he asked of a Rebel, "that we find North Carolina [injured] almost everywhere?" "The only reason we can give for it," answered a young man, "is that they try to wreak *their vengeance* upon us because our State was opposed to going out of the Union. They put us in every dangerous and exposed place, and give us the hard end of everything. Another said, my part of the State was opposed to going out, and they brought an army in on us, and compelled us to go with them."

Cross declared that many of the Confederates from Mississippi and Alabama were also, "decided Union men," and "that they never wanted any better Government than they had, and never expected as good a one again." In the Third Corps hospital he came across a North Carolina private who declared he hoped the U.S. Government would not stop until they brought every "god damn" one of the Southern states back into the Union.

Two identified Tennessee soldiers whom he met were the nephews of Vice President Andrew Johnson. They were James and William Burchett, members of the 8th Virginia, and both had been wounded on July 3. James told Cross that in 1862 they had started out for Kentucky with a group of men to enter the Union cavalry, but were captured on September 10 near Lucky Cove Seminary, Powell Valley, Lee County, Virginia. From there the brothers and their companions were sent to Staunton and put in the 8th Regiment, and had been in the Rebel service ever since. Cross testified that these soldiers were strong Union men, and one summed up their experiences thusly: "[W]e were driven up into *slaughter pens*."[92]

Because of the excellent and kind treatment he received at Camp Letterman, another Confederate officer was so smitten by his captors that he claimed he was theirs to keep. Nurse Emily Souder told this little story:

"The Lieutenant-Colonel of a North Carolina regiment is in the same tent with several...New York boys. He says he shall never again fight against the flag but henceforth belongs to the 64th New York."[93]

Local attorney Robert G. McCreary, verified too the disillusionment of many Confederates. He demonstrated the premise that

[a] great many of the rebel soldiers seemed to have no affection for the service, and would gladly leave it if possible. This we found by conversation with their wounded men in the hospitals, and did space permit, many incidents might be related showing that this feeling is common in the army, and that the soldiers are kept in the ranks solely by force of stern and inexorable military law. A gentleman living in the south end of the town...encountered one of these men alone in the stable, and entered into conversation with him. He [the rebel] declared that he had been compelled to enter the army, and wept when he spoke of his wife and children, from whom he had been forced away; he was anxious to be assisted in getting within our lines; but [at the time] that was impossible; as the intervening space was covered by the fire of the pickets of both armies.[94]

One of the most interesting examples and indications of the status of Southern loyalty comes from a document issued by the provost marshal's office at Point Lookout, Maryland, in the fall of 1863. On this roll is a list of 17 Confederates "desirous of taking the Oath of Allegiance." These prisoners had all been captured during the Gettysburg Campaign at places like Falling Waters, Maryland, Manassas Gap, and Williamsport, Maryland. They were from various regiments, including the 2nd, 13th, and 21st Mississippi, the 12th, 53rd and 55th Virginia, the 11th North Carolina, and others. All of these men claimed different reasons for wanting to take the oath. Two declared they were U.S. citizens illegally taken by the Rebels, some said they were foreign born and were conscripted, one had deserted the Confederacy and was recaptured by his army, another had been a pilot on the Rappahannock River and was forced into service by the 47th Virginia. One man was a civilian who had already been discharged at Richmond, Virginia, and was ordered back in service and was captured at Front Royal, Virginia. All emphasized that they would happily go North or fight for the Union.

Interestingly, one man on the list was Preston Crow of the 53rd Virginia. He had survived the Pickett-Pettigrew charge at Gettysburg on July 3 only to be captured at Falling Waters a week later. He eventually joined the Federal army as a volunteer in January 1864.[95]

The cross-section of personal accounts just covered may help to explain and indicate a small segment of the dissatisfaction, disillusionment, and despair present in the minds of some Confederate soldiers on the rolls of the Army of Northern Virginia during the Gettysburg Campaign. The same stories could likely be found throughout the ranks of Federal regiments as well. These examples again, were not printed to express merely a one-sided view of that army's mental status, nor are they intended to exploit any particular perceived weakness in general Southern morale. They were incorporated to show an opposing view of the oft heard exclamations of a "Solid South," a status that is plainly and fairly not true and is basically unfounded.

◆ ◆ ◆

Experiences of POWs

The final part of this chapter includes a short summary of the experiences of two average unwounded soldiers, both a Federal and Confederate captured at Gettysburg. These commentaries do not follow a particular theme, nor are they intended to make any singular point. The inclusion of two "general" accounts is merely to enhance the reader's perception of how the *mass* of captives was treated, removed from the battlefield, and sent on to their final destinations. The prison experiences themselves shall not be covered, as they do not belong in this short study of the aftermath of Gettysburg.

The typical Confederate who surrendered on the field of battle was invariably marched to the rear of the Union fighting lines. In time the prisoners were sent further southward along the Baltimore Pike to a holding pen or collecting point covered earlier in this chapter. These sites were about a mile down the pike in the vicinity of Nathaniel Lightner's farm, or on ground near the "White Church." When brought to Mark's German Reformed or White Church the POWs were placed in an open field in the hot sun nearly 100 yards from White Run. There the Confederates were allowed to drink the filthy water if they wished that had already been terribly fouled and polluted by cavalry and artillery horses and the mules assigned to the supply wagons. On the evening of July 3 these unfortunate men were given a pointed lecture by General Judson Kilpatrick, who in essence told them: "If you behave yourselves and don't try to get away, I will treat you as prisoners of war, but if you attempt to escape, I'll order my cavalry to charge right and left, and hew you down." According to witnesses, this particular harangue was met with a call of "three cheers for Jeff Davis," afterwhich the general galloped off.[96]

One woman who viewed a large group of captives possibly in this area, was Eliza Farnham. She mentioned that the private soldiers were "destitute, abject looking creatures," and believed there were enough of them to cover a one and one quarter acre lot.[97]

The Confederates in captivity at White Run were awakened early on July 4 to begin the journey to military prisons. They spent only one night in this location, a night interrupted by the sounds of musket and cannonfire in the distance and wagons passing close by on the pike, accompanied by the quiet and measured tread of Union sentinels. The prisoners were fed on that morning, then counted and registered by the provost guard. The day's march of 25 miles began soon afterward and took them through Two Taverns to Littlestown, Pennsylvania, then on to Union Mills, Maryland, and finally to Westminster. There, the *horde* of several thousand men was halted and led into an open space near the depot to await transportation to Baltimore. Less than twelve hours later and upon arrival in that large eastern city, the *majority* of the Confederates was formed into columns and marched through the streets of the city to Fort McHenry; others were immediately placed on connecting trains and shipped northward through Philadelphia to New York and elsewhere, and eventually all were placed in confinement in sundry camps located throughout the Northern states.

A Confederate who left behind a personal recollection of his travels was Captain Benjamin L. Farinholt of the 53rd Virginia, who was wounded on July 3. From Westminster, Maryland, he and other prisoners were taken by railroad to Baltimore and Fort McHenry, where for the first time Farinholt's lacerated leg was properly dressed by a Union surgeon. After a day's stay they embarked on the steamer *Kennebec* for a sail down the Chesapeake, past Fort Monroe, and finally up to Fort Delaware. The captain and others in his group were held there until August under the charge of General Albin F. Schoepf, where conditons he testified, were "miserable in the extreme." In that month all officers were removed across the country to Johnson's Island situated in Lake Erie, Ohio, a place Farinholt escaped from in February 1864.[98]

By the time Farinholt or any other prisoner of war reached Baltimore or New York they were sure to be in "pitiable condition." A New York newspaper described all in this way:

"[The rebels] arrived in a wretched condition—dirty, ragged and covered with vermin—their soiled and torn uniforms...stained and soaked with blood; and their wounds, which had not been dressed [since Gettysburg]...are alive with maggots...."[99]

Union captives at Gettysburg were guarded and collected by the Confederate army primarily in several places close to and throughout the area of the three-day battle. The first days' catch of prisoners was brought together on the west side of the Carlisle Road about three-quarters of a mile north of the Southern battle line which ran east and west across that thoroughfare from the Harrisburg Pike toward the Mummasburg Road. From the sources available, what emerged was that these Yankees were soon marched further northward still on the Carlisle Road for an additional five miles, and there offered a parole near present day Biglerville. Those men accepting parole were pushed onward to Carlisle and then to Harrisburg and/or Philadelphia, ultimately to be exchanged and reunited with their regiments. The remainder of this conglomeration, about 2,500, was pointed back southwest to a farm behind Seminary Ridge and placed in a field through which "a sluggish stream ran." One Union participant said he thought the stream was Marsh Creek, and that it bore marks of fighting "further up." From this evidence, it seems this was probably Willoughby's Run. Furthermore, the soldier remembered the field was off the main road a short distance up a lane, which led to a low, one-story unpainted house where there was a spring, and wounded men were quartered on the opposite side of the lane.[100]

On the west side of the Confederate battle front, most of the Federals captured by General Longstreet's and Hill's Corps were led through a wooded area to an open field, and from there to a "cross road near an old house," which was very dilapidated, and was being employed as a station for some wounded. This description sounds very much like the statement given above, which would indicate that almost all of the National troops were being consolidated at one large general collecting point.

One of the prisoners here felt very gratified to rest for a while, as the trip from the combat zone transpired quickly, and soon wore the men down in the July heat. After a short rest, the captives who had then begun to grow into substantial numbers were marched to "Willoughby's Run at a point where it is crossed by the Hagerstown [or Fairfield] Road." At this site was an open lot south of the pike and east of the stream. Here they halted for the night of July 2, meanwhile being joined by more and more Northerners. All then remained at the creek until late on July 3. During the course of this last day of the battle, the Union troops under Confederate control were offered a parole. This, the reader may recall was discussed previously by 15th Massachusetts infantryman, Roland Bowen. General Graham was present at this meeting and bid the captives not to accept the parole, which turned out to be a poor decision for many.

Finally, on July 4 the thousands of U.S. prisoners were placed in regulation infantry files and started on the road for Fairfield, arriving about 3 p.m. with a hard rain and muddy conditions making the travel slow and torturous. At Fairfield the POWs had an opportunity to see General Lee at a close distance. Lee, as one captured man remarked, "cast an Eagle eye at us, as if to say, I have made a pretty good haul on you Yanks this time...."[101]

Among the Federals taken on July 2 was Dyer B. Pettijohn, a member of the 1st U.S. Sharpshooters, who said that before he got to the holding place on Willoughby's Run, he saw "long lines of Negro cooks baking corn pone for [the] rebel soldiers at the front." Meanwhile he and other captives were robbed at pistol point of clothing, money and other valuables. When issued raw flour on July 4, the prisoners who had no cooking utensils, mixed the flour in their blankets. It was then made into "hoe cakes" and baked by a fire, usually on a flat rock or twisted onto a stick. Pettijohn interjected that this was all done in a driving rain which made it difficult to keep the fires going.[102]

Thomas Taft, 124th New York Infantry, was another soldier who remembered the meager rations. The first commissary issue, he pointed out, was made up of one pint of flour, one-half pound of meat and a little salt. At another time near Williamsport, Maryland, they were given one pint of flour and a small piece of bacon which followed every day or so.[103] An officer of the 26th Wisconsin (one of the most shot up regiments at Gettysburg), Bernhard Domschcke, revealed that his squad's initial rations were handed out by Colonel W.H. French's 17th Virginia Cavalry. Those rations consisted of "raw meat with a handful of wheat flour and a few grains of salt." Domschcke remembered how he rolled dough on an oil cloth and shaped little loaves which were placed on hot stones near a fire, then turned and baked on each side as needed. He added: "[O]nly with disgust could I nibble such bread now; but we wolfed it then and craved more."

On July 3 this hungry parcel of captives "passed in review" in front of General George E. Pickett, whose division became its guard force all the way to the Potomac. Pickett was a man whom Domschcke described as, "[t]he archetype of a Virginia slave baron, [who] strutted briskly, [was] proud in bearing, [with] head lifted in arrogance. Obviously he took pains with [his] appearance—riding boots a glitter, near-shoulder-length hair tonsorially styled—but the color of his nose and upper cheeks betrayed that he pandered the inner man. Pleasures of the bottle left indelible tracks. Indeed, the coarse plebian features in no way matched the efforts at aristocratic airs."[104]

The lot of prisoners, still under the watchful eye of Pickett's Division trekked about 40 miles to Williamsport, Maryland, then was routed through Monterey and Hagerstown, which was six miles from the river. Massachusetts Private Roland Bowen declared that on this part of the journey he passed numerous Rebel hospitals and saw much plunder taken by the Southerners, which added to their already burdened trains.

The tired and famished Yankees arrived at the Potomac River on July 5; their final destination however, was Staunton, Virginia, approximately 200 miles from Gettysburg. At Williamsport Sergeant Taft specified that the only means for crossing the Potomac was an old ferry boat, which could carry only 60 men at a time. Another soldier in the 157th New York, claimed the "old scow" could take 200 at each trip.[105] Either way the crossing was slow, and it took one day and a night to take all the Unionists over; Taft thought 3,000 was the total number ferried across. He also narrated that besides the ferry the Rebels had laid a pontoon bridge across the river two or three miles below Williamsport, but Union cavalry had destroyed it. After the river adventure the men remained on the march 12 to 15 miles to Martinsburg, which several prisoners enthusiastically believed was the most patriotic town they had seen anywhere during the campaign. All of the citizens there crowded in to assist the Federal prisoners, and some even risked bodily injury to hand out food to the men, because the guards were very forceful in pushing back the hordes of people trying to help the boys in blue.

Two days following the bright spot that was Martinsburg, the column reached Winchester on July 12, about 34 miles from the Potomac and 22 from Martinsburg. At Winchester the Yanks were fed a meager ration of flour and beef which was meant to last two or three days, and went into camp two miles south of the town. Between July 13 and 15 the captives passed through Strasburg, then kept up the forced journey along the Valley Pike, which was a "macadamized" or hard surfaced road and was very brutal on the feet of the men. On July 15 they entered Mt. Jackson, drew rations and camped seven miles beyond. A day later the long blue line traveled 22 miles and bivouacked four miles on the south side of Harrisonburg. The 17th found them finally reaching Staunton, a march of 19 miles, where they encamped near a large spring a mile or two out of the city along the Virginia Central Railroad.

Between July 18 and August 6 all of the Gettysburg prisoners were shipped by train from Staunton to Richmond. While awaiting their turn to board the cars the men were placed under guard on a high hill, today called Sears' Hill, overlooking the Staunton depot. Escapes were common along the long route from the battlefield through Pennsylvania, Maryland, and Virginia, and a few Yanks were even able to elude the Confederates while at Staunton; these later ones especially faced a hard journey through enemy country. Fortunately some did make their way back to Union lines at Harpers Ferry and other places.[106]

Thomas Taft said that at Staunton the men were placed in a hot, treeless field two miles south of town, and there they were searched, and all weapons, large knives, tents, rubber blankets, and canteens were confiscated. He remained in this open field five days, alternating between broiling in the sun or being wet to the skin. Each day the prisoners were given one pint of flour, a piece of bacon that was one-and-a-half inches square covered with vermin, and a little salt. On the fourth of August, after another search of their clothing for money, Taft and his companions were finally loaded on the railcars for Richmond. This train he pronounced, consisted of "dirt cars, with an old cattle-box of an engine to haul us."

Very few accounts exist which describe the actual rail journey from Staunton to Richmond, the capital of the Confederacy. In contrast to this scarcity of material on that subject is the diary of William H. Warren of the 17th Connecticut Infantry. On Sunday, July 19, he began a record of his trip with these very descriptive lines:

It was announced that 700 men would be transported to Richmond & the 1st that got in line would go first so of course there was a scattering, jamming, & a great deal of swearing as the line was forming. 8 of our company succeeded in getting in the line & thus was marched down to the depot & embarked on part platform & part box cars. Rickety old things they were too as the box car I was in had no roof on, only the frame & I remember while setting upon the frame that it swayed, back & forth sideways, so that it frightened me & I was expecting every moment to be dumped out by the side of the road & left there. The inside of the car was so full there was not standing room. The rideing was very slow as the cars being so poor, they would not admit of fast travel, besides the road bed being in very poor condition. There was also a halt every little while. The scenery however was truly a remarkable feature, especially after passing beyond the Blue Ridge. The road skirted the summit of a high ridge, giveing a splendid view of the valley beneath & distant mountains. It was very tedious rideing nevertheless. Night brought no relief as it was so crowded as to render sleep of any account out of the question & so the day wore away into the night while we went jogging on to Richmond. We left Stanton at just 11 A.M., the distance to Richmond being 136 miles. The first station we arrived at was Fishersville, 129 [miles] to Richmond. The second station was Wanesborough, 124 miles to Richmond. About halfway between Fishersville & Wanesborough we stopped about 1/2 hour, going up grade. They burnt chestnut & oak wood. Passed through 4 tunnels between 2 stations. First tunnel we were 7 minutes passing through it. I timed it by my watch. We were running lively too. After we got through I had to look almost strait up in the air to see the top of the mountain. The third station was Meashum River, 115 miles to Richmond. Passed a sign board marked "Blairs Park 24 1/2 miles." There were 2 trains on the side track at this station, one a passenger train just arrived, loaded mostly with soldiers. The name of the R.R. is Virginia Central. The name of the passenger train engine was Hero, the name of the other engine was C.S.C. Name [of the] fourth station Ivy. Fifth station Charlottsville, quite a place. Sixth station Shadwell. Here was a brick building & several wooden buildings with the insides all torn out. At this station we run on the side track & waited about one hour for another train. Between this station & the next, we stopped to get wood. At 5 P.M. we were just 90 miles from Richmond. Seventh station not known. 8th station, Lindsays, did not stop here. 9th station, Gordonsville, another road branched off here & went to Culpepper. Several barracks & tents were here put up around & near the depot & filled with wounded. Reached here about dark & stayed about 1 hour for the officers to get their supper, so it was reported. We then went on stopping at the different stations along the road till we arrived at Richmond. I bought 2 blackberry pies for $1.00 & sold one to R.G. Seymour for $1.00. They were very thin, hardly more than the top & bottom crust & hardly berrys enough to color the crust. Pretty poor things but I was very hungry & I bought the first thing I could get hold of.[107]

As most Union captives reached Richmond they were usually paraded through the city to tobacco warehouses along the river. Sergeant Taft counted 300 men to a floor in his temporary prison, with only four small windows present to allow air and light to enter. Within two days most of the enlisted men were moved to Belle Island in the James River about a half mile from the city. Of the six or seven acres on the island, between two and three acres of ground were allotted for the prison, which was overshadowed by a defensive earthwork, guards and cannon. Roland Bowen wrote home that as of December 1863 the island, which was one mile in length and one-half in width, was filled with 6,000 prisoners on only three acres. He was also surprised to find, as he walked through the famous city, that it and its citizens seemed in better condition and appearance than he had been led to believe, following 27 hard months of warfare against them.

According to Thomas Taft there were only 4,000 prisoners on the island with tents for 3,000, but most sources agree with Bowen. At 10 a.m. and 4 p.m. the men were fed, usually being given one-quarter loaf or five ounces of bread each, and 15 pounds of meat, bones included, for a squad of 100 men. This provided a two ounce portion per man, with seven ounces total food constituting breakfast and dinner. The four o'clock meal averaged out at one pint of soup, using beans and rice alternately; it was very thin, usually about two to three spoonfuls of rice or beans in the pint.[108]

Returning to Captain Domschcke we find that after the prison column traversed the river into Virginia, the guards of Pickett's Division were replaced by the mounted infantry of General John D. Imboden, and soon the men were forced to cover 15 to 20 miles a day to keep up with Imboden's horsemen. His remembrances of the trip included camping near Martinsburg in an apple orchard and at Winchester near a spring shaded by the "massive limbs of a gigantic elm hundreds of years old."

Upon arrival in Richmond, this Wisconsin captain recounted how the Federals were formed in a four-file column with guards on either side, and were escorted through the streets all the while under the gaze of hundreds of curious white and black citizens, until they reached Cary Street. There, next to a canal Domschcke was placed with other officers in a three-story building marked with a sign that read: "Libby & Son, Ship Chandlers & Grocers."[109]

Although the preceding accounts surely covered the journey from Pennsylvania to Richmond very thoroughly, this final narrative gives a better picture of the intense suffering of the average Yankee on that long trip. The writer was Captain William Wilkin, 1st West Virginia Cavalry (U.S.) who became separated from his company on July 5 while assisting an artillery crew in action near Hagerstown, Maryland. That night while in search of his regiment, he was picked up by a squad of "about a dozen gray-backs" who were concealed along

"Libby Prison," Richmond, VA. (PBE)

the path he and a comrade were travelling. Here in Wilkin's own words is his story from that moment on:

> I was taken to Williamsport, and put under guard. About ten o'clock I began to have an appetite for my rations, having eaten nothing since early in the morning, and ventured to make some inquiry for supper, when I was informed that I could have nothing to eat that night. The next morning I was politely informed that they had nothing to give me for breakfast. In the evening, however, they gave me 1 pint of flour; this I wet up with water and baked on a stove for supper, breakfast, dinner and supper again next night, but I need not think to stop and particularize. Here my hardships commenced. I had been doing duty before my capture that no one who has been in the cavalry service would believe any man could endure: but never up to now (July 6th) had I endured anything to equal what was just ahead of me. Up to the 10th they kept us near Williamsport on the Virginia side, with almost nothing to eat; at which time we were (over 3,000 in all) started to Richmond, with 130 miles of the way to travel on foot. The first day's march we had nothing to eat; the second day, about noon, we drew just simply one biscuit and half a pound of beef. From that time till we got through, at irregular intervals, we were served with one pint of flour each, and a small piece of beef; and sometimes the flour was so sour that I don't believe a decent well-to-do country dog would eat it. Of course, we suffered intensely. Many fell dead by the roadside; while many others fell down, completely exhausted, and, after being kicked and cursed and bayoneted till it was found they could not possibly proceed, they were paroled and turned loose.
>
> Our march from Williamsport to Staunton comprised the whole length of the Shenandoah valley, which is the best watered region I have ever traveled in; yet we suffered horribly for water. I saw the men, 8 or 10 at once, after having been nearly famished for water, break from the ranks to procure a drink from a spring or a pump by the edge of the road, and, in every case, they were immediately driven back at the point of the bayonet, without having time to get

a drop. It was pitiable, to see them go along, cups in hand, ready to dip and drink from every little mud-puddle or stagnant pool that came within reach; and this, too, in one of the best watered countries in the world....

"And how did you stand it?" That question was asked me more than one-hundred times on the road. I answered that nothing kept me up but the resolution that I had formed—never to give up till I fell dead in my tracks—This I told our men, together with the strong and unconquerable desire I had to get back and fight them (the rebs) again which kept me up, but it was by the hardest that I got through several times I reeled and staggered like a drunken man; my head became dizzy, my sight failed me; I almost sunk to the earth—Once I caught hold of my comrade, and steadied myself for a few minutes, and then traveled on again, staggering at every step till a halt was ordered. Toward the last of the tramp, I suffered very much with my feet, for not being used to walking any in the last two years they soon became so blistered that I could not wear my boots and had to take it barefooted. Being on a McAdamized pike, I soon became badly crippled. My feet took to swelling and every step I took pained me to the very heart—but I must hurry along.

On the 20th we landed in Richmond a little before daylight... At daylight we were marched through the streets and crammed into a large warehouse opposite Castle Thunder. One thousand of us were crowded into this place, the filthiest place I ever saw—and kept there till evening, when we were marched out and over to Bell Island—Here we lay for three days on this sandbar, without any shelter to protect us from the scorching heat of the sun. During these three days I was very sick and being thus exposed I suffered very much. On the 23rd we were loaded into stock cars and joyously started on our way to Chesapeake Bay for a truce....

On the 24th Captain Wilkin and others landed at Annapolis. They were given clean clothes and plenty to eat and there he commenced the above letter to his home.[110]

V

FROM BATTLEFIELD TO
HALLOWED GROUND

"I infer that the ground on which the battle was fought was made for battle and graveyard—the one always requiring the other—for it is good for nothing else."

"Our Town is quite a noted place, it seems to me they will never get done coming to the battlefield."[1]

In leaving behind the several chapters highlighting the battlefield as it appeared soon after the fighting, the many dead and the early and final burials associated with them, the care of the wounded and the field hospitals, and also the prisoners of war, deserters and stragglers, it is now time to conclude this study of the aftermath of Gettysburg. The last chapter is a focus on a variety of topics, which include the government's problem of guarding the huge battle area with all of the assorted military equipment and arms left behind; the collecting of weapons and other useable items; the injuries inflicted upon visitors and residents who were careless in handling abandoned ordnance; the early relic and souvenir hunters and the growth of a thriving business selling war mementoes; a synopsis of the damage claims filed by citizens and farmers who had been devastated by the actions of the two armies; and finally, the construction of an overview following the early movement to memorialize, preserve, and protect the battleground as a national shrine.

If at this time the reader has not read or does not recall the theme of chapter one, it might aid in understanding the upcoming subjects to again contemplate that material so as to become familiar with the amount of destruction wrought by the two forces. A review will enable one to see and experience the foul atmosphere of that festering and melancholy arena, along with the accumulated tons of military hardware left strewn everywhere by the contending antagonists. Those who have perused the entire book in its se-quence already well know the scenes spoken of. Admittedly, perhaps this forthcoming section should have been placed in line following the first chapter, because it follows the natural momentum to proceed from the physical damage and litter to the clean up and protection of property and to other assorted problems associated with those important tasks. In conclusion, however, this section covers such a wide scope of material that its placement here should readily sum up the book and tie together its four previous chapters.

Visitors

The early visitors and curiosity seekers, grave robbers and ghouls, army guards and quartermaster workers hurrying to beat the scavengers and relic hunters from pilfering the rich bounty of booty scattered everywhere, the medical people and their attendant volunteers, in fact anyone who was in direct contact with the 25 to 30 square mile battlefield, were all forced to endure the thousands of hideous sights which abounded on all sides and toward all points of the compass. And they were not limited to sight alone. One soldier described the atmosphere as "air laden with mist and pervaded by that strange musty smell peculiar to battlefields immediately after a battle." Another witness likewise attested: "The air was filled with that indescribably sickening odor never found save on a summer battle-field."[2]

Scenes of decomposing bodies and littered battle debris were common sights long into the aftermath period of Gettysburg. (USLC)

Out of all of the visitors to the field in the month after the clash, one of the more legitimate was an unnamed woman from New England. Her story illustrates the problems many strangers encountered and faced on a daily basis when they entered the unsettled realm of Gettysburg to recover the remains of a loved one or to tend to a wounded family member or friend. For some reason this story attracted wide attention, probably because it had such a pathetic side to it. Those who told and retold it knew it would touch the hearts of anyone hearing it, and all realized the actions of the woman matched those of anyone in the same situation. The first time the account was printed was during the middle of August 1863 by one of the local papers. It read:

Incident Of The Battle-Field

A few days ago the battle-field of Gettysburg was visited by a lady from Massachusetts who had come all the way from that distant State in search of the body of her dead husband. She found the spot upon which her husband fought and fell, all covered over with graves, without marks to show who lay beneath those clods. After opening about 20 graves and failing to find the object of her search, her heart almost failed. She moved on to the next one, when something seemed to say to her—"This is my husband's grave." She had it opened, and imagine her feelings when she discovered that it contained all that was near and dear to her on earth. She recognized the body by a peculiar button on his coat in which he was buried. She marked the grave and weepingly left the spot. Sad, sad indeed, are the associations of a battle-field.[3]

J. Howard Wert, who would soon after become an officer in the army and then a professor of education, was the original guide and benefactor who escorted this grief-stricken woman over the field. In 1907 he reported that the confusion in Adams County after the battle was "indescribable," and, "was a task herculean for sorrowing friends to find any trace of loved ones, either the dead or the wounded." Wert testified that these quests were often carried on for weeks or months and many ended in utter disappointment. According to John Wert, the Massachusetts woman was in search of her spouse on a little rocky ridge west of John Rose's "wheatfield," where the 22nd, 28th, and 32nd, Massachusetts Regiments and the 2nd Company Andrew Massachusetts Sharpshooters had been engaged on July 2. Oddly, in a later publication another version of this story was described. The writer was not J.H. Wert and he claimed that the buried soldier fought with the 13th Massachusetts Regiment on the *first day's field*.

Two other persons escorted by Wert around the bloody ground and through the hospitals in those aftermath days were Annie Roberts and a "Mrs. Harness" of Richland, New York. Mrs. Roberts of 114 Lewis Street, New York City, came looking for her brother Robert Guy and husband Elias Roberts, both who saw service in the 14th Brooklyn Regiment. After contending with many difficulties, Annie Roberts found her sibling in a field hospital with a leg torn off by a shell, while her husband as she later discovered, had been made a prisoner and was marched to Virginia with Lee's army. Mrs. Harness was not so fortunate. Both her son and husband had enlisted in the 147th New York Infantry. Hers was a most tragic ending, for the husband Elias, age 43 and son De Grasse, age 19, were among the dead, one was killed on July 1 and the other succumbed on July 15 of wounds received the same day as his father. As both men were privates of Company C, it is a good guess that they were cut down while fighting side by side. There is hardly any greater tragedy concerning the Battle of Gettysburg than this. The husband is buried in the National Cemetery today, but no trace of her son De Grasse was ever found.[4]

The people with justifiable reasons for being present at Gettysburg like those just noted, were in the minority to the "foolish, mischievous, and excitable characters of both sexes who always congregate where there are scenes of horror and blood to gratify a disgusting morbid curiosity."[5] The former visitor usually hired some resident to guide and assist them in finding a particular grave, or a person confined within the boundaries of a certain field hospital. One commonly used way to locate people or even lost objects, was to place an advertisement or "notice" in one of the several area newspapers. A few examples of these notices exist which often amounted to pleas, and are worthy of insertion here.

The first to be presented is very unusual, as it requested help on July 30 in determining the whereabouts of a valuable family heirloom rather than a person:

Lost

A large size double case gold watch with link chain belonging to Captain W.L. Magruder, C.S.A., who was killed at Gettysburg, July 3; and thought to have been placed in possession of Captain W.D. Nau, Co. B, 11th Miss. Regt., who died, July 13th at 1st Army Corps, 2d Division Hospital, and who, it is supposed, gave it to some one previous to his death for safe keeping. The full value of the watch will be given for its return and the information gratefully received. Apply to Mrs. Mary C. Magruder, 64 Courtlandt Street, Baltimore.

Similarly, through an ad in the November 16th *Compiler*, a Northern man sought a less monetarily valuable article but equally important memento of his lost boy.

Memorandum

The undersigned is informed that some one has found a MEMORANDUM [diary] belonging to his son, JOSEPH H. BALDWIN, Co. D, 149th P.V., who was killed in the first day's fight at Gettysburg, on the Millerstown [or Fairfield] road, near Mrs. [Elizabeth F.] Shultz's residence. The undersigned is very anxious to obtain said Memorandum, and will liberally reward any person who will place it in his possession, or leave it at the *"Compiler"* office. Joseph Baldwin Nov. 16, 1863

And on July 23 this typical case appeared where a person was in search of a relative:

Fort Worth, July 16, 1863.—My brother, Captain S.[L.]E. Pond, Company E, Seventh Wisconsin volunteers, was wounded at Gettysburg. Beyond that I can find no trace of him. Any person that can give any information about him, where he is, or what has become of him, or assist him if alive, will put me under lasting obligations and shall be liberally rewarded.

> Simon Pond
> First Wisconsin Artillery
> Fort Worth; Washington, D.C.

We do not know what the results were of Mr. Pond's advertisement, but Captain Levi Pond was discharged from the service on December 10, 1864.

This next was placed in an October 1, 1863, paper, indicating a long quest for a friend or family member.

"Any person giving information of the grave of James M. Daniel, Twenty-seventh Pennsylvania volunteers, will confer a great favor on an affected family in Philadelphia. Address, Rev. Thomas F. McClure, Oakland Mills, Juniata County, Pa."[6]

As no transcript of Daniel's final resting place is available, it is presumable that he was buried as an "unknown," and the sorrowing family would never gain any shred of solace or peace of mind concerning his fate, except that he was killed on July 1.

Professor Wert stated it best when he concluded that these advertisements most clearly tell of "aching hearts in which the dread void of uncertainty still remained unsatisfied by positive knowledge."

The Gettysburg *Compiler* inserted another appeal on July 27: "Any person giving information at this office where the grave of Corporal Wm. Strong, of the 2d Delaware regiment, can be found will confer a very great favor on his wife, who had been searching in vain for his body during the past week."

The body of Corporal Strong, a member of Company D who was killed on July 2, was eventually discovered as it is now interred in the Delaware plot of the National Cemetery.

The messages kept coming even into late summer and early fall. On September 15 the Adams *Sentinel* printed this one.

Information Wanted

Any person at Gettysburg, who can give information of the exact burial place of Lieut. Humphreville, of the 24th Michigan Inf., will confer a favor upon his sister. Address Mrs. J.S. Whitcomb, Chicago, Ill. Any information left with the Editor of the *Sentinel*, will be promptly communicated.

Second Lieutenant Humphreville, 29, of Company K was shot in the abdomen on July 1. Unfortunately, as Union graves on the first day's field were rarely marked, the body of this officer from Livonia, Michigan, was probably never recovered.

Other advertisements from this chaotic period shed light on the many unusual and confusing situations which developed following the momentous battle. A few more will suffice to give the reader a taste for the unhappy "climate" of that era.

On November 3 a newspaper story was run in the *Sentinel* which made the point that persons had to be careful when disinterring bodies from the field.

Singular Case of Mistaken Identity

In the battle of Gettysburg there was engaged with the Union forces a young man, whose parents reside in Birmingham Allegheny county, Penna. It was announced that he was among the killed in that sanguinary fight, and his friends proceeded to the battle-field to recover his remains. After some difficulty, they managed to recover what they were positive was his body, and brought it home and had it interred in the family burying ground. A few nights since, the house of the parents was visited by a young man from the army, who aroused the household. On entering the house what was the surprise and astonishment of the parents to discover in their visitor their deeply mourned son, whose remains they fancied were resting quietly in the cemetery. It turned out that the body brought on and interred there was that of a rebel, who wore in the battle a United States uniform and whose resemblance to the Union soldier was a very striking one.

Notices like this were a familiar sight in newspapers following the battle. (ACHS)

Information Wanted.

Any person at Gettysburg, who can give information of the exact burial place of Lieut. HUMPHREVILLE, of the 24th Michigan Inf., will confer a favor upon his Sister. Address Mrs. J. S. Whitcomb, Chicago, Ill. Any information left with the Editor of the *Sentinel*, will be promptly communicated.

In that same issue an article appeared on the first page which concerned a dead Federal sergeant who had been encountered on the field with the ambrotype photograph of three children clasped tightly in his hand. Today, the event is a familiar "human interest" story of the battle, but in 1863 it really fueled the imaginations of hundreds of people who read the melancholy account. Later through much publicity given to the photograph the man was identified as 32-year-old Amos Humiston of the 154th New York, who was mortally wounded on July 1. He had been found and then buried along Stratton Street near the railroad tracks on the east side of Gettysburg.[7]

Another poignant story featured in one of the newspapers of the day was that of Private Edward McCarroll who was enrolled in Company E, 69th Pennsylvania Infantry and had been seriously wounded on July 3. After recovering from his injuries during three and one-half months at Camp Letterman, McCarroll was making his way home on furlough to Philadelphia. While in the process of crossing the Lebanon Valley Railroad tracks near the depot at Harrisburg, Pennsylvania, he was hit by a locomotive and "horribly mangled." This unlucky soldier died a few hours later.[8]

Sometimes the notices in the papers concerned local soldiers. Often the news was good; sometimes it was not.

For instance, on August 3 the Gettysburg *Compiler* inserted two short stories about Adams County men. One account revealed that Calvin Hamilton, a member of Co. K, 1st Pennsylvania Reserves, who had been wounded in the late battle, had not lost his leg as was previously reported, but had suffered only a "severe flesh wound, from which he is rapidly recovering."

The second article was not favorable information for the friends of William McGrew of Mummasburg, Pennsylvania, a tiny village just northwest of Gettysburg. As a member of the 1st Reserves, he too had been wounded on July 2, but McGrew died on July 26, and sympathy was expressed by the editor to the mother and family of this young man.

Often the newspapers recorded the medical conditions of prominent wounded officers or even plain, non-descript privates. Of the former, a piece was featured on Lieutenant Colonel William W. Dudley of the 19th Indiana Infantry who was injured on July 1. The article observed that this former captain of Company B, whose parents lived in Connecticut, was "reduced to a mere skeleton" by September 14.

Dudley had been shot in the right leg and carried to the house of Henry J. Stahle, the editor of the Gettysburg *Compiler*. On Saturday July 4 the lieutenant colonel was moved to Littlestown to the town residence of Ephraim Myers, Esq. When the bullet entered Dudley's body it shattered the bone in his lower leg into 15 fragments. The leg would not heal and another operation became necessary. It was performed by Dr. Thomas O. Kinzer of Littlestown, Pennsylvania, who removed the limb. At the time of the news story, Dudley was beginning to improve. He survived and resigned from the service in 1864.[9]

One of the earliest notices came on July 7 in the *Sentinel and General Advertiser*. From this little bare-bones tidbit of information grew one of the most famous and interesting incidents of the Gettysburg battle. Its simplicity hid its importance:

"But withal, we have been called to part with some. We have learned only of the following:—killed, Miss Virginia Wade by our own sharpshooters;..."

And as we now know and have for over a hundred years, Jennie Wade was not killed by Union riflemen but by the misdirected bullet of a Confederate soldier while she was kneading dough for biscuits in her sister's kitchen.

Equally as important was the documentation of the famed exploits of John Burns, the former Gettysburg constable who captured the imaginations of the world. Again, we have a concise, to-the-point depiction in the July 20th *Compiler*:

"Our townsman John L. Burns, was wounded during Wednesday's action. He volunteered his services and advanced into the thickest of the fight, where he fell,

Mary Virginia Wade

receiving a wound in the leg and arm. We hope he will soon recover and enjoy the honors which his bravery merits."[10]

Then there was also the commonplace business of a small town to attend to, such as the needs of farmers and other citizens trying to find, sort out, and return to the rightful owners, hundreds of wandering and missing animals. The July 20 *Compiler* tried to assist this effort by running this circular:

"Judging from the numerous inquiries made after stray cows, hogs, etc., a large number must be running at large throughout the county. Persons should make known at once any strays that may come under their notice, so that the owners may get them as speedily as possible."

A sidelight to this is a story of a cow who returned of her own free will to its residence after an absence of nearly 12 days. The animal was the property of the McCreary family, and one day while they were eating supper a "familiar bellowing in the street" was heard. Everyone ran outside and behold, there stood their old cow "looking as happy as it is possible for a cow to look at being home again." Although she was struck by two bullets, the creature was no worse for wear than before the battle.[11]

✛ ✛ ✛

Legitimate reasons for being present on the former battlefield were sometimes tainted and overshadowed, especially in the eyes of the military men left behind, by the work of the hordes of scavengers who descended on the grounds like flocks of vultures to collect the vast array of castaway arms, clothing, and equipment now mostly forgotten by the departed armies. No one questioned the right of volunteer citizen nurses or concerned relatives of soldiers to be on the former battleground. In the words of Emily Souder it was for them a heart-breaking time, where "[a] constant procession of coffins meets the eye; groups of men standing in the fields searching for the name of some friend or brother. The town has been filled with people on these mournful errands."[12] It was the plunderers who beguiled and befuddled the chief quartermaster of the Army of the Potomac, Rufus Ingalls. He was aware that civilians were walking, riding and driving off the field with much useable government property, but at that point in the crisis there was little he or his representatives could do about it.

In a letter dated July 8 at Frederick, Maryland, to his chief, General M.C. Meigs, the quartermaster-general of the U.S. Army, Ingalls explained: "I saw citizens carrying off arms, and doubt not it will require coercive steps to recover them. A large quantity, though, was already delivered at the depot, which had been gathered from the field. The people there are doubtless loyal, but they seem to be very simple and parsimonious, and evinced but little enthusiasm [for helping us]."[13]

General Rufus Ingalls, chief quartermaster of the Army of the Potomac. His responsibilities for the clean-up of the battlefield were enormous. (USAMHI)

Forthcoming is a comprehensive section on Ingall's solution to these problems, but for now several examples expounding on the work of these scavengers will suffice to illustrate his dilemma.

In actuality there were really three types of battlefield "looters." The first were the normal individuals or family groups who, out of curiosity, came to view the carnage, and upon leaving, took a handful of relics home for souvenirs, or even something quite larger or more valuable such as a rifle or sword. The next category was the country farmers who went in with a wagon and a serious will and collected artillery harnesses or blankets in bulk, or led away a loose horse or mule, or similar miscellaneous pieces of equipment or material which could be put to use on a farm. As a matter of fact, many of these hard-working people had lost greatly from the presence of the two armies in their "backyards," so they naturally felt it only right to regain something of what was taken or destroyed. The third and final set was the semi-professional; those ruffians who came in large groups and numerous conveyances. These "gangs" arrived to methodically and literally strip the field of all useful, valuable and sellable items, in the way of weapons, clothing, lead, brass, iron, soldiers' money, watches, and other personal property, anything which would turn a quick profit for them. Regarding the three varieties of looters, we have an equal number of stories to illustrate their methods and what became of them.

The first interesting anecdote concerns a Pennsylvania Supreme Court judge who, like many others, flocked to the field to see the unusual sights associated with such a large and destructive event. This judge, dressed in broadcloth, immaculate linen, with snowy white collar and cuffs and silk hat, must have looked out of place as he walked across the fields and meadows spread over with filth, stench, and death. Weapons were everywhere; 30,000 to 40,000 of all kinds would be a conservative estimate, and the judicial visitor could not refrain from picking up a fine musket as a sober reminder of his excursion. His honor may even had seen this sign, as many were posted all around Gettysburg.

Special Notice.

CITIZENS visiting the battle-field are warned against carrying away any Government property, and all those having taken such property, either Federal or Confederate, are directed to return the same without delay, to my office in Gettysbutrg, thereby saving themselves from arrest and punishment.

W. WILLARD SMITH.

Capt· Aide de Camp to the Gen. in Chief and acting Provost Marshal.

However, if "his honor" did read the broadside, he chose to ignore it. When asked by a guard to turn over the weapon, he haughtily told the soldier to mind his own business or he would be reported to headquarters. One who was present recalled the conclusion of the meeting between broadcloth and dirty Union blue:

That silly speech was his finish. Martial law respects not persons. It takes no more account of a judge than a hod carrier. So to burying dead horses he went, not of choice, but because the bayonets behind him were sharp.

The day was a hot one. The work was new to the Judge. It was entirely out of his usual line. Soon his hands were woefully blistered. I am sorry to say that, although a Judge, he used profane language about the matter. The guards didn't seem to care a ha' penny if he swore himself blind. At length he paused from exhaustion and to think over the indignity.

"Get busy, you, there," yelled the unfeeling guard.

"Do you know who I am?" screamed the laborer....

"I'm Judge _____"

"Well," was the unfeeling reply, —"I hope you are one of those [goddamn] Supreme Court Judges that say a soldier has no right to vote, and that they keep you here a month. Get busy, or I'll put my bayonet in you...."

The Judge was kept at work, by spells, for forty-eight hours. He left Gettysburg vowing that somebody should suffer for his lacerated feelings and blistered hands....I don't believe that [he] ever hankered after visiting another battlefield.[14]

This next story exemplifies the neighboring citizens whose farms, as J. Howard Wert remarked, "had been wholly or partially devastated and who had lost much in various ways, [and] sought to recoup themselves somewhat by gathering up blankets and other things of which they could make use."

Thomas Knox saw several of these fellows at work near Joseph Sherfy's peach orchard. Said he: "Here in this orchard I find a countryman engaged in cutting the harness from one of the dead battery horses and preparing to carry it from the field. Another has collected a dozen blankets dropped by soldiers in the heat of the engagement. Another walks past me with three of the best muskets he can find on the battlefield."[15]

The experiences of Nathaniel Lightner, a farmer who lived along the Baltimore Pike south of the village, could be added as a companion piece to this version. His farm had been totally wrecked, and he and his family had gathered relics from the land to sell to a New York man to help defray the cost of replanting and rebuilding his farm. Lightner commented on the situation:

"Then...the Government arrested me, I must tell you about that. Soon after [I sold these items] a Colonel [Captain H.B.] Blood, the meanest man in the world, came down to gather up Government property, and he had me arrested. I told him how it was, that we had no idea of doing anything unlawful; but he was determined to make me all the trouble he could. He put me to considerable expense, but my neighbors got me off after a few days. That arrest is the only thing of it all that made me mad, and I am mad about it yet."[16]

Our concluding illustration concerns the more serious "thieves and plunderers who swooped over the ground before the dead were all buried; and who continued their ravages for weeks." These real scourings of nature, Professor Wert pointed out, were "seamed with streakings of innate selfishness, depravity and ruthless disregard of humanity [and] surge to the surface in every great cataclysm." Wert, by the way, who was often seen exploring the battleground and picking up many small relics for himself, revealed that these rogues

came in teams to load up their loot. They traveled day and night, to hasten to the raven's feast. [They came from Spring Forge (Grove) in York County where] there was...a small paper mill located...; and there were through that section a number of nondescript scavengers, of mixed nationalities, who made a living by scouring the country over and collecting rags which were sold to the mill.

These men, with their teams drawn by spavined and disreputable specimens of horseflesh, hastened to Gettysburg, ostensibly to collect the clothing profusely scattered over the field of slaughter and in the environs of the hospitals. But all was fish that came to their net—guns and sabres on the battle ground, supplies for the wounded left unguarded after they had been unloaded, the few remaining chickens of devastated farms, the pigs that had scampered in terror from their shot-torn stys to the woodland and had not been reclaimed. They pilfered from the living and robbed the bodies of the dead. They even resurrected corpses from their shallow entombment in the hope that some valuable might be found on the festering body.

At points a little more remote from the heaviest conflict, where some fragments of fencing were yet standing, they made short cuts by throwing down what yet remained as they drove around in their career of plunder, and thus it was that three of the boldest met their finish.

As the caravan was about to start York county way, loaded with its miscellaneous loot, a farmer's wife expostulated with them about their wanton destruction of what little was left. They cursed her in mongrel English and "Pennsylvania Dutch." Her son, who came up, not feeling competent to fight at close quarters three stalwart men, took a surer and more effective means of revenge. He knew where there was a squad of Captain Smith's men at a short distance and to them he hied.

Fifteen minutes later the cavalrymen swooped down on the marauders. Cursing didn't go; neither did entreaties. Prayers, tears, profanity and "Pennsylvania Dutch" were all wasted articles when it came to dealing with Captain Willard Smith's "Forty Thieves."

The dose the rag gatherers received was an ample sufficiency to give them the shivers for all future life at the barest glimpse of a blue uniform. Their plunder was confiscated; their teams and they themselves put to work. The work they did was hard work; it was menial and repulsive work, but there were glittering bayonets to enforce activity and diligence in their tasks. It was a long time before the trio ever saw Spring Forge. When they did they were sadder men; likewise, wiser. They had lost all desire for battlefield plunder.[17]

In retrospect, it was not only the county farmers and outsiders who committed these acts. The townspeople had their hand at it too, as remembered by Liberty Hollinger. She maintained both groups were at fault, saying: "It was not very long after the battle until the town began to fill with friends and strangers, some intent on satisfying their curiosity, and others, alas! to pick up anything of value to be found. Blankets, sabres, army guns, and many other articles were thus obtained and smuggled away or secreted. Sometime after the battle when the Government began to count up the losses, houses in Gettysburg were searched and shame to say, some yielded up sound and well preserved government property."[18]

Returning to the subject matter of the first chapter it may be recalled that many travellers to Gettysburg remarked on and were either engrossed or repulsed by the sight of so many dead animals, especially horses. And looking back to the previous paragraphs, J. Howard Wert comically described how a judge was forced to bury horses as punishment for his misdeeds. In the cleanup of the battlefield the problem of eliminating the tons of dead animal flesh, including the carcasses of horses, mules, oxen, cows, hogs, and other creatures, was second only in importance to the burial of the humans struck down during the many hours of combat action. Interestingly, a conservative estimate of the total weight of dead horse, mule, cattle, and human carcasses left on the field on July 4 would be over six million pounds.

So to revive our appreciation for the numbers of all army animals present at the battle let us look again at the statistics:

On June 1, 1863, at the beginning of the Gettysburg Campaign, the Union Army of the Potomac recapitulated its forces. Below are the totals present for the seven corps of infantry, one cavalry corps, the artillery reserve, the engineer brigade, the provost marshal's brigade and army headquarters. It must be remembered that these figures *do not* reflect the scores of men, animals, wagons, and the like accompanying the ordnance, quartermaster, medical and subsistent portions of that army, nor do they count any of the Confederate forces and support. Those marked with an asterisk (*) are estimates only.

Officers	7,937
Enlisted men	134,161
Horses	29,276
Horses, total for the entire Union army	43,303*
(one other source says 35,048)	
Mules	21,844
Wagons	4,391
Ambulances	928
Ambulances (entire army)	1,200
Artillery pieces	362
(67 Batteries & 6,100 horses)	
Caissons/Limbers/Battery Wagons	1,200*

As a curious footnote to these sums, a paragraph in the Gettysburg *Compiler* for February 8, 1864, stated that the Army of the Potomac contained "8,000 teams" of animals and wagons, which added up to 32,000 horses and mules, and "[i]f placed in a single line they would extend over sixty miles." Another estimate gave the length of the Army of the Potomac on the march as 83 1/2 miles.

The army's chief quartermaster, General Ingalls, claimed that it took one wagon for every 37-1/4 to 50 men and officers, and this vehicle could normally carry seven days' food, forage, ammunition, baggage, and hospital stores for the above number.[19] (Horses at hard work consume about 26 pounds of feed a day, mostly hay and grain, and from 10 to 15 gallons of water.)

The government agents left on the field had to deal with the problem of dead human and animal flesh, at the same time they were collecting the thousands of muskets,

"Old Bob." One of the nearly 70,000 horses present during the Gettysburg Campaign. He helped to pull a supply wagon for the 14th Vermont Infantry. His caretaker was teamster Private Silas Knight of that regiment. (TSF)

serviceable ammunition, and other items deemed worthy of pick up and reuse. Former Pennsylvania army lieutenant John Wert summed it up this way in 1907.

> One of the most urgent necessities of the field was the burial or burning of the thousands [about 3000] of dead horses littered over it and the partial sanitation in other respects of the hideous aftermath of the battle which, unless promptly disposed of, bore disease and death in its train.
>
> The men at the command of the provost marshal labored incessantly and energetically, but seemed entirely too few in numbers to produce speedy results. Some of the unwounded Confederate prisoners were put to work, but most of these had already been sent on to Baltimore. Those of them that were still on hand worked only when a bayonet was in close proximity.
>
> But the provost guards and the Confederate prisoners had frequent recruits to their ranks from another class of laborers.

Of course, Wert has already told us who these "new recruits" were. Like the judge above, civilians who ran up against the unyielding and hard-hearted provost guards were forced to engage in "the uncongenial task of burying horses on the field or digging great, deep sinks [latrines] at the hospitals." Those arrested usually did duty for 24 or 48 hour shifts, with infrequent rest spells, and they were fed bean soup, hard tack, and coffee.[20]

It seems from the material available that the most common complaint of arrest was for carrying off a musket or "similar trophy." The provost detachment, then under Captain Smith had first tried other means to halt the outflow of property and to clean up the fast decaying animal carcasses. For instance, on July 7, 1863, a broadside was nailed up around town and was also placed by Smith in all of the newspapers. It read:

To all Citizens

Men, Horses and Wagons wanted immediately, to bury the dead and to clean our streets, in such a thorough way as to guard against a pestilence. Every good citizen can be of use by reporting himself, at once, to Capt. W.W. Smith, acting Provost Marshal, Office, N.E. corner Centre Square.

There were few takers, which inherently made it even harder for the soldiers to remember any "good citizens" living in Adams County, Pennsylvania.

With the passage of time all of the dead animals were dealt with; they were either buried, burned, or simply rotted away, and the bones hauled away to be crushed up for fertilizer. Due to the scarcity of workers most of these nonhuman creatures appeared to have been cremated, causing a Pennsylvania soldier to remark that the dead animals, "were burned and the odor from the burning horse flesh made our departure smell like an escape from a hateful charnal house."[21]

Captain Blood, one of the quartermaster officers left in charge of the clean up, wrote in his diary that on July 10 his squad buried "about 100 horses." And on July 11 he casually noted: "Burned Some Horses on the Emmettsburg Road." In reading his diary, it does not take one long to comprehend that the work of destroying these many beasts seemed a failure. The work his men accom-

A page from the diary of Captain Henry Blood. (USLC)

plished in this quarter amounted to very little, as he scribbles only two notations about dealing with the dead horse problem.[22]

Other horses to be dealt with included those found injured, abandoned, or lost. These were often rounded up by the citizenry and put back into shape if warranted, and then illegally taken for their own personal use. This deed was especially frowned on by the provost force. The brother of John C. Will was the owner of one of Gettysburg's hotels. He found this to be especially true. Mr. Will explained.

My brother [Charles] who had just arrived home at the close of the battle on Saturday morning went out over the battlefield and seeing many horses straying around being crippled and wounded, and as he noticed the Government stamp on them he thought that meant they were condemned, cast out, and unfit for further use and as some were slightly injured, he thought by proper care and attention they could be made pretty good horses, he accordingly commenced gathering up some of them. he brought them home and placed them in the "Globe Hotel" stable. he immediately started out on his second trip to get more horses, but in the meantime the Government had placed Guards over the field. now on his second trip they came upon him and arrested him...[but later released him] with a warning not to attempt [it] again.[23]

Some of the horses noted by Will *were* ultimately condemned and sold off by the Federal authorities. A government auction was advertised in the *Sentinel* on August 18, 1863, proposing a sale of broken down mounts, stating:

Condemned Horses and Mules

Quartermaster Smith advertises a sale of 350 condemned U.S. horses and mules, at Gettysburg, on Monday next—sale to be continued from day to day. The terms cash—in U.S. funds.

This was not the only recorded disposal. Again on both March 21, 1864, and May 9, 1864, the *Compiler* printed information concerning government sales of condemned animals. On the latter date the number 100 was mentioned.

Finally, a sizable herd of these poor creatures who had served both faithfully and hard, were deemed unfit for either continued use by the army or even resale to the populace. Several hundred in number, these animals were driven out to a thicket near Rock Creek, probably on the farm of Abraham Spangler (south of his spring), and shot. Their bones remained for a long time afterward as a reminder of the horrible slaughter of life at Gettysburg.

One of the men responsible for this unpleasant duty was 21-year-old Private Hezekiah Weeks, a blacksmith with the Patapsco Guards, an independent Maryland company on guard at Gettysburg from October to December. As part of his duties, Weeks was instructed to examine the hundreds of horses and mules left behind by the government. He doctored and restored to service those he could help, the others he was ordered to shoot.[24]

The inevitable possibility certainly exists that many of these animal bones and the skeletal remains of other creatures and humans were gathered up and sold to be made into fertilizer. It will be remembered that Mrs. Lydia Leister did this very thing. She attested that it took from July of 1863 to early 1865 for the meat to rot from the bones of the 17 dead horses on her property, after which she was able to collect 50 cents a hundred for approximately 750 pounds of bone.[25]

Besides the legal use of bone debris there were other more sinister complaints and accusations concerning the removal of human bones for museum specimens and even for fertilizer use. Recalling the Georgia newspaper article which warned that unless the Confederate bodies were "removed by fall, the owners of the ground have given notice that they 'intend ploughing up the land and grinding the bones for fertilizing purposes....'"[26]

Some human bones were used in more macabre and interesting ways. A black man named Isaac Carter was interviewed in 1915 and described how "[f]or years afterward farmers ploughing would once in a while find a skull, and they'd take those skulls home and have them setting up on the mantel piece for relics. But I didn't want no such relics as that."[27]

Private Frank Stoke saw other uses for these human artifacts. He called parts of the battlefield "a vast bone yard," with scores of skulls being kicked around the field by visitors like "footballs."[28]

But what angered people the most was not as John Wert attested, the premise that even at "the present day human bones are frequently turned up by the plow where their presence was not suspected." It was the notion that medical students and army doctors were traversing the ground actually gathering and assembling boxes of human bones. One such practitioner was Dr. John H. Brinton, who admitted that one of his duties, besides rendering aid to the wounded, was to "collect specimens and histories for the [Army Medical] museum." Jenny E. Jacobs recorded the idea a little more brutally. She declared that these men were going farther than just picking up pieces of the anatomy, but were in fact preparing various parts of the skeleton by boiling the meat off the bones in huge caldrons. Jacobs called these bones "the remains of heroes."[29]

◆ ◆ ◆

Quartermasters at Work

When General George Meade ordered his victorious army away from Gettysburg in the twenty-four hours between July 6 and 7, he had previously arranged for his corps commanders to bury the dead, collect the wounded, and canvass their operational areas for useable arms and accoutrements. By the 7th however, two of these difficult duties had fallen upon the small undermanned detachment of the Quartermaster Department. The head of this department in Washington was General Montgomery C. Meigs, and the chief quartermaster present with the Army of the Potomac was General Rufus Ingalls. But the actual implementation of Meade's orders, now that the bulk of the army was leaving, fell onto the shoulders of Captain William Willard Smith, an Aide-de-Camp on General-in-Chief Henry Halleck's staff, and Captain Henry B. Blood of the U.S. Quartermaster Department. These two officers were not the first to be instructed to "clean up and guard" the substantial battlefield grounds. That lead person had been Captain William C. Rankin, an inefficient staff member under General Ingalls. Ingalls left Rankin behind and in charge to sort out the mess, to recover as much property as possible, and to continue the burials of men and horses; all the while guarding whatever government ordnance and other materials remained from being carted away by civilians. And as this serviceable property was gathered up, especially the horses and wagons, it was to be forwarded immediately to Meade's army in Maryland or Virginia.

Until a proper guard could be established by Rankin, Meade temporarily detached 53-year-old Colonel R. Butler Price and his 2nd Pennsylvania Cavalry from the army's Provost Guard to assist the overwhelmed and ineffective captain. These troopers were supplemented by about 100 additional soldiers from a variety of infantry regiments that had been present during the battle. The task of these 100 men and the 575 cavalrymen was to guard wounded and unwounded prisoners, and protect the abandoned military equipment lying across 25 square miles of former battlefield. Almost immediately on July 3 and shortly afterward, many of the horse-mounted soldiers were put to work conducting thousands of Rebel prisoners to Westminster. Small detachments were then placed on guard and patrol duty across the field, while most of the infantrymen were used as sentries at the many field hospitals throughout the Gettysburg area.

Despite this total of over 600 men (who would soon be reduced to about 100), and the reinforcements which arrived on July 6 and united under Rankin (the 36th Regiment Pennsylvania Militia), disorder and chaos remained the order of the day. In reality, Rankin had done almost nothing to restore any type of control over the situation. So when Captains Smith and Blood arrived late on July 7, confusion ruled supreme.

One of the prime reasons for the turmoil was the ineffectiveness of Captain Rankin. An explanation may be found in his personal habits, for he was eventually court-martialed for drunkenness. Even though Rankin remained on duty until at least July 23, his minor bureaucratic duties were overshadowed by the real field work of Smith and Blood.

Captain Henry B. Blood. He and Captain Smith were the "workhorses" of the quartermaster detachments at Gettysburg. (NA/EJC)

Broadsides had been posted and newspaper notices printed, or at least would be attended to when Smith arrived, all to notify civilians that they were forbidden to visit the battlefield out of mere curiosity. No one was allowed to pass the pickets or guards without a proper permit, and under no circumstances was anyone allowed to carry off government property in the way of trophies and relics. Only friends or relatives of soldiers killed in action would be permitted onto the battlefield to complete the work of removing their dead.[30]

On July 6 Captain Blood received a directive in person from General Meigs to accompany Captain Smith to Gettysburg in order to, as stipulated, "collect gov't property, bury the dead, etc." On July 8 and within ten hours of his arrival Blood commenced his duties. His diary accounts are straightforward and from the journal entries it emerges that he was only in the Gettysburg area the first visit from 4 p.m. of July 7 to the morning of July 13. By this time there were approximately 100 enlisted men left to assist the two officers. Basically Blood's activities can be summarized thusly:

On July 8 he took with him a squad of prisoners to unload subsistence stores at the depot, then later partook of a ride over the battlefield. On July 9, a Thursday, he and a fatigue squad of prisoners buried 337 Rebel soldiers. On the 10th Blood was with the same squad and buried 30 bodies and 100 horses. That day he arrested several civilians for taking government property and put them to work on the field, "or if they had teams we made them haul a load of Arms to town." July 11 the captain accompanied a cavalry escort on their rounds and arrested one or two citizens. They then burned a few horses on the south end of the field. The following day, the 12th, he and a squad of Confederates marched out to the Rebel hospitals to assist in cleaning up and in burying the dead. These hospitals were "in a suffering condition," and Blood left ten prisoners as nurses. Then as noted, he "repaired for Washington" on July 13.

Captain Blood was back in Gettysburg at 2:30 p.m. on July 16. The next day he went out in search of government property, finding "two Wagon loads in one small hut." On the 18th he was present on the Mummasburg Road northwest of town and examined several houses and found U.S. owned material in all of them, including 50 guns, one horse, a wagon, and other items. Sunday, the 19th he had "very little work." On July 20, Captain Blood and his crew went out with a team and brought in "parts of gun carriages, Blankets," etc. Tuesday the 21st was a busy day. He hired a two-horse buggy and went to Cashtown, Pennsylvania, where he directed the inhabitants to bring in all government property in their possession and leave it at the Washington House hotel in Gettysburg. He then visited the Caledonia Iron Works which had been burned by the Rebels prior to the battle. The manager there voluntarily turned in to Blood a couple of sabres, and that act must have impressed the captain, for the man was duly authorized for a fee paid by Federal authorities, to collect additional public property in that area. On the 22nd Blood picked up a Rebel horse from Jake Sheaver in Hilltown, then rode back to Gettysburg with 40 sabres he had found, and by evening he had returned to Cashtown. Word came on the 23rd that Captain Rankin had officially turned the "collection depot" over to Blood, so he went in to Gettysburg by noon of that day, where he made arrangements to formally receive all government property from Rankin. The following morning he and Rankin went out to see the erection of hospital tents, most likely at Camp Letterman. In the same period he put Private George Jackson in charge of animal forage, while on the 27th Blood made an agreement with Jacob Schwartz out near White Run to rent 30 acres of grass for the use of the depot's horses and mules.

Between July 28 and October 14, Blood's diary includes only four entries, but he seems to be still in the county or nearby. October 13 for instance, places him in Emmitsburg with Captain Smith and "two ladies" from Gettysburg, while on the 14th he is at Chambersburg. So apparently Blood and Smith remained at the "post of Gettysburg," the authorized title given the area throughout the hospital and Camp Letterman period, July 4 through December 1863. The diary sequences and quoted passages from Blood give us a rather clear idea of the duties of one of the key men who was placed in charge of all quartermaster activities at Gettysburg.

The person in command of the post after the departure of Captain Rankin was Captain Smith, and he had his own agenda, which at times paralleled Blood's methods and schedule. William Willard Smith, or W. Willard Smith as he preferred to be addressed was born in New York, but appointed to his rank from Iowa in October of 1861. He became a personal aide-de-camp to General Henry W. Halleck and remained so until he was mustered into the 6th United States Volunteer Infantry in March of 1865 as its lieutenant-colonel. Smith held this latter position through November 1866, serving in the Department of the Plains when he was mustered out. It seems realistically accurate to say that for the years 1861 to 1865 he acted as a "trouble-shooter," if we may be permitted to use a modern term, for the General-in-Chief of the U.S. Army Henry Halleck, doing special duty in particular cases where the chief needed or wanted his own "man on the scene."

While Blood kept a personal diary, Smith on the other hand, as the supervisor on-site, was required to telegraph or write his superior General Meigs. Every few days some message from Smith left Gettysburg alerting Meigs to the troubles, activities, and work accomplished by the quartermaster details on and near the battlefield. One of the first reports was sent off on July

7, not by Smith but by General Ingalls. It outlined that the railroad was almost back to its normal schedule, and included information that Captain Rankin was left on the field to collect and forward all arms and other property to headquarters, and that Captains Smith and Blood would be assigned other duties "with troops," as they were not thought to be needed at Gettysburg. As it turned out both these officers did remain in the area for several weeks.

The day following that dispatch and just before General Ingalls rejoined Meade at Middletown, Maryland, he assigned Colonel Price and his 2nd Pennsylvania Cavalry to safeguard the battleground as citizens were "carrying off arms."[31]

On July 9 the first report left Gettysburg from Captain Smith. It was a telegram in which he described to General Meigs how the 2nd Pennsylvania was about to depart the field for Frederick, but the colonel had been persuaded to leave with Smith one squadron to guard 165 Rebel prisoners who were working at various tasks. Seventy-five of these prisoners were included on a detail unloading stores from the trains and assisting hospital attendants to load wounded soldiers for transport out of Gettysburg. Smith also recorded the burial of the above noted 337 Confederate dead using citizen laborers who had been found with U.S. property, plus the rest of the Southern prisoners, all using shovels he had purchased for 90 cents each.

A telegraphic message on July 10 informed Meigs how Smith had posted signs on the battleground and in town warning civilians of the consequences of taking away weapons and equipment. Captain Smith claimed that even after placing these notices on "different parts of the field," visitors continued to carry off material and also to, "mutilate those [items] on the field." That same day which was a Friday, Smith found 20 wagons loaded with stolen government property, and 75 people involved in these activities were detailed to bury horses. His only guard was still the 100 cavalrymen kindly loaned by Colonel Price. At one point, Smith exclaimed: "I could not disarm and unload one tenth the persons carying off arms." Moreover, he outlined how he had been all over the field finding no discarded pistols or sabres, but had collected four sabres from townspeople (both obviously popular souvenir items). By evening Smith and Blood had seen to the burial of 100 horses and 30 Rebels, and had examined 76 wagons, all of them containing miscellaneous government property, while being informed by witnesses that load after load had already been carried into the country. Oddly, many of the muskets he was finding were minus their lockplates, which he reasoned had been recently removed.

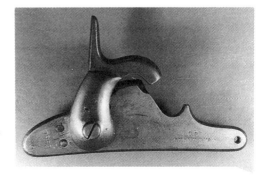

Mysteriously, Captain Smith found that many of the muskets he and his men were gathering were minus their lockplates. (MCW)

By July 11 the warnings and orders proclaimed by Smith and Blood seemed to be getting out to the public, as one farmer freely brought in ten muskets, and other weapons, plus blankets, shirts, pants, and knapsacks. That day Captain Smith himself collected 80 horses which were immediately put to work pulling ambulances, and he suggested that other citizens were beginning to notify him of government material concealed on their farms.

Smith was pleased to let General Meigs know that as of the 15th more useable but injured horses had been corralled, but many required medicines to correct their wounds. He informed his superior that his men were uncovering large quantities of U.S. property, "secreted in barns and garrets of houses," and he was in need of more men and transportation to gather the items.

Coincidentally on this date, Captain W.G. Rankin wrote General Ingalls expressing some of the same information while adding more:

"I am gathering in a good many horses and other property. The provost-marshals are bringing in a good many horses and other property...from a great distance. The farmers came in scores, and took them off to their homes, 50 and 60 miles from here....General [Lorenzo] Thomas [adjutant general of the U.S. Army] is still here. He told Captain Smith that he did not see what use he was here, and ordered him to turn over all property of the Quartermaster's Department to me....

"I will have everything ready to close up here at the earliest moment...."[32]

General Thomas' feelings aside (and Rankin's apparent wishful thinking), Smith and two cavalrymen left Gettysburg on the morning of July 16 to "look into the state of affairs at Farm Houses...." At twelve separate places he discovered guns, blankets, sabres, shelter tents, saddles, artillery harnesses, ammunition, shovels, horse shoes, coats, horses, beef cattle, and axes. In almost every case he came across three to four hundred dollars worth of property hidden at these farms, with guns and blankets being the most popular items taken and concealed by these agriculturalists. The objects he found were "secreted in garrets, between beds, in out-buildings, in fact, in any conceivable hiding place." As he left these farmsteads he ordered the owners out of their fields, and forced them to harness their teams, load up the property, and follow him to headquarters. "I brought in a long train of them," he admonished.

The quartermaster general received word on July 18 from Captain Smith that there were now over 350 horses at Gettysburg which could be placed back in service, many unfortunately first needed proper care and medication for sundry minor or severe wounds received from shell fragments or rifle and musketballs, and some still had sore backs from hard use. With the medicine Smith assumed he could make "speedy cures" upon the animals.

By 8:00 on the following evening Smith was able to gather in 49 more horses and mules, but then the bad news came that the cavalry used to patrol the field had been ordered back to the Army of the Potomac. The captain wondered aloud in his communication how he could continue to recover additional property. On the 19th work continued as usual and his men ferreted out 150 shirts and drawers and 150 pounds of "minnie balls." At Daniel Sheaffer's on the Baltimore Pike (where General Sickles had been taken on July 2), 300 shirts and drawers, 50 blankets, 28 guns, artillery harness, were all cleverly cached in a well dug under the house and in four large sinks filled with water by Sheaffer. The guns were hidden under piles of boards cut at his sawmill, along a fence and in the garret or attic. "Every care seemed to have been taken to prevent detection. I worked the Dutchman hard fishing up and loading the property [but] that is not sufficient punishment, what shall I do with him?" He then lastly requested of Meigs the use of at least 50 mounted militia, if nothing better could be had to accomplish the neverending work.

About a week passed when on July 25 Smith asked General Meigs for several sets of wheel horse harnesses for "light wagons," which would be employed in searching for property at houses and farms and outlying cabins throughout the mountains northwest and west of Gettysburg. Smith claimed that six mule teams were too large and heavy for that section of the county for only "good horses, sabres and guns" had been taken by the civilians there.

That same day he requested chloroform and gum arabic to be used on the horses' back sores to "keep the maggots out," and the captain further informed his chief that the wounds and injuries were healing remarkably fast so that already 127 horses and two dozen mules had been turned over to Captain Rankin. Smith specified also that he had taken possession of two barns full of hay belonging to a "copperhead," plus he was still picking up many serviceable horses, sabres and guns, but they were all located from five to fifteen miles out of town. Smith explained in more detail: "I occasionally find parties who positively refuse to give up the property, in two instances, persons have drawn revolvers to frighten us away, in both instances we got a wagon load of property, I am not very careful how I treat such parties."

In one incident at the farm of George and William Keefauver, the captain and his "forty thieves" confiscated guns, blankets, one coat, axes, picks, etc., but the people bitterly complained that the tools were not military refuse, but personal items. They claimed the coat had come from a soldier on July 3 who traded it for a loaf of bread. Smith quickly interjected that the family should have been ashamed to rob a soldier who had come to fight for them. "I find too many such men here," he sadly lamented.

But that was not the end of the meeting. In October 1863 the Keefauvers hired an attorney who officially petitioned General Meigs to have Smith return the claimed property, and unfortunately, as to the outcome or settlement of this dispute, nothing more is known.

In several instances Smith even found that the farmers he visited had attempted to cut out the U.S. brand from the animal's skin so they could retain the army mules or horses for themselves. Normally when any civilians insisted they had no government property, Smith's soldiers immediately and thoroughly searched the premises and usually found a "wagonload" of army supplies or equipment.

As of the 23rd of July, General Meigs must have been feeling some heat from various complaints turned in against Smith by members of the general populace. For on July 29 the overburdened and harassed captain wrote to his superior to rectify his position:

> ...[I]n complyance to your orders I came to Gettysburg Pa for the purpose of collecting and saving gover[n]ment property.

On my arrival here I found that at the rate property was being carried away, three or four days would clear the field, and the Goverment would find its property, Scattered hundreds of miles....

It was estimated that from Three to five thousand persons visited the battlefield daily, most of them carrying away trophies, the Small force then at my command with hundreds of rebel bodies unburied, hundreds of dead horses Strewn over the battle-field and thousands of rebel prisoners, some of which walked the streets discussing Southern rights, harsh measures was considered best adapted for the emergency....With the immense amount of labor to be performed and the imperitance necessity of immediate action, I could not Stop to hear every gentleman's explanation of what he was doing with goverment property, nor could I, with all the force at my command stop one tenth the persons then carrying away goverment arms.

In his closing paragraphs, Captain Smith alludes to a grievance Meigs must have received from a congressman, "the honorable J.K. Morehead." This politician had protested to Meigs that Smith had arrested three of his constituents for taking U.S. property, and Morehead had threatened to have the captain's shoulder straps torn off. Smith logically explained his actions, and admitted that although his measures were sometimes severe, he insisted upon courteous and respectful treatment to all persons he or his men encountered.

By August 1 the pressure was really mounting against Smith, but he firmly stood his ground. Another set of complaints had been received at the quartermaster general's headquarters in Washington. One aired that Smith's men had broken open a locked trunk in a farmhouse. According to Captain Smith the woman said she did not have the key, so Smith had it pried off, arguing that five minutes work would make it as good as new. The Captain then quoted Meigs' own primary orders to him [Smith] declaring that he had always complied with them to the best of his ability. These instructions are worth recording here in part:

"Examine thoroughly all houses and barns in the county, always asking one member of the family to accompany them [the soldiers] through the house, and in no instance shall more than two men enter the same house; no private property to be unnecessarily disturbed."

Smith also responded to these allegations by asserting that he knew of instances where houses were searched, trunks broken open, etc. but these doings were not by his men, but usually by horse thieves or other outlaws taking advantage of the post-battle situation.

On August 4 Smith and his troops left for Bendersville to search for government owned materials there and in the surrounding mountains. Upon arrival in the community he was informed that these items had already been gathered up and taken to York, Chambersburg, and other places. In the interim, a little boy in the village informed Smith that a local doctor whom he called, a "mean Copperhead" had an army horse. When the doctor was found he swore there was no such horse, so Captain Smith arrested him. The physician was then able to produce the animal, and told Smith if the beast was taken then "he would be damned if I [meaning Smith] should not know where there were more." So the good M.D. turned in another town doctor, plus the local minister, both of whom had stolen government horses. Soon the cavalrymen knew the whereabouts of 41 more and they "obtained them all," even two from Hamilton Myers, a wealthy farmer. In this correspondence Smith asked Meigs if he should also round up private carriages abandoned or sold by the Rebels so they could be claimed by their true owners.

The last communication we have from Captain W. Willard Smith was dated August 22, 1863, and concerned information he had received while on his rounds. This intelligence concerned six brass cannons which supposedly the Southern army had buried in the mountains. A party was sent to recover them, but they found only three limbers, two caissons, one ambulance, and a part of a wagon. From this search came the rumor of some additional gun carriages and army wagons stashed in the same neighborhood. Smith was determined that immediately after the sale of horses and mules on August 24, he would go in person to find the cannons. However, nothing is known of the success or failure of his venture.[33]

In a similar instance Surgeon John Brinton described how one farmer near the field whom he had heard about had "absolutely concealed a six-pound[er] gun, letting it down into his well."[34]

The final paragraph in Smith's last letter complained that he was unable to give General Meigs the *exact* number of weapons collected so far by his men on the battlefield, because an ordnance officer had already shipped them to the main arms and munitions depot in Washington, D.C. without his permission. He regretted not knowing the precise number, but stoically responded "I suppose it will make no material difference who gathered them."[35]

There is little doubt that in the aftermath period Captain Smith's activities did have a great effect on saving much U.S. property and he did much good work to succeed in his task. It is obvious too that as soon as someone began to put "political pressure" on that officer then it may be assumed he was on the right track.

At this juncture in the narrative it might be a good time to observe how one or two members of the local population reacted to Smith's and Blood's tactics. A few personal comments from both the natives of Adams County and visitors should convey a clear picture of the general feelings toward these officers and their diligent squads as their highly unpopular business was carried on.

Earlier we read of the frustration of farmer Nathaniel Lightner, who was arrested by Captain Blood for possessing relics from the field. Lightner remembered that of all the troubles and damages he had suffered throughout the battle, the meeting with Blood was the thing that made him the most angry.

J. Howard Wert gave another excellent account of provost duties, activities, and responsibilities. He testified that,

> [o]n a field like Gettysburg there was a necessity for the strictest military rule, and it was promptly established in all its vigor....[T]here were special commands with the provost marshall of the army that could be left back for just such an emergency as here existed. These were not very showy in point of numbers, but they were thoroughly trained to their work and made up in quickness of movement and efficiency....As soon as possible these troops were reinforced by regiments from the State militia which had been recruited and mustered in for the emergency.

The first provost marshal after the hospital era began...was a certain Captain W. Willard Smith. He knew just what he was there for, and he went about his work very expeditiously, standing not much on ceremony and caring not a picayune whose toes he tramped on....

Now many of the farmers in the vicinity of the battlefield and many of the visitors who came thither out of curiosity knew naught of military rule. To them it was a misty, intangible nothing. Little heed did they take of the Provost Marshal's warning, and hence divers ones of them came to grief. They knew a sight more about it in a few days later, but they paid for their experience.

Many of them whose farms had been wholly or partially devastated and who had lost much in various ways, sought to recoup themselves somewhat by gathering up blankets and other things of which they could make use. Per chance, as these had been nicely washed out and hung up to dry, a couple of Smith's men would come dashing up, seize the articles with scant ceremony and ransack the house for concealed Gover[n]ment property.

So thoroughly detested did these troopers become that the common appellation for them through the countryside was the 'Forty Thieves.' In some cases these arbitrary seizures worked a real injustice to the poor folks who had the blankets and articles of that character, for they were things for which the soldier who originally carried them had been charged by the Goverment on his clothing account; and which the grateful boys in blue had given to some large-hearted farmer's wife for food furnished, wounds bound up, and kindness shown.

Useless though to tell this to Smith's men, for they heeded it no more than the whistling of the wind. The meanest manifestation connected with the progress of the so-called "Forty Thieves" through Adams County was the opportunity it gave for the exhibition of petty neighborhood jealousies and hates.

In more than one case a domiciliary visit from the provost guard and a confiscation of blankets would be in consequence of information secretly given by an envious neighbor.[36]

Franklin Jacob F. Schantz was another who had the opportunity to observe Smith's men at work on a trip he took back to Harrisburg from the battlefield on July 9. On this journey, according to Schantz, they "met soldiers, who halted men on their return from Gettysburg and examined their wagons to learn whether any of the relics carried from the battle field were such as ought to be taken from the visitors. Some visitors fared badly and were obliged to return to Gettysburg. One of our party had placed a rifle in our wagon and he acted wisely in tendering the same to the guard as soon as he approached our wagon. It saved us from a return to Gettysburg."[37]

Surgeon John Brinton who had worked in the hospitals for some time, testified to the efforts of Smith and his command. He recorded this excellent piece:

Crowds of citizens were there from neighboring country and town, and many from Philadelphia. Some of these came under pretext of seeing friends, but many more [were] drawn by curiosity. A great many were in search of relics or "trophies," as they called them, from the battlefield; shot, shell, bayonets, guns, and every sort of military portable property. The gathering and taking away of such objects was strictly forbidden by military proclamation, all articles being regarded as belonging for the time being to the military authorities and under their care. Finally, it was decided to put a stop to this 'trophy' business. Guards were instructed to arrest purloiners, and take away the articles; but even this did not answer, stolen articles were concealed in the clothes and packages. The Provost Marshal (whom I knew, a Captain Smith, a relative of General Halleck's), then determined to put an end to the practice, and therefore ordered the arrest and detention of all persons found with contraband articles in their possession. This order gave much annoyance to visitors, who still attempted to evade it. So the Provost Marshal resorted to the rather summary process of sending delinquents, or those disobeying his orders, out to the field of battle, to assist in burying dead horses, —not a pleasant duty. This gave rise to trouble at once, and to threats of exceeding fierceness. I saw one squad about to start on a march for the field, five or six miles on a hot July morning, —in which was a loquacious gentleman, of portly presence, who had been caught with a U.S. musket, as a battle trophy, in his hands; deep was his wrath and eloquent his protest and fierce his threats at sending him, 'a gentleman and a member of the legislature of this state to do such disgusting work. He promised to have all concerned in issuing the orders dismissed, but he had to make the march all the same, and at least go through the formality of "burying dead horses."

This energetic treatment put a stop to the practice of looting arms. Whether it was worth the trouble and hard feeling excited, I hardly know. It was almost incredible, however, to what an extent this trophy mania had spread.[38]

In a memoir written in 1926, a then much older citizen of Gettysburg, Leander Warren, still must have vividly retained a vision of the activities of the provost, for he accorded them a sentence or two in his book: "There was a man named Captain Blood who came around and collected all blankets and tents. The women washed them, expecting to use them, but he took them to New York and sold them."[39]

Thomas Knox, the New York correspondent, commented that "[s]entries have very properly been posted where they can take from visitors all that is of value to the goverment." But it did not seem to help, for he sighted "[a]ll over the field...numerous men from the county, engaged in gathering whatever is of value. A few are merely in search of relics, but the most of them are bearing away, any and everything that they consider of pecuniary value."[40]

Joseph Parker, a Southern student attending Mount St. Mary's College in Emmitsburg, Maryland, and some of his friends had an opportunity to view the provost guards in action as they were leaving the field one day in late July. He wrote these sentiments in a letter to a friend after their visit:

"Guns and all other things were in such abundance that Fallen and Dallard were induced to take a couple of guns, but after carying [sic] them for about a mile a Yankee took pity on them and relieved them of their load. You can imagine how thankful they must have been to him for saving them the trouble of carying their load any farther. He told them that he had orders to collect all the guns on the field, no doubt but that this was consoling to them, 'but I ain't see it.'"[41]

In replying to people who "did not see it," Captain Smith would have happily quoted an Adams County judge, who when asked if Smith's tactics were too strong, replied emphatically *"No!"* And another prominent citizen in Gettysburg told Smith that he could get a hundred Union men to certify that, "under the circumstances [his] course had not been to [sic] stringent...."[42]

A volunteer nurse proclaimed: the "[g]over[n]ment set a guard over these [items], and for weeks officials were busy in gathering together all the more valuable spoils." Which was a true and necessary business to her mind. And another visitor remarked that, "[a] great portion of these things have been gathered up and taken into the town by the provost guard, and I saw there rooms filled up with them, and wagon loads being carried off." This was clear cut and to the point. It was a visible and shining reminder to all, that Captains Smith and Blood had been successful and detractors aside, these men would always be remembered for the good they accomplished.[43]

When it was all over and history had to be written, the verdict is that Smith and Blood should be complimented. It was an impossible task they took on, the hardest of all work they grappled with, but by their dedication these men managed to save the United States treasury many thousands of dollars worth of useable weapons and other property. They had also scrubbed clean a huge and corrupted parcel of ground, and made it livable again. Their actions prevented disease, and gave the land back to the people and the possibility to sow and plant and reap once more.

At this point, an examination of the regular and militia units is necessary. These organizations were assigned to assist the provost marshal details and quartermaster squads in guarding the battlefield and collecting the valuable and salvageable property thereon.

What is already known is that the first unit on the scene was Price's 2nd Pennsylvania Cavalry, a regiment organized between September 1861 and April 1862 in Harrisburg, Pennsylvania. These troopers were part of General Meade's army headquarters guard and its 500 plus man complement. They were detached temporarily and combined with the 100 infantrymen already spoken of; both "units" remained behind for a few days to secure the battlefield and assist the quartermaster, ordnance, and provost detachments then on the premises. When Colonel Price's men were relieved, Captain W.W. Smith persuaded the colonel to break off 100 of his cavalrymen for continued duty with the provost. While in Gettysburg this regiment bivouacked somewhere on the southeast outskirts of the town. This information came from John Linn who gave the impression that the 2nd was camped in the fields between the German Reformed Church on Stratton Street and Cemetery and Culp's Hills.[44]

On July 20 all 100 of Price's cavalrymen were ordered back to the army, leaving Smith with only the raw militiamen of the 36th Pennsylvania Militia Regiment who remained at the "post" of Gettysburg under Colonel H. Clay Alleman, an officer who saw service previously as lieutenant colonel of the 127th Pennsylvania Infantry. The lieutenant colonel of the 36th, was R.L. Maclay, a former captain in the 49th Pennsylvania. While the 36th was on the battlefield Maclay was appointed "Provost Marshal" at Gettysburg. The Adams *Sentinel* of August 11 remembered that both men while stationed locally had conducted themselves as perfect gentlemen and were respected by the citizens, "...both for their promptness and energy, as well as their courteous deportment."

One of the militia camps located near Gettysburg after the battle. This could be "Camp Harper," the bivouac area of the 36th Pennsylvania Militia along the Baltimore Pike south of the village. (GNMP)

Accordingly, on the day the 36th left the village in the middle of August, several prominent citizens composed a letter to Alleman thanking him and his regiment for their excellent service rendered to the community while on duty in Gettysburg for that past five weeks. These sentiments and Alleman's responding note were printed in the August 25 *Sentinel*.

A rare surviving letter written by militia private George H. Liebig of Company K, 36th Pennsylvania to John Caldwell sheds some light on the duties then being performed by that regiment. Due to its important content, it is quoted here almost in its entirety:

Gettysburg, Camp Harper, July 30, 1863

Dear Sir.

Perhaps a few lines from me would be interesting to you. We are still encamped here and are likely to be for some time to come. We have done and are still doing all kinds of work here. When our regiment (Co. K) came here, the first day's work was to gather arms and accoutrements from off the Battle field, secondly guard duty, next was burn dead horses and so on from one thing to another, some days bringing in rebels from their hospitals in the woods and barns for miles around here, and then again doing guard duty at different places. A squad of men from our company have already been to Baltimore & another will leave here this afternoon, the object in going there is to guard rebel prisoners down.

The battle field of which I spoke above is a very large one, extending for miles around here, and the fight as you have already heard was a very desperate one, the hardest part of which was at Round Top a rocky eminence about two miles from here, but you have doubtless heard a fuller and more accurate description of the Battle than I am able to give you on this small sheet. I have heard several of the rebs give their opinions respecting this fraternal war...Some ten days ago a squad of our company were doing guard duty at one of their hospitals and as we were there three days we had a good chance to speak to them. One intelligent Virginian said that Gen. McClellen would be our next president, we of course told him of his mistake, and that Old Abe was more likely to be, he in return said that he was the cause of this war and it would not be closed as long as he was president of these United States, and many other things have I heard them say some one thing and some another all of which did not amount to anything much. The fall of Vicksburg was to them a bitter Pill, but they were finally compelled to swallow it though they would not believe our newspapers.

Some of the nurses left in charge of the rebel wounded are very intelligent and they seemed very independent too, I thought, for prisoners of war. The military authorities here are sending them off as fast as possible and what our work will be for the next two months I cannot tell you this time. I have gathered several relics from off the field of Battle & which will perhaps be looked at with wonder and interest by friends at home when we return. The other Day one of our men was out on the field and in his rambles found the grave of Jacob Christ, Co. D, 56th P.V. and the next morning our Company moved to have his body taken up and sent home to his family; it will be done I suppose at an early opportunity. The Body of Jno. Reed of our place could not be found, as he was buried with some fifty others in one grave. I forgot to say when I began this letter that I liked soldiering first rate, and would like to [finish] the time out if necessary for the defense of the state, but I do not think the rebels will come back to Pennsylvania very soon again as they were pretty badly whipped in my opinion....Mathias Emes...is going to Baltimore this afternoon with some twenty others as a guard over prisoners....Write soon and direct to Geo. N. Liebig, Gettysburg Camp c/o Capt. Fisk, Co. K, 36th Regt. P.V.M.

Geo. Liebig to Jno. Caldwell[45]

With the departure of the 36th toward the middle part of August, a new militia regiment took its place. This organization was the 51st Pennsylvania Militia also known as the "2nd Coal Regiment." It had also been formed during Lee's invasion in and around Philadelphia, on July 3, 1863, and was mustered out September 1, 1863. The colonel of the 51st was Oliver Hopkinson who had formerly been the lieutenant colonel of the 1st Delaware Infantry but had resigned from that command December 14, 1862. Hopkinson, like his predecessor Alleman, became commander of the "Post of Gettysburg," and his lieutenant colonel, Michael A. Burke, was installed as Provost Marshal. Burke had previously been a captain in the 95th Pennsylvania.

According to the August 25 *Sentinel*, the 51st left Gettysburg for Philadelphia after just a short stay to be mustered out of emergency service. To replace the "Coal Regiment," department headquarters ordered Captain Robert Bell and his Company B, 21st Pennsylvania Cavalry of 80 men to the scene. This force was a six months organization enlisted at Harrisburg and Chambersburg between June 28 and August 1, 1863. They were put to work immediately searching for misappropriated government property under the direction of the quartermaster at Gettysburg. On September 14, 1863, a roster of this company appeared in the *Compiler*, indicating it was still engaged in duties on the battlefield. And a letter written by Dr. Henry Janes from Camp Letterman on December 7, 1863, signified that Bell was still acting as "Provost Marshal."[46]

Captain Bell's "provost" company, as all such entities, worked as "military police," and had various duties to perform, but guarding the general hospital on the York Pike was the most pressing. Their duties ranged from standing as sentinels in the town and hospital, to arresting soldiers who broke the law. Bell's men used the "jail yard" in Gettysburg on East High Street for their prisoners. Offenses committed by men and patients at the Post of Gettysburg include desertion, theft, rape, and drunkenness.[47]

Captain Robert Bell of Company B, 21st Pennsylvania Cavalry. (HCAC)

Bell's company contained several soldiers from Gettysburg and Adams County, and in the entire regiment itself about 40 men hailed from the area. The lieutenants of Company B were James Mickley and Harry G. Scott. Captain Bell was born in Menallen Township in upper Adams County in 1830, and had descended from pre-revolutionary Scots-Irish people, several of whom had been soldiers in the American Revolution. When Bell enlisted his company in June 1863, he was married to Abigail King, and was a farmer. After the war, through which he served until July 1865, the captain continued farming and was also cashier at the town bank. Captain Bell's background made him a perfect choice for the duty assigned as he knew the county well.

When the 51st departed, General Orris S. Ferry took charge of the Post of Gettysburg with Robert Bell as his provost marshal. Gettysburg was included in Ferry's duties as commander of the military post at Chambersburg, where he led a total of 83 officers and 1,500 men who were active as a border militia force. General Ferry, a 40-year-old Connecticut resident and Yale graduate, was a lawyer who had served as the colonel of the 5th Connecticut. He had more recently commanded a brigade in the Fourth Corps. In August 1863, Ferry was temporarily under the direction of General Darius N. Couch who was in charge of the Department of the Susquehanna, a conglomeration of a few regular troops but mostly emergency militia units, totaling nearly 31,000 officers and enlisted men present for duty.[48]

After September, the staffing of the Post of Gettysburg becomes somewhat hazy. The only reference to the organization which replaced Bell's cavalry was published in the Adams *Sentinel* of October 6, 1863, when it reported that, "an infantry company from Maryland arrived last week to take the place of the six month's Pennsylvania unit [21st cavalry] who have been at the General Hospital." It is almost a certainty that this force was part of the "Patapsco Guard" an independent unit, of company size, organized from Howard County, Maryland, and around Ellicott City in 1861. Bell's company was not mustered out until February 20, 1864, and it is positively known that Captain Bell himself did remain in the position of "Provost Marshall" through December. Therefore, it is likely that both Bell's troops and the Marylanders shared duties until the break up of the last hospital in November, and afterward. Records point to a portion of the "Patapsco Guard" performing guard duty in parts of the Department of the Susquehanna including Carlisle, York, Harrisburg, Chambersburg, and Gettysburg. Captain Thomas S. McGowan of the "Guards" was ordered to camp in the last named town in October, and he set up bivouac southeast of the village possibly near the George Spangler farm. The company returned to the post at York in December.

In a letter to Surgeon Henry Janes at Camp Letterman dated October 15, 1863, General Ferry directed the doctor "to have the detailed men at the general Hospital temporarily organized into two companies, properly supplied with non-com. officers & armed with such muskets as you may have. Capt. McGowan will at your suggestion detail two commissioned officers to take charge of the companies. See that their guns are in proper condition and that they are drilled as often as a relief from Hospital duties may allow."

From this correspondence it must be assumed that the general guard force in October and thereafter was going to be made up of not only McGowan's "Patapsco Guards" but also convalescents, nurses and attendants from the camp.[49]

From another existing letter which was written by Frank M. Stoke of that unit, it is believed that his company was only employed as guards within the boundaries of Camp Letterman, for Stoke does not indicate that the old battleground itself was then being patrolled. Evidently by the end of September all property worth saving had been removed, and Bell's men had concluded combing the farms throughout the countryside conducting searches for government animals and material which had been previously removed from the battlefield. The "Guards" may have returned home to Maryland when the general hospital closed in late November 1863.

While the Post of Gettysburg was in operation, the headquarters of various officials and their offices were located in or near the village. They were as follows in order of their appearance on the scene:

Medical officer in charge of the hospitals at Gettysburg	Dr. Henry Janes	Office, upstairs in the Old County building on York Street in the northeast corner of the Diamond (town square)
Provost Marshal	R. Butler Price Wm. C. Rankin W. Willard Smith Robert Bell	Southeast corner of the Diamond in the office of J.C. Neely, Esq. (Smith said "Northeast" corner on July 7.)

Post Commander	R. Butler Price H. Clay Alleman Oliver Hopkinson Orris S. Ferry	In the Office of W.A. Duncan, Esq., on the Diamond. (Ferry may have personally remained in Chambersburg.)
Post Commissary	"Captain Musser" was in this position in July.	Tents located in a, "little field near to a large warehouse," at or near the east bridge over Rock Creek

Hospital Corps of the Adams Express Company	In the storeroom of Michael Spangler on the southwest corner of the Diamond possibly just east of the railroad.
U.S. Christian Commission	In the storehouse of John Shick on the southwest corner of the Diamond (the July 2, actually 9, issue of the *Star and Banner* says S.E. corner)
U.S. Sanitary Commission	In the Fahnestock Brothers store and warehouse on the northwest corner of Baltimore and Middle Streets

"A Harvest of Guns"

The gathering of serviceable weapons was a top priority of the quartermaster corps and a main security concern for the provost marshal guards scattered throughout the battle grounds surrounding Gettysburg. Not only were muskets and pistols, swords and sabres the prime targets of souvenir and relic hunters, but from the beginning of the cleanup period in the aftermath stage of the campaign, these valuable weapons were looked upon as one of the original reasons why General Meade ordered security detachments to remain on the field.

Realistically, the firearms dropped, lost or abandoned by the opposing armies were everywhere, and total estimates for the number of these pieces hovered from between 30,000 to 50,000. Visitors constantly commented on them, and also regularly took them home. To one eyewitness, the aggregates were unforgettable. Along Cemetery Ridge where the first quartermaster squads had methodically stacked up weapons, this man remarked: "I saw piles of Small arms Lying on the field. In Some Instances I Should thin[k], that there were as many as 2000 in a pile."[50]

Near this same area between the low ridge at the famous "angle" and the Emmitsburg Road, an artilleryman "found the ground covered with muskets. Upon picking one up I found it was loaded and cocked, which made it a dangerous weapon to be lying around. I called out to some soldiers near by and told them to be careful with the guns, then stuck the one I had in the ground. I did the same to a number of other muskets, and when I left that locality it very much resembled a large field of bean poles, as every one who picked up a musket, after looking at it stuck it in the ground."⁵¹

A Gettysburg youth underscored that, "[g]reat stacks of muskets that had been thrown aside, were piled like cordwood on the streets, and the salvage corps gathered a great mass of every kind of equipment."⁵²

Because of this unusual "open air warehouse" of arms, individual soldiers or even whole units often exchanged their old firearm for a new rifle, or quickly replaced a lost or damaged weapon with one that had been discarded on the field. This happened to Sergeant Austin Stearns of the 13th Massachusetts. He had been a prisoner from July 1 to 4, but after slipping away from the Rebels on July 5, he needed a musket. Stearns first picked up a sword as a trophy and carried it for awhile, then "threw it away and selected a gun instead."⁵³

Corporal Moses Pugh of the 55th Ohio Infantry did essentially the same thing when he swapped his "old and rusty" piece for a "new bright musket lying by the side of a dead rebel....Upon examination I found it to be a Richmond [Virginia] rifle with the same calibre as the Springfield, the one I had been using...." Pugh was not very careful with his prize. Soon after greasing it with bacon fat to keep it dry he accidentally dropped it and it went off, having been picked up still loaded. The "Johnny ball went through three of my comrades' blouses and killed the colonels' [C.B. Gambee] horse."⁵⁴ Duplicating Pugh's actions was another person who found the exact model of Confederate gun and secured it as a relic of the fight. The man was Amos Stouffer, a civilian from Chambersburg who wrote in his diary on July 9: "We started for home this morning. Each took a rifle and Cartridge box along. Mine is a Virginia gun made in Richmond." Stouffer too, on his visit, had seen "wagon loads of muskets and cartridge boxes."⁵⁵

Sometimes whole companies or regiments made the "weapons switch," as was the case of the 15th New Jersey. On July 4, Colonel William Penrose took his infantrymen to the scene of the conflict of July 2 and, "each man supplied himself with an excellent Springfield musket from among the great number of arms left upon the field. When we marched from Gettysburg, we stacked our old Enfields on the ground, and left them behind. We were now better supplied with the fire-arms of the approved make, yet numbers of our soldiers had learned to love the old Enfields, to which they had grown accustomed, and with which they fancied they could shoot farther, and with more certainty of aim."⁵⁶

Henry N. Blake, an officer in the 11th Massachusetts also felt that "the weapons manufactured in the United States were superior to those which were imported...." He claimed that following the battle, "one regiment in the brigade, that bivouacked near a stack of several thousand arms which had been collected upon the field, threw aside their Belgian rifles, and selected those of the Springfield pattern."

William T. Livermore, a soldier from Maine had similar feelings when he told his brother: "We brought to gether as many as two 6 mule loads of rifles of ours and Rebs. But there [were] thousands that lay everywhere. to see the piles of extra Rifles one would think the whole Army was killed and wounded. Our Regt had the Enfield Rifles. They will shoot as well if not better than Springfield Rifles but double the work to keep them clean. I and every one in Co. B and all but a very few in the Regt threw down our Rifles and picked up others."⁵⁷

Before the Union army evacuated the Gettysburg area between July 6 and 7, a portion of Meade's commanders had begun to gather arms from the tactical positions they had occupied during the fighting. General George Green, who commanded the 3rd Brigade of the 2nd Division, Twelfth Army Corps, documented in his official report that his men collected 2,000 muskets, 1,700 of which were enemy arms. Similarly, General Samuel W. Crawford forwarded to headquarters a complete list of the weapons his division picked up between the "wheat field" and Houck's Ridge. Included in the compilation were 3,672 rifles, smooth-bores, etc.; some being Enfields, Springfields, Remingtons, Austrians, French, and two were described as "fowling pieces." He also added in the 239 Enfields that Colonel Penrose's 15th New Jersey left stacked on the field as noted above. Besides the small arms, Crawford brought in one Napoleon 12-pounder gun and three caissons.[58]

General John W. Geary, a division commander in the Twelfth Corps, interjected in his report to headquarters that in front of his position, besides burying 900 enemy dead, his men knew of "5000 small-arms" that were dropped on the field by the enemy, 2000 of these were gathered and turned in to the division ordnance officer.[59]

First Corps Officer Brigadier General John C. Robinson reported on July 18 that his division ordnance officer, Lieutenant M.S. Smith, "was diligent in the performance of his duty." The lieutenant had seen to the collection and forwarding of 2,251 muskets and a large number of equipments off his section of the battle area, showing that for the short time that the army remained on the contested ground after July 4, they do appear to have used the time in a constructive manner.

General Alexander Hays' 3rd Division of the Second Corps assembled 2,500 "stands of arms from their positions occupied on July 2 and 3, most being in serviceable condition, needing only cleaning, bayonets and ramrods." And one thousand additional but poor quality muskets were "left on the field." On the first day's ground the 1st Brigade, 1st Division, First Corps, collected 1,658 weapons, mostly Springfields, Enfields, and Austrians, 225 of the total were "sent to [the] rear with prisoners."[60]

The Acting Chief Ordnance Officer of the Army of the Potomac, Lieutenant John R. Edie, forwarded the following weapons and equipment from Gettysburg to the Washington Arsenal. These arms and equipment were all amassed by the Ordnance Department's officers and men and by elements of the Second, Fifth, Eleventh, and Twelfth Corps, plus a few cavalry and artillery units. The amounts were impressive:

Muskets	24,864
Bayonets	10,589
Cartridge-boxes	2,487
Sabres	366
Carbines	114
Revolvers	5
Rifled Cannon	2
Gun carriages/Limber	3

There were other equipments credited as well, such as cap pouches, gun slings, and waist-belts, etc.[61]

Sometime by the close of the year 1863, information became public as to the complete sum of muskets that had been collected on the battlefield by army ordnance officers, quartermaster details, and other government agents. This final figure must have been a "hot topic" in those days and still elicits interest today. It must be remembered that this summary does not catalogue the many uncounted small-arms carried off the field by visitors, all of whom usually chose the very best rifles or other weapons they could find, nor the broken or unserviceable pieces left untouched. A man living ten miles north of Gettysburg, sheds some light on this question when he wrote in his diary on July 31, 1863: "Any amount of muskets carried off the battlefield by the visitors passed by this place [Bendersville]."[62]

The February 9, 1864, issue of the Adams *Sentinel and General Advertiser* made the first "official" announcement in the county of this interesting intelligence.

Arms Gathered On The Field of Gettysburg

It is stated that 28,000 muskets have been gathered upon the field of Gettysburg. Of these 24,000 were found to be loaded, 12,000 containing two loads, and 6,000 from three to ten loads. In many instances half a dozen balls were driven in on a single charge of powder. In some cases the former possessor had reversed the usual order, placing the ball at the bottom of the barrel and the powder on top.

The pronouncement that so many of these weapons were still loaded was a major factor in the interest generated by this report, especially the revelation that many of the guns retained *multiple loads*. When this article came out it was reprinted in the *Compiler* and widely circulated elsewhere.

It may be true that not all of the guns overloaded were done unintentionally in the heat of battle, when the noise and confusion around a soldier became so loud and obtrusive that often a man could not tell if his own weapon had been discharged. Therefore many infantrymen kept loading thinking they were firing a round each shot, when in fact as the trigger was pulled only the percussion cap was exploded on the nipple, and the main powder charge along with the bullet remained in the barrel. Then the combatant kept repeating the process, with the same negative results.

A story has survived which may cause one to believe that a handful of men in the ranks of each army for one reason or another, could not bring themselves to take a human life. Attorney Robert G. McCreary of Gettysburg explained how a Confederate rifleman posted on Baltimore Street confided this unusual confession to a townsman living in that neighborhood. The Rebel stressed that he had been forced into the army of the South and hoped for a way to get back to his wife and children. The citizen at the time, possibly doubted the tale the soldier related. But when the battle was over it was verified that the Southerner had either deserted or had been captured or killed, for he left his musket behind in the same position he had occupied during the three days of battle. Picking up this rifle, the civilian found it "two-thirds filled with cartridges, showing that he had refused to fire at the Union troops."[63]

The sounds of battle as mentioned above, such as riflefire or musketry, including artillery detonations were often so loud as to be deafening, but rarely do participants point this out in their letters or memoirs. One who did was U.S. General Alexander Hays. He described how, "[a]t Gettysburg the hearing of one ear was entirely paralyzed, but is now perfectly recovered...." Another soldier, this one a sergeant in the 148th Pennsylvania stated: "Citizen visitors in flocks came to see the field...A number asked me why the soldiers talked so very loud to each other; so fierce when they seemed not angry. I said we were all hard of hearing; nearly deaf, from the awful noise of battle."[64]

With the departure of Meade's army, the ordnance and quartermaster details began their sweeps of the battlefield and all farms in the vicinity. They quickly found the task a daunting one and it could not be accomplished without help. The work of collecting, unloading, and cleaning these assembled weapons prior to transportation to the army ordnance depot in Washington, D.C. was therefore enhanced by the use of a few civilians who were summarily hired by the government to help expedite these duties. Regrettably the name of only one of these contractors is known. He met a tragic fate just hours after the end of active hostilities at Gettysburg. The Tuesday July 7 issue of the *Compiler* gave the sad facts:

"On Friday morning last, Mr. Solomon Warner of York, [Pennsylvania] who was engaged in hauling guns off the battlefield, was killed by the accidental discharge of one of the guns whilst unloading it. He was shot through the heart and died instantly. His remains were taken in charge of by his York friends."

◆ ◆ ◆

Civilian Casualties

With the unfortunate demise of Solomon Warner still solidly in mind, we now enter into a discussion of a rash of similar and equally tragic accidents that injured or claimed the lives of several civilians following the outcome of the Battle of Gettysburg.

It is common knowledge that in addition to the death of 20-year-old Mary Virginia Wade on the morning of July 3, a number of other town and county residents were wounded during the battle by regular infantry fire, or through accidental shots by sharpshooters who plied their deadly trade back and forth both in and across the buildings and streets of the battered little village.

The first regular nonmilitary casualty which occurred during the campaign took place in Bendersville, Pennsylvania, on June 23, 1863. The luckless man was a blacksmith named Charles E. Snedreker, originally from Croton Landing, New York. Snedreker had recently joined a "home defense" force in Bendersville during the threat of the Confederate invasion, and was accidentally shot in the thigh by the discharge of a "buck and ball" round fired from a smoothbore musket in the hands of one of his comrades. Another fellow near him by the name of Myers was also wounded. Believed to be 33, Snedreker died on June 24.[65]

During the battle other noncombatants were injured. They were: John L. Burns who was shot in the arm and leg on July 1 (some sources say he was hit three times); Jacob Gilbert, struck in the upper left arm while walking on Middle Street; Amos M. Whetstone, a Lutheran Seminary student who was hit in the foot on Chambersburg Street by a bullet from a sharpshooter's rifle; and Robert F. McIlhenny wounded in the leg, also Frederick Leman or Lehman of Pennsylvania College who was injured in the right knee on July 1 and treated at the Seminary Hospital.

A second source presents this information in a slightly different manner. He was an unknown reporter with the initials "J.R.D.," who wrote for the Philadelphia *Daily Evening Bulletin*. On July 9 his article was published in that paper, denoting that, "Miss Jennie Wade, a young woman, who, while kneading dough in the kitchen, was instantly killed by a Minié ball entering the back of her neck: R.F. McIlhenny, merchant, wounded in the leg; Amos Whitstone, [*sic*] Theological student, leg; Mr. [T. Duncan] Carson, Cashier of the Bank of Gettysburg, slightly in arm; Mrs. Stauffer, leg. The husband of Mrs. Stauffer is in the Eighty-seventh Pennsylvania Regiment" [Albert D. Stouffer of Co. D].

The only civilian *death* occurred on July 3 between 8 and 8:30 a.m. when Jennie Wade was struck by a stray bullet which pierced the door on the north side of her sister's house on Baltimore Street and hit her in the back, killing her instantly. The first written report of Wade's death came on July 7, and was said to be as a result of gunfire from U.S. sharpshooters. Two days later on July 9, the Gettysburg *Star and Banner* wrote that she was killed "by rebel sharp-shooters posted in the outskirts of town." This article went on to reveal that she was "attending a sick sister at the time," and that her age was 20 years, one month and seven days old, and she was "a young lady of good character and much respected."[66]

These casualty figures may seem low when compared to other wars or battles. In the siege of Vicksburg, Mississippi, for instance, there were 20 women killed along with a number of children and some civilian men.[67] However this siege lasted 47 days and the town was bombarded by Union heavy and naval artillery during the whole interval.

Almost immediately following the Battle of Gettysburg accidents began to happen across Adams and Franklin Counties due to innate human ignorance or carelessness. The reports began to come almost as soon as the fighting had ended. On July 5 a young man, Edward McPherson Woods, the son of Alexander Woods of Gettysburg "was accidently shot...by the discharge of a gun in the hands of an elder brother. The gun had been picked up on the street and was loaded. In handling it, it was discharged, the load passing through the lads body and causing death shortly after....[he] was aged 3 years, 7 months and 1 day...."[68]

After this regrettable death the community newspapers began to print warnings to inform the public of the dangers of these discarded weapons. The *Star and Banner* admonished its readers thus on July 9: "Persons visiting the battle field should be careful in handling the shells and guns strewn over the ground. The accidents, however, that have already occurred here and else-where, should be sufficient warning to put all sensible persons on their guard. No one has any right to carry guns or other property from the battlefield, as will be seen by the notice of the Provost Marshal in another column."

A traveller from Philadelphia who had recently arrived by train on or about Sunday, July 12 was unable or unwilling to heed this good advice. Volunteer nurse Mary A. Brady described the misfortune.

We alighted from the cars...at the edge of an immense pile of muskets, bayonets, ramrods, belts, cartridge boxes, etc., all thrown promiscuously together; another similarly large pile lay at the other end where the cars stopped. Union and rebel implements for destruction of human life were here mingled together, and on some the blood of their former owners still clotted, notwithstanding the rain.

A stranger had pulled at the butt of a French carbine in the tangled mass of small arms, and the trigger of another being thus moved, its contents, consisting of a rebel Minié ball and three buckshot, were discharged into his side, killing him almost instantly, many of the muskets gathered up from the field of battle being found loaded.

At the corner of the streets, also, a number of brass Napoleons, or big guns, lay passive on the spot where they had been last fired. A howitzer still loaded with powder and shell had received from a rebel Whitworth piece a round shot [*sic*] which had struck so exactly the mouth of the former as to penetrate it a couple of inches, and is stuck so fast, the calibre of the projectile being a tight fit or squeeze, the dangerous experiment will have to be resorted to, of firing off the piece to eject its bold invader.[69]

Dabbling with artillery shells and cannonballs seems to have been a common pastime of visitors to the field in the days succeeding the battle. John B. Hege registered some of these bad experiences which had occurred in the Chambersburg area. He aptly underscored the serious problem:

After the rebels had gone, it was dangerous to drive across the roads that they had used, for the reason that many loaded bomb shells were strewn along the road. Quite a number of them were left in the timberland of my father. Here boys were to be seen, placing some of these loaded shells on stumps and then throwing stones, trying to hit the caps [fuses], so that they could see them explode....The boys here all escaped unhurt, but a young Mr. Kile [Kyle], who then resided in the vicinity of Greenwood, was in the act of removing a cap from a loaded shell, when it exploded, and tore away the top of his head, killing him instantly. During the explosion, portions of the same bombshell, badly mutilated both arms of his brother, who was close by. It became necessary to amputate one of his arms....

One of the McFerren boys was also trying to remove a cap from a shell, when it exploded. He was also killed instantly.[70]

On July 28, an article appeared in a newspaper which verified one of the above occurrences. It read:

Accident From A Shell

On Friday morning last, Daniel Kyle and his two sons, Jacob and Henry, residing near Greenwood, Franklin county, Pa., met with a fatal accident in endeavoring to open one of the shells strewn along the road by the rebels in their retreat from Gettysburg. In the attempt to break open the shell it exploded, instantly killing the father and one of the sons. The other son, Henry, was seriously wounded, it being found necessary to amputate one of his hands.[71]

In Fairfield, Pennsylvania, an unusual fatality from negligence occurred after the Confederates had abandoned the tiny hamlet. The teller of the story was a "Mrs. Lewars" who suggested how it happened.

> After the retreat...a few such articles [relics] were picked up by the residents of Fairfield and among them was a fine rifle that was found by a man by the name of William or Hiram Eshelman, who with his wife and two children, lived in [a] house on Main street....
>
> Mr. Eshelman did not seem to prize the gun very highly, but embedded in the stock was a brass or silver plate that he wished to remove. He decided that the best way to get it out was to burn away a part of the wood, and one day he put the rifle in his kitchen stove and made a fire under the gun. When he believed the wood had been well burned away, he removed the rifle from the fire and turned to carry it outdoors. As he turned, a charge in the weapon exploded and one of his children, standing nearby, watching the father, received the shot in the head and was killed instantly. The child's head was nearly blown off. There are a few casualties of war that are not on the battlefield. The father was terribly grieved, because he had not made a careful examination to learn whether or not the rifle was loaded.[72]

The Gettysburg *Compiler* of February 6, 1865, gave another slant to this incident, proving again that one must often be wary of oral traditions, newspaper stories, and even eyewitness accounts. It claimed that Mr. Eshelman's *children* were heating the gun, and that the eldest child had instructed his seven-year-old brother to put his ear to the open end of the barrel to see if he could "hear something." In doing so the contents of the weapon discharged into the child's brain inflicting a mortal wound. It further stated that Hiram Eshelman was absent in the army at the time.

Back closer to Gettysburg a patient at Camp Letterman in a letter sent to his mother in Connecticut on August 11, 1863, made a notation at the close of the page, saying: "I was told last night that a boy in G[ettysburg] was killed by the explosion of a percussion shell while trying to open it."[73]

The months of August and early September must have been deadly ones for these types of calamities. On September 8, the *Sentinel* framed a notice, again cautioning the public:

A Warning

> On Wednesday last, whilst Mr. Michael Crilly, of this place, was engaged in an effort to unload a shell, it exploded, and seriously injured his hand, requiring the amputation of three fingers. The accident is much to be regretted, more especially as Mr. Crilly is a poor man and has a family dependent upon him for support.

The September 14th *Compiler* contained two complete stories of the kind above. Both again involved unstable artillery projectiles, and stupidity.

Another Warning

> We are informed that on Monday week, Mr. William Frame, residing at Harney, Carroll county, Md. lost his life by the explosion of a shell. His brother, George Frame, had the shell screwed in a vice, (in his blacksmith shop) and was attempting to open it with a chisel, when it burst, he escaping harm himself, but William, standing in the far corner, was struck in the breast by several

pieces with such force as to cause his death next day. He was an estimable young man, and his decease is much regretted.

Still Another

A terrible accident occurred on Wednesday evening, in the opening of a shell found on the battlefield, resulting in the death of James M. Culp, an interesting son of Mr. Daniel Culp, of this place. The deceased had opened a number of shells without accident, but...while at work upon another, near the Cemetery grounds, the shell exploded, fearfully lacerating his hands and legs, and a piece entering his abdomen....[T]he body was immediately carried to the residence of his afflicted parents on Baltimore street—death relieved the sufferer in an hour or so. He was in his 17th year....

The *Sentinel* also carried this footnote on the day after, which was the 15th of September, adding: "It is to be hoped that this terrible accident will put an end to this business of opening shells. Several accidents have already occurred and the wonder is that many more have not been killed."

Albertus McCreary may have been a witness to the blast that hurt and led to the death of James Culp. He and his friends often hunted for lead bullets, and shrapnel balls to sell to the metal dealers. He explained how they obtained their products:

The large shells were full of bullets [shrapnel], and we found many of them that had not exploded; we would unscrew the cap [fuse]-end, and, if we were careful, fill the shell with water before we undertook to extract the bullets.

Sometimes boys became careless. A schoolmate of mine, with others of us, had been hunting bullets on Cemetery Hill. He found a shell, and, the contents not coming out fast enough for him, he struck it upon a rock upon which he was sitting, and made a spark which exploded the shell. We carried him to his home, and the surgeons did what they could for him, but he never regained consciousness and died in about an hour. With all my familiarity with horrors, I nearly fainted when I saw the surgeons probing his wound.[74]

James M. Culp was killed as a result of the Battle of Gettysburg. He was not the only such casualty. (GAC)

The day after President Lincoln and Edward Everett made their memorable speeches on Cemetery Hill, Susan Holabough White of Randolph, Ohio, wrote to her husband, Alonzo V. White, describing the dedication ceremonies of November 19. While engaged in composing the missive at a house in Gettysburg, she was interrupted by a knock at the door. When she returned to her paper and pen, she explained the disturbances to her spouse:

"Lonnie the news just come to the door that a little boy was opening a shell and it exploded and cut him [in two] and shot the arms off a man and both his eyes out and he is from Philadelphia. I heard the nois [*sic*] and thought they was fireing."[75]

A more detailed version of this incident can be read in a November 23, 1863, column of the *Compiler*.

Terrible Accident

Mr. Russell M. Briggs, of Philadelphia, who came here to remove the remains of a son killed in the battle [Corporal George E. Briggs, 72nd Pennsylvania who died July 18] and at the same time witness the ceremonies of Thursday, met with a terrible accident on Friday, at the residence of Mr. Solomon Powers. It seems that he had picked up a shell on the battle-field, and undertook to "unload" it. He had the cap taken out, and was striking the shell upon a stone to loosen the powder and thus extract the [shrapnel] balls, when the missile exploded, with a loud report, and so horribly mangled his hands as to require immediate amputation of both, beside otherwise wounding him. When the shell bursted, Allen Frazer, an interesting lad of fourteen, son of T.F. Frazer, deceased, but living with Mr. Powers, was standing near Mr. Briggs, and a fragment striking him in the abdomen, cut him nearly in two, causing death in a few minutes. His remains were interred on Saturday in Ever Green Cemetery. Another warning, and one of the saddest, that the dangerous business of shell opening has yet afforded. May it be the last.

Albertus McCreary was probably again a spectator to misfortune when he described this scene:

The only other accident that I witnessed happened a year [*sic*] after the battle. I was passing along High Street, and had reached Power's stone yard, when I heard a terrible explosion behind me. I turned back to see what had happened. There I saw a young school-mate lying on his back with his bowels blown away. He looked at me for a second, then closed his eyes in death. Near him was a man almost torn to pieces, his hands hanging in shreds. He was promptly cared for, and, although badly wounded, losing both his hands and one leg, he lived. He was a stranger in the place, and was there to visit the battle-field. He was trying to empty a shell he had found on the field. A lady in a house opposite had seen the boy come out of the stone-yard and say to the man that hitting the shell on a stone was a very dangerous thing to do. Just as he spoke, down came the shell on the stone and exploded.[76]

An acquaintance of McCreary's, Charles McCurdy, reminisced years after the battle that they all "had been warned not to experiment with shells that had not exploded, for they were dangerous. Two boys that I knew were killed in trying to open them."[77]

A similar view was held by Hugh M. Ziegler who was ten years old in 1863. He, like McCurdy and the other youngsters in town, knew the dangers and had

Fused artillery shells could be dangerous if handled improperly. Many curious civilians learned a hard lesson through their carelessness. (GAC)

Farmers had to be constantly alert to the hazards of ploughing on the old battlefield. (JSH)

been amply forewarned, yet all appeared to have had personal experiences regarding friends, relatives or strangers who had been killed, injured or suffered close calls in attempting to modify any one of the large quantities of artillery projectiles in proximity to the town.

Ziegler affirmed that he, "with many other of the boys, wandered over the battle field and several of them were killed by tampering with shells that had failed to explode. There were several farmers and their teams killed by [a] plow point coming in contact with unexploded shells."[78]

It has been estimated that between 45,000 and 60,000 of these rounds, i.e., solid shot, shells, case shot and canister, had been carried into the fight or fired by the two forces at Gettysburg, along with perhaps seven million small arms cartridges.

The obvious dangers from this quantity of artillery shells existed long after the year of the battle had come and gone.

On March 1, 1864, the Gettysburg *Star and Sentinel* portrayed yet another sad affair within the borough limits:

"A distressing accident occurred in this place on Monday a week. Several boys, aged about 15 years, were amusing themselves with a gun from the battlefield, (shooting mark, we believe.) when the contents of one of the discharges entered the head of a little colored girl, who was near the spot, inflicting a mortal wound in the head. She died on Wednesday aged about seven years."

And just over three and one half months later, Adam Taney, Jr. "residing in Fairfield, met with a serious accident a few days ago whilst attempting to open a shell, found in one of the fields. The shell exploded while [he was] working with it, and some of the fragments struck him in the feet which may cripple him for life."[79]

It can only be imagined how many other unmindful people throughout the numerous years subsequent to 1863 may have been hurt by these seemingly innocent cylinders and balls of iron, which had laid quietly and harmlessly for so long in the once blood-caked soil of southern Pennsylvania.

Relic Fever

Very often throughout the preceding pages there has been lateral coverage of the collecting of trophies, relics, and souvenirs from the battlefield by the many thousands of visitors who travelled to Adams County in the weeks and months following the encounter at Gettysburg. In the middle of that hectic July, one spectator, a news correspondent, characterized it clearly:

> The country for forty miles around seems to have turned out to view the sad relics of one of the fiercest battles of the war.
>
> Thousands of people are going to the battle-field. Every house and shed and stable in Gettysburg is turned into a lodging house. Every conceivable wheeled vehicle which can carry passengers is dragged to the battle-field.[80]

And nearly all of these multitudes of early explorers took a little something home with them. These remembrances could be any kind of treasure, yet weapons were especially sought after, which, as reported, caused the military guards no amount of problems.

About the third week in July, Sanitary Commission Agent Frederick L. Olmsted was able to illustrate the problem very well. In writing to his superior about his trip to the field, Olmsted reiterated at one point: "The roads for miles about the town, as well as the course of the federal lines are still strewn with wrecks of equipment, muskets, bay[o]nets, caissons, and baggage waggons with broken wheels, although the provost marshall has had parties engaged in collecting them ever since the battle and much must have been carried off by the country people. Ten miles off I met two farmers on horseback each carrying three or four muskets, with some other things."[81]

Weeks prior to Olmsted's comments, people were already hard at work scrounging for trinkets and mementoes of the fighting. Thomas Galwey, a lieutenant in the 8th Ohio, spotted some of them on the morning of July 5, observing:

> Already the civilian souvenir hunters are scattered over the field picking up relics of the battle....The relic hunters, with their satchels slung across their shoulders, provide us a good deal of amusement. Most of them have come from a good distance at the news of the battle, and have gained permission to journey to the field by representing themselves as volunteer nurses for the wounded. Some of them are medical men, some clergymen, and what not. But their innate curiosity is their main motive in visiting the places where anything remarkable occurred during the battle, and to gaze with ludicrous horror at the black and mutilated dead who are strewn everywhere. Cannonballs were especially sought for by these people. And a practical joker of a soldier, seeing a middle-

aged man thrusting his cane into the bloody grass, in search for relics, picked up an unexploded percussion shell and offered it to him. The civilian, who ought to have known better, took it thankfully and put it into his satchel, when another soldier, less jocosely inclined, warned the civilian of the dangerous character of the relic. Fearful lest the terrified greenhorn might throw the treacherous thing to the ground and bring havoc and ruin upon all around, the soldier took it from the satchel and laid it upon the ground as delicately as though it were a child.[82]

The very next day, July 6, Thomas Knox saw many of the same kind of county folk sometimes collecting valuable or reusable items, while, he said "[a] few are merely in search of relics...."[83]

These wandering curiosity seekers, so unmoved by the death and destruction around them, were often reviled by the soldiers who eyed them sauntering their way across the ravaged fields and woods. One civilian who also viewed them in that manner, remarked: "Yet many look upon [the battlefield] without emotion. Many walked about amid the horrid stench of that field unmoved. They turned over the rubbish, picked up bullets and fragments of shells for mementoes, but that was all."[84]

A woman passing through the town shortly afterward named Lizzie J. Belles, illuminated a similar thought: "[T]hose of the visitors [staying at the Eagle Hotel] who had nerve and other bracing necessities to support them went over a great part of the contested ground, and filled their pockets and reticules with bullets and buttons cut off dead soldiers jackets, and such other debris of battle they could carry."[85]

Attorney John B. Linn of Union County, Pennsylvania, after a long stay in Gettysburg returned home with quite a large stock of relics and tokens of the fight. Even within the first moments of arrival Linn began to assemble his cache, for on July 7 two miles east of the village just as he was entering the main battle area he found some torn Confederate money. Shortly thereafter and just south of the borough he removed a ball cartridge out of the cartridge box of a dead Louisianian, and a few steps further, procured a box marked, "3 Second

Cannonballs as relics were especially sought after. This 12-pounder ball struck the side of the George Rose farmhouse, and was kept as a souvenir of the battle. (MCW)

fuzes Richmond Arsenal." By July 8 and while in the vicinity of the George Rose farmhouse, Linn picked up some letters, cards, and cut some buttons off of various Rebel uniforms. One of his companions took an Enfield rifle, while Linn pocketed a testament with the name T.C. Horcraft, 34th Regt. N.Y.S.V. written in it in one place, and "David Mitchel 105 Va Reg" in another. Linn also kept a letter, "from a boy to his father evidently stained with his father's blood, contents very interesting," Linn commenting that, "it is among the relics I have from the field. Also one from a girl to her lover."[86]

Another sightseer Franklin Schantz, upon leaving the Gettysburg locality listed a few items he carried away with him, among them was a bible without a cover, the broken lock of a musket, and a bayonet that was, "greatly bent by hard use." He also collected an envelope addressed to a lady that had been pierced by a bullet. He eventually wrote to the woman who answered him with the news that the envelope had belonged to her brother and that he had survived the battle. Schantz's friend seized, "a solid shot...[and] enclosed [it] in a genuine bandana."[87]

On July 28, the Adams *Sentinel* printed one of their only notations of trophies found or taken from the field. The paper ascribed that a lady in Gettysburg had acquired a souvenir of the battle which belonged to a Louisiana soldier named Wellerford and consisted of several locks of hair and a letter from his wife, Fanny; the hair came from both her and their children.

Many residents of the town and county soon began accumulating mementoes from the three days' battle. One of the first and most famous of these compilers was 22-year-old J. Howard Wert, who actually began picking up souvenirs *during the actual fighting*. He amassed nearly 4,000 of these relics, continuing in this practice for years after the war, even up to his death in 1920. His collection included weapons, medical instruments, original maps and newspapers, photographs, a coffin abandoned by a burial detail, a bowie taken from a dead soldier, buttons, belt plates, shell fragments, bullets, a blood-soaked sash and sword from a corpse on Culp's Hill, and numerous other interesting items.

Many county youths who lived on or near the battle ground and had come through the conflict, caught the relic fever and became very adept at locating these valuable items even long after they had disappeared from the surfaces of the ground, and were no longer in plain view. One boy named Hugh Ziegler declared that "[i]n roving over the battlefield I collected many relics, among them was a sword that had evidently been used, as there was blood marks on the blade."[88]

There was also Charlie McCurdy who is similarly quoted: "I roamed over the fields with other boys looking for relics of various kinds, gathering a store of bullets, particularly prizing those that had been fired and had hit a boulder or a tree, giving them grotesque shapes; making a collection of shells and other things dear to a boy....There was no lack of relics, as we called bullets and shells and grapeshot, and certain parts of the equipment of a soldier. Sword bayonets were particularly prized, for they were not in general use....It was a busy and exciting summer that followed for thousands of visitors flocked to Gettysburg; our relics were in great demand, for everybody wanted a souvenir."[89]

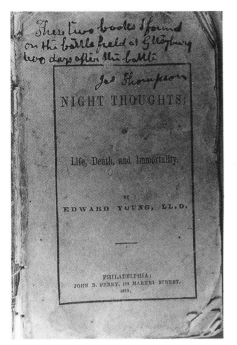

John King of Gettysburg leans on a Confederate sword bayonet he found somewhere on the field at Gettysburg. (MCW)

Booklets, diaries, and testaments were often the preferred choices for battle trophies. This title seems very appropriate for a relic of Gettysburg. (MCW)

Albertus McCreary was probably one of the boys McCurdy spoke about. McCreary had his own version of the common recreation:

> Visitors soon began to come to see the battlefield, and all wanted relics. We were always on the lookout for bullets and pieces of shell, in fact, anything that could be easily handled, to sell to them. We found that a piece of tree with a bullet embedded in it was a great prize and a good seller. Every boy went out with a hatchet to chop pieces from the trees in which bullets had lodged. I found several trees with bullets in them that had met in mid-air and stuck together (these had really collided *inside* the tree). These were considered a great find. Lamps were made of round shells. The caps [fuses] were taken out, a tube for a wick was placed in them, and the shell was fastened to a square block of wood, thus making a very useful and convenient relic.[90]

A version of the McCreary summary was given by another fellow to the town newspaper. It went like this:

CURIOUS RELIC

Mr. Samuel T. Heck shows us an interesting relic of the battle, found by him, the other day, on Culp's Hill, whilst splitting a rotten hickory log. It is composed of two Minie balls, well battered, the end of one so firmly united to the other as to suggest "melting" when they struck. It is hardly to be supposed that they met from two rifles at the same instant in the centre of a large tree. We rather think that the rifle fired contained two charges, both entering the tree simultaneously and the bullets uniting whilst hot. Six other bullets were found in the same log. The battlefield has developed many curious things.[91]

As McCreary suggests above, souvenirs were then even being made *from* battle relics. The Adams *Sentinel and General Advertiser* of April 5, 1864, commented on this new practice:

Our enterprising young neighbor [J.] ALBERTUS DANNER, presented us a few days ago with a match-holder prepared from a shell found upon the battlefield. It is unique in its appearance, and besides has an additional interest in its connection with the great struggle in July. He has a number of articles, both useful and ornamental, made from relics of the battle, and persons wishing such articles, would do well to give him a call, at Danner and Ziegler's store.

There were other men who brought together important groups of battle relics in the Gettysburg area besides J. Albertus Danner, such as Joel A. Danner, L. Mumper, William T. Ziegler, H.T. Collis, and John and George Rosensteel. And ironically, quite often pieces of these early collections become available for sale even today.

Regarding J.A. Danner, Dr. Henry Stewart had this to say:

In the early days [the souvenir business] consisted of "relics" of which there was an abundance. It was a poor sort of a boy who could not pick up a half dozen bullets, mostly "minnie balls," or shell fragments, in an afternoon on a freshly plowed field. They yielded a cent or two, possibly more if it was a particularly deformed bullet.

"Bert" Danner...was the first in this field....He is listed in the 1880 Directory as a tobaccoist, but his main line was "relics." I think he was the first in the relic and souvenir business—no one knows how many times he sold the "bullet which killed General Reynolds." His first place of business was a little brick building, a "lean-to" next to the Fahnestock house...later, he was across the street in [another] building...[on Baltimore Street].[92]

It was not only boys and men who put together treasure troves containing tangible mementoes of the battle either for profit or curiosity. Women and girls were just as interested in this aspect of the aftermath. One such person was

Two bullets that collided inside a tree and fused together are similar to the ones found by Albertus McCreary. (HJS)

Liberty Hollinger who described her sister Annie bringing home a particularly unusual item several weeks after the battle. Annie had "picked up a hand, dried to parchment so that it looked as though covered with a kid glove. There was nothing repulsive about the relic, and we all remarked on the smallness of the fingers. We guessed that it must have belonged to a very young soldier or a Southerner who had never worked with his hands."[93]

On July 17 a woman nurse, Emily Souder, took a respite from her duties in order to walk over the recent scenes of strife. She listed the few items she brought back from her excursion.

"We picked up a tourniquet with which, we are told, all the New Hampshire boys are supplied; an open Testament, still perfect, though wet and somewhat soiled, with 'H.K. Campbell, 145th Reg. P.V.' written in pencil on the blank leaf, —tin cartridge boxes, minnie balls, belt clasps, etc. —These we shall carefully preserve as mementoes."[94]

Tillie Pierce of Gettysburg prized two larger pieces. The first was a gun with the initials P.L.W.T. carved into the stock. The other was an officer's sword and scabbard given initially to her sister by a soldier named Barney M. Kline of the 55th Ohio, who found it in the Pierce orchard along the Taneytown Road. The scabbard had been hit by a bullet or shell fragment or so Tillie recalled.[95]

One of young Pierce's neighbors, Leander H. Warren, also stumbled upon an interesting musket. Not far from the depot near the ice plant, he discovered a dead Confederate who had one of the finest guns he had ever seen. On the stock was engraved a Rebel's name, "T.J. Knight, Co. G, 12th Georgia Vigilantes." Warren kept the weapon for many years until one day it disappeared and was never seen again.[96]

A second nurse who took a turn wandering over the battlefield was Sophronia E. Bucklin. In one place near Round Tops she recollected how the buried bodies under the soft earth could be felt moving as you walked over them.

"We had been shut so much within the limits of the hospital grounds, that we heeded little the space over which we passed, as we went on, and on— gathering fragments of shell, battered bullets; mosses; which had held, among their tiny leaves, the life blood of a hero; scraps of curious stones, which had been loosened by the shot, and tiny wild flowers, which sprung up in the rocky crevices."[97]

The gathering of moss, leaves, and flowers from the battleground was more of an enjoyable past-time than one might imagine. These "natural" relics were often arranged inside shadow box frames and sold or displayed. In the May 30, 1864, *Compiler* an article specified how just such an accumulation was being sent to the U.S. Sanitary Commission's "Great Central Fair" in Philadelphia to raise money for soldiers' relief and aid societies. The gifts included: 35 moss baskets, four pine cone frames, 10 moss crosses, one moss harp, three wreaths of autumn leaves, as well as five shell medallions, one belt buckle, five bayonets, 12 shells, six pieces of shells, two cartridge boxes, one grapeshot, one shell lamp, four dozen dressed canes (battlefield wood, of course) three dozen undressed canes, and one box of relics from School Number 2 in the borough of Gettysburg.

A month earlier the Gettysburg committee members for this fair encouraged their members "to collect and contribute relics and mementoes from our

Dried mosses, leaves, and flowers gathered on the famous battlefield and arranged into a pleasing display. (MCW)

battle-field, by the sale of which in the city fairs, considerable sums can be realized. Such articles are much desired and can be provided at small expense and trouble."[98]

In August, Baltimore pharmaceutical clerk Ambrose Emory spent a few days exploring the field. On his return he took a few souvenirs back to Maryland. On August 24 along Seminary Ridge Emory gathered up a bayonet, a brass epaulette and one or two other little trifles. The next day while on or near the college campus he found a 12-inch solid shot, a piece of shell, and a testament with the name of "R.W. Davis, Virginia." written on the flyleaf. Further on he picked up twenty Minié balls "which had been dropped from some soldiers cartridge box."[99]

The multitude of items being picked off the famous site by people like Emory and others was beginning to show up in places all along the eastern seaboard.

The September 28, 1863, issue of the *Compiler* illuminated the reality that there were many sad relics presently on display in Philadelphia from the battlefield of Gettysburg. In the following month the Adams *Sentinel* of October 6, reiterated that the U.S. Christian Commission office in Philadelphia had on display the "last tokens of dying soldiers," which had been given to many of the delegates, such as bibles, watches, and lockets, almost fifty percent of these objects coming from North Carolina wounded alone.

Some time later on November 16, the *Compiler* printed the following: "The trunks of two trees have been sent from the battle-field of Gettysburg, (Culp's Hill) for the Pennsylvania and Massachusetts Historical Societies. One of them has two hundred and fifty bullet holes in the space of twenty-one feet, and the other one hundred and ten in the same space. These specimens attest [to] the fierceness of the fighting."

Clearly, everyone wanted a relic of Gettysburg. By 1864 the fascination for these historical keepsakes had not died off. Combing the formerly contested countryside in the fall of that year, Isaac Moorhead took a stroll down the Emmitsburg Road where he soon encountered the grandson of Peter Rogers. On the front porch of the Rogers house Moorhead noticed a box "such as one [that] is always found on the hind end of old Pennsylvania wagons for a feed trough. In that box was a quantity of shot, shell, etc. gathered on the farm." The little boy told Moorhead: "Grandpap sold three hundred pounds of minie balls for lead."[100]

This "harvest of lead" was common. Albertus McCreary recalled that during the war lead was very scarce. He remembered that his friends, "could get thirteen cents a pound for it, so all the boys hunted lead bullets. We would go along Culp's Hill, poke among the leaves, and sometimes find what we

Lead musket and Minié balls were dug up and shipped from Gettysburg by the ton. They were also a favorite of relic hunters. (GAC)

called pockets, a lot of bullets in a pile—eight or ten pounds; as it took only eight [bullets] of a certain kind to make a pound, I gathered many pounds myself in this way."[101]

In August 1865 approximately two years following the battle, John Trowbridge pronounced that the trees,

> in certain localities are all seamed, disfigured, and literally dying or dead from their wounds. The marks of balls in some of the trunks are countless. Here are limbs, and yonder are whole tree-tops, cut off by shells. Many of these trees have been hacked for lead, and chips containing bullets have been carried away for relics....
>
> Of the quantities of iron, of the wagon loads of arms, knapsacks, haversacks, and clothing, which strewed the county, no estimate can be made....The harvest of bullets was left for the citizens to glean. Many of the poorer people did a thriving business, picking up these missiles of death, and selling them to dealers; two of whom alone sent to Baltimore fifty tons of lead collected in this way from the battle-field.[102]

By the end of the Civil War, surface relics, which had two years before seemed inexhaustible and in fact had practically carpeted the ground, were now becoming scarce and harder to find. But with luck, perseverance and diligent hunting, it was still possible to locate something worthy enough to take home as a souvenir of the battle.

Frank Firey, a Pennsylvania College student who lived in Gettysburg a few years after the war remembered his jaunts in search of trophies:

> A chum and I went out to hunt relics together on many occasions. We had three ways of knowing where a man was buried. One was that you could see whole rows with the toes of boots sticking out. The Union dead had all been taken up and put in the national cemetery....
>
> But the Confederate dead lay there after the battle. My chum, one Saturday afternoon out between Big and Little Round Top, came to a dark spot of bluegrass and, cutting the sod, found the remains of a Union colonel. On the breast of this officer was a leather pocketbook and inside he found a small tintype picture of a beautiful young lady.
>
> He brought it to the college and sold it to a young fellow by the name of Ackerman for a dollar. This boy advertised it in 'Waverly Magazine.' In due time he received a letter from a young lady in Boston saying that her brother commanded a regiment in the Battle of Gettysburg and that he was killed...in a charge and they had never been able to locate his grave. She asked him if he would not send her the picture, because she knew that he had always carried it with him and if it wasn't hers she would return it to him. He sent the picture to her address in Boston and received a letter...saying that it was her picture and, of course, it was her brother who had been killed, and she wanted to know on what part of the field it was.[103]

If the above incident did occur as described and was not a college prank or a "stretch of the truth," it definitely had to do with a lower ranking officer than a colonel, or possibly even an enlisted man, as there were no Union officers of that rank interred anywhere near the Round Tops.

One unnamed person who commented on the scarcity of relics by the war's end wrote a memoir of a visit to Gettysburg on Saturday, October 14, 1866. The writer described the field and observed this: "...we journeyed along the line passing Meads head quarters viewing shatered breast works intrenchments shatered trees that h[a]d been scard [scarred], picking up relicks which however appeared to be scarce from the fact that hundreds had been there befor us."[104] This barely literate person appeared to be a student, and likely also a resident of the local college, and obviously in dire need of an education.

Three years later in 1869 a Union army veteran by the name of Russell H. Conwell toured Gettysburg. While on Seminary Ridge he found two bullets,

> one driven into the other so far that they could not be pulled apart....When we spoke of this curiosity at the hotel a whole army of relic speculators wished to purchase it. Doubtless the sum which we received for it was trebled when sold to the memento seekers who frequent the town. These speculators do a thriving business in the relic line and have everything to sell from a 100-pound shell to the smallest wares of the toy shop, all in some way connected with the battle.
>
> Canes cut from Culp's Hill or Little Round Top are for sale in many shop windows....This business has become one of great importance to Gettysburg, and it is proposed to introduce machinery for the manufacture of toys from the battlefield wood....
>
> [At Culp's Hill] the breastworks of logs, as well as the trees which lie around, has been pulled to pieces and hacked in every way to get at the tons of bullets which the army left in them. When we were there the axes of the lead and relic hunters made the woods chipper in ever direction.[105]

In 1886 J. Howard Wert, himself a giant in the collecting field, cocked a very wary eye on the people and their wares which made up the local souvenir business, and he explained how to be sure your memento was really from Gettysburg.

> Every visitor to Gettysburg wants a relic. Had they been in these woods [at Culp's Hill in] July, 1863, their wants could have been abundantly gratified. The ground was literally covered with musket-balls, most of them much flattened by contact with rocks. They could be scooped up by the handful. The writer, at various times, picked up along the line...what would amount to a peck-measure filled. Some of these were flattened out to a surface nearly as great as the palm of a man's hand. He saw teams here gathering them up for sale as old lead. It took but a short time to collect as much as the owners could have at a load.
>
> Relic selling, as on any great battlefield, is quite a business. Are they genuine? Many are, for lead and iron were sown thickly all over these miles of farms and woods. Some are not, for cunning will always make a supply where there is a demand. If you can find one yourself you will *know* that it is genuine. Or if you can obtain one from some personal friend or resident who does not make a business of trafficking in them, you can feel pretty safe. Many are still found on the field yearly, especially after a rain or where a field has been freshly ploughed.[106]

To increase the reader's awareness of just how scarce even bullets were becoming by the 1880s, the remarks made by a Massachusetts teenager on an excursion to Gettysburg in July 1889, will serve as an indicator. The boy whose name is not known, kept a diary of his ramblings over the old battleground from Friday, July 12 through Tuesday July 16 of that year. The group of people he was with visited all of the field entirely on foot. During that six days this young man was able to procure two bullets from a little boy who had recently found them in a cornfield on the first day's field. While near Herbst's woods, a woman on the old McPherson farm showed him a "number of relics." He also cut a cane from that famous and by then renamed, "Reynolds Woods." A day or two later he pilfered a piece of tree branch and a leaf out of the "peach orchard." At Little Round Top both he and his friend Will Dorst, found Minié balls among the rocks. On the way back to town one of the men accompanying the two boys picked up a bullet right in the middle of the road. And while crossing a cornfield near the Trostle farm the little Yankee kicked up another Minié ball. Altogether in six days of walking and seeing the entire grounds, only five or six bullets were gathered, plus a few other non-battle or natural relics.[107]

Naturally, actual veterans of the battle were particularly anxious to take home a trophy from their excursions to Gettysburg. One of these parties in June 1886, was ex-members of the 15th Massachusetts who attended a reunion to dedicate two monuments honoring their regiment. On the final day of their visit one veteran who transcribed the activities of his old comrades noted: "The 'relic hunters' went forth in squads and their efforts were quite successful, as many bullets and pieces of shell were picked up on the field where the regiment fought and at other places of special interest."[108]

Several former soldiers found more than the common everyday specimen. A few were even fortunate to make unusual or noteworthy finds. A case in point was that of William E. Miller previously a captain in the 3rd Pennsylvania Cavalry, where in combat at Gettysburg he had won the Medal of Honor. During the action east of town on July 3, 1863, he engaged a Confederate horse soldier in a personal hand-to-hand duel, and in the meleé his sabre blade had been broken off near the hilt. Fourteen years later in 1877, on the same ground where the engagement took place, Miller found, in a pile of useless battle junk collected by the farmer from the surrounding fields, his *very own* sword hilt which had been thrown away on that hot July afternoon so long before.[109]

In a parallel occurrence an ex-Confederate colorbearer, Andrew Wall, took a ten-mile walking tour of the historic ground in 1913, at the age of 72. On July 2 of that reunion year, Wall came to a place where he believed he had been standing in 1863, when the point end of the regimental flag staff he was carrying was shot off by Yankee fire. Searching through the thick accumulation of leaves and dirt, Wall was amazed to discover the metal flag pole tip that had been blown away 50 years before.[110]

George Dietz, a resident of Chester, Pennsylvania, lost his watch at Gettysburg as a young infantryman in 1863. One day in 1899 Dietz, then a jeweler, was fixing a pocketwatch in his jewelry shop. Curious, he asked the young man standing before him where he had gotten it. The owner was Harry Ellis, a Spanish-American War soldier hailing from Kansas, who said that his father had found it on the field at Gettysburg. When Dietz opened the watch case, he was startled to find his *own name* scratched inside. It was the exact timepiece he had dropped in battle 36 years earlier. Dietz admitted he wasted not a moment in making a trade with Ellis.[111]

Another Confederate who had a very unusual experience was Captain F.S. Harris, formerly of the 7th Tennessee Infantry. Out walking on the battlefield one day long after the war, he reached Cemetery Ridge near the place where he had witnessed a member of his regiment, "torn to pieces by a bursting shell" during "Longstreet's July 3 assault." Harris spied a farmer plowing the ground in that particular location at the very moment of his visit, and went up to the man: "I pointed out the spot. The plowman plunged his long, pointed plow very deep, saying: 'I will get you a relic there.' When his plow passed the identical spot, he brought to the surface a

WATCH

... *removed from dead body in railroad cut by J.E. Stahle*

Pocket watches were targeted by battlefield robbers, or "ghouls" as they were called. (MCW)

piece of shell, I am satisfied, from the very nature of the circumstance, that this piece of shell killed this brave Tennesseean."[112]

As time went by and due to the advancing scarcity of battle relics, veterans like everyone else, often left the battlefield disappointed. On July 3, 1888, during the 25th Anniversary of the engagement, a reporter for the *New York Times* recounted the story of an ex-soldier who was seen searching in the mud on Little Round Top for a fragment of the shell that injured him in 1863. "The veteran was so much in earnest," said the correspondent, "that none had the heart to remind him that Gettysburg had been visited by millions of people since the battle, and that every inch of the field had been searched by the relic hunters."

By 1900 the Civil War veterans of Adams County had assembled their own personal group of mementoes from the world-renowned field, which were deposited and displayed in local Post #9 of the Grand Army of the Republic on Middle Street in Gettysburg. In their private collection were such items as a section of hickory tree cut along the banks of Willoughby's Run, complete with a Hotchkiss shell embedded in its center; a small cannon weighing 150 pounds, with one-and-one-half inch bore, made from one of the guns of Henry's North Carolina Rebel Battery that had exploded during the Battle of Gettysburg in front of Round Top; and also a chair which belonged to General R.S. Ewell and was left behind when Lee retreated from Pennsylvania.[113] It can be seen that relics and trophies came in all sizes, shapes and kinds, depending on the whim of the collector.

Eventually, the relic traffic became so important to the town that ultimately it was flooded with numerous shady speculators and their assorted fake merchandise. This led to a winsome sort of backlash which began to take shape against the people of Gettysburg. Several articles that appeared in 1899 took some humorous "pot shots" at these unsavory relic dealers who, like flies, hovered over the famous town and its battle grounds.

A Relic Factory That Supplies Grewsome Souvenirs To Gettysburg's Business Men.

According to a facetious Germantown man, who had just returned from Gettysburg, there is hidden away in the woods, a mile or two from the battlefield, a relic factory. It is a two-story building of brick, 80 by 100 feet; 29 hands are employed in it, and the weekly pay roll averages $300. The value of this year's production will be not far from $20,000, an increase of 40 per cent over that of last year. The relic factory was only built in 1898. The production, the Germantown man says, consists of old bullets, old cannon-balls, soldier buttons, buckles, swords, piece of bone and sabretasches, all, of course, of a very ancient and worn appearance. These are the cheaper products. There are, besides, in the finer and more costly lines, Testaments bored through by bullets, love letters burnt by powder and stained dark with blood; skulls with big leaden balls lodged neatly in the eyesockets or the jaw, and the full uniforms, properly punctured and blood stained, of all the officers slain upon the battlefield. The factory makes nothing in advance, thus avoiding over stocking. It only runs on orders, and by night the customers call for their goods. They are the inn keepers, grocers, the saloon keepers, bakers and real estate men of the town, and whenever it is moonlight they may be seen distributing the rare relics cautiously and judiciously over the field. Visitors there now are more numerous than they used to be. It is no longer usual to poke about all day without unearthing so much as a single bullet, and tourists appreciate this change.

The editor of the Gettysburg *Star and Sentinel* was obviously offended by this article, and did not care to see the lighthearted whimsy in it, for on May 16, 1900, there came a heated retort:

Plenty of Real Relics

The finding of an exploded shell in a lot on North Washington street last week, is another incident showing that real relics are still to be found on the Gettysburg Battlefield, sensational newspapers to the contrary. It is no rare happening. A large number of bullets, pieces of shells and even parts of equipments are found every month on the Battlefield. Every time a field in this locality is plowed, the missiles of war are found and will be found for years to come.

People who come here with incredulous ideas with regard to Battlefield relics know little of the number that have been stored away since the battle and of the many found every year. There are some valuable private collections in Gettysburg which money cannot buy. Those offered by the relic dealers are just as genuine. In many instances they were laid away years ago when they were of little value and are now brought out and sold. Visitors to Gettysburg like to take with them some souvenir of the great battle and it is only natural to suppose that impositions have been practised by unscrupulous persons. But instances of this kind have been remarkably few.

Other newspapers had already seen the droll wit in the original piece and ignored it, or had taken sides with the *Star and Sentinel*. Here are a few of their annotations.

Comments on Relic Libel

"Gettysburg is justly perturbed over a libelous story that was published against that town. It was to the effect that a relic factory, employing twenty-

Sightseers and relic collectors about 1880 share the same eroding Federal trench line on Culp's Hill. Gettysburg is visible in the distance. (FL)

nine hands, exists in the historic county seat of Adams county. There is no truth whatever in the report. There are a certain class of souvenirs made there, such as canes, inkstands, photography, etc., but such things as old bullets, soldier buttons, swords and pieces of shell are still sufficiently abundant, even at this late day, to be unearthed by those who take the trouble to search for them through ploughed grounds and in other places."—*Philadelphia Press.*

"Gettysburg is greatly disturbed over what the Star and Sentinel calls a rank lie. A facetious reporter started a story that the votive city has a relic factory, employing twenty-nine hands and with a weekly pay roll of $300. Everybody knows the story is not true. So much activity would give the old town a greater shake up than the three days' battle in 1863."—Chambersburg *Public Opinion*.

"The Gettysburg *Star and Sentinel* indignantly denies the charge, recently published in a Philadelphia newspaper of unreliable tendencies, that there is in the vicinity of that town a 'factory for the manufacture of relics of the Gettysburg battlefield.' There is, it continues, 'a certain class of souvenirs made here, such as canes, inkstands, souvenir books, photographs, etc., but such things as old bullets, soldier buttons, buckles, swords, pieces of bone and sabretasches are not made here. They are still too abundant to make.' Any visitor to Gettysburg knows that many of the private families there have their own collection of relics, from which they part from time to time, and that even yet bullets, pieces of shells, with an occasional rusty bayonet, are still to be picked up in some quarters of the field. It is also fair to assume that in distant cities bogus 'relics,' purporting to come from that historic scene are palmed off on credulous buyers, but that in nowise touches Gettysburg. The story most likely was intended by some cheap wit as a joke, to whom the Star and Sentinel should pay no further attention."—*Philadelphia Inquirer*[114]

No doubt, the story had "stung" someone when it came a little too close to the truth.

The relic phenomena was out of hand long before this series of articles was written. On April 24, 1864, just nine months after the battle General Alexander Hays heaped fun and sarcasm on the souvenir craze begun by "Sanitary Fair" organizers asking for donations. He cuttingly remarked to John B. McFadden how, "[o]ld clothes have been in much demand, and 'bullet holes' are announced to be worth five dollars each, which is a much higher rate, I assure you, than those who wore the clothes....I think I will propose to exhume my old horses at Gettysburg, [both mortally wounded in the fight] 'Dan' and 'Leet.' There they will find bullet holes, and bullets, and ornaments made from their bones ought to be appreciated by young ladies and 'stay-at-home' people. The bones of poor brutes would prove more devotion to our country than many cowardly humans can show."[115]

In some respects the "defenders" of the town's souvenir and relic businessmen were partly accurate. There have been artifacts found even into the present day. Almost yearly and on many occasions therein between 1863 and the early 20th century Gettysburg newspapers listed accounts of relics or military related items being found in buildings or lifted from the soil of the county battlefields.

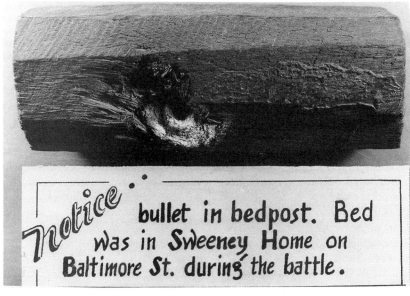

Bullet-struck or blood-stained items were always in high demand as souvenirs of the great battle. (MCW)

The *Compiler*, the *Sentinel* and the *Star and Sentinel* carried some of these pieces. On October 26, 1877, for instance, "M. Crilly" of Gettysburg was reported to have discovered on the farm of John S. Forney along Oak Ridge a "boot heel with a bullet entirely embedded in the solid leather."

And less than a year later on May 15, 1878, an announcement informed the public that an old daguerreotype of a soldier named "H.H. Williams" had been located in the house of A.W. Flemming where it had lain since 1863.

Again, shortly thereafter on December 18, 1879, John Leas ploughed up a cavalry sabre on his land near Granite Hill which was part of the July 3 cavalry field east of town. He then presented it to the "Grand Army" post in Gettysburg.

Three years following this, on August 2, 1882, a soldier's brass clothing identification stencil was unearthed on the battlefield. It was immediately sent to the brother of the former owner who was deceased in Clearfield County, Pennsylvania.

Dr. J.W. Tudor of York Springs, Pennsylvania, owned a sword with a broken blade which had been found three days after the battle and was rediscovered in his house on August 2, 1888. On the partial sword blade was engraved, "Lt. T.L. Livermore." Livermore, strangely, was the ambulance section officer for the Second Corps and recalled losing his weapon on July 2.

More than 40 years after the battle on January 19, 1908, George Hughes was tearing down a house in Gettysburg when he discovered a pair of long riding gloves or gauntlets. "Both have inscribed inside it letters that are very faint now, 'Lieut. Heulings, A.A.Q.M., 1st Army Corps....'" It was Mr. Hughes' desire to return the gloves to the family if anyone could be located.

And so on and on it went for months and years on end, until our present day when after more than 130 years have passed, true battle related artifacts are becoming almost impossible to find.

Relics of any kind were always more attractive and valuable if they were properly labeled with a history and provenance. (GAC)

This critique of the relic trade shall be ended with a poem, which in 1900 summed up the souvenir trade in Gettysburg quite aptly. It is comical, but with the humor is a warning that should still be heeded today.

The Relic Vendor

At Gettysburg, where brave men tried
Their strength upon the foe, and died,
I feel that my unworthy feet
Tread sacred soil—in village street,
In field and wood, on plain and hill;
And to my pulses comes a thrill,
Looking on scenes that met their gaze
On those three bloody July days.

Shell hole and bullet mark are plain
In dwellings where the fiery rain
Fell in its fury; even now,
Three decades afterward, the plow
Turns in the furrow rusted grape;
Trees that have managed to escape
The relic hunter's knife, show well
Where bullets thick as hailstones fell.

A mild, persuasive man, who said
It was his native place (he fled,
Being noncombatant, the day
The troops of Lee began the fray),
Showed me his relics—all for sale.
Of each he told me a thrilling tale
And gave a perfect pedigree
Which greatly interested me.

Scenting my love for souvenirs,
He poured his stories on my ears.
'Now, here,' he came at length to say
In quite a confidential way,
'Is something you'll appreciate
Because it has no duplicate;
This is the very ball that took
The life of gallant General Zook.'

'Yes, 'tis indeed the fatal ball;
A soldier who beheld him fall
Among the Wheatfield's famous dead,
Secured the bit of rebel lead;
I bought it of[f] him for a song,
And, prizing it, have kept it long;'
This was the story he rehearsed-
That man in battle legends versed.

And did I purchase? My reply
Will tell you. When he finished, I,
Mourning somewhat for follies past,
An earnest gaze upon him cast.
'My friend,' I said, 'you need not tell
More details—I recall them well;
When I was here two years ago,
You sold me that same ball, you know!'

Frank Roe Batchelder.[116]

They Had Full Possession:
Damages and Post-Battle Claims in Adams County

The county of Adams, with some of its villages and towns and many of the farms that made up that body, more or less suffered some damages as a result of the Confederate invasion of 1863. An approximate total of major losses claimed by the residents was in the amount of $552,383, making it second only to Franklin County ($838,162) of all county border claims made to and received by the Commonwealth of Pennsylvania in 1868. In a perusal of the State Damage Claim applications, we can find a general breakdown of the *larger* or more important items confiscated by the Confederates in Adams County:

Horses - at least 800
Cattle - at least 1,000
Mules - about 12
Hogs - over 200
Sheep - over 400
Wagons, Buggies, Carriages, etc. - about 160
Personal property about $270,000

It should be remembered that these figures reflect only state claims, not federal, which were a totally different adjudication and once again only the substantial items of property taken out of the county by the Rebel army is quoted. What is not shown in that list are the thousands of smaller possessions lost, destroyed or stolen; nor does this synopsis formulate for us the damage to fences, buildings (both public and private), bridges, roads, railroads, trees, and hundreds upon hundreds of acres of standing crops, either destroyed or eaten, or the unknown hundreds of tons of stored grain, feed, etc. in barns, which was stolen or devoured, or the lost business hours, wages and income and farming time forfeited, all caused by the invading forces. In summary, the above table is only the tip of the iceberg.[117]

In 1861 a bill known as Senate Bill No. 1329 was originated in the Pennsylvania state capital at Harrisburg. It was entitled, "An Act Authorizing the Payment by the State Treasurer, of Certain Warrants Issued by the Auditor General of the Commonwealth of Pennsylvania, for the Payment of Certain Military Claims." This lengthy headed bill was supplemented again both in 1862 and 1863.[118]

The supplement of 1862 followed a raid into Pennsylvania by General J.E.B. Stuart in October of that year. The 1863 "rider" was attached after the momentous summer invasion by Lee's Army of Northern Virginia. A total of 813 people filed affidavits in the latter case (more than 4,000 for both years), stating all damages which incurred during the Campaign and Battle of Gettysburg. Very few of these petitioners received any remuneration for their losses, even after the bill's actual passage in 1868. This was primarily due to opposition from counties which were located north of the border areas and suffered no war damage.

In 1871 a second group of claims was instituted. This occurred when a new state law was written and passed permitting the payment of damages on the condition that the state be reimbursed by the federal government. The resulting affidavits were in essence a carbon copy of the ones sworn to in 1868, however the amounts demanded were somewhat lower in many households, and a few new names appeared on the register as well.

As can be imagined, by 1868 many of the local farmers and townspeople had given up on trying to regain monetary compensation for their losses. Some had failed by then to even file official damage reports. Others had moved or sold their land and farms and a few others had died. But of the 813 who did file, only a handful were keenly specific in the amounts of their damages, losses, and costs. Several businessmen and farmers had suffered heavily, as in the complete destruction of actual structures and buildings, such as warehouses, barns, or houses which were burned by Southern forces. Examples: the warehouse and contents of Daniel Gulden ($5000); the house and/or barns belonging to the families of William Bliss, William Comfort, Alexander Currens, John Herbst, Joseph Sherfy, Alexander Cobean, James Ewing, David Finfrock (Finnefrock), and a "Mr. Little." For instance, Herbst claimed that his barn (80' x 45') was set afire, but not the house, because in it were lying several wounded, one Union and two Confederate soldiers. Currens for one, was told by a Confederate soldier that his house was torched by Union shells which exploded inside the stone structure.[119]

A multitude of stores and warehouses in the area had been looted. At least 17 private and public railroad cars were rifled and burned, and added to that loss was the complete destruction of the railroad bridges and telegraph lines between Gettysburg and Hanover. Public institutions too paid the price of invasion, when great damage was inflicted to the structures of Pennsylvania College (all three buildings), the Lutheran Theological Seminary (again, all three buildings), the Adams County Courthouse and Almshouse, several Public Schools, also many private institutions, including the seven churches and five hotels of Gettysburg, and numerous stores and shops and private dwellings. All these structures bore various injuries inflicted upon them by their use as hospitals, army unit headquarters, bivouac sites or being struck by miscellaneous artillery projectiles, and by soldier vandalism, carelessness or ruthless conduct.

Of the 813 claimants in 1868, 56 as part of their affidavits petitioned the loss of clothing; over 150 listed the theft of horsegear, bridles, and saddles; 150 or more lost grain; cash taken, six, (one of these Samuel Pitzer reported $5,000 stolen in gold and silver coins);[120] jewelry and watches, at least eight; fencing dismantled, damaged or burned, 72; 149 catalogued damage to standing crops including wheat, corn or grasses trodden down during the battle; and 32 decreed a burned or severely damaged building, including the several already mentioned above.[121]

Both the college and seminary, believing that the government was not directly responsible for the ruin of property through battle causes, made local and statewide appeals for monetary assistance to repair war injuries, comprising such problems as the thirteen shell and cannonball holes through the seminary president's house, or the severe wall cracks, and bullet and projectile holes visible in the main edifice. The boards of these institutions set a goal of $5,000 to be raised, and by the end of October they had collected $4,210 which was shared by the two institutions. Hospital use by the government, however, was considered an entirely different situation, and the president and faculty members of the two schools felt the United States was obligated to pay for this type of abuse.[122]

Likewise, in many individual cases a person, family, or business could be compensated for his farmhouse, barn, store or warehouse having been used as a Federal corps hospital, but the government might in the same claim, disavow fields of wheat trampled by that army corps as it battled the Confederates, or breakage to windows by shells or bullets and any looting done by Rebel soldiers.

The forthcoming paragraphs contain a closer inspection of some of the specific damages and losses suffered and claimed by several families whose farms or businesses lay directly in the path of the contending armies on July 1 through 3. They embrace a few familiar names, and some not well known to the average reader. These remain a tiny sample of the over 800 families in Adams County who suffered personal and monetary losses during the six-week campaign and three-day battle.

John S. Forney—Mummasburg Road northwest of Gettysburg

3,891 rails burnt, shell and bullet damage to house and barn, 22 acres of wheat destroyed, window curtains lost, 30 acres of grass, 10 acres of oats used, "buildings were occupied as a field hospital and were greatly damaged by that use and by shells." Fields were trampled and run down, fences used for fuel and much household property carried away or destroyed.

Moses McClean—northwest of Gettysburg, Mummasburg Road

Damage to house and barn, $125; loss of eight acres oats, $30; 13 acres wheat (70 bushels), $84; one ton hay, $12; 4546 rails, $454.60; 35 fenceposts, three acres corn, 40 pounds of ham, 10 pounds of beef. Total claim amounted to $1138.35.

Harriet B. and Charles P. Krauth—Seminary grounds

House used for hospital and first floor filled with wounded; surgeon and a wounded officer upstairs. Contents of house rifled and taken. Four good mattresses destroyed, along with beds and bedding, loss of nine blankets, nine quilts, carpeting, suits, overcoat, underclothing, shirts, drawers, ladies dress goods, necklace, vests, glass and china ware, 36 tumblers, kitchen furniture, utensils, 42 towels, four table cloths, 12 napkins, dried fruit, preserves, butter, meat, pickles, and garden utensils.

The Robert McCurdy and Jeremiah Diehl Warehouse—Gettysburg, near the Railroad Depot

Loss of groceries, three barrels shad, mackerel, molasses, tobacco, matches, buckets, shoe blacking, wagon harness, collars, bridle, lines, grain and gunny sacks. Warehouse was used as hospital, Confederates had complete possession.

Henry G. Carr—Gettysburg; cellar storeroom in David Wills' house

Dry goods and "notions" taken out of store, including ladies' silk stockings, gloves, vests, "Lawn and Mosquito Bars," boots, spices, silverware, gunpowder, violin string, fishing tackle, soap, books, flute, ink, rope, drugs and medicines, whiskey, gin, port, brandy, cider, alcohol, gold pins and rings, playing cards, Union flag (destroyed by Rebels), and two Rockaway carriages. David Wills added that the Confederates broke into the store with an axe, and were constantly looting it during the battle. Other grocers in town however, testified that Carr had no such grand inventory, and never had such a large business.

Samuel Kitzmiller, Jr.—Gettysburg

Had stolen clothing, revolving pistol, two boxes of silver ($5) belonging to his young sons, books, including Byron's "Works," "History of Slavery;" sheets and soap; the "house was stripped of all kinds of goods usually kept in a private house," plus two shells went through the building.

John L. Tate—Eagle Hotel, Chambersburg Street, Gettysburg

"Tate's Hotel" claimed 100 bushels of corn, 200 bushels of oats, harness, 20 gallons best brandy, whiskey, 20 gallons cognac, 20 gallons ginger brandy, 60 gallons gin, 20 gallons cherry wine, two cases of brandy, two horses, two tons of hay, rye straw taken from hotel and stables. A witness, Alfred Scott saw the Rebels roll whiskey barrels out of the cellar and load them onto wagons.

Jacob Hummelbaugh—Taneytown Road

A bay horse taken and used by an Eleventh Corps artillery unit; the house used for hospital and two acres wheat destroyed, value $60; also one acre corn (50 bushels), four acres of grass, $114; three tons of hay at $20 a ton; 12 bushels of potatoes, 330 rails, 26 posts, three bushels of peas and cabbage, vegetables, chickens, three feather beds, 36 yards of carpet, knives and forks, sheets, three quilts, two tin buckets; all taken July 1, by the U.S. Eleventh Army Corps.

Susan Rogers—Emmitsburg Road

Susan and Peter Rogers' house "was on the battlefield; it was struck by shot and shells during the first and second days of the battle, and was occupied by the wounded. [The] buildings etc. were thus damaged, and she alleges her carpets were destroyed and clothing and bedding and furniture taken." Also six panels garden fence lost, $6; damages to growing corn, $20; one horse taken, one bureau (smashed by a shell); total claimed $158.34 (in 1881). In an earlier affidavit written in 1868 Peter and Susan stated that their house was one mile and a half south of Gettysburg and that the location was between the fire of two armies, where some of the most severe fighting was done over their land, including the assault of Pickett's Division on July 3. The carpets were bloodied and ruined and their horse was stolen by a Union cavalryman. The house was occupied as a temporary hospital or aid station.

Catharine and Abraham Trostle—east of Emmitsburg Road and northwest of Little Round Top

This farm was being tilled by George W. Trostle during the war years because Catharine's husband Abraham had become insane and was placed in the Lunatic Asylum. In 1874 Catharine swore out an affidavit asserting that her two-story frame house with brick back-building, all of which contained several rooms and a large basement was used as a temporary hospital during the battle. Her farm was then about 135 acres in size and was occupied by U.S. troops on July 1. The soldiers damaged or appropriated most of the crops on the place, consisting of hay, wheat, oats, corn, and grass, they also stole vegetables, some cattle and a hog. The men destroyed rail fencing which was used for fuel, and ate the stored meat and potatoes, and took many household and personal things. The land was greatly injured by troops who cut roads through the fields, and by the passage of artillery vehicles and guns. The structures themselves were often struck by shells and balls, which went, "crashing through the building and causing great destruction to its contents." In addition 16 dead horses were left "close by the door," and about 100 more around other parts of the farm. The land was fought over several times, driving away or killing the cattle, fowl, cows and other stock.

Their losses included: 20 tons of hay in barn $300; 6400 rails, $512; house and barn used for hospital purposes and damaged by shells, $200; three cows and one heifer killed, $40; one bull, $20; one hog, $15; one sheep, $5; 50 chickens, $12.50; two hives of bees, $14; 15 barrels of flour, $120; family clothes, $20; two barrels of hams and shoulders, 200 pounds, $40; one saddle and two bridles, beds and bedding,

One sheet of Leah H. Sheaffer's battle-damage claim form filled out in 1869. Literally thousands of such pages were processed by the over 800 claimants who suffered losses during Lee's Pennsylvania invasion. (NA)

$50; 32 acres of grass, $650; one acre potatoes, $50; one acre flax, $15; 4 acres of barley, $50; 8 acres of oats, $80; 9 acres of corn, $360; and 27 acres of wheat, $600.

One witness verified that when the family returned after the fighting, they found "their house a perfect wreck; crops and fencing gone, and household articles, farming utencils, etc., broken, and scattered about."

John Slyder—Three miles south of Gettysburg, east of the Emmitsburg Road and just west of Big Round Top

Slyder leased this farm containing 75 acres which belonged to David Study. At the time of his claim in 1868 he was living in Montgomery County, Ohio, having recently married Josephine Miller, adopted daughter of Peter and Susan Rogers, both having moved there soon after the battle. John Slyder claimed that his house near Round Top was occupied by the army (his farm was called "The Granite Farm"), and the property listed below was taken or destroyed. The damages were: seven acres of wheat, $97.50; two acres of grass, $45; destruction of fences and to land, $170; three head of cattle, $100; two boxes of bees and honey, $7; Mattock, $5; saddler and shoemaker tools, $5; Buggy cushions and shafts, $10; ten quilts and comforts, $25; two rifles broken, $15; copper kettle, $3; bedding and carpets, $20; looking glasses and furniture, $38; overcoats and clothing, $20; 16 pieces, ham and bacon, $20; one ton of hay and 30 bushels of corn, $39.

Jacob Weikert—On the Taneytown Road, three miles from Gettysburg and east of Little Round Top

Weikert's farm of 115 acres was taken possession of by the U.S. "Regular" Brigade of the Fifth Corps and they established a hospital in the house and barn for about five days having "as high as 950 dead and wounded at a time." These troops appropriated for their own use, 12 acres of wheat, 16 acres of meadow, 11 acres of oats, 3,500 rails worth $11 per hundred, and cut young timber worth $100. Weikert recorded in his affidavit that during the battle, breastworks were thrown up and entrenchments dug on his place, that troops marched and counter-marched through the fields, and cavalry and artillery and wagon trains passed over the growing crops and fences. Also confiscated or destroyed were bed clothing, pillows, sheets, coverlets, underclothing, kitchen furniture, tin and table ware, and other personal property, all for a grand total of $1,722.[123]

It is indeed an unfortunate fact that of the over 800 claims filed with the Quartermaster General's Office of the War Department under the 1868 law, very few were ever paid. And of those who did receive some compensation, most were awarded only a small fraction of their net claims.

A good study of this situation was George W. and Dorothy Rose who filed a claim in 1878 adding up to $3,306 for damages inflicted by the two armies. Their losses were as severe, if not worse than the Trostle list noted earlier. In 1882 the Quartermaster wrote to Rose's agent relaying that the claim "is dismissed from further consideration in this office...." The quartermaster officer was unable to certify that he was convinced that the stores had been actually received or taken for the sole use of the U.S. Army.

Others were treated just as badly. Adeline and William Bliss' house and barn were burned on July 3 and he and his family lost thousands of dollars in property ($3,256), and hundreds of irreplaceable items, including six family ambrotypes, and other photographs, plus "100 volumes of books." The Bliss estate was eventually notified that they *had* won nearly the full amount, but both he and his spouse went to their deaths without collecting a cent.

When looking back over all of the more than 800 claims which had been fairly and honestly motivated by a law that had been finally passed in 1868, it is clear that the whole process was a huge waste of time for the people involved. Frankly, very few families ever received even the minimal amount due them. Because the ongoing war and Lee's unpredictable 1863 invasion were all events clearly beyond the control of people and governments, we may of course stubbornly allow that perhaps these farmers were not owed or justified any money to begin with, and all such claims, it could be said, should have been disavowed.

However, both the federal and state governments agreed that the citizens were due settlement, but the bureaucrats and officials made the process so difficult and unfair as to render the law practically worthless.[124]

"The ground is to become historic"

Finally, a time arrived in Adams County when the last wounded man had been moved away from Camp Letterman, and the last dead soldier had been buried or reinterred. The *majority* of animal carcasses were buried, burned or removed, and the quartermasters had collected everything that could reasonably be saved, and thousands of visiting civilians, like vultures, picked the remainder of the battlefield clean. Farmers and shopkeepers and townsfolk had assessed their damages, and businesses were opened again, while new crops were planted by the plowmen and farmers who hoped for the chance of a late harvest. The soldiers' cemetery was honorably dedicated, and the conclusive process for completion of the cemetery was in motion as the last bodies were brought to the new burial ground in April of 1864. By this date, the people of Gettysburg and the surrounding county seemed to have put their once normal lives in order again. And as the many and varied armies of north and south maneuvered and clashed across thousands of square miles of Southern territory, Gettysburg became more or less old news, except for a steady but dwindling stream of curious visitors who still made their weary way to south-central Pennsylvania.

On July 24, 1863, the New York *Herald* printed a paragraph which foretold the final chapter in the history of the town and its famous battlefield. "The ground is to become historic," it said, and suggested that, "it will, in the future, be one of the nation's altars...." This conviction would be echoed by many travellers to the site, including a woman who noted: "Like Mount Vernon, it will be a place of pilgrimage for the nation."[125]

Strangers and residents of other states were not the only people to profess that Gettysburg would someday be appreciated and become "hallowed" ground, a place worth saving as one of the premier historic spots in the United States. By the late summer of 1863 a group of concerned Adams County citizens, 26 in all, and many of whom were considered to be the area's best and brightest men, signed a letter addressed to Attorney David McConaughy supporting a plan to initiate and maintain an organization which would purchase and preserve certain parts of the battlefield for all Pennsylvanians and other Americans to enjoy forever. An earlier correspondence from McConaughy had already outlined his thoughts on the subject.

> The Battlefield of Gettysburg
> Gettysburg, August 14, 1863

To the Editor of the Press

Sir:

Immediately after the battle of Gettysburg, the thought occurred to me that there could be no more fitting and expressive memorial of the heroic valor and signal triumphs of our army, on the first, second, and third days of July, 1863, than the battle-field itself, with its natural and artificial defences, preserved and perpetuated in the exact form and condition they presented during the battle.

Acting at once upon this idea, I commenced negotiations, and have secured the purchase of some of the most striking and interesting portions of the battle-ground, embracing among these the heights of Cemetery Hill, on the centre, which resisted the fiercest assaults of the enemy; the granite spur of Round Top, on the left, with its massive rocks and wonderful stone defences, constructed by the Pennsylvania Reserves; and the timber breastworks, on the right, extending for a mile upon the wooded heights of Wolf [Culp's] Hill, whose trees exhibit the fearful effects of our musketry fire.

In pursuance of the original purpose, I now propose to the patriotic citizens of Pennsylvania to unite with me in the tenure of the sacred ground of this battle-field. In order that all may participate who will, at its actual cost, the amount of a single share will be limited to ten dollars.

Committees may be named in the cities and large towns, throughout the State, to whom reference and application can be made.

I respectfully submit the subject to your consideration, and, should it meet the approval of your judgment, invite our active co-operation and influence, with your subscription to the battle-field fund.

It is in contemplation to procure an act of incorporation from the legislature, granting powers similar to those of a Monument Association. It is not designed to limit the number of shares which any citizen may subscribe, as the more generous the fund the more liberal the bounds of this sacred patrimony which it is proposed to perpetuate.

> Very respectfully, etc.,
> D. McConaughy.[126]

The reply of his local supporters follows in part:

> Gettysburg, August 18th, 1863
> D. McConaughy, Esq.

Dear Sir:

We have read with no ordinary interest the delineation of your happy and patriotic conception to commemorate the heroic valor of our national forces in the recent battle of Gettysburg, by the perpetuation of the battle grounds with their natural and artificial defences undisturbed.

We entertain, in common with you, the sentiment that these ever memorable battles, fought on the 1st, 2d, and 3rd days of July last, in which the arms of the United States were crowned with signal victory. So the great joy of the Nation, deserve commemoration to the latest posterity in every way in which such triumphs can be consecrated.

Fought, as they were, in defence of Republican Government and well regulated Freedom, these battle fields are adapted to perpetuate the great principles of human Liberty and just government in the minds of our descendants, and of all men who in all time shall visit them.

We therefore highly approve, and will cheerfully unite in the plan proposed by you, believing it to be the best method of accomplishing the much desired end —the preservation of the standing memorials of the terrible struggles and almost superhuman achievements of our troops in the greatest battle recorded in the annals of the world.

> With sentiments of esteem,
> Your fellow citizens,

C.P. Krauth,	Robert G. Harper,
Charles F. Schaeffer,	R.G. McCreary,
H.L. Baugher,	T.D. Carson,
M. Jacobs,	Charles Horner,
T.P. Bucher,	Edw. G. Fahnestock,
A. Essick,	C.H. Buehler,
David McCreary,	S.S. Schmucker,
J.B. Danner,	M.L. Stoever,
H.S. Huber,	Jacob Zeigler,
D.A. Buehler,	Jno. R. Warner,
Geo. Arnold,	J.L. Schick,
A.D. Buehler,	G. Berkstresser,
Jno. T. McIlhenny,	Jas. F. Fahnestock.[127]

On April 30, 1864, acting on the initiative of McConaughy and his supporters, the Gettysburg Battlefield Memorial Association was formed. By the first week in May the bill incorporating the organization was passed by the Pennsylvania legislature and signed by the governor. This association's opening board was headed by Governor Andrew Gregg Curtin, who was joined in the endeavor by several Union officers, David Wills, and McConaughy himself. A charter outlined the new organization's purpose, which was in general, simply "to hold and preserve the battleground at Gettysburg." In the summer of that year the officers of the G.B.M.A. were listed: President Joseph R. Ingersoll; Vice President, Henry L. Baugher; Treasurer, T. Duncan Carson; and Secretary, David McConaughy. The association also included 13 directors, several of whom were from larger cities throughout Pennsylvania. Plans were made early on to open avenues along the Union lines, but money was not immediately available for this enterprise. One of the few developments completed did not come about until 1878, when George Arnold one of the directors, saw to the erection of a 50-foot observation platform on east Cemetery Hill. This tower became a well-known landmark until 1895.

During the early spring of 1864 the association began an effort to prevent damage from continuing to their holdings. The *Sentinel* of March 1 gave an explanation when it printed this circular:

The Battle Grounds

We are requested by the officers of the Gettysburg Battle-field Memorial Association to remind visitors and others going upon the battle-field that, the cutting of bullets from the trees and otherwise defacing the timber and woods is strictly prohibited. The object of the Association is to preserve the battle grounds and everything connected with them just as they were when the battle was fought. Nothing must be disturbed. It is hoped that this notice will be sufficient without making examples of persons guilty of acts of vandalism upon the timber and grounds.

Within a few years after the end of the Civil War and by the summer of 1867, the Gettysburg Battlefield Memorial Association was well established. Its budget had already enabled the purchase of 140 acres, including the wooded locale where General John Reynolds was shot on July 1, and portions of Little Round Top and Culp's Hill. The president of the association in that year was still J.R. Ingersoll, and included over 50 associates, among them Generals Samuel Crawford and Winfield Hancock. The work of the group was described as "a commendable enterprise," as it concentrated its resources on preserving only the lines occupied by the Union army at Gettysburg.[128]

From 1864 to 1895 the GBMA bought 522 acres of land. When the U.S. Congress authorized and created the Gettysburg National Military Park in that latter year, the Memorial Association property was transferred to the federal government with the War Department having direct jurisdiction over the new park. It was during the years when the Gettysburg Battlefield Memorial Association administered portions of the battlefield lands that most of the state monuments (about 400, 200 constructed before 1888) which today enhance the grounds, were erected. This important work was directed by a superintendent who was employed by the association for over 20 years. He was ex-Union Sergeant Nicholas G. Wilson, a wounded Civil War veteran who had served in an Adams County company of the 138th Pennsylvania Infantry.

This was the first monument erected on the battlefield grounds outside of the Soldiers' National Cemetery. (GAC)

Superintendent Nicholas G. Wilson stands to the left of the cannon near the Baltimore Road entrance to the National Cemetery. (GAC)

The years from 1895 to 1933 under the War Department saw the addition of many federal markers, plaques, cannons and signs which enhanced the story of the great battle in polished bronze, iron, and granite. These federal memorials primarily illustrated only combat action, and the movements and locations of Union and Confederate troops, whereas the state memorials had totally honored Northern regiments and their activities during the battle. The new park was headed by a three-man commission, all battle veterans; John P. Nicholson (28th Pennsylvania), Charles A. Richardson (126th New York), and William M. Robbins, (4th Alabama). Their accomplishments were many, including the construction of 20 miles of semi-permanent avenues, the rebuilding and stabilization of defensive works, the addition of the aforementioned iron and bronze markers and narrative tablets, the placing of 300 cannons around the field, the erection of five steel observation towers, the fabricating of 25 miles of boundary fencing, the restoration of five miles of stone walls, the planting of 17,000 trees, and the acquisition of 800 more acres, in the areas of Devil's Den, the "peach orchard," and on several other important battlefield farms.

These years also saw the peak involvement of Civil War veterans as visitors and users of the park, and the largest reunion took place there in 1913 with the assembly of over 50,000 former soldiers present for the commemoration.[129]

In 1933 the War Department, which had left the most indelible mark on the historic field at Gettysburg, was replaced as chief steward by the newly formed National Park Service of the U.S. Department of the Interior.

The old and barely remembered GBMA had not died out completely. It was reformed in November 1959 as the Gettysburg Battlefield Preservation Association (GBPA) just prior to the Civil War Centennial years of 1961-1965. Its creation came about essentially due to the alarming growth in commercial and residential development occurring on the fringes of the battlefield. This new organization was chartered by the Commonwealth of Pennsylvania and endorsed by President Dwight Eisenhower, a new county resident, and other prominent citizens. By the time it was dissolved in 1981, the GBPA had raised

Gettysburg battlefield commissioners marking Union corps' positions probably with the aid of former army officers. (FL)

more than $200,000 and had purchased 172 acres of land which was donated to the National Military Park. Interestingly, the association was again reorganized a year later because of continuing threats to important parcels of land adjacent to the federally owned battlefield acreage, and also due to the severe cuts in congressional funding for the purchase of such lands. The "new" GBPA highlighted as one of its goals the appropriation of 250 acres of land then threatened by development.

Today the organization is alive and active but still requires the aid of concerned citizens. By joining such associations, one becomes part of a tradition and a long line of dedicated and far-seeing descendants of the original GBMA, who came to the aid of the violated battlefield at a time when the battered and worn veterans of the two armies who had fought there at Gettysburg, were unable to preserve it for themselves.[130]

The memorial association and a host of veterans held sway at Gettysburg for a full fifty years once the battle and the aftermath had come and gone. Each left indelible marks upon the landscape, far more intrusive than three days of simple combat could ever do. Soon monuments and paved avenues imposed upon the scene where splintered trees, battered farm structures, broken and scattered fences, and the military's dead and debris had earlier blighted the trodden and shell-gutted earth. Even to an 1869 visitor all warlike signs had waned on the not yet decade-old battlefield.

> After the thunder storm our heaven is blue:
> Far off, along the borders of the sky,
> In silver folds the clouds of battle lie,
> With soft consoling, sunlight shining through;
> And round the sweeping circles of your hills
> The crashing cannon thrills
> Have faded from the memory of the air;
> And summer pours from unexhausted fountains
> Her bliss on yonder mountains:
> The camps are tenantless, the breastworks bare:
> Earth keeps no stain where hero-blood was poured:
> The hornets humming on their winds of lead,

> Have ceased to sting, their angry swarms are dead,
> And harmless in its scabbard rusts the sword.[131]

And as the years rolled by, for many who were seduced by it, the "sacred ground" began to take on a strange new abstract life fitted to their individual needs and interpretations. Some even added an unearthly dimension to the hallowed place, a feeling quite opposite as remembered by the wide eyed and utterly terrified combatants who were there in the flesh during those ineffable summer days of '63.

> How can I describe the moonlight on Little Round Top and in the weird recesses of the Devil's Den. Personality fades away before the tribute of a nation to her brave, when from the very structure of earth itself her hidden stores have been wrenched to do them honor. There are spiritual presences everywhere, souls that have bridged the space calling unto souls still in mortal frame, this is life eternal. Gettysburg is the apotheosis of an idea, the Nation, the integrity of Pennsylvania and the bond of brotherhood. In this scene of consummated courage, patriotism and self sacrifice...one is proud to belong to the race of man.[132]

Writers, as one might expect, became carried away with the aura of places like Gettysburg. In the main they were men or women who had not faced and cringed at the iron and leaden hail thrown against living bodies on the grim battlefields of history. It was easy to be swept into the atmosphere of an old battle ground and the faded but glorious memories they all seemed to possess. Unfortunately the fields and woods were no longer filled with the vulgar aftermath realities we have so recently examined. There were no young veterans who had been scarred or tormented by war on hand to speak to them of the chaos and terror of the fight. Certainly no ghosts were present, except in overactive or superstitious imaginations, and the singular vision of souls floating in time and space would have been considered ridiculous and childish to all but the most primitive of humans. There had been brotherhood aplenty, but they who shared it were all dead or soon to be. Moreover the nation did not consider applauding the veterans until long after they began to thank themselves. Finally, one would question the absurd idea that anyone would be proud to belong to a race that could create a hellish nightmare like "Gettysburg."

In our million year evolution from low animal into homo sapiens and still further back into the twelve billion year age of the universe, the events at Gettysburg are mighty small and imperceptible. They pale into insignificance even in the context of the 8,000 year history of warfare which spans all of recorded human history. Yet, for the 170,000 soldiers and civilians directly touched by its tragedy, the battle was momentous indeed, and may have been the most all-consuming moment of each of their lives. So for any writer, past or present, to trivialize its sheer horror by perpetuating the glorification of war in any form, is to truly depreciate and misrepresent the participants' motives and memories.

Let us now leave behind the aftermath story with this hope: that for each and every attempt to parade the "pomp and circumstance" of war, we give equal time to the corrupt and merciless monster shielded smugly within, because, "...if the bugler starts to play, we too must dance."[133]

Appendix

"...there was a lot of men killed"

The Battlefield Guides

♦ ♦ ♦

From 1863 to our present day, one particular group related to the Gettysburg battle story has always been at least on the fringes of existence. This one prevailing, and non-failing entity was in some semblance in place long before the Gettysburg Battlefield Memorial Association, the U.S. War Department, or the present day National Park Service. They were the battlefield guides. These "guides" are very peculiar in one sense, as they are at least as old as July 4, 1863, the first day after the battle was fought. Nowhere in the United States has a "guide force" been in effect for so long and still continues. At the first moment when a grieving visitor needed a fairly honest and knowledgeable local person to act as an escort over the field in search of a grave site, or to find one of the isolated field hospitals to search for a wounded friend or relative, or simply when a sightseer asked someone to point out where and what happened in the battle, a guide of some sort has been there. At first, unofficially of course, but they were at least present and able and available to tend to the unusual or singular needs of the casual visitor, the tourists, or to the grieving family member of a deceased soldier.

The first guides were mostly idle farmers or unemployed townspersons who daily could be found lounging around the village hotels, taverns or boardinghouses, "killing time" on the pretext of looking for an odd job. Some of these men would have been uniquely qualified to direct travellers around, as they at least passively knew the area. Lamentably, most were woefully ignorant of the famous battle or its campaign to be much good at relating a true and complete account of the action. As the years passed a few guides did take the time to learn the "story" of the battle itself and more important, the terrain and farms over which it was fought. A few men became aware in the early days following the conflict of the locations of hospitals and what patients were present in them, and also where regimental burial sites or hospital graveyards existed. Most however, could even drive a person to a few obvious or key sites, such as along Cemetery and Seminary Ridges, or to Culp's Hill, Cemetery Hill and the Round Tops.

One of the earliest documented guides was J. Howard Wert, of whom much already has been written. A year after the battle he joined the 209th Pennsylvania Infantry as a second lieutenant, and returned home after his muster out in May 1865. As a civilian prior to his enlistment, he had guided people to graves and field hospitals during the weeks and months following the battle. Contemporary with Wert were other good men such as Samuel Weaver, Dr. John W.C. O'Neal, John R. Frey, also a former soldier, Michael Jacobs, and John Burns who had fought and been wounded in the battle. And there were naturally many other unnamed farmers and town citizens who lived in and around Gettysburg and likewise became engaged in that work.

Much later when Gettysburg evolved into a tourist attraction, and a destination where veterans made periodic pilgrimages, guides were unnecessary as a means to search out a grave or hospital site, but useful more for their entertainment abilities and general battle knowledge. To learn the battlefield itself and its great story, is often a formidable hurdle to first-time visitors. Once its secrets are unlocked, the scenic locale with its deep historic grandeur is as easy to understand and comprehend as one's own backyard. "Unlocking the secrets" said guide Fred Hawthorne, became their most important duty.

To illustrate just how a young man might first become enamored into the guiding trade, this, as told by James Allen Felix during the days of World War I, may prove enlightening:

> Since we were brought up near the Battlefield, it did not hold as much interest to us as to outsiders. I remember one time a carload of people in a Bell touring car spotted me at the ice cream stand [Mr. John Rosensteel's] near Big Round Top. They asked me if I would stand on the running board and take them to Devil's Den and other places. Well, I showed them the places they wanted to see for which they gave me 50 cents. I thought they must be out of their minds to want to see such places, and paying me in the bargain. They had Battlefield Guides then, but you had to have a license to ply your trade, and I was only a boy of 14 or 15. My dad and grandfather [James Anthony] knew the Battlefield about as well as anyone, since they both worked on it, but it never appealed to me UNTIL I left [home], and then it took on more meaning.[1]

In the 1880s an assortment of men were making their exclusive living as "hack drivers" or tour guides, working out of the local hotels and livery stables and the railroad depot. Some of the better known guides between the 1870s and the turn of the century were William D. Holtzworth, James A. Felix (formerly of the 184th Pennsylvania Infantry) William T. Ziegler, A.J. Holtzworth, "Captain" James T. Long, J. Warren Gilbert, John Hoffman, Harry E. Koch, Charles W. Culp, Frank Penn, William M. Shealer, Luther W. Minnigh, and William C. Storrick. By the early 1900s, it has been estimated that there were approximately 50 people engaged in guiding as a "more-or-less permanent occupation." During the years from 1880 to 1900 visitation grew, and by the late 1890s sources indicate that nearly 150,000 sightseers were coming to the battlefield each year.[2]

One of these individuals was a woman who travelled to Gettysburg in 1894 and had some praise for her driver:

> We drove through the little, old-fashioned town out over the battle ground in charge of a guide whom a friend had told us we must not fail to secure. In appearance, and in some peculiarities of speech, he was a good type of a Yankee grafted upon Pennsylvania Dutch stock, of whom evolution had made a very wide-awake citizen without spoiling a very simple-hearted man. A farmer by nature, a soldier when the call came, and now possessed of a thorough knowledge of the field, a sedate sense of humor, and a modest, comfortable and most unsophisticated country hotel in the town.[3]

Five years had passed, when in July 1899 John McElroy gave his own measure of these characters:

> The livery service has been much developed, and now one can be driven to any part of the field for a moderate fee. The drivers of the vehicles are well-informed as to the history of the battle, give a fairly truthful account of the various movements, and are careful to point out all points of interest. Their horses and traps are in good condition, so that a drive about the field is a pleasure.[4]

James Anthony Felix, Battlefield Guide. (MFC)

Due to the growth of the automobile industry which brought more and more people each year to Gettysburg, guiding took on the aura of a full-time and serious business. The occupation, though, was not without its detractors. Because of the quantity of money which could be made off an unwary visitor, a number of unscrupulous guides had begun to offer their services to the public. J. Howard Wert remembered the slow but steady debasement of a once highly regarded calling.

> There are guides and guides at Gettysburg—that is, some that are very good and some that—to put it mildly—are not so good. Of the competent class, William D. Holtzworth, himself a brave soldier, was the pioneer, and he has always had worthy successors....Occasionally [however], a man drifts in from the Lord knows where then goes to driving for someone. He sleeps with a history of the battle beneath his pillow and scans [through] it at odd times in the horsestalls till he gets off a lot of jargon as pat as a parrot with a mouthful of cheese. He imagines he is a guide. He knows more of how the battle was fought than General Meade ever knew, or Colonel [John B.] Bachelder ever found out.[5]

A man who surely encountered this type of "hacker" as described by Professor Wert was Henry Walker of Pittsburgh. He related this little scenario:

> The visitor arrives and is immediately surrounded by guides soliciting patronage. Some of these are good, but most are poor and illiterate. Some years ago there was a guide named Captain [James T.] Long who started out by giving the visitor a brief account of the events leading up to the battle and a short synopsis of its plan. He then followed with each day's fighting step by step, ending with a quite eloquent peroration at the Bloody Angle [*sic*]. When the visitor left he had not only a good idea of the battle but in addition had his patriotism stirred

up to a considerable extent. Now the guide is illiterate and mixes the battle up. On my last visit with some friends the guide took us to the angle first instead of last, and mixed everything else up until, instead of leaving well pleased and impressed, you leave with no clear comprehension of the event except that there was a lot of men killed....[6]

Walker, upon concluding this tirade, suggested that the federal government, who then administered the field, should license the guides, teach them the story and regulate their conduct.

Things had gotten so bad by then that a nearby newspaper, the Hanover *Record Herald*, which was a German oriented paper began eyeing up this nuisance called the "guide profession." In one issue the paper conceded that the one advantage of living at the north pole would be that one would find there no battlefield guides. *The Gettysburg Times* on September 9, 1909, however, cleverly fired back a reply to the German editor's insult, concluding that "there is [also] no sauerkraut up there."

And in essence by 1915, Walker's recommendation was exactly what occurred. The War Department proposed a bill in 1913 to regulate the guides on all National Military Parks, Memorial Battlefields and National Monuments. By October of 1915, 87 tests had been administered and the first licenses issued; 37 had passed the exam of 101 questions with a grade of 70% or better.[7]

From that time hence, guides have been screened, tested, and licensed by the federal government. Today with over a million visitors travelling yearly to Gettysburg, there are more then 100 guides on the National Park Service roster, with about one third of those generally active in the touring "profession." The Licensed Battlefield Guide service remains an important and integral part of the Gettysburg scene, and it is still the best and most logical way to see the grounds and to be assisted in understanding the famous story.

An early U.S. Government issue guide badge. (DST)

NOTES

◆ ◆ ◆

Preface

1. Keenan, Sophie G., "Pere Le Chaise and Gettysburg," Gettysburg *Compiler*. May 29, 1894, p. 1. Wert, J. Howard. *A Complete Hand-Book of the Monuments and Indications and Guide to the Positions on the Gettysburg Battlefield*. Harrisburg, PA: R.M. Sturgeon & Co. (1886): 109. Hereafter cited as Monument Handbook.

    John Howard Wert was born in Adams County, Pennsylvania, in 1841. His father and mother were Adam and Catherine Wert, and the family lived on a farm along White Run on the east side of the Baltimore Turnpike about 2 1/2 miles south of Gettysburg. The Wert or "Wirt" family had been established in the area as early as 1711. J. Howard eventually graduated from Pennsylvania College and later earned a masters degree in education. At the time of the Civil War he was a writer and teacher; and as an Abolitionist had even travelled to Kansas to report on John Brown's anti-slavery activities. When the Confederates invaded his home state he acted as a guide and scout for Union forces. During the Battle of Gettysburg he was present on the field assisting Federal commanders, including General Reynolds, Colonel Vincent, and even General Meade. In the aftermath period Wert and his parents spent many hours assisting the wounded in field hospitals which surrounded or were in close proximity to their farm. By September 1864 J. Howard had enlisted in Co. G, 209th Pennsylvania Infantry. Discharged as a second lieutenant in May 1865 he became superintendent of Adams County schools in 1869. In that same year Wert married 24-year-old Emma L. Aughinbaugh of Gettysburg and they eventually had two children, Anne and Edward. The family moved to Harrisburg where J. Howard was active in education, writing and collecting Civil War relics until his death in 1920.

Introduction

2. Long, E.B. *The Civil War Day by Day, An Almanac, 1861-1865*. Garden City, NY: Doubleday & Company, Inc. (1971): 701-03.

    On page 432-34 of *Confederate Veteran* magazine, vol. IV, Nashville, TN, 1896, the number of eligible males from 18 to 45 years of age is given at 4,285,105 for the entire country, both Union and Confederate states. It appears from this same source, as an example, that North Carolina had 115,369 males available and Virginia had 196,587. Deaths in battle for those two states were: VA, 5,327; NC, 14,522, indicating that some states far outshone their neighbors in the sacrifice of life for the "Cause." These statistics are questioned in vol. V, p. 80, however the case presented is weaker than the original article.

3. Ibid., p. 705.
4. Boatner, Mark M. *The Civil War Dictionary*. New York, NY: David McKay Co., Inc. (1959): 25.
5. "Numbers and Losses" files in the library of the Gettysburg National Military Park, Gettysburg, PA. Hereafter cited as GNMP.
6. Coddington, Edwin B. *The Gettysburg Campaign, A Study in Command*. New York, NY: Charles Scribner's Sons (1968): 248-50.

    Not all sources agree with these figures. For instance although Coddington claims 93,500 in the Union force, he believes that only about 85,500 were present or "effectives" in the battle. Other historians such as Boatner, above, list the Army of the Potomac having 88,289 engaged. John Busey sets the numbers at 89,135 Federals and 69,748 Confederates present at Gettysburg, in the infantry, cavalry, and artillery alone.

7. Faust, Patricia L., ed. *Historical Times Illustrated Encyclopedia of the Civil War*. New York, NY: Harper & Row (1986): 307.

    Here as above, there are many varying estimates of Confederate casualties. Robert R. Krick in *The Gettysburg Death Roster* believes at least 4,572 Southerners were killed or mortally wounded in the battle, with 12,179 wounded and 5,592 missing/prisoners (Dayton, OH: Press of Morningside, 1981). William F. Fox in his *Regimental Losses in the American Civil War* states the Confederate loss at 2,592 killed, 12,706 wounded (including mortally), and 5,510 missing and captured. Jonathan Letterman, M.D., medical director of the Army of the Potomac, quotes specifically that 14,193 U.S. wounded were picked up off of the field by July 4, and 6,802 Rebel injured were left behind by the retreating Southern army to be cared for by Federal medical personnel. John D. Vautier in vol. I of the March 1886 issue of *Southern Bivouac* places the South's casualties at Gettysburg to be around 28,000 and breaks down the losses by corps and day involved. Also see *Blue & Gray* magazine (1989) vol. 6, #4, p. 38, an article by J.B. Mitchell entitled "Confederate Losses at Gettysburg" for a reevaluation of C.S. casualties in the battle. In all of these sources, deserters are never claimed nor estimated.

8. West, John C. *A Texan in Search of a Fight*. Waco, TX: Press of J.S. Hill & Co. (1901): 91.

9. Harrison, Kathleen R. Georg. Notes in the senior historian's files at GNMP, Gettysburg, PA entitled, "Estimated Numbers of Wagons and Horses, Gettysburg Battlefield Vicinity, June-July 1863."

10. Bradsby, H.C. *History of Cumberland and Adams Counties, Pennsylvania*. Chicago, IL: Warner, Beers & Co. (1886): 57-71; 181-204.

11. United States, Department of the Interior, Bureau of the Census. Eight Census of the U.S., 1860, III, p. 721; Agriculture, pp. 124-25; Manufactures, p. 493. Bradsby, H.C., *History of Cumberland and Adams Counties...*, pp. 133-34.

12. Ibid., pp. 84-87.

Chapter One

13. Carter, Robert G. *Four Brothers in Blue*. Austin, TX: University of Texas (1978): 321.

14. Quote from *The Christian Advocate*, vol. LXXXIII, #22, New York, NY, May 28, 1908.

15. Hollinger, Liberty A. (Clutz). *Some Personal Recollections of The Battle of Gettysburg*. Gettysburg, PA: privately printed by author (1925): 14-15.

16. Catton, Bruce, ed. *The Battle of Gettysburg*. (By Frank Haskell). Boston, MA: Houghton Mifflin Company (1969): p. 148. Skelly, Daniel A. *A Boy's Experience During the Battles of Gettysburg*. Probably printed in Gettysburg, PA (1932): 24.

17. Clarke, James F., "A Visit to Gettysburg," *The Christian Register*, vol. 11. Boston, MA, September 18, 1913, p. 900.

18. Fergus, Chuck, "Thornapples," *Pennsylvania Game News*, April 1986, p. 56. The soldier was Private Thomas P. Meyer. Muffly, Joseph W. *The Story of Our Regiment, The 148th Pennsylvania Volunteers....* Des Moines, IA: Kenyon Printing & Mfg. Co. (1904): p. 467.

19. Harrison, Kathleen R. Georg. "The Gettysburg Campaign Daybook," entry for July 8, 1863, in the files of GNMP senior historian, Gettysburg, PA. Hereafter cited as "Daybook."

20. Forbes, Edwin. An undated account of his trip to Gettysburg in the files of the Pierpont Morgan Library, New York, NY, p. 2.

21. Thorn, Elizabeth M., "Mrs. Thorn's War Story," unpublished manuscript in the files of the GNMP Library, Gettysburg, PA, p. 8. See also Gettysburg *Compiler*, July 26, 1905; July 9, 1932.

22. Foster, Joseph H., "Visit To The Battlefield," *Journal of Literature and Politics*, Portsmouth, NH, August 8, 1863.

23. Gardner, Leonard M. *Sunset Memories*. Gettysburg, PA: Gettysburg Times Publishing Co. (1929): 71.

24. Hoke, Jacob. *Historical Reminiscences of the War, or, Incidents Which Transpired In and About Chambersburg During the War of the Rebellion*. Chambersburg, PA: M.A. Foltz, Printer and Publisher (1884): 172.

25. Crozier, Emmet. *Yankee Reporters, 1861-1865*. New York, NY: Oxford University Press (1956): 353.

26. "Special Correspondent." A letter to the editors of the Philadelphia *Public Ledger*, written on Monday July 6 and published on July 15, 1863. Leiper, Thomas J.D. (Lieutenant 58th Pennsylvania Infantry). Extract from a letter written at Kelly's Ford, VA, August 1, 1863, to his father and printed in the August 6, 1863, issue of the Philadelphia *Public Ledger*, p. 1.

27. Knox, Thomas W., "The Battle Field at Gettysburg. Scenes after the Battle. Visit to the Battle-Field," New York *Herald* article written July 6, printed July 9, 1863, p. 1, col. 5.

28. Salomon, Edward S., "Gettysburg," an article in the papers of the Military Order of the Loyal Legion of the U.S. (MOLLUS), California Commandery, Shannon-Conmy Printing Co., San Francisco, CA, 1913. Read January 17, 1912.

29. Carter, Robert G., *Four Brothers in Blue*, p. 326.

30. Moorhead, Isaac, "A Visit to Gettysburg, A Tourist's Account in 1864," *The American Magazine and Historical Chronicle*, vol. 2, Clements Library, Ann Arbor, MI: The University of Michigan, 1985-86, p. 24.

31. Harrison, Kathleen R. Georg, "Daybook" entry for July 2, 1863.

32. Powers, Alice, "Dark Days of the Battle Week," Gettysburg *Compiler*, July 1, 1903.

33. Catton, Bruce, ed. *The Battle of Gettysburg*, p. 154.

34. Emory, Ambrose M. Original unpublished handwritten manuscript record book in the author's collection, p. 4.

    Ambrose M. Emory is believed to have been a descendent of the Emory family of Queen Annes County, Maryland, which dates back to the 17th Century. In 1850 he was known to be a resident of Centreville in that county. On September 13, 1851, Emory left the firm of Martin and Whitely, wholesale druggists at 48th S. Calvert Street in Baltimore to work for Wm. E. Bartlett and Sons or "Bartlett Bros." at 74 Calvert Street who were also druggists. At that time he was married to Mary Bartlett and had a daughter Anna Marie. The 1860 U.S. census lists Emory as a "clerk" living at 96 Park Avenue in the city. Between 1865-69 he resided at 88 1/2 Franklin Street and was employed by Seim & Sindell, who were dealers in paints and glass. In 1880 the name of this firm was changed to "A.M. and A.W. Emory, Glass and Paints" at 88 1/2 Franklin Street which would indicate Emory and a relative had purchased the business from Seim & Sindell.

    A.M. Emory's diary or memoranda book lists various expenses, names of family and friends, memorable events and occasions, trips through the South presumably to purchase or sell pharmaceuticals or glass and paint. His account of visiting the battlefield at Gettysburg dates from August 18 through August 26, 1863, and is a very rare first-hand memoir of a civilian seeing the field and all its horrors and wonders so recently after the combat.

    Previously, this source had been listed as composed by "Edward A. Bird" in other publications (including mine), or in the files of various libraries and or Civil War research facilities. Bird was simply one of the names in Emory's memoranda book, and had been in the past incorrectly identified as the author of the journal. When I obtained the original document in October 1994, the correct verification as to the author was finally ascertained and has now been corrected.

35. Trowbridge, John T. "The Field of Gettysburg." *Atlantic Monthly*, vol. 16. (November 1865): 617-18.

    Yet two other references are available which tells us that some soldiers during the actions of July 1-3, had purposefully taken care not to injure the memorials in the graveyard. "Mrs. C.A. Ehler," a volunteer nurse from Lancaster, PA, stated that in the Evergreen Cemetery, "...our soldiers had carefully laid down the highest monuments." See *Hospital Scenes....* Philadelphia, PA: Henry B. Ashmead, printer (1864): 17-18. Also Michael Jacobs noted this: "It is a matter of no little surprise that but few of the monuments in the citizen's cemetery...sustained any serious injury....Many had been thrown down but it has been said that this was done designedly by our men to prevent greater injury to them." See Michael Jacobs, "Later Rambles Over The Field Of Gettysburg," *United States Service Magazine.* vol. I & II, January & February 1864, p. 166.

36. The large hill on the right flank of the Union "hook-shaped line" was owned jointly by Henry Culp, Peter Raffensperger, Abraham Spangler and others. The small knoll, McKnight's Hill, now known as "Stevens Knoll" was the property of James McKnight who lived about 100 yards west of it and along the Baltimore Pike. See "Land Ownership Map," by Kathleen R. Georg Harrison, senior historian, GNMP, Gettysburg, PA. Culp's Hill was also known as Raspberry Hill in 1863. Emory, Ambrose M., unpublished manuscript diary, p. 1.

37. Knox, Thomas W., "The Battle Field at Gettysburg...," July 9, 1863, p. 1.

38. Catton, Bruce, ed., *The Battle of Gettysburg*, p. 149. Boynton, Henry V. A letter written to the Cincinnati, OH, *Gazette* and published as "A Visit to the Battle Ground," June 30, 1866. Boynton had been a lieutenant colonel in the Civil War with the 35th Ohio Infantry. Later, he served as the chairman of the Chickamauga and Chattanooga (TN) National Military Park Commission, 1897-1905. Stoke, Frank M. Extracted from a letter dated at Gettysburg, October 26, 1863 to his brother, J.M. Stoke. Gettysburg College Library Archives, Gettysburg, PA, p. 2. Stoke was a member of "The Patapsco Guards," an independent company of Maryland volunteers who performed as hospital guards and "provost marshal" squads as needed in the weeks following the battle. The unit was formed in 1861 near Ellicott Mills in Howard County, Maryland. Hoke, Jacob, *Historical Reminiscences of the War...*, p. 172.

39. Jones, Jesse H., "Saved the Day," *National Tribune*, Washington, D.C. vol. XIV, March 7, 1895, p. 2.

40. Wert, J. Howard, *Monument Handbook*, pp. 200-01.

41. Bucklin, Sophronia E. *In Hospital and Camp: A Woman's Record of Thrilling Incidents Among the Wounded in the Late War*. Philadelphia, PA: John E. Potter and Co. (1869): 187-88.

42. Catton, Bruce, ed., *The Battle of Gettysburg*, p. 149.

43. Emory, Ambrose M., unpublished manuscript diary, p. 2.

44. Johnson, Clifton. *Battleground Adventures*. Cambridge, MA: Houghton Mifflin Co., The Riverside Press (1915): 174-75. An interview with Christian Benner, Jr. entitled "The Farmer's Son."

45. Gardner, Leonard M., *Sunset Memories*, pp. 71-72.

46. Forbes, Edwin, undated account, p. 3.

47. Chapman, Horatio D. Excerpt from his original diary in the archives of the Connecticut State Library, Hartford, CT, entry for July 4, 1863.

48. Storrs, John W. *The Twentieth Connecticut, A Regimental History*. Naugatuck, CT: Press of the "Naugatuck Valley Sentinel" (1886): 102-03.

49. Rosensteel, John H. Material in the curator's files and Museum of the Civil War collection of the National Park Service at GNMP, Gettysburg, PA.

50. Knox, Thomas W., "The Battle Field at Gettysburg...," July 9, 1863, p. 1, col. 8.

51. Bucklin, Sophronia E., *In Hospital and Camp...*, pp. 189-90.

52. Knox, Thomas W., "The Battle Field at Gettysburg...," July 9, 1863, p. 1, col. 9.

53. Powell, Richard M., "With Hood At Gettysburg," Philadelphia *Weekly Times*, vol. VIII, Philadelphia, PA, p. 1, col. 1. Coco, Gregory A. *Recollections of a Texas Colonel at Gettysburg*. Gettysburg, PA: Thomas Publications (1990): 21.

54. Boynton, Henry V., "A Visit to the Battle Ground," p. 1.
    Curiously, at Little Round Top on November 18, 1863, a man found a pair of discarded soldiers' trousers. Inside the pocket was a small silver coin and a medal. The medal bore the name of John W. Hershey, 11th Massachusetts Infantry. The soldier was contacted; he had survived the battle, and the identification tag was returned to him. See Franklin J.F. Schantz, "Reflections on the Battle of Gettysburg," ed. by R.S. Shay, Lebanon County Historical Society Publication, vol. 13, #6 (1963). p. 301.

55. Knox, Thomas W., "The Battle Field at Gettysburg...," July 9, 1863, p. 1, col. 5.

56. Campbell, John T., "Sights at Gettysburg," *National Tribune*, Washington, D.C., September 17, 1908, p. 7.

57. Wert, J. Howard, "In the Hospitals of Gettysburg, July 1863," Harrisburg *Telegraph*, Harrisburg, PA, a series of 12 articles published between July 2 and October 7, 1907.

58. Jacobs, Michael, "Later Rambles Over The Field Of Gettysburg," *United States Service Magazine*, vol. I and II, January and February 1864, pp. 70 & 163.

59. Unidentified letter writer to the *Daily Patriot and Union*, Harrisburg, PA, July 11, 1863. Courtesy of Timothy H. Smith, Gettysburg, PA.

60. Carter, Robert G., *Four Brothers in Blue*, pp. 343-44.

61. Foster, John Y., "Four Days at Gettysburg," *Harper's New Monthly Magazine*, February 1864, p. 382.

62. Emory, Ambrose M., unpublished manuscript diary, p. 4-5, 10. A "round about" was a short military jacket favored by the Confederate Army.

63. Moorhead, Isaac, "A Visit to Gettysburg...," pp. 25-26.
    The guide used by Moorhead was John G. Frey, a local farmer who had served an enlistment in the 138th Pennsylvania Infantry. He was one of the first "unofficial guides" on the battlefield, and kept a register/notebook of the field burial locations of many of the Union soldiers who had been killed at Gettysburg. Evergreen Cemetery records indicate that Frey died October 30, 1866, and was survived by his spouse, Elizabeth Carpenter.
    Joseph H. Carter, ed., *Magnolia Journey: A Union Veteran Revisits the Former Confederate States*, by Russell H. Conwell, University, AL: University of Alabama Press (1974): p. 185.
    Russell H. Conwell was a 26-year-old Boston veteran who had served as a captain in the 46th Massachusetts Infantry and the 2nd Massachusetts Heavy Artillery. He was dismissed from the service in February 1864. In 1869 he also saw the carvings on Little Round Top, noticing that "several large flat stones near which officers were killed have been engraved with their names and the dates of their deaths." The second officer so enshrined was General Stephen H. Weed, a casualty of July 2.

64. Boynton, Henry V., "A Visit to the Battle Ground," p. 1, col. 5.

65. Judson, Amos M. *History of the Eighty-third Regiment Pennsylvania Volunteers*. Erie, PA: B.F.H. Lynn (1865): 70.

66. White, Wyman S. Excerpt from his reminiscence which is in the collection of Silas W. White, Fitzwilliam, NH, p. 92. See also a published account of his memoirs edited by Russell C. White and made available by Butternut and Blue, Baltimore, MD, 1991 as *The Civil War Diary of Wyman S. White*.

67. Rosenblatt, Ernie, ed. *Anti-Rebel—The Civil War Letters of Wilber Fisk*. Croton-on-Hudson, NY: Ernie Rosenblatt (1983): 115-16.

68. Musgrove, Richard M. *Autobiography*. Published by Mary D. Musgrove (1921): 94.

69. Ibid., p. 94.

70. Graham, Ziba B. "On To Gettysburg. Ten Days From My Diary of 1863." Detroit, MI: Winn & Hammond, Printers and Binders (1893): 14. A paper read before the Commandery of the state of Michigan and the Military Order of the Loyal Legion of the U.S., March 2, 1889.

71. Johnson, Clifton, *Battleground Adventures*, pp. 195-96.

72. Parker, Joseph A. Excerpt from a letter written to a "friend," in the archives of Mount St. Mary's College, Emmitsburg, MD, p. 3.

73. Carter, Joseph C., ed., *Magnolia Journey...*, p. 189. Keenan, Sophia G., "Pere Le Chaise and Gettysburg," p. 1.

74. Unidentified letter writer, *Daily Patriot and Union*, Harrisburg, PA, July 11, 1863.

75. Wert, J. Howard, *Monument Handbook*, p. 93.

76. Moorhead, Isaac, "A Visit to Gettysburg...," p. 25.

77. Hoke, Jacob, *Historical Reminiscences of the War...*, p. 172.

78. Stoke, Frank M., October 26, 1863, letter, p. 3. Speaking of the crevices a member of the 118th Pennsylvania saw, "[o]ne Confederate in the death grip had seized the sharp edge of a huge rock, and with feet held fast in a cleft of the rock above, hung head downwards between the two." Smith, John L. *History of the Corn Exchange Regiment*. (118th Pennsylvania), Philadelphia, PA (1888): 257.

79. White, Wyman S., reminiscence, p. 92.

80. Houghton, James, 4th Michigan Infantry. Excerpts from his unpublished journal memoir in the archives of the University of Michigan, Ann Arbor, MI, p. 15.

81. Bushman, Emanuel. Excerpt from a letter to Henry J. Stahle, editor of the Gettysburg *Compiler*, August 19, 1884. Brown, Andrew. *Geology and the Gettysburg Campaign*. Commonwealth of Pennsylvania Bureau of Topographic and Geologic Survey, Educational Series, No. 5, (1983), p. 1.

82. Skelly, Daniel A, *A Boy's Experience...*, p. 22.

83. Unidentified letter writer, *Daily Patriot and Union*, Harrisburg, PA, July 11, 1863.

84. McCalmont, Alfred B. *Extracts From Letters....* Franklin, PA: Robert McCalmont (1908): p. 47.

85. Houghton, James, unpublished journal, pp. 16-17.

86. Unidentified letter writer, *Daily Patriot and Union*, Harrisburg, PA, July 11, 1863.

87. Wert, J. Howard, *Monument Handbook*, p. 109. Wert, J. Howard, "'Twas Fifty Years Ago," #13, Harrisburg *Telegraph*, a series of articles written by Wert and printed in that paper from June to December 1913.

88. Carter, Robert G., *Four Brothers in Blue*, pp. 324-25.

89. Linn, John Blair. Excerpt from his diary written from July 6-11, 1863, and located in the files of the Centre County Library and Historical Museum, Bellefonte, PA, pp. 7-8. John B. Linn, obituary, printed in the Keystone *Gazette*, Bellefonte, PA, January 6, 1899.

   John B. Linn was born in Lewisbury, PA, October 15, 1831, the son of James F. Linn a prominent area attorney. He attended both Lewisbury Academy and Marshall College at Mercersburg, PA, graduating in 1848. His law study was conducted in his father's office and he was admitted to the bar in 1851. Linn was married twice, first to Julia J. Pollack in 1857 and later to Mary E.D. Wilson. He had two children.

   John B. Linn was an accomplished local and state historian, and served for several years as Secretary of the Commonwealth. He also practiced law in Sullivan, Union, and Centre counties, making his final home in Bellefonte in 1871. Before his death in 1899 Linn wrote several books on history, law, geneology and the bible. In the latter he made a study of that book in a "practical manner" not in a theoretical way, translating the book from the original Greek for better understanding of its *historical* nature. Friends described him as a man of "more than ordinary wit and intelligence."

90. Emory, Ambrose M., unpublished manuscript diary, pp. 14-16.
91. Sloan, I.O. Excerpt of a letter to G.S. Griffith printed in the Lutheran *Observer*, August 14, 1863. The *Observer* is available on microfilm at the Lutheran Theological Seminary, Gettysburg, PA.
92. Skelly, Daniel A., *A Boy's Experience...*, p. 21.
93. Knox, Thomas W., "The Battle Field at Gettysburg...," p. 1, col. 5.
94. Moorhead, Isaac, "A Visit to Gettysburg...," pp. 27-28. Only two of Armistead's colonels were killed outright on July 3, J.G. Hodges and E.C. Edmonds. The other officers may have been attached to Garnett's or Kemper's Brigades.
95. Durkin, James, ed. *This War is an Awful Thing...The Civil War Letters of the National Guards, The 19th & 90th Pennsylvania Volunteers*. Glenside, PA: J.M. Santarelli Publishing (1994): p. 245. Adams *Sentinel & General Advertiser*, November 22 & 29, 1864.
96. Trowbridge, John T., "The Field of Gettysburg," p. 622. There may have been only one "delapidated tree" present in 1896, but in September 1879, Mr. Sherfy had 1,000 trees in his orchard, all brimming with peaches, which he was very liberal in giving away to visitors. So said a former infantryman of Co. G, 53rd Pennsylvania Infantry, who chronicled his visit to Gettysburg in that year. See the Potter County (PA) *Journal*, September 4, 11, 18, 1879. Hemphill, W.A. "On Gettysburg's Famous Battlefield" in "Gettysburg Newspaper Clippings" file, vol. II, senior historian's office at GNMP, Gettysburg, PA.
97. Twitchell, Joseph H. Letter in the archives of Yale University Library, New Haven, CT, p. 5. Blight, David W., ed. *When This Cruel War Is Over. The Civil War Letters of Charles Harvey Brewster*. Amherst, MA: The University of Massachusetts Press (1992): pp. 239 & 243.
98. Stevens, George T. *Three Years in the Sixth Corps*. New York, NY: D. Van Nostrand, Publisher (1870): pp. 254-55.
99. Haines, Alanson A. *History of the Fifteenth Regiment New Jersey Volunteers*. New York, NY: Jenkins & Thomas, Printers (1883): p. 96.
100. Livermore, William T. Extract from a letter written to Charles Livermore on July 6, 1863, from "camp in the field near Gettysburg, Penna." in the "20th Maine Infantry" file at the GNMP Library, p. 2.
101. Boynton, Henry V., "A Visit to the Battle Ground," p. 1, col. 3.
102. Unknown correspondent, "On The Battlefield," Philadelphia *Weekly Times*, June 8, 1878. This "Indian sign," if it ever existed, is no longer visible on the boulder on which it was carved, or the rock has been removed, as many have been.
103. Nevins, Allan, ed. *A Diary of Battle. The Personal Journals of Colonel Charles S. Wainwright, 1861-1865*. New York, NY: Harcourt, Brace & World, Inc. (1962): 252.
104. White, Wyman S., reminiscence, p. 92.
105. Thompson, Benjamin W. From his personal narrative of the Civil War written in 1910 and in the collection of John A. Thompson, Minneapolis, MN, p. 46. A copy is in the files of the "111th New York Infantry" at GNMP.
106. Hoke, Jacob. *Historical Reminiscences of the War...*, pp. 172-73.
107. Benedict, George G. *Army Life in Virginia*. Burlington, VT: Free Press Association (1895): pp. 190-91.
108. Silliker, Ruth L., ed. *The Rebel Yell & the Yankee Hurrah...* Camden, ME: Down East Books (1985): 107.
109. Catton, Bruce, ed. *The Battle of Gettysburg*, pp. 109-10.
110. Knox, Thomas W., "The Battle Field at Gettysburg...," p. 1, col. 4. The 137th NY grave noted by the author is probably a mis-identification, as this unit was posted at Culp's Hill.
111. Unidentified letter writer, *Daily Patriot and Union*, Harrisburg, PA, July 11, 1863.
112. Clarke, James F., "A Visit to Gettysburg," p. 900.
113. Moore, Jane B. Excerpt from a letter written to G.S. Griffith printed in the Lutheran *Observer*, July 26, 1863.
114. Houghton, James, unpublished journal memoir, p. 16.
115. Skelly, Daniel A., *A Boy's Experience...*, p. 21. The "wounded soldier" may have been General G.K. Warren of Meade's staff who was slightly injured on July 2 while on Little Round Top.
116. Trowbridge, John T., "The Field of Gettysburg," p. 623. In October 1864, almost a year before Trowbridge visited "Meade's Headquarters," Isaac Moorhead was at the house where he observed a pile of bones of 18 horses killed there, which had been collected by Lydia Leister.

117. Stoke, Frank M., October 26, 1863 letter, p. 2.

118. Knox, Thomas W., "The Battle Field at Gettysburg...," p. 1, col. 4.

119. Boynton, Henry V., "A Visit to the Battle Ground," p. 1, col. 4.

120. Boone, Samuel G. Unpublished manuscript in the GNMP Library within the "88th Pennsylvania Infantry" file, p. 27. Boone was a lieutenant in Co. B of that regiment.

121. Linn, John B., diary written from July 6-11, 1863, pp. 3-4.

122. Gardner, Leonard, *Sunset Memories*, p. 73.

123. Hollinger, Liberty A. (Clutz), *Some Personal Recollections...*, p. 15.

124. McCreary, Albertus. *Gettysburg: A Boy's Experiences of the Battle*. Gettysburg, PA: Privately printed (1909): pp. 16-18. Copy in the Adams County Historical Society, Gettysburg, PA:

125. Helffrich, William, "William Helffrich...Horse and Buggy Preacher," Historical Review of Berks County (Fall, 1982): pp. 153-54.

126. "T.W.B." Special Correspondent. Letter to Philadelphia *Public Ledger*, July 5, 1863, printed in that newspaper on July 10, 1863.

127. Hoke, Jacob. *Historical Reminiscences of the War...*, p. 172. Clarke, James F., "A Visit to Gettysburg," p. 900.

128. Gettysburg *Compiler*, July 20, 1863, p. 1, col. 4.

129. McClean, William, "The Days of Terror in 1863," Gettysburg *Compiler*, June 1, 1908, p. 2, cols. 1-3.

130. Alleman, Matilda J. "Tillie" (Pierce). *At Gettysburg, or What a Girl Heard and Saw of the Battle*. New York, NY: W. Lake Borland (1889): pp. 94-95.

131. Croll, Jennie Smyth, ed., "Days of Dread," Philadelphia *Weekly Press*, November 16, 1887, p. 2, col. 3. The article is written about Mary Agnes Horner who lived on Chambersburg Street in Gettysburg. Her father was Dr. Charles Horner.

132. Jacobs, Jenny Eyster. *Memoirs of Jenny E. Jacobs*, Vol. I. Henry E. Horn (1974): pp. 61-62.

133. Shay, Ralph S., ed. "Reflections on the Battle of Gettysburg," vol. XIII, #6, 1963, p. 284, at the Lebanon County Historical Society. Letter from Jennie McCreary, July 22, 1863.

134. King, Sarah B., "Battle Days in 1863," Gettysburg *Compiler*, July 4, 1906, p. 3, col. 6.
    Mrs. King was not the only person to have clothes "exchanged," in her house. Lydia Meals also found that several Confederates had undressed in her house and then walked away in her brother's clean clothing.

135. Powers, Alice. "Dark Days of the Battle Week," Gettysburg *Compiler*, July 7, 1908, p. 2, col. 2.

136. Tyson, Charles J. Extract from a letter printed in the Philadelphia *Weekly Times*, March 29, 1884, p. 1, col. 4-5. The letter was addressed to N.D. Preston, Esq. of Bradford, PA, and written from Flora Dale, PA, on January 16, 1884.

137. Souder, Emily Bliss Thacher. *Leaves From The Battle-Field of Gettysburg, A Series of Letters Written from a Field Hospital and National Poems*. Philadelphia, PA: Caxton Press of C. Sherman, Son & Co. (1864): pp. 22-23. E.B. Thacher was married to Edmund A. Souder.

138. Walker, Joel, "Some Stirring Incidents," Philadelphia *Weekly Times*, March, 17, 1883, p. 2, col. 2-3.

139. Runge, William H., ed. *Four Years in the Confederate Artillery. The Diary of Private Henry R. Berkeley*. Chapel Hill, NC: University of NC Press (1961): pp. 50-51.

140. McClean, William, "The Days of Terror in 1863," p. 2, col. 3.

141. Johnson, Clifton, *Battleground Adventures*. "The Colored Servant Maid," pp. 190-91.

142. Wert, J. Howard, *Monument Handbook*, pp. 162-63.

143. Stiles, Robert. *Four Years Under Marse Robert*. New York, NY: The Neale Publishing Company (1903): 219-20.

144. Gardner, Leonard M., *Sunset Memories*, pp. 73-75.

145. Beller, Lizzie J., "Gettysburg," *National Tribune*, Washington, D.C., March, 17, 1892, p. 2, col. 3.

146. Unidentified letter writer, *Daily Patriot and Union*, Harrisburg, PA, July 11, 1863.

147. Hoke, Jacob, *Historical Reminiscences of the War...*, pp. 171-72.

148. Jacobs, Jenny E., *Memoirs of Jenny E. Jacobs*, p. 61.

149. Brinton, John H., M.D. Extract from a letter to Dr. Henry Janes dated August 15, 1863, in the "Camp Letterman File," GNMP Library, Gettysburg, PA.

150. Stoke, Frank M., October 26, 1863, letter, p. 1.

151. Emory, Ambrose E., unpublished manuscript diary, pp. 9-11.

   The two soldiers mentioned by Emory were Corporal Murray M. Littrell and Sergeant Lewis Williams of Co. A, 47th VA, Infantry. This is the first ever confirmation of their deaths at Gettysburg, as both their personal compiled service records and R.K. Krick's *The Gettysburg Death Roster* do not list them as casualties of the battle.

152. Moorhead, Isaac, "A Visit to Gettysburg...," p. 27.

153. Jacobs, Michael, "Later Rambles...," pp. 66-67.

154. "Mr. Cooke." "Battle of Gettysburg." An article by Special Correspondent "Mr. Cooke" of *The Age*, reprinted in the Gettysburg *Compiler*, July 20, 1863, p. 1, col. 6; p. 2, col. 1.

155. Sparks, David S., ed. *Inside Lincoln's Army. The Diary of Marsena Rudolph Patrick...Provost Marshal General, Army of the Potomac*. New York, NY: Thomas Yoseloff (1924): 268.

   "Copperheads," were Northern democrats who opposed Lincoln's war policy and wanted a negotiated peace instead of continuing the war. However, in this usage, Patrick, like others, was merely referring to citizens who were either Southern sympathizers or those who had no patriotic feeling toward Federal soldiers in general and who took advantage of them whenever possible. The name was taken from the copper pennies or one cent coins they carried for identification. The coins have the head of "Liberty" stamped thereon.

156. Catton, Bruce. ed., *The Battle of Gettysburg*, p. 148.

157. "Mr. Cooke," "Battle of Gettysburg," Gettysburg *Compiler*, p. 2, col. 1. Brown, Edmund R. *The Twenty-Seventh Indiana Volunteers in the War of the Rebellion....* Monticello, IN: R.E. Brown (1899): pp. 394-94.

Chapter Two

1. "Killed and Wounded," Gettysburg *Compiler*, July 7, 1863.

2. *The War of the Rebellion: A Compilation of the Official Records of the Union and Confederate Armies*. Washington, DC: Government Printing Office (1889): vol. 27, part I, p. 378. Hereafter cited as *Official Records*. The notation reads: "Remarks. —[Found dead] One female (private), in rebel uniform." National Archives War Records Office, Record Group 94, Union Battle Reports, vol. 27, boxes 48-52.

3. Foster, Joseph H., "Visit To The Battle Field."

4. As examples of this same attitude, Albert Einstein remarked that, "(n)either can I believe that the individual survives the death of his body, although feeble souls harbor such thoughts through fear or ridiculous egotism." Another great thinker, Thomas Edison, wrote: "My mind is incapable of conceiving such a thing as a soul. I may be in error, and man may have a soul; but I simply do not believe it."

   Busey, John W. *The Last Full Measure: Burials in the Soldiers National Cemetery at Gettysburg*. Hightstown, NJ: Longstreet House (1988): xli.

5. The vulture and buzzard population of the Gettysburg battlefield was present in the county for many years before the battle. Driven away by the noise and smell of gunpowder, these birds returned to find little left to prey upon. Today over 700 of these unique creatures still live in this area, generally south of town near the Round Tops where one of the largest populations on the East Coast survive. In the winter there are up to 800 in residence; in the summer about 200 make their home there. The turkey buzzards forage on wild small animal remains, while the black vultures prefer larger carcasses, such as livestock. None usually roam more than about six miles from their roosts at Big Round Top. See article in the *Town Talk*, Alexandria, LA, June 28, 1986. See also, "Vulture Research Begins at Gettysburg" article by Victoria B. Greenlee in *Park Science*, vol. 4, #1, Fall 1983, p. 12.

6. Warren, Leander H. *My Recollections*. Gettysburg, PA: privately printed (1926): p. 12. Wert, J. Howard. *Monument Handbook*, p. 163. Another source which describes the activities of hogs on the battlefield is found on page 257 of *The History of the Corn Exchange Regiment* by John L. Smith. In it he said: "Wild hogs feeding on the corpses magnified the surrounding horrors [of July 2]." Musgrove, Richard W., *Autobiography*, p. 94. Smith, John L. *History of the Corn Exchange Regiment...*, p. 250-51. Wills, David. Excerpt from a letter written on July 24, 1863, to Governor Andrew G. Curtin. Pennsylvania State Archives. R.G. 26, Executive Correspondence, Department of State, Secretary of the Commonwealth.

7. Schraf, Joannie M. "Murder, they chirped." Excerpt from an article in *U.S. News and World Report*, October 14, 1991, p. 67.

8. Croll, Jennie S., "Days of Dread" article, p. 2, col. 3. Campbell, John, "Sights at Gettysburg," *National Tribune*, September 17, 1908, p. 7. Muffly, Joseph W. *The Story of Our Regiment...*, p. 460.

9. U.S. Government, National Archives Record Group 94, War Records Office, Union Battle Reports, vol. 27, boxes 48-52. "147th Pennsylvania Infantry," unknown diarists of Co. G, entry for July 5, 1863, in the archival files of the "Association of Licensed Battlefield Guides," Gettysburg, PA. Sparks, David S., ed., *Inside Lincoln's Army...*, p. 268.

10. *Official Records*, vol. 27, part I, p. 119. Haines, Alanson A., *A History of the Fifteenth Regiment New Jersey Volunteers*, p. 95.

11. Blood, Henry D., Assistant Quartermaster, U.S.A. Extracts from his unpublished 1865 diary in the collection of the National Archives, Washington, D.C.

12. Brinton, John H. M.D. *Personal Memoirs*. New York, NY: The Neale Publishing Company (1914): 245-46.

13. Schildt, John W. *Roads From Gettysburg*. Chewsville, MD: John W. Schildt (1979): 23.

14. Baird, William (6th Michigan Cavalry). Extract from his unpublished memoirs at the Bentley Historical Library, University of Michigan, Ann Arbor, MI. Parker, John L. *History of the 22nd Massachusetts Infantry*. Boston, MA: The Press of Rand Avery Co. (1887): 345. Carter, Robert G., *Four Brothers in Blue*, p. 325.

15. Osborne, Steven A., "Recollections of Army Life in the Civil War," A series of articles in the Shenango, PA, *Valley News*, 1915.

16. Shuffler, R. Henderson, ed. Decimus et Ultimus Barziza. *The Adventures Of A Prisoner Of War, 1863-1864*. Austin, TX: University of Texas Press (1964): 55.

17. Muffly, Joseph W., *The Story of Our Regiment*, pp. 462 and 465.

18. Blanchard, Charles H. Extract from his memoir of service in the 111th Pennsylvania Volunteers, now housed in the Erie County Historical Society, Erie, PA. See also Muffly, Joseph W., *The Story of Our Regiment*, p. 466.

19. Nye, Wilber S., ed. Thomas F. Galwey. *The Valiant Hours: Narrative of "Captain Brevet" an Irish American in the Army of the Potomac*. Harrisburg, PA: The Stackpole Company (1961): 121.

20. Bloodgood, John D. *Personal Reminiscences of the War*. New York, NY: Hunt & Easto (1893): 149-50.

21. Dickert, D. Augustus. *History of Kershaw's Brigade*. Newberry, SC: Elbert H. Hull Company (1899): 248-49.

22. Author unknown. (He was a member of the 6th New Jersey Infantry). "Scenes and Incidents at Gettysburg." *Harper's Weekly*, January 16, 1864.

23. Willson, Arabella M. *Disaster, Struggle, Triumph; The Adventures of 1,000 "Boys in Blue," from August, 1862 to June, 1865*. Albany, NY: The Argus Company, Printers (1870): 178.

24. White, Wyman S., reminiscence, p. 91.

25. Storrs, John W., *The Twentieth Connecticut...*, p. 102.

26. Author unknown, "3rd Maine Infantry" file, GNMP Library.

27. Houghton, James, unpublished journal memoir, pp. 16-17.

28. Wert, J. Howard, "'Twas Fifty Years Ago," #13. Wert, J. Howard, "In the Hospitals of Gettysburg...," #9.

29. McLaughlin, James, (21st Mississippi Infantry). Confederate compiled service record in the Military Records Division, National Archives, Washington, D.C.

30. Stoke, Frank M., October 26, 1863, letter, p. 2.

31. Jacobs, Michael, "Later Rambles...," p. 70. Another civilian already quoted, William McClean said about this subject: "The work of burial of the dead...was poorly done by details of Rebel prisoners...." See McClean, "The Days of Terror in 1863," p. 2.

32. Unidentified letter writer *Daily Patriot and Union*, Harrisburg, PA, July 11, 1863.

33. Cross, Andrew B. *Battle of Gettysburg and the Christian Commission*. Baltimore, MD: (1865) 26. Emory, Ambrose M., unpublished manuscript diary, p. 10.

34. Ibid., pp. 143-44.

35. Ibid., p. 9.

36. Linn, John B., diary written from July 6-11, 1863, pp. 8, 12-13.

37. Author unknown, article in *The Daily Telegraph*, Harrisburg, PA, July 10, 1863.

38. Nash, Eugene A. *A History of the Forty-Fourth Regiment, New York Volunteer Infantry....* Chicago, IL: R.R. Donnelley & Sons, Co. (1911): 295.

39. Field, T.G. Extract from a letter to M. Braddock, July 4, 1863. Courtesy of Timothy K. Krapf, Licensed Battlefield Guide, Gettysburg, PA.

40. Author unknown, article in Gettysburg *Compiler*, July 27, 1863.

41. The original of this unique map is currently in the Library of Congress in Washington, D.C. It was officially, "entered...in the year 1864...," by S.G. Elliott into the clerk's office, District Court of the Eastern District of Pennsylvania. F. Bourgran & Co., Lithographers of 602 Chestnut Street, Philadelphia printed the original. Elliott states that the map, which perports to locate the graves of several thousand Union and Confederate soldiers, as well as many horses killed in action, was "made from an accurate Survey of the Ground by Transit and Chain." A facsimile of the original may be seen at the GNMP Library or in the senior historian's office, Gettysburg, PA.

    An article in the July 27, 1863, Gettysburg *Compiler* states that, "[a] map of the battlefield has been made which shows the localities of graves." See p. 1, col. 6.

42. *Report of the General Agent of the State of New York for the Relief of Sick, Wounded, Furloughed and Discharged Soldiers*. Albany, NY: Comstock & Cassidy, Printers (1864): 51 & 60.

43. One of the original volumes of the "J.G. Frey Burial List" was in the possession of the Larson family who until January 1995 owned and operated the "General Lee Headquarters Museum." Mr. Andrew Larson was kind enough to donate, through me, a copy to the GNMP Library. The book contains about 1100 names.

44. Advertisement notice in the Adams *Sentinel*, February 24, 1863, and April 7, 1863.

45. Mitchell, Mary H. *Hollywood Cemetery. The History of a Southern Shrine*. Richmond, VA: Virginia State University (1985): 86.

    As a curious sidelight, Dr. O'Neal may have been selling his compiled list or considering having it printed in a local newspaper, possibly to aid families searching for bodies. A receipt is known to exist which states: "Gettysburg, June 23, 1866. Rec'd of Dr. J.W.C. O'Neal five dollars for published list of Confederate marked dead in the Compiler. $5.00 H.J. Stahle." No other information on this cryptic "message" is known at this time. (A copy of the receipt is in the author's files. As far as is known today, the list was never published in any local newspaper.)

46. Elmer, William M.D. *Physicians Hand-Book of Practice for 1863*. New York, NY: W.A. Townsend, Publisher (1862): 197-99. This was O'Neal's personal day-to-day notebook and it is presently in the files of the Adams County Historical Society, Gettysburg, PA.

47. O'Neal, John William C. "Record of Confederate Burials," in the GNMP "Museum of the Civil War" archives. It was donated to the park in November 1943, by "Mrs. J.T. Huddle," who was O'Neal's daughter, and it had been in her possession since the death of O'Neal in April 1913. See also the article in the December 3, 1943, issue of the Gettysburg *Times*. O'Neal, John W.C. "List of Marked Confederates Buried Upon the Battlefield of Gettysburg;" and "List of Graves of Confederate Soldiers Lying On The Battlefield, Still Marked, Taken in May, 1866." These two compilations are in Dr. O'Neal's file in the GNMP Library.

48. Scott, James K.P. *The Story of the Battles at Gettysburg*. Harrisburg, PA: The Telegraph Press (1927): 35.

49. Rose, George W. "Location of Confederate Graves in the Vicinity of the Rose House—From a book found on the battlefield, by George Washington Rose" 1865, pp. 5 & 12. A copy of this book is located in the files of the GNMP library, and the original is in the curator's archives at the National Military Park. There were about 230 graves removed from the Rose farm area in the early 1870s. The reader should be aware that some of the Rebel soldiers' names documented may not be correct as to spelling, units, etc. The senior historian of the park, Kathleen R. Georg Harrison, believes that this book may have been partially or entirely filled in by Samuel Weaver, not Mr. Rose. (Conversation with Ms. Harrison on December 5, 1994.)

50. Bachelder, John B. Extract from a letter to Andrew Curtin. See "Origins of Gettysburg's Soldiers' National Cemetery and Gettysburg Battlefield Memorial Association." May 1982, p. 10. Unpublished manuscript located in the GNMP senior historian's office, Gettysburg, PA.

51. Barker, Daniel. *Losing Faith in Faith*. Madison, WI: FFRF, Inc. (1992): 204. The actual cross of christianity is derived from the ancient Cheldean god Tannuz, being in the shape of the mystic "Tau," or (T) the symbol of his name. All Christian symbols eventually can be traced to earlier pagan religions.

52. Coco, Gregory A., *Wasted Valor*.... pp. 155-56. Harrison, Kathleen R. Georg. "This Grand National Enterprise" August 10, 1863; a copy in the GNMP Library files.

53. Knox, Thomas W., "The Battle Field at Gettysburg," p. 1, cols. 4-5.

54. Author unknown. Extract from an article in the Adams *Sentinel*, Gettysburg, PA, July 21, 1863, p. 1, col. 2.

55. Foster, Joseph H., "Visit to the Battle Field." In speaking of identification tags sometimes used by soldiers to prevent the loss of their identity when buried, one colonel, W.C. Oates of the 15th Alabama ordered company letters and regimental numerals for his men's caps so they would be buried properly. Oates, *The War Between the Union and the Confederacy*.... New York, Neale Publishing Company (1905): p. 678. See also *Maine at Gettysburg*, p. 526.

56. Stone, Martin. Excerpt from his diary, July 7, 1863, in the "Quartermaster Reports" file at the GNMP Library. Stone was a captain in Co. I, 2nd Pennsylvania Cavalry.

57. Author unknown, Harrisburg *Telegraph*, Harrisburg, PA, July 10, 1863.

58. Dickert, D. Augustus, *History of Kershaw's Brigade*, p. 249.

59. Cross, Andrew B. *The War and the Christian Commission*. Baltimore, MD: (1865): 26.

60. Catton, Bruce, ed., *The Battle of Gettysburg*, pp. 149-51.

61. Weaver, Rufus B. "Papers Listing Confederate Dead Exhumed On The Battlefield of Gettysburg and Boxed and Shipped to the Hollywood Memorial Association, Richmond, Virginia." "2d Shipment" "Confederate Burial Files," GNMP Library.

62. Wert, J. Howard. "In the Hospitals at Gettysburg...," #9.

63. Author unknown. Excerpt from November 2, 1863, issue of the Gettysburg *Compiler*. See the *Star and Sentinel*, Gettysburg, PA, November 3, 1863, for more on this subject.

64. Busey, John W. *These Honored Dead*. Hightstown, NJ: Longstreet House (1988): 12.

    Of the four Confederates mis-buried, it is strange that Benjamin Watkins Leigh was taken for a Union soldier. His grave was marked specifically by a Gettysburg minister, John R. Warner, who was commissioned to do so by G.H. Byrd of Baltimore in the month of August 1863. It is possible that since he was a staff officer with no regimental designation able to be placed on his headboard, and the added fact that he was buried near 15 Union soldiers, all caused him to be thought of later as a Federal. If only his name was written on the headboard, as it appears, then this is presumably what occurred. My thanks to local historian Dr. Walter L. Powell of Gettysburg for this information.

    Author John Busey believes that there could be as many as eight Confederates interred in the cemetery today, and others like Roy Frampton and James Cole agree, but place the number even higher. See Busey, *The Last Full Measure*.... pp. xviii-xxii, and Gregory A. Coco, *Wasted Valor*..., p. 161.

65. *State of Pennsylvania. Revised Report of the Select Committee Relative to the Soldiers' National Cemetery Together with the Accompanying Documents, As Reported to the House of Representatives of the Commonwealth of Pennsylvania*; Harrisburg, PA: Singerly & Myers, State Printers (1865): 151.

66. This figure was arrived at by taking the total number of U.S. dead, about 5,100, and subtracting the 3,512 David Wills reported were buried in the Soldiers' National Cemetery, then take away 100 more or less that were never recovered, with a result of approximately 1,488 shipped to Northern homes. The "100 more or less" never recovered is pure conjecture, the true figure is, of course, impossible to ever determine.

67. Busey, John W., *The Last Full Measure*..., p. xxxix. For an excellent overview of the National Cemetery history, the best ever written in my opinion, see John S. Patterson's "Preface," in this fine book.

    The Boston committee which undertook the aforementioned task was led by Alderman Hiram A. Stevens, and consisted of eight delegates. They hired Solomon Powers who, with these men, eventually visited the entire field. Finding only rude headboards on the ground, they attempted to identify as many of the Massachusetts men as possible. In a week's time they re-marked over 135 sites, with Powers adding 20 or 30 more later on. Powers, as we know, was contracted to rebury all Massachusetts soldiers in the National Cemetery, his work being accomplished in accordance with David Wills' specifications, but he kept a separate contract with Massachusetts alone.

68. *Report of the General Agent of the State of New York*..., pp. 60-61.
    Harrison, Kathleen R. Georg. "This Grand National Enterprise," p. 9.

69. *Star and Banner*, Gettysburg, PA. vol. 34 #16, July 2 (actually 9), 1863, p. 3, col. 2.

70. This woodlot was owned by the Zeigler family, whose name was spelled with both the "e" before the "i" and after the "i." The National Military Park now designates the woods "Ziegler's Grove." The Adams County History of 1886 lists two families each using a different spelling; the "Judge" however,

used "Zeigler." The Gettysburg *Compiler* of August 17, 1863, said the cemetery will be in, "Judge [David] Ziegler's woods," but Professor Michael Jacobs at the time of the battle calls them "Zeigler's Woods." So take your pick!

71. Busey, John W., *The Last Full Measure...*, pp. 179-80.

72. The Adams *Sentinel and General Advertiser*, Gettysburg, PA, September 1, 1863.

73. Editor unknown. *Harvard Memorial Biographies*, Vol. II, Cambridge, MA: Sever and Francis (1866): pp. 425-30. The lovely farm where Abbot died is now a golf course and probable future housing development. The original barn is, as of December 1994, being destroyed. The most serious medical cases of Vincent's Brigade, which had fought on Little Round Top, were quartered there.

74. It should be noted that there were in fact several (seven or more) soldiers removed after they had been buried in the National Cemetery. See Busey, *The Last Full Measure...*, p. xxviii.

75. "*Broadside*," drawn up by David Wills on October 15, 1863, and printed at the "Sentinel Office," Gettysburg, PA. The original is presently in the Museum of the Civil War collection of the GNMP.

76. *State of Pennsylvania*, Revised Report...., pp. 14-15.

77. Weaver, Samuel. "Report of Samuel Weaver." *State of Pennsylvania*. Revised Report..., pp. 149-51. Samuel Weaver obviously kept his own burial register, the whereabouts of which is unknown. According to Historian Earl J. Coates, Weaver had several of these books of the dead, and Coates himself recently saw one in the collection of the National Archives. Unfortunately since that time that particular "Weaver burial book" has disappeared again, and the archives staff was unable to locate it for Mr. Coates. According to the senior historian at GNMP, Kathleen R. Georg Harrison, none of Weaver's books have been discovered as yet. (Communications with Earl J. Coates and Kathleen R. Georg Harrison on December 17-18, 1994.)

78. Weaver, Samuel. From a letter to his brother, William, dated November 25, 1863, in the U.S. Patent Office Records, Record Group 241, National Archives, Washington, D.C. Weaver's brother had evidently applied for a patent during the Civil War years for a photographic traveling van or wagon, which he and Samuel owned jointly. See also *Civil War Times* magazine for November 1960, p. 10 and November 1963, p. 21.

79. Warren, Leander H. Excerpt from his unpublished account in the "National Cemetery" file at the GNMP Library.

80. Warren, Leander H. *My Recollections*, p. 19.

81. The Gettysburg *Compiler*. November 2, 1863, p. 1, col. 6.

82. Ibid., January 18, 1864, p. 1, col. 3.

83. *State of Pennsylvania*, Revised Report...., p. 152. The reader may be interested to know what disposition was made and what became of the hundreds of personal items removed from the dead by Weaver, such as watches, diaries, money, photographs, letters, etc. For many years, probably between 1872 and 1933, these pieces were on display in cases inside the cemetery superintendent's gatehouse or lodge near the Baltimore Street entrance to the National Cemetery in hope that they could help visitors or relatives to identify any unknown soldier. In 1933-34 when the National Park Service took over the jurisdiction of the park from the War Department, these effects were shipped to the National Archives in Washington, D.C. The curator of the section where they were stored supposedly went insane at some point, and all of this material and other objects and documents were either lost or destroyed, and no sign of the precious items has been found since. (Conversation with Senior Historian Kathleen R. Georg Harrison, December 5, 1994.)

84. The Gettysburg *Compiler*. November 15, 1864, p. 1, col. 7. The burials were officially completed March 18, 1864.

85. Trowbridge, John T., "The Field of Gettysburg," pp. 617-19.

86. Busey, John W., *The Last Full Measure...*, p. xiv. The notation in the *Compiler* alluded to earlier concerning the 1864 California visitor is paralleled by the recollection of an ex-Company G, 53rd Pennsylvania soldier who wrote of a visit to Gettysburg in 1879. He remembered that some of the graves in the National Cemetery were still marked with wooden headboards that had been carved by their comrades—many were rotted and lying next to the graves. This, we may recall, was 16 years after the battle. The man related, however, that most of the graves did have the granite markers installed that were called for in the early specifications. See the Potter County (PA) *Journal*, September 4, 11, 18, 1879.

87. Boynton, Henry V., "A Visit to the Battle Ground," p. 2, col. 6.
88. Carter, Joseph C., ed., *Magnolia Journey...*, p. 185.
89. The Adams *Star and Sentinel*, Gettysburg, PA, February 2, 1864, p. 1. Even General George Meade had similar kind feelings a few years after the war. In a speech reported in the Gettysburg *Compiler* on July 16, 1869, Meade admonished his listeners: "There is one subject, my friends, which I will mention now, and on this spot where my attention has been called to it, and in which I trust my feeble voice will have some influence. When I contemplate this field, I see here and there marked with hastily dug trenches, the graves in which the dead with whom we fought are gathered. They are the work of my brothers in arms the day after the battle. Above them a bit of plank indicates simply that these remains of the fallen foe were hurriedly laid there by the soldiers who met them in battle. Why should we not collect them in some suitable place? I do not ask that a monument be erected over them. I do not ask that we should in any way indorse their cause or their conduct, or entertain other than feelings of condemnation for their cause. But, they are dead; they have gone before their Maker to be judged. In all civilized countries it is usual to bury the dead with decency and respect, and even to fallen enemies respectful burial is accorded in death. I earnestly hope this suggestion may have some influence throughout this broad land, for this is only one among a hundred crowded battle fields. Some persons may be designated by the government, if necessary, to collect these neglected bones and bury them without commemorative monuments, but simply indicate that below sleep the misguided men who fell in battle for a cause over which we triumphed."
90. Trowbridge, John T., "The Field of Gettysburg," p. 620.
91. *State of Pennsylvania*, Revised Report...., p. 151.
92. Krick, Robert K. *The Gettysburg Death Roster.* Dayton, OH: Press of Morningside (1981): 3. Officially, the Confederates reported 2,592 killed in action; 2,810 died of wounds, total 5,402. There were also 12,709 wounded and 5,150 missing. Many of this latter category were certainly killed. Lee also shows 12,227 taken captive. It should be remembered that in the Southern Army none of their slightly wounded were included in this nominal list. See J.B. Young, *The Battle of Gettysburg.* Dayton, OH: Morningside Bookshop (1971): 332.
93. O'Neal, John W.C. See the notes in his "Physicians Handbook" in the "O'Neal Collection" at the Adams County Historical Society, Gettysburg, PA. Hoke, Jacob. *The Great Invasion of 1863, or, General Lee in Pennsylvania.* Dayton, OH: W.J. Shuey (1887): 495. Toomey, Daniel C. *Marylanders at Gettysburg.* Baltimore, MD: Toomey Press (1994): 44.
94. Nicastro, Anthony M. Extract from an article in the "Battlefield Dispatch," the Licensed Battlefield Guide newsletter, Gettysburg, PA, vol. XII, #6, June 3, 1993, pp. 2-4. Townsend, George E. *Rustics in Rebellion. A Yankee Reporter on the Road to Richmond, 1861-1865.* Chapel Hill, NC: The University of North Carolina Press (1950): 121-22 & 153-54.
95. McCreary, Albertus. *Gettysburg: A Boy's Experiences...*, p. 18. Unknown woman, "E.D.W.," "Gleanings From Gettysburg by A Lady," Philadelphia *Daily Evening Bulletin*, November 21, 1863, p. 10.
96. Will, John, "Battle Days at Globe Inn," Gettysburg *Compiler*, July 21, 1910, p. 31.
97. Wilson, William B. Excerpt from his diary entry for October 28, 1863, in the collection of the Adams County Historical Society, Gettysburg, PA, p. 132.
98. Rider, Alfred J. Extract from a letter written to Colonel John B. Bachelder on October 2, 1885, from Navarre, Stark County, Ohio, in the "Bachelder Papers" on microfilm in the GNMP Library.
99. Marcus, Edward, ed. *A New Canaan Private in the Civil War: Letters of Justus M. Silliman....* New Canaan, CT: New Canaan Historical Society (1984): 44.
100. Page, Evelyn. ed. Frederick L. Olmsted, "After Gettysburg," The Historical Society of Pennsylvania Newsletter, Philadelphia, PA, October 1951, p. 442. Olmsted was the "General Secretary of the U.S. Sanitary Commission" through the summer of 1863.
101. Souder, Emily B.T., *Leaves from the Battlefield...*, p. 22.
102. Ibid., p. 63.

    In speaking of Mr. Garlach's business, a woman who visited Gettysburg in November 1863 stated that Garlach's son had helped his father until he fell ill with typhoid fever. While in a delirious state the boy imagined he was back working on the neverending job of building the coffins for the dead. The eyewitness also mentioned that the aftermath of the battle was very traumatic for many people, particularly an unnamed woman whose brain became so shocked with tension and stress, that she went into an epileptic state, hovering between life and death for many days. It is easy to forget at times that the days during and following the battle were difficult ones for anyone involved in the climactic events.

103. Rider, Alfred J. *Extract from a letter....* Janes, Henry M.D. Extract from a letter to Surgeon W.L. King written at Gettysburg, August 17, 1863, in the "Camp Letterman Papers" file box in the GNMP Library.

104. Roberts, Charles W. "At Gettysburg in 1863 and 1888." (MOLLUS) Maine Commandery, vol. I. Portland, ME: The Thurston Print (1898): 55.

105. Weaver, Samuel. Excerpt from a letter written to "Mrs. C.B. Bedinger" on December 27, 1865, in the burial files of the GNMP Library.

106. Davis, Archie K. *Boy Colonel of the Confederacy—The Life and Times of Henry K. Burgwyn, Jr.* The University of North Carolina Press, Chapel Hill, NC (1985) 335.

107. D. Augustus Dickert, *History of Kershaw's Brigade.* p. 250.

108. O'Neal, John W.C. Letters to Lucy H. Wood, June 10, 1869, and Joseph W. Southall, August 10, 1869, in "O'Neal" File, GNMP Library.

109. O'Neal, John W.C. Letter dated October 5, 1866, and written to C.B. Burns in the "Bodies Discovered Long After The Battle" file at the GNMP Library, Gettysburg, PA.

110. Information obtained from Michael Hofe of Gettysburg, PA, who is currently writing a booklet on McLeod's story, which should be published in 1995.

111. Weaver, Rufus B. Extract from an October 9, 1871, letter to Mrs. E.L. Campbell, Savannah, GA in the "Weaver Family" file at the GNMP Library.

112. *"The Hahnemann Institute."* Philadelphia, PA: Hahnemann Medical College (December 1895): vol. III, #2, pp. 1-2.

113. *The Hawkinsville Dispatch*, Hawkinsville, GA, July 6, 1871.

114. Weaver, Rufus B., extract from October 9, 1871, letter to Mrs. E.L. Campbell, Savannah, Georgia.

115. Ibid.

116. Mitchell, Mary H., *Hollywood Cemetery...,* pp. 83-92.

117. Weaver, Rufus B. Extract from a letter to Dr. J.W.C. O'Neal on February 19, 1887, a copy of which is in the "Weaver" files of the GNMP Library.

118. Harrison, Kathleen R. Georg, "Daybook" for Monday, July 6, 1863. For more on these "out-of-the-way" burials, see Gregory A. Coco, *Wasted Valor...,* pp. 151-53.

119. The Gettysburg *Star and Sentinel*, April 30, 1873.

120. Muller, Charles. Extract from his memoirs in the collection of the Minnesota Historical Society, St. Paul, MN, p. 16a.

121. Keenan, Sophie G., "Pere Le Chaise and Gettysburg," p. 1.

122. All of these citations are derived from the "Bodies Discovered After The Battle" file in the library of the GNMP and from various newspaper sources in the author's "Burial File." Most are from the Gettysburg *Compiler*, Adams *Sentinel and General Advertiser*, the *Star and Sentinel*, and the Gettysburg *Times* all printed between 1870 and 1940.

One other reference to bodies recovered in post-war years comes from an unnamed member of Co. G, 53rd Pennsylvania Infantry writing in the Potter County (PA) *Journal*, September 4, 11, and 18, 1879. He recalled that while on a visit to Gettysburg in early September he met Abraham Trostle who told him that there were many Confederate graves still scattered across his farm which had no marks of identification as such, and while plowing for corn in the spring of 1879 he (Trostle) had uncovered the remains of one of these soldiers.

✛ ✛ ✛

Nicholas G. Wilson, who is several times noted as the superintendent of the Soldiers' National Cemetery, was named to that position on July 1, 1873, shortly after the U.S. Government was deeded ownership of that cemetery.

Wilson was an interesting man. He was born in 1832 at Wilsonville, (near Bendersville), Menallen Township, Adams County. His early occupations were that of teamster and blacksmith. Wilson enlisted in August 1862 into Company G, 138th Pennsylvania Infantry, and as 1st Sergeant was wounded at the Battle of Monocacy, Maryland, in July 1864. After the war he resumed "teaming" until his appointment to the superintendency of the National Cemetery. N.G. Wilson was married twice, once in 1852 and again in 1857, and he had two daughters.

Wilson remained in his post at the National Cemetery for 14 years, when he resigned to accept the work of superintendant of the grounds for the Gettysburg Battlefield Memorial Association, where he stayed until 1895, when those protected and preserved acres were turned over to the War Department. Sergeant Wilson held various positions in local and state government and in the Grand Army of the Republic, until his death in December 1907. At the time of his passing, Wilson was one of the most loved and respected men in Adams County; he was popularly known by veterans from coast to coast as a modest, "whole-souled" fellow, and an esteemed companion.

Chapter Three

1. Haines, Alanson A. *A History of the Fifteenth Regiment New Jersey Volunteers*, pp. 94-95. Cort, Cyrus. Excerpt from his diary in the files of the GNMP Library. Cort was a native of Altoona, PA.
2. Wert, J. Howard. "In the Hospitals of Gettysburg," #1.
3. Sheely, Aaron. Unpublished book of collected stories and newspaper clippings. vol. I. Courtesy of Sam Small, Gettysburg, PA.
4. McFarland, Baxter. "Losses of the Eleventh Mississippi Regiment at Gettysburg," *Confederate Veteran*, vol. 31, 1923, p. 259. Vollum, Edward P. Extract from a one-page report dated "Washington, D.C., July 29, 1863" in his compiled service records at the National Archives in Washington, D.C.
5. Read, Thomas (5th Michigan Infantry). Extract from an August 20, 1863, letter to his parents from a U.S. general hospital in Chester, PA, in the collection of the University of Michigan, Ann Arbor, MI.
6. For more on this subject see Thomas Livermore, "Numbers and Losses in the Civil War;" Robert K. Krick, *The Gettysburg Death Roster*; Joseph B. Mitchell's article in *Blue and Gray* magazine vol. 6, #4, 1989, entitled, "Confederate Losses at Gettysburg;" and E.B. Coddington, *Gettysburg - A Study in Command*, chapter 10; also John Busey and David Martin, *Regimental Strengths and Losses at Gettysburg*, p. 1.
7. *United States. The Medical and Surgical History of the War of the Rebellion, 1861-1865*. Appendix to Part I, "Reports of Medical Directors and Other Documents" Washington, D.C.: Government Printing Office (1870): 140-47. Hereafter cited as "Medical and Surgical History."
8. Duncan, Louis C. *The Medical Department of the United States Army in the Civil War*. Washington, D.C.: U.S. Government Printing Office (1910): 215-22. Gettysburg *Compiler*, March 14, 1864. Linn, John B., diary written from July 6-11, 1863, p. 8.
9. Taylor, William H. *Some Experiences of a Confederate Assistant Surgeon*. Transactions of the College of Physicians of Philadelphia, PA, vol. 28 (1906): 114-16.
10. Duncan, Louis C., *The Medical Department...*, pp. 225-26.
11. *Official Records*, vol. 27, part 3, p. 523.
12. Fiske, Samuel W. *Mr. Dunn Browne's Experiences in the Army*. Boston, MA: Nichols and Noyer (1866): 218.
13. Davis, George B., et. al. *The Official Military Atlas of the Civil War*. New York: Arno Press (1978): Plate CLXXIV. Duncan, Louis C., *The Medical Department...*, p. 225.
14. Commager, Henry S., ed. *The Blue and The Gray*, Vol. II. Indianapolis, IN: The Bobbs-Merrill Co., Inc. (1950): 195-96.
15. Phillips, Marion G. and Valerie P. Parsegian, eds. *Richard and Rhoda: Letters from the Civil War*. Washington, D.C.: Legation Press (1981): 32. Fulton, II, William F. *The War Reminiscences of....* Gaithersburg, MD: Butternut Press, Inc. (1984): 80.
16. Clendening, Logan. *The Romance of Medicine*. Garden City, NY: The Garden City Publishing Co. (1933): 385-93.
17. Halsey, Jr., Ashley. *Who Fired The First Shot?* Greenwich, CT: Fawcett Publications, Inc. (1963): 173-74.
18. Bradsby, H.C., *History of Cumberland and Adams Counties...*, p. 171.
19. Edwards, William B. *Civil War Guns*. Harrisburg, PA: The Stackpole Company (1962): 437.
20. Janes, Henry M.D. Excerpt from a letter written to the editor of the Baltimore *Sun*, October 27, 1899. A copy is in vol. 6 of the "Gettysburg News Clippings" files in the senior historian's office at the GNMP Library.
21. Monteiro, Aristides. *Confederate Surgeon*. New York, NY: Dodd, Mead & Co. (1969): 128-32.
22. *The Medical and Surgical History...*, Appendix, pp. 509-10.
23. Duncan, Louis C., *The Medical Department...*, p. 232.
24. Bradsby, H.C., *History of Cumberland and Adams Counties...*, p. 171.
25. Sheads, Annie. Extract from a letter in the GNMP "Museum of the Civil War" collection.

26. Duncan, Louis C., *The Medical Department...*, p. 230.

27. *United States Christian Commission for the Army and Navy. Work and Incidents, First Annual Report.* Philadelphia, PA (1863): 70-71. Hereafter cited as *The U.S.C.C. for the Army and Navy....*

28. Cross, Andrew B., *The War...*, p. 15.

29. *United States Christian Commission, Second Report of the Committee of Maryland.* Baltimore, MD: Sherwood and Company (1863): 24. Hereafter cited as *The U.S.C.C. Maryland Report.*

30. Ibid., p. 91.

31. Jones, Horatio G. *To The Christian Soldiers and Sailors of the Union.* Philadelphia, PA: Lippincott's Press (1868): 180. (This was a U.S. Christian Commission publication.)

32. Colston, F.M. From an article in *Confederate Veteran*, vol. V, 1897, p. 553. Colston was a captain in Alexander's artillery of the First Corps, Army of Northern Virginia.

33. *The U.S.C.C. Maryland Report*, pp. 104-07.

34. Davidson, Nathaniel, "Our Wounded at Gettysburg," New York *Herald*, July 24, 1863.

35. Unidentified Confederate officer, "College Hospital in Gettysburg," *The Land We Love*, vol. II, November-April 1866-67, Charlotte, NC, Hill, Irwin & Co., p. 291.

36. Harris, Isaac. Extract from his personal diary in the files at the GNMP Library. Harris may have been at some time attached to or a member of the 13th New York National Guard Infantry or the 13th Pennsylvania Reserves.

37. Bellows, Henry W. Extract from a letter dated "New York, July 14, 1863" and printed in *The Sanitary Reporter*, vols. I and II, May 15, 1863 to August 15, 1865, New York, NY, 1866, published at Louisville, KY, p. 43.

38. Leiper, Thomas J., letter to his father, dated August 1, 1863. See also Nicholson, John P. (editor & compiler). *Pennsylvania at Gettysburg.* Address by Joseph A. Moore. Vol. II, William Stanley Roy, State Printer, Harrisburg, PA: (1904): 718. This source recalls the death of another injured soldier who took his own life. Coco, Gregory A. ed. *Recollections of a Texas Colonel*, p. 21.

39. Fisher, Mary C., "A Week on Gettysburg Field," *Grand Army Scout and Soldiers Mail*, 1883, vol. II, #12, pp. 2 & 6.

40. McKay, Charlotte Elizabeth. *Stories of Hospital and Camp.* Philadelphia, PA: Claxton, Remsen & Haffelfinger (1876): 54-55.

41. Brinton, Daniel G., "From Chancellorsville to Gettysburg, A Doctors Diary." *The Pennsylvania Magazine of History and Biography.* Historical Society of Pennsylvania, Philadelphia, PA, vol. 89, 1965, pp. 312-15. Another source stated that Armistead, who died shortly after Brinton mentions him, was not wounded very seriously and could have lived, but his mental and physical exhaustion and uneasiness in Union hands caused his premature death. See the "J.F. Crocker" article in the *History of Gettysburg College*, by S.G. Hefelbower, Gettysburg, PA, (1932): 429-30.

42. Stevens, George T., *Three Years in the Sixth Corps*, pp. 251-52.

43. Souder, Emily B.T., *Leaves from the Battle-Field...*, p. 34.

44. Page, Evelyn, ed. "On the Escape of Lee" by Frederick L. Olmsted, p. 443.

45. Bucklin, Sophronia E., *In Hospital and Camp...*, p. 146.

46. Wafer, Francis M. Extract from his diary which is in the archives of Douglas Library, Queen's University at Kingston, Kingston, Ontario, Canada, p. 48-49.

47. Foster, John Y., "Four Days at Gettysburg," pp. 382 & 385.

48. Fatout, Paul, ed. *Letters of a Civil War Surgeon.* Lafayette, IN: Purdue University Studies (1961): 70-71.

49. Adams, John G. *Reminiscences of the Nineteenth Massachusetts Regiment.* Boston, MA: Wright & Potter Printing Company (1899): 71.

50. Haines, Alanson A., *A History of the Fifteenth Regiment New Jersey Volunteers*, pp. 94-95.

51. Schurz, Carl. "The Battle of Gettysburg," *McClure's Magazine.* vol. XXIX, May to October 1907, The S.S. McClure Co. New York, NY (1907): 285.

52. Houghton, James, unpublished memoir journal, p. 15.

53. Fuller, Charles A. Extracts from a series of letters written to the editor of the *News*, Sherburne, NY, October-December, 1906, now in the Sherburne, NY, Public Library and loaned through the courtesy of Herb Crumb, Norwich, NY.

54. Weygant, Charles H. *History of the One Hundred and Twenty-fourth Regiment, N.Y.S.V.* Newburgh, NY: Journal Printing House (1877): 182-85.

55. Johnston, David E. (7th Virginia Infantry). *Four Years A Soldier*. Princeton, WV (1887): 218.

56. Shuffler, R. Henderson, ed. *The Adventures Of A Prisoner Of War...*, pp. 54-55.

57. James, Bushrod W. *Echoes of Battle*. Philadelphia, PA: Henry T. Coates & Co. (1895): 104-5.

58. Alleman, Matilda J. "Tillie" (Pierce), *At Gettysburg*, ... pp. 72-74.

59. Buehler, Fannie J. *Recollections of the Rebel Invasion and One Woman's Experience During the Battle of Gettysburg*. Gettysburg, PA: Star and Sentinel Printing (1896): 26.

60. Fahnestock, Gates D. Excerpt from his "Recollections of the Battle of Gettysburg," unpublished but written in 1933-34, p. 2. Copy in the Adams County Historical Society, Gettysburg, PA.

61. Ward, W.C. "Incidents and Personal Experiences on the Battlefield at Gettysburg," *Confederate Veteran*, Nashville, TN, vol. VIII, 1900, pp. 348-49.

62. Runge, William H., ed., *Four Years in the Confederate Artillery...*, p. 52.   Blacknall, Charles C. Excerpt from a "memoir" written by his son, Oscar W. in the North Carolina State Department of Archives and History, Raleigh, NC, p. 31.

63. Durkin, Joseph T., ed. *John Dooley, Confederate Soldier, His War Journal*. Washington, D.C.: Georgetown University Press (1945): 113.

64. Nickerson, Azor H., "Personal Recollections of Two Visits to Gettysburg," vol. XIV, *Scribner's Magazine*, New York, NY: Charles Scribner's Sons (1893): 22.

65. *Official Records*, vol. 27, part II, p. 364. Unidentified author. (Colonel, Chief Records and Pension Office, U.S. War Department, Washington, D.C.) Letter to J.P. Nicholson, Philadelphia, PA, September 17, 1898, in the "Hospital Marker" record book in the senior historian's office at the GNMP Library, p. 57-59.   Baruch, Simon M.D., "A Surgeon's Story of Battle and Capture," *Confederate Veteran*, vol. XX, 1914, p. 546.

66. Letterman, Jonathan M.D. "Report on the Operations of the Medical Department during the Battle of Gettysburg," October 3, 1863 in the *Medical and Surgical History*, #CXXX, p. 140.

67. New, George W., M.D. Extract of letter dated September 8, 1865, at New Orleans, LA to John B. Bachelder, in the "Field Hospital" files of the GNMP Library.

68. Farnham, Eliza W. "Description of Scenes After The Battle Of Gettysburg." A letter printed in *Common Sense*, August 22, 1874. Courtesy of Eric A. Campbell, Gettysburg, PA.

69. Duncan, Louis C., *The Medical Department...*, p. 235. See the U.S. Government bronze hospital tablet across from the "White Church" site on the Baltimore Pike.   Coco, Gregory A. *A Vast Sea of Misery: A History and Guide to the Union and Confederate Field Hospitals at Gettysburg, July 1 -November 20, 1863*. Thomas Publications, Gettysburg, PA: (1988) pp. 3-27 and 83-89.

70. Livermore, Thomas L. *Days and Events, 1860-1866*. Boston, MA: Houghton, Mifflin Co. (1920) 254.

71. Dwinell, Justin M.D. "Report of Surgeon Justin Dwinell...at the Battle of Gettysburg." MS C129, National Library of Medicine, Bethesda, MD, p. 1.   Duncan, Louis C., *The Medical Department...*, p. 236. Norris, William F., M.D. "A Hospital at Gettysburg." *The General Magazine and Historical Chronicle*, vol. 45 (1942-3): 35.

72. Livermore, Thomas L. *Days and Events*, pp. 258-59.

73. Moore, Frank, ed., *The Rebellion Record: A Diary of American Events*. New York, NY: G.P. Putnam (1861-1868) "Report of Dr. J.H. Douglas:" 128.

74. *Report of the General Agent of the State of New York...*, pp. 52-53.

75. Dwinell, Justin., "Report of Surgeon Justin Dwinell...," p. 4.   Souder, Emily B.T., *Leaves from the Battle-Field...*, p. 57.

76. Dwinell, Justin M.D., "Report of Surgeon Justin Dwinell...," pp. 5-6.

77. Duncan, Louis C., *The Medical Department...*, p. 239.

78. Ibid., pp. 239-40.

79. Wert, J. Howard, "In the Hospitals of Gettysburg...," #1.

80. Davidson, Nathaniel, "Our Wounded at Gettysburg."

81. U.S. Government Hospital Marker, Third Corps, located on Goulden Road several hundred yards east of the Rock Creek bridge.

82. Moore, Frank, ed., *The Rebellion Record...*, p. 128.

83. *Report of the General Agent of the State of New York...*, p. 54.

84. Brady, Mary A. Extract from a letter written on July 22, 1863, from the Third Corps Hospital near Gettysburg, PA, and printed in the July 23, 1863, issue of the Philadelphia *Daily Evening Bulletin*.

85. Duncan, Louis C., *The Medical Department...*, p. 239. Other sources available report that the Third

Corps had only about 10,000 present for duty on July 2.   Moore, Frank, ed., *The Rebellion Record...*, p. 128.

86. Duncan, Louis C., *The Medical Department...*, pp. 242-43.
87. Ibid., p. 245.
88. Wert, J. Howard, "In the Hospitals of Gettysburg...," #1.
89. U.S. Government Hospital Marker, Fifth Corps, located on Goulden Road, south side, 100-200 yards east of the Third Corps marker.
90. Duncan, Louis C., *The Medical Department...*, p. 246.
91. *Report of the General Agent of the State of New York...*, pp. 54-55.   Davidson, Nathaniel, "Our Wounded at Gettysburg."   Moore, Frank, ed., *The Rebellion Record...*, p. 128.
92. Clark, A.M., M.D. Extract from a letter to David McConaughy of Gettysburg, PA, written from White Plains, NY on August 16, 1869, in the "Field Hospital Marker" file in the senior historian's office at the GNMP Library.
93. Bowen, James L., "On the Gettysburg Field," Philadelphia *Weekly Times*, vol. VIII, no. 19, June 28, 1884, p. 1, col. 2.
94. *Report of the General Agent of the State of New York...*, p. 54.
95. Moore, Frank, ed., *The Rebellion Record...*, p. 128.
96. Cross, Andrew B. *The War and the Christian Commission*, p. 27.
97. Ibid.
98. Davidson, Nathaniel, "Our Wounded at Gettysburg."
99. *Report of the General Agent of the State of New York...*, pp. 51-52.
100. Marcus, Edward, ed. *A New Canaan Private...*, p. 44.
101. Schantz, Franklin J.F., "Reflections on the Battle of Gettysburg," pp. 296-97.
102. Muller, Charles, *Memoirs*, pp. 19-20.
103. Coco, Gregory A., *A Vast Sea of Misery...*, pp. 73-76.   *Report of the General Agent of the State of New York...*, p. 52.
104. Duncan, Louis C., *The Medical Department...*, pp. 11-12.
105. Toombs, Samuel. *New Jersey Troops in the Gettysburg Campaign*. The Evening Mail Publishing House, Orange, NJ (1888) pp. 322, 325.
106. *Report of the General Agent of the State of New York...*, p. 52.
107. Wert, J. Howard, *In the Hospitals of Gettysburg...*, #1.   Eliason, Talcot, M.D., Extract from a letter to H.B. McClellan written July 23, 1885, in the files of the GNMP Library. Eliason was one of Stuart's cavalry divison surgeons.   King, Sarah B. Memoir published in the Gettysburg *Compiler*, July 4, 1906, p. 2, cols. 1-3, and p. 3, cols. 4-6.   Duncan, Louis C., *The Medical Department...*, p. 256. Bachelder, John B., "Notes on the Service of Troops at the Battle of Gettysburg." In the collection of the Huntington Library, San Marino, CA. Cowles, Luther E. *History of the Fifth Massachusetts Battery*. Luther E. Cowles, Boston, MA (1902): 658. Author unknown. New York *Herald*, July 24, 1863.
108. Duncan, Louis C., *The Medical Department...*, pp. 251-52.
109. Moore, Frank, ed., *The Rebellion Record...*, p. 127.
110. Baruch, Simon M.D., "A Surgeon's Story of Battle and Capture," pp. 545-46.
111. Cunningham, Mary ("Mrs. J. Paxton" Bigham), "The Scotts and Cunninghams See the Battle," The Gettysburg *Times*, April 22, 1941.
112. Duncan, Louis C., *The Medical Department...*, p. 254.   O'Neal, John W.C., M.D., "Record of Confederate Burials," ledger book in the GNMP "Museum of the Civil War" collection.
113. Ibid., p. 154.
114. Moore, Frank, ed., *The Rebellion Record...*, p. 127.   Duncan, Louis C., *The Medical Department...*, p. 256.
115. Johnson, Clifton, *Battleground Adventures*, p. 189.   U.S. Sanitary Commission's "Hospital Map" published in 1863, a copy of which is reproduced in *A Vast Sea of Misery....* This "grove" hospital site was noted only on the U.S. Sanitary Commission hospital map published after the battle, q.v.
116. Coco, Gregory A., *A Vast Sea of Misery...*, pp. 127-31, 153.
117. Duncan, Louis C., *The Medical Department...*, p. 255.   Moore, Frank, ed., *The Rebellion Record...*, p. 127.   Peeler, A.J., (Lieutenant, 5th Florida Infantry), letter headed "College Hospital" and in that regiment's file at the GNMP Library.
118. Coco, Gregory A., *A Vast Sea of Misery...*, pp. 134-37.

119. Ibid., pp. 133-34, 137-40.
120. *The U.S. Sanitary Commission. A Sketch of Its Purposes and Its Work.* Boston, MA: Little, Brown & Company (1863): 145. Hereafter cited as *The U.S.S.C. A Sketch....*
121. Duncan, Louis C., *The Medical Department...*, p. 256.
122. *Official Records*, vol. 27, part I, pp. 24-28.
123. Foster, Joseph H., "Visit To The Battlefield."
124. *The U.S.S.C. A Sketch...*, p. 51.
125. Norris, William F., M.D., "A Hospital at Gettysburg," pp. 39-40. See also *Maine at Gettysburg*, p. 527.
126. *U.S.C.C. Maryland Report*, p. 19. Gettysburg *Compiler*, August 10, 1863. Adams *Sentinel & General Advertiser*, August 18, 1863.
127. Ludlow, James P. Extract from a letter dated August 6, 1863, at Gettysburg, and published in the August 15, 1863, issue of the *Democrat and American*, Rochester, New York. Courtesy of Brian A. Bennett, Scottsville, NY.
128. Norris, William F., M.D., "A Hospital at Gettysburg," pp. 39-40.
129. *The U.S.S.C. A Sketch...*, pp. 145-46.   A Christian Commission source, however, claimed that the Sanitary Commission had three tents and only 12 delegates. See *U.S.C.C. Maryland Report*, p. 85.
130. Gettysburg *Compiler*, November 16, 1863.
131. Unidentified author. (Colonel, Chief, Records and Pension Office), pp. 58-59.
132. Way, William C. Extract from a letter written by Way, the chaplain of the 24th Michigan, in Gettysburg, August 7, 1863, and printed in the August 14, issue of the Detroit *Advertiser and Tribune*, p. 4, col. 8.
133. Stoke, Frank M., October 26, 1863, letter, p. 1.
134. U.S. Government. National Archives, RG94, stack 9W3, rows 8-12, vols. 558-560.   *U.S.C.C. Maryland Report*, pp. 27-32.
135. Bucklin, Sophronia E., *In Hospital and Camp...*, pp. 146-49, 166, 172, 181, 193.
136. Hancock, Cornelia. *South After Gettysburg*. Philadelphia, PA: University of Pennsylvania Press (1937): 15-18. Ms. Dix was appointed to the position of "Superintendent of Female Nurses" by Abraham Lincoln in June 1861. While at Gettysburg, she stayed in the house of Henry Rupp.
137. Holstein, Anna M. *Three Years in the Field Hospitals of the Army of the Potomac*. Philadelphia, PA: J.B. Lippincott & Co. (1867): 43-45.
138. Silliman, Justus M. Extracts from letters written to his mother from Camp Letterman on August 11 and 19, 1863, in the collection of the New Canaan Historical Society, New Canaan, CT.
139. Blood, Henry B. Extract from a letter to Dr. Henry Janes from "Ass't Quarter Masters Office, York, Pa. February 10, 1864," pp. 1-2, in the author's collection. Courtesy of Len Rosa, Gettysburg, PA.
140. Silliman, Justus M., letters written to his mother from Camp Letterman. See note 138 above.
141. Smith, Henry H. Extract from a letter written at "U.S. General Hospital," Gettysburg, PA: August 17, 1863, and published in the August 26 issue of the *Democrat and American*, Rochester, NY. Courtesy of Brian A. Bennett, Scottsville, NY.
142. Gettysburg *Compiler*, November 16, 1863.
143. Bachelder, John B. *Business Enterprise*. Boston, MA: Privately published (1878): 74.
   As this is now written in December, 1994, the last remaining vestiges of Camp Letterman are fast being destroyed. The old hospital grounds are surrounded on all sides by unsightly and unremitting development, with only about 10 acres of the original 80 remaining. These few acres have just recently been donated to a private college near Dillsburg, PA. Only time will tell what fate has in store for this important historic site.
144. Skelly, Daniel A., *A Boy's Experience...*, p. 25. After its closure, Letterman became a temporary encampment for the soldiers who came for the cemetery dedication in late November 1863. See Souder, E.B.T., *Leaves from the Battlefield*, p. 137.
145. Janes, Henry, M.D. Extract from a letter dated Philadelphia, February 15, 1864, to Surgeon C.C. Cox in the "Camp Letterman Papers," file at the GNMP Library.
146. Dwinell, Justin, M.D., "Report of Surgeon Justin Dwinell...," p. 6.
147. Letterman, Jonathan, M.D., "Report on the Operations of the Medical Department...," pp. 155-59. Adams *Sentinel and General Advertiser*, Gettysburg, PA, August 18, 1863.
148. Dwinell, Justin, M.D., "Report of Surgeon Justin Dwinell," p. 3.
149. *Official Records*, vol. 27, part 3, p. 521. There was also an Alexander Spangler who owned a warehouse near the railroad.

150. U.S. Government "Hospital Fund" receipt to farmer Peter Conover. A copy is in the "Camp Letterman Papers" file, GNMP Library. Conover's farm on the Baltimore Pike south of "White Church" was a division hospital site of the First Corps.

151. Baird, William, (7th Michigan Cavalry), unpublished memoirs, p. 37.

152. Adams *Sentinel and General Advertiser*, Gettysburg, PA, September 1, 1863. Samuel Fahnestock had died in 1861, but the family still owned the store and warehouse in 1863.

153. Moore, Frank, ed., *The Rebellion Record...*, pp. 122-24.

154. *The U.S.S.C. A Sketch...*, p. 131.

155. *The U.S.C.C. for the Army and Navy...*, p. 67.

156. Ibid., pp. 76-78.

157. Beauchamp, Virginia W., "The Sisters and the Soldiers," *Maryland Historical Magazine*, vol. 81, #2, Summer 1986, p. 131.

158. Keifer, William R. *History of the One Hundred and Fifty-third Regiment Pennsylvania Volunteer Infantry... 1862-1863*. Easton, PA: Press of the Chemical Publishing Company (1909): 223-24. For more information on this negative attitude of Civil War soldiers toward religion, see John R. Sellers, compiler, *Civil War Manuscripts: A Guide to Collections in the Manuscript Division of the Library of Congress*. Washington, D.C.: Library of Congress (1986): xi.

159. *The U.S.S.C. A Sketch...*, p. 63.

160. Silliman, Justus M. Extract from a letter to his cousin dated September 9, 1863, from Camp Letterman Hospital in the collection of the New Canaan (CT) Historical Society, p. 1.

161. Bacon, Jr., Cyrus, M.D. Extract from his diary, July 6, in the Department of Radiology and Microbiology, The University of Michigan, Ann Arbor, MI.

162. Fatout, Paul, ed., *Letters of a Civil War Surgeon*, p. 70.

163. Brinton, John H., M.D. *Personal Memoirs*. p. 244.

164. "Ehler, Mrs. C.A.," *Hospital Scenes...*, pp. 55-56.

165. Graham, Ziba B., "On To Gettysburg...," p. 13.

166. Thompson, Benjamin W., personal narrative, p. 49.

167. Silliker, Ruth L., ed., *The Rebel Yell and the Yankee Hurrah*, p. 108.

168. *The U.S.S.C. A Sketch...*, p. 133.

169. Nevins, Allan, ed., *A Diary of Battle...*, p. 254.

170. Storrs, John W., *The Twentieth Connecticut...*, p. 104.

171. Walker, C.N. & R., ed. *Diary of the War, by Robert S. Robertson*. Excerpt from his published diary in the "93rd NY Infantry" file at the GNMP Library, p. 113.

172. Catton, Bruce, ed., *The Battle of Gettysburg*, p. 148.

173. Sparks, David S., ed., *Inside Lincoln's Army...*, 268.

174. Bandy, Ken & Florence Freeland (compilers). *The Gettysburg Papers*, Vol. II. Dayton, OH: Press of Morningside Bookshop (1978): 519.

175. Fiske, Samuel W., *Mr. Dunn Browne's Experiences...*, pp. 207-08.

176. Creveling, Lewis M. Extract from a letter in the collection of Lewis Leigh, Jr., Fairfax, VA and used through his generosity.

177. "Young Captain of Infantry," an unidentified North Carolina officer, "Northern Prison Life," *The Land We Love*, Charlotte, NC (November 1866): 40.

Chapter Four

1. Moore, Gilbert C. Jr., ed. *Cornie. The Civil War Letters of Lt. Cornelius L. Moore, Co. I, 57th Regiment, New York State Volunteers*. Chattanooga, TN: G.C. Moore, Jr. (1989): 120.

2. Hesseltine, William B., ed. *Civil War Prisons*. Kent, OH: The Kent State University Press (1962): 6.

3. *Official Records*, vol. 27, part 1, p. 187 and part 2, p. 346. Taylor, Frank H. *Philadelphia in the Civil War 1861-1865*. Published by the city (1913): 246.

4. *Official Records*, vol. 27, part 2, pp. 309 & 325.

5. This compilation was provided through the kindness of James M. Cole, Gettysburg, PA, a Licensed Battlefield Guide. A partial list of these "hostages" was also printed in the local papers following the battle. It appears that many of these men were "captured" by the Confederates because they were U.S. government representatives, such as local postmasters. In relation to this topic, it should be documented that the Federal government itself, through its army representatives that remained after the

battle, also arrested some citizens, these mainly for "disloyalty." In one incident, the editor of the *Compiler*, Henry J. Stahle, was seized by the provost marshal, "for pointing out the refuge of Union Soldiers to Rebel Officers...." Another witness to this affair stated that Stahle had merely gone to the courthouse hospital to obtain assistance from the Confederates for several wounded men in his house. The "Copperhead editor" as he was called by Union authorities, was taken to Baltimore for imprisonment but was later released. See David Sparks, ed., *Inside Lincoln's Army*..., p. 268-69, and "Mrs. Gilbert's Story," in the Gettysburg *Compiler*, September 6, 1905, p. 2, cols. 1 and 2. Bradsby, H.C., *History of Cumberland and Adams Counties*..., p. 454.

6. *Official Records*, vol. 27, part 3, p. 514.
7. Coco, Gregory A., ed. *From Ball's Bluff to Gettysburg and Beyond: The Civil War Letters of Private Roland E. Bowen, 15th Massachusetts Infantry, 1861-1864.* Gettysburg, PA: Thomas Publications (1994): p. 207.
8. Boynton, Jonathan W.W., his unpublished memoirs in the "157th New York Infantry" file at the GNMP Library, pp. 17-18.
9. Trautmann, Frederick, ed. *Twenty Months in Captivity: Memoirs of a Union Officer in Confederate Prisons.* Cranbury, NJ: Fairleigh Dickinson University Press (1987): 28. "Losses in the Regiment, etc., etc.," Brooklyn *Eagle*, July 7, 1863.
10. Harrison, Kathleen R. Georg, "Daybook" entry for July 4, 1863.
11. Harris, Isaac, diary entry for July 5, 1863.
12. *Official Records*, series II, part 6, pp. 78-79. Harrison, Kathleen R. Georg, "Daybook" entry for July 19, 1863.
13. "Prisoners of War With Particular Reference to the Battle of Gettysburg," a "handout" of the National Park Service at GNMP, p. 2. *Confederate Veteran*, vol. IV, 1896, p. 434. Taylor, Frank H., *Philadelphia in the Civil War*..., p. 352.
14. Small, Abner R. *The Road To Richmond*. Berkeley, CA: University of California Press (1939): 108.
15. Hoke, Jacob., *The Great Invasion*..., pp. 87-88. Schildt, John W., *Roads From Gettysburg*, pp. 43, 76 & 79.
16. "Prisoners of War...," a "handout" of the GNMP, p. 2.
17. Alleman, Matilda J. "Tillie" (Pierce), *At Gettysburg*..., pp. 87-88. Tyson, Charles J. Extract from an unpublished letter to N.D. Preston, Esq.
18. Hubbard, Robert M.D. Extract of a letter written on July 9, 1863, from Gettysburg and located in the "17th Connecticut Infantry" file at the GNMP Library, p. 65.
19. Linn, John B., diary written from July 6-11, 1863, p. 14.
20. Wilkin, William P. (1st W. VA Cavalry). Extract from his letter dated July 31, 1863, at Annapolis, MD and printed in West Virginia's *The Athens Messenger*, August 13, 1863, vol. 20, #32.
21. Buck, Andrew. Excerpt from his unpublished diary, a copy of which is in the "7th Michigan Cavalry" file at the GNMP Library.
22. Powell, David. Extract from his diary, the entry written about July 5, 1863, a copy of which is in the "3rd West Virginia Infantry" file at the GNMP Library. Harrison, Kathleen R. Georg, "Daybook" entries for July 4 and 5, 1863.
23. Schaff, Philip, "The Gettysburg Week," *Scribner's Magazine*, vol. XVI, July-December, Charles Scribner's Sons, New York, NY, 1894, p. 27. Veterans Association. *History of the 71st Regiment, N.G.N.Y.* New York: The Veterans Association, Press of the Eastman Publishing Co. (1919): 263.
24. Harrison, Kathleen R. Georg, "Daybook" entries for July 5 and July 8, 1863. *Official Records*, vol. 27, part 2, pp. 214-15.
25. *Official Records*, vol. 27, part 2, p. 580. Hoke, Jacob. *The Great Invasion*..., pp. 506-07.
26. Wilson, William B. Diary entry of July 4, 1863, p. 130.
27. Minor, Berkeley. "The Night After Gettysburg," *Confederate Veteran*, vol. XXXIII, 1925, p. 140.
28. Harrison, Kathleen R. Georg, "Daybook" entry for July 14 and 17, 1863.
29. Schildt, John W., *Roads From Gettysburg*, p. 15.
30. Harrison, Kathleen R. Georg, "Daybook" entries for July 10 and 24, 1863.
31. Wilson, William B. Diary entry of July 5, 1863, p. 130.
32. Follman, John. Extract from his unpublished diary in the "16th Pennsylvania Cavalry" file at the GNMP Library.
33. Reeves, Henry. Extract from a letter written from Chambersburg, PA on July 4, 1863, to his sister "Lizzie." Courtesy of John P. Pannick, Gettysburg, PA.

34. Hoke, Jacob., *The Great Invasion...*, pp. 494-95. Major Donald M. McLeod's remains were recovered in April 1866 by his brother-in-law and a black man who had been the major's servant. The body was taken up, carried to a place near Martha and Jacob Snyder's spring, and boxed for shipment home.
35. *The U.S.C.C. Maryland Report*, p. 95.   *The U.S.C.C. for the Army and Navy...*, p. 78.
36. Forbes, Edwin, undated account, p. 3.
37. Moore, Frank, ed., *The Rebellion Record...*, p. 122.
38. Schaff, Philip. "The Gettysburg Week," p. 58.
39. Klein, Frederick S., ed. *Just South of Gettysburg*. Lancaster, PA: Wickersham Printing Company (1974): 84-85, 103.
40. Cross, Andrew B. *Battle of Gettysburg and the Christian Commission*, p. 11.
41. Sparks, David S., ed., *Inside Lincoln's Army...*, pp. 266-69, 271, 279.
42. Jacobs, Michael, "Later Rambles...," p. 70.   McClean, William, "The Days of Terror in 1863."
43. McCreary, Albertus, *Gettysburg: A Boy's Experiences...*, p. 19.
44. Coates, Earl J., "A Quartermaster's Battle of Gettysburg," *North South Trader*, vol. V, no. 1, November-December 1977, p. 19. One of the men present in the ranks of the 36th was none other than a veteran of the War of 1812. He was 74-year-old Peter Hileman of Co. F. See *Adams Sentinel*, August 11, 1863.
45. "Ehler, Mrs. C.A.," "Hospital Scenes...," pp. 36, 46, 49, 51.
46. Jones, Charles. *Confederate Veteran*, vol. IX, 1901, p. 503.
47. Croll, Jennie S. ed., "Days of Dread."
48. Hollinger, Liberty A. (Clutz), *Some Personal Recollections...*, p. 12.
49. Coddington, Edwin B., "A Vignette of Gettysburg," *The Historian*, vol. 25, #2, February 1963, pp. 195-199.   *Official Records*, vol. 27, part 3, p. 991.
50. Crocker, James F., "Prison Reminiscences," *Confederate Veteran*, vol. XIV, 1906, p. 503.
51. Douglas, Henry K. *I Rode With Stonewall*. Chapel Hill, NC: The University of North Carolina Press (1940): 257.
52. Johnson, H.L. Excerpt from a letter to Surgeon Henry Janes written on October 8, 1863, from York, PA in the "Camp Letterman Papers" file at the GNMP Library.
53. Hollinger, Liberty A. (Clutz), *Some Personal Recollections...*, p. 14.
54. Holstein, Anna M., *Three Years in the Field Hospitals...*, pp. 44-45.   Hadley, John L. Letter to Dr. Henry Janes dated November 22, 1863, in the "Camp Letterman Papers" file at the GNMP Library.
55. Reeves, Henry. Extract from a letter written on July 4, 1863, to his sister "Lizzie."
56. Coddington, Edwin B., *The Gettysburg Campaign...*, p. 154. Hoke, Jacob, *The Great Invasion...*, pp. 121, 131, 174. Isaac and Nancy Strite lived about a mile east of Guilford Springs, PA. The men who killed the 45-year-old farmer were from General A.G. Jenkin's Virginia cavalry brigade. The murderers were soon caught by Union troops and hanged on the spot. See *Warm Welcomes* Magazine, February 1994, pp. 14-16.
57. Hoke, Jacob., *The Great Invasion...*, pp. 153, 176-77.
58. Mohr, James C., ed. *The Cormany Diaries: A Northern Family in the Civil War*. Pittsburgh, PA: University of Pittsburgh Press (1982): 339.
59. Sparks, David S., ed., *Inside Lincoln's Army...*, see entries for the days indicated in text.
60. "Unidentified 47th NC officer," p. 293.
61. Sparks, David S., ed., *Inside Lincoln's Army...*, p. 275.
62. Smart, James G., ed. *A Radical View: The "Agate" Dispatches of Whitelaw Reid, 1861-1865*. Memphis, TN: Memphis State University Press (1976): 12-13.
63. Scott, James K.P., "The Story of the Battles at Gettysburg," p. 30.
64. *Official Records*, vol. 27, part 3, pp. 620-21.
65. Harrison, Kathleen R. Georg, "Daybook" entry for July 12, 1863.
66. Ibid.
67. Wiley, Bell I. *The Life of Johnny Reb*. New York, NY: The Bobbs-Merrill Company (1943): 143-44.
68. Harrison, Kathleen R. Georg, "Daybook" entry for July 22, 1863. See also the Adams *Sentinel* for August 4, 1863, p. 2, col. 2. The editor of the Raleigh *Standard* had openly denounced President Davis, and furthermore the paper declared that "North Carolina has sacrificed forty thousand men in this 'causeless war,' and suggests the sending of a delegation to Washington to enable [the state] to re-enter the Union."

69. Adams *Sentinel and General Advertiser*, Gettysburg, PA, issues of July 28 and August 4, 1863.

70. Goldsborough, William W., "After the Battle," Gettysburg *Compiler*, January 1, 1901. This unit is often called the 2nd Maryland Infantry Battalion, which is incorrect, as it was the "First Maryland." The tragic incident between the deserters and the adjutant occurred on August 28, 1863, near Scottsville, VA. There were supposedly only seven men in the party, and all were hanged or shot on September 5, 1863. See Walter Clark, *Histories of the Several Regiments and Battalions from North Carolina in the Great War 1861-65....* Published by the State: Goldsboro, Nash Brothers printer (1901). (3rd Infantry and 47th Infantry).

71. Harrison, Kathleen R. Georg, "Daybook" entry for July 30, 1863.

72. Mohr, James C., ed., *The Cormany Diaries...*, pp. 337-41.

73. Wilson, William B., diary entry for July 1, 1863.

74. Bayly, Harriet. "Mrs. Joseph Bayly's Story of the Battle," an unpublished memoir in the civilian accounts files of the GNMP Library, p. 4. See also *Star and Sentinel*, September 25, 1888.

75. Crotty, Daniel G. *Four Years Campaigning in the Army of the Potomac.* Grand Rapids, MI: Dygert Bros. & Co. Printers (1874): 94-95.

76. Balsley, Joseph R., "A Gettysburg Reminiscence," *National Tribune*, May 19, 1898, p. 3.

77. Toomey, Daniel C., *Marylanders At Gettysburg*, p. 47.

78. Judson, Amos M., *History of the Eighty-Third Regiment Pennsylvania Volunteers*, p. 69.

79. Kiefer, William R., *History of the One Hundred and Fifty-third Regiment...*, pp. 218-19.

80. Kent, Arthur A., ed. *Three Years With Company K.* Rutherford, NJ: Fairleigh Dickinson University Press (1976): 183.

81. Liebig, George H. Extract from a letter to John Caldwell written on July 30, 1863, from Camp Harper in Gettysburg, in the collection of Lewis Leigh, Jr., Fairfax, VA, and used through his generosity. Another unit guarding and transporting POWs immediately after the battle was the 10th Maine Battalion, under Captain John D. Beardsley. See *Maine at Gettysburg*, pp. 526-527.

82. Cort, Cyrus, diary entry for July 10, 1863.

83. Linn, John B., diary written from July 6-11, 1863, p. 9.

84. Unknown New York Volunteer. "A Penitent Rebel," *The Grand Army Scout and Soldiers Mail*, vol. IX, 1889, p. 3.

85. McNeil, Alexander. Extract from a letter to David G. Porter written from Bristowburg, VA, on August 16, 1863. A copy is presently in the "14th Connecticut Infantry" file at GNMP Library.

86. "Interesting War Statistics," *Confederate Veteran*, vol. IV, 1896, pp. 432-33. See also *Confederate Veteran*, vol. V, 1897, p. 80.

87. *Report of the General Agent of the State of New York...*, p. 47.

88. Cunningham, Mary ("Mrs. J. Paxton" Bigham), "The Scotts and Cunninghams See The Battle," The Gettysburg *Times*, April 22, 1941.

89. Foster, John Y., "Four Days at Gettysburg," pp. 384 and 387.

90. Hoke, Jacob, *Historical Reminiscences of the War...*, p. 171.

91. Hubbard, Robert, M.D., July 9, 1863, letter, "17th Connecticut Infantry" file at the GNMP library. p. 64.

92. Cross, Andrew B., *Battle of Gettysburg and the Christian Commission*, pp. 28-30.

93. Souder, Emily B.T., *Leaves from the Battle-field...*, p. 53.

94. *The U.S. Christian Commission for the Army and Navy...*, p. 65.

95. Patterson, J.N. (Captain and provost marshal at Point Lookout, MD). Excerpts from a 16" x 20" document found in his personal effects. Used through the courtesy of Sam Small, Gettysburg, PA.

96. Long, Roger, "The Confederate Prisoners of Gettysburg," *Gettysburg Magazine*, Issue #2, January 1990, p. 108. For an excellent summary of the adventures and misfortunes of several Confederates captured at Gettysburg, Mr. Long's fascinating article is highly recommended.

97. Farnham, Eliza W., "Descriptions of the Scenes After the Battle...."

98. Farinholt, Benjamin L., "Battle of Gettysburg—Johnson's Island," *Confederate Veteran*, vol. V, 1897, p. 470.

99. Long, Roger, "The Confederate Prisoners of Gettysburg," p. 109.

100. Northrop, Rufus P. (90th Pennsylvania), "Good-by Hoecake," *National Tribune*, March 23, 1911. Boynton, Jonathan W.W., unpublished memoirs, pp. 15-19.

101. Coco, Gregory A., ed., *From Ball's Bluff to Gettysburg and Beyond...*, p. 208.

102. Pettijohn, Dyer B. *Gettysburg and Libby Prison*. Privately printed by Harriet P. Crawford circa 1970, pp. 6-8.
103. Taft, Thomas (124th New York), "Experiences in Captivity," Gettysburg, PA, Adams *Sentinel*, October 30, 1863, p. 1.
104. Troutmann, Frederick, ed., *Twenty Months in Captivity*, pp. 29-30.
105. Taft, Thomas, "Experiences...," p. 1.   Boynton, Jonathan W., unpublished memoirs, p. 19.
106. Taft, Thomas, "Experiences...," p. 1.
107. Warren, William H. Extract from his unpublished diary in the "17th Connecticut Infantry," file at the GNMP Library.
108. Taft, Thomas, "Experiences...," p. 1. For a very detailed look at everyday life in Belle Island prison, see Roland Bowen's account in *From Ball's Bluff to Gettysburg and Beyond...*, pp. 173-184. This book contains an excellent account by a prisoner who escaped from Staunton, VA and describes his many adventures along the way until his recapture. After several months in prison, Bowen was paroled, captured again, and eluded the Rebels for good in 1864.
109. Trautmann, Frederick, ed., *Twenty Months in Captivity...*, pp. 34-36.
110. Wilkin, William P., July 31, 1863, letter.

Chapter Five

1. Unknown correspondent, *Daily News Express*, Lancaster PA, July 20, 1863.   Sheads, Annie. Extract from an unpublished letter written on August 14, 1863, to "Mary" in the collection of the GNMP Museum of the Civil War.
2. Cavada, Alfodo F. (Union staff officer and captain in the 23rd Pennsylvania Infantry). Extract from his diary of July 2, a copy of which is in the files of the GNMP Library.   Bardeen, Charles W. (1st Massachusetts Infantry). *A Little Fifer's War Diary*. Syracuse, NY: Charles W. Bardeen (1910): 238.
3. Gettysburg *Compiler*, August 17, 1863.
4. Wert, J. Howard, *Monument Handbook*, p. 162.   Wert, J. Howard, "In the Hospitals of Gettysburg...," # 2.   Wert, J. Howard, "'Twas Fifty Years Ago," #13.   Busey, John W., *These Honored Dead*, p. 165.
5. Dwinell, Justin M.D., "Report of Surgeon Justin Dwinell...," p. 8.
6. Wert, J. Howard, "In the Hospitals of Gettysburg...," #9. Wert claimed that he collected over 100 of these and similar notices in July and August newspapers of the period.
7. Ibid., #9.   Busey, John W., *These Honored Dead*, p. 214.   Wert, J. Howard, "In the Hospitals of Gettysburg...," #10.
8. Adams *Sentinel and General Advertiser*, Gettysburg, PA, October 13, 1863.
9. Gettysburg *Compiler*, September 14, 1863.
10. In February 1864, John Burns was voted a pension of $8 a month by the U.S. Senate for his actions at Gettysburg. See the Gettysburg *Compiler*, February 22, 1864.
11. McCreary, Albertus, *Gettysburg: A Boy's Experiences...*, pp. 16-17.
12. Souder, Emily B.T., *Leaves from the Battle-Field...*, pp. 52-53.
13. *Official Records*, vol. 27, part 3, p. 607.
14. Gettysburg *Star and Banner*, July 30, 1863. Wert, J. Howard, "In the Hospitals of Gettysburg...," #10.
15. Ibid., #10.   Knox, Thomas W., "The Battle Field at Gettysburg...," p. 1, col. 6.
16. Lightner, Nathaniel, "Horrors of Battle. The Story of Gettysburg Told By A Farmer," Gettysburg *Compiler*, November 21, 1893, p. 2, col. 2. This article was written by correspondent "A.F.C." of the Washington *Star* which first published it on November 4, 1893.
17. Wert, J. Howard, "In the Hospitals of Gettysburg...," #11.
18. Hollinger, Liberty A. (Clutz), *Some Personal Recollections...*, p. 14.
19. *Official Records*, vol. 27, part 3, pp. 1, 213, 652-53.   Harrison, Kathleen R. Georg. "Estimated Numbers and Vital Statistics" file, and notes therein by Colonel Alfred B. Johnson, (USMA Class of 1913), in the GNMP senior historian's office.
20. Wert, J. Howard, "In the Hospitals of Gettysburg...," #9. For another slant on the "judge's" story see John H. Brinton, M.D., *Personal Memoirs*, p. 244. Brinton witnessed the same basic scene, but believed that the person involved was a member of the state legislature.
21. Simpson, William T. (28th Pennsylvania Infantry). "The Drummer Boys of Gettysburg," Philadelphia *North American*, June 29, 1913.

22. Blood, Henry B., diary entries from July 6 through October 1863. Original diary is in the National Archives in Washington, D.C.
23. Will, John C. "Battle Days at Globe Inn," Gettysburg *Compiler*, July 21, 1910.
24. Toomey, Daniel C., *Marylanders at Gettysburg*, p. 46. Notes in file on "Horses" in senior historian's office at GNMP.
25. Trowbridge, John T., "The Field of Gettysburg," p. 623.
26. *The Hawkinsville Dispatch*, Hawkinsville, GA, July 6, 1871.
27. Johnson, Clifton, *Battleground Adventures*, p. 185.
28. Stoke, Frank M., October 26, 1863, letter, p. 2.
29. Wert, J. Howard, *Monument Handbook*, p. 163. *Report of the General Agent of the State of New York...*, p. 49. Brinton, John H., M.D., *Personal Memoirs*, pp. 244-46. Horn, Henry E., ed. *Memoirs of Jenny Eyster Jacobs*. Privately printed (1974): 61.
30. *Official Records*, vol. 27, part 3, pp. 568-69, 591, 706. Coates, Earl J., "A Quartermaster's Battle of Gettysburg," pp. 17-19. Harrison, Kathleen R. Georg, "Daybook" entry for July 6, 1863.
31. *Official Records*, vol. 27, part 3, p. 706.
32. "U.S. Army Quartermaster Department Reports." This file in the GNMP Library contains telegrams and other correspondence relating to Captain Smith's activities after the Battle of Gettysburg. The preceding information on Smith's episodes was taken from this file. This folder also contains correspondence of Rufus Ingalls and W.G. Rankin.
33. Ibid.
34. Brinton, John H., M.D., *Personal Memoirs*, p. 244.
35. "U.S. Army Quartermaster Department Reports" file.
36. Wert, J. Howard, "In the Hospitals of Gettysburg...," #10.
37. Schantz, Franklin J.F., "Reflections on the Battle of Gettysburg," p. 291.
38. Brinton, John H., M.D., *Personal Memoirs*, pp. 243-44.
39. Warren, Leander H., *My Recollections*, p. 17.
40. Knox, Thomas, W., "The Battle Field at Gettysburg...," p. 1, col. 5 & 6.
41. Parker, Joseph A., letter to a friend, pp. 1-2.
42. "U.S. Army Quartermaster Department Reports" file. Correspondence dated August 1, 1863.
43. Trowbridge, John T., "The Field of Gettysburg...." p. 624. Foster, John H., "Four Days at Gettysburg," col. 2.
44. Linn, John B., diary written from July 6-11, 1863, p. 4. In March 1864, the 20th, 21st and 22nd Pennsylvania cavalry regiments were camped west of Gettysburg. See Gettysburg *Compiler*, March 14, 1864.
45. Liebig, George H., unpublished letter. Private Jacob Christ was buried in the Soldiers' National Cemetery. Reed's body was never identified.
46. Janes, Henry, M.D. Unpublished letter in the "Camp Letterman Papers" file at the GNMP Library dated December 7, 1863.
47. Wade, John James, unpublished journal now in the collection of Dr. Walter L. Powell, Gettysburg, PA and used initially through the generosity of Sam Small. Wade was a member of Robert Bell's Co. B, 21st Pennsylvania Cavalry, was a resident of Gettysburg and the brother of the slain Mary Virginia "Jennie" Wade.
48. Bradsby, H.C., *History of Cumberland and Adams Counties...*, pp. 181, 349. *Official Records*, vol. 27, part 3, pp. 811-15.
49. Toomey, Daniel C., *Marylanders at Gettysburg*, pp. 45-46. Ripley, George C. (Lieutenant 10th Connecticut Infantry), unpublished letter to Dr. Henry Janes from York, PA, October 15, 1863, in the author's collection. Also thanks to Len Rosa, Gettysburg, PA.
50. Stone, Martin. Excerpt from diary, July 7, 1863, p. 1. in "U.S. Army Quartermaster Department Report" file at the GNMP Library.
51. Aldrich, Thomas M. *The History of Battery A, First Regiment Rhode Island Light Artillery....* Providence, RI: Snow & Farnham, Printers (1904): 221.
52. McCurdy, Charles M. *Gettysburg, A Memoir*. Pittsburgh, PA: Reed & Witting Company (1929): 28.
53. Kent, Arthur A., ed., *Three Years With Company K*, p. 204.
54. Keesy, William A. *War as Viewed From the Ranks*. The Experiment and News Co., Norwalk, OH: (1898) 185.

55. Piston, William G., ed. "The Rebs Are Yet Thick About Us." The Civil War Diary of Amos Stouffer of Chambersburg. *Civil War History*. vol. 38, #3. The Kent State University Press, Kent, OH: (1992): 220-21.

56. Haines, Alanson A., *A History of the Fifteenth Regiment New Jersey Volunteers*, p. 94.

57. Blake, Henry N. *Three Years in the Army of the Potomac*. Boston, MA: Lee and Shepard (1865): 219. Livermore, William T. Letter to Charles Livermore written July 6, 1863, p. 2.

58. *Official Records*, vol. 27, part 1, p. 656.

59. Ibid., p. 831.

60. Ibid., p. 291. Potter, M.E. (Ordnance officer). Letter to Capt. D.W. Flagler, Chief of Ordnance, Army of the Potomac, July 7, 1863. National Archives, RG94, War Records Office, vol. 27, boxes 48-52.

61. *Official Records*, vol. 27, part 1, p. 225.

62. Wilson, William B., diary entry, p. 130.

63. *The U.S.C.C. for the Army and Navy...*, p. 66.

64. Fleming, George T. ed. *Life and Letters of Alexander Hays*.... Edited and Arranged with Notes and Contemporary History by G.T.F. from data compiled by Gilbert A. Hays. Pittsburgh, PA: (1919): 474. Muffly, Joseph W., *The Story of Our Regiment*, p. 467.

65. Gettysburg *Star and Banner*, July 2 (actually 9), 1863, p. 1, col. 5.

66. Adams *Sentinel*, Gettysburg, PA, July 7, 1863, p. 1, col. 2. Lehman, the student, was treated by doctors in the "Seminary Hospital." Gettysburg *Star and Banner*, July 2 (actually 9), 1863, p. 3, col. 2.

67. Adams *Sentinel & General Advertiser*, August 18, 1863.

68. Gettysburg *Star and Banner*, July 2 (actually 9), 1863, p. 3, col. 2. Recently I found a notation in a file at the GNMP Library that in the 1870s the U.S. Army had a regulation or some type of printed "handout" issued on how to prevent deaths in the field from handling and disposing of Civil War artillery shells. However, no citation or other source was named.

69. Brady, Mary A. Extract from a letter written by her on July 22, 1863, from the field hospital of the Third Corps near Gettysburg, PA, and printed in the July 23, 1863, issue of the *Daily Evening Bulletin*, Philadelphia, PA.

70. Hege, John B., Article in the *Public Opinion*, Chambersburg, PA, "Gettysburg News Clippings," vol. 3, p. 100 in the senior historian's office at GNMP Library.

71. Adams *Sentinel & General Advertiser*, July 28, 1863.

72. Lewars, Mrs., "Fairfield is Scene of Many Interesting Army Incidents During Battle Here in 1863," Gettysburg *Times*, July 1940.

73. Silliman, Justus M., letter of August 11, 1863, p. 3.

74. McCreary, Albertus, *Gettysburg: A Boy's Experiences...*, pp. 19-20.

75. White, Susan Holabaugh, unpublished letter in the Museum of the Civil War collection of the GNMP, dated November 20, 1863, written from the home of Lavenia Bollinger in Gettysburg, PA.

76. McCreary, Albertus, *Gettysburg: A Boy's Experiences...*, pp. 20-21.

77. McCurdy, Charles, *Gettysburg, A Memoir...*, p. 28.

78. Ziegler, Hugh M., "Reminiscences of...," unpublished manuscript written in May 1933, now in the files of the Adams County Historical Society, Gettysburg, PA, p. 5.

79. Gettysburg *Compiler*, June 20, 1864. As an example of the tremendous number of artillery rounds fired during the battle, one need only read the report of Battery "L," 1st New York Light Artillery in the *Official Records*, vol. 27, part 1, p. 364. This unit alone fired at least 1,200 rounds in action between July 1-3. If all the guns at Gettysburg (630) fired 200 rounds each, the total amount of ordnance spent would have been 126,000 rounds. And if every soldier in the ranks (150,000) shot off only the 40 rounds available in his cartridge box the sum of small-arms bullets expended would be approximately 6,000,000. Gettysburg *Star and Sentinel*, June 21, 1864. These accounts remind me of a time when I was a boy growing up on the Avoyelles Prairie near Mansura, LA, where a battle had been fought on May 16, 1864, during the Red River Campaign of that year. Our family farm contained relics from this battle, and in the barn was a pile of old cannonballs and shells plowed up throughout the years. One day I was severly scolded by my uncle who caught me on top of the barn methodically throwing down a fused 6-pounder cannonball onto the concrete pavement below. I was about 10, and was hoping the severe blows would explode the projectile. It never did, and the old ball is still on one of my bookcases.

80. "Mr. Cooke," "Battle of Gettysburg," Gettysburg *Compiler*, July 20, 1863.

81. Page, Evelyn, ed., "On the Escape of Lee," p. 442.

82. Nye, W.S., ed., *The Valiant Hours*, pp. 121-22.

83. Knox, Thomas W., "The Battle Field at Gettysburg...," p. 1, col. 5-6.

84. "Mr. Cooke," "Battle of Gettysburg," Gettysburg *Compiler*, July 20, 1863.

85. Beller, Lizzie J., "Gettysburg," p. 2, col. 3.

86. Linn, John B., diary written from July 6-11, 1863, pp. 3 & 8.

87. Schantz, Franklin J.F., "Reflections on the Battle of Gettysburg," p. 291.

88. "Phelps, Mrs. Lincoln." ed. *Our Country, In Its Relations To The Past, Present and Future.* Baltimore, MD: John D. Toy (1864): 269-70. The writer of the actual memoir and the person who found the relics was Thomas E. Van Bebber. Courtesy of Daniel Toomey, Linthicum, MD.   Ziegler, Hugh M., "Reminiscences of...," p. 5.

89. McCurdy, Charles M., Gettysburg, *A Memoir*, pp. 29-30.

90. McCreary, Albertus, *Gettysburg: A Boy's Experiences...*, p. 51.

91. Sheely, Aaron, unpublished book of stories.

92. Danner, J. Albertus. Obituary, April 27, 1904, in the files of the Adams County Historical Society, Gettysburg, PA.

93. Hollinger, Liberty A. (Clutz), *Some Personal Recollections...*, p. 15.

94. Souder, Emily B.T., *Leaves from the Battle-Field...*, pp. 28-29.   Hiram K. Campbell, a member of the 145th Pennsylvania Infantry, Co. H, was captured at Gettysburg on July 2 and died at Annapolis, MD on January 8, 1864.

95. Alleman, Matilda J. "Tillie" (Pierce), *At Gettysburg...*, p. 107.

96. Warren, Leander H., *My Recollections*, p. 12.

97. Bucklin, Sophronia E., *In Hospital and Camp...*, p. 190.

98. Gettysburg *Compiler*, April 4, 1864.

99. Emory, Ambrose M., unpublished manuscript diary, pp. 9-10.

100. Moorhead, Isaac, "A Visit to Gettysburg...," p. 28.

101. McCreary, Albertus, *Gettysburg: A Boy's Experiences...*, pp. 19-20.

102. Trowbridge, John T., "The Field of Gettysburg," pp. 619 & 624. Often in later years shells were placed in natural holes in trees and allowed to grow "tight" for a few years. These staged "war logs" as they are now called, brought high relic prices when sold to the unsuspecting buyer, as they do now.

103. Firey, Frank P., "Boy's Story of the Gettysburg Retreat," *National Tribune*, November 7, 1929, p. 6, col. 2-3.

104. Unknown author. "My Rambol." October 14, 1866. Excerpt from an unpublished memoir in the "Early Visitation" file at the GNMP Library.

105. Carter, Joseph C., ed., *Magnolia Journey...*, pp. 184-85.

106. Wert, J. Howard. *Monument Handbook.* p. 205.

107. Unknown Massachusetts author. Excerpt from a diary kept while on a visit to Gettysburg by a Gloucester, MA, youth between July 12-16, 1889, now in the "Early Visitation" file at the GNMP Library.

108. Earle, David M. *History of the Excursion of the Fifteenth Massachusetts Regiment and Its Friends....* Worcester, MA: Press of Charles Hamilton (1886): 47.

109. Gilmore, D.M. (Captain, 3rd Pennsylvania Cavalry). "With General Gregg at Gettysburg," MOLLUS-MINN. St. Paul, MN: H.L. Collins Co. (1898).

110. Ibid.

111. Ibid.

112. Harris, Fergus S. "Captain Fergus S. Harris," *Confederate Veteran*, vol. XIII, 1905, p. 177.

113. Bradsby, H.C., *History of Cumberland and Adams Counties*, p. 202.

114. "Gettysburg Newspaper Clippings," vol. 3, in the senior historian's office at GNMP, pp. 14-25.

115. Fleming, George T., ed., *Life and Letters of Alexander Hays*, p. 591.

116. Batchelder, Frank R., "The Relic Vender," A poem in the author's research file, "Relics."

117. Harrison, Kathleen R. Georg. "Summary of State Damage Claims," compiled June 9, 1982, and available in the senior historian's files at GNMP. The total amount claimed as stated in the Gettysburg *Star and Sentinel* on April 23, 1869, p. 3 for Adams County is $507,797.37.   Commonwealth of Pennsylvania, *Records of the Department of the Auditor General.* Record Group 2 (Pennsylvania Archives) of the Board of Claims, 1862-70 Damage Claims Applications, 1871-79, 53 boxes, boxes 1-12, folders 1-162. Hereafter cited as "Pennsylvania State Board of Claims RG2." U.S. Government.

"Index of Federal Claims," National Archives, Record Group 92 Quartermaster General Claims Files, Adams County, PA.

118. Commonwealth of Pennsylvania. "Papers of the Governors, 1858-71," vol. 8, Pennsylvania Archives IV, (1902), pp. 629-634.

119. Gettysburg *Star and Banner*, July 2 (actually 9), 1863, pp. 1 & 3. Pennsylvania State Board of Claims, RG2.

120. Pennsylvania State Board of Claims, RG2, Emanuel Pitzer claim, Box 8, Folder 109. McCurdy, Charles M. *Gettysburg, A Memoir*, p. 24-25. Linn, John B., diary written from July 6-11, 1863, pp. 7-8, Gettysburg *Compiler*, August 19, 1884.

121. Pennsylvania State Board of Claims, RG2.

122. Gettysburg *Star and Banner*, July 23, 1863, p. 3.

123. These individual claims and cited histories are part of the "Battle Claims Files" in the GNMP Library.

124. Pennsylvania State Board of Claims, RG2.

125. Souder, Emily B.T., *Leaves from the Battle-Field...*, p. 64.

126. Adams *Sentinel*, Gettysburg, PA, August 14 and 18 and September 8 and 15, 1863. For more detail on the GBMA see also Adams *Sentinel*, March 22, 1864 and Gettysburg *Compiler*, May 16, 1864.

127. Adams *Sentinel*, September 15, 1863.

128. Gettysburg *Star and Sentinel*, June 26, 1867. "Gettysburg Battlefield Preservation Association" brochure, circa 1988, in the collection of Dean S. Thomas, Gettysburg, PA, p. 1. For a complete list (all seven sections) of the bylaws of the GBMA and its members, see the May 16, 1864, issue of the Gettysburg *Compiler*.

129. Wihoff, Jerold, ed., "Gettysburg *Compiler*, 125th Commemorative Edition," Gettysburg, PA: Times & News Publishing Co. (1988): 28-34. Harrison, Kathleen R. Georg. "A Fitting and Expressive Memorial, The Development of Gettysburg National Military Park," Gettysburg *Compiler*, 125th Commemorative Edition, p. 28.

130. GBPA 1988 brochure, pp. 1-2.

131. Bradsby, H.C., *History of Cumberland and Adams Counties....*p. 180-181. The author of the poem is Bayard Taylor.

132. Unknown correspondent, The Adams County *Independent*, Littlestown, PA, August 7, 1897.

133. "Soldiers," by Benny Andersson and Bjorn Ulvaeus, Countless Songs, Lts., USA and Canada, copyright 1981.

Appendix

1. Felix, James Allen. Extract from his memoir, kindly provided to me by Marilyn Felix Campbell of Carmel, IN.

2. Hawthorne, Frederick W. *A Peculiar Institution: The History of the Gettysburg Licensed Battlefield Guides*. Privately published by The Association of Licensed Battlefield Guides, Gettysburg, PA, 1991, pp. 2-3.

3. Keenan, Sophie G., "Pere Le Chaise and Gettysburg," The Gettysburg *Compiler*, May 29, 1894, p. 1.

4. McElroy, John, "Gettysburg—Thirty-Six Years After," *National Tribune*, July 13, 1899, p. 1.

5. Wert, J. Howard, "Little Stories of Gettysburg," #4, Harrisburg *Telegraph*, August 6, 1907.

6. Hawthorne, Frederick W., *A Peculiar Institution...*, p. 8.

7. Ibid., p. 13.

BIBLIOGRAPHY

◆ ◆ ◆

Books

Adams, John G. *Reminiscences of the Nineteenth Massachusetts Regiment.* Boston, MA: Wright & Potter Printing Company (1899).

Aldrich, Thomas M. *The History of Battery A, First Regiment Rhode Island Light Artillery....*Providence, RI: Snow & Farnham, Printers (1904).

Alleman, Matilda J. "Tillie" (Pierce). *At Gettysburg, or What a Girl Saw of the Battle.* New York, NY: W. Lake Borland (1889).

Bachelder, John B. *Business Enterprise.* Boston, MA: John B. Bachelder (1878).

Bandy, Ken & Florence Freeland (compilers). *The Gettysburg Papers,* Vol. II. Dayton, OH: Press of Morningside Bookshop (1978).

Bardeen, Charles W. *A Little Fifer's War Diary.* Syracuse, NY: Charles W. Bardeen (1910).

Barker, Daniel. *Losing Faith in Faith.* Madison, WI: FFRF, Inc. (1992).

Bellows, Henry W. *The Sanitary Reporter.* Vols. I and II, May 15, 1863 to August 15, 1865. New York, NY. Louisville, KY (1866).

Benedict, George G. *Army Life in Virginia.* Burlington, VT: Free Press Association (1895).

Blake, Henry N. *Three Years in the Army of the Potomac.* Boston, MA: Lee and Shepard (1865).

Blight, David W., ed. *When This Cruel War Is Over. The Civil War Letters of Charles Harvey Brewster.* Amherst, MA: The University of Massachusetts Press (1992).

Bloodgood, John D. *Personal Reminiscences of the War.* New York, NY: Hunt & Easto (1893).

Boatner, Mark M. *The Civil War Dictionary.* New York, NY: David McKay Company, Inc. (1959).

Bradsby, H.C. *History of Cumberland and Adams Counties,* Pennsylvania. Chicago, IL: Warner, Beers & Co. (1886).

Brinton, John H., M.D. *Personal Memoirs.* New York, NY: The Neale Publishing Company (1914).

Brown, Andrew. *Geology and the Gettysburg Campaign.* Commonwealth of Pennsylvania Bureau of Topographic and Geologic Survey, Educational Series, No. 5, (1983).

Brown, Edmund R. *The Twenty-Seventh Indiana Volunteers in the War of the Rebellion....*Monticello, IN: R.E. Brown (1899).

Bucklin, Sophronia E. *In Hospital and Camp: A Woman's Record of Thrilling Incidents Among the Wounded in the Late War.* Philadelphia, PA: John E. Potter and Co. (1869).

Buehler, Fannie J. *Recollections of the Rebel Invasion and One Woman's Experience During the Battle of Gettysburg.* Gettysburg, PA: Star and Sentinel Printing (1896).

Busey, John W. *The Last Full Measure: Burials in the Soldiers' National Cemetery at Gettysburg.* Hightstown, NJ: Longstreet House (1988).

Busey, John W. *These Honored Dead.* Hightstown, NJ: Longstreet House (1988).

Carter, Joseph H., ed. *Magnolia Journey: A Union Veteran Revisits the Former Confederate States.* By Russell H. Conwell. University, AL: University of Alabama Press (1974).

Carter, Robert G. *Four Brothers in Blue.* Austin, TX: University of Texas Press (1978).

Catton, Bruce, ed. *The Battle of Gettysburg.* By Frank Haskell. Boston, MA: Houghton Mifflin Company (1969).

Clark, Walter. *Histories of the Several Regiments and Battalions from North Carolina in the Great War*

*1861-'65....*Goldsboro, NC: Published by the State, Nash Brothers, printer (1901).

Clendening, Logan. *The Romance of Medicine.* Garden City, NY: The Garden City Publishing Co. (1933).

Coco, Gregory A., ed. *From Ball's Bluff to Gettysburg and Beyond: The Civil War Letters of Private Roland E. Bowen, 15th Massachusetts Infantry, 1861-1864.* Gettysburg, PA: Thomas Publications (1994).

Coco, Gregory A. *On The Bloodstained Field, I.* 130 Human Interest Stories of the Campaign and Battle of Gettysburg. Gettysburg, PA: Thomas Publications (1987).

Coco, Gregory A. *On The Bloodstained Field, II.* 132 More Human Interest Stories of the Campaign and Battle of Gettysburg. Gettysburg, PA: Thomas Publications (1989).

Coco, Gregory A., ed. *Recollections of a Texas Colonel at Gettysburg.* Gettysburg, PA: Thomas Publications (1990).

Coco, Gregory A. *A Vast Sea of Misery: A History and Guide to the Union and Confederate Field Hospitals at Gettysburg, July 1-November 20, 1863.* Gettysburg, PA: Thomas Publications (1988).

Coco, Gregory A. *War Stories: A Collection of 150 Little Known Human Interest Accounts of the Campaign and Battle of Gettysburg.* Gettysburg, PA: Thomas Publications (1992).

Coco, Gregory A. *Wasted Valor: The Confederate Dead at Gettysburg.* Gettysburg, PA: Thomas Publications (1990).

Coddington, Edwin B. *The Gettysburg Campaign, A Study in Command.* New York, NY: Charles Scribner's Sons (1968).

Commager, Henry S., ed. *The Blue and The Gray,* Vol. II. Indianapolis, IN: The Bobbs-Merrill Co., Inc. (1950).

Cowles, Luther E. *History of the Fifth Massachusetts Battery.* Boston, MA: Luther E. Cowles (1902).

Cross, Andrew B. *Battle of Gettysburg and the Christian Commission.* Baltimore, MD: (1865).

Cross, Andrew B. *The War and the Christian Commission.* Baltimore, MD: (1865).

Crotty, Daniel G. *Four Years Campaigning in the Army of the Potomac.* Grand Rapids, MI: Dygert Bros. & Co. Printers (1874).

Crozier, Emmet. *Yankee Reporters, 1861-1865.* New York, NY: Oxford University Press (1956).

Davis, Archie K. *Boy Colonel of the Confederacy—The Life and Times of Henry K. Burgwyn, Jr.* Chapel Hill, NC: The University of North Carolina Press (1985).

Davis, George B., et. al. *The Official Military Atlas of the Civil War.* New York, NY: Arno Press (1978).

Dickert, D. Augustus. *History of Kershaw's Brigade.* Newberry, SC: Elbert H. Hull Company (1899).

Douglas, Henry K. *I Rode With Stonewall.* Chapel Hill, NC: The University of North Carolina Press (1940).

Duncan, Louis C. *The Medical Department of the United States Army in the Civil War.* Washington, D.C.: U.S. Government Printing Office (1910).

Durkin, James, ed. *This War is an Awful Thing...The Civil War Letters of the National Guards, The 19th & 90th Pennsylvania Volunteers.* Glenside, PA: J.M. Santarelli Publishing (1994).

Durkin, Joseph T., ed. *John Dooley: Confederate Soldier, His War Journal.* Washington, D.C.: Georgetown University Press (1945).

Earle, David M. *History of the Excursion of the Fifteenth Massachusetts Regiment and Its Friends....* Worcester, MA: Press of Charles Hamilton (1886).

Edwards, William B. *Civil War Guns.* Harrisburg, PA: The Stackpole Company (1962).

"Ehler, Mrs. C.A.," (Patriot Daughters of Lancaster). *Hospital Scenes After the Battles of Gettysburg, July 1863.* Philadelphia, PA: Henry B. Ashmead, printer (1864).

Elmer, William M.D. *Physicians Hand-Book of Practice for 1863.* New York, NY: W.A. Townsend,

Publisher (1862).

Fatout, Paul, ed. *Letters of a Civil War Surgeon.* Lafayette, IN: Purdue Research Foundation, Purdue University Studies (1961).

Faust, Patricia L., ed. *Historical Times Illustrated Encyclopedia of the Civil War.* New York, NY: Harper & Row (1986).

Fiske, Samuel W. *Mr. Dunn Browne's Experiences in the Army.* Boston, MA: Nichols and Noyer (1866).

Fleming, George T. ed. *Life and Letters of Alexander Hays....* Edited and Arranged with Notes and Contemporary History by G.T.F. from data compiled by Gilbert A. Hays. Pittsburgh, PA: (1913).

Fox, William F. *Regimental Losses in the American Civil War, 1861-1865.* Albany, NY: Brandon Printing Co. (1898).

Fulton, William F., II. *The War Reminiscences of....* Gaithersburg, MD: Butternut Press, Inc. (1984).

Gardner, Leonard M. *Sunset Memories.* Gettysburg, PA: Gettysburg Times Publishing Co. (1929).

Graham, Ziba B. *On To Gettysburg. Ten Days From My Diary of 1863.* Detroit, MI: Winn & Hammond, Printers and Binders (1893).

Haines, Alanson A. *History of the Fifteenth Regiment New Jersey Volunteers.* New York, NY: Jenkins & Thomas, Printers (1883).

Halsey, Jr., Ashley. *Who Fired The First Shot?* Greenwich, CT: Fawcett Publications, Inc. (1963).

Hancock, Cornelia. *South After Gettysburg.* Philadelphia, PA: University of Pennsylvania Press (1937).

Harvard Memorial Biographies, Vol. II. Cambridge, MA: Sever and Francis (1866).

Hawthorne, Frederick W. *A Peculiar Institution: The History of the Gettysburg Licensed Battlefield Guides.* Gettysburg, PA: The Association of Licensed Battlefield Guides (1991).

Hesseltine, William B., ed. *Civil War Prisons.* Kent, OH: The Kent State University Press (1962).

Hoke, Jacob. *Historical Reminiscences of the War, or, Incidents Which Transpired In and About Chambersburg During the War of the Rebellion.* Chambersburg, PA: M.A. Foltz, Printer and Publisher (1884).

Hoke, Jacob. *The Great Invasion of 1863, or, General Lee in Pennsylvania.* Dayton, OH: W.J. Shuey (1887).

Hollinger, Liberty A. (Clutz). *Some Personal Recollections of The Battle of Gettysburg.* Gettysburg, PA: Liberty A. Hollinger (1925).

Holstein, Anna M. *Three Years in the Field Hospitals of the Army of the Potomac.* Philadelphia, PA: J.B. Lippincott & Co. (1867).

Horn, Henry E., ed. *Memoirs of Jenny Eyster Jacobs. Vol I.* By Jenny Eyster Jacobs. Henry E. Horn (1974).

James, Bushrod W. *Echoes of Battle.* Philadelphia, PA: Henry T. Coates & Co. (1895).

Johnson, Clifton. *Battleground Adventures.* Cambridge, MA: Houghton Mifflin Co., The Riverside Press (1915).

Johnston, David E. *Four Years A Soldier.* Princeton, WV: David E. Johnston (1887).

Jones, Horatio G. *To The Christian Soldiers and Sailors of the Union.* Philadelphia, PA: Lippincott's Press (1868).

Judson, Amos M. *History of the Eighty-third Regiment Pennsylvania Volunteers.* Erie, PA: B.F.H. Lynn (1865).

Keesy, William A. *War As Viewed From The Ranks.* Norwalk, OH: The Experiment and News Co. (1898).

Keifer, William R. *History of the One Hundred and Fifty-third Regiment Pennsylvania Volunteer

Infantry.... 1862-1863. Easton, PA: Press of the Chemical Publishing Company (1909).

Kent, Arthur A., ed. *Three Years With Company K*. Rutherford, NJ: Fairleigh Dickinson University Press (1976).

Klein, Frederick S., ed. *Just South of Gettysburg*. Lancaster, PA: Wickersham Printing Company (1974).

Krick, Robert K. *The Gettysburg Death Roster*. Dayton, OH: Press of Morningside (1981).

Livermore, Thomas L. *Days and Events, 1860-1866*. Boston, MA: Houghton, Mifflin Co. (1920).

Long, E.B. *The Civil War Day by Day, An Almanac, 1861-1865*. Garden City, NY: Doubleday & Company, Inc. (1971).

Marcus, Edward, ed. *A New Canaan Private in the Civil War: Letters of Justus M. Silliman....* New Canaan, CT: New Canaan Historical Society (1984).

McCalmont, Alfred B. *Extracts From Letters....* Franklin, PA: Robert McCalmont (1908).

McCreary, Albertus. *Gettysburg: A Boy's Experiences of the Battle*. Gettysburg, PA: Albertus McCreary (1909).

McCurdy, Charles M. *Gettysburg, A Memoir*. Pittsburgh, PA: Reed & Witting Company (1929).

McKay, Charlotte Elizabeth. *Stories of Hospital and Camp*. Philadelphia, PA: Claxton, Remsen & Haffelfinger (1876).

Mitchell, Mary H. *Hollywood Cemetery. The History of a Southern Shrine*. Richmond, VA: Virginia State University Press (1985).

Mohr, James C., ed. *The Cormany Diaries: A Northern Family in the Civil War*. Pittsburgh, PA: University of Pittsburgh Press (1982).

Monteiro, Aristides. *Confederate Surgeon*. New York, NY: Dodd, Mead & Co. (1969).

Moore, Frank, ed., *The Rebellion Record: A Diary of American Events*. New York, NY: G.P. Putnam (1861-1868).

Moore, Gilbert C. Jr., ed. *Cornie. The Civil War Letters of Lieutenant Cornelius L. Moore, Co. I, 57th Regiment, New York State Volunteers*. Chattanooga, TN: Gilbert C. Moore, Jr. (1989).

Muffly, Joseph W. *The Story of Our Regiment, The 148th Pennsylvania Volunteers....* Des Moines, IA: Kenyon Printing & Mfg. Co. (1904).

Musgrove, Richard M. *Autobiography*. Published by Mary D. Musgrove (1921).

Nash, Eugene A. *A History of the Forty-Fourth Regiment, New York Volunteer Infantry....* Chicago, IL: R.R. Donnelley & Sons, Co. (1911).

Nevins, Allan, ed. *A Diary of Battle. The Personal Journals of Colonel Charles S. Wainwright, 1861-1865*. New York, NY: Harcourt, Brace & World, Inc. (1962).

Nicholson, John P., editor and compiler. *Pennsylvania at Gettysburg, Vol. II*. Harrisburg, PA: W.M. Stanley Ray, State Printer (1904).

Nye, Wilber S., ed. *The Valiant Hours: Narrative of "Captain Brevet" an Irish-American in the Army of the Potomac*. By Thomas F. Galwey. Harrisburg, PA: The Stackpole Company (1961).

Oates, William C. *The War Between the Union and the Confederacy....* New York, NY: Neale Publishing Company (1905).

Parker, John L. *History of the 22nd Massachusetts Infantry*. Boston, MA: The Press of Rand Avery Co. (1887).

Pettijohn, Dyer B. *Gettysburg and Libby Prison*. Harriet P. Crawford (c. 1970).

"Phelps, Mrs. Lincoln," ed. *Our Country, In Its Relations To The Past, Present and Future*. Baltimore, MD: John D. Toy (1864).

Phillips, Marion G. and Valerie P. Parsegian, ed. *Richard and Rhoda: Letters from the Civil War*.

Washington, D.C.: Legation Press (1981).

Report of the General Agent of the State of New York for the Relief of Sick, Wounded, Furloughed and Discharged Soldiers. Albany, NY: Comstock & Cassidy Printers (1864).

Rosenblatt, Emil, ed. *Anti-Rebel - The Civil War Letters of Wilber Fisk.* Croton-on-Hudson, NY: Emil Rosenblatt (1983).

Runge, William H., ed. *Four Years in the Confederate Artillery. The Diary of Private Henry R. Berkeley.* Chapel Hill, NC: University of NC Press (1961).

Schildt, John W. *Roads From Gettysburg.* Chewsville, MD: John W. Schildt (1979).

Scott, James K.P. *The Story of the Battles at Gettysburg.* Harrisburg, PA: The Telegraph Press (1927).

Sellers, John R., compiler. *Civil War Manuscripts: A Guide to Collections in the Manuscript Division of the Library of Congress.* Washington, D.C.: Library of Congress (1986).

Shuffler, R. Henderson, ed. *The Adventures Of A Prisoner Of War, 1863-1864.* By Decimus et Ultimus Barziza. Austin, TX: University of Texas Press (1964).

Silliker, Ruth L., ed. *The Rebel Yell & the Yankee Hurrah. The Civil War Journal of a Maine Volunteer.* Camden, ME: Down East Books (1985).

Skelly, Daniel A. *A Boy's Experience During the Battles of Gettysburg.* Gettysburg, PA: Daniel A. Skelly (1932).

Small, Abner R. *The Road To Richmond.* Berkeley, CA: University of California Press (1939).

Smart, James G., ed. *A Radical View: The "Agate" Dispatches of Whitelaw Reid, 1861-1865.* Memphis, TN: Memphis State University Press (1976).

Smith, John L. *History of the Corn Exchange Regiment.* (118th Pennsylvania). Philadelphia, PA: Survivors' Association, John L. Smith (1888).

Souder, Emily Bliss Thacher. *Leaves From The Battle-Field of Gettysburg, A Series of Letters Written from a Field Hospital and National Poems.* Philadelphia, PA: Caxton Press of C. Sherman, Son & Co. (1864).

Sparks, David S., ed. *Inside Lincoln's Army. The Diary of Marsena Rudolph Patrick, Provost Marshal General, Army of the Potomac.* New York, NY: Thomas Yoseloff (1924).

State of Pennsylvania. Revised Report of the Select Committee Relative to the Soldiers' National Cemetery Together with the Accompanying Documents, As Reported to the House of Representatives of the Commonwealth of Pennsylvania. Harrisburg, PA: Singerly & Myers, State Printers (1865).

Stevens, George T. *Three Years in the Sixth Corps.* New York, NY: D. Van Nostrand (1870).

Stiles, Robert. *Four Years Under Marse Robert.* New York, NY: The Neale Publishing Company (1903).

Storrs, John W. *The Twentieth Connecticut, A Regimental History.* Naugatuck, CT: Press of the "Naugatuck Valley Sentinel" (1886).

Taylor, Frank H. *Philadelphia in the Civil War 1861-1865.* Published by the city (1913).

Toombs, Samuel. *New Jersey Troops in the Gettysburg Campaign.* Orange, NJ: The Evening Mail Publishing House (1888).

Toomey, Daniel C. *Marylanders at Gettysburg.* Baltimore, MD: Toomey Press (1994).

Townsend, George E. *Rustics in Rebellion. A Yankee Reporter on the Road to Richmond, 1861-1865.* Chapel Hill, NC: The University of North Carolina Press (1950).

Trautmann, Frederick, ed. *Twenty Months in Captivity: Memoirs of a Union Officer in Confederate Prisons.* Cranbury, NJ: Fairleigh Dickinson University Press (1987).

United States Christian Commission for the Army and Navy. Work and Incidents, First Annual Report. Philadelphia, PA (1863).

United States Christian Commission, Second Report of the Committee of Maryland. Baltimore, MD: Sherwood and Company (1863).

United States. *The Medical and Surgical History of the War of the Rebellion, 1861-1865.* Washington, D.C.: Government Printing Office (1870).

United States. *War of the Rebellion: A Compilation of the Official Records of the Union and Confederate Armies.* Washington, DC: Government Printing Office, Vol. 27, Parts 1-3 (1889).

U.S. Sanitary Commission, A Sketch of Its Purposes and Its Work. Boston, MA: Little, Brown & Company (1863).

Veterans Association. *History of the 71st Regiment, N.G.N.Y.* New York, NY: The Veterans Association, Press of the Eastman Publishing Co. (1919).

Warren, Leander H. *My Recollections.* Gettysburg, PA: Leander H. Warren (1926).

Wert, J. Howard. *A Complete Hand-Book of the Monuments and Indications and Guide to the Positions on the Gettysburg Battlefield.* Harrisburg, PA: R.M. Sturgeon & Co. (1886).

West, John C. *A Texan in Search of a Fight.* Waco, TX: Press of J.S. Hill & Co. (1901).

Weygant, Charles H. *History of the One Hundred and Twenty-fourth Regiment, N.Y.S.V.* Newburgh, NY: Journal Printing House (1877).

White, Russell C., ed. *The Civil War Diary of Wyman S. White.* Baltimore, MD: Butternut and Blue (1991).

Wihoff, Jerold, ed. *Gettysburg Compiler, 125th Commemorative Edition.* Gettysburg, PA: Times & News Publishing Co. (1988).

Wiley, Bell I. *The Life of Johnny Reb.* New York, NY: The Bobbs-Merrill Company (1943).

Willson, Arabella M. *Disaster, Struggle, Triumph: The Adventures of 1,000 "Boys in Blue," from August, 1862 to June, 1865.* Albany, NY: The Argus Company, printers (1870).

Young, J.B. *The Battle of Gettysburg.* Dayton, OH: Morningside Bookshop (1971).

Journals

Baruch, Simon M.D., "A Surgeon's Story of Battle and Capture," *Confederate Veteran*, Nashville, TN, 1914, vol. XX.

Beauchamp, Virginia W., "The Sisters and the Soldiers," *Maryland Historical Magazine*, Summer 1986, vol. 81, #2.

Brinton, Daniel G., "From Chancellorsville to Gettysburg, A Doctors Diary," *The Pennsylvania Magazine of History and Biography.* Historical Society of Pennsylvania, Philadelphia, PA, 1965, vol. 89.

Civil War Times Illustrated, Historical Times, Inc., Gettysburg, PA, November 1960 and November 1963.

Clarke, James F, "A Visit to Gettysburg," *The Christian Register*, Boston, MA, September 18, 1913, vol. 11.

Coates, Earl J., "A Quartermaster's Battle of Gettysburg," *North South Trader*, November-December 1977, vol. V, no. 1.

Coddington, Edwin B., "A Vignette of Gettysburg," *The Historian*, February 1963, vol. 25, no. 2.

Colston, F.M., "Gettysburg as We Saw It," *Confederate Veteran*, Nashville, TN, 1897, vol. V.

Crocker, James F., "Prison Reminiscences," *Confederate Veteran*, Nashville, TN, 1906, vol. XIV.

Farinholt, Benjamin L., "Battle of Gettysburg—Johnson's Island," *Confederate Veteran*, Nashville, TN, 1897, vol. V.

Farnham, Eliza W., "Description of Scenes After The Battle Of Gettysburg," *Common Sense*, August

22, 1874.

Fergus, Chuck, "Thornapples," *Pennsylvania Game News*, April 1986.

Fisher, Mary C., "A Week on Gettysburg Field," *Grand Army Scout and Soldiers Mail*, 1883, vol. II, #12.

Foster, John Y., "Four Days at Gettysburg," *Harper's New Monthly Magazine*, February 1864, vol. 28.

Foster, Joseph H., "Visit To The Battlefield," *Journal of Literature and Politics*, Portsmouth, NH, August 8, 1863.

Gilmore, D.M., "With General Gregg at Gettysburg," The Military Order of the Loyal Legion of the U.S., (MOLLUS), Minnesota Commandery, H.L. Collins Co., St. Paul, MN, 1898, vol. 4.

Greenlee, Victoria B., "Vulture Research Begins at Gettysburg," *Park Science*, Fall 1983, vol. 4, #1.

"Hahnemann Institute," Hahnemann Medical College, Philadelphia, PA, December 1895, vol. III, #2.

Harper's Weekly, "Scenes and Incidents at Gettysburg," January 16, 1864. (Written by an unknown member of the 6th New Jersey Infantry.)

Harris, Fergus S., "Captain Fergus S. Harris," *Confederate Veteran*, Nashville, TN, 1905, vol. XIII.

Hefelbower, S.G., "J.F. Crocker," *The History of Gettysburg College*, Gettysburg, PA, 1932.

Helffrich, William, "William Helffrich...Horse and Buggy Preacher," *Historical Review of Berks County*, Fall, 1982.

"Interesting War Statistics," *Confederate Veteran*, Nashville, TN, 1896, vol. IV.

Jacobs, Michael, "Later Rambles Over The Field Of Gettysburg," *United States Service Magazine*, January and February 1864, vols. I and II.

Long, Roger, "The Confederate Prisoners of Gettysburg," *Gettysburg Magazine*, January 1990, Issue #2.

McFarland, Baxter, "Losses of the Eleventh Mississippi Regiment at Gettysburg," *Confederate Veteran*, Nashville, TN, 1923, vol. XXXI.

Minor, Berkeley, "The Night After Gettysburg," *Confederate Veteran*, Nashville, TN, 1925, vol. XXXIII.

Mitchell, J.B., "Confederate Losses at Gettysburg," *The Blue & The Gray*, 1989, vol. 6, #4.

Moorhead, Isaac, "A Visit to Gettysburg, A Tourist's Account in 1864," *The American Magazine and Historical Chronicle*, Clements Library, The University of Michigan, Ann Arbor, MI, 1985-86, vol. #2.

Nicastro, Anthony M., an article in *The Battlefield Dispatch*, Newsletter of the Licensed Battlefield Guides, Gettysburg, PA, June 3, 1993, vol. XII, #6.

Nickerson, Azor H., "Personal Recollections of Two Visits to Gettysburg," *Scribner's Magazine*, Charles Scribner's Sons, New York, NY, 1893, vol. XIV.

Norris, William F., M.D., "A Hospital at Gettysburg," *The General Magazine and Historical Chronicle*, 1942-43, vol. 45.

Page, Evelyn. ed., "After Gettysburg," by Frederick L. Olmsted, *Historical Society of Pennsylvania Newsletter*, Philadelphia, PA, October 1951.

Piston, William G., ed., "'The Rebs Are Yet Thick About Us,' The Civil War Diary of Amos Stouffer of Chambersburg." *Civil War History*. The Kent State University Press, Kent, OH, 1992, vol. XXXVIII, no. 3.

Roberts, Charles W., "At Gettysburg in 1863 and 1888," MOLLUS, Maine Commandery, The Thurston Print, Portland, ME, 1898, vol. I.

Salomon, Edward S., "Gettysburg," MOLLUS, California Commandery, Shannon-Conmy Printing Co., San Francisco, CA, 1913.

Schaff, Philip, "The Gettysburg Week," *Scribner's Magazine*, Charles Scribner's Sons, New York, NY, July-December 1894, vol. XVI.

Schraf, Joannie M., "Murder, they chirped," *U.S. News and World Report*, October 14, 1991.

Schurz, Carl, "The Battle of Gettysburg," *McClure's Magazine*, The S.S. McClure Co., New York, NY, May to October 1907, vol. XXIX.

Shay, Ralph S., ed., "Reflections on the Battle of Gettysburg," by Franklin J.F. Schantz, Lebanon County Historical Society Publication, 1963, vol. 13, #6.

Taylor, William H., M.D., "Some Experiences of a Confederate Assistant Surgeon," Transactions of the College of Physicians of Philadelphia, PA, 1906, vol. 28.

The Christian Advocate, New York, NY, May 28, 1908, vol. LXXXIII, #22.

Trowbridge, John T., "The Field of Gettysburg," *Atlantic Monthly*, November 1865, vol. 16.

Unidentified Confederate officer, "College Hospital in Gettysburg," *The Land We Love*, Hill, Irwin & Co., Charlotte, NC, November-April 1866-67, vol. II.

Unidentified North Carolina officer, "Young Captain of Infantry," "Northern Prison Life," *The Land We Love*, Hill, Irwin & Co., Charlotte, NC, November 1866.

Unknown New York Volunteer, "A Penitent Rebel," *The Grand Army Scout and Soldiers Mail*, 1889, vol. IX.

Vautier, John D., "The Loss at Gettysburg," *The Southern Bivouac*, March 1886, vol. 4.

Walker, Charles N. & Rosemary, ed., "Diary of the War by Robert S. Robertson," *Old Fort News*, vol. 28, (four parts) January-December 1965.

Ward, W.C., "Incidents and Personal Experiences on the Battlefield at Gettysburg," *Confederate Veteran*, Nashville, TN, 1900, vol. VIII.

Manuscripts (Diaries, Letters and Memoirs)

Bachelder, John B., letter to Andrew Curtin in "Origins of Gettysburg's Soldiers' National Cemetery and Gettysburg Battlefield Memorial Association," unpublished manuscript, senior historian's office, GNMP, Gettysburg, PA.

Bachelder, John B., "Notes on the Services of Troops at the Battle of Gettysburg," Huntington Library, San Marino, CA.

Bacon, Cyrus Jr., M.D., personal diary, July 1863, the Department of Radiology and Microbiology, The University of Michigan, Ann Arbor, MI.

Baird, William, unpublished memoir, Bentley Historical Library, University of Michigan, Ann Arbor, MI.

Bayly, Harriet, "Mrs. Joseph Bayly's Story of the Battle," unpublished memoir, "Civilian Accounts" file, GNMP Library.

Blacknall, Charles C., "memoir" written by his son, Oscar W., North Carolina State Department of Archives and History, Raleigh, NC.

Blanchard, Charles H., memoir of service in the 111th Pennsylvania Volunteers, Erie County Historical Society, Erie, PA.

Blood, Henry B., Assistant Quartermaster, U.S.A., unpublished 1863 diary, Library of Congress, Washington, D.C.

Blood, Henry B., letter to Dr. Henry Janes from "Ass't Quarter Masters Office," York, PA, February 10, 1864, "Quartermaster Reports" file, GNMP Library.

Boone, Samuel G., unpublished manuscript in the GNMP Library within the "88th Pennsylvania Infantry" file.

Boynton, Jonathan W.W., unpublished memoirs, "157th New York Infantry" file, GNMP Library.

Brinton, John H., M.D., letter to Dr. Henry Janes dated August 15, 1863, "Camp Letterman File," GNMP

Library, Gettysburg, PA.

Buck, Andrew, unpublished diary, "7th Michigan Cavalry" file, GNMP Library.

Cavada, Alfodo F., diary entry July 2, GNMP Library.

Chapman, Horatio D., original diary, archives, Connecticut State Library, Hartford, CT.

Clark, A.M., M.D., letter to David McConaughy of Gettysburg, PA, written from White Plains, NY on August 16, 1869, "Field Hospital Marker" file, senior historian's office, GNMP.

Creveling, Lewis M., unpublished letter in the collection of Lewis Leigh, Jr., Fairfax, VA.

Dwinell, Justin M.D., "Report of Surgeon Justin Dwinell...at the Battle of Gettysburg," MS C129, National Library of Medicine, Bethesda, MD.

Eliason, Talcot, M.D., letter to H.B. McClellan written July 23, 1885, in the files of the GNMP Library.

Emory, Ambrose M., original unpublished handwritten manuscript record book and diary in the author's collection.

Fahnestock, Gates D., "Recollections of the Battle of Gettysburg," unpublished, written in 1933-34; Adams County Historical Society, Gettysburg, PA.

Felix, James Allen, memoir, in possession of Marilyn Felix Campbell of Carmel, IN.

Field, T.G., letter to M. Braddock, July 4, 1863, in the collection of Timothy K. Krapf, Licensed Battlefield Guide, Gettysburg, PA.

Follman, John, unpublished diary, "16th Pennsylvania Cavalry" file, GNMP Library.

Forbes, Edwin, an undated account of his trip to Gettysburg, the Pierpont Morgan Library, New York, NY.

Fuller, Charles A., a series of letters written to the editor of the *News*, Sherburne, NY, October-December 1906, Sherburne, NY Public Library.

Hadley, John L., letter to Dr. Henry Janes dated November 22, 1863, "Camp Letterman Papers" file, GNMP Library.

Harris, Isaac, U.S. Sanitary Commission, personal diary, GNMP Library.

Houghton, James, unpublished journal-memoir, archives, University of Michigan, Ann Arbor, MI.

Hubbard, Robert M.D., letter written on July 9, 1863, from Gettysburg, "17th Connecticut Infantry" file, GNMP Library.

Janes, Henry, M.D., letter from Philadelphia dated February 15, 1864, to Surgeon C.C. Cox, "Camp Letterman Papers," file, GNMP Library.

Janes, Henry M.D., letter to Surgeon W.L. King written at Gettysburg, August 17, 1863, "Camp Letterman Papers" file, GNMP Library.

Janes, Henry, M.D., unpublished letter dated December 7, 1863, "Camp Letterman Papers" file, GNMP Library.

Johnson, H.L., letter to Surgeon Henry Janes dated October 8, 1863, from York, PA, "Camp Letterman Papers" file, GNMP Library.

Liebig, George H., letter to John Caldwell written on July 30, 1863, from Camp Harper, Gettysburg, PA, Lewis Leigh, Jr. collection, Fairfax, VA.

Linn, John Blair, original diary, July 6-11, 1863, Centre County Library and Historical Museum, Bellefonte, PA.

Livermore, William T., letter to Charles Livermore written on July 6, 1863, from "camp in the field near Gettysburg, Penna.," "20th Maine Infantry" file, GNMP Library.

McNeil, Alexander, letter to David G. Porter written from Bristowburg, VA on August 16, 1863, "14th Connecticut Infantry," GNMP Library.

Muller, Charles., personal memoir in the collection of the Minnesota Historical Society, St. Paul, MN.

New, George W., M.D., letter dated September 8, 1865, at New Orleans, LA to John B. Bachelder, "Field Hospital" files, GNMP Library.

O'Neal, John W.C., letter dated October 5, 1866, and written to C.B. Burns, "Bodies Discovered Long After The Battle" file, GNMP Library.

Parker, Joseph A., letter written to a "friend," July 22, 1863, archives, Mount St. Mary's College, Emmitsburg, MD.

Peeler, A.J., Lt., letter headed "College Hospital," "5th Florida Infantry" file, GNMP Library.

Powell, David, diary entry about July 5, 1863, "3rd West Virginia Infantry" file, GNMP Library.

Read, Thomas, August 20, 1863, letter to his parents from the U.S. general hospital in Chester, PA, in the collection of the University of Michigan, Ann Arbor, MI.

Reeves, Henry, letter written from Chambersburg, PA on July 4, 1863, to his sister "Lizzie," copy in author's collection.

Rider, Alfred J., letter written to Colonel John B. Bachelder on October 2, 1885, from Navarre, Stark County, Ohio, "Bachelder Papers" on microfilm, GNMP Library.

Ripley, George C., unpublished letter to Dr. Henry Janes from York, PA, October 15, 1863, in the author's collection.

Sheads, Annie, unpublished letter written on August 14, 1863, to "Mary," GNMP Museum of the Civil War collection.

Sheely, Aaron, unpublished book of collected stories and newspaper clippings, vol. I, inventory of The Horse Soldier Civil War Shop, Gettysburg, PA.

Silliman, Justus M., original letters written to his mother from Camp Letterman on August 11 and 19, 1863, New Canaan Historical Society, New Canaan, CT.

Stoke, Frank M., letter dated October 26, 1863, at Gettysburg to his brother, J.M. Stoke, Special Collections, Gettysburg College Library, Gettysburg, PA.

Stone, Martin, diary, July 1863, "U.S. Army Quartermaster Department Reports" file, GNMP Library.

Thompson, Benjamin W., personal memoir, 1910, collection of John A. Thompson, Minneapolis, MN.

Thorn, Elizabeth M., "Mrs. Thorn's War Story," unpublished manuscript, GNMP Library.

Twitchell, Joseph H., letter, archives, Yale University Library, New Haven, CT.

Unidentified author (Colonel, Chief Records and Pension Office, U.S. War Department, Washington, D.C.), letter to J.P. Nicholson, Philadelphia, PA, September 17, 1898, "Hospital Marker" record book, senior historian's office, GNMP.

Unknown author, "My Rambol," October 14, 1866, unpublished memoir, "Early Visitation" file, GNMP Library.

Unknown diarists of Co. G, 147th Pennsylvania Infantry, diary, July 1863, Association of Licensed Battlefield Guides, Gettysburg, PA.

Wade, John James, unpublished journal, collection of Dr. Walter L. Powell, Gettysburg, PA.

Wafer, Francis M., original diary, archives, Douglas Library, Queen's University at Kingston, Kingston, Ontario, Canada.

Warren, Leander H., unpublished account of burial activities, "National Cemetery" file, GNMP Library.

Warren, William H., unpublished diary, "17th Connecticut Infantry" file, GNMP Library.

Weaver, Rufus B., letter to Dr. J.W.C. O'Neal on February 19, 1887, "John W.C. O'Neal" file, GNMP Library.

Weaver, Rufus B., letter to "Mrs. E.L. Campbell," Savannah, GA, October 9, 1871, "Weaver Family" file, GNMP Library.

Weaver, Samuel, letter written to Mrs. C.B. Bedinger on December 27, 1865, "Burial" files, GNMP Library.

White, Susan Holabaugh, unpublished letter in the GNMP Museum of the Civil War collection.

Wills, David, letter written on July 24, 1863, to Governor Andrew G. Curtin. Pennsylvania State Archives. R.G. 26, Executive Correspondence, Department of State, Secretary of the Commonwealth.

Wilson, William B., diary July through October 1863, Adams County Historical Society, Gettysburg, PA.

Ziegler, Hugh M., "Reminiscences of...," unpublished manuscript written in May 1933, Adams County Historical Society, Gettysburg, PA.

Newspaper Articles and Printed (or Published) Letters

Balsley, Joseph R., "A Gettysburg Reminiscence," *National Tribune*, Washington, D.C., May 19, 1898.

Beller, Lizzie J., "Gettysburg," *National Tribune*, Washington, D.C., March, 17, 1892.

Bowen, James L., "On the Gettysburg Field," *Philadelphia Weekly Times*, vol. VIII, no. 19, June 28, 1884.

Boynton, Henry V., "A Visit to the Battle Ground," *Cincinnati Gazette*, Cincinnati, OH, June 30, 1866.

Brady, Mary A., *Philadelphia Daily Evening Bulletin*, July 23, 1863, published letter written on July 22, 1863 from the Third Corps Hospital near Gettysburg, PA.

Bushman, Emanuel, *Gettysburg Compiler*, August 19, 1884, letter to Henry J. Stahle, editor of that newspaper.

Campbell, John T., "Sights at Gettysburg," *National Tribune*, Washington, D.C., September 17, 1908.

"Cooke, Mr." "Battle of Gettysburg," *Gettysburg Compiler*, July 20, 1863.

Croll, Jennie Smyth, ed., "Days of Dread," *Philadelphia Weekly Press*, November 16, 1887.

Cunningham, Mary ("Mrs. J. Paxton" Bigham), "The Scotts and Cunninghams See The Battle," *Gettysburg Times*, April 22, 1941.

Davidson, Nathaniel, "Our Wounded at Gettysburg," *New York Herald*, July 24, 1863.

"E.D.W.," "Gleanings From Gettysburg by A Lady," *Philadelphia Daily Evening Bulletin*, November 21, 1863.

Firey, Frank P., "A Boy's Story of the Gettysburg Retreat," *National Tribune*, Washington, D.C., November 7, 1929.

Goldsborough, William W., "After the Battle," *Gettysburg Compiler*, January 1, 1901.

Harrison, Kathleen R. Georg, "A Fitting and Expressive Memorial, The Development of Gettysburg National Military Park," *Gettysburg Compiler, 125th Commemorative Edition*.

Janes, Henry M.D., *Baltimore Sun*, Baltimore, MD, October 27, 1899, letter to the editor.

Jones, Jesse H., "Saved the Day," *National Tribune*, Washington, D.C., March 7, 1895.

Keenan, Sophie G., "Pere Le Chaise and Gettysburg," *Gettysburg Compiler*, May 29, 1894.

King, Sarah B., "Battle Days in 1863," *Gettysburg Compiler*, July 4, 1906.

Knox, Thomas W., "The Battle Field at Gettysburg. Scenes after the Battle. Visit to the Battle-Field," *New York Herald*, July 9, 1863.

Leiper, Thomas J.D., *Philadelphia Public Ledger*, August 1 letter from Kelly's Ford, VA to his father published on August 6, 1863.

"Lewars, Mrs.," "Fairfield is Scene of Many Interesting Army Incidents During Battle Here in 1863,"

Gettysburg Times, July 3, 1940.

Lightner, Nathaniel, "Horrors of Battle. The Story of Gettysburg Told By A Farmer," *Gettysburg Compiler*, November 21, 1893.

Linn, John B., obituary, *Keystone Gazette*, Bellefonte, PA, January 6, 1899.

Ludlow, James P., *Democrat and American*, Rochester, New York, August 15, 1863, letter dated August 6, 1863, at Gettysburg, PA.

McClean, William, "The Days of Terror in 1863," *Gettysburg Compiler*, June 1, 1908.

McElroy, John, "Gettysburg—Thirty-Six Years After," *National Tribune*, Washington, D.C., July 13, 1899.

Moore, Jane B., *The Lutheran Observer*, July 26, 1863, letter written to G.S. Griffith.

Northrop, Rufus P., "Good-by Hoecake," *National Tribune*, Washington, D.C., March 23, 1911.

Osborne, Steven A., "Recollections of Army Life in the Civil War," a series of articles, Shenango, PA *Valley News*, 1915.

Powell, Richard M., "With Hood At Gettysburg," *Philadelphia Weekly Times*, Philadelphia, PA, December 13, 1884.

Powers, Alice, "Dark Days of the Battle Week," *Gettysburg Compiler*, July 1, 1903, and July 7, 1908.

Simpson, William T., "The Drummer Boys of Gettysburg," *Philadelphia North American*, Philadelphia, PA, June 29, 1913.

Sloan, I.O., *The Lutheran Observer*, August 14, 1863, letter to G.S. Griffith.

Smith, Henry H., *Democrat and American*, Rochester, NY, August 26, 1863, letter written at "U.S. General Hospital," Gettysburg, PA, August 17, 1863.

Taft, Thomas, "Experiences in Captivity," *Adams Sentinel & General Advertiser*, Gettysburg, PA, October 30, 1863.

"T.W.B." Special Correspondent, letter to *Philadelphia Public Ledger*, July 5, 1863, printed in that newspaper on July 10, 1863.

Tyson, Charles J., *Philadelphia Weekly Times*, Philadelphia, PA, March 29, 1884, letter.

Unknown author, "On The Battlefield, The Graves of the Confederate Dead," *Philadelphia Weekly Times*, Philadelphia, PA, June 8, 1878.

Unknown correspondent, "Losses in the Regiment, etc., etc.," (84th New York Infantry), *Brooklyn Eagle*, Brooklyn, NY, July 7, 1863.

Unknown letter writer. *Daily Patriot and Union*, Harrisburg, PA, July 11, 1863.

Walker, Joel A., "Some Stirring Incidents," *Philadelphia Weekly Times*, Philadelphia, PA, March, 17, 1883.

Way, William C., *Detroit Advertiser and Tribune*, Detroit, MI, August 7, 1863, letter to the editor published on August 14, 1863.

Wert, J. Howard, "In the Hospitals of Gettysburg, July 1863," *Harrisburg Telegraph*, Harrisburg, PA, series of 12 articles printed between July 2 and October 7, 1907.

Wert, J. Howard, "Little Stories of Gettysburg," *Gettysburg Compiler*, August 6, 1907, June 8, 1908, #9, from the *Harrisburg Star-Independent*.

Wert, J. Howard, "'Twas Fifty Years Ago," *Harrisburg Telegraph*, Harrisburg, PA, series of articles from July to December, 1913.

Wilkin, William P., *The Athens Messenger*, West Virginia, letter to the editor, August 13, 1863.

Will, John C. "Battle Days at Globe Inn," *Gettysburg Compiler*, July 21, 1910.

Miscellaneous

Batchelder, Frank R., "The Relic Vender," a poem in the author's research file, "Relics."

Commonwealth of Pennsylvania, "Papers of the Governors, 1858-71," vol. 8, Pennsylvania Archives IV, (1902).

Commonwealth of Pennsylvania, Records of the Department of the Auditor General. Record Group 2 (Pennsylvania Archives) of the Board of Claims, 1862-70 Damage Claims Applications, 1871-79, 53 boxes, boxes 1-12, folders 1-162.

Danner, J. Albertus, obituary, April 27, 1904, Adams County Historical Society, Gettysburg, PA.

Frey, John G., "Burial List," copy, GNMP Library.

"Gettysburg Battlefield Preservation Association" brochure, circa 1988, Dean S. Thomas collection, Gettysburg, PA.

"Gettysburg Newspaper Clippings," several volumes, senior historian's office, GNMP.

Harrison, Kathleen R. Georg, "Estimated Numbers of Wagons and Horses, Gettysburg Battlefield Vicinity, June-July 1863" notes, senior historian's files, GNMP.

Harrison, Kathleen R. Georg, "Land Ownership Map," senior historian's office, GNMP.

Harrison, Kathleen R. Georg, "Numbers and Losses" files, GNMP Library.

Harrison, Kathleen R. Georg, "Summary of State Damage Claims," compiled June 9, 1982, senior historian's files, GNMP.

Harrison, Kathleen R. Georg, "The Gettysburg Campaign Daybook," senior historian's files, GNMP.

Harrison, Kathleen R. Georg, "This Grand National Enterprise" copy, GNMP Library.

Hege, John B., article, *Public Opinion*, Chambersburg, PA, "Gettysburg News Clippings," file, senior historian's office, GNMP.

Hemphill, W.A., "On Gettysburg's Famous Battlefield" in "Gettysburg Newspaper Clippings" file, vol. 2, senior historian's office, GNMP.

McLaughlin, James, Confederate compiled service record, Military Records Division, National Archives, Washington, D.C.

National Archives, War Records Office, Record Group 94, Union Battle Reports, vol. 27, boxes 48-52.

O'Neal, John William C. "List of Marked Confederates Buried Upon the Battlefield of Gettysburg;" and "List of Graves of Confederate Soldiers Lying On The Battlefield, Still Marked, Taken in May, 1866." "John W. C. O'Neal" file, GNMP Library.

O'Neal, John W.C., "Record of Confederate Burials," GNMP Museum of the Civil War collection archives.

"Prisoners of War With Particular Reference to the Battle of Gettysburg," a "handout" of the National Park Service at GNMP.

Rose, George W., "Location of Confederate Graves in the Vicinity of the Rose House." Containing the names of marked graves on his farm. The booklet was reportedly found on the battlefield by George Washington Rose in 1865. GNMP Museum of the Civil War collection.

Rosensteel, John H., file, GNMP Museum of the Civil War collection.

Smith, W. Willard, Reports, Office of the Quartermaster General, National Archives, RG92, entry 122NA, QMD, p. 128.

United States. "Army Quartermaster Department Reports" file, GNMP Library.

United States. National Archives, Department of Interior, Bureau of the Census. Eight Census of the U.S., 1860, III.

United States. National Archives, "Index of Federal Claims, National Archives, Record Group 92 Quartermaster General Claims Files, Adams County, PA.

Vollum, Edward P., one-page report dated "Washington, D.C., July 29, 1863" in his compiled service record at the National Archives in Washington, D.C.

Weaver, Rufus B., "Papers Listing Confederate Dead Exhumed On The Battlefield of Gettysburg and Boxed and Shipped to the Hollywood Memorial Association, Richmond, Virginia." "2d Shipment" "Confederate Burial Files," GNMP Library.

Newspapers

Adams County Independent, Littlestown, PA

Adams Sentinel & General Advertiser, Gettysburg, PA

Brooklyn Eagle, Brooklyn, NY

Daily Evening Bulletin, Philadelphia, PA

Daily Express, Lancaster, PA

Detroit Advertiser and Tribune, Detroit, MI

Gettysburg Compiler, Gettysburg, PA

Gettysburg Star and Banner, Gettysburg, PA

Gettysburg Star and Sentinel, Gettysburg, PA

Gettysburg Times, Gettysburg, PA

Harrisburg Telegraph, Harrisburg, PA

Hawkinsville Dispatch, Hawkinsville, GA

Lancaster Evening Express, Lancaster, PA

Lebanon Courier, Lebanon, PA

New York Herald, New York, NY

New York Times, New York, NY

New York Tribune, New York, NY

Philadelphia Inquirer, Philadelphia, PA

Philadelphia Public Ledger, Philadelphia, PA

Potter County Journal, Coudersport, PA

Richmond Dispatch, Richmond, VA

Town Talk, Alexandria, LA

INDEX

◆ ◆ ◆

Richmond Association, 141
Rider, Alfred J., 132
Rife, Isaac, 224
Riley, D.A., 143
Rinehart, Elizabeth A., 121
Rittenhouse, Benjamin F., 252
Roberts, Annie, 305
Roberts, Elias, 305
Robertson, Jerome B., 32, 217
Robertson, Robert S., 252
Robbins, J.B., 43, 95
Robbins, William M., 371
Robinson, John C., 189, 335
Robinson, Samuel, 148
Rock Creek, 19, 21, 24, 25, 35, 68, 82, 170, 171,
    187, 194, 195, 197, 203, 207, 210, 211, 217,
    225, 243, 317
Rock Hill, 26
Rock Island, IL, 260
Rock Top Hill, 26
Rodes, Robert E., 221
Rodes' Division
    number of wounded, 221
Rogers, Peter, 47, 48, 58, 351, 364, 366
Rogers, Susan, 364, 366
Rose, Dorothy, 366
Rose Farm, 38, 40, 41, 42, 45, 58, 83, 90, 93, 95, 96,
    101, 139, 216, 305, 345
Rose, George, 38, 40, 43, 101, 216, 345, 346, 366
Rose Hill Confederate Cemetery, 147
Rose, John, 42, 46
Rosensteel, George D., 23, 348
Rosensteel, John H., 23, 348, 375
Round Hill, 26
Round Top Museum, 23
Round Tops, 26, 34, 36, 40, 45, 47, 48, 52, 57, 93,
    114, 139, 199, 200, 204, 329, 349, 353, 368, 374
Rowley, Thomas A., 189
Ruch, Reuben, 248, 288, 289
Rulison, William H., 191, 213
Rummel, John, 212

Sachs, John, 217
Salisbury, NC, 257, 263
Salomon, Edward S., 12
Satterlee U.S. General Hospital, 167
Saunders, William, 112, 113, 116, 117
Savannah Memorial Association, 136
Scales, Alfred M., 224
Scarborough, J.S., 100
Schantz, Franklin, 209, 346
Schoepf, Albin F., 295
Schriver, David, 221
Schultz, C., 223
Schurz, Carl, 168, 180, 207

Schwartz, Jacob, 106, 139, 141, 176, 180, 195, 203,
    320
Schwietzel's farm, 203
Scott, Alfred, 364
Scott, Harry G., 331
Scott's Prison, 263
Sear's Hill, 297
Second Corps (U.S.), 30, 40, 57, 81, 84, 142, 155,
    170
Second Corps Hospital (U.S.), 106, 162, 171, 173,
    178, 179, 180, 184, 194-196, 213, 217, 234,
    246, 289
Sedgwick, John, 207
Seminary Ridge, 46, 50, 68, 71, 75, 144, 219, 220,
    221, 222, 229, 295, 350, 374
Semmes, Paul J., 214, 216
Sensebaugh, William, 107
Seymour, Horatio, 110
Seymour, John F., 97
Seymour, R.G., 299
Shank, Christian, 224
Sheads and Buehler Hall, 227
Sheads, Annie, 169
Sheads, Robert, 191
Sheaffer, Daniel, 193, 197, 198, 199, 200, 213, 322,
    323
Sheaffer, Leah H., 365
Shealer, Martin, 220
Shealer, William, 375
Shearer, F.F., 268
Sheaver, Jake, 320
Sheely, Aaron, 193, 271
Shellman, Mary, 270
Sherfy Farm, 48, 49, 52, 107
Sherfy, Joseph, 37, 38, 47, 66, 141, 312, 362
Sherman, Eldridge, 211
Sherman, William T., 24
Shick, John, 246, 333
Shiloh, TN, 24
Ship Island, MS, 261
Shoemaker, S.M., 240
Shriver, David, 139
Shriver, Isaac T., 195
Shultz, Elizabeth F., 306
Sickles, Daniel E., 196, 197, 198, 199, 200, 322
Sign of Seven Stars, 224
Silliman, Justus, 235, 237
Sim, Thomas, 197, 204
Sisters of Charity, 191, 240
Sixth Corps Hospital, 131, 207-209
Skelly, Daniel, 8, 37, 40, 46, 58
Slentz, John, 72
Sloan, I.O., 45
Slocum, Henry W., 24
Slyder, John, 133, 145, 216, 366

Gregory A. Coco was born in Marksville, Avoyelles Parish, Louisiana in 1946. He attended colleges in South Carolina, Maryland, and Louisiana, and earned his degree in history in 1972. Drafted into the army in 1967, he spent a tour of duty in Vietnam as both a POW interrogator and an infantryman. He was wounded twice while overseas and was awarded a bronze star in 1968. He has held many vocations since 1972 and is currently a seasonal employee of the Gettysburg National Miliary Park. He is devoted to the research and investigation of the American Civil War, specifically the Battle of Gettysburg, and intends to continue with his writing.

OTHER BOOKS BY GREGORY A. COCO

Through Blood and Fire (1981)

On the Bloodstained Field (1987)

A Vast Sea of Misery (1988)

On the Bloodstained Field II (1989)

Wasted Valor (1990)

Recollections of a Texas Colonel at Gettysburg (1990)

Killed in Action (1992)

War Stories (1992)

From Ball's Bluff to Gettysburg...and Beyond (1994)

Cindy Small and Greg Coco